IMPORTANT.

W9-BZC-512

HERE IS YOUR REGISTRATION CODE TO ACCESS
YOUR PREMIUM McGRAW-HILL ONLINE RESOURCES.

ONLINE RESOURCES

For key premium online resources you need THIS CODE to gain access. Once the code is entered, you will be able to use the Web resources for the length of your course.

If your course is using **WebCT** or **Blackboard**, you'll be able to use this code to access the McGraw-Hill content within your instructor's online course.

Access is provided if you have purchased a new book. If the registration code is missing from this book, the registration screen on our Website, and within your WebCT or Blackboard course, will tell you how to obtain your new code.

Registering for McGraw-Hill Online Resources

то gain access to your мcGraw-нill web resources simply follow the steps below:

1. USE YOUR WEB BROWSER TO GO TO: **http://www.mhhe.com/arends6e**

2. CLICK ON **FIRST TIME USER**.

3. ENTER THE REGISTRATION CODE* PRINTED ON THE TEAR-OFF BOOKMARK ON THE RIGHT.

4. AFTER YOU HAVE ENTERED YOUR REGISTRATION CODE, CLICK **REGISTER**.

5. FOLLOW THE INSTRUCTIONS TO SET-UP YOUR PERSONAL UserID AND PASSWORD.

6. WRITE YOUR UserID AND PASSWORD DOWN FOR FUTURE REFERENCE. KEEP IT IN A SAFE PLACE.

TO GAIN ACCESS to the McGraw-Hill content in your instructor's **WebCT** or **Blackboard** course simply log in to the course with the UserID and Password provided by your instructor. Enter the registration code exactly as it appears in the box to the right when prompted by the system. You will only need to use the code the first time you click on McGraw-Hill content.

тhank you, and welcome to your мcGraw-нill online Resources!

 Mc Graw Hill **Higher Education**

REGISTRATION CODE

1F4J-SGFK-K18B-HA1H-ZUA5

Mc Graw Hill **Higher Education**

* YOUR REGISTRATION CODE CAN BE USED ONLY ONCE TO ESTABLISH ACCESS. IT IS NOT TRANSFERABLE.

0-07-292351-2 ARENDS: **LEARNING TO TEACH, 6E**

Learning to Teach

SIXTH EDITION

Richard I. Arends
Central Connecticut State University

Boston   Burr Ridge, IL   Dubuque, IA   Madison, WI   New York   San Francisco   St. Louis
Bangkok   Bogotá   Caracas   Kuala Lumpur   Lisbon   London   Madrid   Mexico City
Milan   Montreal   New Delhi   Santiago   Seoul   Singapore   Sydney   Taipei   Toronto

The McGraw·Hill Companies

LEARNING TO TEACH, SIXTH EDITION

3 4 5 6 7 8 9 0 QPD/QPD 0 9 8 7 6 5 4

ISBN 0–07–256454–7

Vice president and editor-in-chief: *Thalia Dorwick*
Publisher: *Jane E. Karpacz*
Developmental editor: *Cara Harvey*
Senior marketing manager: *Pamela S. Cooper*
Project manager: *Christine Walker*
Manager, New book production: *Sandra Hahn*
Media technology producer: *Lance Gerhart*
Designer: *Sharon Spurlock*
Cover/interior designer: *Ellen Pettengell*
Cover designer: *Joan Greenfield*
Cover, top left: © *Michelle Bridwell/PhotoEdit*
Cover, top right: © *David Young Wolff/PhotoEdit*
Cover, bottom: © *Mary Kate Denny/PhotoEdit*
Art editor: *Emma Ghiselli*
Manager, Photo research: *Brian J. Pecko*
Senior supplement producer: *David A. Welsh*
Compositor: *Carlisle Communications, Ltd.*
Typeface: 9.5/12 *Palatino*
Printer: *Quebecor World Dubuque, IA*

The credits section for this book begins on page C-1 and is considered an extension of the copyright page.

Library of Congress Cataloging-in-Publication Data

Arends, Richard.
    Learning to teach / Richard I. Arends. -- 6th ed.
        p.   cm.
    Includes bibliographical references and index.
    ISBN 0–07–256454–7 (alk. paper)
    1. Teaching. 2. Effective teaching. I. Title

LB1025.3 .A74 2004
371.102--dc21

                                        2003037960

www.mhhe.com

About the Author

Richard I. Arends is Professor of Educational Leadership at Connecticut State University, where he also served as Dean of the School of Education for nine years. Before coming to Connecticut, Professor Arends was on the faculty and chaired the Department of Curriculum and Instruction at the University of Maryland, College Park. He received his Ph.D. in education from the University of Oregon, where he was on the faculty from 1975 to 1983. A former elementary, junior high, and high school teacher, his special interests are teacher education, organizational development, and school improvement.

Professor Arends has authored or contributed to over a dozen books on education, including the *Second Handbook of Organization Development in Schools, Systems Change Strategies in Education, Classroom Instruction and Management,* and *Exploring Teaching.* He has worked widely with schools and universities throughout North America, in Jamaica, and in the Pacific Rim, including Australia, Samoa, Palau, and Saipan.

The recipient of numerous awards, he was selected in 1989 as the outstanding teacher educator in Maryland and in 1990 received the Judith Ruskin Award for outstanding research in education from the Association for Supervision and Curriculum Development. From 1995 to 1997, Professor Arends held the William Allen (Boeing) Chair in the School of Education at Seattle University. Currently, he divides his time between West Hartford, Connecticut and Portland, Oregon.

Brief Contents

v

Contents

Part 2

The Leadership Aspects of Teaching 93

Chapter 6

Assessment and Evaluation 212

Part 3

The Interactive Aspects of Teaching 259

Chapter 7

Presenting and Explaining 262

3/30/05

Lisa - conference call

Cara Harvey, McGraw Hill   taping April 28th
Dick

Looking for:

- Concepts Attainment
  (attachment) 1 or 2 pages
- Table - putting it All Together

- Sentimental Textbook
  - Major methodologies of teaching
  * Concept teaching
    * How everything comes together
      planning
      assessment

Video 1 [parent permission ? (1 Day)]

Concept Attainment Lesson —
Chapter 9 ? (science)
(examples of topics)
* science
teach & adapt as needed
(footage needed) in material

lead in one class (10-13 minutes)

Video (part 2) —
Book 6 Strategies
vinette
*Use several strategies w/ same
group of kids

Beginning → explain what is expected
then to small group work
* Video of small group
* conduct whole class discussion
after small group
* assessment - could be staged
(test, project)

*teacher interview
standard? obj
intro self & class?
how plan?

Chapter 12

Classroom Discussion   422

Part 4

The Organizational Aspects of Teaching   457

Chapter 13

School Leadership and Collaboration   458

Resource Handbook

Preface

Learning to be a teacher is a long and complex journey full of excitement and challenge. It begins with the many experiences we have with our parents and siblings; it continues as we observe teacher after teacher through 16 to 20 years of schooling. It culminates, formally, with professional training but continues through a lifetime of teaching experiences.

Purpose and Audience

This is the sixth edition of *Learning to Teach*. It is intended for teacher candidates taking a course commonly labeled General Methods of Teaching, and offered through the elementary, secondary, or general education programs. A variety of other course titles—Analysis of Teaching, Study of Teaching, Principles and Practices of Teaching, or Strategies of Teaching—are sometimes used. Whatever its title, the course's content normally focuses on general models, strategies, and tactics that apply to teaching in all subject areas and at all grade levels.

Although these courses vary somewhat among institutions, most of them seem to share the following general goals. Most instructors want their students to:

- Develop a repertoire of basic teaching models, strategies, and tactics.
- Understand the dynamics of teaching, both inside and outside the classroom.
- Develop an awareness and appreciation of the knowledge base that supports current practices in teaching.
- Appreciate the opportunities and challenges of teaching in classrooms characterized by diversity.
- Acquire skills with which to observe, record, and reflect on teaching.

To help students achieve these general course goals, this textbook takes those who are learning to teach "behind, instead of in front of, the teacher's desk" and provides a realistic view of what teaching is all about. I hope I have done that in a way that will be stimulating and will provide multiple opportunities for engagement and reflection.

Content of the Sixth Edition

In the sixth edition of *Learning to Teach,* I have tried to provide a comprehensive and balanced view of teaching. To accomplish this, I organized the book into four parts. Part 1 consists of two chapters. The first chapter, "The Scientific Basis for the Art of Teaching," introduces the book, explores the meaning of effective teaching, and considers the processes and stages beginning teachers go through on the way to becoming accomplished teachers. Chapter 1 also lays out the major themes of the book as well as the contemporary social context that has an impact on teachers and their work. Chapter 2, "Student Learning in Diverse Classrooms," describes how classrooms belong to all students and how teachers help each student realize his or her learning potential.

Parts 2, 3, and 4, the heart of the book, are organized around concepts of what teachers do. These sections assume that all teachers have three important responsibilities: (1) They lead a group of students—the *leadership aspects of teaching;* (2) they provide students with direct, face-to-face instruction—the *interactive aspects of teaching;* and (3) they work with colleagues and parents to perform the *organizational aspects of teaching.* Readers will soon find that these different aspects of a teacher's job are not always discrete; the teacher does not always perform one independently of the others. These different aspects, however, are convenient organizers for helping teacher candidates make sense out of the bewildering array of events associated with teaching in today's complex society.

Theory-Practice Connections

Learning to Teach strives to provide readers with the theory and rationale that underlie and support specific principles and practices. Readers are also shown why a recommended principle or procedure works the way it does, not just how to execute it effectively. Because models, principles, and procedures of teaching were not invented yesterday, a short history lesson is sometimes provided. A good example of this approach is found in the discussions of cooperative and problem-based learning. Even though significant developments have helped refine these approaches to teaching during the past decade, readers will find that the basic models, including the theory and rationale, are lodged firmly in the mainstream of democratic thought and reach as far back as Horace Mann and John Dewey.

Knowledge Base Focus

Because *Learning to Teach* strives to develop the point of view that there is a knowledge base that can and should guide teaching practice, each chapter has a section entitled "Theoretical and Empirical Support." This section provides a broad sampling of the research that underlies and supports the recommended teaching practices found in the latter part of each chapter. In addition, each chapter contains a boxed "Research Summary" of an important research study pertaining to the chapter topic. The studies have been selected to illustrate not only some aspect of the knowledge base that supports the topics under discussion, but also particular modes of inquiry practiced by educational researchers. Some of the studies are more traditional empirical studies, whereas others represent contemporary, qualitative approaches. Many of the studies are considered classics, and together they cover 50 years of educational research. Although highly compressed, these summaries are truthful to the investigators' methods and conclusions and, collectively, they reflect the variety and richness of methods used by educational researchers over time and around the world. This is an important feature of *Learning to Teach.* Much progress has been made in clarifying and organizing the knowledge base on teaching. It is important for teachers in the twenty-first century to have a command of the specialized knowledge that has accumulated over the past half century and more. This will set them apart from the average person and provide them, as professionals, with some guarantees that they are using best practice.

Finally, the Resource Handbook found at the end of the text contains two research-oriented units. The first of these offers a succinct guide to reading and understanding the research literature available through professional journals. Anyone planning to be a serious student of teaching must learn to consume this literature, and this handbook unit provides a good beginning. The second unit provides a guide to action research, a practice that has become increasingly common as teachers become inquirers into their own practice and as the professionalization of teaching continues its long evolution.

New in the Sixth Edition

As with previous editions, revisions were based on my own experience in teaching the text as well as on systematically gathered feedback from users across the country and from colleagues at my own university. Although the general goals, themes, and features of the previous editions have remained constant, many revisions have been made in response to user feedback, as well as to developments in the expanding knowledge base on teaching, significant societal changes now occurring, and new technologies that can enhance teaching.

Expanded Coverage and Thorough Update of All References

Much has been learned about teaching and learning since the first edition of *Learning to Teach*. I have strived particularly hard in both the fifth and sixth editions to include new concepts and research in the field and to update all references. This goal has resulted in *over 100 new references*, as well as new discussions on several topics including *alternative assessment, use of portfolios in student assessment, the way research is conceived and conducted, cognitive/constructivist views of teaching and learning, self-regulated learning, scaffolding, how the brain works, motivation,* and *portfolio development for teachers*. I have also revised content of several chapters to reflect the recent major revision of *Bloom's Taxonomy*.

Increased Emphasis on Diversity and Inclusion

Users of *Learning to Teach* were unanimous in their feedback that more was needed on the topics of diversity and inclusion, found in Chapter 4, "Multicultural Education" in the fifth edition. As a result, the chapter on multicultural education has been completely rewritten and refocused on "student learning in diverse classrooms." It contains extensive new content including sections on education for the gifted, multiple intelligences, gender equity, race, and culture. New sections have also been added to several chapters that focus on student learning and diversity. These sections describe how teachers can adapt or differentiate their instructional practices to the wide range of abilities, to diverse cultural backgrounds, and to students with special needs. An icon alerts readers to these important sections.

Expanded Emphasis on Technology

As more computers are found in classrooms, as more instructional materials become available on CD-ROMs, and as the Internet becomes more and more available to students, teachers must remain abreast of these exciting and important developments. It is particularly important for new teachers to be able to step into their first classroom equipped with the knowledge and skills to use computer and telecommunication technologies. It is beyond the scope of *Learning to Teach* to provide a comprehensive introduction to educational technology. However, this edition includes a feature in each chapter titled "Enhancing Teaching with Technology." This feature has been expanded from previous editions and highlights software and other computer technologies pertaining to the particular chapter topic. It also describes how teachers have used these technologies and directs readers to resources and websites for more information.

New Cases for Reflection and Portfolio

Although many aspects of teaching can be guided by the knowledge base, many other aspects have more than one point of view and require teacher problem solving and reflection. *Learning to Teach* includes several applied features that allow teacher candidates to reflect on important issues, compare their ideas and opinions to those of experienced teachers, and practice what they are learning. The "Reflecting On" feature provides a scenario or questions for the student to reflect on in preparation for the chapter's content. Each chapter concludes with a classroom case or teaching situation, and reactions to the situation from two classroom teachers, in the "Reflections from the Classroom" feature. Both features can be used as springboards for class discussion and have been designed so a reflective essay developed from either can become an exhibit in the candidate's professional portfolio. Finally, each of the teaching models described in Chapters 7 to 12 is accompanied by interactive "Case Exercises and Practice Tasks" on the *Interactive Student CD-ROM.* These interactive case exercises and practice tasks include background information about a real classroom (context, student descriptions, and video clips), aimed at helping teacher candidates apply what they are learning by giving them the opportunity to plan lessons and engage in a variety of practice exercises.

Expanded Interactive Resources

The sixth edition of *Learning to Teach* has become an interactive textbook, connecting readers to an array of technological and print resources aimed at making the process of learning to teach more interactive, more applied and, I hope, more enjoyable. The sixth edition is accompanied by three key student resources: *Interactive Student CD-ROM,* an *Online Learning Center* at **www.mhhe.com/arends6e,** and a *Guide to Field Experiences and Portfolio Development.* Each resource was designed to allow students to interact with, apply, and extend what they learn in *Learning to Teach.* For a full description of the contents of each of these resources, see xvii.

Portfolio Resources

Many teacher candidates today are required to have a professional portfolio. *Learning to Teach* makes available a variety of features and resources to assist students in portfolio development. To help students with the construction of portfolios, *Learning to Teach* provides an introduction to portfolios, and guides students as to how to use the features and resources of the text in the construction of their portfolios. Reader responses to *"Reflections from the Classroom"* can become portfolio exhibits. Mapping the INTASC principles to each chapter also serve as a source for portfolio development, as do many activities listed in the *Guide to Field Experiences and Portfolio Development.* Finally, a special *Learning to Teach* framework (portfolio template) has been constructed in McGraw-Hill's *Folio*Live—an electronic portfolio tool. For more information on portfolios and using the *Learning to Teach* resources to create student portfolios, see page xxii.

Expanded Accompanying Video

The *Teaching Methods in the Classroom* video that accompanies *Learning to Teach* has been revised and expanded. The video depicts the different models of instruction and helps them come alive for those learning to teach. New footage of Discussion and Direct Instruction has been added, and the video has been expanded to include new segments on Presentation, Assessment, and Classroom Management.

Pedagogical Features of Learning to Teach

To increase the accessibility and readability of *Learning to Teach,* previous pedagogical features have been maintained and some new ones added:

- **Graphic Organizer (new).** Each chapter begins with a visual outline of the chapter's topics to help students prepare for the content to follow.
- *INTASC Considering Standards* **(new).** This new feature highlights the INTASC principles most closely associated with the chapter's content.
- *Interactive and Applied Learning* **(new).** This feature at beginning of each chapter directs readers to the technology resources located on the Interactive Student CD-ROM. Additionally, the feature lists the topics of the *PowerWeb* articles and newsfeeds available for the chapter on the Online Learning Center at **www.mhhe. com/arends6e.**
- *Reflecting On. . . .* This chapter-opening feature provides a scenario and series of questions designed to prompt readers to reflect on their own lives and classroom experiences to prepare them for the content to follow. Readers can respond to the questions through the Online Learning Center.
- **Highlighted, Integrated Diversity Coverage (new).** Coverage of diversity-related topics has been integrated throughout the text, and is highlighted by a special icon.
- *Enhancing Teaching with Technology* **(expanded).** Each chapter includes an "Enhancing Teaching with Technology" box that focuses on technology related to the chapter's topic.
- *Research Summary.* The "Research Summary" included in each chapter provides a summary of important and relevant research.
- *Check, Extend, Explore* **(expanded).** Found in the previous edition as "Check for Understanding," this feature has been expanded to a *Check-Extend-Explore* feature. Located at the end of each major chapter section, this feature includes "Check" questions to help the reader review the content covered; "Extend" questions prompt reflection and also ask "poll questions" that the reader can respond to on the Online Learning Center; and "Explore" listings of related website topics located on the Online Learning Center.
- **Marginal Notes.** Throughout the chapters, marginal notes continue to highlight main ideas and define important concepts.
- *Reflections from the Classroom—***Case Study (expanded).** The final feature of the chapter text allows students the opportunity to apply what they just learned. A brief case study is following by reflections on the situation by an elementary teacher and a secondary teacher.
- *Chapter Review* **(new).** This feature, found at the end of each chapter, lists the student study guide materials available on the Online Learning Center and *Interactive Student CD-ROM.*
- **Summary.** A precise, point-by-point summary concludes each chapter.
- **Key Terms.** Key terms with page references are listed at the end of each chapter. Definitions are listed in the book-ending Glossary.

- *Portfolio and Field Experience Activities* **(new).** This new feature lists portfolio activities related to the chapter that are available in the *Guide to Field Experiences and Portfolio Development* that accompanies the text.
- *Books for the Professional.* This feature lists important professional books for further study. Annotations of the books are available on the Online Learning Center at **www.mhhe.com/arends6e** and on the Interactive Student CD-ROM.

Supplements

This edition of *Learning to Teach* is accompanied by an expanded number of supplemental resources and learning aids for instructors and students.

For the Instructor

- **Instructor's Resource CD-ROM** with the Instructor's Manual, Test Bank, and PowerPoint slides
- *Teaching Methods in the Classroom* original video with examples of teaching models, assessment, and classroom management; and engaging segments of teachers reflecting on their classrooms and teaching.
- **Instructor's Online Learning Center** at **www.mhhe.com/arends6e**
- *Folio*Live: *Folio*Live is an online portfolio tool students can use to create an electronic portfolio in three easy steps: (1) Use a template to create a homepage; (2) choose to create a custom framework or frameworks to structure your portfolio; and (3) add exhibits or artifacts to your portfolio by uploading existing files (from Word to PowerPoint to Video), linking to artifacts posted elsewhere on the Web, or by creating an artifact through *Folio*Live embedded forms. Go to **www.foliolive.com** for more information.

For the Student

Some aspects of teaching cannot be learned by merely studying theory-based or research-based knowledge. To truly understand what effective teaching is all about, teacher candidates must actively observe others teach, engage in dialogues about teaching, and reflect on both their own and others' teaching experiences. To help promote such active learning experiences, several student resources are available.

- *Interactive Student CD-ROM.* Free with new copies of the text, this CD-ROM contains extensive case study materials and practice exercises to extend mastery of content found in the text and/or to develop important exhibits for a portfolio. The *Interactive Student CD-ROM* also contains audio clips of teachers discussing chapter topics in relation to their own classrooms and teaching experiences and video clips of actual classrooms. Additionally, the CD-ROM contains a study guide with practice quizzes (with feedback).
- **Online Learning Center** at **www.mhhe.com/arends6e** The Online Learning Center contains a student study guide with practice quizzes (with feedback), links to the websites listed throughout the text, and a means for readers to respond to questions posed in the text. Access to *PowerWeb* articles and newsfeeds is available by using the passcode card included free with new copies of the text.

- *Guide to Field Experiences and Portfolio Development.* Organized by chapter, this guidebook—free with new copies of the text—includes over 100 pages of field experience activities and suggestions for portfolio development. These resources constitute a helpful field guide that assists teacher candidates in gathering and interpreting data, examining their own experiences, and developing a professional portfolio.
- *Folio***Live.** *Folio*Live is an online portfolio tool you can use to create an electronic portfolio in three easy steps: (1) Use a template to create a homepage; (2) choose to create a custom framework or frameworks to structure your portfolio; and (3) add the artifacts to build your portfolio by uploading existing files (from Word to PowerPoint to Video), linking to artifacts posted elsewhere on the Web, or creating an artifact through *Folio*Live embedded forms. Go to **www.foliolive.com** for more information.

Student and Instructor Feedback

As with previous editions, I encourage students to provide feedback about any and all aspects of the text. Please e-mail me at arends@CCSU.edu.

Acknowledgments

Because the field of teaching and learning is becoming so comprehensive and so complex, I have relied on colleagues to assist in writing about topics outside my own area of expertise. Outstanding contributions were made in previous editions by chapter authors Dr. Richard Jantz, Dr. Virginia Richardson, and Dr. Nancy Winitzky.

I also want to acknowledge and extend my thanks to the many students in my Principles of Teaching classes at the University of Maryland, particularly those in the Master's Certification Program, for their willingness to ask questions and provide reactions to every aspect of the book. Similarly, my co-teachers and colleagues over the years—Drs. Hilda Borko, Sharon Castle, Shelley Ingram, Lenore Cohen, Pat Christensen, Neil Davidson, Margaret Ferrara, Paulette Lemma, Ronald Moss, Susan Seider, Carole Shmurak, Nancy Hoffman, Karen Riem, Jim Henkelman, Frank Lyman, Joe McCaleb, Kathy Rockwood, Roger Zieger, and Linda Mauro—have not only been a source of support but have provided important input for early versions of the manuscript as well as for this revision.

My graduate assistant, Elizabeth Hayes, has made significant contributions to the fifth and sixth editions by working on the margin notes, tracking down permissions, identifying websites, and writing most of the study questions on the *Interactive Student CD-ROM*.

I want to extend a special thanks to Dr. Sharon Castle, a colleague from George Mason University, who was the primary developer of the case exercises and practice tasks on the *Interactive Student CD-ROM*. Dr. Castle was also responsible for much of the development and editing of the audio and video clips.

The "Reflections from the Classroom" and "Teachers on Teaching" features are brought to life by the following classroom teachers who share their experiences. Thank you.

Angela Adams
Faye Airey
Ian Call
Amy Callen

Diane Caruso
Lynn Ciotti
Ellen Covell
Sandra Frederick

Kendra Ganzer
Mike Girard
Dennis Holt
Jason O'Brien

Patricia Merkel
Jennifer Patterson
Addie Stein
Vickie Williams

Many reviewers also contributed useful reactions and critiques that have resulted in a much improved text. I would like to extend a special thanks to the reviewers who provided feedback during the revision of this new edition:

Donna D. Amstutz, University of Wyoming
Anita S. Baker, Baylor University
Sally R. Beisser, Drake University
Nona M. Burney, Roosevelt University
Barbara Davis, Southwest Texas State University
Sarah Edwards, University of Nebraska at Omaha
Laurie M. Hawke, Tarleton State University
Jan Guidry Lacina, Stephen F. Austin State University
Lola LeCounte, Bowie State University
Jon Margerum-Leys, Eastern Michigan University
Elizabeth Brock McBride, University of Memphis
Renee Myers, University of Pittsburgh
Karen Peterson, Governors State University
Judy Reinhartz, The University of Texas at Arlington
Lisa Anne Rizopoulos, Manhattan College
Molly Romano, University of Arizona
Amany Saleh, Arkansas State University
Richard T. Scarpaci, St. John's University
Gary Stiler, University of Southern Indiana
David J. Tarver, Angelo State University
Jian Wang, University of Nevada, Las Vegas
Saundra L. Wetig, University of Nebraska at Omaha
Carl B. Williams, Flagler College
Vickie Rey Williams, University of Maryland, Baltimore County
Raydine Pruitt Yarbrough, The University of Memphis

My current editor, Cara Harvey, has been outstanding throughout the revision process. She has been a constant source of encouragement, support, and great ideas. She also gently pushed me along as deadlines approached and we were pressed to get the book out.

Finally, thanks to the bookteam whose work has supported the book's development, production, and marketing: Jane Karpacz, Publisher; Lance Gerhart, Media Producer; Pamela Cooper, Senior Marketing Manager; Christine Walker, Project Manager; Sandra Hahn, New Book Production Manager; Sharon Spurlock, Designer; Emma Ghiselli, Art Editor; Brian Pecko; Photo Research Manager; and Dave Welsh, Senior Supplements Producer.

Your Portfolio

What Is a Portfolio?

Many pre-service and beginning teachers today are preparing what are known as "professional portfolios." A professional portfolio is a collection of ideas and exhibits that provide an authentic means for teachers to represent their views on teaching, their work as teachers, and their students' work.

Portfolios are not just something you create one time. Instead, they are useful for keeping a record of professional growth over a lifetime of learning to teach. Many teacher education programs require teacher candidates to build a portfolio early in their program so it can evolve and mature as the candidate grows and changes and so it can be used by teacher candidates to demonstrate their effectiveness. Some states require portfolios as part of the evaluation process for beginning teachers. A portfolio can also be useful for displaying work when interviewing for a teaching position.

What Goes Into a Portfolio?

In many cases, your instructor or program may present you with a list of requirements or suggested exhibits for your portfolio. Items most teacher candidates put into their portfolios include reflective essays showing how they think about teaching and learning, artifacts such as sample units of work or lesson plans, and samples of their students' work, particularly work that shows how the teacher has impacted student learning. Some teachers also include photos and videos showing classroom teaching and student interaction. Basically, the exhibits in your portfolio should represent you as a teacher—your beliefs, what you have learned and how you can teach.

How Should I Format My Portfolio?

There is no particular format to follow in a portfolio. However, the portfolio should represent you. You can create a paper portfolio or an electronic portfolio. Electronic portfolios can be presented as a website, on a CD-ROM, or through another form of electronic delivery.

What Portfolio Development Resources Does *Learning to Teach* Provide?

Learning to Teach is accompanied by a *Guide to Field Experiences and Portfolio Development*.[1] This manual includes several exercises or activities for each chapter that you can complete as exhibits for your portfolio. At the end of each chapter of *Learning to Teach*,

---

[1]The *Guide to Field Experiences and Portfolio Development* is packaged with new copies of the text. If you purchased a used text, you can purchase this guide by calling McGraw-Hill Customer Service at 1-800-338-3987.

you will find a feature called *Portfolio and Field Experience Activities.* This feature lists portfolio activities in the *Guide* related to the chapter. Additionally, forms for some of the guide's activities are available on the Online Learning Center.[2] A suggested portfolio table of contents (or framework) has been developed for *Learning to Teach* and can be accessed through the *Online Learning Center* (under Portfolio Resources) or through *Folio*Live.

How Do I Organize My Portfolio Around Standards?

Standards—both state and national—are playing an increasing role in the preparation of teachers. It may be useful to organize your portfolio around a set of standards to demonstrate that you have met each of the standards. A suggested INTASC portfolio table of contents (or framework) has been developed for *Learning to Teach* and can be accessed through the *Online Learning Center* (under Portfolio Resources) or through *Folio*Live.

What Is *Folio*Live and How Can I Use It to Create an Electronic Portfolio?

*Folio*Live is an electronic portfolio tool that allows you to create an electronic portfolio in three simple steps:

1. Use a template to create a homepage.
2. Choose to create a custom framework (portfolio organization) or use a *Folio*Live framework to structure your portfolio.
3. Add artifacts to build your portfolio by uploading existing files (from Microsoft Word to PowerPoint to video), linking to artifacts posted elsewhere on the Web, or creating an artifact through a *Folio*Live form.

The two *Learning to Teach* portfolio frameworks mentioned above have been added to *Folio*Live for easy portfolio development. Use the electronic forms for the *Learning to Teach* portfolio activities to create your exhibits, and then upload them into the frameworks. You may also create your own framework or use one developed by your teacher education program.

Go to **www.foliolive.com** to learn more about *Folio*Live and for ordering information.

[2]The portfolio forms are part of the Online Learning Center's premium content that are accessible using the passcode card packaged with new copies of the text. If you purchased a used text, you can purchase a passcode card by calling McGraw-Hill Customer Service at 1-800-338-3987.

Student Guide to Learning to Teach

Welcome to the sixth edition of *Learning to Teach.* Join us for a walk through the text's features.

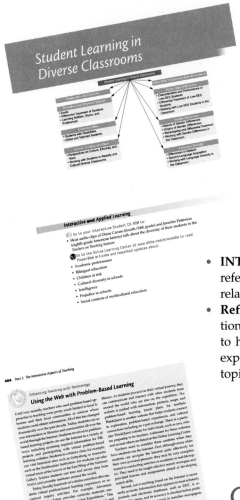

Chapter Opening Features

The chapter-opening features are designed to prepare you for the chapter ahead.

- The **Graphic Organizer** provides a visual listing of the chapter's main content.
- **Interactive and Applied Learning** lists the extension activities and resources available on the *Interactive Student CD-ROM,* and the *PowerWeb* articles and newsfeed topics for the chapter.

- **INTASC Considering Standards** references the INTASC principles related to the chapter's content.
- **Reflecting On. . .** presents questions or a short scenario designed to help you reflect on your own experiences related to chapter topics.

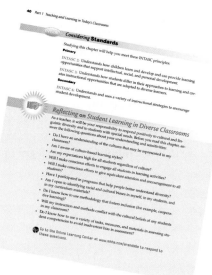

Chapter Features

The chapter features work to provide you with the ability to check your understanding of the main ideas of the chapter, take a closer look at important content, and apply what you are learning.

- The **Enhancing Teaching with Technology** box highlights how technology can be used to help teachers teach and students learn.
- **Marginal Notes** highlight key information.

- The **Research Summary** box provides a summary of a piece of important research related to the chapter.

Research Summary
What Do Teachers Do to Create Well-Managed Classrooms?

Kounin, J. S. (1970). *Discipline and group management in classrooms.* New York: Holt, Rinehart & Winston.

The most challenging aspect of teachers' work is developing and maintaining a well-managed classroom. This challenge has led many researchers to examine how effective teachers manage their classrooms. The interesting result that stems from all this research is that good classroom managers actually prevent problems from occurring through the way they plan for and pace their lessons and the means they use to nip misbehavior in the bud. The classic study on this topic was done by Jacob Kounin in the 1960s.

Problem and Approach: After several years of trying to understand discipline in classrooms, Jacob Kounin started to consider that perhaps the key was not so much the way teachers disciplined individual students but, instead, the way they managed the whole classroom group. So, he decided to study group management. This is an interesting and important study because Kounin was one of the first researchers to go directly into classrooms and observe exactly what was going on. His study was also one of the first to use a video camera as an observation tool.

Sample: The sample of Kounin's study reported here consisted of forty-nine teachers and their students in upper elementary classrooms.

Procedures: Kounin developed elaborate procedures for observing classrooms, including videotaping teacher and student interaction and transcript analysis. Many variables were measured in the complete study. Here, only a few of the more important variables are described.

Dependent Variables: For Kounin, managerial success

Contextual Variables: Kounin observed two types of learning activities: recitations and seatwork.

Independent Variables: Kounin conceptualized eight different variables for describing the group management behavior of teachers.

1. *"With-itness."* The ability to accurately spot deviant behavior, almost before it starts.
2. *"Overlappingness."* The ability to spot and deal with deviant behavior while going right on with the lesson.
3. *Smoothness.* Absence of behaviors that interrupt the flow of activities.
4. *Momentum.* Absence of behaviors that slow down lesson pacing.
5. *Group alerting.* Techniques used by teachers to keep noninvolved students attending and forewarned of forthcoming events.
6. *Accountability.* Techniques used by teachers to keep students accountable for their performance.
7. *Challenge arousal.* Techniques used by teachers to keep students involved and enthusiastic.
8. *Variety.* The degree to which various aspects of lessons differed.

Pointers for Reading Research: Up to this point in presenting statistics, researchers depended on mean scores and *t* tests or analysis of variance (*f* tests) to see if mean scores between two groups were significant. To understand Kounin's study, a new statistic—the *correlation coefficient*, described in the Resource Handbook section on understanding research—needs to be reviewed. Remember, correlation refers to the extent of a relationship that exists between pairs of measures. The coefficient can range from +1.00 through .00 to −1.00. The sign does not have the traditional mathe-

away opportunities for student initiative and self-direction. At the same time, if the teacher finds that students are unclear about the directions or that they cannot complete planned tasks, then direct intervention and assistance are required.

Check, Extend, Explore

Check
- What are the major planning tasks associated with cooperative learning lessons?
- How does planning for cooperative learning lessons differ from planning for direct instruction?
- What factors should teachers consider when they are choosing a particular cooperative learning approach? When choosing how to form learning groups?
- What are the six phases of a cooperative learning lesson? What kinds of teacher behaviors are associated with each phase?
- How does the teacher's role in cooperative learning differ from the teacher's role in direct instruction?

Extend
- Think about the various subjects you will be teaching. Which would lend themselves to cooperative learning lessons?
- Do you agree or disagree that it is a teacher's responsibility to teach social skills to students? Go to the "Extend Question Poll" on the Online Learning Center to respond.

Explore
- Go to the Online Learning Center at www.mhhe.com/arends6e for links to websites related to Planning for and Using Cooperative Learning.

Adapting Cooperative Learning Lessons for Diverse Learners

As with other approaches to teaching, teachers who use cooperative learning must find ways to adapt lessons to meet the needs of a diverse group of students. Many features of adapting for diversity that were described in earlier chapters hold true for cooperative learning. However, this model presents some unique opportunities and some particular challenges for teachers.

The most important opportunity inherent in cooperative learning is the chance for students with special needs and from diverse backgrounds to work together in cooperative groups and on special projects. Cooperative learning is an important way for students with disabilities to participate fully in the life of the classroom, just as it is for students from varying racial and ethnic backgrounds to develop better understanding of each other.

However, teachers must adapt cooperative learning lessons to meet the needs of all students. Some examples of appropriate adaptations include:

- Remember that before students can work effectively in cooperative learning groups, they must learn about each other and respect individual differences. Students in any class will possess varying amounts of understanding and respect, so instruction on these topics will need to vary.
- Make available more visual assists and explanations for students with disabilities who may help them make transitions from whole-group to small-group work.
- Be prepared to give assistance and supportive feedback to students who may be having difficulty but who are on the right track.
- Help regular students understand how their peers with disabilities differ and what they can expect as they work together in learning groups. Point out the strengths and competencies all students bring to group tasks.
- Help all students understand cultural norms of various ethnic and racial groups and how these might affect group interaction and cooperation.
- Help all students become familiar with aids used by students with particular disabilities, such as hearing aids, sign language, and the assistive technologies described in Chapter 2.

Managing the Learning Environment

Unlike models described in the previous chapters, cooperative learning is a student-directed approach to teaching, and a cooperative learning environment requires attention to a unique set of rather difficult management tasks. For example, describing to students how to accomplish a complex group project is much more difficult than assigning them problems at the end of a textbook chapter. It is more difficult to organize students into study teams and to get them to cooperate than it is to get them to line up for recess or to sit and listen to the teacher. Consider, for example, the problems faced by Ken* when he tried to use cooperative learning as a student teacher:

*Ken's story is a true one. It was told by Ken while he was doing his student teaching and was described by Weinstein and Migano (1993).

- **Check, Extend, Explore** concludes each major section in the chapter. It includes "check" questions that help you confirm you understood the main ideas of the section; "extend" questions that prompt you to reflect on the chapter, and sometimes include a polling question to respond to online; and an "explore" section that lists the Web links related to the section that you can link to from the Online Learning Center at **www.mhhe.com/arends6e.**

- Coverage of **Diversity** has been integrated throughout the chapters (in addition to being the primary focus in Chapter 2). An icon highlights this coverage.

Reflections from the Classroom
Teacher's Work

At the beginning of this chapter, you read about the busy work lives of two beginning teachers. Both are highly involved, not only with their students, but also with schoolwide activities.

Think about all aspects of a teacher's work and write a reflective essay on school leadership and collaboration. Consider the following questions: What are your views on the noninstructional aspects of a teacher's work? Are these aspects important? Or do they take valuable time that could be spent with students? What about the effective school research? Do you believe that synergy can be created and student achievement enhanced when teachers work together? Or do you believe that the best way to improve student learning is to allow maximum autonomy for teachers? When you begin your teaching career, which aspects of a teacher's work will you value the most? Which aspects will you find most troublesome? Do you look forward to working with colleagues and parents? Or do you think you will resent this type of work because it takes time away from your students? You may wish to illustrate your reflections with photographs of schools, videos, papers, and other artifacts that will demonstrate your understanding of the school as a place where teachers work and the features that make some schools more effective than others. Approach the situation from the perspective closest to the grade level you are preparing to teach. Finally, place this work in your professional portfolio and compare it with the following views of two experienced teachers.

Amy Callen
Lyndon Pilot School, 4th and 5th Grade Loop
Boston, MA

Whether you are a first-year teacher or have twenty years of experience, the day does not end when the last child steps on the school bus. There are papers to correct, bulletin boards to design, new units to research, parents to call, conferences to

classroom. Allow yourself time to get comfortable with who you are as a teacher, and begin to balance that with who you are outside of school. Do not forget that there is a life outside the school walls.

After a few years, your classroom responsibilities will seem automatic to you. You will know your curriculum inside and out, and you will be ready to share your knowledge and time with the community. This is the time to join the PTO, to

- **Reflections from the Classroom** ends each chapter with a brief case study and reactions to the scenario from two experienced classroom teachers.

Chapter-Ending Features

The chapter-ending features provide tools and resources for study, and expansion resources.

- The **Chapter Review** lists the chapter review and practice materials available on the *Online Learning Center* and *Interactive Student CD-ROM*.
- The **Summary** provides a detailed, point-by-point review of the chapter's main points.
- **Key Terms** lists the chapter's key terms along with page references.
- **Books for the Professional** provides a brief bibliography of books for further reading. Annotations of these titles are located on the *Online Learning Center* and *Interactive Student CD-ROM*.
- **Portfolio and Field Experience Activities** lists the activities in the *Guide to Field Experiences and Portfolio Development* related to the chapter.

Student Resources

The resources that accompany *Learning to Teach* include:

- The *Interactive Student CD-ROM** with **Case Exercises and Practice Tasks;** a **Student Study Guide** with quizzes; *Teachers on Teaching* **audio clips; video clips,** and resources referred to in the text. Each **Case Exercises and Practice Tasks** module includes background information about a real classroom (context, student descriptions and video clips), and then a series of activities and tasks (with supporting information and resources) that lead you through each step of preparing a lesson using the particular methodology.
- The Online Learning Center at **www.mhhe.com/arends6e** includes a **Student Study Guide with quizzes** (with immediate feedback), chapter review materials, and practice with key terms; *PowerWeb* **articles and newsfeeds*;** and **annotated Web links.**
- The *Guide to Field Experiences and Portfolio Development** includes activities and resources to guide you through field experiences and developing your portfolio.
- *Folio*Live**—an online portfolio tool you can use to easily create an electronic portfolio. Go to **www.folio-live.com** to learn more about this product or to purchase a one-year account.

*The Interactive Student CD-ROM, *Guide to Field Experiences and Portfolio Development*, and access to *PowerWeb* are free with new copies of the text. If you purchased a used copy of the text, and would like access to either, please call McGraw-Hill Customer Service at 1-800-338-3987.

**If your professor did not order *Folio*Live, you can purchase access by calling McGraw-Hill Customer Service at 1-800-338-3987 and requesting ISBN 0-07-283582-6, or by going to www.foliolive.com to purchase access online.

Part 1 *Teaching and Learning in Today's Classrooms*

Part 1 of *Learning to Teach* is about teachers and teaching; students and learning. The aim of the chapters in Part 1 is to provide you with background information about teaching and learning that will serve as a foundation for understanding later chapters that describe a variety of teaching models, strategies, and tactics.

Chapter 1, "The Scientific Basis for the Art of Teaching," provides a brief historical perspective on teaching from colonial times to the present and strives to show how expectations for teachers have been characterized by both constancy and change. As you will read, some aspects of teaching are not much different than they were one hundred years ago. Others have changed dramatically over the past two decades, particularly those aspects of the role needed to address the new and important teaching challenges of the twenty-first century.

Most important, Chapter 1 outlines the overall perspective about the purposes and conceptions of effective teaching that has influenced the plan and content of *Learning to Teach.* This perspective is one that argues that teaching is both an art and a science and that effective teachers base their practices in both traditions. On one hand, effective teachers use research on teaching and learning to select practices known to enhance students' learning. On the other hand, teaching has an artistic side based on the collective wisdom of experienced teachers. Experienced teachers know that there is no one best way to teach. But instead, effective teachers have repertoires of practices known to stimulate student motivation and to enhance student learning. Particular practices are selected depending upon the goals teachers are trying to achieve, the characteristics of particular learners, and community values and expectations.

Chapter 2, "Student Learning in Diverse Classrooms," tackles one of the most difficult challenges faced by teachers today, how to ensure that every child reaches his or her potential regardless of the abilities or backgrounds they bring with them to school. This chapter examines the challenges and opportunities diversity presents and describes how, unlike earlier times, today's classrooms are characterized by many different kinds of students and are governed by societal beliefs that the learning potential of all children must be realized: "no child can be left behind." Diversity at both ends of the spectrum of students labeled exceptional are described—those with learning disabilities and those who are gifted. Similarly, differences in race, ethnicity, culture, language, and gender are also described in some detail. The varying forms of diversity are not only described, the chapter provides rather extensive methods and guidelines for teaching and working with diverse groups of students in inclusive classrooms.

Chapter One

The Scientific Basis
for the Art of Teaching

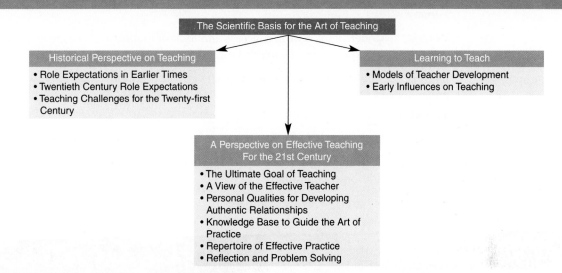

Interactive *and* Applied Learning

Go to your Interactive Student CD-ROM to:

- Hear audio clips of Amy Callen (fourth/fifth grade) and Ronald Moss (twelfth grade social studies) talk about what it means to be an effective teacher in the *Teachers on Teaching* feature
- Watch the video clip: Reflection on Teaching
- Take a Learning Styles Assessment
- Read the McGraw-Hill Study Skills Primer
- Read the McGraw-Hill Internet Primer

Go to the Online Learning Center at www.mhhe.com/arends6e to read *PowerWeb* articles and newsfeed updates about:

- The aims of education
- Cultural diversity in education
- Education
- Education standards
- Excellence and education
- The future of education
- Ethics and teaching
- Learning
- Teachers' attitudes
- Technology and education
- The World Wide Web

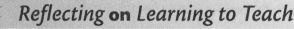

INTASC *Considering* **Standards**

Studying this chapter will help you meet four INTASC* principles:

Primary

INTASC 1: Understands central concepts and tools of inquiry and can create meaningful learning experiences of subjects taught.

INTASC 9: Values reflective practice and actively seeks opportunities to grow professionally.

Secondary

INTASC 4: Understands and uses a variety of instructional strategies.

INTASC 10: Understands the importance of fostering relationships with colleagues, parents, and the larger community.

*Interstate New Teacher Assessment and Support Consortium

Reflecting **on** *Learning to Teach*

If you are like many students, you begin this book and this course with a sense of excitement and challenge, perhaps also some concerns. You have decided you want to be a teacher, but you also know some of the challenges teachers face today, and you know you have a lot to learn if you are going to meet these challenges. Before you read this chapter, take a few minutes to think about teachers, teaching, and education today.

- Think about the best teachers you have had. Do you still know their names? Why were they good teachers? How did they influence your life?

- Think about teachers you didn't think were very good. Why didn't you consider them good teachers? Regardless of how good they were, did they have any influence on your life?

- Which aspects of teaching do you look forward to the most? Which aspects give you the greatest concern? What do you see as the major challenges facing teachers today?

- Think about education in general. Do you believe most schools are doing a good job? Or do you believe schools are in lots of trouble and need serious reform? Do you see yourself as a person who can help schools become better?

OLC Go to the Online Learning Center at www.mhhe.com/arends6e to respond to these questions.

Teaching offers a bright and rewarding career for those who can meet the intellectual and social challenges of the job. Despite the spate of reports over the past decade critical of schools and teachers, most citizens continue to support schools and express their faith in education. The task of teaching the young is simply too important and complex to be handled entirely by parents or through the informal structures of earlier eras. Modern society needs schools staffed with expert teachers to provide instruction and to care for children while parents work.

In our society, teachers are given professional status. As experts and professionals, they are expected to use **best practice** to help students learn essential skills and attitudes. It is no longer sufficient for teachers to be warm and loving toward children, nor is it sufficient for them to employ teaching practices based solely on intuition, personal preference, or conventional wisdom. Contemporary teachers are held accountable for using teaching practices that have been shown to be effective, just as members of other professions, such as medicine, law, and architecture, are held to acceptable standards of practice. This book is about how to learn and to use best practice—practice that has a **scientific basis.** It is aimed at helping beginning teachers master the knowledge base and the skills required of a professional.

> Teaching has a scientific basis—its practices are based on research and scientific evidence.

This book also explores another side of teaching: the **art of teaching.** Like most human endeavors, teaching has aspects that cannot be codified or guided by scientific knowledge alone but instead depend on a complex set of individual judgments based on personal experiences. Nathaniel Gage (1984) of Stanford University, one of the United States' foremost educational researchers, some years ago described the art of teaching as:

> an instrumental or practical art, not a fine art aimed at creating beauty for its own sake. As an instrumental art, teaching is something that departs from recipes, formulas, or algorithms. It requires improvisation, spontaneity, the handling of hosts of considerations of form, style, pace, rhythm, and appropriateness in ways so complex that even computers must, in principle, fall behind, just as they cannot achieve what a mother does with her five-year-old or what a lover says at any given moment to his or her beloved (p. 6).

Notice some of the words chosen by Gage to describe the art of teaching—*spontaneity, pace, rhythm.* These words describe aspects of teaching that research cannot measure very well but that are nonetheless important characteristics of best practice and are contained in the wisdom of experienced and expert teachers. This book strives to show the complexity of teaching—the dilemmas faced by teachers and the artistic choices that effective teachers make as they perform their daily work. It also presents an integrated view of teaching as a science and as an art, and emphasizes that what we know about teaching does not translate into easy prescriptions or simple recipes.

> Teaching is also an art based on teachers' experiences and the wisdom of practice.

This chapter begins with a brief historical sketch of teaching, because the basic patterns of teaching today are intertwined in the web of history and culture, which impact the processes of learning to teach. This introduction is followed by the perspective about effective teaching that has guided the design and writing of *Learning to Teach.* The final section of the chapter describes a portion of what is known about the processes of learning to teach. It tells how beginners can start the process of becoming effective teachers by learning to access the knowledge base on teaching, accumulating the wisdom of practice, and reflecting on their experiences.

> "The dream begins with a teacher who believes in you, who tugs and pushes and leads you onto the next plateau."
>
> Dan Rather

Historical Perspective on Teaching

Conceptions of teaching reflect the values and social philosophy of the larger society, and as these change, so too does society's view of its teachers. To understand the role of the teacher in today's society requires a brief historical review of some of the important changes that have taken place in teaching and schooling over the past three centuries.

Role Expectations in Earlier Times

The role of teacher, as we understand it today, did not exist in the colonial period of our national history. Initially, literate individuals, often young men studying for the ministry, were hired on a part-time basis to tutor or teach the children of the more wealthy families in a community. Even when schools started to emerge in the eighteenth century, the teachers selected by local communities did not have any special training, and they were mainly middle-class men who chose to teach while they prepared for a more lucrative line of work.

Common, or public, schools came into existence in the United States between 1825 and 1850. During this era and for most of the nineteenth century, the purposes of schools were few and a teacher's role rather simple, compared to today. Basic literacy and numeracy skills were the primary goals of nineteenth-century education, with the curriculum dominated by what later came to be called the three Rs: reading, writing, and arithmetic. Most young people were not required (or expected) to attend school, and those who did so remained for relatively brief periods of time. Other institutions in society—family, church, and work organizations—held the major responsibility for child rearing and helping youth make the transition from family to work.

Standards for teachers in the nineteenth century emphasized the conduct of their personal lives over their professional abilities.

Vast changes in the nineteenth century determined many elements of the educational system we have today.

Teachers were recruited mainly from their local communities. Professional training of teachers was not deemed important, nor was teaching necessarily considered a career. Teachers by this time were likely to be young women who had obtained a measure of literacy themselves and were willing to "keep" school until something else came along. Standards governing teaching practice were almost nonexistent, although rules and regulations governing teachers' personal lives and moral conduct could, in some communities, be quite strict. Take, for example, the set of promises, illustrated in Figure 1.1, that women teachers were required to sign in one community in North Carolina. This list may be more stringent than many others in use at the time, but it gives a clear indication of nineteenth-century concern for teachers' moral character and conduct and apparent lack of concern for teachers' pedagogical abilities.

Twentieth-Century Role Expectations

By the late nineteenth and early twentieth centuries, the purposes of education were expanding rapidly, and teachers' roles took on added dimensions. Comprehensive high schools as we know them today were created, most states passed compulsory attendance laws that required all students to be in school until age 16, and the goals of education moved beyond the narrow purposes of basic literacy. Vast economic changes during these years outmoded the apprentice system that had existed in the workplace, and much of the responsibility for helping youth to make the transition from family to work fell to the schools. Also, the arrival of immigrants from other countries, plus new migration patterns from rural areas into the cities, created large, diverse student populations with more

I promise to take a vital interest in all phases of Sunday-school work, donating of my time, service and money without stint for the benefit and uplift of the community.

I promise to abstain from dancing, immodest dressing, and any other conduct unbecoming a teacher and a lady.

I promise not to go out with any young man except as it may be necessary to stimulate Sunday-school work.

I promise not to fall in love, to become engaged or secretly married.

I promise to remain in the dormitory or on the school grounds when not actively engaged in school or church work elsewhere.

I promise not to encourage or tolerate the least familiarity on the part of any of my boy pupils.

I promise to sleep eight hours a night, eat carefully...

Figure 1.1 *Sample Nineteenth-Century Teacher Contract*
Source: Brenton (1970), p. 74

extensive needs than simple literacy instruction. Look, for example, at the seven goals for high school education issued by a committee appointed by the National Education Association in 1918, and notice how much these goals exceed the focus on the three Rs of earlier eras:

1. Health
2. Command of fundamental processes
3. Worthy home membership
4. Vocational preparation
5. Citizenship
6. Worthy use of leisure time
7. Ethical character*

Such broad and diverse goals made twentieth-century schools much more comprehensive institutions as well as places for addressing some of the societal reforms that characterized the twentieth century. Schools increasingly became instruments of opportunity, first for immigrants from Europe and later for African Americans, Hispanics, and other minority groups who had been denied equal access to education. Expanding their functions beyond academic learning, schools provided such services as health care, transportation, extended day care, and breakfasts and lunches. Schools also took on various counseling and mental health functions—duties that earlier belonged to the family or the church—to help ensure the psychological and emotional well-being of youth.

Obviously, expanded purposes for schooling had an impact on the role expectations for teachers. Most states and localities began setting standards for teachers that later became requirements for certification. Special schools were created to train teachers in the subject matters they were expected to teach and to ensure that they knew something about **pedagogy.** By the early twentieth century, teachers were expected to have two years of college preparation; by the middle of the century, most held bachelor's degrees. Teaching gradually came to be viewed as a career, and professional organizations for teachers, such as the National Educational Association and the American Federation of Teachers, took on growing importance, both for defining the profession and for influencing educational policy. Teaching practices of the time, however, were rarely supported by research, and teachers, although expected to teach well, were judged by vague global criteria, such as "knows subject matter," "acts in a professional manner," "has good rapport," and "dresses appropriately." However, progress was made during this period, particularly in curriculum development for all the major subject areas, such as reading, mathematics, social studies, and science. Also, major work was accomplished in helping to understand human development and potential as well as how learning occurs.

> The study of the art and science of teaching is called pedagogy.

Teaching Challenges for the Twenty-first Century

No crystal ball can let us look fully into the twenty-first century, which we have just begun. Certain trends, however, are likely to continue, and some aspects of education and teaching will remain the same, while others may change rather dramatically (Figure 1.2). On one hand, the tremendous changes occurring in the way information is stored and

---

*These goals were named the Seven Cardinal Principles. Some historians believe that they were symbolic statements of hope that reveal what schools in the new industrial society aspired to do rather than descriptions of reality.

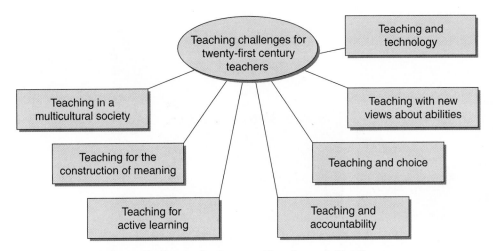

Figure 1.2 *Teaching Challenges for Twenty-First Century Teachers*

accessed with computers will certainly change many aspects of education. Today and in the future, the Internet has the potential of connecting students to a vast array of resources not previously available. Many believe that the Internet will become, if it hasn't already, the primary medium for information and will substantially redefine other forms of print and visual publications. This in turn will cause educators to redefine many lessons and assignments they give to students.

On the other hand, it is likely, at least in the immediate future, that society will continue to require young people to go to school. Education will remain committed to a variety of goals and some new ones may be added, but **academic learning** will remain the most important. It is not likely that the physical space called *school* will change drastically in the foreseeable future. Organizing and accounting for instruction will change, but if history is a guide, this change will come slowly. Schools will likely continue to be based in communities, and teachers will continue to provide instruction to groups of children in rectangular rooms.

Contemporary reform efforts show the potential of bringing new and radical perspectives about what academic learning means and how it can best be achieved. New perspectives also are emerging as to what constitutes *community* and its relationship to the common school. The nature of the student population and the expectations for teachers are additional factors that likely will change drastically in the decades ahead.

Teaching in a Multicultural Society. The United States is a multicultural society. Today, this situation is no longer a question of values or policy. It is a fact, a condition of our culture. The challenge for teachers in the twenty-first century is to transform schools and approaches to teaching that were created at a time when most of the students had a Western European heritage and spoke English to meet the needs of a much more diverse student population. Harold Hodgkinson (1983) wrote that "every society is constructed on a foundation of **demographic assumptions.** When these assumptions shift, as they do from time to time, the result is a major shock throughout the society" (p. 281). Schools in the United States have been experiencing such a demographic shock over the past thirty years, and it will continue to affect schools and teachers well into the twenty-first century. The most important demographic shift involves the increasing number of students who have ethnic or racial heritages that are

We live in a multicultural society; it is a condition of our culture.

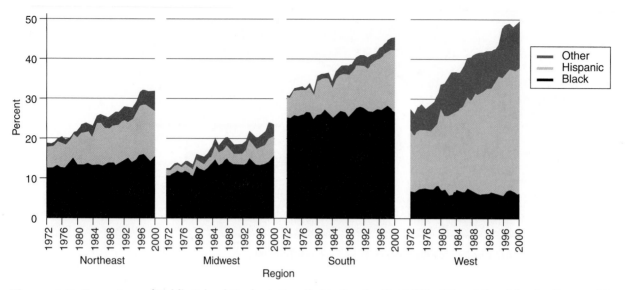

Figure 1.3 *Percentage of Public School Students Enrolled in Grades K–12 Who Were Minorities, by Geographic Region: 1972–2000*

Source: U.S. Department of Commerce, Bureau of Census. As cited in *Conditions of Education* (2002), p. 45

non-European, for whom English is a second language, and who live in poverty. As illustrated in Figure 1.3, the proportion of these minority students in schools has increased from less than one-fifth in the early 1970s to over one-third today. It is predicted that students from minority groups will comprise over 40 percent of the student population by the year 2010 (*Conditions of Education,* 2001, 2002). As shown in Figure 1.3, the percentage of minority students has reached over 50 percent in the western United States and approaches that proportion in the South.

Linguistic diversity constitutes one of the most rapidly growing shifts, as an increasing number of non-English-speaking children enter the public schools. The number of limited-English students has doubled nationwide over the past two decades (*Conditions of Education,* 2000, Mercado, 2001), with 3.2 million now enrolled in public schools. At the beginning of the twenty-first century, almost 20 percent of children had a first language other than English. The majority of these children speak Spanish as their first language, but many other languages are represented, including Arabic, Vietnamese, Russian, and Tagolog.

> Today, almost 20 percent of children in school have a first language other than English.

A trend throughout the history of schools has been to extend educational opportunities to more and more students. Compulsory attendance laws enacted early in the twentieth century opened the doors to poor white children; the now-famous Supreme Court decision, *Brown* v. *Board of Education of Topeka* (1954), extended educational opportunities to African American children. The Education for All Handicapped Children Act of 1975 (now called The Individual with Disabilities Education Act) brought to an end policies that prevented children with disabilities from getting an education and changed the enrollment patterns in schools. For example, in the mid 1970s, when the Disabilities Act was passed, only about 8 percent of children in schools were identified and served for their disability, whereas by the mid 1990s, this statistic rose to 13 percent (*Conditions of Education,* 1996, 2000). Similarly, more and more students with disabilities are being served in regular rather than special classes. As shown in Figure 1.4, 47 percent of disabled children spent 80 percent or more of their day in regular classrooms,

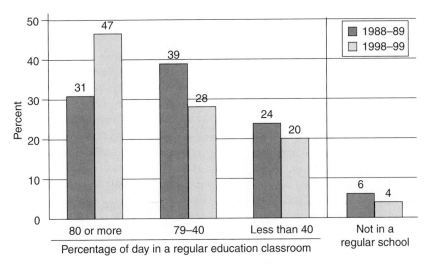

Figure 1.4 *Percentage Distribution of Students Ages 6–21 with Disabilities by Educational Environment between 1988–1989 and 1998–1999.*

Schools today must accommodate a wide variety of learning and cultural differences.

an increase from 31 percent ten years earlier. Note also that the percentage of children with disabilities educated in separate schools or facilities declined during the ten-year period.

Another demographic factor that affects schools and teachers is that many children who attend public schools today live in poverty. In fact, some observers argue that poverty has replaced race as the most urgent issue facing the nation and that poverty is at the core of most school failure. Figure 1.5 shows the percentage of children living

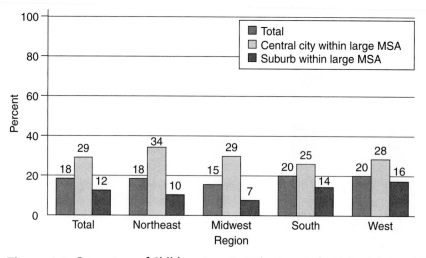

Figure 1.5 *Percentage of Children Ages 5–17 in Poverty by Urbanicity and Region, 1997*

Source: U. S. Department of Commerce, Bureau of Census. As cited in *Conditions of Education* (2002), p. 46

in poverty in 1997 (the latest available data by region). As of 2001, however, it was reported (*Conditions of Education,* 2002) that 15 percent of children ages 5–17 lived in households in which the family's annual income was below the poverty line. The problem of child poverty is most severe in the central cities, where the averages are about 29 percent, compared to less than 13 percent in the suburbs. Child poverty is most pronounced in the Northeast and least in the West and South. The only good news in this picture is that the percentage of children who lived in poverty decreased slightly between 1994 and 2001 (*Conditions of Education,* 2002, p. 46).

These demographic trends have significance for teaching and for those preparing to teach in at least three important ways.

First, for both social and economic reasons, many people in the larger society will remain committed to providing educational opportunities to all children. Society will also demand that minority and students with disabilities do well in school. Some of these students will come from homes of poverty; others will come from homes in which parents do not speak English; some will be emotionally or physically different from their classmates. These students will experience school differently than those whose parents were educated in our schools and who have prepared their children for them. Working with youth from diverse cultural backgrounds and with various special needs will necessitate that teachers have a repertoire of effective strategies and methods far beyond those required previously. Teachers will also have to be able to adapt curriculum and instruction to make them more suitable for those who may find school devastatingly difficult or irrelevant to their lives.

> Today's schools require teachers who have a repertoire of effective teaching strategies so the needs of all children can be met.

Second, it is likely that schools will continue to be scrutinized for racial and ethnic balance in their student and teacher populations. This means that during the next several decades, teachers can expect to experience complex social and organizational arrangements in which school enrollment boundaries will be changed, efforts will be made to diversify student populations through open enrollment and magnet school programs, and teachers themselves may be moved from school to school more often than in the past.

Finally, and perhaps most important, the voices of minority and immigrant communities and those who don't speak English will no longer be ignored. Parents of these children will no longer tolerate schools with inadequate materials and untrained teachers. They will not allow their children to be automatically grouped by ability and placed in noncollege-bound tracks. They will demand a curriculum and approaches to teaching that will ensure the same academic and social success for their children as for children in the mainstream. Listening to the voices of a multicultural community and providing effective learning experiences for all students will be the most difficult, but also the most interesting, challenge of your generation of teachers.

Teaching for the Construction of Meaning. The schools you attended were, for the most part, very similar to the schools attended by your parents and perhaps even your grandparents, because the schools that evolved in the late nineteenth century were built around a set of assumptions about the nature of knowledge and how knowledge is acquired. Also factored in was a corresponding set of beliefs about how best to ensure that all young citizens acquire this knowledge and, in turn, become productive adult citizens and workers.

Our contemporary educational system has its roots in the late nineteenth and early twentieth centuries and is based on a factory model of schooling and an **objectivist perspective** of knowledge and learning. Schools, like the factories of the time, were places where instruction or tasks could be standardized and teachers could pass on information to their students in the form of known "truths." Knowledge, from an objectivist perspective, was somewhat constant and unchanging. Teachers, from an objectivist perspective, were individuals who had acquired a "chunk" of important knowledge in particular disciplines. Their role was to transmit that knowledge, in the form of facts, concepts, and principles, to students. Since knowledge was known and fixed (relatively speaking), formal schooling governed by this perspective aimed to organize what was known into a set curriculum for all students to learn. In turn, school success was demonstrated through student mastery of the curriculum, as measured by standardized achievement tests. This perspective led to the statewide testing movement observed over the past two decades and in recent national legislation labeled "leave no child behind." Every state is required to test students and show that they have mastered specified knowledge and skills. Increasingly, those students who do not pass their state's mastery tests are held back from promotion to the next grade and required to attend summer school. School districts that do not meet minimum requirements for *all* students will be sanctioned and, in some instances, have their federal funds restricted.

> The traditional view of knowledge holds that there are "truths" and an objective reality that humans have access to and can learn through discovery.

An alternative to the objectivist perspective, and one that has gained respectability in educational circles over the past two decades, is known as **constructivism.** Rather than viewing knowledge as fully known, fixed, and transmittable, the **constructivist perspective** holds that knowledge is somewhat personal, and meaning is constructed by the learner through experience. Learning is a social and cultural activity in which learners construct meaning that is influenced by the interaction of prior knowledge and new learning events. Tobin (1992) wrote that from a constructivist perspective, "learning should focus . . . not only on the manner in which an individual attempts to make sense of phenomena, but also on the role of the social in the mediation of learning" (p. 3). The school's curriculum, from this perspective, is no longer considered a document of important information but instead a set of learning events and activities through which students and teachers negotiate meaning jointly.

> A constructivist perspective holds that learning is a social and cultural activity, that knowledge is somewhat personal, and that learners construct meaning through interaction with others.

Teaching for Active Learning. The system of schooling created in the nineteenth century rested on a perspective that learning was a passive activity. Rectangular rooms, fixed seating, and blackboards and lecterns at the front of classrooms were designed for the effective transmission of knowledge from teachers as their students sat quietly taking notes.

Learning from a constructivist perspective is not viewed as students passively receiving information from the teacher but instead as actively engaging in relevant experiences and having opportunities for dialogue so meaning can evolve and be constructed. Learning takes place not in passive classrooms but in communities characterized by high levels of participation and engagement. We will repeatedly come back to the idea that learning is the process of making sense out of experience in *Learning to Teach,* and you will come to see that teaching for active learning will require drastic changes in teacher behavior as contrasted to the teachers you have observed for most of your life.

Teaching with New Views about Abilities. Traditional theories and practices have held that individuals have specific mental abilities. At the turn of the nineteenth century, psychologists such as Alfred Binet in France and Lewis Terman at Stanford University developed tests aimed at measuring human intelligence and abilities. These tests were used widely in Europe to determine who could benefit from advanced schooling. In the United States, they were soon employed to help place students in instructional groups based on their abilities as well as to help determine who was fit to serve in the army. Even though IQ tests have fallen into disfavor over the past half century, tests of basic skills and those that measure more general knowledge, such as the Scholastic Aptitude Test (SAT), have replaced them and are used widely to make decisions about where students should be placed in school and where they can go to college. Over a century of work has left us with three unresolved questions: Is intelligence one or many things? Is intelligence inherited? And, can intelligence be accurately measured?

Many practicing educators today believe that IQ tests and tests of general knowledge have little to do with an individual's ability or capacity for learning but instead reflect one's social and cultural background. Children from families and communities that reflect the cultural mainstream, for instance, often do better on these tests than the children of parents who live in poverty or who just immigrated to the United States and whose primary language is not English.

Finally, some contemporary psychologists, such as Howard Gardner (1983, 1993) and Sternberg (1985, 1999), challenge the idea that there is general intelligence, as suggested by Spearman (1927). Instead, this research has shown that intelligence and ability are much more than the single dimension of language usage and logical thinking as measured by most intelligence and aptitude tests. We will come back to this issue in much more detail in Chapter 2.

Teaching and Choice. Once we move away from notions of fixed curriculum and fixed ways of knowing, we can also start questioning the efficacy of the standardized school. For example, do all students need to be exposed to the same ideas in particular subjects, at the same time and in the same manner? Should all students be required to go to the same type of school with the same curriculum and for the same lengths of time? An increasing number of policymakers and educators are saying no to these types of questions, and alternatives are being sought to the standard public school.

Alternatives to the standard school are found in many areas of the country today. Normally, these alternatives consist of magnet or special-focus schools, where curriculum is designed around the performing arts or science and technology. This type of alternative is financed by public funds, but students and their parents can choose the alternative over other, more traditional schools in the community.

A trend more pronounced in schools situated in the larger cities in the United States, where student populations are most diverse and where resources to support public education are scarcest, is privatization and charter schools. For instance, several large city school systems from Florida to California have contracted with private firms to run some of their schools, with the intent of making a profit. In the spring of 1992, the president of Yale University resigned to manage Whittle Industries' Edison Project. Today, Edison runs for-profit schools all over the country.

Another trend over the past decade related to choice has been the home schooling movement. Many reasons have prompted parents to take on the responsibility of educating their own children. Some belong to fundamental religious groups that fear that the secular nature of public schools will dilute their children's faith. Others want to keep their children separated from youth culture and the drugs and violence perceived to characterize the public schools in their communities. Still others want to express their right to have their children experience a "monocultural" rather than a multicultural community. An article in *Education Week* (Gewertz, 2001) estimated that almost one million children, or close to 2 percent of the school population, are now schooled at home.

The latest trend in school choice has been the charter-school movement. Charter schools are publicly funded schools conceived and started by parents, citizens, or teachers; in some ways, they operate like private schools in that they are independent of the local public school districts and exempt from many of the local and state regulations imposed on public schools. After individuals or groups obtain a charter from a school district or the state government, they are then given public monies to operate the school and are held accountable by the chartering agency for meeting prespecified standards. Currently, over twenty-five states had enacted charter-school laws, and over seventeen hundred charter schools had been started.

> Giving parents a choice in the schools their children attend challenges the traditional concept of the standardized public school.

School choice and privatization have their critics as well as their advocates. Advocates maintain that private, profit-driven schools will introduce an element of competition into the educational system and that schools, once freed from the bureaucratic structures and political processes that have come to characterize many large city schools, will provide superior education for students for the same or lower cost through innovative programming and more effective use of human resources. Many people are willing to allow these experiments to proceed because of beliefs that the public schools simply are not functioning as they should.

On the other hand, many educators and concerned citizens worry that private schools will not accept the more difficult-to-teach students, thus making the public schools more and more the home for the most helpless and hopeless young people in our society. Some research evidence seems to bear this out. Others are concerned about the values and moral system reflected, either formally or informally, in for-profit schools. Still others are afraid that the best teachers in the country will be drawn to for-profit schools, leaving the less capable to teach those students who need good teachers the most.

Teaching and Accountability. Until very recently, teachers had minimal preparation and few expectations as to performance. However, the twentieth-century standard's movement began to emphasize liberal arts preparation and some exposure to pedagogy. During the early part of the twenty-first century, this trend is accelerating

> Today's teachers are held accountable for their teaching practices and for what their students learn.

The best teachers show concern for their students and feel responsible for their learning.

rather dramatically. Beginning teachers will increasingly be required to demonstrate their knowledge of pedagogy and subject matter prior to certification, and they will be held **accountable** for using best practice throughout their careers. For instance, as of 2000, all but one state required some type of testing before issuing an initial certificate to teach. Most states are using the Praxis tests developed by the Educational Testing Service (ETS), but alternative and more performance-based tests are being considered in a number of states.

Current trends in teacher testing are likely to continue and to lead to extended training programs for teachers. Many of you using this book may be in extended programs now. Most extended programs are characterized by the teacher candidate obtaining a bachelor's degree with a subject matter major, followed by a master's degree in pedagogy.

Before getting a license to teach, you may be required to demonstrate through examination your knowledge and skill in teaching. Competency in academic subject matter will no longer be sufficient, particularly for teaching in classrooms that are culturally diverse and contain students with various special needs. Neither will liking children, in and of itself, be enough for tomorrow's teachers. Twenty-first-century teachers will be required to have a command of various knowledge bases (academic, pedagogical, social, and cultural) and to be reflective, problem-solving professionals. The following description of teachers appeared in *A Nation Prepared: Teachers for the Twenty-First Century,* sponsored by the Carnegie Forum on Education and the Economy (1986):

> Teachers should have a good grasp of the ways in which all kinds of physical and social systems work; a feeling for what data are and the uses to which they can be put; an ability to help students see patterns of meaning where others see only confusion; an ability to foster genuine creativity in students; and the ability to work with other people in work groups that decide for themselves how to get the job done. They must be able to learn all the time, as the knowledge required to do their work twists and turns with new challenges and the progress of science and technology. Teachers will not come to the school knowing all they have to know, but knowing how to figure out what they need to know, where to get it, and how to help others make meaning out of it.
>
> Teachers must think for themselves if they are to help others think for themselves, be able to act independently and collaborate with others, and render critical judgment. They must be people whose knowledge is wide ranging and whose understanding runs deep (p. 25).

Arthur Wise (1995), the president of the National Council for the Accreditation of Teacher Education (NCATE), made a similar statement about the knowledge and skills teachers will need to demonstrate in the future:

> Teachers should be able to use strategies for developing critical thinking and problem solving. They should be able to use formal and information evaluation strategies to ensure continuous student learning. They should be versed in educational technology, including use of the computer and other technologies for instruction and student evaluation. Prospective teachers should be skilled in classroom management and be able to collaborate effectively with parents and others in the community. They should know and use research-based principles of effective practice proven to be effective. In other words, teachers should be able to explain why they decide to use a certain strategy or teach a particular idea in a certain way. In short, prospective teachers should demonstrate competence, needed knowledge, and acceptable proficiency (p. 5).

In 1986, the Carnegie Task Force on Teaching as a Profession recommended establishing a career ladder for teachers and the creation of a National Board for Professional Teaching Standards (NBPTS). NBPTS was formed the following year and is currently governed by a sixty-three-member board of directors, mostly K–12 teachers but also includes administrators, curriculum specialists, state and local officials, union and business leaders, and college and university professors. The national board has designed procedures to assess the competence of experienced teachers, and it issues a national teaching certificate to those who meet its rigorous standards. National certification is voluntary, and the national certificate is not intended to replace the continuing or advanced certificate offered by the states. Currently, no specific extrinsic rewards, such as a higher salary, accompany national certification. However, some teacher groups argue that a reward system will be required if national certification is to become more widespread.

When fully realized, the national board will offer certificates in more than thirty fields, categorized by subject matter and developmental level of students. Certification will be available to teachers either as generalists or specialists in subject areas or special education.

Teaching and Technology. It is likely, as our society completes its transition into the informational age, that schools will change just as they did when we moved from an agrarian to an industrial society during the nineteenth century. Although we certainly don't know exactly how schools will look by the mid-twenty-first century, futurists have argued that formal schooling, as currently conceived and practiced, will be as out-of-date in the enterprise of learning as the horse and buggy are in the modern transportation system.

Throughout *Learning to Teach,* you will find box summaries on particular aspects of technology. These boxes are included to help you see how almost everything teachers do today is influenced by technology and how many aspects of teaching can be enhanced by technology. The Enhancing Teaching with Technology box in this chapter provides an overall perspective about technology. Boxes in later chapters will highlight particular technologies related to the chapter's content.

A Perspective on Effective Teaching for the Twenty-first Century

Central to the process of learning to teach are views about how children learn, the primary goals of teaching, and definitions of an effective teacher. The goals of teaching in a complex society are diverse, and trying to define an effective teacher has long occupied

Check, Extend, Explore

Check
- How have teacher roles evolved over the years, and what forces have contributed to these changes?
- What demographic shifts have led to changes in the student population, and how have these trends impacted schools and teachers?
- What are major teaching challenges of the twenty-first century?

Extend
- What revisions to traditional schooling do you foresee in the next ten years? twenty years?
- Do you agree or disagree that it is fair to hold teachers accountable for the learning of every student? Why? Go to "Extend Question Poll" on the Online Learning Center to respond.

Explore
- Go to the Online Learning Center at www.mhhe.com/arends6e for links to websites related to *Teaching in the 21st Century.*

the thoughts of many. For example, in the media we have traditional images of effective teachers, such as the kindly Miss Dove and the bumbling but caring Mr. Chips. More recently, the effectiveness of the rigid and authoritarian Joe Clark has been described, as has that of James Escalante of *Stand and Deliver* fame, who was able to get his low-achieving Latino students in Los Angeles to learn advanced algebra and accomplish extraordinary feats. Dave Holland of *Mr. Holland's Opus* is another example of how an ordinary person can be an extraordinary teacher by helping his students achieve their goals through music.

Within the educational community there has been a remarkable diversity in the definition of effective teaching. Some have argued that an effective teacher is one who can establish rapport with students and a nurturing, caring environment for personal development. Others have defined an effective teacher as a person who has a love for learning, a superior command of a particular academic subject, and an ability to transmit his or her subject effectively to students. Still others argue that an effective teacher is one who can activate student energy to work toward a more just and humane social order.

The content of a teacher education curriculum is itself a statement about what effective teachers need to know. Clinical experiences and tests for certification, such as Praxis I or Praxis II, make similar statements, as do the assessment systems used in schools to evaluate and mentor beginning teachers.

> Central to learning to be a teacher are views about how children learn and definitions of the effective teacher.

The purposes of teaching and conceptions of the effective teacher are also central to writing a book about learning to teach and influence its plan, its organization and unifying themes, and the choice of topics to include. The following sections describe the point of view of *Learning to Teach* on these matters.

The Ultimate Goal of Teaching

Citizens in a diverse and complex society such as ours expect their schools to accomplish many different goals. For example, here are a few that appear regularly in the popular press: teach basic academic skills, build student self-esteem, prepare students for college, promote global understanding, prepare students for work, transmit cultural heritage. The multiple purposes of education can become overwhelming unless teachers can focus their teaching goals. *Learning to Teach* takes the position that the ultimate purpose of teaching is *to assist students to become independent and self-regulated learners.* This purpose does not negate other purposes of education, but instead it serves as an overarching goal under which all other goals and teacher activities can be placed. This primary purpose stems from two underlying assumptions. One is the contemporary view that knowledge is not entirely fixed and transmittable but is something that all individuals, students and adults alike, actively construct through personal and social experiences. The second is the perspective that the most important thing that students should learn is *how to learn.*

> The ultimate purpose of teaching is to help students become independent and self-regulated learners.

Peanuts By Charles M. Schulz

PEANUTS reprinted by permission of United Feature Syndicate, Inc.

Enhancing Teaching with Technology

Perspective on Technology

Over the past several decades, methods of processing and using information have undergone a dramatic technological revolution. This revolution is not over and, indeed, may be only in its infant stages in the field of education. Providing a quality education to students in an information age requires teachers to stay abreast of technological developments and, in some cases, to "keep up" with their students. It is particularly important for new teachers to have the requisite technological skills so they can harness the power of computers and related technologies for effective teaching. They also need to be aware of possible negative side effects characteristic of any innovation.

It is beyond the scope of *Learning to Teach* to provide a comprehensive introduction to technology. However, the text does provide a feature in each chapter called "Enhancing Teaching with Technology." This feature is not aimed at describing everything you must know and be able to do with technology. Instead, it highlights particular technologies pertaining to the chapter's topic and explains how teachers can integrate these technologies into their teaching repertoire to enhance meaningful student learning. This feature for Chapter 1 provides an overall perspective about *teaching, learning,* and *technology.*

Currently, the technological revolution is a topic on many people's minds and also one for which there are quite divergent opinions about what the future holds. For example, over a decade ago, L. Perelman (1992) wrote a provocative book arguing that the *new technologies* would bring about the end to schools as we know them. He developed the thesis that technologies in the form of computers, information networks, and multimedia would give everyone in society access to learning, something not possible when today's schools were created. Instead of learning occurring within the "classroom box," learning in the future, according to Perelman, will permeate every form of social activity. Instead of learning being confined to children, it will be the province of everyone at every age. Perelman argued that it makes no sense to reform schools, and current reform efforts such as school choice or higher standards only serve as a diversion from the main things that need to happen, including:

- Complete privatization of education
- Replacement of school buildings with learning channels and information superhighways
- Abolition of all credentialing systems (including those for teachers), which he believed choked progress
- Creation of national technological schools that will exist without campuses or formal faculty

Perelman's wrote *School's Out* in 1992, and some of his predictions seem to have come true. Home schooling, distant learning, Web-based instruction, and e-learning have made schools as formal organizations somewhat less dominant. Today, a great deal of learning occurs informally through families, peer groups, work organizations, and computer networks.

On the other hand, schools and teachers have not been replaced, and most education still occurs in classrooms similar to those you, your parents, and your grandparents attended. Some individuals are critical of the new technologies and their potential negative impact on education. Ingrid Banks (1998), for instance, has argued, "reliance on technology threatens the very essence of teaching," which for her is face-to-face interaction between a caring teacher and his or her students. Barbara Means (2000) lamented the weaknesses of the Internet and the uneven quality and excessive advertising on the World Wide Web. Others, such as Tapscott (2000), who has coined the term "digital divide," worry about how we may be creating a society of information "haves" and one in which the "have nots" will not fare so well.

David Tyack and Larry Cuban (2000) recently predicted that we should not expect an educational "moonshot" through technology. Instead, they argue that computers and related technologies can be powerful teaching and learning tools when in the hands of teachers who know how to integrate them appropriately into their day-to-day interaction with their students.

Although the effects of technology on student learning remain unclear, most agree with Latham (1999) that "technology can and does matter" and that the evidence is starting to show positive relationships between technology use and student outcomes.

The perspective offered in *Learning to Teach* is similar to that held by Tyack and Cuban. Computers and telecommunication technologies will have a significant impact on teaching for your generation of teachers, partly because they have become so pervasive in other aspects of our lives, but also because they offer important advantages over other educational tools. For example, multimedia presentations are more interesting and effective than scratching a few words on the chalkboard. A CD-ROM can enrich students' understandings of things far away and in the distant past far better than can the printed words. At the same time, it is doubtful that schools will disappear, at least during the early years of your career. You will continue to meet students face-to-face and you will still use print materials. Although many of your teaching practices will be modified to take advantage of technology, many will remain the same. You and your students will remain at the center of the instructional process.

A View of the Effective Teacher

The concept of effective teaching that has guided the planning and writing of *Learning to Teach* does not include any of the stereotypes embodied in Mr. Chips, Joe Clark, or Miss Brooks; neither does it include an argument about whether academic competence is more important than nurturance or vice versa. Effective teaching requires at its baseline individuals who are academically able, who have command of the subjects they are required to teach, and who care about the well-being of children and youth. It also requires individuals who can produce results, mainly those of student academic achievement and social learning. These characteristics are prerequisites for teaching, but they are insufficient without four higher-level attributes:

1. Effective teachers have *personal qualities* that allow them to develop **authentic** human relationships with their students, parents, and colleagues and to create democratic, **socially just classrooms** for children and adolescents.
2. Effective teachers have positive dispositions toward knowledge. They have command of at least three, broad **knowledge bases** that deal with subject matter, human development and learning, and pedagogy. They use this knowledge to guide the science and art of their teaching practice.
3. Effective teachers command a **repertoire** of teaching practices known to stimulate student motivation, to enhance student achievement of basic skills, to develop higher-level thinking, and to produce self-regulated learners.
4. Effective teachers are personally disposed toward **reflection** and problem solving. They consider learning to teach a *lifelong process,* and they can diagnose situations and adapt and use their professional knowledge appropriately to enhance student learning and to improve schools.

These attributes of effective teachers are illustrated in Figure 1.6.

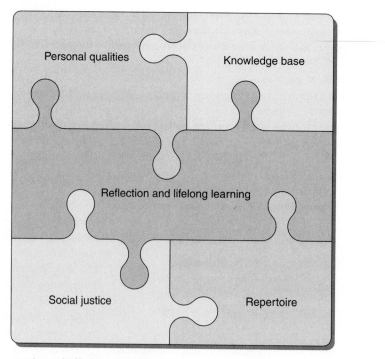

Figure 1.6 *A View of Effective Teachers*

In *Learning to Teach,* these attributes of an effective teacher are crucial themes and have been woven into each of the chapters in the book. The word *theme* is used here as it is used to describe a theme song in a Broadway musical—a song that recurs often throughout the production and becomes associated with the main ideas and characters in the play. Readers will find the themes summarized here referred to again and again throughout the book.

> Effective teaching requires careful and reflective thought about what a teacher is doing and the effects of his or her action on students' social and academic learning.

Personal Qualities for Developing Authentic Relationships

For many years, people believed that a teacher's personal qualities were the most important attributes for effective teaching. In general, teachers who were warm and loving were thought to be more effective than those who were perceived to be cold and aloof. Like most beliefs, this one had a measure of truth to it. It also left an incomplete picture, because effective teaching requires much more than being warm and loving toward children.

Our perspective encompasses a view that it is important for teachers to have caring dispositions toward children and youth and to believe in the abilities of all children to learn. As will be described in later chapters, all too often teachers do not hold high expectations for all children. Instead, they sometimes have perceptions that some students, mainly those from minority groups, are not capable of learning, and as a result, they restrict these students' opportunities to learn. It is critical that tomorrow's teachers break the cycle of failure built into our educational system by creating classroom learning communities that are democratic and socially just.

Our perspective encompasses the view that teachers must possess sufficient interpersonal and group skills to establish authentic relationships with their students and their colleagues. They must also have a "passion" for learning that can be translated into inspiration for their students to learn. Horace Mann said it a long time ago, "a teacher who is attempting to teach without inspiring the pupil with a desire to learn is hammering on cold iron." Similarly, it is from authentic relationships with colleagues and passion that schoolwide goals are developed and accomplished.

> Establishing authentic relationships with students is a prerequisite to everything else in teaching.

Knowledge Base to Guide the Art of Practice

Effective teachers have control over a knowledge base that guides what they do as teachers, both in and out of the classroom. In fact, professionals by definition have control over information (the knowledge base) that allows them to deal with certain matters more insightfully and more effectively than the average person. At the same time, no professionals, including doctors, engineers, and lawyers, have a complete knowledge base from which to find answers to every question or problem. Not every problem can be solved by the use of best practice—patients die, design ideas fail, and legal cases are lost. The same is true in teaching. Despite the use of best practice, some students do not learn and others drop out of school.

It is important for those learning to teach to understand what is meant by the *knowledge bases* for teaching and to understand the strengths and limitations of the scientific research that informs the current knowledge bases for teachers. It is also important to point out that, though the knowledge bases for teaching are still young and not yet complete, in contrast to the fragmentary and inconsistent knowledge bases of two or three decades ago, the situation today is vastly improved.

Three questions about the knowledge base for teaching are important to consider: (1) What does it mean to have a knowledge base about teaching, and what domains of knowledge are most relevant? (2) How do teachers access and use knowledge? (3) What are the limits of current knowledge on teaching and learning?

Nature and Domains of Knowledge. Scientific knowledge is essentially knowledge about relationships between variables. In the social sciences or applied fields (such as education), this means that knowledge exists about how one variable is related to another and, in some instances, how one set of variables under certain conditions affects others. In education, the variables that have been most studied, and those most relevant to learning to teach, are those associated with student learning and with how student learning is affected by teacher behavior. Lee Schulman (1987) has attempted to organize the important domains of knowledge for teachers into seven categories:

There are several domains of knowledge that inform teaching, some of which stem from research and others from the experiences of practicing teachers.

1. *Content knowledge,* or knowledge of the particular subjects to be taught such as mathematics, English, history.
2. *Pedagogical content knowledge;* that is, the special amalgam of content and pedagogy that is uniquely the province of teachers; their own special form of professional understanding.
3. *Knowledge of learners* and their characteristics.
4. *General pedagogical knowledge,* with special reference to those broad principles and strategies of classroom management and organization that appear to transcend subject matter.
5. *Knowledge of educational contexts,* ranging from the workings of the group or classroom, to the governance and financing of school districts, to the character of communities and cultures.
6. *Curriculum knowledge,* with particular grasp of the materials and programs that serve as "tools of the trade" for teachers.
7. *Knowledge of educational ends, purposes, and values* and their philosophical and historical grounds (pp. 2–3).

Learning to Teach explores primarily the knowledge bases associated with categories 3, 4, and 5. In particular, it synthesizes and describes the enormous body of knowledge that has been created in the past forty years and informs our understanding of how students learn; the factors that motivate learning; how leadership can be provided to manage complex instructional settings; and, specifically, the links that have been found between teacher expectations and behaviors and student achievement. At one time, what we knew about these topics and relationships was very limited. Currently, we can be confident of considerable knowledge in several areas, some of which have been validated experimentally and replicated under varying conditions.

Teacher Use of Knowledge. Educational philosopher Gary Fenstermacher (1986) has proposed that the major value of educational research for teachers is that it can lead to the improvement of their **practical arguments.** His argument for this position goes something like the following.

A practical argument is the reasoning, based on knowledge and beliefs, that is used by teachers as they make pedagogical decisions.

The knowledge and beliefs that teachers, as well as other professional practitioners, hold are important not only for their own sake but also because they prompt and guide action. Actions taken by practitioners are guided by a number of premises—beliefs held to be just and true and linked together in some logical format. Sometimes these premises and the underlying logic have been made explicit by the practitioner; many times, however, they are not consciously aware of their practical arguments. Fenstermacher (1986) provides the following example of a teacher's practical argument used to support the methods she used to teach reading:

1. It is extremely important for children to know how to read.
2. Children who do not know how to read are best begun with primers.
3. All nonreaders will proceed through the primers at the same rate (the importance of learning to read justifies this standardization).

4. The skills of reading are most likely to be mastered by choral reading of the primers, combined with random calling of individual students.
5. This is a group of nonreaders for whom I am the designated teacher.

   Action: (I am distributing primers and preparing the class to respond in unison to me.) (p. 46)

In this example, premise 1 is a statement of value, on which most people concur. Premise 5 is a statement of fact, presumed to be accurate. Premises 2, 3, and 4, however, are beliefs held by the teacher about how children learn and about pedagogy. These beliefs influence the actions of using primers and choral reading. In this particular instance, these beliefs are simply not supported by the research on reading instruction.

Fenstermacher pointed out that the results of research, and knowledge of "best" practice, if known, could lead this teacher to doubt her beliefs and subsequently rethink the premises undergirding her pedagogical behavior and instructional practices. Knowing about and using research becomes a process of understanding, doubting, and challenging the beliefs we hold about how children learn and about the best practices to employ to enhance this learning. It is in contrast to taking actions based on tradition, conventional wisdom, or folklore.

Research on teaching, then, can dispel old wives' tales about teaching, just as other research can dispel myths about aspects of the physical and social world outside education. For this reason, it is important for teachers to have a firm grasp of the knowledge base on teaching, including its application in various settings. Everyone, however, should be cautious and remember that teaching is a tremendously complex process that continually departs from fixed recipes and formulas. We should also remember the limits of educational research and current knowledge about teaching.

The Limits of Research. There are several reasons why research can inform classroom practice in some instances and not in others.

No Fast Formulas or Recipes. Even though principles and guidelines for best practice exist for today's teachers, beginning teachers should not jump to the conclusion that principles based on research will work all the time, for all students, or in all settings. That simply is not true. Instead, teaching and learning are very situational. What works with one group of students in one setting will not necessarily work with another group someplace else. Similarly, strategies and approaches used by expert, experienced teachers cannot necessarily be emulated by a novice teacher. Teachers must take explanations and principles and apply them within the capacity of their own abilities and skills and within the contextual confines of particular groups of students, classrooms, and communities.

> There are no easy prescriptions or simple recipes for teaching effectively.

Explanations Are Not Automatically Recommendations. Practicing teachers often ask researchers to make recommendations based on their research. Some examples of the types of questions they ask include: Should we use ability groupings in third-grade classrooms? What are the best concepts to teach in tenth-grade social studies? How can I motivate John, who comes to school tired every morning? The reply to such questions has to be that research alone cannot provide answers to such specific practical problems. For example, take the question about what to teach in tenth-grade social studies. Even though a researcher might provide empirical information about what other school districts teach in the tenth grade or about the abilities of most 15-year-olds to understand historical concepts, this would not tell a teacher what concepts to teach, given a particular group of students, the goals of a particular social studies curriculum or teacher, and the community values—all crucial factors to consider.

> Societal views and community values influence what and how teachers teach.

Explanations Are Not Inventions. A final limitation of research is that it focuses on existing practice. The descriptions and explanations about what teachers currently do are valuable but should not preclude the invention or use of new practices. The two examples that follow may help to highlight the importance of this point.

Many of the research-based practices for classroom management stem from studies in which researchers compared the classroom management procedures used by researcher-defined effective teachers with those used by less-effective teachers. From this research, patterns of effective classroom management practices have emerged. However, these results do not mean that better practices are not to be invented. It simply means that compared to the range of current practices, we can say that some classroom management procedures are better than others under certain conditions.

Along the same line, much of the research on effective teaching has been done in classrooms that represent the more traditional patterns of teaching—a single teacher working with whole groups of students for the purpose of achieving traditional learning objectives—student acquisition of basic information and skills. Although this research, like the classroom management research, can inform us about best practices within the confines of the traditional paradigm, it does not tell us very much about worthwhile innovations and new paradigms that may exist in the future.

Repertoire of Effective Practice

Effective teachers have a repertoire of best practices. *Repertoire* is a word used mainly by people in music and the theater to refer to the number of pieces (such as readings, operas, musical numbers) a person is prepared to perform. Obviously, more experienced and expert performers have larger, more diverse repertoires than novices do. This is also true for teachers.

This book emphasizes that effective teachers have diverse repertoires and are not restricted to a few pet practices. This is in contrast to some arguments from earlier eras intended to prove the superiority of one approach to another—for example, inductive versus deductive teaching, the lecture versus discussion method on the use of phonics to teach reading versus a whole-language approach. This debate is futile and misdirected. No single approach is consistently superior to any other in all situations. Instead, many teaching approaches are appropriate, and the selection of a particular model depends on a teacher's goals, the characteristics of a specific group of learners, and community values and expectations.

The teaching practices described in this book comprise a minimum number of models, strategies, and procedures that should be in a beginning teacher's repertoire. Some are large and complex models of teaching; others are rather simple procedures and techniques. The practices described are obviously not all that exist; effective teachers add to their repertoires throughout their careers.

The concept of repertoire carries with it the idea that a course of action is linked to various aspects of the job. To use the music analogy again, an accomplished musician may have one repertoire for performances of classical music, one for appearances in nightclubs or pop concerts, and perhaps another for family get-togethers. Just as this text was designed around a particular perspective of teaching, so too was it constructed around a conception of what teachers do and the repertoire required in three domains of their work.

Teachers, regardless of their grade levels, their subject areas, or the types of schools in which they teach, are asked to perform three important functions. They provide leadership to a group of students, they provide direct, face-to-face instruction to stu-

Figure 1.7 *Three Aspects of Teaching*

dents, and they work with colleagues, parents, and others to improve classrooms and schools as learning organizations. These three aspects of teachers' work are illustrated in Figure 1.7. Obviously, these aspects are not always discrete, nor does the teacher always perform one aspect of the job independently of the others. These labels, however, are convenient organizers for helping beginning teachers make sense out of the bewildering array of events associated with teaching in a complex school setting.

Leadership. In many ways, a contemporary teacher's roles are similar to those of leaders who work in other types of organizations. Leaders are expected to plan, to motivate others, to coordinate work so individuals can work interdependently, and to help formulate and assess important organizational goals.

The **leadership** view of teaching has sometimes been criticized. Critics argue that it grew out of the industrial age concept of the efficient manager and that this image makes people think about schools the same way they think about factories and, thus, overemphasizes the technical and skill side of teaching. The "teacher as leader" metaphor can also lead to excessive attention to control, orderliness, and efficiency at the expense of creativity and spontaneity.

Regardless of past misuse of the "teacher as leader" metaphor, there are indeed many parallels between the work performed by both teachers and leaders in other fields. *Learning to Teach* presents these leadership skills in a manner that does not violate the artistic side of teaching—that is, teacher creativity and spontaneity.

> Teachers provide leadership to their students through planning, motivation, and the facilitation of learning.

Instructional. When most people think about what teachers do, they think of the day-by-day **instruction** of students. The overall framework for thinking about this aspect of teaching comes mainly from three sources: (1) the "models of teaching" concept developed by Bruce Joyce and Marsha Weil (1972) and Joyce, Weil and Calhoun (2000), (2) the teaching strategies and procedures that have resulted from the research on teaching over the past forty years (Gage, 1963; Richardson, 2001; Travers, 1973; Wittrock, 1986), and (3) the wisdom of practice contained in the repertoire of experienced teachers.

Over the years, many different teaching approaches have been created. Some were developed by educational researchers investigating how children learn and how teaching behavior affects student learning. Others were developed by classroom teachers experimenting with their own teaching in order to solve specific classroom problems. Still

> The most important aspect of teachers' work is providing face-to-face instruction to students in classrooms.

Table 1.1 *Classification of Six Models of Teaching*

Traditional/Teacher-Centered	Constructivist/Student-Centered
Lecture/presentation	Cooperative learning
Direct instruction	Problem-based learning
Concept teaching	Classroom discussion

others were invented by psychologists, industrial trainers, and even philosophers such as Socrates.

The term *teaching model* is used to describe an overall approach to or plan for instruction. The attributes of teaching models are a coherent theoretical framework, an orientation toward what students should learn, and specific teaching procedures and structures.

Joyce and Weil (1972), and Joyce, Weil, and Calhoun (2000) labeled each of these approaches a **teaching model.** A model, as defined here, is more than a specific method or strategy. It is an overall plan, or pattern, for helping students to learn specific kinds of knowledge, attitudes, or skills. A teaching model, as you will learn later, has a theoretical basis or philosophy behind it and encompasses specific teaching steps designed to accomplish desired educational outcomes.

Each model differs in its basic rationale or philosophical base and in the goals the model has been created to achieve. Each model, however, shares many specific procedures and strategies, such as the need to motivate students, define expectations, or talk about things.

Teachers need many approaches to meet their goals with a diverse population of students. A single approach or method is no longer adequate. With sufficient choices, teachers can select the model that best achieves a particular objective, the model that best suits a particular class of students, or the models that can be used in tandem to promote student motivation, involvement, and achievement.

In *Models of Teaching* (2000), Joyce, Weil, and Calhoun identify and describe over twenty major models or approaches to teaching. But how many of these should there be in a beginning teacher's repertoire? Obviously, it is unrealistic to ask a beginner to master all the models—that is a lifelong process. To require command of only a single model is equally unrealistic. It seems fair and practical to ask beginning teachers to acquire a modest repertoire during the initial stages of their career. Therefore, we have selected six models that, if learned well, can meet the needs of most teachers. These are: presentation, direct instruction, concept teaching, cooperative learning, problem-based learning, and classroom discussion. In Table 1.1, you will find that the first three teaching models—presentation, direct instruction, and concept teaching—are based on more traditional perspectives about student learning and rest on teacher-centered principles of instruction. Cooperative learning, problem-based instruction, and discussion, on the other hand, stem from more constructivist perspectives of learning and learner-centered approaches to teaching.

In addition to working with students, teachers today are expected to work with other adults in the school setting for the purpose of schoolwide planning and coordination.

Organizational. The common view of teaching focuses mostly on classroom interactions between teachers and students, and as such it is insufficient for understanding the reality of teaching in contemporary schools. Teachers not only plan and deliver instruction to their students; they also serve as **organizational** members and leaders in a complex work environment.

Not only are schools places where children learn; they are also places where adults carry out a variety of educational roles—principal, teacher, resource specialist, aide,

Working with other teachers is an important aspect of a teacher's job.

and so forth. Schools are both similar to and different from other workplaces. Similarities include the ways coordination systems are designed to get the work of the school accomplished. Beginning teachers will find that adults who work in schools are pretty much like adults who work in any other organization. They strive to satisfy their own personal needs and motives in addition to achieving the mission of the school. At the same time, those of you who have worked in other organizations (perhaps during the summer or in a previous career) will find some unique aspects of the school workplace. These include norms that give teachers a great deal of autonomy in their work but isolate them from their colleagues; clients (students) who do not participate voluntarily in the organization; and because the school is highly visible politically, diverse and unclear goals that reflect the multiple values and beliefs of contemporary multicultural society.

Schools are also places, like other organizations, that need to be changed as things change in the larger society around them. Many people preparing to teach have strong idealistic drives to make education and schools better. This idealism, however, is not always supported with sound strategies for putting good ideas into practice, even though the knowledge base on educational change and school improvement has increased substantially over the past two decades. A knowledge base now exists to explain why many earlier education reform efforts failed, and this knowledge can be applied to school improvement ideas you may want to implement.

Building a repertoire of organizational skills is important for two main reasons. First, your ability to perform organizational roles and to provide leadership within the school as well as the classroom will greatly influence your career. It is through performing organizational roles well that beginning teachers become known to other teachers, to their principals, and to parents. For example, few colleagues observe a teacher's classroom while he or she is teaching. However, they have many opportunities to see the teacher speak up in faculty meetings, volunteer for important committee

Student learning not only depends on what teachers do in their classrooms; it is also strongly influenced by what teachers and parents in particular schools do in concert.

work, and interact with parents in open houses or meetings of the Parent-Teacher Association. Through these other opportunities, teachers become influential professionally with their colleagues and beyond the confines of their schools. Conversely, a beginning teacher's inability to perform organizational functions effectively is the most likely reason for dismissal. Many teachers who are terminated in their early years are dismissed not for instructional incompetence but for their inability to relate to others or to attend to their own personal growth and psychological well-being within a complex organizational setting.

A second reason for learning organizational skills is because researchers and educators are starting to understand that student learning is related not only to what a particular teacher does but also to what teachers within a school do in concert. To work toward schoolwide effectiveness requires such organizational skills as developing good relationships with colleagues and parents, engaging in cooperative planning, and agreeing on common goals and common means for achieving those goals. The effective teacher is one who has a repertoire for entering into schoolwide and communitywide dialogue about important educational issues, and one who can join and team with colleagues for the purpose of working together to enhance student learning.

Reflection and Problem Solving

Many of the problems faced by teachers are situational and characterized by their uniqueness. Unique and situational cases call for "an art of practice," something that cannot be learned very well from reading books. Instead, effective teachers learn to approach unique situations with a problem-solving orientation and learn the art of teaching through reflection on their own practice.

In addition, many of the problems facing teachers become problems of values and priorities that scientific knowledge can help explain but cannot help decide. An observation from Schön (1983) underscores the value-laden world of practicing teachers.

> Practitioners are frequently embroiled in conflicts of values, goals, purposes and interests. Teachers are faced with pressure for increased efficiency in the context of contracting budgets, demands that they rigorously "teach the basics," exhortation to encourage creativity, build citizenship, and help students to examine their values (p. 17).

If knowledge cannot provide a complete guide for effective practice, how do practitioners become skilled and competent in what they do? Again Schön (1983) provides valuable insights. He argues that there is an irreducible element in the art of professional practice and that gifted practitioners, whether they are engineers, scientists, managers, or teachers, display their artistry in their day-to-day practice. And, though we don't always know how to teach the art of practice, we do know that for some individuals it is learnable.

Learning to Teach strives to present its textual information in such a way as to alert you to the areas of teaching where our knowledge is fragmented and incomplete and to possible teaching situations in which you will be required to exhibit individual problem solving and reflection. Many of the learning aids found in the Field Experience and Portfolio Manual that accompanies this text, in the Interactive Student CD-ROM and in the Online Learning Center will assist you in become problem oriented and reflective about your teaching practice. Reflection and problem solving are complex dispositions and skills and are not easily learned. However, as you read previously, the art of professional practice is learnable, and it is experience, coupled with careful analysis and reflection, that produces this learning.

Check, Extend, Explore

Check
- What are the major characteristics of effective teachers?
- What specific personal qualities are typically exhibited by effective teachers?
- Why should a teacher's repertoire of strategies be as diverse and flexible as possible?
- What are the three major aspects of a teacher's job?

Extend
- At this stage in your development, do you think you will tend to use mainly teacher-centered or student-centered approaches? Go to "Extend Question Poll" on the Online Learning Center to respond.
- What views do you hold about the organizational aspects of a teacher's job? Do you value these? Why? Why not?

Explore
- Go to the Online Learning Center at www.mhhe.com/arends6e for links to websites related to *Effective Teaching*.

Learning to Teach

Some teachers, like fine wines, keep getting better with age. Others do not improve their skills even after years of practice and remain at about the same skill level they possessed the day they first walked into a classroom. Why is it that some teachers approach the act of teaching critically and reflectively; are innovative, open, and altruistic; are willing to take risks with themselves and their students; and are capable of critical judgment about their own work? Conversely, why do others exhibit exactly the opposite traits?

Becoming truly accomplished in almost any human endeavor takes a long time. Many professional athletes, for example, display raw talent at a very early age, but they do not reach their athletic prime until their late twenties and early thirties and then only after many years of dedicated learning and practice. Many great novelists write their best pieces in their later years only after producing several inferior and amateurish works. The biographies of talented musicians and artists often describe years of pain and dedication before the subjects reached artistic maturity. Becoming a truly accomplished teacher is no different. It takes purposeful actions fueled by the desire for excellence; it takes an attitude that learning to teach is a lifelong developmental process in which one gradually discovers one's own best style through reflection and critical inquiry.

> Becoming a truly accomplished teacher takes a long time, fueled by an attitude that learning to teach is a lifelong process.

This section describes some of the things we know about the process of learning to teach and emphasizes that learning to teach is a lifelong and developmental process, not one limited to the period of time between the first methods class and the date a teaching license is acquired. Few effective teachers are born that way. Rather, they become increasingly effective through attention to their own learning and development of their own particular attributes and skills.

Models of Teacher Development

As you will read later, contemporary views about how children learn also apply to how teachers learn. As applied to teaching, it means that individuals develop cognitively and affectively through stages. As we learn to teach, we process experiences through our existing cognitive structures. Obviously, individuals entering teaching have a rather complex cognitive structure about teaching because they have spent so many hours observing teachers during their years in school. As we gain new experiences, growth occurs and we progress to a more complex stage. Growth, however, is not automatic and occurs only when appropriate experiences provide a stimulus to a person's cognitive and emotional growth. When environmental conditions are not optimal—that is, too simple or too complex—then learning is retarded. In other words, as people learning to teach become more complex themselves, their environments must also become correspondingly more complex if they are to continue developing at an optimal rate. Although it is not possible to readily change many of the environments you will experience as you learn to teach, you can, nonetheless, try to seek out environments and experiences that will match your level of concern and development as a teacher.

What this means is that becoming a teacher, like becoming anything else, is a process in which development progresses rather systematically through stages with a chance of growth remaining static unless appropriate experiences occur. The following are specific developmental theories about how people learn to teach.

Stages of Development and Concern. The late Frances Fuller studied student teachers, beginning teachers, and more experienced teachers at the University of Texas in the late 1960s and early 1970s. During the 1980s, Sharon Feiman-Nemser (1983), then a researcher at Michigan State University, also identified several stages that **novice teachers** go through in the process of becoming **expert teachers.** Her stages are similar to those of Fuller, and the two are combined in the following list.

Novice teachers go through rather predictable stages in the process of becoming accomplished.

1. *Survival stage.* When people first begin thinking about teaching and when they have their first classroom encounters with children from in front of rather than behind the desk, they are most concerned about their own personal survival. They wonder and worry about their interpersonal adequacy and whether or not their students and their supervisors are going to like them. Also, they are very concerned about classroom control and worry about things getting out of hand. In fact, many beginning teachers in this initial stage have dreams about students getting out of control.

2. *Teaching situation stage.* At some point, however—and this varies for different individuals—beginning teachers start feeling more adequate and pass beyond the survival stage. Various aspects of controlling and interacting with students become somewhat routinized. At this stage, teachers begin shifting their attention and energy to the teaching situation itself. They start dealing with the time pressures of teaching and with some of the stark realities of the classroom, such as too many students, inappropriate instructional materials, and perhaps their own meager repertoire of teaching strategies.

3. *Pupil concern and mastery stage.* Eventually, individuals mature as teachers and find ways of coping or dealing with survival and situational concerns. During this stage, teachers master the fundamentals of teaching and classroom management. These become effective and routine. It is only then that teachers reach for higher-level issues and start asking questions about the social and emotional needs of students, being fair, and the match between the teaching strategies and materials and pupil needs. Most importantly, it is during this stage that teachers have concern and assume full responsibility for *student learning.*

Over the past few years there has been a gradual shift away from the stage theory described above and replaced with a more flexible view about how teacher development occurs. (Griffiths and Tan, 1992, Richardson and Placier, 2001). This more flexible perspective posits that developmental process for teachers are evolutional and gradual and not as precise as suggested in the Fuller and Feiman-Nemser model. However, the Fuller and Feiman-Nemser models are useful for thinking about the process of learning to teach. Their principles help to put present concerns in perspective and to prepare beginners to move on to the next and higher level of concern. For example, a beginning teacher who is overly worried about personal concerns might seek out experiences and training that build confidence and independence. If class control takes too much mental and emotional energy, a beginning teacher can find ways to modify that situation. A questionnaire to measure your concerns at this point in your career is included in the *Guide to Field Experiences and Portfolio Development* and on the Online Learning Center.

Implications of Developmental Models for Learning to Teach. As beginning teachers go through the process of learning to teach, the developmental models have numerous implications. First, these models suggest that learning to teach is a developmental process in which each individual moves through stages that are simple and concrete at first and later more complex and abstract. Developmental models thus provide a framework for viewing your own growth.

Second, you can use the models to diagnose your own level of concern and development. This knowledge can help teachers to accept the anxiety and concerns of the beginning years and, most important, to plan learning experiences that will facilitate growth to more mature and complex levels of functioning.

Early Influences on Teaching

It appears that some aspects of learning to teach are influenced by the experiences that people have with important adult figures, particularly teachers, as they grow up and go through school. In the early 1970s, Dan Lortie, a sociologist at the University of Chicago, spent several years studying why people become teachers, what kind of a profession teaching is, and what experiences affect learning to teach. As part of his study, he interviewed a rather large sample of teachers and asked them what experiences most influenced their teaching. Many experienced teachers told Lortie that early authority figures, such as parents and teachers, greatly influenced their concepts of teaching and their subsequent decision to enter the field. Lortie's study and his results are summarized in the "Research Summary" on page 32.

This is the first example of the research summaries you will find in each chapter of *Learning to Teach.* These summaries are included to help you get a feel for some of the research that has been carried out in education and to help you develop an appreciation for the knowledge base on teaching. The boxed research summaries, such as the Lortie study, were chosen either because they are considered classics in particular fields or because they illustrate the variety and richness of method found in educational research.

The format used to present Lortie's research is one that will be followed throughout the book when research reports are summarized. The problem the researcher addressed is presented first, followed by brief descriptions about who was studied and the types of procedures used. When needed, pointers are provided to help you read the research. Each research summary concludes with a description of important findings and statements about the implications of the research for practice.

This format is used because it is important that you become knowledgeable about the research base on teaching and learning, and it is equally important that you learn how to read, critique, and use research. At the end of this book is a special section called "Reading and Using Research." This section provides further insight into the nature of research on teaching and a practice exercise for reading research; you may want to read it before going on.

A great deal is known about the process of learning to teach that goes beyond the scope of this chapter. However, by way of summary, those learning to teach should enter the process valuing the experiences they have had and recognize that they already know a lot about teaching. At the same time, they should also accept that they have much to learn. Effective teachers must learn to execute complex and particularly effective procedures and methods. They must also challenge their existing perceptions and learn how to think like experienced teachers. This is not always easy because expert and novice teachers think differently. Mastering the behaviors and thought processes of teaching are among the most important challenges of learning to teach and, when accomplished, can bring the most cherished rewards.

Our parents and teachers have had important influences on our desire to teach and on our perspectives about what constitutes effective teaching.

Research Summary

How Do Early Experiences Influence Our View of Teaching?

Lortie, D. (1975). School-teacher: A sociological study. Chicago: University of Chicago Press.

What do we know about the influences on our decision to become teachers, and how do all those experiences we have as students influence our view of teaching? These were among several questions asked by Daniel Lortie in what has become a classic study about teachers and teaching.

Problem and Approach: Lortie was interested in a variety of issues about teaching as an occupation, particularly the organization of the teacher's work, the sentiments teachers have about their work, and the "ethos" of the teacher's occupation as contrasted to other occupations.

Sample and Setting: Lortie collected information from a number of sources. The focus here is on the data he collected through extensive interviews with ninety-four teachers from five towns in the Boston metropolitan area and from a national survey conducted by the National Education Association in the late 1960s.

Procedures: By Lortie's own account, his methods included "historical review, national and local surveys, findings from observational studies by other researchers, and content analysis of intensive interviews" (p. ix). His sample from the five towns around Boston included selecting school systems that were broadly representative of American education; he then randomly selected teachers from within the five systems. He interviewed the teachers about the attractions of teaching and various other features of their careers, using techniques he developed in earlier studies on the legal profession.

Pointers for Reading Research: The researchers who carried out many of the studies used in this book reported their results in numeric form and summarized them in data tables. Lortie's data are presented not in tabular format but, instead, as direct quotes from the people he interviewed. Information quoted directly from interviews is quite easy to read and to understand. However, readers of this type of research information always need to ask themselves questions about the data, such as: Did the researcher conduct the interviews in such a way that respondents provided honest and accurate information? From many possibilities, did the researcher select quotes that were representative of what the total sample reported, or did he or she select quotes to represent a particular point of view or bias? Are the conclusions reached by researchers using interview data consistent with the information the data contain?

Results: Lortie's study is large and complex and has many insights into teaching and teachers. Here are some of his findings about why people go into teaching and the influence of early experiences on their teaching.

Interview Data: One teacher interviewed shows the influence of early adult figures on her decision to teach:

> My mother was a teacher, her sisters were teachers—it's a family occupation. I always wanted to go into teaching. I can't remember when I didn't want to. . . . I remember as a little girl sometimes seeing teachers have a hard time. I thought, well, I will be careful because some day I'll be on the other side of the desk (p. 61).

Lortie also found that teaching is one of the few professions in which the practitioner has been in the client (student) role for an extended period (several hours each

Check, Extend, Explore

Check
- What are the stages that teachers typically go through during the process of becoming an effective teacher?
- What forces seem to influence many teachers when they initially make the decision to enter the profession? What are the advantages and disadvantages of this situation?

Extend
- Think about your own experiences. What individuals or forces influenced you to enter teaching? How did they influence your views about teaching?
- Have you ever had teachers who did not continue to develop and grow? Why do you think this happens to some teachers? What safeguards can you take to make sure it doesn't happen to you?

Explore
- Go to the Online Learning Center at www.mhhe.com/arends6e for links to websites related to *Learning to Be a Teacher.*

day for sixteen years) before switching to the professional role. It comes as no surprise that teachers told Lortie that their own teaching was greatly influenced by the teaching they had received as students. The following excerpts from Lortie's interviews illustrate this influence.

> The teacher I had in sixth grade was good, interesting. There are a few things I used this year that I remember having done in her room (p. 63).

> There was one particular teacher in my eighth and ninth grades. She was very hard, very strict, and used to say, "I know some of you don't like me since I'm so strict; but when you get out of school and think back, a lot of you will probably think of me as being the best teacher." She really was. She probably taught me how important classroom discipline was (p. 64).

> My second-grade teacher was kind. She knew it was a terrific change for me to come all the way from Iowa and she'd take the time to talk to me, to take away some of the fright. I never forgot that and when new youngsters come into my room I always try to team them up with someone. I have a special word for them (p. 64).

> I had a college professor. . . . This is the man who had more to do with my techniques than any other person (p. 64).

> I had her in United States history and she whetted my appetite for history. . . . I may be one of her products. I think I am (p. 64).

Discussion and Implications

It is obvious that prior experiences with their own teachers have affected and will continue to influence the ways teachers think and act about teaching. In some ways this is positive, since it provides beginners with many models over the years. However, relying too completely on these early experiences may make teachers rather conservative in trying new approaches. Many of the standard practices used by former teachers may not represent best practices, given current knowledge about teaching and learning. Also, if beginning teachers rely too heavily on their prior experiences, that may prevent them from being sufficiently reflective and analytical toward their work.

Sylvia Ashton-Warner was a person who cared deeply about her teaching and about the children she taught.

Reflections **from the** *Classroom*

You have just completed your first year of teaching, and the professor at the local university where you graduated last year has asked you to provide your perspective on *effective teaching* to her teaching strategies class. You feel honored that the professor has asked you to do this. At the same time, you know that coming up with a definitive answer about what constitutes effective teaching is no easy task. So, you start asking yourself: What is the perspective that guided my actions while I was student teaching? During my first year of teaching? How were my teaching practices tied to my views about student learning? How were my teaching practices influenced by research? How did my own experiences or those of my cooperating teachers or teacher colleagues influence my practice? How has my practice changed over the past year?

Reflect on answers to these questions as you prepare your presentation and compare them to the following views expressed by experienced teachers. Approach this situation from the perspective closest to the grade level or subject area you are preparing to teach. You may want to turn your presentation into a reflective essay and an exhibit on effective teaching for your portfolio.

Diane Caruso

Saltonstall School, 4th and 5th Grade
Salem, MA

Effective teaching and best practices are phrases that have been essential components of my planning and teaching for years. Reflection of my own teaching, that of my colleagues, and of research is a constant, necessary element of my continuous growth as a teacher. When mentoring new teachers, I always stress that, although there are certain qualities and skills that will always be part of effective teaching, in order to encourage the success and welfare of our students, our own fulfillment, and to counteract the many frustrations teachers face on a daily basis, we must remain lifelong learners.

As I reflect upon the philosophy that has guided my teaching over the past 25 years, it includes certain qualities and skills such as dedication, sensitivity, inquiry, literacy, logic, and many more. The basic belief that all children can learn, and that they can experience success and a sense of self-worth while enjoying the process that leads to those goals remains consistent. I believe good teachers make sincere efforts to communicate with students, parents, colleagues, and administrators, as well as with their network of educational professionals. They also strive to provide their students with the most rewarding educational experience possible.

In summary, I would advise the members of a teaching strategies class that effective teaching involves:

1. Holding the belief that every child can learn and experience success;

2. Remaining open to new ideas and techniques through professional development opportunities and lifelong learning; and

3. Communicating effectively at all levels. Perhaps, most of all, teachers must be willing to learn from their students. Learn who they are, what they're about (personally and culturally), what their needs are, and what excites their thirst for knowledge.

Theresa Carter

10th Grade

If I were asked to provide students in a methods class my perspective on effective teaching, I would emphasize two important things: knowledge and passion for my subject, and ability to relate to students. Mainly, I hold a constructivist perspective about how students learn. This means that it is not enough merely to present information to students, have them take notes, and then give it back to me on a test. I want students to build and develop their own knowledge and meaning. This requires that I know my subject well enough so I understand the nuances of the field and so I can create lessons that connect new subject matter to what my students already know. Also, I need to be able to explain things in response to student questions and in ways they understand.

I think effective teachers must also show students that they really care about them as individuals. It is the kind of caring where teachers hold high expectations for the student's work, where they take the time to provide each student with in-depth and constructive feedback, and where they pay attention to what students are doing in aspects of their lives that extend beyond the classroom.

Chapter Review

Go back to the "Interactive and Applied Learning" feature at the beginning of the chapter for a listing of interactive and applied activities. Go to the Online Learning Center at **www.mhhe.com/arends6e** or your Interactive Student CD-ROM to take practice quizzes over the content of this chapter and receive immediate feedback. You can also review chapter content and main ideas, practice with key terms, and find annotated Web links on topics associated with this chapter.

Summary

The Scientific Basis for the Art of Teaching

- Teaching has a scientific basis that can guide its practice; it also has an artistic side.

Historical Perspective on Teaching

- The role of the teacher is a complex one that has been shaped by historical and contemporary forces. Expectations for teachers have changed. In the eighteenth and nineteenth centuries, the primary concern was the teacher's moral character, whereas today we are more concerned about the teacher's pedagogical abilities.
- Today, almost one-third of our students come from non-Western European backgrounds, many speak English as their second language, and a large proportion of them are poor. These three factors in combination are reshaping the teacher's role. Teachers are expected to work in complex multicultural educational settings and to provide good educational experiences for all children.
- Teachers today are expected to help students construct their own knowledge and to be actively involved in their own learning.
- Increasingly, teachers are expected to have advanced preparation and to demonstrate their knowledge of both subject matter and pedagogy.

A Perspective on Effective Teaching for the Twenty-first Century

- Effective teachers possess personal qualities for developing authentic relationships with their students, understand the knowledge base on teaching and learning, can execute a repertoire of best practices, have attitudes and skills necessary for reflection and problem solving, and consider learning to teach a lifelong process.

- The scientific basis of teaching is learned mainly through studying research and the wisdom of practice accumulated by the profession. From scientific knowledge certain teaching principles and propositions have been derived that can inform best teaching practices.
- Principles based on research, however, cannot be translated directly into fixed recipes and formulas that will work all the time. This is true because teaching is situational, and the characteristics of particular students, classrooms, schools, and communities affect what works and what doesn't.
- Repertoire refers to the number of strategies and processes teachers are prepared to use. Effective teachers develop a repertoire of methods and skills to successfully carry out various aspects of their work.
- A teacher's work can be conceptualized around three main functions: leadership, instructional, and organizational.
- The leadership aspects of teaching refer to the leadership roles teachers are expected to play in their classrooms, such as providing motivation, planning, and allocating scarce resources.
- The instructional aspects of teaching refer to methods and processes teachers employ as they provide day-by-day instruction to students.
- The organizational aspects of teaching refer to teachers' work in the school community, including work with colleagues, parents, and school leadership personnel.
- Effective practice includes abilities to approach classroom situations in reflective and problem-solving ways.

Learning to Teach

- Learning to teach is developmental and a lifelong process. Teachers go through predictable stages. At first they are concerned about survival, later about their teaching situation, and finally about the social and academic needs of their pupils.

- Parents and teachers often influence a person's decision to enter teaching and affect a teacher's vision of teaching. Memories of favorite teachers, however, may not be the best models for developing one's own teaching style, because these teachers may not have been as effective as they seemed.

- Learning to teach is a complex process, and information that is useful to experienced teachers may not have the same value for beginners.

Key Terms

academic learning 9	demographic assumptions 9	novice teachers 30	reflection 20
accountable 16	expert teachers 30	objectivist perspective 13	repertoire 20
art of teaching 5	instructional aspects of teaching 25	organizational aspects of teaching 26	scientific basis of teaching 5
authentic relationship 20	knowledge bases 20	pedagogy 8	socially just classrooms 20
best practice 5	leadership aspects of teaching 25	practical arguments 21	teaching model 26
constructivism 13			
constructivist perspective 13			

Portfolio and Field Experience Activities

This feature has been designed to help you learn from your field experiences and to assist you in the preparation of artifacts for your professional portfolio on topics and standards associated with Chapter 1.

1. Complete the "Reflections from the Classroom" exercise at the end of this chapter and use the recommended presentation or reflective essay as an exhibit of your views of effective teaching.

2. Use Activity 1.1 in the *Guide to Field Experiences and Portfolio Development* to assess your current efforts at learning to be a teacher. Summarize the results as an exhibit for your portfolio.

3. Use Activity 1.4 in the *Guide to Field Experiences and Portfolio Development* to observe what teachers do. Use the recommended reflective essay to communicate your views about the various teaching roles and place it in your professional portfolio.

4. Complete Activity 1.5 in the *Guide to Field Experiences and Portfolio Development* to develop a "teaching platform" that describes your current thinking about teaching and learning.

Books for the Professional

Go to the Online Learning Center at www.mhhe.com/arends6e or your Interactive Student CD-ROM for an annotated version of this list.

Ashton-Warner, S. (1963). *Teacher.* New York: Simon & Schuster.

Bennett, B., and Rolheiser, C. (2001). *Beyond Monet: The Artful Science of Instructional Integration.* Toronto, Ontario: Bookation, Inc.

Danielson, C. (1996). *Enhancing Professional Practice: A Framework for Teaching.* Alexandria, VA: Association for Supervision and Curriculum Development.

Gage, N. L. (1978). *The Scientific Basis of the Art of Teaching.* New York: Teachers College Press.

Joyce, B., Weil, M., and Calhoun, E. (2000). *Models of Teaching* (6th ed.). Boston: Allyn & Bacon.

Richardson, V. (ed.). (2001). *Handbook of Research on Teaching* (4th ed.). Washington, DC: American Educational Research Association.

Schön, D. A. (1983). *The Reflective Practitioner.* San Francisco: Jossey-Bass.

Warren, D. (ed.). (1989). *American Teachers: Histories of a Profession at Work.* New York: Macmillan.

Weiner, L. (1999). *Urban Teaching: The Essentials.* New York: Teachers College Press.

Chapter Two

Student Learning in
Diverse Classrooms

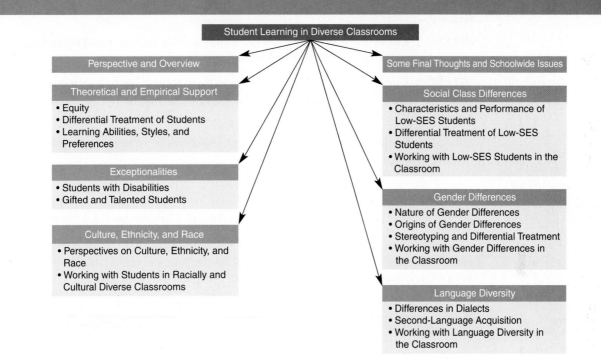

Student Learning in Diverse Classrooms

Perspective and Overview

Theoretical and Empirical Support
- Equity
- Differential Treatment of Students
- Learning Abilities, Styles, and Preferences

Exceptionalities
- Students with Disabilities
- Gifted and Talented Students

Culture, Ethnicity, and Race
- Perspectives on Culture, Ethnicity, and Race
- Working with Students in Racially and Cultural Diverse Classrooms

Some Final Thoughts and Schoolwide Issues

Social Class Differences
- Characteristics and Performance of Low-SES Students
- Differential Treatment of Low-SES Students
- Working with Low-SES Students in the Classroom

Gender Differences
- Nature of Gender Differences
- Origins of Gender Differences
- Stereotyping and Differential Treatment
- Working with Gender Differences in the Classroom

Language Diversity
- Differences in Dialects
- Second-Language Acquisition
- Working with Language Diversity in the Classroom

Interactive **and** *Applied Learning*

Go to your Interactive Student CD-ROM to:
- Hear audio clips of Diane Caruso (fourth/fifth grade) and Jennifer Patterson (eighth grade American history) talk about the diversity of their students in the *Teachers on Teaching* feature

Go to the Online Learning Center at www.mhhe.com/arends6e to read *PowerWeb* articles and newsfeed updates about:
- Academic performance
- Bilingual education
- Children at risk
- Cultural diversity in schools
- Intelligence
- Prejudice in schools
- Social contexts of multicultural education

INTASC *Considering* **Standards**

Studying this chapter will help you meet three INTASC principles:

Primary

INTASC 2: Understands how children learn and develop and can provide learning opportunities that support intellectual, social, and personal development.

INTASC 3: Understands how students differ in their approaches to learning and creates instructional opportunities that are adapted to diverse learners.

Secondary

INTASC 6: Understands and uses a variety of instructional strategies to encourage student development.

Reflecting **on** *Student Learning in Diverse Classrooms*

As a teacher, it will be your responsibility to respond positively to cultural and linguistic diversity and to students with special needs. Before you read this chapter, answer the following questions about your understanding and sensitivities:

- Do I have an understanding of the cultures that may be represented in my classroom?
- Am I aware of culture-based learning styles?
- Are my expectations high for all students regardless of culture?
- Will I make conscious efforts to engage all students in learning activities?
- Will I make conscious efforts to give equivalent attention and encouragement to all students?
- Have I participated in programs that help people better understand diversity?
- Am I open to identifying racial and cultural biases in myself, in my students, and in my curriculum materials?
- Do I know how to use methodology that fosters inclusion (for example, cooperative learning)?
- Will my instruction and methods conflict with the cultural beliefs of any students in my classroom?
- Do I know how to use a variety of tasks, measures, and materials in assessing student competencies to avoid inadvertent bias in assessment?

Go to the Online Learning Center at www.mhhe.com/arends6e to respond to these questions.

Perspective and Overview

Schools, as we have come to know them in the twentieth century, were created at a time when most students were of Western European heritage and spoke English. Only a small portion of children and youth attended school. Immigrant and farm children were expected to work or help their families. Children who were physically disabled and those with severe learning problems either stayed home or were taught in special schools. Girls, until the post World War II era, were *not* expected to finish high school or go to college. The monocultural schools created in the nineteenth century suffered under the assumption that learning potential was genetically and culturally derived, that teachers were relatively powerless to do anything about these conditions, and that society could tolerate low levels of achievement by some students.

Today, this has all changed. All children are expected to be in school. These children and youth bring with them a wide range of cultural backgrounds, talents, and needs. Many come from homes where support and encouragement are in short supply. This is true for impoverished and wealthy homes alike. Some students are learning disabled; others are gifted. It is no longer acceptable to allow some students to be placed in special classrooms, to let others drop out, and to allow still others to pass from grade to grade without having mastered basic literacy and numeracy skills. Instead, schools belong to all children, and the learning potential of each child must be realized. Diversity in classrooms is no longer a question of policy, values, or personal preferences. It is a fact!

Recognizing the diversity among students and understanding how students learn are among the most important challenges you will face as a teacher. Fortunately, you will be assisted with new and provocative theories about how students learn and a growing knowledge base about diversity and how teachers can create culturally responsive classrooms where every student is respected and where *every student can learn.*

> Understanding students in a diverse classroom is one of the most important challenges in teaching.

The primary goal of this chapter is to help you understand how students learn in today's diverse classrooms so you can meet the diversity challenge. Let's begin by looking into an experienced teacher's classroom and the students she meets every day.

> Ms. Caliendo loves her seventh-grade science class. In her fifth year of teaching, she has been highly successful in raising her students' achievement and is considered one of the best teachers in the school. Part of her success stems from her understanding of her students and her unrelenting respect for each one of them. Ms. Caliendo has spent hours in the community attending cultural events and meeting with parents. This is no small feat when one observes the diversity found in her classroom, as portrayed in Table 2.1.
>
> Ms. Caliendo has firm understandings and keen sensitivities of the various cultures and native languages her students bring with them to school. She strives to make her curriculum and pedagogy culturally relevant. She is careful to never silence any student's voice and to always make all students feel comfortable while expressing themselves regardless of their language skills. Most importantly, Ms. Caliendo has created a community of learners and has made deep and meaningful connections to each of her students.

The variety of students found in Ms. Caliendo's class in not an exception; it is the norm. Working with them as Ms. Caliendo does is not something that happens automatically either. Instead, her teaching practices result from a deep understanding of diversity and how students learn. This chapter introduces you to the diversity found in classrooms like Ms. Caliendo's and to the understandings and skills she has for working successfully in this type of classroom. The first two sections examine the nature of today's classrooms, the challenges and opportunities diversity presents, and a theoretical framework for

Table 2.1 *Ms. Caliendo's Seventh-Grade Science Class*

Name	Ethnicity	Native Language	Father's Occupation	Mother's Occupation
Low Socioeconomic Status				
Jacques	Haitian American	French	Migrant laborer	Migrant laborer
Hannah	African American	Ebonics	Not available	Waitress
Joe	Bohemian American	English	Seaman	Not available
Dontae	African American	English	Not available	Not available
Tammy	Scotch Irish	Appalachian	Custodian	Wife and mother
Juanita	Mexican American	Spanish	Farmhand	Cleaning lady
Working Class				
Tran	Vietnamese	Vietnamese	Truck farmer	Truck farmer
Tomas	Mexican American	Spanish	Carpenter	Office worker
Maria	Puerto Rican American	Spanish	Restaurant cook	Waitress
Komiko	Japanese American	English	Salesman	Store clerk
Grace	Mexican American	English	Taxi driver	Not available
Patricia	African American	English	Longshoreman	Data entry
Howard	African American	English	Unemployed	Teacher's aide
Middle Class				
Ritchie	African American	Bidialectal	Minister	Nurse
Wei-ping	Chinese	Mandarin	Architect	Wife and mother
Yoshi	Japanese American	English	Computer specialist	Teacher
Peter	German American	English	Banker	Social worker
Natasha	Russian American	Russian	Professor	Teacher
Elaine	African American	English	Store manager	Store clerk
Anna	Irish American	English	Doctor	Nurse
Kate	Scottish American	English	TV announcer	Daycare director
Ricardo	Mexican American	Spanish	Teacher	Teacher
Upper Class				
Houa	African (Niger)	Tribal/French	Diplomat	Wife and mother
Abdul	Kuwaiti American	Arabic/French	Oil executive	Wife and mother

Source: Adapted from Cushner, McClelland, and Safford (2003)

understanding these challenges. The third section describes differences found at both ends of the spectrum of those students labeled as *exceptional*—students who have learning disabilities as well as those who have exceptional talents. Later sections describe other kinds of differences found in classrooms: differences in *race, ethnicity,* and *culture; language* diversity; and *gender* and *social class* differences. Each of these sections will present the best scientific knowledge about the differences that exist and provide guidelines for teaching and working with diverse groups of students. The chapter concludes with a very important discussion pointing out how teachers by themselves *cannot* solve all the problems alone and how schoolwide reform is required.

It is important to note that the categories used to organize this chapter are social constructions that are culturally determined. While membership in any one category may be based on physical characteristics such as skin color or disability, they are categories we have devised. The characteristics of people in different categories may take on more or less significance in other cultures. For example, in the United States, a person with any African ancestry is usually considered black; in Puerto Rico, however, the same person may be classified as white if his or her social standing is high. A disability may or may not constitute a limitation depending on social factors. Ease in manipulating symbols, for example, is important in technological societies but less so in agrarian communities; a person lacking this skill is considered learning disabled in one society but not in another. Similarly, no individual exists in a single category. We are not just men or women, black or white, affluent or poor. In real life, we are members of many groups.

> The categories in which we place individuals are social constructions and culturally influenced.

Finally, it is important to learn how to use the right language when you discuss diversity and when you refer to racial groups or to students with special needs. This has become increasingly significant as our society becomes more sensitive to individuals with different heritages and disabilities. It is very important to use "African American" when referring to students whose parents have African heritage and to use correct language in describing students with Hispanic or Asian backgrounds. Most people today believe that it is not appropriate to refer to someone as "handicapped" because of the term's evolution. At one time, according to Friend and Bursuck (2002), people with disabilities had to resort to begging and were referred to as "cap-in-handers." Later, they were called "hand-in-cappers," a term obviously similar to the contemporary term **handicapped.** Some also prefer the term **challenged** or *differently abled* instead of **disability** when referring to students with special needs. For example, a person who cannot walk might be said to be *physically challenged*; a learning-disabled student could be referred to as *cognitively challenged.* Some hold this preference because the term *challenge* communicates an obstacle that can be overcome, whereas *disability* seems to convey a condition that is permanent. The term **disability,** however, remains acceptable, and you will find it used in most textbooks, other documents, and in this book.

> Using appropriate language when discussing diversity or referring to students' backgrounds and abilities is critical.

Check, Extend, Explore

Check
- How have society's expectations changed over the past century in regard to who should be educated?
- Why is using the right language important when discussing differences and referring to students' backgrounds and abilities?

Extend
- Think back to your own schooling. What kind of diversity existed in your classrooms? How did you respond to this situation as a student?

Explore
- Go to the Online Learning Center at www.mhhe.com/arends6e for links to websites related to *Perspectives about Diversity.*

Theoretical and Empirical Support

Values, philosophical perspectives, and politics influence teaching practices in diverse classrooms, and these are matters with which beginning teachers need to be concerned. At the same time, teachers must pay attention to a substantial knowledge base that describes what actually happens to special-needs children and those from diverse cultures when they attend school, as well as the best practices for working with these children and youth. Equity and the differential treatment of children have provided the impetus for much of the research on diversity. Similarly, a substantial knowledge base exists about the nature of students' learning abilities and their learning styles and preferences. These topics will be discussed in this section.

Equity

A serious and troubling gap exists between the achievement of white students and that of students in most other racial groups.

Schools that ensure impartial, fair, just, and equal conditions for all students exhibit **equity**. Historically, equitable conditions have not existed in our schools. Even as we begin the twenty-first century, many students have restricted opportunities. Textbook shortages still exist in many schools (Pyle, 1997), and some schools attended by African American and Latino students still have limited access to computers, the Internet, and advanced courses required for college. Teachers in schools attended by minority students too often focus on basic skill instruction instead of developing inquiry and problem-solving skills. These teachers are also less likely to be qualified—some lack degrees or majors in education or in the subjects they teach (Darling-Hammond, 1996). Most important, however, is the fact that minority students do less well in school than do students from European backgrounds. SAT averages rose for most racial and ethnic groups between 1990 and 2000 (College Board, 2000). However, according to Jackson (1999) and the College Board (2000), African American and Hispanic high school students score, on average, between 50 and 100 points lower than white students on SATs. African American and Hispanic students also lag behind whites on the National Assessment of Educational Progress and on many locally developed achievement tests (see *The New York Times,* March 28, 2002). While more African American and Hispanic students are completing high school than ever before, an important gap remains. For example, the African American high school completion rate increased from 59 to 87 percent between 1971 and 1997. White students, however, still have a higher (93 percent) rate of high school completion. This gap remains troubling to many (U.S. Department of Education, 1998).

Poverty is another problem. The United States and other parts of the world experienced great economic prosperity in the 1990s. However, all individuals and groups did not advance equally. The overall poverty rate has been increasing and the middle class is shrinking. Recent Bureau of the Census estimates of poverty indicate that 32.9 million Americans live below the poverty line—a twenty-eight-year high—and most of them are children, 11.7 million under 18. Reed and Sautter (1990) reported over a decade ago that the United States had the highest rate of childhood poverty among industrial nations. Although the rate has decreased slightly, it still remains high, with more than 15 percent of children living in poverty. Projections (U.S. Census Bureau, 2001; Pallas, Natriello, & McDill, 1989) predict that by 2020, close to 20 percent of U.S. children will live in poverty.

In a multicultural and diverse world, teachers really have no choice but to create classrooms that are inclusive and equitable.

Homelessness is another troubling equity issue. Families now account for one-third of the homeless; as many as half a million children in this country are homeless. Although beliefs about rugged individualism incline us to blame individuals for their distressing situations, studies indicate that economic achievement is best predicted by educational achievement, which in turn depends primarily on family socioeconomic status. This means that if you are poor, the educational and economic deck is stacked against you, making success much more difficult to attain.

Some of you may be asking why teachers should concern themselves with the larger social problem of equity. It may be unfair, even unrealistic, to expect teachers and schools to remedy inequities that have existed in the larger society for a long time. At least two arguments can be advanced in response: The first is that these issues should be of major concern to every citizen—it is incumbent on us as citizens to work toward the public good by trying to ameliorate these problems. Educators can do their part by ensuring that every young person gets equal opportunities to learn. The second argument is that Americans have a strong belief in the power of education as the route to later success in life—economically, politically, and culturally. This belief is supported by research, which consistently shows that education is related to income. The argument has intuitive appeal as well, in that educated people are equipped with the tools to escape from poverty and to participate fully in our economic and political systems. As teachers, it is part of our responsibility to help them accomplish their escape.

> Educators have a responsibility to ensure that every young person gets equal opportunities to learn.

Differential Treatment of Students

Whereas one body of research has documented the inequities that exist in education as a whole, another has documented the **differential treatment** of students by teachers within classrooms. Differential treatment occurs partially because teachers, consciously or unconsciously, have different expectations for some students as contrasted to others. Let's look at how this works.

> Differential treatment refers to the differences in educational experiences of the majority race, class, culture, or gender to those of minorities.

Self-Fulfilling Prophecy. In 1968, Robert Rosenthal and Lenore Jacobson published *Pygmalion in the Classroom.* This book, instantly popular with professional and lay audiences, introduced the concept of the **self-fulfilling prophecy** and the effects of teacher expectations on student achievement and self-esteem. In their research, Rosenthal and Jacobson provided teachers in a particular elementary school information about several students in each of their classes. They told teachers that a few students had been identified through a new test as "bloomers" and that they could expect these students to make large achievement gains during the coming year. In fact, these students had been identified at random—no special test information existed. As the year progressed, however, the identified bloomers, particularly those in the early grades, made significant gains in achievement. Rosenthal and Jacobson argued that these gains could be attributed to the differential treatment received from the teachers as a result of their false expectations—thus, the self-fulfilling prophecy, a situation in which inaccurate perceptions of students' abilities and subsequent acting on these perceptions make them come true over the years.

> Self-fulfilling prophecy refers to situations in which teachers' expectations and predictions about student behavior or learning causes the behavior to happen.

Teacher Expectations. Rosenthal and Jacobson's study, although faulted because of its methodological weaknesses (see Brophy & Good, 1974; Claiborn, 1969), aroused the interest of the research community about the effects of **teacher expectations** on student achievement. Over the past three decades, researchers have found that although the effects of teacher expectations on students are not quite so straightforward as suggested in the Rosenthal-Jacobson study, they are, nonetheless, real. Teacher expectations create a cyclical pattern of behaviors on the part of both teachers and students. Drawing from the work of Good and Brophy (1987; see also Oakes & Lipton, 2003), this cyclical process is illustrated in Figure 2.1.

There are two important questions to ask about this process: How are expectations created in the first place? How do they get communicated to students?

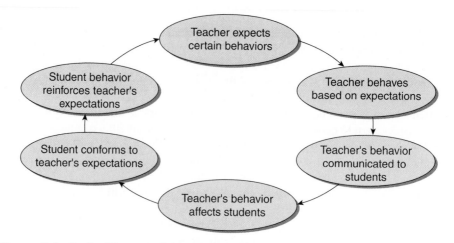

Figure 2.1 *Cyclical Process of Teacher Expectations*

In the classroom, as in all other aspects of life, people make impressions on us. The way students dress, the language they use, their physical features, as well as their interpersonal skills, influence teachers. Information about a student's family or information gleaned from the school's records can also create impressions and expectations, even before the teacher meets the student. As long as initial impressions are accurate, there is no problem. But when initial impressions are translated into inaccurate expectations about students and then used in differential treatment toward them, there is a problem.

Once expectations (positive or negative) are formed, they are communicated to students in numerous ways. You can probably recall several instances when a particular teacher communicated expectations to you that influenced your attitude and work in his or her class. You may remember high expectations a teacher held for you. From the first day of class, she chose to single you out for important assignments; she wrote positive comments on your papers; and she called on you to answer difficult questions. It is likely that you worked hard for this teacher, perhaps even beyond your potential. Or you may remember an instance when a teacher had low expectations for you. He seldom acknowledged your work publicly, and even though you raised your hand, he seldom called on you. If this teacher's behavior persisted, it is likely that you started to ignore your work in his class and concentrated your energies elsewhere.

Table 2.2 shows some of the ways that teachers communicate their expectations to students and how they behave differentially toward those for whom they hold high and low expectations.

The discussion up to this point has focused on expectations in situations wherein teachers hold inaccurate beliefs about particular students. There is actually a second expectation effect that is called the **sustaining expectation effect.** This effect exists when a teacher accurately reads a student's ability and behaves accordingly toward the student but does not alter the expectation when the student improves or regresses over time. You can probably recall instances of this happening to you in classrooms as well as in other places. Perhaps you were an excellent English student. The essays you wrote for the teacher were always meticulous. You wrote with clarity and you showed considerable creativity in how you created beautiful images with words. You always received an "A" for your effort. One week, however, you were recovering from the flu and were overwhelmed with other schoolwork. You had to write your essay in haste and with little thought or care. When the paper was returned marked with an "A" and a comment from

Sustaining expectation effect occurs when teachers do not change their expectations about a student, even after the student's performance has changed.

Table 2.2 *How Teachers and Schools Communicate Differential Expectations to Students*

Teaching or School Practice	For Students Perceived to be More Capable	For Students Perceived to be Less Capable
Curriculum, Procedures, Pacing, Qualities of the Environment	More opportunities to perform publicly on tasks; more enrichment and resources; more opportunities to think	Less opportunity to perform publicly on meaningful tasks; fewer enrichment opportunities; less opportunity to think; work aimed at practice
Grouping Practices	Assigned to higher-ability groups with assignments aimed at understanding	Assigned to lower-ability groups with more worksheet and drill-like assignments
Responsibility for Learning	More autonomy and more choices	Less autonomy and frequent teacher direction and monitoring
Feedback and Evaluation Practices	More opportunity for self-feedback and evaluation	Less opportunity for self-evaluation
Motivational Strategies	More honest, direct, and contingent feedback	Less honest and more gratuitous feedback
Teacher Quality	More qualified and experienced teachers	More uncertified and inexperienced teachers
Quality of Teacher Relationships	More respect for learners as individuals with unique needs	Less respect for learners as individuals with unique needs

Source: Adapted from Good and Brophy (2003); Good and Weinstein (1986); and Oakes and Lipton, (2003)

the teacher, "Another superb piece of writing," you knew that your work had been judged not on its current value but on your previous history of producing good essays.

You can also probably think of instances when the sustaining expectation effect worked the other way. Perhaps you were notorious for not keeping up with your reading assignments in history. Every time the teacher called on you, you answered with silly and careless answers. This behavior made your classmates laugh and covered up your unpreparedness. You decided one day to stop this behavior. You started to read your assignments very carefully, and you came prepared to discuss your ideas in class. You raised your hand in response to the teacher's questions over and over, but someone else was always selected to recite. When you did get your chance, everyone started to laugh, including the teacher, before you could complete your point. You had changed your behavior, but the teacher sustained her past expectations.

Tracking and Ability Grouping. Differential treatment also results from ability grouping and tracking. Low-socioeconomic status (SES) and minority students are disproportionately placed in low-ability groups and low-track classes. Instructional quality is often poorer in these groups than in the higher groups. The criteria used to guide placement decisions are sometimes of dubious merit. Those used most often are standardized aptitude test scores (the type administered in large groups, deemed least valid by test developers) and teachers' judgments. Unfortunately, teachers' judgments are influenced by race and class, and even when ability and teacher recommendations are equivalent, race and class are often the most likely determining factors in placing children.

Tracking (formal or informal) limits educational opportunities for students placed in the lower tracks.

Learning Abilities, Styles, and Preferences

A third major theoretical perspective about the diversity that classroom teachers need to consider is the differences observed in student abilities, their talents, and their learning styles. This section explores how learner abilities are defined and how students will vary widely in their abilities. It also discusses how students vary in their approaches to learning and in how they process cognitive and emotional information.

Learner Abilities and Intelligence. The belief that people vary in learning abilities is not new. In fact, the early Greeks puzzled over these differences, as have many others over the past several thousand years. One important step in understanding students and learning in diverse classrooms is to understand differences in learning abilities and how these abilities have been defined and measured.

General Intelligence. Traditional theories have held that individuals have specific **mental abilities** as measured by performance on particular cognitive tasks such as analyzing word associations, doing mathematical problems, and solving certain kinds of riddles. At the turn of the twentieth century, psychologists such as Alfred Binet in France and Lewis Terman in the United States developed the first tests aimed at measuring human intelligence and abilities. These theorists saw **intelligence** as being mainly a single ability. Binet, for example, wanted to find ways to measure learning ability so children could be provided special help rather than being dismissed from school, as was the practice in France and other European countries at that time. Out of Binet's work came the idea of **mental age.** A child who could pass the same number of test items as passed by other children in the child's age group would have the mental age of that age group. The concept of **intelligence quotient** (IQ), according to Woolfolk (2002), was added after Binet's test was brought to the United States. An IQ score became the computation of a person's mental age divided by his or her chronological age and multiplied by 100, as in the following example:

> Intelligence refers to the ability or abilities to solve problems and adapt the physical and social environments.

> Intelligence quotients compare individuals' mental and chronological ages.

$$\text{Intelligence quotient} = \frac{\text{Mental age (10)}}{\text{Chronological age (10)}} \times 100 = 100$$

Performance on a variety of intelligence tests designed during the first two decades of the twentieth century was highly correlated and thus offered support to the single ability theory. These tests were used widely in Europe to determine who could benefit from advanced schooling. In the United States, they were soon employed to help place students in instructional groups, to determine who was best fit to serve in the army, and who should go to college. Even though IQ tests have fallen into disfavor, tests of academic achievement and those that measure more general knowledge, such as the Scholastic Aptitude Test (SAT), have replaced them and are used widely to make decisions about where students should be placed in school and where they can go to college.

Multiple Intelligences. Over the past two decades, several contemporary psychologists, such as Howard Gardner (1983, 1999) and Robert Sternberg (1985, 1999a, 1999b) have challenged the idea that there is general or singular intelligence. Instead, their research has shown that intelligence and ability are much more than the single dimension of logical thinking and language. Sternberg maintained that there are three types of intelligence: analytical, creative, and practical. **Analytical intelligence** involves an individual's cognitive processes. **Creative intelligence** is an individual's insight for coping with new experiences. **Practical intelligence** is an individual's ability to adapt and reshape his or her environment. Sternberg argues that "intelligent behavior" may vary from one occasion or setting to another. It depends on the environmental context, one's prior experiences, and particular cognitive processes required of the task or setting. Success in life, according to Sternberg, depends not on how much of each of the three intelligences individuals have, but on understandings individuals have of their own strengths and weaknesses, how to use their strengths to an advantage, and how to compensate for their weaknesses. Success also depends on individuals drawing from their past experiences to deal with new situations and adapting their behavior appropriately to fit particular environments. In some instances, intelligent behavior requires selecting an environment conducive to a particular individual's success. This latter idea helps explain why individuals are successful in one college and not another or in one job and not another.

Howard Gardner is the best-known contemporary theorist of intelligence being more than a singular ability. Gardner's theory of **multiple intelligences** proposes eight separate intelligences: linguistic, logical-mathematical, spatial, musical, bodily-kinesthetic, interpersonal, intrapersonal, and naturalist. These different intelligences and their attributes are displayed in Table 2.3. According to Gardner, individuals differ in their strengths in the various intelligences. Some may be strong in logical and mathematical reasoning, whereas others may have exceptional musical talent or physical dexterity. Gardner and his disciples believe that teachers and schools should expand the range of abilities they value and teach in ways that accommodate different kinds of intelligence. Unfortunately, many schools today continue to emphasize success as determined by language and mathematical abilities and largely ignore the other forms of intelligence. We will come back to this issue throughout *Learning to Teach*.

Sternberg and Gardner have posited the view that intelligence is more than a single ability but instead encompasses many abilities and talents and is contextual.

Table 2.3 *Gardner's Eight Types of Intelligence*

Type	Description
Logical-mathematical	Ability to discern logical and numerical patterns and to manage long chains of reasoning
Linguistic	Sensitivity to the sounds, rhythms, and meanings of words and to the different functions of language
Musical	Ability to produce and appreciate pitch, timbre, rhythm, and the different forms of musical expression
Spatial	Ability to perceive the visual-spatial world accurately and to perform transformations on one's perceptions, both mentally and in the world
Bodily-kinesthetic	Ability to exert great control over physical movements and to handle objects skillfully
Interpersonal	Capacity to discern and respond appropriately to the moods, temperaments, motivations, and desires of others
Intrapersonal	Perceptiveness about one's own emotional state and knowledge of one's own strengths and weaknesses
Naturalist	Ability to discriminate among living things and sensitivity to features of the natural world

Emotional Intelligence. A final type of intelligence of interest to teachers is **emotional intelligence** (EQ) (Goleman, 1995). EQ is the ability to recognize and manage one's own emotions, to recognize emotions in others, and to handle relationships. This concept has become quite popular in the preparation of leaders in all types of fields; evidence shows that leader success is perhaps more dependent on EQ than on cognitive skills (Goleman, McKee and Bayatzis, 2002). The field that interprets brain research for classroom practice (Sousa, 2001; Wolfe, 2001) has also started to recognize the interaction between the cognitive and the emotional in all matters of human functioning. The important thing about EQ for teachers is to recognize emotion as an ability and realize that it can be influenced like other abilities. Teaching students to be in touch and to manage strong emotions such as anger provides the focus for many human relations lessons. Teaching students to work toward desired goals rather than act on emotional impulse is another example of how EQ has become part of the schools' curriculum.

> Most psychologists believe that one's intelligence and capacity to learn result from both inherited traits and environmental influences.

Nature or Nurture? A debate has existed for years over whether intelligence(s) result from heredity (nature) or from the environment (nurture). On the one side of the argument are those who believe that we are born with a set amount of intelligence that can be unfolded but not exceeded (Herrnstein & Murphey, 1994). On the other side are those such as Perkins (1992; 1995), who view intelligence as a "capacity to learn" that is mostly environmentally determined. Most psychologists today take a middle road and view intelligence as resulting from both heredity and the environment. Heredity establishes a range of abilities, but environment heavily influences what individuals do with it.

Today, many practicing educators believe that the results of IQ tests and tests of general knowledge have little to do with an individual's ability or capacity to learn, but instead they reflect one's social and cultural background. Children from families and communities that reflect the cultural mainstream, for instance, do better on these tests than do the children of parents who live in poverty, those who recently immigrated to the United States, or those whose primary language is not English. It is important for teachers to remember that all understandings and skills are improvable and that many differences, particularly those among older students, result from what and how students have been taught in schools.

Differences in Cognitive and Learning Styles. Another especially important area for teacher awareness is cognitive and learning style variations, mainly in the ways that students perceive their world and in how they process and reflect on information. Some of these variations seem to be caused by differences in the brain, others by individual preferences, and still others by culture. Many different cognitive and learning styles and preferences have been described; a few of these follow.

Cognitive Styles. For a long time, psychologists have observed that people differ in how they perceive and process information (Wapner & Demick, 1991). Some individuals appear to be **field dependent**—they perceive situations "as a whole" rather than "in parts." They are likely to see the big picture in most problem

"Well, Dad, my guess would be that heredity played a part in those bad grades."

© Adam Stoller. Reprinted with permission

situations. Other people are **field independent**—they tend to see the separate parts of the whole instead of the whole itself. In general, field-dependent individuals are more people oriented; social relationships are important to them, and they work well in groups. Individuals who are field independent, on the other hand, have strong analytical abilities and are more likely to monitor their information processing rather than their relationships with others. The classroom implications are obvious. It is likely that field-independent students will need assistance in seeing the "big picture" and may prefer working alone, whereas field-dependent students will prefer working on longer-term and problem-based assignments.

Learning Styles. Individuals also approach learning in different ways. One important **learning style** difference has been labeled "in-context and "out-of-context" style. These differences appear, to some extent, to be culturally influenced. In some cultures and domestic subcultures, teaching and learning are conducted **in-context,** whereas in mainstream American schools, the predominant mode is **out-of-context.** What does "in-context learning" mean? It means that children acquire skills and knowledge at the point that they are needed and in real-life situations. For example, children may learn to use a paring knife in the context of helping their parents prepare meals, or they may learn how to multiply fractions in the context of doubling a recipe when company is coming. "Out-of-context" learning means that learning is unconnected to a real, immediate need. When parents play "what's this" games with infants or when math is broken down into discrete algorithms, each drilled separately before application to real math problems, then out-of-context learning is happening. Both kinds of teaching and learning are important, and both can clearly "work," but children accustomed to in-context learning are often confused by out-of-context teaching.

Learning Preferences. Finally, some evidence suggests that students have preferences for particular kinds of learning environments and modalities. A widely popular conceptualization of **learning preferences** was developed some years ago by Dunn and Dunn (1978, 1987). They argue that students differ in preferred learning environments (sound, light, seating patterns), in the amount of required emotional support, and in the degree of structure and peer interaction. Learners, according to the Dunns, also differ in their preferred learning modality. Some students are more visually oriented while others prefer to obtain information through auditory channels.

Obviously, it is important for teachers to recognize that students differ in the ways they process information and in their preferred ways of learning. They should make an effort to adapt their instruction to learning styles and preferences and to how the brain works (Kotulak, 1996; Wolfe, 2001). Successful, experienced teachers have known this for a long time. However, three caveats are in order for beginners: (1) At the present time, there is no consensus about which of the several cognitive and learning styles are most important for teachers to pay attention to. (2) Some students may communicate that their preferred learning style is the one that is easiest for them or one for which they have no alternative. They may have to be helped to develop a repertoire of learning styles and taught how to select the most appropriate one for particular learning situations. And, finally (3) there are real drawbacks to planning completely around learning style differences. The number of different styles sometimes are too varied to make it practical for teachers to accommodate every student's style. However, that doesn't mean that teachers shouldn't attend to style and preference differences and learn to diversify strategies to meet the varying needs of students.

Check, Extend, Explore

Check
- Why should teachers be concerned about equity and classrooms that are inclusive and equitable?
- Contrast "self-fulfilling prophecy" with the "sustaining expectation effect."
- Give some examples of how teachers treat students for whom they hold high expectations as compared to those for whom they hold low expectations.
- Contrast the traditional definition of IQ with the views held by Robert Sternberg and Howard Gardner.
- Why are the concepts of cognitive and learning styles important when thinking about diverse classrooms?

Extend
- Think of situations in your own schooling when teachers had inaccurate expectations about you. Why did they hold these expectations? How did you respond?
- What proportion of ability do you think results from nature? From nurture? Go to "Extend Question Poll" on the Online Learning Center to respond.

Explore
- Go to the Online Learning Center at www.mhhe.com/arends6e for links to websites related to *Teacher Expectations, Multiple Intelligences and Learning Styles.*

Exceptionalities

Student exceptionalities account for some of the greatest diversity found in today's classrooms. In any one classroom, teachers may find students with severe learning disabilities or other special needs as well as students who are gifted and possess special talents. This section describes students who have disabilities and those who are gifted. It also provides you with strategies for working with all kinds of exceptionalities.

Students with Disabilities

Students who have learning disabilities or who are challenged have special needs that must be met if they are to successfully function in and out of school. Before the post-World War II era, not much attention was paid to this group, and those who did receive an education were more likely to do so in special schools. This has changed dramatically over the past twenty-five years as a result of legislation and court action. The landmark event was the passage of Public Law 94-142, the Education for All Handicapped Children Act. Now called the Individuals with Disabilities Education Act (IDEA), it was amended in 1983, 1986, and 1990. It was reauthorized in 1997 as Public Law 105-17. IDEA now protects the rights of all individuals with cognitive, emotional, or physical disabilities from birth to age 21. These laws, along with numerous court decisions, were enacted in response to inequalities and discrimination in services provided to children and adults with disabilities and special needs. In the case of education, some jurisdictions had barred children from attending school because of their special needs; in others, the education such children received was often segregated and inferior. This legislation has changed all of this. As shown in Figure 2.2, there has been a dramatic increase in the number of children with disabilities who were served by federally supported programs between 1977 and 2000.

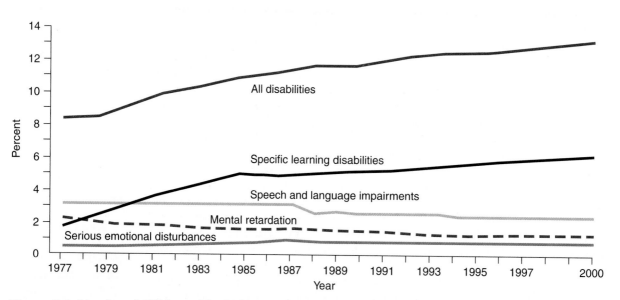

Figure 2.2 *Number of Children with Disablties Who Were Served by Federal Programs as a Percentage of Total Public K–12 Enrollment*

Source: *Conditions of Education* (1998, 2000)

Features of Special Education Today. The aim of the Individuals with Disabilities Education Act was to ensure a free and appropriate public education for all children in a setting that was most suitable for their needs. It also guaranteed due process. This legislation introduced the concept of **mainstreaming,** a strategy to move children out of special education and into regular classrooms (the mainstream) to the degree possible. At first, only children who had mild disabilities were placed in regular classrooms. The concept of **inclusion** followed on the heels of mainstreaming and promoted a wider goal—including all students, even those with severe disabilities, into regular classrooms. Unlike mainstreaming, inclusion begins with students in regular classrooms and makes provisions for pulling them out for services as needed.

Mainstreaming and inclusion are important even if law did not mandate them. Other educational benefits accrue in addition to alleviating discrimination. For example, children with special needs in regular classrooms have the opportunity to learn appropriate social and academic behaviors by observing and modeling other children. Children without disabilities also benefit by seeing firsthand the strengths and potential contributions, as well as the limitations, of their disabled peers. The school environment and society at large are thereby enriched.

Public Law 94-142 and subsequent legislation rested on four premises: (1) students should be educated in the least restrictive environment; (2) each child with a special need should have an individual education plan; (3) evaluation procedures should be fair and nondiscriminatory; and (4) right should be guaranteed through due process.

Children are to be educated within the **least restrictive environment.** This means that to the extent possible, children with disabilities should be included in the regular classroom. Those with very mild physical, emotional, and learning disabilities are to spend their entire school day in the regular classroom. Those with slightly more serious problems are to receive extra assistance from a special educator, either in or out of regular classrooms. As the disabilities grow more serious, the responsibility of the regular classroom teacher normally is reduced, and the child receives a larger portion of his or her education in more specialized settings. In practice, the majority of children with learning or physical disabilities attend regular classes for at least part of the day.

Each child with a disability is to have an **individualized educational plan** (IEP). IEPs are developed by a committee composed of the regular classroom teacher, the child's parents, the special education teacher, and other staff who may be helpful, such as psychologists, speech therapists, or medical personnel. IEPs describe the child's current level of academic performance and set goals for future development. The IEP, and the teacher's role in the process, will be described in more detail in the next section, Working with Students Who Have Disabilities.

School systems receive special federal funds for each child with a disability, so the process of categorizing looms large in schools. Controversy reigns, however, about the desirability of labeling per se and the validity of current means for evaluating exceptionality. Advocates of labeling contend that it helps educators meet the special needs of the student and brings additional funding to bear where it is most needed. While they acknowledge the weaknesses of the current system of evaluation and placement, they argue that eliminating labeling amounts to throwing the baby out with the bath water.

Opponents counter that labeling creates more problems than it solves. For example, questions about equity arise because of the differential placement of boys, students of lower socioeconomic status, and minorities into special education programs and because the incidence of disabilities varies widely from state to state and from district to

> Inclusion is the practice of placing students with mild and rather severe disabilities into regular classrooms and pulling them into special classrooms only as needed.

> Least restrictive environment refers to the placement setting for students with disabilities that is most like the regular classroom.

district. Opponents also contend that labeling causes teachers to view problem behaviors as deficiencies that are inherent in the child; teachers who hold this view could overlook deficiencies in the learning environment. Labels tend to become permanent—once students are placed in a special education program, they tend to stay there.

Finally, there exist few, well-validated methods of instruction that are tied to the categories, and distinctions between the categories are blurry. No special interventions for the mildly mentally retarded, for instance, are distinct from those that might be used with any student experiencing academic difficulty (Reynolds, Wang, & Walberg, 1987; Wang, Reynolds, & Walberg, 1995).

Working with Students Who Have Disabilities. Most beginning teachers worry about what they can do in the classroom to assist students who have disabilities. They can take several steps. First, it is important for beginning teachers to know district policies pertaining to students with special needs and the teacher's role in the referral, screening, and IEP process. Familiarize yourself with district policies and procedures for referral and screening. Be alert for students with problems or special potential. Do you have any students whose academic work is well below or well above grade level? Do you have students whose behavior is well below or above the maturity level of their age mates? Do any of your students demonstrate especially low or high persistence at learning tasks? Typically, districts expect teachers to refer students who exhibit these characteristics—unusual academic performance, behavior or emotional problems, lack of persistence—to appropriate colleagues for further evaluation.

A student's individualized learning plan (IEP) specifies his or her functioning, long- and short-term goals, and how the student will be evaluated.

Also, teachers need to be aware of the specific categories of disabilities as prescribed by federal law. Students who have one of the disabilities described in Table 2.4 are eligible for special education services. Schools are required to have an individualized educational plan (IEP) for each student identified with a disability. In most school districts, IEPs are developed by a committee composed of the regular classroom teacher, the child's parents, the special education teacher, and any other staff who may be helpful. IEPs should contain information about the child's current level of academic performance, a statement of both long- and short-term educational goals, a plan for how these goals will be achieved, the amount of time the child will spend in the regular class, and an evaluation plan. The IEP is revised annually. Figure 2.3 shows an example of a completed IEP.

Evaluation procedures used to assess special-needs students are tied to the IEP process and, by law, must be nondiscriminatory. In screening a child for special services, school officials are required to use a variety of tests and must consider the child's cultural background and language. The involvement of parents in the evaluation process is mandated, and no major educational decisions may be made without their written consent. Parents must be informed of intended school actions in their own language.

For specific lessons, teachers can develop learning materials and activities commensurate with the abilities of children with special needs, much as they adapt lessons to the individual differences of all students. In doing so, they should expect to work closely with resource teachers and other support personnel. Most schools have such support services readily available. Cooperative learning strategies can also be used often, both to facilitate achievement and to help exceptional and regular students accept and appreciate each other.

Two perspectives currently exist about the best approach to use with students most likely to be included in regular classrooms—the mildly learning disabled and the behaviorally or emotionally disabled. Turnbull and Colleagues (2002), and Tomlison

Table 2.4 *Summary of Students with Disabilities*

Federal Disability Category	Characteristic	Percentage of All Students Receiving Special Education Services
Learning disabilities (LD)	Dysfunctions in processing information; average intelligence; problems learning how to read, write, compute	51%
Emotional disturbance (ED)	Difficulties in social and emotional areas; trouble with social relationships	9%
Speech or language impairment	Disordered speech that interferes with communication	21%
Mental retardation	Significant, below-average mental functioning and cognitive abilities	12%
Hearing impairment	Significant hearing loss; amount can vary	1.3%
Visual impairment	Significant vision loss; amount can vary	0.5%
Deaf-blindness	Significant vision and hearing disabilities	0.1%
Orthopedic impairment	Serious physical disabilities; impaired ability to move around	1.2%
Traumatic brain injury (TBI)	Intellectual and physical impairments resulting from brain injury	0.1%
Autism	Developmental disability characterized by impairments in communication and social interactions	0.5%
Multiple disabilities	Two or more interwoven disabilities	1.8%
Other health impairments	Conditions resulting from chronic health problems or disease	2.2%

(1999), who favor a somewhat structured and direct instruction approach, offer the following recommendations:

- Use highly structured materials. Tell students exactly what is expected. Avoid distractions.
- Allow alternatives to the use of written language, such as tape recorders or oral tests.
- Expect improvement on a long-term basis.
- Reinforce appropriate behavior. Model and explain what constitutes appropriate behavior.
- Provide immediate feedback and ample opportunities for drill and practice.

As you will see, these practices are *not* very different from many of the effective teaching behaviors described in Chapter 8.

Not all agree, however, that these are the only effective teaching strategies for this population. Many, such as Curtis and Shaver (1980), Haberman (1991), and Slavin (1996), believe that instruction for students with disabilities should stem from their interests and that strategies used by teachers should not emphasize basic information but should instead promote the student's ability to solve problems and think critically. They recommend strategies that resemble those recommended for gifted

Quentinburg Public Schools— Special Education Department

Individualized Education Program

Student Name: Jillian Carol   **Date of Birth**: 4/2/87
School: Jefferson Elementary   **Grade:** 5
Primary lang.: Home-English Student-English   **Date of meeting:** 8/28/97
Program start date: 8/28/97   **Review date:** 8/28/98

Services Required

General Education   Full-time participation with support from
                        paraprofessional or special education teacher
                        at least three hours weekly

Resources   Incidental as needed
Self-Contained   Speech/language therapy for language development
Related Services   40 minutes/week
Other

Justification for Placement (include justification for any time spent not in general education): Student's needs indicate that learning can appropriately take place in the general education classroom with appropriate supports provided. Support will include adapted materials as well as adult assistance up to three hours per week. Incidental time noted in the resource room is intended to preserve the option of one-to-one assistance on specific goals and objectives as needed, as determined by the teachers.

Tests Used

Intellectual   WISC-III (Full Scale IQ = 64)
Educational   Woodcock Reading, Keymath
Behavioral   NA
Speech/language
Other
Vision   Within normal limits
Hearing   Within normal limits

Strengths (present level of functioning)

Jillian enjoys talking with peers and adults.
Jillian is polite and well-mannered.
Jillian generally responds appropriately to directions.
Jillian likes to tell stories she creates.

Weaknesses (present level of functioning)

1. Below grade level in word identification (3.1) and reading comprehension (3.2)
2. Below grade level in vocabulary usage (2.1)
3. Below grade level in math computation and problem solving (1.6)

(continued)

Figure 2.3 *Sample Individualized Education Plan*
Source: Friend and Bursuck (1999), pp. 55–56

Annual Goal: Jillian will improve her reading skills to approximately a 3.9 level.

    STO 1: Jillian will read from a 3rd grade reader at 80 words per minute with fewer than 3 errors per minute.

    STO 2: Jillian will answer with 80% accuracy comprehension questions about reading passages at a third-grade level.

    Evaluation: Oral performance **Person(s):** Special education teacher

Annual Goal: Jillian will use vocabulary at approximately a 3.0 level

    STO 1: Jillian will tell a story using vocabulary from third-grade reading materials.

    STO 2: Jillian will use third-grade vocabulary when talking about her out-of-school activities.

    STO 3: Jillian will learn at least 40 vocabulary words by using a word bank.

    Evaluation: Oral performance, checklist **Person(s):** Special education teacher
                                                     Classroom teacher

Annual Goal: Jillian will compute and problem solve at approximately a 2.5 level.

    STO 1: Jillian will write answers to basic addition and subtraction facts with 100% accuracy.

    STO 2: Jillian will accurately compute two-digit addition and subtraction problems without regrouping with 90% accuracy.

    STO 3: Jillian will correctly solve word problems written at her reading level and at approximately a 2.5 difficulty level with 90% accuracy.

    Evaluation: Written performance **Person(s):** Special education teacher
                                                     Classroom teacher

Team Signatures

LEA Representative	*Eva Kim*
Parent	*Julia Carol*
Special Education Teacher	*Vera Delaney*
General Education Teacher	
Psychologist	*Nadine Showalter*
Counselor	
Speech/Language Therapist	*Ed Briggs*
Other	
Other	

Figure 2.3 *(Continued)*

Diagnosis and evaluation are important aspects of the IEP process.

children—group investigation, community problem solving, problem-based learning, and activities that emphasize active learning. Approaches such as cooperative learning and reciprocal teaching convey to all students that they can learn, that all students can make a contribution to the learning process, and that all perspectives are valued. Community problem solving (described later) tells students that teachers care about their lives and their communities and provides opportunities for complex, meaningful, and motivating academic work.

Teachers also need to carefully think through the physical layout of their classrooms and make any changes that will facilitate easy movement for all students, particularly those who require wheelchairs or special walking devices. They need to consider scheduling and time constraints and how these might affect special students—for example, the transition time between lessons may need to be extended for a student who is physically disabled. Teachers also need to consider how to manage the downtime created for the students without disabilities—highly able students will accomplish learning tasks very quickly, and thought must be given to how they can use their extra time meaningfully. Routines and procedures for such contingencies must be planned and taught to the whole class. Teachers may also be called upon to assist students with special equipment, a topic that is highlighted in this chapter's Enhancing Teaching with Technology box.

As always, teachers must accommodate individual differences and maintain communication with parents. They must help exceptional and regular students work and play together. Like all students, students with special needs model their teachers' intended and unintended behaviors, and they often live up to teachers' expectations, whether positive or negative. Positive, even-handed regard for exceptional students is a prerequisite for effective teaching, as are making the curriculum relevant, employing strategies known to work with students who have special needs, and using the resources of special education teachers and personnel.

Assistive Technologies

Computers are an important part of today's inclusive classroom. Of particular importance are **assistive technologies** that help students with special needs learn to perform tasks associated with learning and daily living. Some assistive technologies make it possible for students with disabilities to have access to computers; others make available a wide variety of educational opportunities not previously offered.

Among the most important assistive technologies are those that provide students with disabilities access to computers and other modern communication technologies. Keyboards can be modified, for example, so one-handed or one-fingered typists can use them. Voice recognition programs allow students with physical disabilities to input text into a computer by speaking. Joysticks have been developed that allow individuals to control the computer by pointing with their chin or their head.

A wide variety of assistive devices exist today that make available a wider range of educational opportunities than would otherwise be possible. For example, computer-assisted large print and Braille translations can assist communication for students who have visual impairments. Braille translation software can convert text into correctly formatted Braille. Screen-magnification software increases the size of text and graphics, similar to captioning and real-time graphic display on television, which relay the dialogue and action in television programs and movies via printed text.

Computer speech synthesizers can generate spoken words artificially. Speech recognition software can assist students who can only speak a few sounds to perform a variety of tasks. An individual is taught a few "token" sounds that can be responded to by a specially programmed computer. The computer recognizes the sounds and performs everyday and school-based functions, such as turning on the TV, starting a videotape, or accessing appropriate school curriculum on a CD-ROM. Other advanced devices react to brain signals that are in turn translated into digital commands and actions.

Other technologies, such as adaptive equipment and special switches, afford students with physically disabilities to increase their functional mobility by turning on appliances and controlling other devices like lamps or radios. Computerized "gait trainers" can help individuals with poor balance or those who lack control of their bodies learn how to walk. Radio-controlled devices can open doors and operate telephone answering machines.

A particularly interesting piece of technology has been designed for students who are sick and must be hospital-ized. PC Pal, a special computer and LCD screen, can be made available in hospital rooms. This device provides games and Internet access and allows hospitalized students to keep up with their homework and remain in contact with their friends.

Special websites have been created that are noted for their ease of use for students with disabilities. The most prominent are those developed and promoted by the Center for Applied Special Technology (CAST), an organization whose mission is to expand opportunities for people with disabilities through the use of computers and assistive technologies. CAST offers a website (called "Bobby") and Web-based tools that analyzes Web pages for their accessibility. You can access this website and others like it through the *Learning to Teach* Online Learning Center.

Because more and more students with disabilities are being included in regular classrooms, it is very likely that you will encounter students who require the use of assistive technology. You will not be alone, however, in making decisions about the appropriate technologies to use. Schools are required to assist individuals with disabilities to identify, obtain, and learn how to use appropriate assistive devices. These devices are identified during the development of a student's IEP. You will be expected to work with appropriate personnel in the school to develop the IEP. Once the student is provided an assistive device, you and others will be expected to help the student use it appropriately.

Computers provide valuable assistance to students with special needs.

Gifted and Talented Students

In addition to students who are challenged and unable to meet regular curricular expectations, teachers will also have students in their classrooms who have exceptional abilities. **Gifted and talented** students demonstrate above-average talent in a variety of areas including those defined by the Gifted and Talented Students Education Act passed by Congress in 1987: intellectual ability, creativity, leadership, and special talents in the visual or performing arts.

There is less support and consensus for how gifted students should be served as contrasted to serving students with disabilities. Several reasons account for this. Some people believe that having special classes or providing extra support for gifted students is undemocratic and elitist and that it takes scarce resources from students of lesser abilities who need them the most. This is compounded by the fact that many gifted students go unnoticed in schools (Gallagher & Gallagher, 1994). Students may hide their talents fearing ridicule from peers or, in some instances, because they prefer *not* to have the additional work that may come with harder challenges. Also, many gifted students, particularly those who are at risk or those who are culturally different, are often under-identified because of bias in teacher expectations.

There is also a lack of consensus among educators about who should be identified as gifted and talented. At one time, the gifted were identified primarily through traditional IQ scores. Those with scores above 125–130 were perceived to have advanced cognitive functioning and, thus, were considered "gifted." However, as you read earlier, researchers and theorists such as Sternberg (1985, 1999) and Gardner (1983, 1993) have questioned the singularity of intelligence and have proposed instead the idea of multiple intelligences, thus raising the question of whether the gifted should be identified in each of the domains of multiple intelligences.

Finally, giftedness is culturally defined and may take different forms in different cultures. For example, very talented athletes are not identified in most schools for "gifted and talented" classes, yet special academies have been established for them in some countries, such as India. Students who have special interpersonal skills or sensitivities are normally not identified as gifted in American schools, but these attributes are valued highly in some Native American and African cultures.

Characteristics of Gifted and Talented Students. Students who are gifted and talented can have a wide range of characteristics, particularly if we accept the concept of multiple intelligences. These include extraordinary cognitive functioning, the ability to retain lots of information, flexible thought processes, creative problem-solving skills, large vocabularies, extensive knowledge of particular subjects, advanced artistic or physical talents, excellent metacognitive skills, and high standards for performance. Turnbull and colleagues (2002, p. 231) organize these characteristics into five categories to provide teachers with clues about what to watch for in identifying gifted students who may be in their classes:

- *General intellect.* Students with above-average general intellect can grasp complex and abstract concepts readily. They often have advanced vocabularies, ask lots of questions, and approach problems in unique and creative ways.
- *Specific academic ability.* Gifted students often have information and skills in particular academic subjects well in advance of their peers. They normally acquire this advance understanding in mathematical reasoning, scientific inquiry, or writing because they are avid readers and have been reading adult materials from an early age.

There is less consensus for how gifted students should be served as contrasted to serving students with disabilities.

Some aspects of giftedness are culturally defined.

- *Creative productive thinking.* Gifted students are often highly creative. This quality demonstrates itself in traits that are intuitive, insightful, curious, and flexible. Students come up with original ideas and see relationships often missed by others. Their creativity may express itself in risk taking and sometimes in an extraordinary sense of humor.
- *Leadership ability.* Gifted individuals sometimes display advanced inter- and intra-personal skills along with the ability to motivate and lead others.
- *Visual or performing artistry.* Some gifted students have advanced visual, physical, or performing arts talents. They master physical and artistic skills quickly and well ahead of their peers. Students with certain cognitive, emotional or physical disabilities may have very highly developed visual or performing arts skills. You know of many examples: musician, Stevie Wonder, artist, Vincent van Gogh, and John Nash, the Nobel prize winner in economics depicted in the award-winning movie, *A Beautiful Mind.*

Gifted and talented individuals vary widely in their emotional and social skills as they are growing up. Some are very popular, well-balanced emotionally, and are school leaders. Other gifted individuals lack social skills and may have serious emotional problems. They may see themselves as different and may be reluctant to join with others for social events or classroom group lessons. This lack of social skills and/or emotional maturity can sometime mask the exceptional talents some students possess—another reason many go unnoticed. Many gifted individuals do poorly in school and are not popular with their teachers, and only as adults are their talents recognized—well-known historical examples include Edison, Einstein, Mozart, and Gandhi.

Working with the Gifted and Talented. Guidelines and programs for working with the gifted and talented vary enormously from district to district and from state to state. Some states identify large portions (as many as 10 percent) of their students as gifted, whereas other states may identify less than 1 percent. Some districts have extensive programs for the gifted and talented; other districts have none. Districts that have such programs normally employ three types of strategies: acceleration, enrichment, and novelty. Examples of these types of programs are provided in Table 2.5.

Table 2.5 *Strategies for Working with Gifted Students*

Strategy	Math	Science	Language Arts	Social Studies
Acceleration	Taking algebra in fifth grade	Taking physics or chemistry early	Learning grammatical structure early	Taking world history early
Enrichment	Changing bases in the number system	Doing advanced experiments	Writing short stories and poetry	Reading original sources and writing history
Novelty	Using probability and statistics	Writing about the impact of science on society	Rewriting a Shakespearian tragedy with a different ending	Creating hypothetical future societies

Source: Ideas adapted from Gallagher & Gallagher, 1994, p. 100

On a day-to-day basis, particularly in districts or schools where special programs do not exist, it is the classroom teacher who must remain alert for students with special talents, identify these talents, and find ways to meet their special needs. Unfortunately, this doesn't always happen, as shown in the following case reported by Gardner (1983):

> People like me are aware of their so-called genius at ten, eight, nine . . . I always wondered, "Why has nobody discovered me? In school, didn't they see that I'm more clever than anybody in school? That the teachers are stupid, too? That all they had was information I didn't need?" It was obvious to me. Why didn't they put me in art school? Why didn't they train me? I was different, I was always different. Why didn't anybody notice me? (p. 115)

Regardless, of districtwide programs, there are numerous strategies teachers can use to meet the needs of gifted and talented students in their own classrooms.

Differentiate Instruction for Gifted Students.   Instruction or curriculum that has been modified to meet the needs of particular students is called **differentiation.** Most often this occurs when teachers modify particular standard lessons or their curriculum to accommodate students with learning disabilities. However, differentiation is also an effective means for working with gifted and talented students. In her book on differentiated instruction, Carol Ann Tomlinson (1999) wrote that teachers need to be:

Differentiation refers to instruction that has been modified from a standard approach to meet the need of particular students.

> well aware that human beings share the same basic needs for nourishment, shelter, safety, belonging, achievement, contribution and fulfillment. [They] also know that human beings find those things in different fields of endeavor, according to different timetables, and through different paths. [They] understand that by attending to human differences (they) can best help individuals address their common needs. . . . In the differentiated classroom, the teacher unconditionally accepts students as they are, and . . . expects them to become all they can be.

Create a Rich Learning Environment with a Variety of Opportunities.   Many gifted students, with appropriate guidance and opportunities, will seek out challenges on their own. Classrooms with rich learning environments will contain print materials (books and magazines) that the gifted will find interesting and challenging as well as computers that will allow them access to the rich array of information available on the Internet. In elementary classrooms, these materials might be organized in "learning centers," where both remedial and advanced materials and activities are available. In secondary schools, materials will more likely be available in the school's library, subject-specific resource centers, and computer laboratories.

Use Flexible Groupings.   **Flexible grouping** is an important strategy for meeting diversity and for developing talent, particularly in elementary schools. This practice groups gifted students with students (regardless of age) who have similar talents and interests, not for the full day, but for part of the day. As the name implies, these groups are flexible and can change as teachers and students identify new needs, interests, and challenges.

Compact the Curriculum and Instruction.   If students have a sound grasp of the knowledge and skills associated with particular lessons, teachers can compact the curriculum for these lessons. This normally means reviewing the content of the lesson quickly and then allowing students to move on to more complex and higher-level ideas, concepts, and skills.

Use Tiered Activities. Teachers can use what Tomlinson (1999) has called **tiered activities** so that all students can focus on the same understanding and skills, but at different levels of abstraction and complexity. When teachers use tiered activities, it is important that they increase the level of challenge for students who have special knowledge or skills in particular areas.

Consider Independent Study and Learning Contracts. Independent assignments and learning contracts are additional strategies that challenge gifted students. The author used this strategy while teaching a course on the history of the Pacific Northwest to a group of ninth graders. Two students in the class were incredibly bright. They had advanced analytical reasoning skills, were excellent writers, and were very well read in history for their age. Instead of attending class, they went to the library at a local university a few blocks away. Their task, agreed upon in a learning contract, was to write their own version of the history of their community between the time the first settlers arrived in the mid 1850s to 1900. They were to use only original sources. The product of their efforts was outstanding, and it was published in the local newspaper.

Use Group Investigation and Problem-based Learning. Group investigation (described in Chapter 10) and problem-based learning (Chapter 11) are excellent strategies for working with all students, but particularly the gifted. These strategies allow students with special talents to identify problems of their own choosing and to design projects that address these problems in authentic and challenging ways.

Hold Gifted Students to High Standards. All students need the teacher's help in setting standards appropriate to their needs. This is particularly true for students who have special talents. Even though these students may be capable of high performance and achievement, they will not automatically set high goals for themselves—nor, in some instances, will their peers or families. Teachers can assist these students by showing them what a truly outstanding performance is in a particular field. Teachers can encourage students to aim toward an outstanding level of performance rather than be content with a level that may be observed in many of their peers.

Culture, Ethnicity, and Race

The United States has a rich history of cultural diversity and interaction among cultural groups. This interaction started when the first European settlers made contact with Native American populations and continued with each new wave of immigrants in the four centuries that followed. Currently, we are experiencing an increased movement of diverse groups of people into the United States, and we have become more aware and sensitive of the impact of cultural diversity for both newcomers and for the groups who have been here for a long time. Today, almost one-third of Americans are of non-European heritage. By 2020, it is predicted that 45 percent of all students in the public schools will be students of color. By 2050, every person in the United States will be a member of a minority group (Conditions of Education, 1998, Grant & Sleeter, 1989). The predominate minority student populations in today's schools are African Americans and Hispanics, although Asians and children of immigrants from all over the world are present in large numbers, as described in Chapter 1. Diversity in culture, ethnicity, and race presents difficult instructional challenges for teachers, particularly because the racial and ethnic inequalities and issues of intolerance that persist in society are mirrored in schools and classrooms. As described earlier, accumulated evidence has shown that many minority

Check, Extend, Explore

Check
- What are the main features of inclusion as defined by legislation and judicial decisions over the past quarter-century?
- What is an IEP and what are features of the IEP process?
- What strategies can teachers use when working with students with disabilities?
- What are the characteristics commonly observed in gifted students?
- What strategies can teachers use when working with gifted and talented students?

Extend
- What are your views about placing children with learning disabilities in regular classrooms?
- Do you think scarce resources should be used on students who are gifted and talented? Go to "Extend Question Poll" on the Online Learning Center to respond.

Explore
- Go to the Online Learning Center at www.mhhe.com/arends6e for links to websites related to *Special Education and Gifted Education.*

students receive a lower-quality education as a result of differing enrollment patterns, an unequal curriculum, tracking, and differential classroom interactions with teachers. Minorities are disproportionately placed in vocational and special education programs and are underenrolled in college preparatory and gifted programs. Even when the coursework is ostensibly the same, there are inequalities (Oakes, 1985; Oakes & Lipton, 2003).

Perspectives on Culture, Ethnicity, and Race

Although culture, ethnicity, and race are treated together in this section, it is important to point out that these terms do not mean the same thing. **Culture,** as used here, is a term that describes a group's total way of life—its histories, traditions, attitudes, and values. "Culture" is how members of a group think and the ways they go about resolving problems in collective life. Culture is learned and is ever changing; it is not static. In the United States, we belong to all kinds of groups that have distinctive cultures—racial, ethnic, religious, social class. Organizations, such as schools and businesses, also have cultures. Cultures are not groups; they are created by groups.

Ethnicity, on the other hand, refers to groups that have common language and identities such as nationality. Individuals of Polish, Irish, or Italian descent, for instance, may be classified as ethnic groups even though they are a subset of a larger Western European culture. **Race** is a term reserved for groups that have common biological traits. We all belong to many different groups and are influenced by many different cultures, as illustrated in Figure 2.4. We are influenced the most by those groups with which we have the closest identification. It is important to point out that all three of these terms are socially constructed and their use somewhat controversial. For instance, some scholars (Miles, 1989) have argued for rejecting the use of the term "race" and replacing it with "ethnic group." Others, such as Omi and Wilnant (1994), however, say that this is not a good idea because race plays a significant role in our society and children and youth are racially conscious from a very young age. (See also Mercado, 2001.)

> Culture refers to the way members of groups think about social action and problem resolution, whereas ethnicity refers to groups that have a common heritage. Race refers to groups that have common biological traits.

Figure 2.4 *Multigroup Membership in the United States*

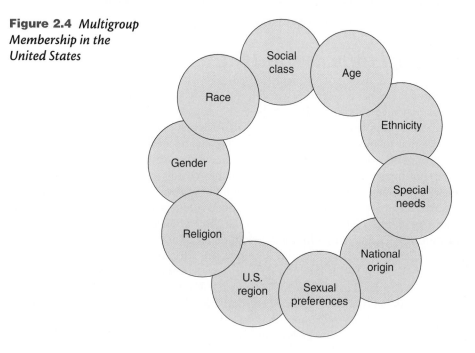

Melting Pot or Salad Bowl? Many immigrants, perhaps many of your parents or grandparents, came to the United States in the late nineteenth and early twentieth centuries. At that time, newcomers were expected to assimilate—that is, forsake their own cultures and melt into the dominant American culture. The **melting pot** was the metaphor often used to describe this blending process. Today, however, many prefer the concept of **cultural pluralism,** a perspective that acknowledges the existence of a dominant American culture but also recognizes the permanence of diversity. This view normally purports that each cultural, racial, or ethnic group will accept some of the common elements of the dominant culture as it interacts with that culture, but will also inject into the culture new elements for the benefit of all. Thus, the "melting pot" metaphor, with its implications of homogeneity, has been replaced with the "salad bowl" metaphor, in which each ingredient is distinct and valued by itself, while at the same time contributes to the whole and binds together with a common dressing—that is, the dominant culture.

> Today we prefer the "salad bowl" metaphor to think about cultural pluralism, a situation wherein each ingredient is valued for itself but also binds together to make something different.

Cultural Deficits versus Cultural Differences. Until recently, students who did not become fully blended or assimilated were often considered to be culturally disadvantaged. Differences in achievement between minority and majority student were accounted for by the **cultural deficit theory.** Various deficit theories were posited. Minorities were said to be genetically deficient in intelligence or they had some other inherent defect (dysfunctional family, poor nutrition) that interfered with their ability to be successful in school. For example, Harvard psychologist Arthur Jensen (1969) argued that children who came from poor families were intellectually inferior. A quarter of a century later, Herrnstein and Murray (1994) wrote *The Bell Curve: Intelligence and Class Structure in American Life,* a book that argued that African Americans inherited lower IQs than whites.

These theories have been discredited, partly because of analyses done by a variety of scholars over the past decade. For example, Gould (1996), in *The Mismeasure of Man,* points out the statistical flaws in IQ testing. Jerome Bruner, in *Acts of Meaning* (1990) and *The Culture of Education* (1996), has shown how learning is social and cultural and how intelligence grows as people interact with one another in society. Robert Sternberg and Howard Gardner have provided important perspectives about how individuals, regardless of race or culture, possess many different abilities rather than the one or two measured by the more traditional IQ and aptitude tests.

Villegas (1991) elaborated on the **cultural difference theory** to account for the achievement difficulties experienced by minority students in schools. He maintained that language is the vehicle for interaction in school, and if language is used by a subculture in ways different from the mainstream, then members of the subculture are at a disadvantage. Villegas explained:

> Cultural difference theory holds that low achievement of minorities is explained by the discontinuity between home culture and school culture and not by some cultural defect.

> Children whose language use at home corresponds to what is expected in the classroom have an advantage in the learning process. For these students, prior experience transfers to the classroom and facilitates their academic performance. In contrast, minority children frequently experience discontinuity in the use of language at home and at school. They are often misunderstood when applying prior knowledge to classroom tasks (p. 7).

Villegas (1991) and Villegas & Watts (1991) have also criticized the work that blames school failure on home-school disjunctures and argued that this view diverts attention from the existing inequalities that sustain the widespread failure of minority students. Villegas argued that the negative relationship between school and society is the problem and that solutions require finding more culturally sensitive political links among the school, its communities, and the larger society.

Cultural Discontinuity. Teachers and their students often occupy various cultures, each with unique beliefs and values and different ways of communicating. This leads to **discontinuity** and miscommunication between the home and the school. For example, Phillips (1972) studied how Native American children learned at home and compared it to the way they were expected to learn in school. She observed that these children were silent in classroom lessons, sometimes even when asked a direct question by the teacher. Most Americans would assume that these children were extremely shy or that they had learning or linguistic disabilities—in the latter case, referring them to low-ability or special classes would make sense. However, Native American children are expected to learn by watching adults, not by interacting with them. Their culture instructs them to turn to older siblings, not adults, when they need assistance; and they are accustomed to a great deal more self-determination at home than is permissible in the school environment. In light of this information, their classroom behavior can be properly interpreted as an example of cross-cultural discontinuity rather than a deficiency.

Another example of cultural discontinuity and miscommunication comes from a landmark study by Heath (1983), who documented the diverging communicative styles of working-class African Americans, middle-class African Americans, and Euro-Americans in the Piedmont region of the Carolinas. One of the many cultural differences she found involved the use of questions. At home, working-class African American adults didn't ask children very many questions, and when they did, they were *real* questions—really seeking information that the adult didn't have. In school, however, teachers expected children to answer questions all the time, and the questions themselves were artificial in that the adults already knew the answer. From the students' perspective, these questions didn't make any sense at all, and there was difficulty bridging the cultural gap. These results have been replicated many times over the past decade and have been summed up nicely by Darder (1991).

> [Bicultural students have experienced] an enculturation process that is distinct from that of Anglo-American students. This distinction is derived from the fact that bicultural students, throughout their development, must contend with: (1) two cultural systems whose values are very often in direct conflict, and (2) a set of social-political and historical forces dissimilar to those of the mainstream of the Anglo-American students and the educational institutions that bicultural students must attend (as cited in Mercado, 2001, p. 676).

Working with Students in Racially and Culturally Diverse Classrooms

Beginning teachers worry a lot about what they can do in the classroom to work effectively with a culturally diverse group of students. Fortunately, a wealth of strategies is available for developing classrooms that respond to the needs of students, regardless of their racial or ethnic backgrounds. Beginning teachers are encouraged to work first on their own knowledge and attitudes and to battle biases, stereotypes, and myths they may hold. Equally important, teachers need to make sure their curriculum is fair and culturally relevant and that they are using teaching strategies known to be effective and culturally responsive.

Developing Cultural Understandings and Self-Awareness. The first part of a teacher's strategy for working effectively in classrooms with a culturally diverse group of students is to develop wider cultural understandings and more self-awareness. Beginning teachers can work to improve their own knowledge and attitudes toward peo-

Perhaps the most important thing teachers do to work successfully with minority children is to have deep cultural understandings and sensitivities.

ple who are different from them by taking the initiative to learn about the cultures represented in their student's communities and by striving to uncover and conquer their own biases.

To familiarize themselves with local cultures, teachers should find and read books, magazines, and research articles, or take a course or workshop. The following excerpts from research shed light on the effects of culture in the classroom and provide the mainstream culture with a glimpse of what it looks like to a member of a minority culture.

A Navajo woman described her first school experience:

> Well, my first deal is just getting to school. Just when you live all Navajo culture and you first start school and first see the brick buildings, you don't know what's inside them buildings. Especially when you've only been to trading post twice in your life before school. It's when you get there you see these long lines of kids with their mamas. All the kids throwing fits and cryin, hangin onto their mom. And your mom's standin there beside you sayin, "You can't be like them. You can't cry cause you're big girl now. You gotta go to school. Don't, don't shame me at the beginning. You gotta make me proud . . .
>
> So she took all of us to school, and she dropped me off there. . . . The ceilings were so high, and the rooms so big and empty. It was so cold. There was no warmth. Not as far as "brrr I'm cold," but in a sense of emotional cold. Kind of an emptiness, when you're hanging onto your mom's skirt and tryin so hard not to cry. And you know it just seems so lonely and so empty. Then when you get up to your turn, she thumbprints the paper and she leaves and you watch her go out the big, metal doors. The whole thing was a cold experience. The doors were metal and they even had this big window, wires running through it. And these women didn't smile or nothin. You watch your mama go down the sidewalk, actually it's the first time I seen a sidewalk, and you see her get in the truck, walk down the sidewalks. You see her get in the truck and the truck starts moving and all the home smell goes with it. You see it all leaving (McLaughlin, 1996, pp. 13–14).

An educational anthropologist's description of elementary classrooms in Mexico can provide insights into the culture of many Hispanic students:

> Characteristic of instruction in the *Primaria* was its oral, group interactive quality. . . . Students talk throughout the class period; teachers are always available to repeat, explain, and motivate; silent seat work is rare; and often a crescendo of sound . . . is indicative of instructional activity. The following observation of a first-grade classroom illustrates this pattern of verbal and physical activity:
>
> As she instructs children to glue sheets of paper in their books and write several consonant-vowel pairs, the teacher sometimes shouts her directions to compete with the clamor of kids asking for glue, repeating instructions to each other, sharing small toys, sharpening pencils, asking to go to the bathroom, etc. This activity and "noise" is compounded by the large number in the classroom, 35, but things somehow seem to get done by some, if not all, students. Then teacher has the children recite the word pairs taped to the chalkboard. They shout these out loudly as a group as she points to each combination with an old broken broom handle. Sometimes she calls out the pairs in order; other times, out of order to check their attention. Then she calls individual children to the board, gives them the stick, they choose a pair of sounds, but then have to pronounce them loudly and quickly as she presses them for correct responses (Macias, 1990, p. 304).

There are a number of areas of cultural difference that seem to consistently cause trouble. Beginning teachers need to be alert to these. Cultures differ, for instance, in their attitudes toward work and the appropriate balance between being on task and socializing. Middle-class American culture tends to be very task-oriented, but many other

Teachers need to be sensitive to the basis of cultural differences and how they can affect a student's classroom behavior.

cultures give more attention to social interaction. Cultures also vary in their sense of time. For many Americans, punctuality is an unquestioned virtue, and children in school are penalized for tardiness, turning work in late, and so on. But in many non-Western cultures, people are much more relaxed about time—they do not regard punctuality as particularly sacred and do not pay strict attention to deadlines. The amount of physical space deemed proper between people who are conversing and norms about making eye contact are other key areas of difference.

Another area of possible misunderstanding is the relative weight put on the needs of the group versus the needs of the individual. American culture is very oriented to the individual, whereas Japanese and some Native American and Hispanic cultures place more emphasis on the group. Many Native American children, for example, do not want to be singled out for praise and attention—a situation that can be very disconcerting to their teachers.

Cultures also differ in their attributions, or judgments, about the causes of behavior. A polite smile that conveys friendliness in one culture may constitute a cold rebuff in another. Giving a friend academic assistance can mean helpfulness to one person and cheating to another. Erroneous attributions can obviously hinder the development of rapport among people of different cultures.

Finally, people of different cultures categorize and differentiate information differently—that is, they chunk information, combining and separating bits, in a variety of ways. A simple example comes from language comparisons. In English, there are the separate verbs *to like* and *to love,* while in French, one word, *aimer,* means both, and in Italian, no verb meaning *to like* exists. Speakers of these different languages categorize and differentiate experiences differently. It is easy to imagine the difficulties in communicating clearly when the interacting parties, even though both may be speaking English, are relying on such divergent conceptions.

With so many areas of divergence, it is easy to see how students and teachers from different cultures could come into conflict with each other. Simply being aware of these potential sources of misunderstanding will reduce the risk that miscommunication will occur. Familiarize yourself with the cultures and backgrounds of your students and reach out to people in the community to try to understand their points of view. Talk to your students and get to know them. When students and parents observe your efforts, they will feel that you do, indeed, value their experience and respect their uniqueness.

Reaching out to parents and others in the school's community is an important avenue for understanding students and their cultural differences.

Creating a Culturally Relevant and Multicultural Curriculum. In addition to attending to their own understandings and attitudes, beginning teachers need to be prepared to make curriculum decisions that will help their classrooms be culturally relevant and multicultural. It is beyond the scope of this book on teaching strategies to go into depth about multicultural education. However, in general, **multicultural education** is defined as curriculum and pedagogical approaches that teach students to *respect and value diversity.* Multicultural education has a wide variety of meanings and approaches. However, many prefer the perspective offered by James Banks (2001), which is illustrated in Figure 2.5.

The *contribution* approach, according to Banks, consists of devoting lessons to the heroes of various cultures, celebrating holidays of various cultures, and recognizing the art, music, literature, cuisine, and language of different cultures. For example, a third-grade teacher might have a Mexican American theme party on Cinquo de Mayo, with a piñata and tacos, and might teach the children a few Spanish words. In another method, the *additive* approach, the teacher sets aside lessons or units on specific groups or cultures or brings in literature or books that convey different cultural perspectives.

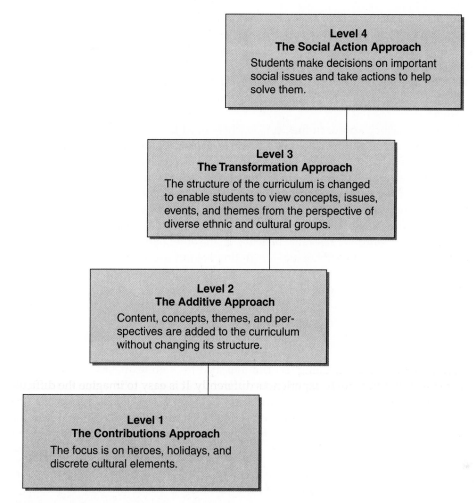

Figure 2.5 *Approaches to Multicultural Curriculum Reform*
Source: Banks (2001)

Although these can be very worthwhile educational activities, both the contribution and additive approaches have limitations. They emphasize differences between groups, not similarities, and may have the undesired side effect of widening cultural gaps rather than bringing cultures closer together. Both approaches can also be quite superficial and fragmented.

A third curricular strategy is called the *transformational* approach. When teachers use this method, they strive to transform the curriculum by incorporating a series of concepts associated with cultural pluralism into ongoing lessons. This approach identifies important concepts (for example, pluralism, interdependence, or communication) appropriate to a particular subject or grade level and then uses these concepts as the basis for lessons to promote understanding of cultural diversity. The major goal of this approach is to help students understand people from diverse ethnic and cultural perspectives. For example, the concept of pluralism could be infused into an intermediate school lesson on bar graphs; students plot the proportions of various ethnic and other groups in their community. The concept of interdependence could be infused into an elementary science unit on ecology. A secondary social studies lesson on voting rights could infuse the concept of exploitation.

A final approach defined by Banks is the *social action* approach, which encourages students not only to examine problems associated with diversity but to pursue projects that hold potential for taking social action. The problem-based model of instruction described in Chapter 11 is an appropriate teaching strategy to facilitate the social action approach.

No matter which approach they use, teachers need to review their curricular decisions to ensure that they demonstrate to their students they are valued people and that they provide a complex curriculum—one that is challenging and culturally relevant to students. A **culturally relevant curriculum** includes everyone and provides the voices of diverse people, particularly those who have been traditionally left out. For young black or Latino students, a curriculum lacking black or brown faces, traditions, literature, or music tells them that they don't count; it gives students from other groups the same message. Culturally relevant curricula, on the other hand, convey both value and challenge. They are often thematic, integrating subject areas from diverse traditions and, most importantly, they arise out of students' own questions and experiences.

A final aspect of creating a culturally relevant and multicultural curriculum is to ensure that the curriculum is free of bias. Normally, this requires teachers to move beyond the standard canons and become more inclusive in their choice of content. For example, English teachers could include literary works by prominent African American, Hispanic, and Asian authors in an American literature class.

Much of a school's curriculum is communicated through textbooks and other print materials. Researchers have identified curricular bias in many of the materials traditionally used in classrooms. Although progress has been made in eliminating bias over the past three decades, teachers nonetheless need to be on the lookout and ensure that the materials they use are free of bias and stereotyping. Forms of bias to watch for include:

1. *Stereotyping* is found in some materials—for example, white boys are depicted as brave, active, and successful, while boys of color and girls all of ethnicities are shown in more passive and dependent situations.
2. *Invisibility* is another way that cultural and gender bias finds its way into materials. Females and people of color are simply omitted or greatly underrepresented in both text and illustrations.
3. *Imbalance* is a related problem that refers to the situation in which only one aspect or interpretation of an issue or group of people is presented.
4. *Unreality* is another form of bias found in some textbooks and curriculum materials. In an attempt to avoid controversy, texts sometimes present an unrealistic picture of modern life, showing a nuclear family as typical, perhaps, instead of single-parent or blended families.
5. *Fragmentation* occurs when information about minorities is not integrated into the body of a text but is presented in a separate chapter or box. This conveys the idea that minority contributions are tangential to the mainstream and are not important.
6. *Linguistic gender bias* occurs when masculine terms and pronouns are used to refer to all people. This is easy to spot and easy to remedy. Simply replacing *he* with *he/she*, *mankind* with *people*, and so on corrects the problem.

The websites annotated on the Online Learning Center also have many examples of lessons that are multicultural and describe ways to deal with bias.

When teachers work with materials that contain bias, they can supplement them with additional materials that redress the bias. By the same token, when teachers make presentations, they need to supply examples and illustrations that are grounded in a variety of cultures. Finding such examples and illustrations demands great initiative.

One resource is practitioner journals; journals for teachers such as *Instructor, Arithmetic Teacher, Art Education, Social Studies, Language Arts Journal,* and *Mathematics Teacher* are helpful. One issue of *Arithmetic Teacher* (February, 1991) describes a unit on teaching the geometry concept of tessalation through Native American art forms. The January 1995 issue of *Education Leadership* was devoted to the topic of the inclusive school, and the April 1999 issue to race, class, and culture.

Alternatively, teachers can raise the issue of bias and discuss it directly with their students. Students can analyze curriculum materials for bias and share their findings with peers. Class discussions can focus on the emotional impact of the various forms of bias, on the political conditions that give rise to bias, or on action that can be taken to correct it. Chapter 12 provides guidelines for organizing effective discussions.

Using Culturally Relevant Pedagogies. The heart of working with cultural diversity is the teacher's ability to *connect the world of his or her students and their cultures to the world of the school and the classroom.* It is finding ways to embed the culture of the student into every lesson and every act. The strategies described in Part 2 of *Learning to Teach* form the basis for teaching in culturally diverse classrooms. For example, direct instruction has been used widely and found effective for teaching basic skills to students with special needs. Cooperative learning has been shown to be effective in all kinds of urban classrooms with diverse student populations and in changing the attitudes of students of different cultures positively toward their peers. Therefore, attention here is on instructional strategies that are aimed particularly at culturally diverse classrooms. The discussion draws heavily on the work of Gloria Ladson-Billings (1995a, 1995b), Jame Banks and Cherry Banks (1996), and Jeannie Oakes and Martin Lipton (2003). All of these educators have argued for a curriculum and a pedagogy that is culturally relevant and committed to social justice.

> It is important for teachers to connect to the world of their students' culture.

Making Connections to Prior Knowledge. Teachers can anchor instruction in students' prior knowledge and help them construct links between what they know and what they are to learn. By doing this, teachers help students see commonalities and differences among cultures and assist students in developing multicultural awareness. To do this effectively, though, teachers must actively seek out information about students' prior knowledge. They must spend time understanding their students' cultures and sizing up what they know and what they don't know.

Using Flexible Grouping. When teachers group students for instructional purposes, they can lean heavily on heterogeneous grouping and minimize ability grouping. The deleterious effects of tracking and the poor-quality instruction generally found in lower-ability groups and classes are well documented (see Oakes, 1985; Oakes & Lipton, 2003). Teachers should ensure that there are students of high, middle, and low ability in each learning group and strive to achieve racial and ethnic balance. Membership in ability groups should be flexible; group composition should change as students progress or as new and different needs are identified.

Paying Attention to Learning Styles. Teachers can also design learning activities that mesh with a variety of learning styles. As described earlier, there are several style dimensions along which teachers can vary their instruction. One route is to incorporate visual, auditory, tactile, and kinesthetic modalities into lessons. Teachers can also apply cooperative as well as individualistic task and reward structures. Further, teachers can vary their lessons by making them more or less concrete or abstract and more or

Table 2.6 *Learning Styles of African American, Hispanic, and Native American Learners*

African American Learners Tend To	Hispanic Learners Tend To	Native American Learners Tend To
Respond to things in terms of the whole instead of isolated parts	Prefer group learning situations	Prefer visual, spatial, and perceptual information rather than verbal
Prefer inferential reasoning as opposed to deductive or inductive	Be sensitive to the opinions of others	Learn privately rather than in public
Approximate space and numbers rather than adhere to exactness or accuracy	Be extrinsically motivated	Use mental images to remember and understand words and concepts rather than word associations
Focus on people rather than things	Prefer concrete representations to abstract ones	Watch and then do rather than employ trial and error
Be more proficient in nonverbal than verbal communication		Value conciseness of speech, slightly varied intonations, and limited vocal range

Source: Irvine and York (1995) as cited in Dilworth and Brown (2001) p. 656.

less formal or informal and by emphasizing in-context as well as out-of-context learning. Table 2.6 provides a summary of learning styles (or preferences) taken from the work of Irvine and York (1995) of three groups of bicultural students. It is important to point out there is a great deal of variation in regard to learning style within any group and that styles and preferences can be learned and unlearned.

Assigning Competence. A related consideration in planning and presenting lessons is to capitalize on students' existing abilities. This is particularly crucial for culturally different children who may be ascribed low status for whatever reason. Teachers can use a technique called **assigning competence** (Lotan & Benton, 1990). To assign competence, teachers first carefully observe their students while they work at a variety of tasks and then identify the special abilities of each student—verbal reasoning, drawing, visual or spatial abilities, for example. Teachers then publicly and specifically draw the class's attention to the student's special competence. Children who have been troubled by a lack of motivation and/or low achievement often bloom after teachers assign them competence. The story presented in Figure 2.6 illustrates the impact of assigning competence to one student.

Employing Strategy Instruction. Strategy instruction is an instructional element that should be an important part of teaching. One of the characteristics that distinguishes good learners from poor learners is their ability to use a variety of **learning strategies** to read and write, to solve problems involving numbers, and to learn successfully. When teachers help at-risk students acquire the strategies they need to learn effectively, they

Alicia, a rather tall, bilingual Spanish-English-speaking second grader, was the type of youngster whom people barely noticed. She was not a discipline problem; she did not make demands on the teacher or the other students, nor did she actively participate in interactions. Alicia seldom raised her hand to answer questions, and she rarely voiced her opinions.

One day in April, while videotaping group interactions in Alicia's classroom, we focused on students who frequently exhibited low-status behavior. While working on the coordinates and measurement unit, Alicia had teamed up with another child in her group, Aneke. Their task was to draw life-sized representations of their bodies. The girls took turns, lying on large sheets of butcher paper and then outlining each other's bodies with a thick, felt-tip pen. After making the outlines, the children had to cut out the replicas and then color in their features and clothing.

Aneke had possibly the highest academic status in this second-grade classroom, She was petite, precocious, and popular. She knew the answer to almost every question the teacher asked. Her hand flew up at every opportunity. She was a delightful, outgoing child, who seemed to be skilled at everything she was asked to do.

Among the important skills needed by students in the second grade is the ability to use scissors and to cut accurately. However, as Alicia and Aneke set about to cut out their butcher paper bodies, it became apparent that Aneke, who was so accomplished academically, did not know how to use scissors properly, nor did she know how to follow the outline of the body to cut it out accurately. Aneke was distressed. She feared she would cut off her paper arms and legs. Patiently and expertly, Alicia guided Aneke through the procedure, coaching her exasperated partner on how to use the scissors and follow the outline.

When Alicia's teacher viewed the videotape of this incident with one of the authors, the teacher commented on the fact that this was the first time since school started that she had seen Alicia show real mastery on a skill relevant to a classroom task. During the next orientation, the teacher shared her observation with the class. She wanted all the children to realize that Alicia was particularly skilled at using scissors and that if they ever needed help cutting, they could turn to Alicia as a resource.

Coincidentally, the school was getting ready to present a musical called "Let George Do It." This colonial play required that each class be responsible for making a number of three-cornered hats. The second-grade teacher decided to put Alicia in charge of making these hats for her class. Alicia was to pick children to be on the committee, decide on what materials were needed, get the pattern from the teacher in charge of costumes, and see to it that the hats were made to specification. Since Alicia was perceived as the most accomplished "cutter" in her classroom, the committee looked to her for guidance.

Alicia took to the making of the three-cornered hats with tremendous enthusiasm. Again, it was the first time since September that her teacher had seen Alicia talking and working with other children in such an animated and empowered way. Alicia was now raising her hand more often during wrap-up, answering questions frequently and accurately. During this same period of time, the teacher also discovered that Alicia had good spatial reasoning and visual thinking skills. For example, when the task for her group was to draw a map of the classroom to scale, Alicia drew the map and then created an impressive three-dimensional model of the room. The teacher made sure that Alicia was assigned competence for this accomplishment also.

After the beginning of the next academic year, the opportunity arose to talk with Alicia's third-grade teacher. This teacher said that she would have never guessed that Alicia had been a low-status student for a large part of her second grade. Particularly during Finding Out/Descubrimiento, but also during many other parts of the day, Alicia interacted frequently and effectively with her classmates, raised her hand and answered questions correctly, and expressed her opinions readily. Children listening to Alicia were often observed going along with her suggestions. Alicia was greatly valued by her teachers and her classmates for her artistic and organizational skills. It appeared that Alicia was also performing better academically in almost every curricular area.

SOURCE: Lotan and Benton (1990), pp. 60–62.

Figure 2.6 *A Story about Assigning Competence*

give them the tools for school success. Many programs are available to support teachers in this goal. Palinscar (1991) and Palinscar and Brown (1984) have documented the effectiveness of reciprocal teaching—an approach to reading instruction used in both elementary and secondary classrooms in which peer teaching is used to help students master basic reading skills and become better strategic readers.

Check, Extend, Explore

Check
- Contrast the meanings of the terms *culture*, *ethnicity*, and *race*.
- How do the "melting pot" and "cultural pluralism" perspectives differ?
- Contrast the theory of cultural deficits with the cultural differences theory.
- Describe actions teachers can take to develop cultural understandings of the students in their classrooms.
- Why is it important for teachers to use culturally relevant pedagogies?

Extend
- What are your own personal views about the cultural deficit as contrasted to the cultural difference theory?
- Some have argued that teachers and students must be of the same race to work effectively together. Do you agree or disagree with this view? Go to the "Extend Question Poll" on the Online Learning Center to respond.

Explore
- Go to the Online Learning Center at www.mhhe.com/arends6e for links to websites related to *Culture, Ethnicity and Race, Multicultural Education,* and *Culturally Relevant Pedagogies.*

Motivation is also a major concern. You will read in Chapter 3 about theories of motivation and alterable factors that impinge on students' willingness to engage and persist in learning tasks. Researchers have also studied specific strategies that promote motivation for at-risk students. The HOTS program (Pogrow, 1990, 1999) was developed for elementary students in remedial pull-out programs. Rather than providing additional drill on basic skills, as most pull-out programs do, students were challenged with difficult, ambiguous problems and were expected to discuss, question, and resolve problems for themselves with only modest help from the teacher. The program has been very effective in helping students succeed in school, and part of the reason is that students find challenge and interaction much more motivating than continuous "drill-and-practice."

Abi-Nader (1991) described a successful program for Hispanic high school students that focused on priming them for college, in part through future-oriented classroom talk. These students had been oriented to getting by day-by-day, and they were unaccustomed to planning and setting goals. Program classes are filled with references to the future, from specific lessons that prepare students for future experiences (such as filling out sample financial aid forms), to describing situations they may encounter in college or in a professional career, to telling stories about graduates from the program and their successes in college and careers.

Finally, *community problem solving* is a strategy similar to problem-based learning (described in Chapter 11) that has been effective in culturally diverse classrooms. When using this strategy, teachers encourage students to identify concerns they have about their community or neighborhood and help them plan and carry out independent projects. In one case, students at a low-income-area elementary school decided to tackle the problem of a hazardous waste site in their neighborhood. In the process of confronting this problem, students had to plan, read up on environmental issues, and understand the danger of the various chemicals on their doorstep. They wrote to their legislators and investigated the political process. Students organized and presented their arguments for action effectively to a variety of audiences, and raised and managed money. In the context of a meaningful, important, and engaging activity, students developed skills in reading, writing, math, social studies, science, design and layout, and interpersonal communication.

The Research Summary for Chapter 2, *Dreamkeepers,* is a very important study conducted by Gloria Ladson-Billings that speaks directly to strategies shown to be successful for working with African American students.

Language Diversity

Language diversity represents one of the significant shifts in the demographics of schools in the United States (see Chapter 1). Today, almost 20 percent of the students in public schools speak a first language other than English (Mercado, 2001). Many other students come to school speaking what might be considered local dialects of English. Teacher must recognize that language is a big factor in schooling and develop ways to work with students who speak different dialects or languages as their first language.

Differences in Dialects

Not surprisingly, the United States enjoys a rich diversity of languages and dialects. Black English, or **Ebonics;** Hawaiian Creole; and Spanglish are a few of the major, indigenous dialects. In the past, these and other dialects were considered inferior to

Research Summary

How Do Successful Teachers Work with African American Children?

Ladson-Billings, Gloria (1994). *The Dreamkeepers: Successful Teachers of African American Children.* San Francisco: Jossey Bass.

Of the many challenges facing education, none has been more difficult than improving the academic achievement of African American students. Everyone seems to agree that success requires "culturally relevant teaching." However, there has been a paucity of research-based knowledge about what this entails. Gloria Ladson-Billings's study, highlighted here, goes a long way in helping us understand culturally relevant teaching practices. Ladson-Billings's work is interesting for two reasons: for the insights it provides and for the research methods she used. *The Dreamkeepers* represents a very nice piece of qualitative research that breaks with a scholarly convention: *objectivity.* In addition to her study of successful teachers of African American children, Ladson-Billings takes the liberty as a researcher to write and provide insights into the problems gleaned from her own life experiences and her memories of being an African American student.

Problem and Approach: The purpose of Ladson-Billings's study was to describe the practice of "highly effective teachers of African American students." The study was based on three premises: (1) effective teachers are capable of describing their practice contrary to the belief held by some that they operate intuitively; (2) African American students and their parents act rationally and normative, and (3) it was OK for the researcher (Ladson-Billings) to insert her own beliefs and experiences into the research process.

Methods: This was an ethnographic study with four components: teacher selection, teacher interviews, classroom observations and videotaping, and collective interpretation and analysis.

Teacher Selection. The teachers who participated in the study were selected through a "nomination" process. Community members were asked to nominate teachers they believed worked effectively with their children. Sev-

enteen teachers were nominated. To cross-check community members' perceptions, Ladson-Billings consulted with several elementary school principals and teachers. They were asked the same question: "Who works effectively with African American students?" The principals and teachers identified twenty-two individuals. Nine teachers who were nominated by both groups were selected to participate in the study; one declined to participate. Of the eight teachers in the final study, five were African American and three were white. All were experienced, ranging from twelve to forty years in the classroom.

Interviews. Ladson-Billings interviewed each teacher with a set of predetermined questions. She reported, however, that she allowed teachers to converse freely about their concerns and their teaching practices. Interviews were taped and transcribed.

Classroom Observations and Videotaping. Over a two-year period, Ladson-Billings visited and observed the teachers' classrooms for ninety minutes to two hours once a week. She reported that she visited each classroom over thirty times. She audiotaped and wrote notes during the visits. During some visits, she also functioned as a participant-observer—in addition to observing the class, Ladson-Billings also participated as a tutor, a teacher's aide, and sometimes as a member of a student group. Many ethnographers like to engage in this type of participation because it helps them build rapport with the people they are studying and they learn things they seldom learn in an observer-only role. During the end of the first year, each teacher was videotaped.

Collective Interpretation and Analysis. Ladson-Billings met with the eight teachers and worked collectively with them to analyze and interpret their interview data and the audio- and videotapes collected in their classrooms. Together, they developed their model of "culturally relevant teaching practices." Involving participants this way is also quite unique in educational research.

(continued)

Research Summary

How Do Successful Teachers Work with African American Children? (Continued)

Results: An abbreviated description of the results of Ladson-Billings's study cannot do justice to the rich ethnographic data described in the full study. If you are interested, you should obtain *Dreamkeepers* and read the whole book. However, following are some of the main ideas and conclusions reached by Ladson-Billings and her eight teachers. These conclusions are broken down into the four categories found in the study, which later became chapter titles for her book.

1. *"Seeing Color, Seeing Culture."* The successful teachers in Ladson-Billings's study rejected the "equity of sameness." They *saw and valued* their students' racial and ethnic differences. They loved their work and saw themselves as part of the community. These teachers helped students see themselves as members of the community, but also helped them make connections to larger national and global communities. They believed strongly that all students can *succeed.*

2. *Developing "We Are Family."* The successful teachers in Ladson-Billings's culturally responsive classrooms encouraged a *community of learners.* They made deep and flexible connections with each of their students and cultivated relationships beyond the boundaries of the classroom. They encouraged students to learn cooperatively and to teach and take responsibility for each others' learning.

3. *Having Passion for Knowledge.* The successful teachers held a constructivist view about knowledge and the curriculum—a view that knowledge is not static but instead is continuously evolving and changing. Teachers were *passionate* about their content, but also viewed excellence as a complex standard in which student differences were taken into account. These teachers spent lots of time helping students develop learning skills and building *scaffolds* for bridging the curriculum of the school and the knowledge students brought with them to school.

4. *Focusing on Literacy and Numeracy.* The teachers in Ladson-Billings's study had strong literacy and math programs. These programs did not use more traditional "drill-and-practice" approaches, but instead emphasized communal activities and ways to make learning to read, write, and compute meaningful for African American students. Students were apprenticed in the community, and their real-life experiences were "legitimized" as part of the official curriculum. Students in these classrooms were treated as competent and were moved from "what they know" to what they need to know.

Discussion and Implications Ladson-Billings's study tells the story of eight teachers who were successful in one of the most difficult challenges in education: improving the academic achievement of African American students. It has a happy ending. Teachers who engage in culturally responsive practices—recognizing and valuing the racial and ethnic backgrounds of their students, creating vibrant learning communities characterized by mutual respect and collaboration, and having a passion for knowledge—can produce great results. The significant question that stems from this study is "How do we get all teachers who work with African American students (and all students, for that matter) to use the practices found to be so successful in the classrooms of the eight teachers in Ladson-Billings's study?"

Your Reflections Which of the findings from Ladson-Billings's study are congruent with beliefs you already hold? Which are new or incongruent? Do you think it is possible to get all teachers to teach the way the teachers in Ladson-Billings's study taught? Why? Why not?

English, and educators blamed the use of these "substandard" languages for childrens' poor academic performance (another manifestation of the cultural deficit theory). The school's remedy was to attempt to eliminate the use of the home dialect. This approach has not worked—children do not improve academically when their language is suppressed or when the language of their family is degraded. In fact, many may suffer negative emotional and cognitive consequences from these acts.

It is important to emphasize that people speaking a dialect are not speaking an error-ridden form of standard English. They are using a distinct language with its own complexity and its own rules. Use of the double negative, for example, an anathema in standard English, is correct in black English, as it is in many romance languages. The following is a further sampling of rules for black English (Jordan, 1988):

The dialect used by some African Americans is called Ebonics.

- Use a minimal number of words for every idea; this is the source for the aphoristic and poetic force of the language.
- Eliminate use of the verb *to be* whenever possible. This leads to the deployment of more descriptive and, therefore, more precise verbs.
- Never use the *-ed* suffix to indicate the past tense of a verb. (*Standard English:* She closed the door. *Black English:* She close the door. Or, she have close the door.)
- In black English, unless you keenly want to underscore the past tense nature of an action, stay in the present tense and rely on the overall context of your ideas for the conveyance of time and sequence (pp. 368–369).

The whole issue of the use of dialects can become politically charged, as evidenced when the Oakland, California School Board made Ebonics the language of instruction. The Board later rescinded this policy and then introduced it again in 2002, but only after considerable debate and cultural warfare. The important thing for teachers to remember is to be sensitive and *not* to make negative judgments about students' abilities based on their use of particular dialects. Teachers should not assume that students whose language is different than English lack the intellectual capital to be academically successful. One teacher chose to deal with the language her students brought with them to school in the following way:

> I vowed never to deliberately silence my students' voices. This vow is not easy to keep; it is something I struggle with daily. I am committed to creating a safe environment within my classroom, where my students feel comfortable expressing themselves regardless of the language that they bring with them, be it Ebonics, Spanglish, or other English dialects. But, to facilitate my students' acquisition of mainstream English, all of their assignments must be written in "standard" English. The majority of the time, I communicate with my students using standard English, but I feel that it is also necessary to model code switching in the classroom. I validate my students' primary language, but I do not feel the need to teach it. They come to class equipped with this language (Oakes & Lipton, 1999, p. 21).

Second-Language Acquisition

In addition to dialect diversity, the United States is home to a number of people for whom English is a second language. These students are referred to as **ESL** (English as a second language) or **LEP** (limited English proficiency) students. There are over 200 Native American languages spoken in the United States, and a large proportion of the U.S. population speaks Spanish. The influx of immigrants in recent years has brought many speakers of Vietnamese, Farsi, Korean, Russian, and dozens of other languages. For millions of American students, English is not their native tongue. The ten most frequently spoken languages in the Untied States in addition to English are listed in Table 2.7.

ESL is the acronym for "English as a second language." LEP refers to "limited English proficiency."

Table 2.7 *The Ten Most Frequently Spoken Languages in the United States Not Including English*

(out of a population of 230,466,777)	
Spanish	17,339,172
French	1,702,176
German	1,547,099
Italian	1,308,648
Chinese	1,249,213
Tagalog	843,251
Polish	723,483
Korean	626,478
Vietnamese	507,069
Portuguese	429,860

Source: Crawford, 1997 as cited in Mercado, 2001, p. 673

How do these children approach the problem of learning English? It is not an easy task, as you know if you have ever tried to learn a foreign language. Communicative competence in any language consists of more than simply knowing its phonology (pronunciation), morphology (word formation), syntax (grammar), and lexicon (vocabulary). The speaker also must understand how to organize speech beyond the level of single sentences; know how to make and interpret appropriate gestures and facial expressions; understand the norms surrounding use of the language in accordance with roles, social status, and in different situations; and finally, know how to use the language to acquire academic knowledge (cognitive-academic language proficiency).

In first-language learning, these abilities are acquired over an extended period of time and in meaningful social interaction with others. It is estimated that non-English speakers require two years to attain basic communication skills but need five to seven years to develop academic language proficiency. Children can get along on the playground and in social situations very readily, but they need much more time to become skillful in learning academic content in the medium of English. It appears that the task of learning a second language is a creative one. Second-language learners do not passively soak up a new language—they must listen attentively, rely on social and other context cues to help them make guesses about how to use the language, test out their guesses, and revise accordingly. All of this takes time.

Working with Language Diversity in the Classroom

The submersion approach is the practice of placing LEP students in regular classrooms and expecting them to pick up English on their own.

Schools are legally required to assist language-different children in learning English and other school subjects. Bilingual education gained support when Congress passed the Bilingual Education Act in 1972. Instruction for language-different students gained further ground as a result of the 1974 Supreme Court ruling in *Lau* v. *Nichols,* a class action suit brought by Chinese students in San Francisco against the school district. The Court reasoned that instruction presented in a language students could not understand amounted to denying them equal access to the educational system. The district's practice, common to many districts, had been simply to place LEP students in regular classrooms with native speakers. This **submersion approach,** allowing language-minority students to sink or swim on their own, is no longer permissible.

Schools have responded to the *Lau* v. *Nichols* mandate in a variety of ways. The most common is to provide ESL instruction in a pull-out program that places ESL students in regular classrooms for most of the day but in separate classes in English instruction for part of the day. Another approach is to provide a **transitional bilingual program** for non-English-speaking students. In these programs, instruction is initially provided in the native language, with gradual increases in English usage until the student is proficient. ESL is a part of these programs, too. **Full bilingual programs,** in which the goal is full oral proficiency and literacy in both languages, are rare. Interestingly, research suggests that bilingualism brings with it several cognitive advantages, including heightened cognitive flexibility and a greater ability to analyze language (McCown & Roop, 1992).

Happily, researchers have also illuminated some methods that more effective teachers use to help language-minority students learn English and subject matter. Allen (1991) reports that effective teachers:

- Simplify their language, use gestures, and link talk to a strong context;
- Make language comprehensible by keeping the learner's special needs in mind; and
- Use the native language judiciously when necessary.

Guidelines for teachers can also be gleaned from the second-language learning literature. To learn to speak, read, and write in English requires a high input of English speech and print. Teachers who structure learning tasks and classroom interaction to maximize comprehensible English input help their students master the language. For example, effective teachers structure more teacher-student interaction and less peer interaction in a classroom in which most of the students are LEP, but in a classroom that is evenly divided between native speakers and LEP students, more peer interaction is appropriate.

The research on how children acquire English as a second language is often forced to take a backseat to political pressures. Many parents oppose bilingual programs, believing that the approach hinders their children's progress in learning English. A number of states have recently passed legislation (such as laws passed in California in 1998 and in Massachusetts in 2002) restricting bilingual programs and the use of a student's native language in schools, replacing them with programs that emphasize English and less transition time.

Gender Differences

Even though women predominate in education, gender bias and differential treatment of girls have been problems in American classrooms. Issues of **gender bias** have focused mainly on girls, how they are socialized, whether gender differences exist in verbal and mathematical abilities, and whether these differences are the result of nature or differential socialization. However, within the last decade, concern has also been expressed regarding how boys may be lagging behind in their verbal skills and college attendance as a result of what happens to them in school.

Check, Extend, Explore

Check

- What types of language diversity are teachers likely to find in their classrooms?
- Why is it critical that teachers be supportive of language differences?
- How do children approach the problem of learning English if it is not their native language?
- Contrast transitional bilingual programs with full bilingual programs.

Extend

- In some states, legislation has been passed that limits how much instruction can be provided to students in their native language. What do you think of this type of legislation?
- Suppose that all of the students in a school in Los Angeles spoke Spanish as their first language. Should the school provide all instruction in Spanish? Go to "Extend Question Poll" on the Online Learning Center to respond.

Explore

- Go to the Online Learning Center at www.mhhe.com/arends6e for links to websites related to *Language Diversity and ESL Programs.*

Nature of Gender Differences

One important question for teachers and many others in society has been how do boys and girls, men and women differ? This question has been thoroughly investigated over a long period of time and though there are disagreements, some general trends appear to have emerged. Most studies have not found major, inherent differences between boys and girls in general cognitive abilities. In a persuasive meta-analysis (a technique for synthesizing and summarizing results from many individual studies, described further in Chapter 11), Linn and Hyde (1989) concluded that differences between boys and girls "were always small, that they have declined in the last two decades, that differences arise in some contexts and situations but not in others, and that educational programs can influence when differences arise" (p. 17). Other studies such as Adelman (1991) and Ma (1995) have reached similar conclusions. However, Diane Halpern (1995; 1996) reached a slightly different conclusion and argued that some differences do exist. She reported that girls do better in the language arts, reading comprehension, and written and oral communication, whereas boys seem to excel slightly in mathematics and mathematic reasoning. Finally, others have pointed out that gender differences in regard to cognition and achievement may be situational. Differences vary with time and place (Biklen and Pollard, 2001) and may interact with race and social class (Pollard, 1998).

In terms of personality and physical features, differences are more pronounced and the research is somewhat more consistent. Men appear to be more assertive and have higher self-esteem as compared to women who are more open and trusting. Two decades ago, Carol Gilligan's (1982) landmark study described the drop of self-esteem in girls during their adolescent years and how they became less intellectually and socially confident. Banks (2001), however, argued that Gilligan's findings are modified by race and class and cites research that shows that African American girls do not experience the same drop in self-esteem as do the middle-class white girls studied by Gilligan. Obviously, men and women differ in physical features. Girls reach puberty before boys. Boys grow taller and with more muscle tissue than girls.

Ormund (2000) has summarized the research over the past 30 years on gender differences and the implication of this research for teachers. Table 2.8 shows the result of her work. It summarizes similarities and differences between boys and girls and suggests the educational implications of these similarities and differences.

Origins of Gender Differences

A second important question about gender differences is their origins. The nature-nurture debate described earlier in the chapter to explain differences in ability also applies to explaining gender differences and gender role identity. The best evidence is that biology and hormones (nature) affect the kinds of play and activities pursued by young children with boys preferring more aggressive and active play. At the same time, studies have shown that both mothers and fathers play more roughly (socialization) with their sons than with their daughters (Lytton & Romney, 1991). Other adults in a child's life—neighbors, siblings, teachers—also hold beliefs about what it means to be a man or a woman and they act on these beliefs and interact differently toward girls than boys. For example, boys are given more freedom and independence; girls are provided more protection. Boys may be given model cars and legos; girls get dolls and play houses. The media can also be a source of gender stereotyping (Sadker and Sadker, 1994). Males

Table 2.8 *Gender Differences and Educational Implications*

Feature	Differences/Similarities	Implications for Education
Cognitive Abilities	Boys and girls appear to have similar cognitive abilities. Girls are slightly better at verbal tasks; boys may have slightly better visual-spatial skills. Achievement differences in particular subjects are small and have become very similar in recent years.	Expect boys and girls to have similar cognitive abilities
Physical	Before puberty boys and girls have similar physical capabilities. After puberty boys have an advantage in height and muscle strength.	Assume both genders have potential for developing physical and motor skills, especially during the elementary years.
Motivation	Girls are generally more concerned about doing well in school. They tend to work harder on assignments but also take fewer risks. Boys exert more effort on "stereotypically male" subjects such a math, science, and mechanics.	Encourage both boys and girls to excel in all subjects; avoid stereotyping.
Self-Esteem	Boys are more likely to have self-confidence in their abilities to control and to solve problems; girls are more likely to see themselves more competent in interpersonal relationships. Boys have a tendency to rate their own performance more positively than girls even when actual performance is the same.	Show all students that they can be successful in counter-stereotypical subject areas.
Career Aspirations	Girls tend to see themselves as college bound more than boys. Boys, however, have higher long-term expectations for themselves particularly in stereotypically "masculine" areas. Girls tend to choose careers that will not interfere with their future roles as spouses or parents.	Expose all students to successful male and female models in all fields. Show people who successfully juggle careers and families.
Interpersonal Relationships	Boys tend to exhibit more physical aggression; girls tend to be more affiliative and form more intimate relationships. Boys feel more comfortable in competitive situations; girls prefer cooperative environments.	Teach both genders less aggressive ways to interact and provide cooperative environments to accommodate girl's affiliative tendencies.

Source: This table has been adapted from Ormrod (2000), pp. 146–147

are shown in more dominant roles; woman in passive roles. So, what may have started as biological differences soon are influenced significantly by the socialization process as children interact with their parents, their peers, and other adults. An important perspective for teachers about the origin of gender differences is the one held by Zambo and Hess (1996)—some gender difference may exist at birth, but that they are not fixed and can be changed by experience.

Stereotyping and Differential Treatment

Boys and girls learn about becoming men and women in school just as they do in their families. For many years, curriculum materials fostered a gender bias by portraying men and women in stereotyped roles. Studies (Sadker, Sadker, & Klein, 1991; *Women on Words and Images*, 1975) found that men were more likely to be portrayed in active and professional roles while women were seen more often in passive and homemaker roles. Similarly, a series of studies spread over two decades (Baker, 1986; Sadker & Sadker, 1994; Serbin & Oleary, 1975) showed that teachers interact differently with boys than they do with girls. They ask boys more questions, give them more praise, and allow them to use equipment in science labs more frequently. The reason behind differential treatment is complex. Some argue that it results from gender stereotyping (AAUP, 1992), while others maintain that teachers pay more attention to boys than girls because boys are more active and more likely to cause trouble if left unattended. (See David's action research study in the Handbook at the end of this book.)

Gender bias and differential treatment of girls remain a problem. However, there have also been some successes over the past thirty years. Eccles (1989) and Ormrod (2000) report that schools and teachers have increasingly strived to treat boys and girls the same. Today, boys' and girls' sports receive equal financial support, and in some regions of the country they receive equal publicity in the local media. Since 1971, girls have made definite strides in terms of graduating from high school and attending and graduating from college. In 1971, only about 78 percent of girls finished high school compared to almost 90 percent of boys. By 1996, this figure had essentially reversed. Also, in 1971, less than 40 percent of women had completed one year of college and less than 20 percent had graduated. In comparison, over 60 percent of men had completed one year of college and 30 percent had graduated. In 1996, almost 70 percent of women were going to college, compared to 50 percent of men. Also, a larger proportion of women than men was graduating from college in 1996 (*Conditions of Education*, 1998; Koerner, 1999).

In the last decade, a number of educators have written about the problems experienced by boys and young men in school. Kleinfield (1999) argued that the attention paid to girls since the passage of Title IX in 1972 has resulted in the neglect of boys, especially African American boys. Others (Gurian, 1996; Hoff, 2000), point out that the majority of students who are referred to special education are boys. Boys have a higher dropout rate as compared to girls, and they are more likely to fall behind in verbal skills and college attendance. Today, only 45 percent of college students are men. Like concern for differential treatment of girls, those concerned about boys point out that teachers should be knowledgeable and sensitive about the unique needs of ALL students.

Working with Gender Differences in the Classroom

Many of the guidelines provided for teachers who work with students of various races and ethnic groups also apply to working with boys and girls, and young men and young women:

1. *Be aware of your own beliefs and behavior.* Sometimes, particularly in mathematics, boys are the norm for which girls much catch up. Reject this idea—it is the same as the cultural deficit theory described earlier. If assignments are differentiated, make sure they are based on the needs of particular students and not on gender stereotyping.

2. *Monitor the frequency and nature of your verbal interaction.* Treating boys and girls the same in your expectations, questioning, and praise. More about discourse patterns and the use of questioning and praise will be provided in Chapter 12.
3. *Make sure your language and curriculum materials are gender-free and balanced.* Most current curriculum materials have been scrutinized for sexual stereotyping, However, it is still a good idea to submit all materials and your own speech to scrutiny regarding what was described in the previous section as "linguistic gender bias." Do not use masculine pronouns to refer to all people. Make sure boys and girls and men and women are portrayed in a variety of active and positive roles and that show career and parenting roles equally.
4. *Show respect for all students and challenge both boys and girls appropriately.* As with matters of race and ethnicity, all students should be shown respect and that they are valued. All of your actions should show both boys and girls that you have confidence in their abilities and have high expectations for all aspects of their work.

Social Class Differences

For a long time, social scientists have studied variations among individuals with regard to wealth, status, power, and prestige. They use the term **socioeconomic status** (SES) to refer to these differences and have categorized individuals in Western societies into four socioeconomic classes: upper class, middle class, working class, and lower class. Several characteristics account for an individual's social class identification: occupation, income, political power, education, neighborhood, and, sometimes, family background. Boundaries between SES lines, however, are not always clearly defined. An individual may be high in one characteristic and not so high in another. College professors and teachers have fairly high status as a result of their occupation, but they may have low incomes, relatively speaking. A representative in Congress may have a substantial amount of power, but not very much money. A successful entrepreneur may be very wealthy, live in an elite neighborhood, and yet lack formal education.

The fact that an individual's socioeconomic status overlaps with race and ethnicity further complicates efforts at defining precise SES categories. For example, middle-class whites and African Americans often have more in common than they do with lower-class members of their own race. Educated, working-class Americans may live in the same community and find they have much in common with their middle-class neighbors. Because of the legacy of discrimination in the United States, low-SES African Americans and Hispanics may be treated differently and exhibit different values and behaviors as compared to low-SES individuals who have not experienced racial or ethnic discrimination.

Characteristics and Performance of Low-SES Students

Many children of working-class parents and almost all children of low-SES families live in poverty. Many are raised in single-parent households by an adult who lacks education, language proficiency, and job skills. Many low-SES children are also children of first-generation immigrants who are likely to have limited formal education and, perhaps, limited command of either English or their native language. Many suffer from malnutrition and poor health. Often, these are the children who come to school without breakfast, wearing old clothes, and speaking a language different than the one used in school.

Check, Extend, Explore

Check
- How is gender bias still a problem in the classroom?
- Discuss gender differences in regard to personality and abilities.
- Contrast gender differences attributed to nature as compared to socialization.
- What kinds of differential treatment in regard to gender are most likely to be found in schools?

Extend
- Some have argued for same-sex schooling as a way to reduce gender bias and to enhance the self-esteem of girls. Other have argued the same for African American boys.
- Do you agree or disagree with having same-sex or same-race schools? Go to "Extend Question Poll" on the Online Learning Center to respond.

Explore
- Go to the Online Learning Center at www.mhhe.com/arends6e for links to websites related to *Gender Differences.*

Most importantly, there is an achievement gap between low-SES and middle-class students. Just as in the case of racial and ethnic minority students, low-SES students, regardless of race, show less achievement than their high-SES peers and they often suffer under unequal curriculum, tracking, and differential classroom interactions with teachers. They, too, are underenrolled in college preparatory courses and are less likely to go to college. Research, three decades ago, demonstrated dramatically the differences that SES can have on school learning. Cazden (1972) examined speech patterns, specifically sentence length, under differing contexts for a working-class (low-SES) child and a middle-class (middle-SES) child. She found that while all the children gave their shortest utterances in the same context—an arithmetic game—their longest sentence context varied. The middle-class child, for example, spoke more extensively during a formal, story-retelling situation. The working-class child, however, spoke longer during informal, out-of-school conversations. In an earlier study, Heider, Cazden, and Brown (1968) found that while working-class and middle-class students' descriptions of animal pictures contained the same number of key attributes, working-class students required more prompts from the adult interviewer than did middle-class students. If the interviewer hadn't persisted in requesting more information, student knowledge would have been underestimated.

These studies and those conducted subsequently indicated that low-SES students have verbal abilities that may not be accessed by typical classroom tasks. As with any cultural group, people of each socioeconomic status behave in ways appropriate to their subculture. Middle-class teachers expect middle-class behavior, and when low-SES students behave differently, as these studies document, teachers' expectations about their students' abilities are affected negatively. Differing expectations result in differential student-teacher interactions, which result in poorer academic performance for low-SES students.

> **Socioeconomic status (SES) refers to variations among people based on income, family background, and relative prestige within society.**

Differential Treatment of Low-SES Students

Differential treatment provides one explanation of the lower achievement of low-SES students. Teachers hold low expectations for these children and stereotype their abilities because of the clothes they wear or their ungrammatical language. As described earlier, teachers' low expectations for students can lead to the children's low self-esteem and low expectations for their own work.

Perhaps the most serious problem for low-SES students is ability grouping and tracking. Low-SES students are disproportionately placed in low-ability groups and low-track classes where instructional quality is poorer than in the higher groups. The criteria used to guide placement decisions are sometimes of dubious merit, as described in a landmark study by Ray Rist (1970). Rist studied a single class of children in an urban area over a three-year period. He documented that kindergarten teachers used nonacademic data—namely, who was on welfare, a behavioral questionnaire completed by the children's mothers, teachers' own experiences with and other teachers' reports about siblings, and the children's dress—to make initial ability grouping decisions. The teacher used this information to place children in low-, middle-, and high-ability groups on the eighth day of kindergarten. Children of like "ability" were seated together and received like instruction throughout the year. The teacher gave more positive attention to the children in the high-ability group and spent more instructional time with them. She reprimanded the children in the low-ability group more often.

When the students entered first grade, their new teacher also divided them into low-, middle-, and high-ability groups and seated them together. All the kindergarten highs became first-grade highs (group A), the former middle and low children became middle children (group B), and children who were repeating first grade constituted the new low group (group C). Only the group-A children had completed the kindergarten curriculum and were able to start right away with the first-grade material. Groups B and C children spent the early part of their first-grade year completing kindergarten lessons.

The second-grade teacher continued the low-middle-high grouping practice. Group A students became "Tigers," group B and C students became "Cardinals," and repeating second graders became "Clowns." By now, however, the teacher had test score data on which to base her decisions, as well as parental occupation and other social-class information. Of course, low children were at a disadvantage on these tests because they had not been exposed to the same curriculum as the high children. The three groups were assigned different books for reading instruction and could not advance to the next book until they completed the previous one. Thus, low children were locked into the low group, making it nearly impossible to advance into the higher group. Rist summed up his results with this statement: *"The child's journey through the early grades of school at one reading level and in one social grouping appeared to be pre-ordained from the eighth day of kindergarten"* (p. 435).

Rist's findings shocked the educational community at the time. He had demonstrated that teachers' expectations and instructional decisions and actions were profoundly influenced by the social-class characteristics of children and that children who did not fit the middle-class mold suffered academically and emotionally. In the thirty years since the publication of Rist's study, other researchers (Anyon, 1980; Goodlad, 1984; Hallinan & Sorensen, 1983; Oakes, 1985, Oakes & Lipton, 2003; Rosenbaum, 1976; Sorensen & Hallinan, 1986) corroborated his disturbing findings. However, recent experiments by Robert Slavin and his colleagues with "Success for All" have demonstrated that schools and classrooms can be organized with programs and processes that offset the impact of poverty and social class (Stevens & Slavin, 1995).

Working with Low-SES Students in the Classroom

Many of the strategies recommended for working with students from different racial or ethnic backgrounds or for dealing with gender or language differences are appropriate for working with low-SES students. They, too, respond to teachers who show respect for them regardless of their dress and language patterns. They, too, benefit from challenge rather than low expectations and from instruction that is differentiated according to their unique needs and aspirations.

In many schools, low-SES students (unless they have been identified as troublemakers) are nearly invisible. They are unlikely to participate in extracurricular activities and special programs that exist for identified racial groups or for girls. Low-SES students can benefit schoolwide when teachers pay attention to them, help them become involved, and advocate for their rights to get an equal education.

Check, Extend, Explore

Check
- How do social scientists define the term *socioeconomic status* (SES)?
- What specific problems are faced by students of low economic status? Out of school? In school?
- How can teachers prevent the negative situations described in the Rist study?

Extend
- Many teachers believe they can teach students better if students are placed in ability groups. Do you agree or disagree? Go to "Extend Question Poll" on the Online Learning Center to respond.

Explore
- Go to the Online Learning Center at www.mhhe.com/arends6e for links to websites related to *Social Class and Education*.

Some Final Thoughts and Schoolwide Issues

We conclude with an admonition that all problems regarding diversity cannot be solved by teachers working alone. Instead, schoolwide actions are required that will make schooling more sensitive to students from diverse backgrounds and those with special needs. A number of approaches hold promise.

One of the most consistent findings from research is that tracking by ability or retention does not promote achievement. Further, it has damaging consequences for minority students. A good place to start reform, then, is to reduce or eliminate tracking. Many schools are beginning to experiment with reorganizing into teams of teachers and students. Some schools are developing interdisciplinary curricula, relying heavily on cooperative learning in heterogeneous groups, alternatives to standardized testing, and flexible grouping (Kohn, 1996; Oakes, 1992; Oakes & Lipton, 2003).

There are also school-level actions that can be taken to address the difficult life circumstances of students considered "at risk" due to poverty. Most schools offer free and reduced-price lunches for students, but only about 50 percent of these schools also offer free and reduced-price breakfasts. A smaller number of districts provide meals over the summer through the federal Summer Food Service Program. The connection between student learning and basic nutrition is not only self-evident, but also well documented, so it behooves schools and districts that lack these basic programs to implement them.

School programs that target early intervention are also helpful. The effectiveness of one such program—Head Start—is well established. For every dollar invested in Head Start, many more are saved later on in reduced need for discipline and remediation, welfare, and criminal justice. Yet, only a relatively small proportion of eligible children are served. The process of establishing a Head Start center is long and complex, but as a beginning teacher, you can lend your support to existing centers by promoting awareness among colleagues and parents and by lobbying for increased funding so that more low-income children can be served. Early identification and intervention with children who have been exposed prenatally to drugs and alcohol are also very important. To establish new programs or support existing ones, link with health and special education professionals in your school or district.

During the last decade a move toward interagency collaboration has begun among educators concerned about at-risk students. As Guthrie and Guthrie (1991) argued a decade ago, "a wide assortment of social service agencies has been organized to serve children and youth at risk; but the services often overlap, agencies are compartmentalized, and children are incorrectly referred" (p. 17). To improve services, they advocate that these agencies coordinate their work with schools to provide assistance that is comprehensive, preventive,

Schools can be organized to offset the negative impact of poverty.

and child-centered. Again, linking with health, special education, and social service professionals is the first step in streamlining interagency collaboration.

Another important avenue to improve the educational outcomes of low-income students is parent and community involvement. When parents and other community members are involved in the life of the school through tutoring programs, mentoring programs, school improvement committees, parent education, site-based governance, or other activities, students benefit (Epstein, 1995, Nettles, 1991). This is a topic that will receive more attention in Chapter 13.

Three schoolwide intervention programs are especially noteworthy: Accelerated Schools (Levin, 1997), Success for All (Madden et al., 1992; Stevens & Slavin, 1995), and James Comer's School Development Program (1998). These programs share characteristics such as parent involvement, decentralized decision making, and application of research-based instructional innovations. All three have proven quite effective in raising the achievement of at-risk students if implemented in appropriate ways. All three also have critics.

Underlying all the recommendations made in this chapter is the importance of teachers individually and collectively valuing each and every student and challenging them to reach their highest potential. Claude Steele (1992) highlighted the themes of value and challenge: "If what is meaningful and important to a teacher is to become meaningful and important to a student, the student must feel valued by the teacher for his or her potential and as a person." If anything going on in the school—curriculum cast as remediation, or instruction cast as the pedagogy of poverty—diminishes students' sense of themselves as valued people, students will be disinclined to identify with the goals of the school. Intellectual challenge goes hand in hand with valuing. "A valuing teacher-student relationship goes nowhere without challenge, and challenge will always be resisted outside a valuing relationship" (p. 78).

Reflections from the *Classroom*

Student Tensions

During your first year of teaching, you have been assigned to the school's interdisciplinary team (this could be in either a middle or high school). With one other teacher, you are responsible for teaching literature, writing, and history to a group of forty-seven students. You meet with your students in eighty-minute blocks of time three times a week.

You like this assignment, but it presents you with some real challenges. Students in your classroom are about equally mixed among three racial and ethnic groups. In the larger community, these groups have traditionally *not* gotten along very well with each other. In addition, three of your students have been diagnosed as having behavior disorders; two have learning disabilities; and one student has a physical disability.

The major problem you face is that the students just don't seem to get along with one another. Students from the three racial and ethnic groups hang out mostly with members of their own group. It's not that they are impolite to one another—they simply ignore anyone outside their own group. From time to time, some students make fun of the students with behavior

(continued)

Reflections **from the** *Classroom, (Continued)*

disorders. Although things are not out of control from a classroom management perspective, the overall climate is not positive. It is not the type of learning environment you or your colleague want for your classroom.

What would you do to make the learning environment more productive and to help students in your group get along better? Where would you start? Which of your actions would involve instruction? Group development? Are there outside resources that you might call upon? Write a reflective essay for your portfolio on this problem and then compare what you write to what the following experienced teachers have said they would do. Approach this situation from the perspective closest to the grade level or subject area you are preparing to teach.

Cassandra Garcia
5th and 6th Grade

This is the type of situation that demands action on two fronts, one short-term, the other more long-term. For the short term, I would have some of the special education and counseling personnel provide human relations training for students in the class. I would want them to emphasize how to get along with one another, how to communicate in positive ways, and how to resolve conflict situations without resorting to anger or force. I would also like them to provide students with experiences through which they would get to know each other on a personal level. I think this would help students listen to each other a little better and display less indifference toward one another.

On a longer-term basis, I would work to establish an environment of trust between the students and myself and among the various groups of students. I would use "classroom meetings" to help students discuss their problems and differences. I would start using cooperative learning groups on a regular basis. I would make sure that each group had representatives from the three racial and ethnic groups and that each group had one of the special-needs students. I would make sure that all assignments were set up in such a way that students had to work together and each student's success was tied to the group's accomplishments.

I know that it will take a long time to develop the type of learning environment I envision. I will have to remain patient and to expect many setbacks along the way.

Dennis Holt
Tampa Bay Technical High School, 11th and 12th Grade Hillsborough, FL

I teach in the most ethnically diverse high school in my district so I understand classrooms made up of students from a variety of racial and ethnic backgrounds and with any number of behavioral/learning disabilities. It is important at the beginning of the year to mold these students into an academic team. A first-step that I have found to be successful is to focus on identifying the variety of learning styles and multiple intelligences evident among my students. The theory of multiple intelligences is based on the work of Howard Gardner and suggests that individuals have eight different intelligences. Also, I have utilized a number of learning style inventories that are readily available via the Internet or through commercial sources. Since learning styles cut across racial, ethnic, and gender boundaries, students quickly comprehend that a variety of different learning styles are evident among members of "their" group and that they share similar learning styles with members of other groups. It is fun for me to become aware, along with my students, that the girl who had been tapping her pencil on the desk is primarily a musical-rhythmic learner and that the body-kinesthetically inclined "dumb jock" is not so dumb after all. I never hesitate to share my own primary visual-spatial learning style with my students. This exercise in self-analysis and appreciation of diverse learning styles has been a valuable first-step in team building. The next step is to assign students to mixed race/gender/learning-style teams of four to five to engage in cooperative work or problem-solving activities. I would suggest that the group work be something that the students consider to be "fun" rather than academic. Remember, at this point the idea is to build a sense of "team" among your students. Once a cooperative atmosphere is established in your classroom the academic work will follow. Establishing a team-oriented classroom is so important that I suggest you consider devoting as much time as you need to team-building activities. I have begun my school year this way for several years now and have found this method to be very successful. Good luck.

⊙⊙ *Chapter Review*

Go back to the "Interactive and Applied Learning" feature at the beginning of the chapter for a listing of interactive and applied activities. Go to the Online Learning Center at **www.mhhe.com/arends6e** or your Interactive Student CD-ROM to take practice quizzes over the content of this chapter and receive immediate feedback. You can also review chapter content and main ideas, practice with key terms, and find annotated Web links on topics associated with this chapter.

Summary

Perspective and Overview

- Over the past half century, the student population in American schools has changed dramatically. Understanding diversity and helping each student are teaching challenges of the twenty-first century.
- Using appropriate language when discussing diversity or referring to students' backgrounds and abilities is critical.

Theoretical and Empirical Support

- Much of the research and concern with diversity has focused around three topics: equity, differential treatment, and variations of the learning abilities of students.
- Equity refers to the making conditions in schools impartial and equal for everyone. Historically, these conditions have not existed. Some students have been provided restricted opportunities because of their race or abilities.
- Differential treatment refers to the differences in educational experiences of the majority race, class, culture, and gender and those of minorities.
- Studies over the years have shown that minority students receive a lower-quality education as a result of enrollment patterns, tracking and grouping patterns, and differential interactions with teachers.
- Teachers' expectations affect relationships with students, what they learn, and students' perceptions of their own abilities. Teachers can learn to be aware of and minimize their biases about students of different backgrounds.
- Students vary in their abilities to learn. For many years, human intelligence was conceived as a single ability.
- Modern theorists view ability and intelligence as more than a single ability and propose the theory multiple intelligences.
- Debates have existed for a long time over whether ability to learn is inherited (nature) or is a result of the environment (nurture). Today, most psychologists believe it is a

combination of both and also recognize that an individual's capacity to learn reflects cultural backgrounds.
- Learners vary in the way they process information and also in their preferred styles of learning. It is important to tailor instruction to student's learning styles and preferences. However, this is not always possible because the different styles in a classroom are simply too varied to make it practical for teachers to accommodate every student's style.

Exceptionalities

- Students who have learning disabilities have special needs that must be met if they are to successfully function in and out of school. Traditionally, these students have received an inferior education. Current efforts to mainstream and include students with special needs are aimed at correcting this situation.
- Inclusion is an effort to extend regular classroom educational opportunities to students with special needs, a group that traditionally has been segregated and has received inferior educational opportunities.
- Public Law 94-192 specified that students with disabilities must be educated in the least restrictive environment and that each much have an individualized educational plan (IEP).
- Teachers' responsibilities for working with special-needs students include helping with the IEP process and adapting instruction and other aspects of teaching so all students can learn.
- Perspectives differ on how best to work with students with disabilities. Some advocate highly structured approaches whereas others argue that instruction should stem from the student's interest and emphasize problem solving and critical thinking.
- There is lack of consensus about how to identify and educate students who have special gifts and talents. Some

- believe that paying attention to the gifted takes resources away from students who need them more.
- Characteristic of gifted students can include extraordinary cognitive functioning, the ability to retain lots of information, flexible and creative thought processes, large vocabularies, and advanced artistic talents.
- Effective strategies for working with gifted students include differentiating instruction, creating rich learning environments, using flexible groupings, compacting curriculum and instruction, using independent study, and helping gifted students set high standards for themselves.

Culture, Ethnicity, and Race

- Contemporary perspectives reject ideas about cultural deficits and instead embrace cultural differences theories and cultural discontinuity to account for the difficulties minority students experience in school.
- To work effectively with students in culturally and racially diverse classrooms, teachers must recognize, understand, and appreciate cultural groups, whether based on racial, ethnic, language, gender, or other differences.
- Becoming aware of one's own bias and developing understandings and sensitivities of students' cultures is an important first step for successful teaching in culturally diverse classrooms.
- Effective teachers of racially and culturally different students know how to create culturally relevant and multicultural curricula and how to use culturally relevant pedagogies.
- Specific teaching models and strategies available to accomplish multicultural learning goals include direct instruction, cooperative learning, reciprocal teaching, and community problem solving.

Language Diversity

- Teachers will find significant language diversity in today's classrooms. This includes diversity in dialects spoken as well as many students who speak English as their second language.
- Second-language acquisition is a difficult and long-term process for students. It includes not only learning phonology, morphology, syntax, and vocabulary, but also how to interpret gestures and facial expressions, learning the norms that surround language usage, and using language to acquire cognitive knowledge.

- Language diversity must be respected and bilingual skills must be encouraged and developed for students who do not speak the dominant language.

Gender Differences

- Even though education has been a field dominated by women, gender bias and differential treatment of girls have been problems in schools.
- Most studies show that there are few major, inherent differences between the abilities of men and women. However, some evidence exists that girls do better in language arts, reading, and oral and written communication whereas boys seem to excel slightly in mathematical reasoning.
- Although some aspect of female and male personality and behavior can be attributed to nature, socialization likely plays a more important role in role identity.
- Traditionally, teachers have interacted differently with boys and girls. They ask boys more questions, give them more praise, and afford them greater independence.
- Effective teacher's are aware of their own possible gender bias, show respect, challenge all students, and make sure their language and curriculum materials are gender free and balanced.

Social Class Differences

- Low-SES students, for the most part, come from families who are poor, have limited formal education, and who often speak English as second language. They come to school in poor health, with old clothes, and speak a language other than English.
- Socioeconomic status has rather dramatic effects on school learning, mainly because of tracking and grouping and because of differential interactions with teachers.
- Low-SES students respond to teachers who show them respect, who challenge them by holding high expectations for their academic learning, and who will be advocates for their rights to an equal education.

Some Final Thoughts and Schoolwide Issues

- Teachers alone cannot solve all the problems faced by schools today. Many of the challenges of providing equal opportunities can be met only through community and schoolwide actions and reform.

Key Terms

analytical intelligence 48	disability 43	inclusion 53	mental age 48
assigning competence 72	discontinuity 66	in-context 51	multicultural education 68
assistive technologies 59	Ebonics 74	individualized education	multiple intelligences 49
challenged 43	emotional intelligence 50	plan 53	out-of-context 51
community problem	equity 44	intelligence 48	practical intelligence 49
solving 74	ESL 77	intelligence quotient 48	race 64
creative intelligence 48	ethnicity 64	learning styles 51	self-fulfilling prophecy 45
cultural deficit theory 65	field dependent 50	learning preferences 51	socioeconomic status 83
cultural difference theory 65	field independent 51	learning strategies 72	submersion approach 79
cultural pluralism 65	flexible grouping 62	least restrictive	sustaining expectation
culturally relevant	full bilingual programs 79	environment 53	effect 46
curriculum 70	gender bias 79	LEP 77	teacher expectations 45
culture 64	gifted and talented 60	mainstreaming 53	tiered activities 63
differential treatment 45	handicapped 43	melting pot 65	transitional bilingual
differentiation 62		mental abilities 48	program 79

Portfolio and Field Experience Activities

This feature has been designed to help you learn from your field experiences and to assist you in the preparation of artifacts for your professional portfolio on topics and standards associated with Chapter 2.

1. Complete the "Reflections from the Classroom" exercise at the end of this chapter. The essay will provide insight into your views about diversity and strategies you might use to resolve student conflicts and tensions that may arise in diverse classrooms.

2. Complete Activity 2.1 in the *Guide to Field Experiences and Portfolio Development.* Use the product of this work as an artifact for describing your understanding of diversity and student learning. Identify how you plan to grow professionally in this area.

3. Complete Activities 2.2 and 2.4 in the *Guide to Field Experiences and Portfolio Development.* These activities will help you produce important artifacts about your understanding of special-needs students and those who are culturally different than you. Describe how you might go about differentiating instruction for them.

4. Complete Activity 2.6 in the *Guide to Field Experiences and Portfolio Development* to provide evidence about your understanding of multicultural education and inclusion.

Books for the Professional

Go to the Online Learning Center at www.mhhe. com/arends6e or your Interactive Student CD-ROM for an annotated version of this list.

Banks, J. A. (2001). *Cultural diversity in education: Foundations, curriculum and teaching.* (4th ed.). Boston: Allyn and Bacon.

Cushner, K. A., McClelland, & P. Safford. (2000). *Human diversity in education: An integrative approach.* (3rd ed.). New York: McGraw Hill.

Friend, M., and Bursuck, W. (2002). *Including Students with Special Needs.* (2nd ed.). Boston: Allyn and Bacon.

Oakes, J., and Lipton, M. (2003). *Teaching to Change the World.* (2nd ed.). New York: McGraw-Hill.

Obiakor, F. E., Algozzine, B., & Rueda, R. (2001). *It Even Happens in 'Good' Schools: Responding to Cultural Diversity in Today's Classrooms.* Thousand Oakes, CA: Corwin Press.

Pang, V. O. (2001). *Multicultural education: A caring-centered reflective approach.* New York: McGraw-Hill.

Tomlinson, C. A. (1999). *The Differentiated Classroom: Responding to the Needs of All Learners.* Alexandria, VA: Association for Supervision and Curriculum Development.

Weiner, Lois (1999). *Urban Teaching: The Essentials.* New York: Teachers College Press.

Winebrenner, P. E. (ed.). (2000). *Teaching Gifted Kids in the Regular Classroom.* Minneapolis, MN: Free Spirit Press.

Part 2 *The Leadership Aspects of Teaching*

This part of *Learning to Teach* is about the leadership aspects of teaching. Teachers, like leaders in other settings, are expected to provide leadership to students and to coordinate a variety of activities as they and students work interdependently to accomplish the academic and social goals of schooling. Teacher leadership is critical because if students are not motivated to participate in and persist with academic learning tasks, or if they are not managed effectively, all the rest of teaching can be lost. Yet, these complex functions must be performed in classrooms characterized by fast-moving events and a large degree of unpredictability, and unlike many of the instructional aspects of teaching that cannot be planned ahead of time. Many teacher leadership roles require on-the-spot judgments.

Part 2 focuses on five important leadership functions: planning, motivating students, building productive learning communities, managing classroom groups, and assessing and evaluating student progress. Even though each function is described and discussed separately, in the real day-to-day life of teaching, the distinctions are not nearly so tidy. When teachers plan, as described in Chapter 3, they are also setting conditions for allocating time, determining motivation, and building productive learning communities, the subjects of Chapter 4. The way students behave and how they are managed on any particular day, the focus of Chapter 5, cycles back to influence future plans and resource allocation decisions, as does assessment and grading, the focus of Chapter 6.

There is a substantial knowledge base on each aspect of teacher leadership that can provide a guide for effective practice. There is also considerable wisdom that has been accumulated by teachers over the years to help beginning teachers get started with learning to plan, to allocate resources, and to deal with students in group settings.

You will discover as you read and reflect on the leadership aspects of teaching that providing leadership in classrooms is no easy matter and cannot be reduced to simple recipes. Instead, leadership is tightly connected to specific classrooms and schools and to your own leadership style, and what works in general may not work in any specific case. Learning to read specific situations and to act on them effectively in real classrooms through reflection and problem solving is one of the most important challenges facing beginning teachers. When mastered, this is a most rewarding ability.

Chapter Three

Teacher Planning

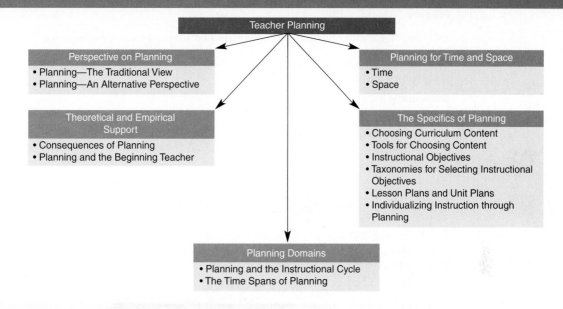

Teacher Planning

Perspective on Planning
- Planning—The Traditional View
- Planning—An Alternative Perspective

Planning for Time and Space
- Time
- Space

Theoretical and Empirical Support
- Consequences of Planning
- Planning and the Beginning Teacher

The Specifics of Planning
- Choosing Curriculum Content
- Tools for Choosing Content
- Instructional Objectives
- Taxonomies for Selecting Instructional Objectives
- Lesson Plans and Unit Plans
- Individualizing Instruction through Planning

Planning Domains
- Planning and the Instructional Cycle
- The Time Spans of Planning

Interactive **and** *Applied Learning*

Go to your Interactive Student CD-ROM to:

- Hear audio clips of Jason O'Brien and Angella Transfeld (tenth grade English) talking about teacher planning in the *Teachers on Teaching* feature
- See sample lesson plans and do a lesson plan exercise

Go to the Online Learning Center at www.mhhe.com/arends6e to read *PowerWeb* articles and newsfeed updates about:

- Constructivist curriculum
- Curriculum
- Instruction
- Technology and education
- World Wide Web

Considering **Standards**

Studying this chapter will help you meet four INTASC principles:

Primary

INTASC 3: Creates instructional opportunities adapted to diverse learners.

INTASC 7: Plans instruction based on knowledge of subject matter, students, the community, and curriculum goals.

Secondary

INTASC 1: Creates learning experiences to make subject matter meaningful.

INTASC 2: Provides learning opportunities that support student development.

Reflecting **on** *Teacher Planning*

Think about personal experiences you have had in your life that required considerable planning. Examples might be planning what college to attend, for a wedding, or for an extended trip. They might also include experiences for which you did not plan. Divide these experiences into two categories: experiences that were well planned and experiences that were not well planned. Now consider the following questions:

- What did the well-planned experiences have in common?
- What did the poorly-planned experiences have in common?
- What were the consequences, if any, of good planning? Of poor planning?

Now think about your own planning skills. Are you the type of person who likes to plan? Do you make to-do lists? Do you think through each step of an activity before you begin? Or are you the type of person who feels more at home with allowing experiences to go unplanned and letting things evolve?

How do you think your own attitudes toward planning might influence your teaching and the planning required of teachers?

 Go to the Online Learning Center at www.mhhe.com/arends6e to respond to these questions.

ven though planning and making decisions about instruction are demanding processes that call for rather sophisticated understanding and skills, teachers do not have to feel overwhelmed. Most of you have planned trips that required complicated travel arrangements. You have planned college schedules, made to-do lists, and survived externally imposed deadlines for term papers and final examinations. Graduation celebrations and weddings are other events most people have experienced that require planning skills of a high caliber. Planning for teaching may be a bit more complex, but the skills you already have can serve as a foundation on which to build.

This chapter describes some of what is known about the processes of teacher planning and decision making. The rationale and knowledge base on planning, particularly the impact of planning on student learning and on the overall flow of classroom life, are described, as are the processes experienced teachers use to plan and make decisions. Also included is a rather detailed explanation of specific planning procedures and a number of aids and techniques used for planning in education and other fields. The discussion that follows strives to capture the complexity of teacher planning and decision making and to show how these functions are performed by teachers under conditions of uncertainty. Although the chapter's emphasis is on the planning tasks carried out by teachers in solitude prior to instruction, attention is also given to the varied in-flight decisions teachers make in the midst of teaching lessons to students.

Perspective on Planning

People today express great confidence in their ability to control events through sophisticated planning. The importance given to planning is illustrated by the many special occupational roles that have been created for just this purpose. For example, a professional cadre of land-use planners, marketing specialists, systems analysts, and strategic planners, to name a few, work full-time putting together detailed, long-range plans to influence and direct the economy and ensure appropriate military efforts. Family planning, financial planning, and career planning are topics taught to students in high schools and universities and to adults in many settings.

Planning is also vital to teaching. One measure of the importance of planning is illustrated when you consider the amount of time teachers spend on this activity. Clark and Yinger (1979), for example, reported that teachers estimate they spend between 10 percent and 20 percent of their working time each week on planning activities. The importance of planning is illustrated in another way when you consider the wide variety of educational activities affected by the plans and decisions made by teachers, as described by Clark and Lampert (1986):

> **Good planning involves allocating the use of time, choosing appropriate methods of instruction, creating student interest, and building a productive learning environment.**

> Teacher planning is a major determinant of what is taught in schools. The curriculum as published is transformed and adapted in the planning process by additions, deletions, interpretations, and by teacher decisions about pace, sequence, and emphasis. And in elementary classrooms, where a teacher is responsible for all subject matter areas, planning decisions about what to teach, how long to devote to each topic, and how much practice to provide take on additional significance and complexity. Other functions of teacher planning include allocating instructional time for individuals and groups of students, composing student groupings, organizing daily, weekly, and term schedules, compensating for interruptions from outside the classroom and communicating with substitute teachers (p. 28).

Indeed, the process of learning to teach is described by some as that through which teacher candidates learn to decide what curriculum content is important for students

Careful planning is required for many aspects of modern life.

to learn and how it can be enacted in classroom settings through the execution of learning activities and events (Doyle, 1990; Stronge, 2002).

This chapter will emphasize the importance of planning and highlight that there is much more to planning than good lesson plans. Most important, it will attempt to convey the message that planning is complex and that effective teachers believe "plans are made to be bent."

Planning—The Traditional View

The rational-linear approach to planning focuses on setting goals first and then selecting particular strategies to accomplish these goals. Nonlinear planning turns this around. Planners start by taking action and attach goals at some later time.

The planning process in all fields, including education, has been described and studied by many researchers and theorists. The dominant perspective that guides most of the thinking and action on this topic has been referred to as the **rational-linear model.** This perspective puts the focus on goals and objectives as the first step in a sequential process. Modes of action and specific activities are then selected from available alternatives to accomplish prespecified ends. The model assumes a close connection between those who set goals and objectives and those charged with carrying them out. Figure 3.1 illustrates the basic linear planning model.

This model owes its theoretical base to planners and thinkers in many fields. In education, the basic concepts are usually associated with early curriculum planners and theorists, such as Ralph Tyler (1950), and with later instructional designers, such as Mager (1962, 1997), Gagné and Wager (1992), and Eby (1992). For both groups, good educational planning is characterized by carefully specified instructional objectives (normally stated in behavioral terms), teaching actions and strategies designed to promote prescribed objectives, and careful measurements of outcomes, particularly student achievement.

Planning—An Alternative Perspective

During the last twenty-five years, many observers have questioned whether the rational-linear model accurately describes planning in the real world (Fullan, 2001; Weick, 1979, for example). The view that organizations and classrooms are goal-driven has been challenged, as has the view that actions can be carried out with great precision in a world characterized by complexity, change, and uncertainty.

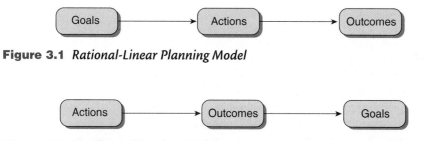

Figure 3.1 *Rational-Linear Planning Model*

Figure 3.2 *Nonlinear Planning Model*

Check, Extend, Explore

Check
- Contrast the traditional, rational-linear view of planning with nonlinear perspectives.
- In what ways do planning and decision-making activities impact other aspects of teaching?

Extend
- Which perspective of planning most closely fits the way you plan?

Explore
- Go to the Online Learning Center at www.mhhe.com/arends6e for links to websites related to Approaches to Planning.

Note that the rational-linear model found in Figure 3.1 is turned upside down in the **nonlinear model,** in which planners start with actions that in turn produce outcomes (some anticipated, some not) and finally summarize and explain their actions by assigning goals to them. Proponents of this model of planning illustrated in Figure 3.2 argue that plans do not necessarily serve as guides for actions but instead become symbols, advertisements, and justifications for what people have already done. As will be shown later, this model may describe the way many experienced teachers actually approach some aspects of planning. Although they set goals and strive to get a sense of direction for themselves and their students, teachers' planning proceeds in a cyclical, not a straight linear, fashion, with a great deal of trial and error built into the process. Indeed, experienced teachers pay attention to features of both the linear and nonlinear aspects of planning and accommodate both.

Theoretical and Empirical Support

The research on teacher planning and decision making is substantial and has grown significantly in the past three decades. It has shown that planning has consequences for what students learn, that beginning teachers and experienced teachers plan differently, and that experienced teachers do not always plan as expected. This research also illustrates the complexity of teacher planning and how certain kinds of planning can produce unanticipated and surprising results.

Consequences of Planning

Both theory and common sense suggest that planning for any kind of activity improves results. Research also favors instructional planning over undirected events and activities, but as you will see, some types of planning may lead to unexpected results.

Planning processes initiated by teachers can give both students and teachers a sense of direction and can help students become aware of the goals implicit in the learning tasks they are asked to perform. Two important studies done at about the same time highlight the effects of planning on teacher behavior and its consequence for students.

Duchastel and Brown (1974) were interested in the effects of instructional objectives on student learning. At the time of their study, previous research results were contradictory, and some had failed to support the contention that clear objectives lead to higher student achievement. The researchers randomly assigned college students taking a course in communications at Florida State University into two groups. Subjects were asked to study several units on the topic of mushrooms. Twenty-four objectives

Planning and the use of objectives have a focusing effect on students and their learning.

had been written for each unit, and a specific test item had been written to correspond to each objective. Students in group 1 were given twelve of the twenty-four objectives to use as a study guide. Students in group 2 were not given any of the objectives, but they were told to learn as much as they could from the mushroom materials.

When the subjects were tested later, the researchers found that both groups scored the same on the total test. What is interesting and important, however, is the fact that the students who were given twelve of the twenty-four objectives to focus their learning outscored other students on test items associated with these twelve objectives. Of equal interest is that students without any objectives as study aids outscored their counterparts on the items associated with the other twelve objectives.

Duchastel and Brown concluded that learning objectives have a focusing effect on students, which leads to the recommendation that teachers make students aware of the objectives they have for their lessons. On the other hand, the researchers caution teachers to be careful because the study also illustrated how focusing too much on objectives may limit other important student learning.

John Zahorik (1970), working about the same time as Duchastel and Brown, was interested in the effects of planning on *teacher behavior,* particularly planning behaviors associated with identifying objectives, diagnosing student learning, and choosing instruction strategies. He wanted to find out if teachers who planned lessons were less sensitive to pupils in the classroom than teachers who did not plan.

Zahorik studied twelve fourth-grade teachers from four suburban schools near Milwaukee, Wisconsin. The twelve teachers in the study were randomly divided into two groups designated "teachers who planned" and "teachers who did not plan." Teachers in the planning group were given a lesson plan with objectives and a detailed outline on the topic of credit cards. They were asked to use it with their classes. Teachers in the nonplanning group were asked to reserve an hour of classroom time to carry out some unknown task—the task later to be announced as teaching about credit cards. All lessons were tape-recorded, and teacher behaviors were coded using a system designed to categorize the teachers' sensitivity to students.

Zahorik found *significant* differences between the teachers who had planned and those who had not planned. Teachers who planned were less sensitive to student ideas and appeared to pursue their own goals regardless of what students were thinking or saying. Conversely, teachers who had not planned displayed a higher number of verbal behaviors that encouraged and developed student ideas. Zahorik concluded that goal-based planning may inhibit teachers from being as sensitive to students as they could be.

> Planning can also have the unintended consequence of causing teachers to be insensitive to student needs and ideas.

The question that immediately arises from this study is, if goal-based planning makes teachers less sensitive to students, should teachers eliminate planning? Zahorik concluded that the answer is obviously no. Elimination of planning might "also bring about completely random and unproductive learning. If a lesson is to be effective, it would seem that some direction in the form of goals and experiences, no matter how general or vague, is needed" (p. 150).

Both the Duchastel and Brown and the Zahorik studies are interesting, because together they show the importance of goal-based planning; but they also warn that this type of planning can lead to unanticipated consequences that are not always desirable. To resolve this dilemma, Zahorik recommends that teachers establish goals that focus on their own behavior. He states, "Along with the typical plan, which can be described as a plan for pupil learning, develop a teaching plan that identifies types and patterns of teacher behaviors to be used during the lesson" (p. 150).

Another consequence of teacher planning is that it produces a smoothly running classroom with fewer discipline problems and fewer interruptions. Chapter 5 is de-

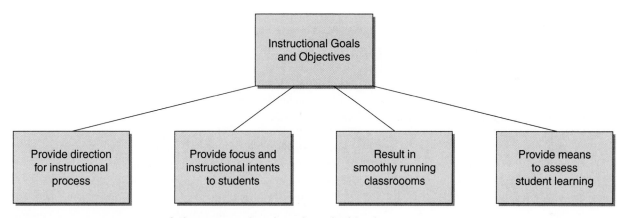

Figure 3.3 *Consequences of Clear Instructional Goals and Objectives*

voted to classroom management, so the research on this topic will not be highlighted here. It is important to note, however, that educational research for the past three decades has consistently found that planning is the key to eliminating most management problems. Teachers who plan well find they do not have to be police officers because their classrooms and lessons are characterized by a smooth flow of ideas, activities, and interactions. Such planning encompasses the rules and goals teachers establish for their classrooms and emphasizes how responsible and businesslike classroom behavior is an integral part of learning. Figure 3.3 summarizes the consequences of having clear instructional goals and objectives.

Careful planning by teachers can lead to smoothly running classrooms.

Planning and the Beginning Teacher

Researchers and educators also have puzzled over why it seems so difficult for beginning teachers to learn some of the important planning skills. One insight gleaned over the past few years is that it is difficult to learn from experienced teachers, not only because they think differently about planning, but also because they approach planning and interactive decision making differently. Three interesting studies highlight these differences.

Housner and Griffey (1985) were interested in comparing differences in planning and decision making of experienced and inexperienced teachers. They studied sixteen physical education teachers. Eight of the subjects had more than five years' experience; the other eight were preservice teacher candidates. The teachers were given sixty minutes to plan a lesson on how to teach soccer and basketball dribbling to 8-year-olds. The teachers then taught their lessons and were videotaped. Later the teachers viewed their lessons and told the researchers what they were thinking and the decisions they made while teaching. The results of their study are highlighted in this chapter's Research Summary.

Gael Leinhardt (1989) conducted a similar study and compared planning and lesson execution skills of experienced and inexperienced math teachers. Leinhardt found that experienced teachers had more complete "mental notepads" and agendas compared to inexperienced teachers. They also built in and used many more checkpoints to see if students were understanding the lesson than did the inexperienced teachers. The experienced teachers, according to Leinhardt:

> weave a series of lessons together to form an instructional topic in a way that consistently builds upon and advances materials introduced in prior lessons. Experts also construct lessons that display a highly efficient within-lesson structure, one that is characterized by

Research Summary

Experience Makes a Difference in Planning

Housner, L. D., and Griffey, D. G. (1985). Teacher cognition. Differences in planning and interactive decision making between experienced and inexperienced teachers. Research Quarterly for Exercise and Sport, 56, 45–53.

Problem: Housner and Griffey were interested in the differences in planning and decision making of experienced and inexperienced teachers.

Sample and Setting: The researchers studied sixteen physical education teachers. Eight of the subjects had more than five years of teaching experience; the other eight were preservice teachers training to be physical education teachers.

Procedures: The teachers were given sixty minutes to plan a lesson on how to teach soccer and basketball dribbling skills to 8-year-old children. They were to teach two lessons, one for each of the skills. Subjects were told they could ask for more information if they needed it and to think aloud while planning so their thought processes could be recorded. Teachers then taught their lessons to students in groups of four. Lessons were videotaped, and teachers viewed their lessons with the researchers and told them what they were thinking and the decisions they made while teaching.

Points for Reading Research: Often researchers are interested mainly in presenting descriptive information about their study. You will find this situation in the data tables from the Housner and Griffey study. The re-

searchers counted teacher behaviors in various categories and described these for the reader using straight percentage figures.

Results: Table 3.1 lists data about the kinds of decisions experienced and inexperienced teachers made during the planning period. The researchers divided these into two broad sets—activity decisions and instructional decisions; each set has several subsets.

Table 3.2 shows the types of cues that experienced and inexperienced teachers attended to as they taught the lesson and made in-flight decisions.

Discussion and Implications Table 3.1 shows that experienced and inexperienced teachers differed in the percentage of their thinking that went into four categories: adaptations, management, verbal instructions, and assess/feedback. Experienced teachers planned ahead for more adaptations that might be needed in a lesson as it got underway and were more concerned than inexperienced teachers with establishing rules for activities and means for giving students feedback. Inexperienced teachers devoted a larger percentage of their planning to verbal instructions.

Table 3.2 shows that experienced and inexperienced teachers varied in the types of cues they attended to while teaching the lesson. The experienced teachers were most attentive to student performance, whereas inexperienced teachers attended most often to student interest and were more interested in keeping the class on task. This study suggests that beginning teachers would do well to consider the following:

(continued)

fluid movement from one type of activity to another. . . . Novice teachers' lessons, on the other hand, are characterized by fragmented lesson structures with long transitions between lesson segments. . . . Their lessons do not fit well together within or across topic boundaries (p. 73).

Finally, in a study that is now considered a classic, Peterson and her colleagues (1978) found that experienced teachers do not always use what might be considered "best planning practices." Researchers gave twelve experienced elementary teachers objectives and materials and asked them to plan three lessons on a town in France. Their study produced important and interesting results. Experienced teachers in the study did not follow the common recommendation to start with objectives and learner outcomes. Instead, they planned content and instructional activities first, then came

- When planning, submerge a natural tendency to think about verbal instructions and think more about ways to structure rules and routines, give feedback to students, and plan for contingencies.

- When teaching, pay attention to student performance as a basis for making in-flight decisions rather than the stated interests of students or their requests for changes in the lesson.

Table 3.1 *Comparison of Types of Activity and Instructional Strategy Decisions Made by Experienced and Inexperienced Teachers*

Activity Decisions	Exp.	Inexp.	Instructional Strategy Decisions	Exp.	Inexp.
Structure	42.6%	54.5%	Management	13.4%	4.8%
Procedures	24.6	28.0	Assess/feedback	22.8	15.9
Formations	4.9	1.5	Demonstrate	7.9	7.9
Time	9.0	6.8	Transitions	5.5	6.4
Adaptations	18.9	9.1	Focus attention	18.9	19.1
			Equipment use	7.9	7.9
			Verbal instruction	19.7	34.9
			Time	3.9	3.2

Source: Adapted from L. D. Housner and D. G. Griffey (1985), p. 48

Table 3.2 *Types of Cues Heeded by Experienced and Inexperienced Teachers during Interactive Teaching*

Cues	Experienced	Inexperienced
Student performance	30.1%	19.0%
Student involvement	27.4	22.6
Student interest	11.8	27.3
Student requests	3.2	7.7
Student mood/feelings	3.2	6.5
Teacher's mood/feelings	5.3	1.7
Other	19.0	15.2

Source: Adapted from L. D. Housner and D. G. Griffey (1985), p. 49

back to the objectives. This raises an interesting question about whether or not these planning patterns represent best planning practices.

The fact that experienced teachers attend to different planning tasks and cues from those attended to by inexperienced teachers presents some challenging problems for a beginning teacher. Unlike other acts of teaching, most teacher planning occurs in private places, such as the teacher's home or office. Also, by their very nature, planning and decision making are mental, nonobservable activities. Only the resulting actions are observable by others. Even when written plans are produced, they represent only a small portion of the actual planning that has gone on in the teacher's head. The private nature of planning thus makes it difficult for beginning teachers to learn from experienced teachers. Beginning teachers may ask to look at lesson plans, or they may talk to experienced teachers

Planning skills can sometimes be difficult for beginning teachers to learn because the process itself cannot be directly observed.

Check, Extend, Explore

Check
- What are the benefits and consequences of good planning?
- How did Zahorik's study demonstrate that planning possibly impedes a teacher's level of sensitivity and flexibility? Does his research suggest that planning should be eliminated? Why or why not?
- In what ways do planning approaches of new teachers differ from those used by experienced teachers? How do you explain this, and what can the novice teacher do to improve planning?

Extend
- From your own experiences, what consequences have you observed as a result of planning? Were these positive or negative?
- On a scale of 1 to 10, how detailed do you think a teacher's plans should be? Go to "Extend Question Poll" on the Online Learning Center to respond.

Explore
- Go to the Online Learning Center at www.mhhe.com/arends6e for links to websites related to *How Teachers Plan.*

about planning and decision-making processes. However, many experienced teachers cannot describe in words the novice can understand the thinking that went into specific plans and decisions. This is particularly true of moment-to-moment planning decisions that characterize the rapid flow of classroom life, such as those described in the studies by Housner and Griffey and by Leinhardt. Teacher planning and decision making may be one of the teaching skills for which research can be of most assistance in helping beginning teachers learn about the hidden mental processes of the experienced expert.

Planning Domains

Teacher planning is a complex process. Planning interacts with all other aspects of teaching and is influenced by many factors. Understanding the planning process and mastering the specifics of planning are important skills for beginning teachers.

Planning and the Instructional Cycle

Teacher planning is a multifaceted and ongoing process that covers almost everything teachers do. It is also part of an overall instructional cycle. It is not just the lesson plans that the teachers create for the next day, but also the in-flight adjustments they make as they teach as well as the planning done after instruction as a result of assessment. Figure 3.4 illustrates the overall flow of planning as it is connected to the instructional cycle.

Notice in Figure 3.4 how some aspects of planning precede instruction and, in turn, precede assessment of student learning. The whole planning process, however, is cyclical. Assessment information influences the teacher's next set of plans, the instruction that follows, and so on. Further, the mental processes of planning vary from one phase of the cycle to the next. For example, choosing content can only be done after careful analysis and inquiry into students' prior knowledge, the teacher's understanding of the subject matter, and the nature of the subject itself. Most postinstructional decisions, such as the type of test to give or how to assign grades, can also be made as a result of consideration. Planning and decision making during instruction itself, on the other

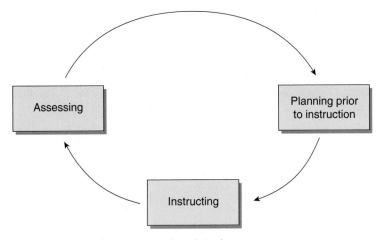

Figure 3.4 *Planning and the Instructional Cycle*

hand, most often must be done spontaneously, on the spur of the moment. Examples of decisions made at each phase of the cycle are listed in Table 3.3.

The Time Spans of Planning

Teachers plan for different time spans, ranging from the next minute or hour to the next week, month, or year. If schoolwide planning or one's own career planning is involved, time spans may even cover several years. Obviously, planning what to do tomorrow is much different from planning for a whole year. However, both are important. Also, plans carried out on a particular day are influenced by what has happened before and will in turn influence plans for the days and weeks ahead.

Robert Yinger (1980) conducted an interesting and important study that provides teachers with a model for thinking about the time dimensions of teacher planning. Yinger made a detailed study of one first- and second-grade elementary school teacher in Michigan. Using participant-observation methods, he spent forty full days over a five-month period observing and recording the teacher's activities. From this work, Yinger was able to identify the five time spans that characterized teacher planning: daily planning, weekly planning, unit planning, term planning, and yearly planning. Figure 3.5 illustrates these five time spans of planning and plots their occurrence across the school year.

> Teachers plan for different time spans ranging from a few minutes to a full year.

Table 3.3 *Three Phases of Teacher Planning and Decision Making*

Before Instruction	During Instruction	After Instruction
Choosing content	Presenting	Checking for understanding
Choosing approach	Questioning	Providing feedback
Allocating time and space	Assisting	Praising and criticizing
Determining structures	Providing for practice	Testing
Determining motivation	Making transitions	Grading
	Managing and disciplining	Reporting

Check, Extend, Explore

Check
- What are the three primary phases of the overall instructional cycle? What types of plans and decisions do teachers make at each phase?
- For what time spans must teachers establish plans?

Extend
- Why do you think it is important to develop unique plans for different time spans? How might these plans interrelate with each other, requiring modification as lessons evolve?

Explore
- Go to the Online Learning Center at www.mhhe.com/arend6e for links to websites related to *Instructional Planning*.

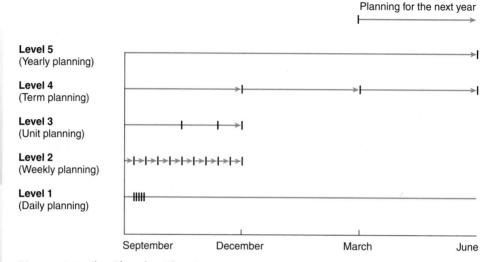

Figure 3.5 *Five Planning Time Spans*

The Specifics of Planning

By now it must be obvious that planning is important and that teachers must consider a broad range of planning tasks. In this section, the primary tasks associated with teacher planning are described in some detail, starting with choosing what to teach and the use of instructional objectives and followed by the use of long-range and short-range plans and the tools available to teachers to accomplish planning tasks.

Choosing Curriculum Content

Deciding what to teach is among the most difficult aspects of teacher planning because there is so much that could be learned and so little time.

The curriculum in most elementary and secondary schools is currently organized around the academic disciplines—history, biology, mathematics, and so forth—used by scholars to organize information about the social and physical worlds. And even though some curriculum reformers have repeatedly argued that this is an inappropriate way to organize content for young people, the current structures are likely to remain for some time. Consequently, an important planning task for teachers will continue to be choosing the most appropriate content from the various subject matter areas for a particular group of students. This is no small feat, because there is already much more to teach on any topic than time allows, and new knowledge is being produced every day.

Beginning teachers are often bewildered about where content comes from and the role teachers play in selecting it. In today's schools, deciding what to teach is no longer done by teachers independently. Instead, what-to-teach decisions are influenced by many factors, some of which are described here and portrayed in Figure 3.6.

Learned Society Standards. Curriculum has traditionally been drawn from the various academic disciplines deemed central to an individual's education. Core disciplines have included English, history, geography, foreign languages, mathematics, and the sciences. Content from these subjects is sequenced over students' twelve years of schooling, and specific accomplishments in each subject are required for high school graduation. Each subject has a learned society or professional association that makes

Planning Tools and Software Evaluation

Technology is related to teacher planning in two important ways: (1) It can be a powerful tool for organizing learning activities, keeping attendance records, and for creating lesson plans and learning materials. (2) It presents an important planning task for teachers in deciding how to integrate technology into particular lessons and how to evaluate particular technologies such as computer software, CDs, and Web-based materials.

Planning Tools

Tools that are available to assist teacher planning include:

- *Lesson planning software*—Software designed to organize lesson plans and to tie particular plans to learning objectives.
- *Worksheet and puzzle tools*—Software designed to create worksheets and puzzles and link these to learning objectives.
- *Concept mapping tools*—Software for organizing ideas into conceptual maps or webs and showing relationships among various ideas.
- *Certificate production software*—Software for creating certificates that can be given students to reward achievement and special effort.
- *Poster and bulletin board production tools*—Software that enables teachers to create and print posters and other devices to post on bulletin boards and classroom walls.
- *Time and meeting management tools*—Software and hand-held computers that allow teachers to plan, keep track of, and organize meetings, schedules, things to do, telephone numbers, and so on.

More general tools like database software and spreadsheets included in software suites such as Clarisworks and Microsoft Office can also be helpful to teachers for keeping records, summarizing information, and for a variety of other planning and organizing activities. Examples of planning tools and websites where they can be accessed can be found in the *Learning to Teach* Online Learning Center.

Software Review

As with any educational material or resource, teachers must review and evaluate technological tools such as computer software, CDs, and websites for their quality and their appropriateness for particular groups of students. Numerous criteria have been developed to evaluate technological-based teaching resources. Following are some questions that can be used to evaluate computer software and websites:

Quality Questions

- Is the particular software/website the best medium to use to accomplish your goals?
- Is the software/website content aligned with your curriculum or learning standards?
- Is the content accurate?
- Is the content free of bias, stereotypes, and violence?
- Is the level of difficulty appropriate for your students?
- Is the software or website student friendly? Easy to access? Easy to navigate?
- Is the software/website designed for individuals or groups of students?
- If designed for individuals, can students use it independently?
- If designed for groups of students, does it support cooperative learning?
- Does the software/website provide useful feedback to students?
- Does the software/website have sufficient motivational appeal?

Technical Questions

- Can your school's computers access the website and/or have sufficient memory to use the software?
- Is the software easy to install and free from error?
- Does the software or Web resource have good instructions for teachers?

More information about evaluating software and websites, along with a form for evaluating software, can be found in the *Learning to Teach* Online Learning Center.

So many software programs, CDs, and websites exist today that it is impossible for teachers to review each and every piece or site. Fortunately, special groups have been formed for the purpose of reviewing software and websites. You might think about and use these groups the same way you do *Consumer Reports*—these groups test a wide variety of technology products and provide evaluation information for teachers. Some of the most widely used groups are listed here and can be accessed through the *Learning to Teach* Online Learning Center.

- Active Learning Associates
- SuperKids Educational Software Review
- Children's Software Review

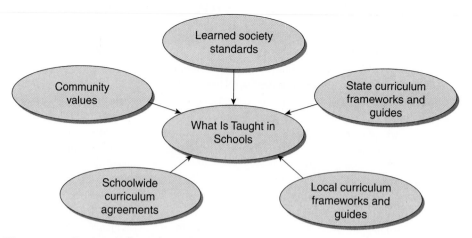

Figure 3.6 *Factors Influencing What Is Taught in Schools*

Performance standards define what students should know and be able to do and at what level they are expected to perform in various subjects.

recommendations about what should be taught. Sometimes these recommendations are made in the form of **performance standards** for what students should learn.

State Curriculum Frameworks and Mastery Tests. Over the past decade, state departments of education have exerted an increasing amount of influence over what is taught in schools. Today, most states have curriculum guides or frameworks, as they are often called, that define what students should know and be able to do as they proceed through the various levels of schooling. Curriculum frameworks in most states exist for each subject area and each grade level. Table 3.4 provides an illustration of performance standards found in one state's science framework. Note how the overall goal for learning about the "evolution of scientific thought" is divided into specific performance standards for each level of instruction—early elementary, middle school, and high school. It is expected that teachers will provide learning experiences for students at the various levels that will ensure that students can meet the standards and ultimately the overall goal.

State frameworks have an important influence on what is taught in schools because mastery tests are usually built around the performance standards identified in the frameworks. These tests are administered to students on a regular basis. Student scores are summarized by schools and/or school districts. Scores on mastery tests often are published in local newspapers so parents and citizens know how students in their school compare to students elsewhere in the state. It should be obvious that this situation heightens the influence of state curriculum frameworks.

Deciding what to teach is value-laden and influenced greatly by societal and community viewpoints.

Community Values and Local Curriculum Frameworks. Community values and societal viewpoints have an important influence on what is taught in schools, particularly in subjects that contain topics that are controversial. Larger societal views influence the content and standards that appear in the frameworks developed by professional associations, and local community values impact local curriculum frameworks. Movements in many communities to get schools "back to the basics" or to use a "phonetic approach" to teaching reading are two examples of how beliefs get translated into curriculum decisions at the local level. Actions in 1999 by the Kansas State Board of Education had the effect of reducing the amount of attention paid to evolution in that state's science curriculum, an issue that has been controversial for most of the past century.

Table 3.4 *Illustration of Goals and Performance Standards in Science*

Overall goal: Students will learn the evolution of scientific thought, how science has influenced culture and society, and how groups from many countries have contributed to the history of science.

K–12 Performance Standards

Educational experiences in **grades K–4** will ensure that students:	Educational experiences in **grades 5–8** will ensure that students:	Educational experiences in **grades 9–12** will ensure that students:
Recognize (in grades K–2) that science is an adventure that people everywhere can take part in, as they have for many centuries	Recognize important contributions to the advancement of science, mathematics, and technology that have been made by men and women in different cultures at different times	Recognize that many Western as well as non-Western cultures (e.g., Egyptian, Chinese, Hindu, Arabic, Mayan) have developed scientific ideas and solved human problems through technology

Many content decisions are made by experienced teachers and curriculum specialists in particular districts long before the student or first-year teacher steps into a classroom. Textbooks are selected and curriculum guides are often planned to parallel state frameworks. When this has occurred, such guides provide excellent tools for a beginning teacher to use. The experts who prepare these materials have taken considerable time to ask what should be taught and how various topics should be sequenced over time—both during the course of a year and over several years—as well as how local community values should be reflected in the school's curriculum. The job of beginning teachers becomes mainly that of making sure they understand the scope and sequence of this content and finding ways to interpret and teach it effectively to a particular group of students.

Some beginning teachers, however, may find themselves facing the time-consuming task of having to select content themselves. For instance, textbooks in some schools may no longer reflect current knowledge. In such a case, it is the beginning teachers' responsibility to plan ways to incorporate new knowledge into the curriculum, an action that generally requires taking something else out.

Tools for Choosing Content

When beginning teachers face a situation in which they have to make content decisions without much assistance, they need to be aware of ideas and tools that can help them do this.

Use Concepts of Economy and Power. It has been observed that most teachers try to teach too much information and too much information that is irrelevant. Students are hampered in learning key ideas because of verbal clutter. Bruner (1962), a long time ago, argued that teachers should strive for **economy** in their teaching. Using economy means being very careful about the amount of information and the number of concepts presented in a single lesson or unit of work. The economy principle argues for taking a difficult concept and making it clear and simple for students, not taking an easy concept

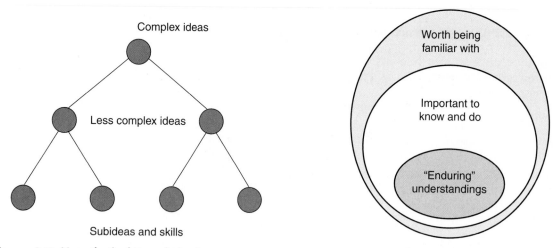

Figure 3.7 *Hypothetical Knowledge Structure*

Figure 3.8 *Establishing Curricular Priorities*
Source: Adapted from Wiggins and McTighe (1998)

and making it difficult. It means helping students examine a few critical ideas in depth rather than bombarding them with unrelated facts that have little chance of making an impact on learning.

Bruner also described how the principle of **power** should be applied when selecting content. A powerful lesson or unit is one in which basic concepts from the subject area are presented in straightforward and logical ways. It is through logical organization that students come to see relationships between specific facts and among the important concepts of a topic.

Attend to Knowledge Structures. In every field there is much more to learn than is possible to master in a single year or even a lifetime. Teachers must choose content based on the basic ideas and **structures of knowledge** for a particular field, taking into account, of course, their students' prior knowledge and abilities. In all fields of knowledge, advanced concepts and understandings are built in a more or less pyramid fashion on simpler ones, as illustrated in Figure 3.7. Notice how information is divided into more complex and abstract ideas and into simpler, less complex concepts and skills. Notice also that relationships exist among various subsets of ideas and understandings. We will discuss knowledge structures in more detail in later chapters.

Grant Wiggins and Jay McTighe (1998) have provided a simple but very useful framework for putting into operation the economy, power, and structure of knowledge principles, as illustrated in the nested rings shown in Figure 3.8. The background of the illustration represents the whole field of possible contents, which obviously can't be covered. The largest of the rings represents knowledge and skills that a teacher might determine that students should be familiar with, whereas the middle ring would be that knowledge that is determined to be very important. The students' education would be incomplete if they do not master these essentials. The third ring in the framework represent the "enduring" understandings, the big ideas that should remain with students after they have forgotten most of the details. Wiggins and McTighe offer four questions for teachers to ask as they select what to teach.

Question 1: To what extent does the idea, topic, or process represent a big idea having enduring value beyond the classroom?

Question 2: To what extent does the idea, topic, or process reside at the heart of the discipline?

Question 3: To what extent do students have misconceptions about the idea, topic, or process and find it difficult to grasp?

Question 4: To what extent does the idea, topic, or process offer potential for engaging students?

Curriculum Mapping. Even though teachers work together in the same school or school districts, they usually have only a sketchy knowledge about what each other teaches. Even teachers next door to one another lack information about what each is teaching. And although curriculum frameworks may list overall goals and standards, too often they remain mute on what teachers are doing day to day.

Heidi Hayes Jacobs (1997) has offered the idea of "curriculum maps" as a way for teachers in particular buildings or school districts to chart what they are doing and to help make sure neither gaps in important skills and understanding nor too much over-lap and repetition occur.

Curriculum mapping begins with each teacher describing the processes and skills he or she emphasizes, the essential concept and topics he or she teaches, and the kind of learner outcomes expected. Then, depending on the situation, these descriptions are shared with other teachers across the school, and maps are constructed showing the school's curriculum, including gaps that may exist and topics that are unnecessarily taught more than once. Although beginning teachers will not be asked to be in charge of this process, understanding that it exists will help them enter into curriculum map-ping and gain a clearer understanding of what is really going on in other teachers' classrooms and how what they are teaching fits in. Figure 3.9 illustrates two curricu-lum maps: One shows how literature and social studies are integrated in a fifth-grade class; the other shows the life science program taught by a ninth-grade interdiscipli-nary team.

Instructional Objectives

By definition, teaching is a process of attempting to promote growth in students. Stu-dent learning is the "bottom line" for teachers and for schools. The intended growth may be far-reaching, such as developing a whole new conceptual framework for thinking about science or acquiring a new appreciation for literature. It may be as precise and simple as learning how to tie a shoestring. Teachers' intentions for stu-dent learning are called a variety of names. In the past, they have been referred to as *aims, purposes, goals,* or *outcomes* (Bobbitt, 1918; Rugg, 1926; Taylor, 1949). Today, they are often referred to as *content* or *curriculum standards.* In *Learning to Teach,* the term **instructional objective** is used to describe the teacher's intention for students' growth and change. You will find that instructional objectives are like road maps: They help teachers and their students know where they are going and when they have arrived at their destination. Like different kinds of road maps, some instruc-tional objectives are simple. They are easy to make and to read. Others are more com-plex. For this reason, there are several different approaches to guide the writing of instructional objectives and a variety of formats to use. A major issue (sometimes controversial) has been differences among theorists and teachers about how specific or general instructional objectives should be.

> Instructional objectives describe a teacher's intent about what students should learn.

Fifth-Grade Integrated Curriculum Map

ORGANIZING CONCEPTS	NEW BEGINNINGS →	→	BALANCE →	→	EXPANSION →	→	INTERDEPENDENCE →	→
MONTHS	AUGUST/ SEPTEMBER	OCTOBER	NOVEMBER	DECEMBER	JANUARY	FEBRUARY	MARCH	APRIL	MAY/JUNE
Related Literature	The Talking Earth	Author Study	Witch of Blackbird Pond —→	→		Caddie Woodlawn	Hatchet???	Lit Set on Various Cultures —→	Independent Reading ↑
Seminar Selections									
Field Studies	Sequoyah-Energy Connections		Williamsburg Jamestown	Nutcracker Ballet		Channel 3 TV Station		D.A.R.E. Picnic	
Forum/Current Events	Focus on people and countries making new beginnings			Focus on our struggle for independence		Focus on immigration effects on our country	Focus on government regulation and its effects on citizens	Focus on USA events and how we live together as a nation	Focus on exploration in various fields (medicine, law, etc.)
Social Studies	5 themes of Geography Explorers Native Americans	Colonization —→	→	Declaration of Independence Bill of Rights and Constitution Branches of Government	Exploration Westward Expansion	Immigration to Ellis Island		USA supply geography states and capitals	Interdependence of North Am. countries Interdependence of regions

Ninth-Grade Interdisciplinary Life Science Curriculum Map

SUBJECT THEMES	QUARTER 1: TRUST	QUARTER 2: COMMUNICATION	QUARTER 3: TOLERANCE	QUARTER 4: RESPONSIBILITY
Health 9	Drug Education (physiology & prevention)	Family Living (Role models, sex, birth control, AIDS prevention)	Drug Education (physiology & prevention)	Family Living (Role models, sex, birth control, AIDS prevention)
Biology 9	Characteristics of Life (cells, biochemistry, metabolism)	Continuity of Life (reproduction & genetics)	Homeostasis (anatomy & physiology)	Patterns of Organization (evolution, ecology, & environment)
PA/Fitness	Cardiovascular Fitness (muscular strength & endurance)	Project Adventure (problem-solving skills)	Cardiovascular Fitness (muscular strength & endurance)	Project Adventure (problem-solving skills)

Figure 3.9 *Two Examples of Curriculum Maps*

Source: Adapted from Jacobs (1997)

The Mager Format of Behavioral Objectives. In 1962, Robert Mager wrote a book titled *Preparing Instructional Objectives* that set off a debate over the most desirable "form of a usefully stated objective" (p. i). The general message of Mager's work was the argument that for instructional objectives to be meaningful, they must clearly communicate a teacher's instructional intent and should be very specific. Objectives written in the Mager format became known as **behavioral objectives** and required three parts:

- *Student behavior.* What the student will be doing or the kinds of behavior the teacher will accept as evidence that the objective has been achieved.
- *Testing situation.* The condition under which the behavior will be observed or expected to occur.
- *Performance criteria.* The standard or performance level defined as acceptable.

A simple mnemonic for remembering the three parts of a behavioral objective is to think of it as the STP approach: student behavior (S), testing situation (T), and performance criteria (P). Table 3.5 illustrates how Mager's three-part approach works and provides examples of each.

When teachers write behavioral objectives using the Mager format, the recommendation is to use precise words that are *not* open to many interpretations. Examples of precise words include *write, list, identify, compare.* Examples of less precise words are *know, understand, appreciate.* There are also recommendations about how to link the three parts of the instructional objective together using the following steps: Begin by noting the testing situation, follow this by stating the student behavior, and then write the performance criteria. Table 3.6 illustrates how behavioral objectives written in this format might look.

Table 3.5 *Sample Behavioral Objectives Using Mager's Format*

Parts of the Objective	Examples
Student behavior	Identify nouns
Testing situation	Given a list of nouns and verbs
Performance criteria	Mark at least 85 percent right
Student behavior	List five causes of the Civil War
Testing situation	Essay test without use of notes
Performance criteria	Four of five reasons

Table 3.6 *Three Parts of Behavioral Objectives Applied*

Testing Situation	Student Behavior	Performance Criteria
Given a map . . .	The student will be able to:	At least 85 percent
Without notes . . .	Identify	Four of five reasons
With the text . . .	Solve	Correct to nearest percentages
	Compare	
	Contrast	
	Recite	

Mager's behavioral approach has been widely accepted among teachers and others in the educational community over the past three decades. Well-written behavioral objectives give students a very clear statement about what is expected of them, and they help teachers when it comes time to measure student progress, as you will see in Chapter 6. The behavioral approach, however, is not free from criticism.

Critics have argued that Mager's format leads to reductionism and, when used exclusively, it leads to neglect of many of the most important goals of education. Putting an emphasis on precision and observable student behaviors forces teachers to be specific in their objectives. To accomplish this specificity, they must break larger, more global educational goals into very small pieces. The number of objectives for almost any subject or topic could run well into the thousands, an unmanageable list for most teachers. The teacher also runs the risk of paying attention only to specific objectives, which are of minor importance in themselves, while neglecting the sum total, which is more important than all the parts.

Critics have also pointed out, and rightfully so, that many of the more complex cognitive processes are not readily observable. It is easy, for instance, to observe a student add two columns of numbers and determine if the answer is correct. It is not easy to observe the thought processes or the mathematical problem solving that goes into this act. Along the same line, it is rather easy to observe students recall the major characters in a Tolstoy novel. It is not so easy to observe and measure their appreciation of Russian literature or the novel as a form of creative expression. Critics worry that the emphasis on behavioral objectives may lead to the neglect of the more important aspects of education merely because the latter are not readily observed and measured.

More General Approaches. Several curriculum theorists, as well as measurement specialists, have developed alternative approaches to the behavior objective. Gronlund (1999), for example, illustrated how objectives can be written first in more general terms, with appropriate specifics added later for clarification. Gronlund, unlike the strict behaviorists, is more willing to use words such as *appreciate, understand, value,* or *enjoy* with his approach. He believes that although these words are open to a wide range of interpretations, they nonetheless communicate more clearly the educational intents of many teachers. Table 3.7 illustrates how an objective might look using the Gronlund format.

Notice that the initial objective is not very specific and perhaps not very meaningful or helpful in guiding lesson preparation or measuring student change. It does, how-

Table 3.7 *More General Approach to Writing Objectives*

Format	Example
Overall objective	Understands and appreciates the diversity of the people who make up American society.
Subobjective 1	Can define diversity in the words of others and in his or her own words.
Subobjective 2	Can give instances of how diverse persons or groups have enriched the cultural life of Americans.
Subobjective 3	Can analyze in writing how maintaining appreciation for diversity is a fragile and difficult goal to achieve.

ever, communicate the overall intent the teacher wants to achieve. The subobjectives help clarify what should be taught and what students are expected to learn. They provide more precision, yet are not as precise as the three-part behavior objective.

A third approach for writing objectives has been developed by scholars who recently revised Bloom's *Taxonomy of Educational Objectives,* a topic of the next section, Taxonomies for Selecting Instructional Objectives. The Bloom revisionists Anderson et al., 2001) argue that objectives that use more traditional frameworks have focused only on content and skills of instruction and have ignored the cognitive—the "way-students-think" dimension of teaching and learning. They have identified a standard format for stating objectives that requires only a *verb* and a *noun.* The verb generally describes the intended cognitive process and the noun describes the knowledge students are expected to acquire. Take the following as examples of what an objective would look like using the taxonomy framework:

- The student will *learn to distinguish* (verb for cognitive process) among *federal and unitary systems of government* (noun for knowledge).
- The student will *learn to classify* (verb for cognitive process) different types of *objectives* (noun for knowledge).
- The student will *be able to analyze* (verb for cognitive process) various types of *social data* (noun for knowledge).

This approach will become clearer to you after reading the next section on Bloom's Taxonomy.

Which Approach to Use? The form and use of instructional objectives, as with many other aspects of teaching, are likely to remain subject to controversy and inquiry for a long time. The approach teachers use will be influenced somewhat by schoolwide policies, but in most instances, considerable latitude exists for individual preference and decisions. It is important to remember that the purposes behind instructional objectives are to communicate clearly to students a teacher's intents and to aid the teacher in assessing student growth. Common sense, as well as the research summarized earlier, suggests adopting a middle ground between objectives stated at such a high level of abstraction that they are meaningless and a strict adherence to the behavioral approach. Gronlund's approach of writing a more global objective first and then clarifying it and getting as specific as the subject matter allows is probably the best advice at this time. Similarly, after reading the next section, you will see the importance of identifying not only the content to be learned but also the cognitive process associated with the learning.

Some educators advocate first writing global objectives and then writing specific objectives that are consistent with the larger (usually unobservable) ones.

Taxonomies for Selecting Instructional Objectives

Taxonomies are devices that classify and show relationships among things. You already know about a variety of taxonomies; for instance, those that classify plants and animals in science, and those that classify food groups, the colors, and the periodic table of the elements. One taxonomy that has been a very useful tool for making decisions about instructional objectives and for assessing learning outcomes has been Bloom's *taxonomy for educational objectives.* This taxonomy was initially developed by Bloom and his colleagues in the 1950s (Bloom, 1956). Recently, it has been revised by a group of Bloom's students (Anderson et al., 2001) and renamed *taxonomy for learning, teaching, and assessing.* As the name implies, the revised taxonomy provides a framework for classifying learning objectives and a way for assessing them.

Bloom's revised taxonomy is two-dimensional. One dimension, the **knowledge dimension,** describes different types of knowledge and organizes knowledge into four categories: factual knowledge, conceptual knowledge, procedural knowledge, and metacognitive knowledge. These categories lie along a continuum from very concrete knowledge (factual) to the more abstract (metacognitive). The second dimension, the **cognitive process** (ways of thinking) **dimension,** contains six categories: remember, understand, apply, analyze, evaluate, and create. Like the knowledge dimension, the categories of the cognitive process dimension are assumed to lie along a continuum of cognitive complexity. For example, understanding something is more complex than simply remembering it; applying and analyzing an idea is more complex than understanding the idea. Table 3.8 shows the two dimensions of the taxonomy and the relationship between the knowledge and cognitive process dimensions.

Categories of the Knowledge Dimension. The revised taxonomy divides knowledge into four categories: **Factual knowledge** includes the basic elements that students need to know to be acquainted with a topic. **Conceptual knowledge** is knowledge about the interrelationships among basic elements. **Procedural knowledge** is knowing how to do "something." **Metacognitive knowledge** is knowledge about one's own cognition as well as knowing when to use particular conceptual or procedural knowledge. Table 3.9 explains the four major types of knowledge and provides examples of each type.

Table 3.8 *The Taxonomy Table*

The Knowledge Dimension	The Cognitive Process Dimension					
	1. Remember	**2. Understand**	**3. Apply**	**4. Analyze**	**5. Evaluate**	**6. Create**
A. Factual Knowledge						
B. Conceptual Knowledge						
C. Procedural Knowledge						
D. Metacognitive Knowledge						

Source: Anderson, L. W. et al. (2001), p. 28

Table 3.9 *Major Types of Knowledge in the Knowledge Dimension*

Major Types and Subtypes	Examples
A. Factual Knowledge—The basic elements students must know to be acquainted with a discipline or solve problems in it.	
A_A. Knowledge of terminology	Technical vocabulary, music symbols
A_B. Knowledge of specific details and elements	Major natural resources, reliable sources of information
B. Conceptual Knowledge—The interrelationships among the basic elements within a larger structure that enable them to function together	
B_A. Knowledge of classifications and categories	Periods of geological time, forms of business ownership
B_B. Knowledge of principles and generalizations	Pythagorean theorem, law of supply and demand
B_C. Knowledge of theories, models, and structures	Theory of evolution, structure of Congress
C. Procedural Knowledge—How to do something, methods of inquiry, and criteria for using skills, algorithms, techniques, and methods	
C_A. Knowledge of subject-specific skills and algorithms	Skills used in painting with water colors, whole-number division algorithm
C_B. Knowledge of subject-specific techniques and methods	Interviewing techniques, scientific method
C_C. Knowledge of criteria for determining when to use appropriate procedures	Criteria used to determine when to apply a procedure involving Newton's second law, criteria used to judge the feasibility of using a particular method to estimate business costs
D. Metacognitive Knowledge—Knowledge of cognition in general as well as awareness and knowledge of one's own cognition	
D_A. Strategic knowledge	Knowledge of outlining as a means of capturing the structure of a unit of subject matter in a text book, knowledge of the use of heuristics
D_B. Knowledge about cognitive tasks, including appropriate contextual and conditional knowledge	Knowledge of the types of tests particular teachers administer, knowledge of the cognitive demands of different tasks
D_C. Self-knowledge	Knowledge that critiquing essays is a personal strength, whereas writing essays is a personal weakness; awareness of one's own knowledge level

Source: Anderson, L. W. et al. (2001), p. 29

Categories of the Cognitive Process Dimension. The cognitive dimension provides a classification scheme of various **cognitive processes** that might be included in an instructional objective. These processes lie along a continuum that ranges from the rather simple (remembering) to the more complex (creating). As shown in Table 3.10, **remember,** according to the taxonomy's creators, means to retrieve relevant information from long-term memory, whereas **understand** means to construct meaning from instructional messages. **Apply** means to carry out or use a procedure; **analyze** means to break material into its constituent parts and determine how the parts relate to one another. **Evaluate** and **create,** the two categories situated at the more complex end of the continuum, mean to make judgments based on criteria, and to put elements together to form a new pattern or structure, respectively. Notice also in Table 3.10 that each process category is associated with two or more specific cognitive processes. "Remember," for example, includes the cognitive processes of recognizing and recalling. "Evaluate" includes the cognitive processes of checking and critiquing.

Bloom's revised taxonomy a taxonomy table helps us to understand and classify objectives and, also, as described later in Chapter 6, how to assess them. Figure 3.10 shows how a particular objective can be classified. Note that the objective "the student will learn to apply the reduce-reuse-recycle approach to conservation" is classified as procedural knowledge (how to do something) and requires the cognitive process of apply (carry out or use a procedure).

The ability to classify objectives with this tool allows teachers to consider their objectives from the wide range of available possibilities and provides a way of remembering the "integral relationship between knowledge and cognitive processes inherent in any objective" (Anderson et. al., 2001, p. 35). Also, categorization of objectives helps point out consistencies or inconsistencies among an array of objectives for a given unit of study and, as will be described later, helps teachers deal more effectively with assessment of their instructional objectives.

Teachers spend most of their time on objectives related to the cognitive domain. However, it is important to remember that other objectives for education exist that fall into the affective domain and the psychomotor domain.

The Affective Domain. Bloom's original taxonomy divided objectives in the **affective domain** into five categories. Each category specified the degree of commitment or emotional intensity required of students. The five categories are:

The affective domain in Bloom's taxonomy classifies objectives for emotional responses.

Receiving—The student is aware of or attending to something in the environment.
Responding—The student displays some new behavior as a result of experience and responds to the experience.
Valuing—The student displays definite involvement or commitment toward some experience.
Organization—The student has integrated a new value into his or her general set of values and can give it its proper place in a priority system.
Characterization by value—The student acts consistently according to the value and is firmly committed to the experience.

The Psychomotor Domain. We normally associate psychomotor activity most closely with physical education and athletics, but in fact, many other subjects require physical movement of one kind or another. Obviously, handwriting and word processing are tightly connected to all subjects. Work in laboratories for science students requires intricate use of complex equipment. Eye coordination is required for viewing all forms of

Table 3.10 *The Cognitive Process Dimension and Related Cognitive Processes*

Process Categories	Cognitive Processes and Examples
1. Remember—Retrieve relevant knowledge from long-term memory.	
1.1 Recognizing	(e.g., Recognize the dates of important events in U.S. history)
1.2 Recalling	(e.g., Recall the dates of important events in U.S. history)
2. Understand—Construct meaning from instructional messages, including oral, written, and graphic communication.	
2.1 Interpreting	(e.g., Paraphrase important speeches and documents)
2.2 Exemplifying	(e.g., Give examples of various artistic painting styles)
2.3 Classifying	(e.g., Classify observed or described cases of mental disorders)
2.4 Summarizing	(e.g., Write a short summary of the events portrayed on videotapes)
2.5 Inferring	(e.g., In learning a foreign language, infer grammatical principles from examples)
2.6 Comparing	(e.g., Compare historical events to contemporary situations)
2.7 Explaining	(e.g., Explain the causes of important eighteenth-century events in France)
3. Apply—Carry out or use a procedure in a given situation.	
3.1 Executing	(e.g., Divide one whole number by another whole number, both with multiple digits)
3.2 Implementing	(e.g., Determine in which situations Newton's second law is appropriate)
4. Analyze—Break material into constituent parts and determine how parts relate to one another and to an overall structure or purpose.	
4.1 Differentiating	(e.g., Distinguish between relevant and irrelevant numbers in a mathematical word problem)
4.2 Organizing	(e.g., Structure evidence in a historical description into evidence for and against a particular historical explanation)
4.3 Attributing	(e.g., Determine the point of view of the author of an essay in terms of his or her political perspective)
5. Evaluate—Make judgments based on criteria and standards.	
5.1 Checking	(e.g., Determine whether a scientist's conclusions follow from observed data)
5.2 Critiquing	(e.g., Judge which of two methods is the best way to solve a given problem)
6. Create—Put elements together to form a coherent or functional whole; reorganize elements into a new pattern or structure.	
6.1 Generating	(e.g., Generate hypotheses to acount for an observed phenomenon)
6.2 Planning	(e.g., Plan a research paper on a given historical topic)
6.3 Producing	(e.g., Build habitats for certain species for certain purposes)

Source: Anderson, L. W. et al. (2001), p. 31

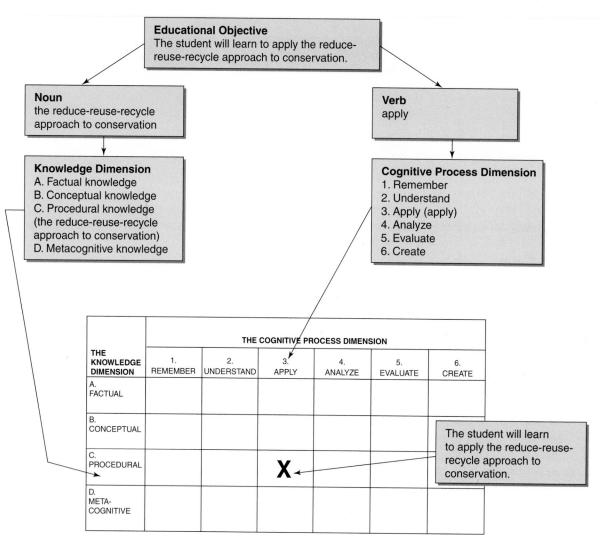

Figure 3.10 *Classifying an Objective in the Taxonomy Table*

Source: Anderson et. al. (2001), p. 32

The psychomotor domain in Bloom's taxonomy classifies objectives in the area of physical movement and coordination.

visual art; hand coordination is required for producing this art. Moving from student to student, using audiovisual equipment, and communicating intentions with facial and hand gestures are examples of teacher skills in the psychomotor domain. Following are the six categories of objectives in the **psychomotor domain.** Notice that the categories range from simple reflex reactions to complex actions that communicate ideas and emotions to others.

Reflex movements—Student's actions can occur involuntarily in response to some stimulus.

Basic fundamental movements—Student has innate movement patterns formed from a combination of reflex movements.

Perceptual abilities—Student can translate stimuli received through the senses into appropriate desired movements.

Physical abilities—Student has developed basic movements that are essential to the development of more highly skilled movements.

Skilled movements—Student has developed more complex movements requiring a certain degree of efficiency.

Nondiscursive communications—Student has the ability to communicate through body movement.

The original taxonomies for affective and psychomotor objectives have never been revised.

Bloom's initial taxonomy was not free from criticism. Some misinterpreted that certain, less complex types of knowledge are not as important as those that are more complex. This was not Bloom's intent. Others challenged the hierarchical ordering of the instructional objectives. It is likely that the same criticisms will occur with the revised taxonomy, particularly in regard to the new complexity continuum. Finally, critics have argued, and rightfully so, that the taxonomy and the ordering of categories do not fit all fields of knowledge equally well.

Regardless of the criticism and identified weaknesses in the original taxonomy, it remains popular with teachers. It is likely that the revised version of the taxonomy will find an equally receptive educator audience because it provides a valuable way of thinking about instructional intents and assessment and, thus, is viewed as a valuable planning tool. The taxonomy provides a good reminder that we want students to learn a variety of knowledge and skills and be able to think and act in a variety of straightforward as well as complex ways

Lesson Plans and Unit Plans

Instructional objectives are used in conjunction with **lesson plans,** and, as you saw from Yinger's research, teachers construct both short-term and long-term plans.

Daily lesson plans normally outline the content to be taught, motivational techniques to be used, materials needed, specific steps and activities, and evaluation procedures.

Daily Planning. A teacher's daily plan is the one that receives most attention. In some schools, it is required. In other schools, even the format for daily plans is prescribed. Normally, daily plans outline what content is to be taught, motivational techniques to be used, specific steps and activities for students, needed materials, and evaluation processes. The amount of detail can vary. During student teaching, cooperating teachers may require a beginning teacher to write very detailed daily plans, even though their own plans may be briefer.

Most beginning teachers can understand the logic of requiring rather detailed daily plans at first. Think of the daily lesson plan as similar to the text of a speech to be delivered to a large audience. Speakers giving a speech for the first time need to follow a set of detailed notes or perhaps even a word-for-word text. As they gain experience, or as their speeches are gradually committed to memory from repeated presentations, they find less and less need for notes and can proceed more extemporaneously. Or think of using the plan as being similar to using a road map. Going to a location the first time requires careful and continuous attention to the map. After several trips, it can be discarded.

Daily plans can take many forms. The features of a particular lesson often determine the lesson plan format. For example, each of the teaching models described in Chapters 7 through 13 requires a somewhat different format, as you will see. A beginning teacher will find, however, that some schools have a preferred format that they require of all teachers. Usually, that format contains most, if not all, the features included in the sample lesson plan developed by faculty at Augsburg College and illustrated in Figure 3.11.

```
Lesson topic/subject_____ Grade level_____

Preinstructional Planning


    Objectives:                              Domains:
    _____         Cognitive
    _____         Affective
    _____         Motor/Skill


    Materials/special arrangements/individual modifications:


During Instruction

    Introduction/establishing set:

    Sequence (syntax) of learning activities:


    Closure:

    Assignment:


Postinstructional

    Evaluation of student learning:

        Formal:

        Informal:

    Evaluation of the lesson (How did the lesson go?
    Revisions needed.)
```

Figure 3.11 *Sample Lesson Plan Format*

Source: Fleener (1989)

Observe that this lesson format includes a clear statement of objectives and a sequence of learning activities for the lesson, beginning with a way to get students started and ending with some type of closure and assignment. The lesson format also provides a means to evaluate student learning as well as the lesson itself.

Weekly and Unit Planning. Most schools and teachers organize instruction around weeks and units. A unit is essentially a chunk of content and associated skills that are perceived as fitting together in a logical way. Normally more than one lesson is required to accomplish a unit of instruction. The content for instructional units might come from chapters in books or from major sections of curriculum guides. Examples of units include such topics as sentences, the Civil War, fractions, thermodynamics, note taking, the heart, Japan, and the short stories of Hemingway.

Unit planning is, in many ways, more critical than daily planning. The unit plan links together a variety of goals, content, and activities the teacher has in mind. It determines the overall flow for a series of lessons over several days, weeks, or perhaps even months. Often it reflects the teacher's understanding of both the content and processes of instruction.

Most people can memorize plans for an hour or a day, but they cannot remember the logistics and sequencing of activity for several days or weeks. For this reason, teachers' unit plans are generally written in a fair amount of detail. When unit plans are put into

> Most teachers organize instruction around units that require multiple lessons spread over several days.

```
Title of unit_____

Unit rationale and introduction_____
_____

Overall Unit Objectives

        General Objective 1
        Specific objective:_____
        Specific objective:_____
        General Objective 2
        Specific objective:_____
        Specific objective:_____


Unit Content

        Major Content and Topics to Cover


Syntax For Unit

        Major Activities and Overall Flow of Lessons
        Day 1
        Day 2
        Materials and Other Resources Required


Major Assignments

        Long-range
        Short-term
        Bibliography and Other Student Aids

Assessment and evaluation _____
_____
```

Figure 3.12 *Sample Unit Plan Format*

writing, they also serve as a reminder later that some lessons require supporting materials, equipment, motivational devices, or evaluation tools that cannot usually be obtained on a moment's notice. If teachers are working together in teams, unit planning and assignment of responsibilities for various unit activities are most important. The content usually contained in a unit of instruction can be found in the sample unit plan illustrated in Figure 3.12.

Unit plans can also be shared with students because they provide the overall road map that explains where the teacher or a particular lesson is going. Through the communication of unit goals and activities, students can recognize what they are expected to learn. Knowledge of unit plans can help older students allocate their study time and monitor their own progress.

Over time, experienced teachers develop unit plans and supporting materials that can be reused. However, most beginning teachers will have to rely on textbooks and curriculum guides. There is nothing wrong with doing this, and the beginning teacher should not feel guilty about it. Most curriculum guides have been developed by experienced teachers, and even though their approach to subjects cannot be expected to fit the preferences of an individual teacher, they do provide a helpful overall design to follow. Curriculum frameworks developed by most state departments of education can also provide valuable assistance with unit planning.

Two notes of caution are worth mentioning, however. First, some beginning teachers, particularly in middle schools and high schools, rely heavily on their college textbooks

Unit plans should be put in writing, since they function as maps that connect several lessons and give teachers, students, and others an idea of where lessons are going.

or the course and unit plans of their college instructors. These plans and materials are not ever appropriate for younger learners, who are not ready for the advanced content found in college courses. Second, there are teachers who, after several years of experience, still rely on textbooks for planning and sequencing their instruction. Teaching and learning are creative, evolutionary processes that should be keyed to a particular group of students at a particular point in time. Only when this is done can lessons rise above the humdrum and provide students with intellectual excitement.

Yearly Plans. Yearly plans are also critical but, because of the uncertainty and complexity in most schools, cannot be done with as much precision as daily or unit plans. The effectiveness of yearly plans generally revolves around how well they deal with the following three features:

Most teachers have a few long-term global goals that can be achieved only by infusing them into many lessons and units during the year.

Overall Themes and Attitudes. Most teachers have some global attitudes, goals, and themes they like to leave with their students. Perhaps a teacher in a mixed-race elementary classroom would like his or her students to end the term with a bit less bias or misunderstanding and a bit more tolerance of people who are racially different. No specific lesson or unit can teach this attitude, but many carefully planned and coordinated experiences throughout the year can. Or perhaps a high school biology teacher would like students to understand and embrace a set of attitudes associated with scientific methods. A single lesson on the scientific method will not accomplish this goal. However, personal modeling and formal demonstrations showing respect for data, the relationships between theory and reality, or the process of making inferences from information can eventually influence students to think more scientifically. As a last example, a history teacher may want students to leave her class with an appreciation of the very long time frame associated with the development of democratic traditions. Again, a single lesson on the Magna Carta, the Constitution, or the Fourteenth Amendment will not develop this appreciation. However, building a succession of lessons that come back to a common theme on the "cornerstones of democracy" can achieve this end.

Coverage. There are few teachers who run out of things to do. Instead, the common lament is that time runs out with many important lessons still to be taught. Experienced teachers carry many of their yearlong plans in their heads. Beginning teachers, however, will have to take care to develop yearlong plans if they want to get past the Civil War by March. Planning to cover desired topics requires asking what is really important to teach, deciding on priorities, and attending carefully to the instructional hours actually available over a year's time. In most instances, teachers strive to teach too much, too lightly. Students may be better served if a reduced menu is planned. In short, most beginning teachers overestimate how much time is actually available for instruction and underestimate the amount of time it takes to teach something well. Careful planning can help minimize this error in judgment.

Cycles of the school year can have strong effects on the plans teachers make.

Cycles of the School Year. Experienced teachers know that the school year is cyclical and that some topics are better taught at one time than another. School cycles and corresponding emotional or psychological states revolve around the opening and closing of school, the days of the week, vacation periods, the changes of season, holidays, and important school events. Some of these can be anticipated; some cannot. Nonetheless, it is important to plan for school cycles as much as possible. Experienced teachers know that new units or important topics are not introduced on Friday or the day before a holiday break. They know that the opening of school should emphasize processes and structures to facilitate student learning later in the year. They know that the end of the school year will be filled with interruptions and decreasing motivation as students anticipate summer vacation. They also know that it is unwise to plan for a unit examination the night after a big game or the hour following the Halloween party.

As beginning teachers, you will know something about these cycles and corresponding psychological states from your own student days. You can use this information, along with information provided by experienced teachers in a school, as you proceed with making long-range, yearly plans.

Time-tabling Techniques to Assist Unit and Yearly Planning. There are several techniques to assist teachers in making clear and doable instructional plans that extend over several days or weeks or that include many specific, independent tasks to be completed before moving on. One such technique is **time-tabling.** A time table is a chronological map of a series of instructional activities or some special project the teacher may want to carry out. It describes the overall direction of activities and any special products that may be produced within a time frame. The most straightforward time-tabling technique consists of constructing a special chart called a Gantt chart. A **Gantt chart** allows you to see the work pieces in relation to each other—when each starts and finishes. Gantt charts can be used similarly to previously described curriculum maps to show how particular content is to be covered over a period of time, such as a semester. They can also be used to plan logistics for instructional activities, such as the one illustrated in Figure 3.13 used by a teacher to plan a field trip to a local museum.

There are many formats for making time tables. Some teachers believe in evolving processes and prefer a more open and nonspecific approach. Others prefer just the opposite and write everything down in great detail. One's own personal philosophy and work style influence the exact approach and level of detail required. Regardless of the

> Time tables are chronological maps showing how a series of instructional activities are carried out over time.

TASK	TIME			
	Mar 10–15	Mar 18–23	Mar 26–31	April 3–7
Call museum director	xx			
Talk to principal	xx			
Request bus for field trip	xx			
Introduce unit on art history	xxxxxxxx			
Prepare field trip permission slips	xx			
Send permission slips home		xx		
Require slips to be returned			xx	
Teach unit on art history		xxxxxxxxxxxxxxxxxxxxxxxx		
Go over logistics of field trip				xxxxxxxx
Discuss what to look for on trip				xxxx
Take trip				x
Follow up trip in class				xxxx
Write thank-you letters				xxx

Figure 3.13 *Gantt Chart, Museum Trip*

It is often important for teachers to communicate their plans to parents.

extent to which you choose to make time tables a part of your planning, it is at least important to consider their use because they help planners recognize the limits of a very important and scarce resource—time.

The Enhancing Teaching with Technology box on page 107 described several tools that can assist teachers with planning and time-tabling.

Other Planning Decisions. Most of this discussion has been devoted to how teachers choose curriculum content, instructional objectives, and learning activities. There are, however, other decisions teachers make about their classroom that require advanced planning. For example, classroom teachers and students are expected to perform certain housekeeping activities such as taking attendance, keeping the classroom space safe and livable, making assignments, collecting papers, and distributing and storing materials. These tasks, like instructional tasks, require careful planning. Experienced teachers plan housekeeping tasks so thoroughly and efficiently that the naïve observer may not even notice they are occurring. A beginning teacher who has not planned efficient ways to accomplish housekeeping routines will suffer from ongoing confusion and wasted instructional time. The following planning guidelines for routines derive from effective teachers' practice and from experience.

Guideline 1. Make sure detailed written plans exist for taking roll, giving assignments, collecting and distributing papers, and storing books and equipment.

Guideline 2. Distribute these written plans and procedures to students the first time a housekeeping activity occurs in a particular year or with a particular class.

Guideline 3. Provide students with time to practice routines and procedures, and give them feedback on how well they are doing.

Guideline 4. Post copies of the housekeeping plans on the bulletin board or on chart paper to serve as public reminders about how particular activities are to be carried out.

Guideline 5. Train student helpers immediately to provide leadership and assistance in carrying out routines. Students at all ages can and like to be in charge of taking roll, picking up books, getting and setting up the movie projector, and the like.

Guideline 6. Follow the plan that has been developed consistently, and make sure that plenty of time exists to carry out each activity, particularly early in the year.

Guideline 7. Be alert to ways to make housekeeping activities more efficient and seek feedback about how students think the housekeeping activities are going.

Individualizing Instruction through Planning

Teachers can use planning to individualize instruction and meet the needs of every student. By planning carefully, teachers can provide more time for students to complete assignments, adjust the level of difficulty of instructional materials, and provide varied learning activities. In some instances, they can also vary what students are expected to learn.

Keep Learning Objectives the Same for All Students. Sometimes content taught to students is so important that teachers do not have the luxury of tailoring their objectives to meet the needs of particular students. For example, all students are expected to know the answers to specific questions that appear on required mastery tests. These questions normally cover the basics in core curriculum areas: mathematics, reading and writing, the sciences, and history. Because students do not come to class with the same backgrounds and abilities in these subjects, the teacher's plan must reflect ways to help them make progress according to their abilities. Normally, teachers do this by varying one of three aspects of instruction: time, materials, or learning activities.

Vary Time. Every experienced teacher knows that it takes some students longer than others to master particular content. To accommodate these differences, teachers devise plans with a common assignment but provide more time for students who need it to complete the assignment. To make this work, however, teachers must plan for the students who are likely to complete their work ahead of others. Generally, this means providing enrichment activities for students who complete the assignment quickly or making technology centers available to these students so they can pursue advanced topics of their choosing.

Adapt Materials. Teachers can also tailor their instruction through planning by varying the level of difficulty of the instructional materials. Some schools provide a variety of textbooks that are written at different levels. In other schools, teachers will have to make their own adjustments. Materials can be adapted by rewriting, although this can be very time-consuming. Other ways to adapt materials include providing students with specially designed study guides or notes that make the materials easier to understand or making flashcards and other practice devices available.

Use Different Learning Activities. As described in Chapter 2, students vary in the way they prefer to learn. Some students can glean a great amount of information from text, while others are more adept at listening to the teacher explain things. Some students like to deal with abstract ideas, while others are more successful when they are working with hands-on materials and projects. Still others learn as they talk about their ideas with each other. Effective teachers vary the teaching strategies they use and provide students with options for the learning activities they can use in pursuit of common learning goals.

Vary the Learning Objectives. In some instances, teachers can vary the learning objectives they hold for students. For instance, students can be allowed to select topics that interest them within a unit of study or they can choose projects that are consistent with their own abilities. The risk of this approach, like the risk of grouping students by ability, is that students in the slower groups or those who pursue less difficult or less complex projects may fall farther and farther behind in the essential core content of the curriculum and never accomplish the objectives of their peers. These are decisions that each teacher will have to make for particular students and situations.

Planning for Time and Space

An additional, overall aspect of teacher planning has to do with the use of time and space, resources over which teachers have considerable control. This includes how much time to spend on academic tasks in general, how much time to allocate to particular subjects,

Check, Extend, Explore

Check
- What are the major factors that influence teachers' decisions about what to teach?
- What is the primary purpose of a curriculum map?
- How do the various approaches to writing objectives vary? What have been the major criticisms of the behavioral approach to writing objectives?
- What are taxonomies? What are the category schemes in Bloom's revised taxonomy?
- What are the differences between unit plans and daily plans?
- How can teachers adapt instruction to meet the individual needs of their students?

Extend
- Do you think teachers should be required to hand in their lesson plans to the principal? Go to "Extend Question Poll" on the Online Learning Center to respond.

Explore
- Go to the Online Learning Center at www.mhhe.com/arends6e for links to websites related to particular *Performance Standards Developed by Professional Organizations* and for sites related to *Writing Objectives and Preparing Lesson Plans.*

and where to place students, materials, and desks. Because there is much useful research on the relationship between teachers' use of classroom time and student achievement, we now look more carefully at this topic. Following that, we briefly consider the topic of classroom space. A more thorough discussion about the use of space can be found in Chapters 7 through 12, where particular teaching models are examined.

Time

Research has validated that time available for instruction is far less than one might believe, even though it seems plentiful at the beginning of the year.

The management of classroom time is a complex and difficult task for teachers, although on the surface it appears to be a rather simple and straightforward matter. Fortunately, there is a well-developed knowledge base on the use of classroom time that can guide teacher planning in this area. Essentially, the research validates what experienced teachers have always known: The time available for instruction that appears to be so plentiful when the year begins soon becomes a scarce resource. Too often, inexperienced teachers find themselves racing through topics in as little time as possible in order to cover targeted content. Unfortunately, what appears to them as efficient use of time often produces little, if any, student learning. This suggests that the effective use of time is just as important as the amount of time spent on a topic. Current interest in the use of classroom time stems mainly from thought and research done in the 1970s and 1980s. A number of studies during that era produced three important findings (Fisher et al., 1980; Rosenshine, 1980; Stallings & Kaskowitz, 1974).

A direct relationship exists between time engaged in academic tasks and high achievement gains.

1. Time allocated and used for specific tasks is strongly related to academic achievement. What the researchers found was that regardless of the specific methods used by teachers in particular programs, classrooms in which students spent the most time *engaged in academic work* were those in which students were making the highest achievement gains in reading and mathematics.
2. Teachers varied considerably in the amount of time they allocated to particular studies. For instance, in one study, researchers found some fifth-grade classrooms allocated sixty minutes each day to reading and language arts whereas others spent almost two and a half hours on these subjects.
3. Regardless of the amount of time a teacher allocated to a particular topic, the amount of time students were actually engaged in learning activities varied considerably. A large proportion of time was found to be devoted to nonacademic, noninstructional, and various housekeeping activities.

These time studies led Carol Weinstein and Andrew Mignano (2002) to differentiate instructional time into seven categories:

1. *Total time.* This is the total amount of time students spend in school. In most states, the mandated time consists of one hundred eighty days of school per year and from six to seven hours of school each day.
2. *Attended time.* This is the amount of time that students actually attend school. Sickness, broken heating systems, and snow days reduce the amount of attendance time from the total time required by law.
3. *Available time.* Some of the school day is spent on lunch, recess, pep rallies, and other extracurricular activities and, consequently, is not available for academic purposes.
4. *Planned academic time.* When teachers fill in plan books, they set aside a certain amount of time for different subjects and activities, called *planned academic time.*

Opportunity to learn is the time a teacher actually spends on academic tasks and activities.

5. *Actual academic time.* The amount of time the teacher actually spends on academic tasks or activities is called *allocated time.* This is also called **opportunity to learn** and

is measured in terms of the amount of time teachers have their students spend on a given academic task.

6. *Engaged time.* The amount of time students actually spend on a learning activity or task is called **engaged time,** or **time on task.** This type of time is measured in terms of on-task and off-task behavior. If a teacher has allocated time to seatwork on math problems and the student is working on these problems, the student's behavior is on task. Conversely, if the student is doodling or talking about football with another student, the behavior is counted as off task.

> Time on task is the amount of time students actually spend on a particular subject or learning activity.

7. *Academic learning time (ALT).* The amount of time a student spends engaged in an academic task at which he or she is successful is **academic learning time.** It is the aspect of time most closely related to student learning.

> Academic learning time is when students are engaged in academic subjects or activities at which they are successful.

The graph illustrated in Figure 3.14, developed by Carol Weinstein and Andrew Mignano (2002), shows how much time is available in each of the seven categories. Based on the time studies described previously, this figure shows how the almost eleven hundred hours of mandated time for schooling is reduced to slightly over three hundred hours when it comes to actual academic learning time, because there is slippage each step of the way. Thus, although there is great variation in the way school and classroom time is managed, the lesson from the research on how time is used clearly shows that far less academic learning time is available to teachers and students than initially meets the eye.

Time studies done by prominent educational researchers gained worldwide attention from both practitioners and researchers alike. If strong relationships existed between time on task and academic achievement, the obvious follow-up research would be to discover what some teachers do to produce classrooms with high on-task ratios and what can be done to help other teachers improve in this direction. Two domains of immediate concern were the ways teachers organized and managed their classrooms and the particular teaching methods they employed. More is said about these two topics in Chapters 7–12.

Space

The arrangement of classroom space is critical and does not have simple solutions. Most important, the way that space is used influences how classroom participants relate to

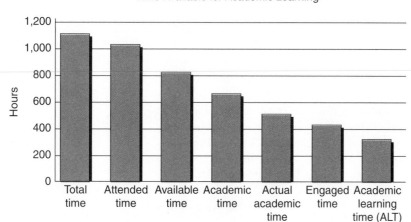

Figure 3.14 *How Much Time Is There, Anyway?*

Source: After Weinstein and Mignano (2002)

one another and what students learn. Consider, for example, how a teacher might conduct a discussion with students. The teacher and students could be arranged in a circle that permits equal communication among all parties or, as is more usual, the students could be arranged in straight rows with all information directed to and from a central figure (the teacher). In the latter arrangement, the discussion does not occur among students but between the students and the teacher. As this example shows, the way space is designed influences not only communication patterns but also power relationships among teachers and students. These relationships are important because they may affect the degree to which students take ownership of the lesson and become independent learners.

Arrangements of students, desks, and chairs not only help determine classroom communication patterns and interpersonal relationships, but also influence a variety of daily decisions teachers must make concerning the management and use of scarce resources. The choices involved are not clear-cut. Fortunately, a substantial body of research provides guidelines for teachers as they think about these decisions. Space arrangements to facilitate particular teaching models are described in some detail in Chapters 7–12.

Check, Extend, Explore

Check

- What does research show about how teachers vary as to the amount of time they spend on similar subjects and work activities?
- What are the seven categories of instructional time as defined by Weinstein and Mignano?
- How might different types of lessons affect the way a teacher arranges classroom space?

Extend

- Some educators argue that we pay too much attention to the way time is spent and that we have gone overboard in insisting on sets amount of ALT, even to the point of doing away with recess. Do you agree or disagree that we should eliminate recess? Go to the "Extend Question Poll" on the Online Learning Center to respond.

Explore

- Go to the Online Learning Center at www.mhhe.com/arends6e for links to websites related to *Planning for Classroom Space and Time.*

Reflections **from the** *Classroom*

To Plan or Not to Plan

Considerable debate has existed over the years about best practice in regard to teacher planning. On one side of the debate are those who hold more behaviorist views about teaching and learning and who see planning as a rational, linear process. This view would argue for detailed delineation of content and skills to be taught and careful use of behavioral objectives. On the other side of the debate are those who hold a more constructivist view of teaching. This view holds that planning is not always linear and should take into account the complexity and serendipity of teaching and learning.

Write a reflective essay that gives your views on teacher planning in a way that would provide a principal who is considering hiring you insight into the type of planner you will be. Approach this situation from the perspective of the grade level or subject area you are preparing to teach. Compare your views with those of the following two teachers. You may want to include your essay in your professional portfolio.

(continued)

Donald Early
5th Grade

In my teacher education program, my professors emphasized the importance of tying all instructional activities to student learning outcomes. In an ideal world, I agree with this approach. However, in the real world, it just doesn't seem to work that way. As I plan, I normally start with big ideas I want students to understand. Sometimes I write these out; sometimes I don't. Also, over the years, I have developed many lessons that I know will interest the students and keep them engaged. I try to incorporate these highly motivational lessons into my teaching on a regular basis. Finally, I believe that students are mainly responsible for their own learning. My job is not to cram information and ideas into their brains. Instead, my job is to create learning experiences that will allow them to discover things on their own and to build knowledge out of experience. This calls for a different kind of planning that I find difficult to explain to others.

Angela Adams
Jacksonville Middle School, 7th and 8th Grade
Jacksonville, TX

During my first year of teaching, lesson planning was the most overwhelming aspect of my job. Several things have to be considered when planning lessons such as individual education plans, school curriculum requirements, national and state standards, and available resources. Many mornings I woke up with my first thought, "What are we going to do today?" Never a good way to start the day. Gradually I learned to develop integrated units that lasted a long period of time and also allowed for flexibility when standardized test days, pep rallies, or assemblies were scheduled.

A goal I set for my second year was to plan for the entire year in the summer to alleviate stress once the school year started. Once again, I began to feel overwhelmed and did not know where to begin. So, I divided the year into teaching units and planned objectives for each unit. This helped me design a flexible scope and sequence in my head that could be developed more fully later in the school year.

Lesson planning is a source of stress for even the best, most experienced teachers. Every teacher has to develop a system of lesson planning that fits his or her needs and resources.

Chapter Review

Go back to the "Interactive and Applied Learning" feature at the beginning of the chapter for a listing of interactive and applied activities. Go to the Online Learning Center at **www.mhhe.com/arends6e** or your Interactive Student CD-ROM to take practice quizzes over the content of this chapter and receive immediate feedback. You can also review chapter content and main ideas, practice with key terms, and find annotated Web links on topics associated with this chapter.

Summary

Perspective on Planning

- Planning and making decisions about instruction are among the most important aspects of teaching because they are major determinants of what is taught in schools and how it is taught.
- It is sometimes difficult to learn planning skills from experienced teachers because most of their planning activities are hidden from public view.
- The traditional perspective of planning is based on rational-linear models characterized by setting goals and

taking specific actions to accomplish desired outcomes. The knowledge base suggests that teacher planning and decision making do not always conform to rational-linear planning models. Newer perspectives on planning put more emphasis on planners' actions and reflections.

Theoretical and Empirical Support

- Studies have shown that planning has consequences for both student learning and classroom behavior. It can enhance

student motivation, help focus student learning, and decrease classroom management problems.

- Planning can have unanticipated negative effects as well;
for example, it can limit self-initiated learning on the part
of students and make teachers insensitive to student ideas.

- Experienced teachers and beginning teachers have different
planning approaches and needs. Experienced teachers are
more concerned with establishing structures ahead of time
to guide classroom activities and plan ahead for the adaptations needed as lessons get under way. In general, beginning teachers need more detailed plans than experienced
teachers do. They devote more of their planning to verbal
instructions and respond more often to student interests.

Planning Domains

- Teacher planning is multifaceted but relates to three
phases of teaching: prior to instruction, in which decisions
are made about what will be taught and for how long; the
instructional phase, in which decisions are made about
questions to ask, wait time, and specific orientations; and
after instruction, when decisions are made about how to
evaluate student progress and what type of feedback to
provide.

- Planning cycles include not only daily plans but also plans
for each week, month, and year. The details of these various plans differ, however. Plans carried out on a particular
day are influenced by what has happened before and will
in turn influence future plans.

The Specifics of Planning

- One of the most complex planning tasks is choosing curriculum content. Standards and frameworks developed by
professional societies and by state and local curriculum
committees assist in making these decisions. A number of
planning tools also can help teachers, including curriculum mapping.

- Curriculum mapping is a planning tool that allows groups
of teachers to chart what they are teaching across grade
levels and content fields. This type of planning identifies
gaps and overlaps.

- Instructional objectives are statements that describe the
student changes that should result from instruction. Behavioral objectives include statements about expected student behavior, the testing situation in which the behavior
will be observed, and performance criteria. An objective
written in a more general format communicates the
teacher's overall intent but lacks the precision of a behavioral objective.

- Taxonomies are devices that help classify and show relationship among things. Bloom's taxonomy has been
widely used in education to classify objectives in three
domains—the cognitive, the affective, and the psychomotor. The original taxonomy for the cognitive domain, developed in the 1950's, has recently been revised
to reflect new perspectives and research about the relationships between types of knowledge and the cognitive
processes.

- Formats for lesson plans can vary, but in general, a good
plan includes a clear statement of objectives, a sequence of
learning activities, and a means of evaluating student
learning.

- Unit plans cover chunks of instruction that can span several days or weeks. Like lesson plans, the format can vary,
but a good unit plan includes overall objectives for the
unit, major content to be covered, syntax or phases of the
unit, major assignments, and assessment procedures.

- Time-tabling techniques, such as making a chronological
map of a series of instructional activities, can assist with
long-range planning tasks.

- Effective teachers know how to make good formal plans.
They have also learned how to make adjustments when
plans prove to be inappropriate or ineffective.

- Through the planning process, teachers can vary time, materials, and learning activities to meet the needs of every
student in the class.

Planning for Time and Space

- Time and space are scarce commodities in teaching, and
their use should be planned with care and foresight.

- Research on time shows considerable variation from
teacher to teacher on the amount of time allocated to different subject areas.

- The amount of time students spend on a task is related to
how much they learn. Students in classrooms in which allocated time is high and a large proportion of students is
engaged learn more than in classrooms where allocated
time is low and students are found off task.

- Space—the arrangement of materials, desks, and students—
is another important resource that is planned and managed by teachers. The way space is used affects the learning
atmosphere of classrooms, influences classroom dialogue
and communication, and has important cognitive and emotional effects on students.

- The use of time and space is influenced by the demands of
the learning tasks. Effective teachers develop an attitude
of flexibility and experimentation about these features of
classroom life.

Key Terms

Portfolio and Field Experience Activities

This feature has been designed to help you learn from your field experiences and to assist you in the preparation of artifacts for your professional portfolio on topics and standards associated with Chapter 3.

1. Complete the "Reflections from the Classroom" exercise at the end of this chapter. The recommended reflective essay will provide insight into your views and approach to teacher planning.

2. Complete Activity 3.4 in the *Guide to Field Experiences and Portfolio Development*. This activity provides guidelines for discovering the internal structure of an experienced teacher's lesson.

3. Complete Activity 3.5 in the *Guide to Field Experiences and Portfolio Development*. This activity will provide you an artifact for your portfolio that demonstrates your understanding and skill for planning lessons and units.

Books for the Professional

Go to the Online Learning Center at www.mhhe.com/arends6e or your Interactive Student CD-ROM for an annotated version of this list.

Anderson, L. W., and Krathwohl, D. R. (eds. and with P. W. Airasian, K. A. Cruikshank, R. E. Mayer, P. R. Pintrich, J. Raths, and M. C. Wittrock) (2001). *A Taxonomy for Learning, Teaching, and Assessing: A Revision of Bloom's Taxonomy of Educational Objectives.* New York: Longman.

Gronlund, N. E. (1999). *How to Write and Use Instructional Objectives* (6th ed.). New York: Macmillan.

Jacobs, H. H. (1997). *Mapping the Big Picture.* Alexandria, VA: Association for Supervision and Curriculum Development.

Mager, F. R. (1997). *Preparing Instructional Objectives: A Critical Tool in the Development of Effective Instruction.* Los Angeles: Center for Effective Instruction.

Wiggins, G., and McTighe, J. (1998). *Understanding by Design.* Alexandria, VA: Association for Supervision and Curriculum Development.

Chapter Four

Classrooms As Learning Communities

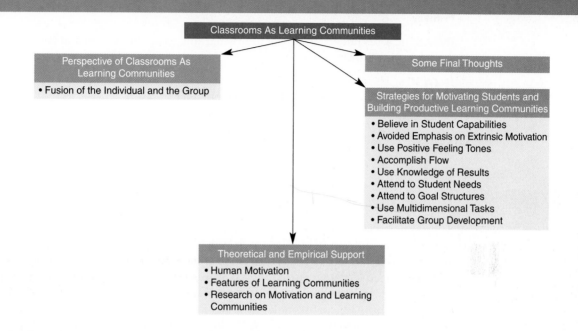

Classrooms As Learning Communities

Perspective of Classrooms As Learning Communities
- Fusion of the Individual and the Group

Some Final Thoughts

Strategies for Motivating Students and Building Productive Learning Communities
- Believe in Student Capabilities
- Avoided Emphasis on Extrinsic Motivation
- Use Positive Feeling Tones
- Accomplish Flow
- Use Knowledge of Results
- Attend to Student Needs
- Attend to Goal Structures
- Use Multidimensional Tasks
- Facilitate Group Development

Theoretical and Empirical Support
- Human Motivation
- Features of Learning Communities
- Research on Motivation and Learning Communities

Interactive **and** *Applied Learning*

Go to your Interactive Student CD-ROM to:

- Hear audio clips of Diane Caruso (fourth/fifth grade) and Angela Adams (seventh/eigth grade) talk about creating learning communities in the *Teachers on Teaching* feature
- Watch the video clip *Reflections,* which presents experienced teachers discussing the importance of motivation

Go to the Online Learning Center at www.mhhe.com/arends6e to read *PowerWeb* articles and newsfeed updates about:

- Classroom climate
- Cultural diversity in education
- Emotions
- Ethics and teaching
- Moral development
- Morality and schooling
- Nonviolent conflict resolution
- Social contexts of multicultural education
- Technology and education

INTASC *Considering* **Standards**

Studying this chapter will help you meet three INTASC principles:

Primary

INTASC 5: Uses understanding of individual and group motivation and behavior to create positive learning environment.

INTASC 6: Uses knowledge of verbal and nonverbal communication to foster inquiry, collaboration, and supportive classroom interaction.

Secondary

INTASC 2: Provides learning opportunities that support student development.

Reflecting **on** *Classrooms As Learning Communities*

Before you read this chapter, think for a moment about some of the classrooms you were in when you were in elementary or high school or, for that matter, classrooms you have been in as a college student. Some of these classrooms were definitely teacher-centered places where teaching practices were characterized by transmitting knowledge to students. Some were efficient, and students were well behaved. Others may have been out of control. Still others were places where students were friends with one another and where everyone worked hard to learn things that had meaning for them.

Make two lists, one describing the attributes of classrooms that you thought led to positive learning communities and the other detailing attributes that were negative and prevented the development of a learning community.

Positive Attributes	Negative Attributes
_____	_____
_____	_____
_____	_____

Now analyze your lists and reflect on what you think teachers did to make those classrooms the way they were. Consider other factors that may have influenced the situation such as the type of student, physical conditions, and so on.

Go to the Online Learning Center at www.mhhe.com/arends6e to respond to these questions.

Making one's classroom a learning community is one of the most important things a teacher can do, even more important perhaps than the practices used in the more formal aspects of instruction. The classroom learning community influences student engagement and achievement, and it determines how a teacher's class will evolve from a collection of individuals into a cohesive group characterized by high expectations, caring relationships, and productive inquiry. Creating positive learning communities, however, is no simple task, nor are there easy recipes that will ensure success. Instead, it is a process of doing many things right and well and of having the courage to create classrooms that are different from many now found in schools. Let's begin this process by looking at two teachers who do this aspect of their work very well:

Carolyn Barnes has come to love her fifth-grade class. She is now in her third year of teaching at Woodville School. Her class is organized as a learning community, and she is pleased to be able to focus on the real learning needs of her students rather than being preoccupied with classroom management problems. She believes that her class is a democratic society in which she and the students are devoted to learning about themselves and the world around them. She sees herself as playing two roles—instructional leader and participant—in the community of scholarship they are building together. Barnes believes that what is learned must be socially constructed and that what is constructed affects what it is possible to learn. She finds herself reflecting frequently on the balance between initiating actions and responding to student initiatives within the class.

One of Barnes's students, Steve, is a good example of the payoff of her approach to teaching. Steve had a low opinion of himself and of schooling in general before he started in Carolyn's fifth-grade class. He didn't seem to care about anything. In fact, his favorite response to most everything was, "Who cares?" However, in Carolyn's learning community, students learn to trust their ability to think through problems in many areas of the curriculum. Steve first became excited when he discovered that he could solve simple algebraic problems. Later on, he found that he could apply his problem-solving skills in the social arena. The leadership Steve developed within his study team in dealing with mathematical problems helped him when he was faced with social problems within the team. Success in one area spread to other areas.

How did Carolyn Barnes get Steve to change so radically from a bored and indifferent nonparticipant to an enthusiastic learner? "It wasn't what I did so much," Carolyn says, "as what Steve's done for himself." Steve, however, thinks differently. He says, "Ms. Barnes's class is like a continuous debate. It's nothing like any class I've ever known." Steve is referring to the continuing discussions that characterize Barnes's class. No matter what the subject, students are involved in defining concerns, focusing on issues, gathering information, suggesting hypotheses, and defending their theories. Instead of focusing on facts and rote learning, students in Barnes's class strive to make sense of what they experience and to communicate that sense to others.

Mark Hicks now teaches social studies in the Walden Middle School in his midwestern home state. He found out about this job when he visited his parents during summer vacation several years after he started teaching. Walden is a professional development school associated with a nearby midwestern research university and located in an urban setting in a medium-size city. Hicks is a team leader in a . . . learning community that consists of 60 students. His team includes two interns from the university; an aide who is a specialist in reading; . . . a university professor who teaches language arts; and a graduate student who works as a researcher and documenter. The students are organized into study groups, and the whole group is organized into a cooperative learning community. The students leave their groups when it is time for them to take their mathematics, science, art, and physical education classes in different rooms and different groups. However, for half the day, the students are all together in one area of the school. Hicks is the instructional leader for social studies (including civics, history, geography, and economics), and the professor is the instructional leader for the language arts (literature, writing, speech, and drama). Mark also teaches one history class in the afternoon, for another learning-community group.

The whole group is also considered the home room for all 60 students. Insofar as possible, Hicks and his teaching colleagues organize their instruction themes around interdisciplinary issues. The students keep journals in which they write their thoughts and feelings about what they are studying and what is happening in the class. Their entries give Hicks insights into their fears and other emotions, as well as their cognitive development. Hicks is particularly interested in what the students understand and can use conceptually to build new ideas about the world they live in. The students are challenged to connect what they are studying in school with the outside world. For example, during a national election campaign one fall, the students organized into research groups and followed particular candidates, read their speeches, watched them on television, checked on their positions, and compared their voting records. The study groups prepared presentations for the whole group and made predictions about the election outcome.

After the elections, the students studied the results and compared them with their predictions. Where they missed the mark, the groups tried to find reasons for the difference between the outcomes and their predictions. This project combined many areas of knowledge and gave the students a feeling that what they were doing was relevant to the world around them (after Putnam & Burke, 1992).

Classrooms like Carolyn's and Mark's do not happen by chance. Instead, they are the result of skillful planning and execution by their teachers. The intent of this chapter is to give you the understandings and skills to develop classrooms like Carolyn's and Mark's. The first section of the chapter, Perspectives of Classrooms As Learning Communities, provides an overview of motivation and the concept of learning com-

Productive learning communities do not happen automatically. They require a lot of hard work on the part of teachers.

munities. This overview is followed by a discussion of the theoretical and empirical support for these topics. The focus of the chapter then shifts to a discussion of specific actions teachers can take to motivate their students and to build productive learning communities. Several of these ideas were introduced in Chapter 2, where the focus was on the nature of classrooms with students from diverse backgrounds, and will be revisited in Chapter 5, Classroom Management.

You will discover as you study these three chapters that concepts that lead to productive learning communities are strongly connected to those that describe how teachers think about their students and about the diversity that characterizes today's classrooms. They also relate to how teachers go about creating approaches to classroom management that are caring and democratic.

Perspective of Classrooms As Learning Communities

The process of developing classrooms as learning communities necessitates that teachers attend to many features of their students and their classrooms. Some of the ideas that inform this work date back many years. Other ideas are more recent. This section discusses three topics. First, a rather old perspective is presented, one that conceives of classrooms as places where individual and group needs are played out and where daily activity mirrors life outside of school. Second, a brief description is offered of human motivation and how teachers' choices of motivational strategies influence the development of learning communities. Finally, the concept of learning community itself and attributes that contribute to positive learning communities are described. An effort will be made throughout this section, and elsewhere in the chapter, to describe the nature of most learning communities today while pointing out how these can be changed for the future, particularly a future characterized by diversity.

Fusion of the Individual and the Group

The relationship between individuals and the group is complex in any setting and often fraught with dilemmas. In some ways, it mirrors the dilemma we have built into our larger system of government and economics in the United States. For instance, Americans value collective action, and we have built an elaborate system around democratic principles aimed at ensuring that the voices of citizens are heard and that actions are based on the will of the majority. We have many traditions such as singing the "Star-Spangled Banner" and saying the Pledge of Allegiance that define and promote our groupness. At the same time, we value liberty and have ensured through the Bill of Rights and subsequent laws that individuals can say what they want, believe what they want, bear arms, and pursue their lives without interference of others. This is the individual aspect of our lives.

The same dilemma exists in classrooms. We find a situation where, on the one hand, we want to establish communities that provide encouragement, safety, and support for individual learners. John Dewey (1916) observed a long time ago that children learn as they participate in social settings. More recently, scholars such as Jerome Bruner (1996) have argued that people create meaning out of relationships and membership in particular cultures. So groups and learning communities become an important aspect of learning. On the other hand, group life can limit an individual's initiative and promote

There are always built-in dilemmas in our society and in our classrooms between the needs of the group and the rights of individuals.

Check, Extend, Explore

Check
- What are the two major aspects of classroom life?
- What is the most important factor related to the individual aspect of classroom life? Why?
- What is the main feature of a classroom learning community?

Extend
- In your own life, how do you resolve the tension between individual and group needs?

Explore
- Go to the Online Learning Center at www.mhhe.com/arends6e for links to websites related to *Learning Communities.*

norms opposed to creativity and academic learning. Let's look more closely at the relationships between these two features of classroom life.

Thinking about the individual-group connection stems from the work of early social psychologists, led by the famous Kurt Lewin (1939, 1951) and many of his colleagues who were interested in how a combination of individual needs and environmental conditions explain human behavior. Getzels and Thelan (1960) applied this work to education and developed a two-dimensional model for considering the relationship between the needs of individual students and the conditions of classroom life. The first dimension of the model describes how, within a classroom, there are individuals with certain motives and needs. This perspective can be labeled the *individual dimension* of classroom life. From this perspective, particular classroom behavior results from the personalities and attitudes of students and their actions to satisfy their individual needs and motives.

The second dimension of the model describes how classrooms exist within a social context and how certain roles and expectations develop within that setting to fulfill goals of the system. This dimension can be labeled the *group dimension* of the classroom. From this perspective, classroom behavior is determined by the shared expectations (norms) of the school and the classroom. Classroom life, thus, results from individually motivated students and teachers responding to each other in a social setting. It is out of this sustained development and interaction that learning communities evolve and produce desired social and academic learning.

For teachers, the most important factor on the individual side of the model is *motivation.* This is true because, unlike a student's personality and other individual features that are rather stable and enduring, features of motivation are alterable, as will be described later in the chapter.

The concept of *learning community* is the most important factor on the social dimension of classroom life. A learning community, as contrasted to a collection of individuals, is a setting in which individuals within the community have mutual goals, have common relationships, and show concern for one another. It is a place in which people share tendencies and norms to feel and act in certain ways. These features are summarized in Table 4.1. Developing productive learning communities with these features is no easy task. However, for teachers who meet this challenge, no aspect of the job is more rewarding.

Table 4.1 *Individual and Group Features of Productive Learning Communities*

Individual	Group
• Students and teachers share common goals.	• Norms exist for expecting everyone to do their intellectual best.
• Students see themselves as feeling competent and self-determining.	• Norms exist for getting academic work done.
• Students see themselves as colleagues with high levels of attraction for one another.	• Norms exist for helping and being helped.
• Students and teachers reflect on past experiences and celebrate accomplishments.	• Norms support open communication and dialogue.

Theoretical and Empirical Support

Human Motivation

Motivation is usually defined as the processes that stimulate our behavior or arouse us to take action. It is what makes us act the way we do. Think about this definition for a minute, and consider what arouses you to take action. What prompted you to get up this morning? Why did you choose to eat or ignore your breakfast? Why are you reading this book now rather than earlier or later? Is it because you find it interesting? Are you preparing for a classroom discussion on the topic? Or perhaps for a test? All these factors and more have the potential to arouse action. And, as you will discover later, often several factors combine to motivate individuals to act.

Psychologists make the distinction between two major types of motivation—intrinsic and extrinsic—as illustrated in Figure 4.1. When behavior is sparked internally by one's own interest or curiosity or just for the pure enjoyment of an experience, this is called **intrinsic motivation.** Lingering to watch the sun go behind the horizon on a beautiful evening is an example of intrinsic motivation. In contrast, **extrinsic motivation** kicks in when individuals are influenced to action from external or environmental factors, such as rewards, punishments, or social pressures. Intrinsic and extrinsic motivation are both important in classrooms. How teachers can use both to accomplish desirable behavior and learning is discussed more thoroughly later in the chapter.

> Intrinsic motivation causes people to act in a certain way because it brings personal satisfaction or enjoyment.

Many theories have been proposed over the years that help explain human motivation. Some of these date back to the early part of the twentieth century, whereas others are of more recent origin. Here, our discussion of motivation is selective and follows the recent work of Graham and Weiner (1996), Spaulding (1992), and Stipek (1996). In general, the discussion is limited to those aspects of motivation that help explain behavior within academic or achievement situations rather than behavior within a full range of situations. The discussion concentrates on four perspectives: reinforcement theory, needs theory, cognitive theory, and social learning theory.

> Extrinsic motivation is when individuals work for rewards that are external to the activity.

Reinforcement Theory. In the early twentieth century, **reinforcement theory** and behavioral theory dominated thinking about motivation. This approach to motivation

Figure 4.1 *Intrinsic and Extrinsic Motivation*

emphasized the centrality of external events in directing behavior and in the importance of reinforcers (Skinner, 1956). Reinforcers, whether positive or negative, are stimulus events that occur contingent with a behavior and increase the likelihood of particular behaviors. Reinforcers can be either positive or negative. **Positive reinforcers,** following desired behaviors, enhance the probability that the behavior will be repeated. **Negative reinforcers,** on the other hand, are stimulus events removed after particular behaviors. These stimuli also increase the likelihood of the behavior being repeated. In other words, people or animals repeat behavior to keep the negative reinforcer away—rats push a bar to avoid electric shock or kids do homework to avoid nagging by their parents or teachers. It is important to make distinctions between negative reinforcers and **punishments.** Punishments decrease the likelihood of a behavior being repeated, or at least are intended to do so. For instance, if a rat removes the shock by pushing the bar, it will continue to push the bar, and that is negative reinforcement; if the rat gets a shock when it pushes the bar, it will stop pushing the bar, and that is punishment. If a student misbehaves and gets to leave class as a result, that is negative reinforcement; the student will continue to misbehave, assuming the class is more annoying than going to the principal's office. If a student misbehaves and gets detention after school, that is punishment, and it is supposed to stop the misbehavior.

Educators have embraced reinforcement theory for a long time, and many of the practices found in contemporary classrooms stem from this perspective. The use of good grades, praise, and privileges are examples of incentives and rewards teachers have at their disposal to get students to develop desirable habits and to behave in certain ways. Negative reinforcers, such as bad grades, punishments, and loss of privileges, are used to discourage undesirable tendencies or actions. Behavior modification programs, the use of token economies, and assertive discipline (Canter & Canter 1976, 2002; Cohen 1973) are formal programs that have developed based on reinforcement theory and have been used widely in classrooms during the past thirty years. Although ideas stemming from behavioral theory still dominate many practices found in classrooms, they are increasingly in disrepute among reformers such as Kohn (1966, 1995), Noddings (1992, 2001), and Oakes and Lipton (2003), believe these practices contribute to many of the problems schools face today.

Needs Theory. Developed in the middle part of the twentieth century in part as a reaction to reinforcement theory, **needs theory** emphasizes that individuals are aroused to action by innate needs and intrinsic pressures, rather than by extrinsic rewards or punishments. There are several major variations within this overall theory, but three are of the most importance to classroom teachers.

Abraham Maslow, one of America's foremost mid-twentieth century psychologists, posited that human beings have a hierarchy of needs that they strive to satisfy. These needs were categorized by Maslow into seven levels. At the lower levels, needs exist to satisfy basic physiological requirements, such as food and shelter, to be safe, and to belong and be loved. The needs at the higher level of Maslow's hierarchy are more complex and refer to human growth needs, such as self-understanding, living up to one's potential, and self-actualization. Maslow's hierarchy of needs is illustrated in Figure 4.2.

According to Maslow, it is only when basic physical needs and the needs for love and self-esteem are met that individuals strive to meet higher-order needs. The classroom implications of this situation are clear. Children who come to school without lower-level needs for food and security satisfied are unlikely to spend much energy in satisfying their higher-level needs for knowing and understanding. Students who lack a sense of belonging, either at home or at school, are less likely to seek knowledge of mathematics or history than they are to search for friends and colleagues.

A positive reinforcer is a stimulus such as a reward intended to get individuals to repeat desirable behavior.

A negative reinforcer is a stimulus that is removed, and also intends to get individuals to repeat desired behaviors.

Needs disposition theory posits that people are motivated to take action to satisfy basic and higher-level needs.

The desire to take action and to excel for the purpose of experiencing success and feeling competent is called achievement motivation.

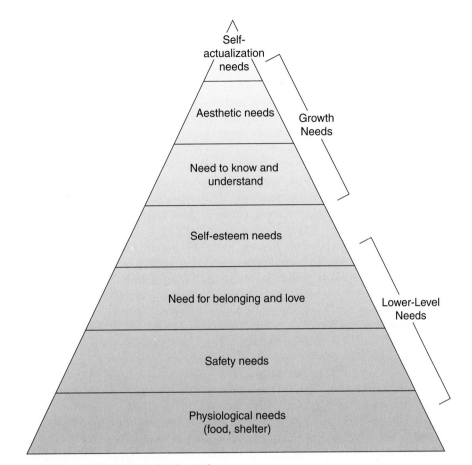

Figure 4.2 *Maslow's Needs Hierarchy*

David McClelland (1958), Atkinson and Feather (1966), and Alschuler and his colleagues (1970) took Maslow's more general needs theory and applied it to the specific needs relevant to teaching and classrooms. Sometimes called *needs disposition theory,* this theory of motivation suggests that individuals are motivated to take action and to invest energy in pursuit of three outcomes: achievement, affiliation, and influence.

The desire for achievement is evident when students try hard to learn a particular subject or when they strive to reach the objectives of particular tasks. Teachers manifest **achievement motives** as they strive to provide good instruction and act as competent professionals. **Affiliative motives** become important when students and teachers come to value the support and friendship of their peers. The motivation toward **influence** can be seen in those students who strive to have more control over their own learning and in those teachers who strive to have a larger say in the way schools are run. Students' feelings of self-esteem are related to feelings they have about their competence, affiliation, and influence. When these emotional states are frustrated by the activities in a classroom or a school, students become less involved in the school. When these states are frustrated for teachers, teachers are likely to feel incompetent, lonely, and powerless. Achievement motivation, or a student's "intent to learn," is the most important aspect of this theory of motivation for classroom teaching.

A third cluster of ideas about the relationship between human needs and motivation is associated with the work of deCharms (1976), Deci and Ryan (1985), and

Csikszentmihalyi (1990). Although the ideas of these theorists differ in significant ways, they have in common the idea that people strive to satisfy needs for choice and self-determination in what they do and that actions taken as a result of internal pressures are more satisfying than those resulting from external influences.

DeCharms used the concepts of *origin* and *pawn* in his analysis. Pawns are persons who have no control over what happens to them. They are aroused to action not from intrinsic values but from a sense of obligation or from external rewards. They always feel they are doing what others want them to do. Origins, on the other hand, are in charge of their own behavior. They behave in particular ways because of themselves, not because of others. As origins, they resist external pressures such as orders and rules. DeCharms believed that tasks imposed externally, such as by a teacher, make people feel like pawns and dampen the internal motivation they may have to perform the task on their own. The implication of this point of view for classroom practices is considered in more detail later.

University of Chicago psychologist and educator Mihaly Csikszentmihalyi (1976, 1990) views the importance of self-determination in regard to motivation differently. For over two decades, Csikszentmihalyi has studied what he calls "states of optimal experience," defined as times in people's lives when they experience total involvement and concentration as well as strong feelings of enjoyment. These types of experiences are called **flow experiences,** because the respondents Csikszentmihalyi studied often reported that what they were doing during the experience was so enjoyable "it felt like being carried away by a current, like being in a flow" (p. 127).

Perhaps you can think about a time in your life when you were doing something you became totally involved in. It could have been climbing a mountain, reading a novel, working on an old car, playing chess, engaging in a challenging run, or writing a poem. If you experienced flow, you were totally absorbed and concentrating on the activity alone, even to the point of losing track of time. In Csikszentmihalyi's (1990) words, "actor and action become one," and participation is sustained because of intrinsic rather than extrinsic motivation (p. 127).

Obviously, the concept of flow has implications for education and for teaching. In fact, Csikszentmihalyi concluded that the main obstacles to student learning do not

During flow experiences, individuals experience pure enjoyment and total involvement.

stem from the cognitive abilities of students but instead from the way we structure schools and from learning experiences that inhibit intrinsic motivation and corresponding flow experiences. Emphasis on external rules and evaluation and on rewards such as grades deters flow experiences for students. Similarly, standardized curricula and lessons that keep students in passive roles inhibit involvement and enjoyment.

Cognitive Theory. Cognitive theories provide a third perspective about human motivation. Like cognitive learning theorists, described elsewhere in this text, cognitive motivation theorists believe that individuals are aroused to action by their thinking. It is not external events or whether individuals are rewarded or punished that is important in explaining behavior, but instead it is the beliefs and attributions they hold about the event.

Bernard Weiner is a major cognitivist theorist, and his **attribution theory** is of particular importance to teachers. Attribution theory is based on the proposition that the ways individuals come to perceive and to interpret the causes of their successes or failures are the major determinants of their motivation, rather than innate needs or fixed earlier experiences. According to Weiner (1986, 1992), students attribute their successes or failures in terms of four causes: ability, effort, luck, and the difficulty of the learning task. Attributions can be classified as *internal* or *external.* Internal attribution occurs when individuals explain success or failure in terms of themselves; external attribution occurs when they give external causes. Attributing success to ability and effort are examples of internal attributions; luck and circumstances are external examples.

Attribution theory has several important implications for teachers. Students with high achievement motivation tend to associate their successes with their abilities and their failures with lack of effort. Conversely, students with low achievement motivation tend to attribute their successes to luck and their failures to lack of ability. There are ways in which teachers can change students' perceptions of themselves and the things around them. For instance, students can be taught to attribute their successes and failures to internal causes, such as effort, rather than to external causes, such as luck.

Attribution theories emphasize the way individuals come to perceive and Interpret the causes of their successes and failures.

Social Learning Theory. A final perspective about motivation that has importance for teachers is Bandura's (1977) **social learning theory.** In some ways, social learning theory has similarities to both reinforcement and attribution theories. However, the important idea for teachers stems from Bandura's assertion that motivation is the product of two things: an individual's expectations about his or her chances of reaching a particular goal and the degree of value or satisfaction that will accrue if the individual achieves the goal. For instance, if a student who is working on a project for the local science fair believes that the project will win an award (high expectation) and if that reward is something he or she badly wants (high value), then motivation to work and persist until the project is done will be high. On the other hand, if either the expectation for success or the value of the reward is low, then perseverance will be low. The implications of this theory to teaching are clear. It is important to provide learning tasks that students value and have a high chance of completing successfully.

The four perspectives about motivation are summarized in Table 4.2. Lessons for teachers and strategies that stem from these theories are described later.

Features of Learning Communities

Now let's turn to the social dimension of classrooms and explore theories that explain the community aspect of classroom life. Let's do this by first looking into the classroom of Marie Cuevas, a sixth-grade teacher at Martin Luther King Middle School. She meets

Table 4.2 *Four Perspectives of Motivation*

Theory	Theorists	Main Idea
Reinforcement	Skinner	Individuals respond to environmental events and *extrinsic* reinforcement.
Needs	Maslow, Decl, McClelland, Csikszentmihalyi	Individuals strive to *satisfy* needs such as self-fulfillment, self-determination, achievement, affiliation, and influence.
Cognitive	Weiner	Individuals' actions influenced by their *beliefs and attributions,* particularly attributions about success and failure situations.
Social learning	Bandura	Individuals' actions influenced by the value particular *goals* hold for them and their *expectations* for success.

daily with her students in an integrated science and language arts class. The students in her class have been heterogeneously grouped, meaning that all ability levels are represented. If we were to visit Ms. Cuevas's classroom on a typical day, we would likely see the following things going on.

Ms. Cuevas sits with a cluster of students in one corner of the room discussing a story they have just read on the life cycle of the Pacific Coast salmon, while several other students are working alone at their desks. They are writing their own stories about how salmon are threatened with extinction because hydroelectric activities have disturbed their breeding grounds. In another corner, a special education teacher is working with Brenda, a young girl who still reads at a second-grade level. Elsewhere, Ms. Cuevas's aide is administering a test to three children who were absent the previous Friday. At a far science table, a pair of students who are supposed to be practicing with a microscope are really discussing yesterday's football game. Overhearing their discussion, Ms. Cuevas stops to get them back on task. At the same moment, a squabble erupts between two students who are returning from the library. Ms. Cuevas asks the teacher's aide to resolve the conflict, then returns to the life-cycle discussion, in which irrelevant comments from Joey about last week's fishing trip with his father has caused it to drift.

As the class period draws to a close, the principal slips in to remind Ms. Cuevas that they have a short meeting scheduled during the lunch break and also to ask if she objects to having a small group of parents visit her next period. All this occurs as learning materials are being returned and readied for the next class, as today's homework assignments are collected, and as the squabble between the two students continues (after Arends, 1996).

This scenario is not an atypical situation. Classrooms everywhere are extremely busy places, characterized by a variety of simultaneous activities: individual and group instruction, socializing, conflict management, evaluation activities, and in-flight adjustments for unanticipated events. In addition to being a specially designed learning community, classrooms are social settings where friendships form and conflicts occur. They are settings for parties, visits, and a myriad of other activities. Three basic ideas can help us understand the complexity of the classroom and will provide guidance on

Enhancing Teaching with Technology

Using Technology As a Motivational Tool

As you have read in this chapter, motivation is not a simple topic and there is no single approach for teachers to take to ensure student interest and engagement. However, most teachers who use computers and related technologies in their classrooms report the strong motivational aspects of computers and Internet resources. Although the findings are not completely consistent, several important studies have confirmed the motivational elements of teaching practices that make use of technology. For example, an essential element for improving basic skills such as spelling and math operations is keeping students interested and engaged. Several recent studies have demonstrated that computers can motivate students to stay engaged in learning tasks. Hatfied (1996) found that the use of computer stations in classrooms increased student computer use and overall motivation. Terrell and Rendulic (1996) found that feedback via the computer had a positive effect on student motivation. In a rather large-scale study of the Apple Classrooms of Tomorrow (ACOT), Ringstaff, Sandholtz, and Dwyer (1995) found that students in technology-rich classrooms worked together more often and, in turn, were more interested in school. Students in these classrooms went beyond expectations of particular assignments and often chose to explore topics and projects during their free time.

The theories of motivation described in this chapter help to partially explain the motivation qualities of computers. Many software programs are developed to use reinforcement theory. When the user identifies a correct answer or exhibits desirable behavior, a reward is provided to reinforce and get the individual to repeat the behavior. Other software programs are developed to satisfy an individual's achievement motivation and aim at being both entertaining and educational. These software programs with gamelike and competitive features are motivational to most students and can be used not only in schools but also purchased by parents for use at home. For instance, Math Magic software has an arcade-game format to help students learn basic math skills such as addition and subtraction. The aim of the game is to help Wizrow free an enchanted dragon from an evil dungeon. To free the dragon, students use a magic wand and must solve math problems correctly. The fantasy setting and arcade format of the software challenge students and seem to make them willing to spend considerable more time doing math this way than they would doing worksheets.

Motivation to achieve meaningful learning and higher-level goals is also important. Achieving higher-level goals requires students to do hard mental work and bear most of the responsibility for their own learning. This type of motivation is often highly personal and stems from needs and cognitive theories of motivation. Working through tutorials, interacting with computer simulations, or creating websites help provide interesting challenges to students and help them sustain the required mental activity to process and learn meaningful information and ideas.

Many teachers use educational software with gamelike qualities, such as *The Oregon Trail* or *Where in the World Is Carmen Sandiego?* or allow time on the Internet to reward students who have worked hard or have completed their work early. The fact that students perceive "working on the computer" as rewarding is perhaps the best evidence of the motivational qualities of computers and related technologies.

---

how to build a more productive learning community. These three dimensions are highlighted in Figure 4.3 and described in the following text.

Classroom Properties. One way to think about classrooms is to view them as **ecological systems** in which the inhabitants (teachers and students) interact within a specific environment (the classroom) for the purpose of completing valued activities and tasks. Using this perspective to study classrooms, Walter Doyle (1986) has pointed out that classrooms have six properties that make them complex and demanding systems.

An ecological perspective views classrooms as places where teachers, students, and others interact within a highly interdependent environment.

Multidimensionality. This refers to the fact that classrooms are crowded places in which many people with different backgrounds, interests, and abilities compete for

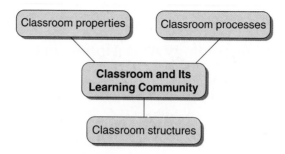

Figure 4.3 *Three Dimensions of Classrooms*

scarce resources. Unlike a dentist's or an optician's office where a narrow range of predictable events occur, a multitude of diverse events are planned and orchestrated in classrooms. Teachers explain things, give directions, manage conflict, collect milk money, make assignments, and keep records. Students listen, read, write, engage each other in discussion and conversation, form friendships, and experience conflict. Teachers must learn to take these multidimensional activities into account and accommodate them in some manner.

Simultaneity. While helping an individual student during seatwork, a teacher must monitor the rest of the class, handle interruptions, and keep track of time. During a presentation, a teacher must explain ideas clearly while watching for signs of inattention, noncomprehension, and misbehavior. During a discussion, a teacher must listen to a student's answer, watch other students for signs of comprehension, and think about the next question to ask. Each of these situations illustrates a basic feature of classroom life—the simultaneous occurrence of difficult events that effective teachers must be able to recognize and manage.

Immediacy. A third important property of classroom life is the rapid pace of classroom events and their immediate impact on the lives of teachers and students. Teachers have hundreds of daily exchanges with their students. They are continuously praising, reprimanding, explaining, scolding, and challenging. Students also have hundreds of interactions with their teachers and with each other. Pencils are dropped, irrelevant comments are made, squabbles surface, and conflicts are resolved. Many of these events are unplanned, and their immediacy gives teachers little time to reflect before acting.

> Distinctive features of classrooms—such as multidimensionality, simultaneity, immediacy, unpredictability, publicness, and history—are called classroom properties.

Unpredictability. Classroom events not only demand immediate attention, many take unexpected, unpredictable turns. Distractions and interruptions are frequent. Sudden illnesses, announcements over the intercom, and unscheduled visitors are common. Consequently, it is difficult to anticipate how a particular lesson or activity will go on a particular day with a particular group of students. What worked so well last year may be a complete flop this year. Even a lesson that produced enthusiasm and full participation first period may be greeted with stony silence during sixth period.

Publicness. In many work settings, people work mostly in private or in view of only a few others. Doctors' diagnoses of patients' illnesses happen in the privacy of their offices; clerks and waitresses attend to their customers without much attention from others; technicians and accountants do their work unobstructed by an observing public. The classroom, however, is a very public place, and almost all events are witnessed by others. Teachers describe their existence as "living in a fishbowl." This feature of publicness or lack of privacy is just as acute for students. Student behavior is constantly being scrutinized by teachers, many of whom seem (from the students' perspective) to have eyes in the back of their heads. Students also watch each other with considerable interest. It is very difficult, therefore, for any aspect of one's classroom life, whether it is the score on the latest test or a whisper to a neighbor, to go unnoticed.

History. Classrooms and their participants gradually become a community that shares a common history. Classes meet five days a week for several months and thereby accumulate a common set of experiences, norms, and routines. Early meetings shape events for the remainder of the year. Each classroom develops its own social system with particular structures, organization, and norms. Though classrooms may look alike from a distance or on paper, each class is actually as unique as a fingerprint. Each class develops its own internal procedures, patterns of interaction, and limits. It is as if imaginary lines guide and control behavior within the group. In spite of day-to-day variation, there is a certain constancy in each class that emerges from its individual history.

Classroom properties directly affect the overall classroom environment and shape the behavior of participants. They have profound effects on teaching. As you will learn, some of these features can be altered by teachers, others cannot—at least not significantly. This aspect of teaching is revisited later in this chapter in the discussion of how teachers can provide leadership to students and help them manage group life.

Classroom Processes. Richard Schmuck and Patricia Schmuck (2001) developed a slightly different framework for viewing classrooms. They highlight the importance of interpersonal and group processes in the classrooms.

The Schmucks believe that positive learning communities are created by teachers when they teach students important interpersonal and group-process skills and when they help the classroom develop as a group. The Schmucks identify six group processes that, when working in relation to one another, produce a positive classroom community.

Expectations. In classrooms, people have expectations for each other and for themselves. The Schmucks are interested in how expectations become patterned over time and how they influence classroom climate and learning.

Leadership. This refers to how power and influence are exerted in classrooms and their impact on group interaction and cohesiveness. The Schmucks view leadership as an interpersonal process rather than as a characteristic of a person, and they encourage leadership to be shared in classroom groups.

Attraction. This refers to the degree to which people in a classroom have respect for one another and how friendship patterns within classrooms affect climate and learning. The Schmucks encourage teachers to help create classroom environments characterized by peer groups free from cliques, with no student left out of the friendship structure.

Norms. Norms are the shared expectations students and teachers have for classroom behavior. The Schmucks value classrooms with norms that support high student involvement in academic work but at the same time encourage positive interpersonal relationships and shared goals.

Communication. Most classroom interaction is characterized by verbal and nonverbal communication. The Schmucks argue for communication processes that are open and lively and have a high degree of participant involvement.

Interpersonal and group processes that help classroom participants deal with issues of expectations, leadership, attraction, norms, communication, and cohesiveness are important ingredients in developing productive learning communities.

Figure 4.4 *Three Types of Classroom Structures and Their Relationship to Classroom Lessons and Activities*

Cohesiveness. The final process refers to the feelings and commitments students and teachers have to the classroom group as a whole. The Schmucks advocate peer group cohesiveness but point out that it is important for this cohesiveness to be in support of academic work and member well-being.

Unlike the *properties* described by Doyle, classroom *processes* are highly influenced by the teacher's actions and can be altered to build productive classroom communities, as you will see later in this chapter.

Classroom structures are the ways classrooms are organized around learning tasks and participation and the ways goals and rewards are defined.

Classroom Structures. The structures that shape classrooms and the demands particular lessons place on students offer an additional perspective on classrooms. Researchers, such as Gump (1967), Kounin (1970), and, more recently, Doyle (1986, 1990) and Doyle and Carter (1984), believe that behavior in classrooms is partially a response to the structures and demands of the classroom. This view of classrooms attends closely to the kinds of structures that exist within classrooms and to the activities and tasks students are asked to perform during particular lessons. Figure 4.4 shows how the lesson and its activities can vary in three important ways: structures of the learning task, structures for participation, and goals and reward structures.

Unlike the classroom properties described earlier, which are mostly fixed, or classroom processes, which are highly alterable, the three structures highlighted in Figure 4.4 are sometimes fixed by tradition, but they can also be altered if a teacher chooses to do so. In fact, one might compare classroom structures to the design of a house. The way space in a house is designed and partitioned can be thought of as the house's structure. This structure influences how people in the house normally interact with one another. For example, if all the rooms are small and closed off, it is difficult to have a party where lots of people can move around and interact easily. Conversely, if the house is wide open, it is difficult for individuals to find privacy. These structures influence certain types of behavior, but they do not guarantee or prevent specific behaviors. For example, you know of instances in which good parties have occurred in small spaces; you also know of instances in which ideal structural conditions have not produced positive interactions. Structures, however, can be changed. Using the house analogy again, walls can be removed to encourage wider interaction, or screens can be stationed to provide privacy. Classroom structures can also be changed. The following sections describe the three classroom structures in more detail.

Task Structures. The academic and social tasks and activities planned by teachers determine the kinds of work students carry out in classrooms. In this instance, *classroom tasks* refers to what is expected of students and the cognitive and social demands placed upon them to accomplish the task. **Classroom activities,** on the other hand, are the things students can be observed doing: participating in a discussion, working with other students in small groups, doing seatwork, listening to a lecture, and so forth. Classroom tasks and activities not only help shape the way teachers and students behave but also help determine what students learn.

Task structures differ according to the various activities required of particular teaching strategies or models used by teachers. As described in later chapters, lessons organized around lectures place far different demands on students than do lessons organized around small-group discussions. Similarly, the demands of students during discussion periods differ from those associated with seatwork.

Whereas some learning tasks and the demands they place on teachers and students stem from the nature of the learning activities themselves, others are embedded in the subjects being taught. Sometimes the academic disciplines (their concepts, organizing frameworks, and methods of revealing new knowledge) provide the basis for these differences. To understand this idea, think about the college classes you have taken in various disciplines and the demands placed on you as a learner in various situations. For instance, the task demands and your behavior when you were doing an experiment in the chemistry lab were different from the demands placed on you as you provided thoughtful analysis of a Shakespearean tragedy. Similarly, the task demands placed on you in anthropology to understand preliterate cultures were different from those required of you to understand the industrial revolution in European history.

Sometimes different task demands exist within particular academic subjects. A lesson aimed at teaching multiplication tables in arithmetic, for instance, makes a different set of demands on learners than does a lesson aimed at increasing skill in mathematical problem solving. Learning the names and locations of the major cities of the world requires different behaviors and actions for learners and teachers than a geography inquiry lesson exploring the importance of location in determining standard of living. A literature lesson on character development makes different demands than a spelling lesson.

The important thing to remember is that classroom task structures influence the thoughts and actions of classroom participants and help determine the degree of student cooperation and involvement. As later chapters emphasize, students need to be taught specific and appropriate learning strategies to help them satisfy the task demands being placed on them in classrooms.

Goal and Reward Structures. A second type of classroom structure is the way goals and rewards are structured. Chapter 3 introduced the concept of instructional goals, which, as you remember, were desired states a teacher had for students, such as being able to spell a list of words or solve a mathematics problem. The concept of goal structure is different from that of instructional goals. **Goal structures** specify the type of interdependence required of students as they strive to complete learning tasks—the relationships among students and between an individual and the group. Johnson and Johnson (1999) and Slavin (1995) identified three different goal structures.

Cooperative goal structures exist when students perceive that they can achieve their goal if, and only if, the other students with whom they are working can also reach the goal.
Competitive goal structures exist when students perceive they can reach their goal only if other students do not reach the goal.
Individualistic goal structures exist when students perceive that their achievement of a goal is unrelated to achievement of the goal by other students.

The concept of goal structure is illustrated in Figure 4.5.

Classroom rewards can be categorized in the same manner as goals. **Reward structures** are competitive, cooperative, and individualistic. Grading on a curve is an

The work students are expected to do in classrooms and the cognitive and social demands placed on them as they perform particular lessons are called task structures.

Goal structures determine the degree of interdependence sought among students. There are three different types of goal structures: cooperative, competitive, and individualistic.

| Cooperative | Competitive | Individualistic |

Figure 4.5 *Three Different Goal Structures*

example of a competitive reward structure, in that students' efforts are rewarded in comparison with other students. Winners in most field and track events are similarly competitive. In contrast, cooperative reward structures are in place when individual effort helps a whole group succeed. The reward system for a football team's effort (winning) is an example of a cooperative reward structure, even though the team as a whole is in competition with other teams.

Classroom goal and reward structures are at the core of life in classrooms and influence greatly both the behavior and learning of students. Regardless of a teacher's personal philosophy on the use of rewards, the current reality is that student motivation centers around the dispensation of grades. In fact, Doyle (1979) argued that the primary features of classroom life are the way students engage in academic work and how they "exchange [their] performance for grades." The way teachers organize goal and reward structures determines which types of goals are accomplished and how the exchange occurs.

Classroom Participation Structures. Additionally, teaching and learning are influenced by classroom **participation structures.** Participation structures, according to Cazden (1986 and Burboles & Bruce, 2001), determine who can say what, when, and to whom. These structures include the way students take turns during group lessons and the way they ask questions and respond to teacher queries. These structures also vary from one type of lesson to another. During a lecture, for example, student participation is limited to listening to the teacher and perhaps individually taking notes. A discussion or recitation connected to a lecture, on the other hand, requires students to answer questions and to give their ideas. Listening to one another is another expectation for students during a discussion or a recitation, as is raising one's hand to take a turn. When the teacher plans seatwork for students, the prescribed participation is normally to work alone and to interact one-on-one with the teacher when help is required. Small-group and cooperative learning activities obviously require a different kind of participation on the part of students. Small-group activities require that students talk to each other, and cooperative learning activities require joint production of academic tasks. Chapters 10, 11, and 12 provide additional information about participation structures and describe steps teachers can take to increase the amount of student participation in their classrooms.

Sociocultural Perspective. A final perspective and the most contemporary one about classrooms as learning communities stems from sociocultural theorists and school reformers who have been heavily influenced by the work of Dewey, Piaget, and Vygotsky. This perspective views the traditional classroom as a place designed to promote certain types of formal learning and envisions classroom settings in the future that will be modeled after more informal settings in which individuals learn naturally. Often

Reward structures determine the ways in which rewards can be distributed within a classroom. There are three types: competitive, cooperative, and individualistic.

Participation structures help determine who can say what, when, and to whom during classroom discourse.

these settings are described as those that enhance authentic learning, where students are involved in inquiry that helps them construct their own meaning, and where talk and action by teachers and students strive for social justice. Authentic learning is defined as students' accomplishments that have significance and meaning in the real world, not just in the classroom. Constructing one's own knowledge means being actively involved in inquiry that builds on what one already knows, rather than being treated to fixed knowledge defined and transmitted by the teachers.

Oakes and Lipton (2003) have summarized the sociocultural perspective. They argue that the pedagogy associated with this perspective cannot be translated into a "proven set of best practices" but instead evolves from "qualities of the learning relationships among teachers and students . . . and practices cannot be judged independently of the cultural knowledge students bring with them to school" (p. 215).

They do, however, posit a set of guidelines, not too much different than those described by the Schmucks, that teachers can use to construct learning communities that are authentic and socially just. These include:

- Teachers and students are confident that everyone learns well.
- Lessons are active, multidimensional, and social.
- Relationships are caring and interdependent.
- Talk and action are socially just.
- Authentic assessment enhances learning.

Research on Motivation and Learning Communities

The research literature on classrooms and motivation is extensive and represents scholarship from many fields: psychology, social psychology, group dynamics, and social context of teaching. This section provides interesting studies to give beginning teachers insights into the way some of this research is carried out and to provide examples of some important findings. The studies cover a span of a half century and focus on the effects of classroom environments on motivation, how teacher behaviors influence motivation and group life, and how students themselves can influence each other and their teachers.

Relationship between Classroom Environments and Motivation. One of the most difficult aspects of teaching is to get students to persist at learning tasks. Some students persist longer than others, and some tasks appear to be more interesting than other tasks to some students. Researchers have been interested for a long time in how classroom environments influence student motivation. The general finding is that environments characterized by mutual respect, high standards, and a caring attitude are more conducive to student persistence than other environments.

> Students persist longer in their studies and learning tasks if the learning environment is happy and positive.

In an interesting and unique study conducted in the 1970s, Santrock (1976) studied the relationships between some of the dimensions of the classroom environment—happy and sad moods—and students' motivation to persist on learning tasks. Santrock randomly assigned first- and second-grade children into different treatment groups. On the way to a classroom, students were told a happy story and a sad story. The experimenter acted happy in relating a happy story and sad in relating the sad story. The various classrooms involved were decorated in one of two ways: with happy pictures or with sad pictures. In the room, the children were asked to work at a task at which they were interrupted from time to time and asked to think either happy or sad thoughts. Students could stop working on the task whenever they liked.

Students thinking happy thoughts who experienced a happy experimenter in a happy room persisted much longer at the learning task than did students thinking sad thoughts with a sad experimenter in a sad room. This type of result is important because it indicates that persistence at a task for a student is not simply a function of the child's self-control or interest but can be influenced by the environment and by aspects of the environment under the teacher's control—room decor and happy moods.

Relationship between Leadership and Group Life. For many years, teachers have known that what they do influences the behavior of their students. Furthermore, many educators believe that a teacher's behavior should be "democratic" in character, thus reflecting the larger societal values about the way people should interact with one another. Take, for example, the following comments written by John Dewey over eighty years ago:

> We can and do supply ready-made "ideas" by the thousand; we do not usually take pains to see that the one learning engages in significant situations where his own activities generate, support, and clinch ideas—that is, perceived meanings or connections. This does not mean that the teacher is to stand off and look on; the alternative to furnishing ready-made subject matter and listening to the accuracy with which it is reproduced is not quiescence, but participation, sharing, in an activity. In such shared activity the teacher is a learner, and the learner is, without knowing it, a teacher—and upon the whole, the less consciousness there is, on either side, of either giving or receiving instruction, the better (Dewey, 1916, p. 176).

But what effects do democratic behaviors and procedures have on students and group life? This question was first explored well over a half century ago in a set of classic studies conducted by Kurt Lewin, Ron Lippitt, and Richard White (Lewin, Lippitt & White, 1939; Lippitt & White, 1963). The researchers studied 11-year-old boys who volunteered to form clubs and to participate in a series of club projects. Clubs such as the Sherlock Holmes Club, Dick Tracy Club, and Secret Agents Club were formed, and club leaders (teachers) were taught to exhibit three different forms of leadership: authoritarian leadership, democratic leadership, and laissez-faire (passive) leadership. The boys were observed as they participated in club activities, including a time when the leader purposely left the boys on their own.

The researchers found that the boys reacted to authoritarian leadership by becoming rebellious and that they were much less involved than the boys under democratic leadership. What was most telling, however, was the boys' behavior when the leaders were out of the room. Boys under authoritarian and laissez-faire leadership stopped working as soon as the leader was absent. Boys in the democratic group, on the other hand, kept working, and certain boys even stepped in and provided leadership to the group.

Many educators have concluded from this and many similar studies over the past fifty years that teacher behavior has important influences on students' willingness to cooperate and stick to learning tasks. Teachers who are too strict and directive may get a lot of work from their students if they are physically present, but that involvement will drop off once close supervision is removed.

Certain motivational strategies used by teachers have also been the focus of considerable research, particularly over the past two decades. Of particular interest have been those strategies used by teachers that support student motivation to learn. An example of this research is highlighted in the Research Summary for this chapter.

Effects of Students' Behavior on Each Other and on Their Teachers. Studies such as the one described in the Research Summary focus on the influence that teacher behavior has on students. Influence in the classroom group, however, does not always flow just from the teacher. Students also influence each other and can even influence their teachers. One particularly interesting line of inquiry over the years has been research that investigates how the student peer group, through both formal and informal inter-

Researchers have known for a very long time that students respond more favorably to teachers who are democratic than to teachers who are authoritarian.

The peer group has important influences on students' behavior and their motivation to engage in learning activities.

Check, Extend, Explore

Check
- Contrast reinforcement, needs, and cognitive and social learning theories of motivation.
- What are the differences between extrinsic and extrinsic motivation?
- Contrast the classroom properties defined by Doyle with the classroom processes described by the Schmucks.
- How can classroom task-and-reward structures vary?
- Contrast the sociocultural perspective of learning communities with more traditional views.

Extend
- In your own experiences as a student, what are the most important factors that motivate you to persevere in academic tasks?
- Some educators believe that too much emphasis is put on the use of extrinsic motivation. Do you agree or disagree with this view? Go to the "Extend Question Poll" on the Online Learning Center to respond.

Explore
- Go to the Online Learning Center at www.mhhe.com/arends6e for links to websites related to *Motivation and Learning Communities*.

actions, affects attitudes and achievement. Peer group influences have been documented in studies of college dormitories and living houses (Newcomb, 1961, for example) and in many different public and private school settings. Much of the research shows that many students conform to peer group norms and that all too often these norms are in contradiction to those held by educators and teachers. James Coleman (1961) studied ten American high schools in the 1950s. He found many instances wherein the adolescent peer group supported norms for being popular and being athletic over the school's norms in support of academic achievement. This finding has been replicated in American high schools in every decade since Coleman's original work (see, for example, Ogbu, 1995; 1997). Today, peer group pressure is used often to explain high dropout rates and low achievement of many inner-city youth.

Strategies for Motivating Students and Building Productive Learning Communities

Building productive learning communities and motivating students to engage in meaningful learning activities are major goals of teaching. Yet, many ingredients make up a student's motivation to learn. Success depends on using motivational strategies stemming from each of the perspectives described previously as well as on employing strategies that help a group of individuals develop into a productive learning community. Motivational and group development strategies, however, cannot be reduced to a few simple guidelines. No single dramatic event will produce motivation and a productive learning community. Instead, effective teachers employ strategies interdependently until motivation is a permanent aspect of their classrooms, where students' psychological needs are met, where they find learning activities that are interesting and meaningful, and where they will know they can be successful. Strategies to attain this type of classroom situation are described in the sections that follow.

Believe in Students' Capabilities and Attend to Alterable Factors

There are many things that students take with them to school that teachers can do little about. For example, teachers have little influence over students' basic personalities,

Research Summary

Can Particular Strategies Influence Students' Motivation to Learn?

Marshall, H. H. L. (1987). Motivational strategies of three fifth-grade teachers. *Elementary School Journal* 88, 135–150.

An enduring concern among teachers is how to motivate students. Keen observers of classrooms have long recognized subtle differences among classroom environments. Some are friendly; others are not. Some are learning oriented; in others, students avoid work. But how do environments get that way, and how do teachers' use of learning and motivational strategies influence the learning orientations of their classrooms? These were questions that Hermine Marshall explored in a very interesting and provocative study.

Problem and Approach: Marshall was interested in strategies used by teachers that motivate students to learn. Her study is important for two reasons. One, the questions she asked are central to teachers' work. And two, her findings provide concrete recommendations for teachers' actions. Her study is also interesting because it illustrates what can be learned when researchers choose to study a few teachers in depth rather than many superficially.

Sample and Setting: In earlier studies, Marshall developed the idea that classrooms can be classified as having one of three orientations toward learning.

- *Learning-oriented classrooms.* Classroom in which teachers emphasized to students the challenges and enjoyment of learning.
- *Work-oriented classrooms.* Classrooms in which teachers motivated students to complete their work for external reasons (e.g., rewards such as grades or threats such as detention).
- *Work-avoidance classrooms.* Classroom in which teachers seemed not to care and accepted minimal effort and incomplete work from their students.

Marshall selected three fifth-grade classrooms to participate in her study. Each one revealed one of the three motivational orientations. The three teachers in the study were experienced (a minimum of nine years' experience), and students in the three classrooms had similar backgrounds and abilities.

Procedures: To get acclimatized, trained observers visited the selected classrooms over a period of two to four

weeks. They then observed each teacher for at least twelve hours during reading and math lessons and during selected whole-class instruction times. Observers kept a running record of classroom events, and they used an observation form that recorded teacher behavior in three categories: the way the teacher "framed" (began) lessons, the way the teacher refocused students' attention after the lesson was initiated, and the way the teacher encouraged students to take responsibility for their own learning. In addition, all three teachers were interviewed, and their students' achievement test scores in reading were analyzed.

Results: Table 4.3 displays Marshall's analysis of statements made by the three teachers to frame their lessons and statements made once the lesson had begun to maintain attention and engagement. Framing statements were divided into two categories: endogenous statements and exogenous statements. **Endogenous statements** emphasized the personal relevance of learning activities and communicated to students they were going to have fun and do well. **Exogenous statements,** on the other hand, included those that promised positive rewards, such as good grades, for getting work done, and sanctions, such as threats, if work was not completed. Refocusing statements were classified as being either positive or negative in their tone. The data displayed in Table 4.3 reveal some striking differences in the three classrooms and the ways teachers framed and refocused their lessons.

Teacher X framed her lessons with statements defined by the researchers as having mostly endogenous qualities. She emphasized the personal relevance of the lesson to students and told them they were going to have fun and that she expected everyone in class to do well. To maintain student engagement after initiating the lesson, Teacher X used positive motivational statements that challenged students to think (such as "I challenge you . . ."), or statements that alerted students to what was going to happen next, or statements that expressed enthusiasm or humor (such as "look bright-eyed and bushy-tailed, because this next part is going to present you with a real challenge").

Teacher Y, on the other hand, framed her lessons with exogenous statements. She made demands on students, promising rewards if they did well and punishment if they did not. Teacher Y was not observed using any strategies

Table 4.3 *Comparison of Lesson-Framing and Lesson-Refocusing Statements*

	Teacher X		Teacher Y		Teacher Z	
	N	%	N	%	N	%
Framing Statements:						
Endogenous	17	55	3	11	6	13
Exogenous	3	10	7	26	10	28
Management Refocusing:						
Positive	43	53	9	9	6	5
Negative	2	5	56	58	34	28

Percentages of each type are of the total statements in the lesson and thus do not add up to 100 percent.

that alerted students and few that challenged them to think. Most of Teacher Y's refocusing statements merely redirected students to the task at hand. A large proportion of Teacher Y's refocusing statements, according to the researcher, had negative tones as contrasted to the positive tones associated with Teacher X's refocusing statements.

Teacher Z made few framing statements at all. She tended to begin lessons with matter-of-fact statements, such as "Open your books to page 382" or "All right, let's get started." Students were not encouraged to do well, nor were they threatened with punishment if their work was not completed. As you can see in Table 4.3, Teacher Z made few refocusing statements, and of those that were made, almost all were negative in tone.

Researchers reported that students in Teacher Z's classroom were often off task and wandered around the classroom while the teacher was trying to teach. In contrast, students in Teacher X's classroom appeared to be engaged almost all the time and on several occasions were observed asking the teacher for more work.

Marshall and her assistants also interviewed each teacher and compared student gains made in reading between the beginning and the end of the school year. Interviews revealed that Teacher X believed all students have ability and can learn. Teacher Y, on the other hand, believed that she was the one responsible for student learning. Teacher Z didn't take responsibility for learning, nor did she think it was the students' responsibility.

In classroom X, students demonstrated almost a full year's growth in reading during the course of the year. In contrast, students in classroom Y gained almost a year and a half. Students in classroom Z made no gains in reading during the school year.

Discussion and Implications Marshall's study points directly to the importance of teachers' expectations of their students and the relationships they built for getting them to engage in learning activities. Students in Teacher X's classroom were much more engaged and took on more responsibility for their own learning than did students in the other two classrooms. This led Marshall to make the following observations about effective teachers in regard to the motivational strategies they employ.

1. Effective teachers view students as able and responsible and encourage students to take responsibility for their own learning.
2. Effective teachers begin and frame lessons with statements that challenge students. They convince their students that they are going to enjoy the lesson and that they will be successful in learning it.
3. As lessons proceed, effective teachers use encouragement, humor, and group-alerting statements to keep students interested and engaged.

At the same time, it is important to point out that it was the students in classroom Y who made the largest gains as measured by standardized achievement tests—the classroom in which the teacher made the most use of extrinsic and negative motivational strategies. This is an interesting finding and raises questions about motivation strategies, student engagement, and student learning outcomes.

Teachers are more effective if they concentrate their efforts on things they can do something about.

their home lives, or their early childhood experiences. Unfortunately, some teachers attend only to these aspects of their students, and such attention is mostly unproductive. It is true that social factors, such as students' backgrounds or their parents' expectations, influence how hard they work in school. Similarly, their psychological well-being, anxieties, and dependencies also affect effort. However, there is not much teachers can do to alter or influence these social and psychological factors. Instead, teachers are more effective in enhancing student motivation if they concentrate their efforts on factors that are within their abilities to control and influence.

The most important things that teachers can control are their own attitudes toward and beliefs about children, particularly those they may have about students who come from different backgrounds than they do. Believing that every child can learn and that every child sees the world through his or her own cultural lens can shift the burden of low engagement and low achievement from the child's background to where it often belongs—a nonunderstanding classroom and school.

Avoid Overemphasizing Extrinsic Motivation

Most beginning teachers know much about how to use extrinsic motivation because many common-sense ideas about human behavior rest on reinforcement principles, particularly on the principles of providing extrinsic rewards (positive reinforcers) to get desired behavior and using punishment to stop undesirable behavior. This theory of motivation is pervasive in our society. Parents get their children to behave in particular ways by giving them weekly allowances. They withhold these allowances or use "grounding" when their children behave inappropriately. People who work hard at their jobs are given merit raises; those who don't are fired. We give individuals medals for acts of bravery and put them in jail for acts of crime. Good grades, certificates of merit, praise, and athletic letters are extrinsic rewards used by teachers to get students to study and to behave in desirable ways. Poor grades, demerits, and detention are employed to punish undesirable behaviors.

Although reinforcement theory is pervasive in our culture, effective teachers find ways to minimize its potentially harmful effects.

On the surface, reinforcement theory makes good common sense, and certainly there may be instances in all aspects of life in which extrinsic supports are necessary. At the same time, extrinsic rewards do not always produce the intended results. For instance, providing extrinsic rewards for learning tasks that are already intrinsically interesting can actually decrease student motivation (see Chapter 6). Further, for any reward or punishment to serve as a motivator, it must be valued or feared. Many students in today's schools don't care about good grades. If that is so, then grades will not cause students to study. Similarly, if getting demerits or being assigned to detention are considered "badges of honor," as they are to some students, then they will not deter undesirable behavior. Effective teachers use extrinsic rewards cautiously and learn to rely on other means to motivate their students. Table 4.4 details particular strategies teachers can use to minimize the negative effects of extrinsic motivational strategies.

Create Learning Situations with Positive Feeling Tones

Needs and attributional theories of motivation stress the importance of building learning environments that are pleasant, safe, and secure and in which students have a degree of self-determination and assume responsibility for their own learning.

The overall learning orientation and tone of the classroom are critical. As observed in studies summarized in the previous section, teachers' attitudes and orientations toward particular learning situations have considerable influence on how students respond to

Table 4.4 *Minimizing the Negative Effects of Extrinsic Motivation*

Strategies for minimizing the negative effects of rewards on students' intrinsic motivation

I. Use extrinsic rewards when there is no intrinsic motivation to undermine.
   A. Use extrinsic rewards when students feel too incompetent to experience intrinsic interest in the task at hand.
   B. Use extrinsic rewards when the task is one for which no person is likely to find much intrinsic interest in completing.
II. Use extrinsic rewards in such a way that the likelihood of undermining students' perceptions of self-determination and control is minimal.
   A. Emphasize the informative, not the controlling, nature of extrinsic rewards.
      1. Tie grades given on specific assignments to detailed descriptive comments about the quality of the students' performance on the task.
      2. Use symbolic rewards, such as the teacher's initials, as record-keeping devices.
   B. Make the extrinsic reward the opportunity to make choices, to be self-determining.

Source: Spaulding (1992), p. 56

learning situations. Some (e.g., Hunter 1982; 1995) use the term **feeling tone** to describe this aspect of the learning environment and provide the following examples of simple things teachers can say to establish a positive, neutral, or negative feeling tone:

Positive: "You write such interesting stories, I'm anxious to read this one."
Negative: "That story must be finished before you're excused for lunch."
Neutral: "If you aren't finished, don't worry; there'll be plenty of time later."

Students put forth more effort in environments with positive feeling tones and less in environments that are negative. An important point for teachers to consider, if they choose to use unpleasant feeling tones to motivate students to complete a difficult learning task, is to return as soon as possible to a positive one: "I really put a lot of pressure on you, and you've responded magnificently," or "I know you were angry about the demands being made, but you should be proud of the improvement in your performance." Feeling tones in the classroom are not only the result of specific things teachers say at a particular moment; they are also the result of many other structures and processes created by teachers to produce productive learning communities, as later sections of this chapter describe.

> Students put forth more effort in environments where particular learning tasks are perceived as pleasant.

Build on Students' Interests and Intrinsic Values

Needs and attributional theories of motivation stress the importance of using intrinsic motivation and building on the students' own interests and curiosity. A teacher can do a number of things to relate learning materials and activities to students' interests. Here are some examples:

- *Relate lessons to students' lives.* Find things that students are interested in or curious about, such as popular music, and relate these interests to topics under study (Mozart, for instance).
- *Use students' names.* Using students' names helps personalize learning and captures students' attention. For example: "Suppose Maria, here, were presenting an argument

for electing her friend, and Charles wished to challenge her position . . ., "or "John, here, has the pigmentation most commonly associated with Nordic races, whereas Roseanne's is more typical of Latinos."

- *Make materials vivid and novel.* A teacher can say things that make the ordinary vivid and novel for students. For example: "When you order your favorite McDonald's milkshake, it won't melt even if you heat it in the oven. That's the result of an emulsifier made from the algae we're studying," or "Suppose you believed in reincarnation. In your next life, what would you need to accomplish that you didn't accomplish satisfactorily in this life?"

Using games, puzzles, and other activities that are inviting and carry their own intrinsic motivation is another way teachers make lessons interesting for students. Similarly, a variety of activities (field trips, simulations, music, guest speakers) and instructional methods (lecture, seatwork, discussion, small-group) keep students interested in school and their schoolwork.

It is important to highlight two cautions in using student interests for motivational purposes. Stressing the novel or vivid can sometimes distract students from learning a topic. Similarly, new interests are formed through learning about a new topic. Teachers who expose their students only to materials in which they are already interested prevent them from developing new interests.

Structure Learning to Accomplish Flow

Schools and teachers can structure learning activities to emphasize their intrinsic value so students become totally involved and experience the type of flow described earlier. However, such total involvement, according to Csikszentmihalyi, is only possible with learning experiences that have certain characteristics.

First, flow experiences require that the challenge of a particular learning activity corresponds to the learner's level of skill. All of the learner's skill is required, yet the activity cannot be so difficult that the participant becomes frustrated. Perhaps rock climbing can provide a good example of the need to match the degree of challenge and skill. If you are an advanced beginning rock climber, you will be bored if you are asked to climb the slightly sloping, 15-foot-high rock in your backyard. This would not require use of your skills or provide you with challenging practice. On the other hand, as an advanced beginner, you will become very frustrated and stressed if you are asked to climb El Capitan, one of the most challenging climbs in the United States. You will read later how experienced teachers plan lessons in which they balance the level of difficulty and the amount of challenge.

The definition of clear and unambiguous goals is another characteristic of learning experiences likely to produce flow. As you read in Chapter 3, lessons that make clear to students what is expected of them and what they are supposed to accomplish are more likely to produce extended engagement and involvement than are lessons with unclear goals and expectations. Finally, people who report having had flow experiences say they gained relevant and meaningful feedback about their activity as they were doing it, a feature of motivation discussed next.

Establishing "flow" may not be as easy as it may seem, particularly in classrooms that are culturally and linguistically diverse. For instance, learning activities that may appear to be interesting and challenging to middle-class teachers may have little meaning to students with different cultural heritages or who speak English as a second language. Failing to make meaningful connections with students can leave teachers frustrated with the lack of engagement on the part of students and students feeling that their voices are not being heard.

Use Knowledge of Results and Don't Excuse Failure

Feedback (also called *knowledge of results*) on good performance provides intrinsic motivation. Feedback on poor performance gives learners needed information to improve. Both types of feedback are important motivational factors. To be effective, feedback must be more specific and immediate than a grade a teacher puts on a report card every six to nine weeks. In Chapter 8, Direct Instruction, specific guidelines for giving feedback are provided. This topic is also covered in Chapter 6, Assessment and Evaluation. It is enough to say here that feedback should be as immediate as possible (handing back corrected tests the day after an exam), as specific as possible (comments in addition to an overall grade on a paper), and nonjudgmental ("Your use of the word *that* is incorrect—you should have used *which* instead" rather than "What's wrong with you? We have gone over the difference between *that* and *which* a dozen times."). Additionally, feedback should focus on and encourage internal attributions—such as effort or lack of effort—rather than external attributions—such as luck or lack of ability. Feedback should help students see what they *did not* do rather than what they *cannot* do.

> Feedback or knowledge of results is information given to students about their performance.

Sometimes teachers, particularly inexperienced teachers, do not want to embarrass students by drawing attention to incorrect performance. Also, it is sometimes easier to accept students' excuses for failure than to confront them with the fact of their failure. These kinds of teacher actions are most often counterproductive. Teachers should not impose severe punishments for failures or use feedback that is belittling. At the same time, effective teachers know that it is important to hold high expectations for all students and that if things are being done incorrectly, this incorrect performance will continue and become permanent unless teachers bring it to the students' attention and provide instruction for doing it right.

Feedback is important to eliminate incorrect performance— and to enhance student learning.

Attend to Student Needs, Including the Need for Self-Determination

You read in the discussion of needs theory that individuals invest energy in pursuit of achievement, affiliation, and influence as well as to satisfy needs for choice and self-determination. Most motivational research has focused on achievement motivation, and less is known about influence, affiliation, and the role of choice. All of these motives, however, play a role in determining the type of effort students will expend on learning tasks and how long they will persist. In general, students' influence and self-determination needs are satisfied when they feel they have some power or say over their classroom environment and their learning tasks. Cheryl Spaulding (1992) related an interesting story about how important choice and self-determination are to most people. Imagine the following scenario:

> You are a person who loves to travel, and your favorite form of traveling is by car. Each summer you take off on a vacation, driving to and through some of the interesting places in this country. You prefer this sort of vacation because you enjoy discovering for yourself country inns and bed-and-breakfast homes run by unusual people in out-of-the-way places. This year an anonymous benefactor has awarded you with an all-expenses-paid, two-month driving tour through parts of the northeastern United States and Canada, a trip you have long wanted to take. To assist you, this benefactor has gone ahead and planned your itinerary, down to the minutest detail. Your travel route, including the specific roads on which you will travel, has been thoroughly mapped out so that you will never get off course. All your room and dinner reservations have already been made. Even your meals have been preordered for you. All you have to do to take advantage of this wonderful offer is agree to follow the planned itinerary down to the last detail. Would you accept this offer? Would this vacation be as enjoyable as your usual tours through the states? (p. 22)

Spaulding writes that the answers to these questions are likely to be no, because much of the pleasure derived from a driving tour comes from the freedom of being able to make choices on a moment-to-moment basis rather than having these decisions made by someone else.

Here are a few specific examples of how teachers can provide students choice and a sense of self-determination:

- Hold weekly planning sessions with students, assessing how well the previous week has gone and what they would like to see included in next week's lessons. Some experienced teachers use a technique called "pluses and wishes." On large newsprint charts, the teacher makes two columns and labels them as shown in Table 4.5. Together, students and teachers list their suggestions for all to consider. The teacher can use information from this list in his or her own planning and can come back to it to show students that particular lessons and activities were influenced by their input.
- Assign students to perform important tasks, such as distributing and collecting books and papers, taking care of the aquarium, taking roll, acting as tutors to other students, taking messages to the principal's office, and the like.
- Use cooperative learning and problem-based instructional strategies (see Chapters 10 and 11), because these approaches allow students considerable choice in the subject they study and the methods they use.

Table 4.5 *Pluses and Wishes Chart*

Pluses	Wishes
The lecture on cells was clear.	We wish we had had more time on the experiment.
The group work was interesting.	We wish more students would cooperate.
We enjoyed the principal's visit.	We wish the test had been fairer.

Satisfying affiliative needs is also important. In most schools, it is the peer group that students look to for satisfying their affiliation needs. Unfortunately, norms for peer group affiliation often conflict with the strong achievement norms teachers would like to see. In some instances, very competitive cliques that exclude many students from both the academic and social life of the school are found. In other instances, peer group norms exist that apply negative sanctions to those students who try to do well in school work. Teachers can make needs for affiliation work in a positive way by following some of these procedures.

Students look mainly to each other to satisfy their affiliation needs.

- Make sure that all the students in the class (even in high school) know one another's names and some personal information about each student.
- Initiate cooperative goal and reward structures, as described in Chapter 10.
- Take time to help the students in the classroom develop as a group, using procedures described in the following section.

Attend to the Structure of Learning Goals and Difficulty of Instructional Tasks

Social learning theory reminds us of the importance of the ways learning goals and tasks are structured and carried out. Two aspects of learning goals and tasks should be considered here: goal structures and task difficulty.

You read earlier about three types of classroom goal structures: competitive, cooperative, and individualistic. Competitive goal structures lead to comparisons and win-lose relationships among students and make a student's ability, rather than effort, the primary factor for success. Cooperative goal structures, on the other hand, lead to social interdependence, and shared activity makes student effort the primary factor for success. Chapter 10 goes into greater detail about how to set up cooperative goal structures.

Closely connected to the ways goals are structured is the level of difficulty of goals students choose for themselves. Students who set very high goals that are unachievable can be encouraged to rethink what might be more realistic goals. Similarly, students who always set low goals can be encouraged to raise their sights. The important thing for teachers to remember is that students are motivated to persevere longer in pursuing goals that are realistic and achievable.

An additional factor that can influence a student's motivation is associated with the actual degree of difficulty of the learning task and the amount of effort required to complete it. As described previously, tasks that are too easy require too little effort and produce no feelings of success and, consequently, are unmotivational. At the same time, tasks that are too difficult for students, regardless of the effort they expend, will also be unmotivational. Effective teachers learn how to adjust the level of difficulty of learning tasks for particular students. Sometimes this means providing special challenges for the brightest in the class and providing more support and assistance for those who find a particular task too difficult. Effective teachers also help students see the connections between the amount of effort they put into a learning task and their successes and accomplishments. This is done by discussing with students why particular efforts led to success and, conversely, why in other instances they led to failure.

Learning tasks that are too easy require too little effort and produce little feeling of success.

Use Multidimensional Tasks

As described previously, classrooms today are characterized by great diversity. One way for teachers to tailor their instruction for a diverse group of students is to make opportunities available so students can work together on community activities and to pursue tasks that are motivational and challenging. Elizabeth Cohen (1994) and Oakes and Lipton (2003) have called this type of learning situation *using multidimensional tasks.* This approach emphasizes students working together on interesting tasks and problems. Students can make contributions according to their own backgrounds, interests, and abilities. According to Elizabeth Cohen, multidimensional tasks:

- Are intrinsically interesting, rewarding, and challenging.
- Include more than one answer or more than one way to solve the problem.
- Allow different students to make different contributions.
- Involve various mediums to engage the senses of sight, hearing, and touch.
- Require a variety of skills and behaviors.
- Require reading and writing.

Following is an example of how Kim Man Thi Pham uses multidimensional tasks in her eleventh-grade history classroom:

> The room is alive with activity. Desks are pushed to the edge of the classroom, accommodating various groups. Some students discuss how to share their recent experience of working with migrant farm workers in the fields. One student patiently charts a graph showing the economic breakdown of maintaining a large farm. Two students and I plan the presentation order. Other students complete a poster on the United Farm Workers, focusing on the leadership of Cesar Chavez and Philip Ver Cruz. Their photographs, news clippings, and markers are sprawled across the floor. Laughter erupts from the back of the room where four students debate the idea of dressing up as fruit while presenting information on the movement of farm workers across the state following the peak harvest times of the fruit and vegetable season. Someone asks me if she can give her classmates a test after the presentation. "Certainly," I reply, "but consider—'What do you want them to know?'" The student thinks about the question while slowly returning to the group. Activity continues unabated until the final minutes. I remind students to document progress with a short journal entry highlighting individual concerns and feelings. Students write until the end of class (Oakes & Lipton, 2003, pp. 230–231).

Facilitate Group Development and Cohesion

Developing a positive classroom environment will lead to enhanced motivation and heightened achievement. This requires attending to the social and emotional needs of students as well as their academic needs. Also, it requires helping students grow as a group. Sometimes people may not notice, but groups, like individuals, develop and pass through discernible stages in the process. Several social psychologists have studied classrooms and found that classroom groups develop in similar patterns (Putnam & Burke, 1992; Schmuck & Schmuck, 2001). The following stages of **group development** represent a synthesis of their ideas, with particular attention to the ideas identified by the Schmucks.

Stage 1: Facilitating Group Inclusion and Psychological Membership. Everyone wants to feel that they belong, that they are accepted by significant others. This is especially important in a classroom setting because being a learner is a risky business. In order to have the courage to make the mistakes that are a natural part of learning, students need to feel they are in a safe environment. This feeling of safety comes only when students feel accepted and liked by those in their class. Therefore, early in classroom life, students will seek a niche for themselves in the classroom group. They will

Classroom groups go through stages in the process of developing into cohesive and effective groups.

Calvin and Hobbes by Bill Watterson

likely be on their good behavior and present a positive image. Teachers have considerable influence during this period because of their assigned authority. During this period, teachers should spend considerable time forging personal connections with students, helping them learn each others' names, and assisting them in building relationships with each other. When new students enter the group, special efforts must again be made to ensure their acceptance. What teachers do during the initial period of group development represents key first steps in creating a positive learning environment for students.

Stage 2: Establishing Rules and Routines. Think about when you become associated with a new group. Like most people, you are generally very concerned about what is expected of you and how you should behave toward others. Students always want to understand how a class will operate. What are the rules, procedures, policies, and expectations for behavior in the classroom? Sometimes this stage follows stage 1, but it can and often does happen concurrently. Effective teachers conduct lessons early in the year that weave academic expectations with interpersonal and behavioral expectations. They strive to establish an environment in which students can expect to work hard but also feel safe and supported. One day or one lesson is not sufficient to cement these norms; the process takes considerable time spread over several weeks. More about this aspect of classroom life is discussed in Chapter 5 under the topic of Classroom Management.

Stage 3: Establishing Shared Influence and Collaboration. It does not take very long, even with very young children, to facilitate psychological membership and establish rules and routines. However, inevitably, there will be problems. Members of the class soon enter into two types of power struggles. One struggle tests the authority of the teacher; the other establishes the peer group pecking order. These are signals that the classroom has entered stage 3, in which individuals begin struggling to establish their influence within the group. At this stage, it is important for teachers to show students that they have a voice in classroom decision making and that classroom life will be more satisfying if tensions among students can be resolved. Several techniques for dealing with tensions and conflict in the classroom are described in Chapters 5 and 6 and include classroom meetings, conflict resolution, active listening, and dealing with

Well-developed groups are ready to work productively on academic goals.

misbehavior. At this point, it is enough to know that such unpleasant experiences as challenges to the teacher's authority, fights between students, and off-task behavior are all normal occurrences on the road to establishing a positive classroom environment. A caution, however, is in order. If these tensions cannot be resolved and power relationships balanced, the group will not be able to move toward collaboration or into the next stage.

Stage 4: Pursuing Individual and Academic Goals. At this stage, the classroom group is functioning smoothly and productively. Students feel comfortable in the class and are confident that difficulties can be worked out. The frequency of conflicts and off-task behavior decreases, and when they do happen, they are dealt with quickly and effectively. At this time, the classroom enters a stage of development for working productively on academic goals. Students during this stage are very good at setting goals and accomplishing work. They "know the ropes," and little time is lost in miscommunication, conflict, or confusion. Teachers recognize this stage of their group's development and know that this is the time that the best teaching takes place. It is a time to communicate high expectations for students and to encourage them to aspire to high individual and group achievement. Good teachers are also aware that the group can also be pulled back into earlier stages during this period. If that happens, academic work will slow down as membership and power issues are again resolved.

Stage 5: Accomplishing Self-Renewal, Transition, and Closure. As the school year proceeds, teachers should help class members think about their continuous growth and about how to take on new and more challenging tasks. As the semester or year comes to an end, so too does the classroom group. Having worked side by side for several months, students develop close ties with each other, and teachers must address the heartache involved in the breaking of those ties. Similar moments of emotional strain can happen during the year as students move to new schools or as long vacations cause separations. The teacher's job in stage 5 is to watch for these emotional changes, to be ready to assist the group in revisiting and reworking previous stages as needed, and to aid students in synthesizing and bringing to closure the bonds they have formed. Ad-

Table 4.6 *Schmucks' Stages of Classroom Development*

Stage	Group and Member Needs and Behaviors
Stage 1: Inclusion and membership	Early in classroom life, students seek a niche for themselves in the peer group. Students want to present a good image and are on their good behavior. Teachers have great influence during this period because of their assigned authority.
Stage 2: Rules and routines	Members are very concerned about what is expected of them. Students want to understand the way the class will operate and the rules that will govern their behavior.
Stage 3: Influence and collaboration	Members of the class enter into two types of power struggles. One tests the authority of the teacher; the other establishes the peer group pecking order. If tensions cannot be resolved and power relationships balanced, the group cannot move along productively to the next stage.
Stage 4: Individual and academic achievement	The classroom enters a stage of development for working productively on academic goals. Students during this stage can set and accomplish goals and work together on tasks. The classroom can also be pulled back into earlier stages during this stage.
Stage 5: Self-renewal/transition/closure	At this stage, members can think about their continuous growth and about taking on new and more challenging tasks. This is also a stage that can produce conflict, because change in tasks will perhaps upset earlier resolutions around membership.

Source: After Schmuck and Schmuck (2000)

ditionally, teachers must help prepare students for what is to come next—the next grade, teacher, or school. Table 4.6 summarizes the five stages of classroom development.

The Schmucks, as well as others who study classroom groups, are quick to point out, and rightfully so, that the stages of classroom development are not always sequential. Instead, they are often cyclical in nature, with many of the stages repeating themselves several times during the school year. When new students are placed in classrooms, membership issues again become important. Student growth in interpersonal skills keeps influence issues unstable and in constant flux. Larger societal issues cause change and a need to renegotiate norms associated with academic goals and performances.

The stages of classroom group development also have no *definite* time frames associated with them. The time it takes each group to work out issues associated with membership, influence, and task accomplishment depends on the skill of individual members within the class and the type of leadership the teacher provides. *General* time frames, however, can be inferred from the statements of experienced teachers. They report that membership issues consume students during the first month of school and that the most productive period for student learning and attention to academic tasks is between November and early May.

Teachers assist the development of the classroom group at each stage in the ways described and also by helping students understand that groups grow and learn in the same ways that individuals do. It is critical that teachers recognize that positive communication and discourse patterns are perhaps the single most important variable for building groups and productive learning environments. It is through classroom discourse that norms are established and classroom life defined. It is through discourse that the cognitive and social aspects of learning unite. Much more about this important topic is included in Chapter 12.

Check, Extend, Explore

Check
- Contrast the major strategies for accomplishing motivation and a productive learning community.
- Why should teachers focus on controllable factors when attempting to heighten student motivation?
- When and how should extrinsic motivation be used? What cautions should be used?
- What is meant by *flow*? Why are flow experiences often missing in formal education?
- How does a teacher's role as facilitator evolve through each stage of the classroom group's development?

Extend
- Some teachers believe they are responsible for only their students' academic learning and not for students' personal or social development. Do you agree or disagree with this view? Go to "Extend Question Poll" on the Online Learning Center to respond.

Explore
- Go to the Online Learning Center at www.mhhe.com/arends6e for links to websites related to *Enhancing Motivation and Developing Learning Communities.*

Some Final Thoughts

Many teachers and schools have developed positive learning communities where students are interested in school and motivated to learn. However, this is not the situation everywhere. A recent poll of twelfth-grade students revealed that only slightly more than 25 percent found schoolwork "meaningful," only 20 percent found courses "interesting," and only 39 percent perceived school learning to be "important" in later life. These data, collected by the University of Michigan Institute of Social Research, are summarized in Figure 4.6.

What is perhaps most interesting in these statistics is the steady decline in all responses between 1983 and 2000. For example, 40 percent of the twelfth graders reported schoolwork to be meaningful in 1983 compared to only 28 percent in 2000. Course interest also declined during this period from 35 percent to 21 percent.

How do we explain this decline, particularly over a two-decade period when many attempts have been made to increase student effort and interest in education?

Some educators argue that outdated school organizational structures and curricula are mainly to blame for students' lack of interest in schools. They agree with Csikszentmihalyi, who, as you read earlier, feels that structuring middle and high schools around many subjects taught for short periods of time inhibits intrinsic motivation and that reliance on external rewards and grades deters flow experiences. Standardized curricula and external testing may also keep students in passive roles that inhibit enjoyment, interest, and commitment.

Perhaps your generation of teachers will find ways to stop this trend and provide opportunities for all students to be educated in learning communities that are interesting and meaningful. Do you think this is possible?

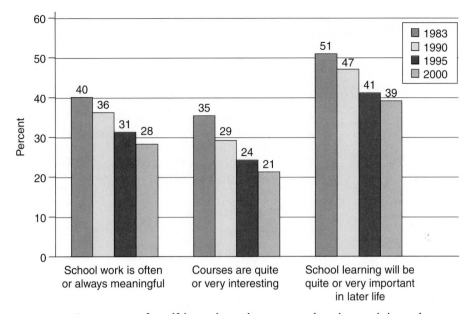

Figure 4.6 *Percentage of twelfth graders who expressed various opinions about their school experience: 1983, 1990, 1995, and 2000.*

Source: Monitoring the Future, 12th Grade Study: 1983, 1990, 1995, 2000 as cited in the *Conditions of Education* (2002), p. 72

Reflections from the *Classroom*

The Lonely Student

It's mid-November, and Patti is sitting by herself again at lunch. Patti came to your school last year after her parents moved to the community from Florida. You have Patti in your homeroom and also for language arts. She is a pretty good student and moderately attractive, but she just hasn't been able to connect with other students or make any friends. You have noticed on several occasions when friendships seem to be forming between someone and Patti, that she goes overboard and gets too demanding. Soon the emerging friendship disappears. At other times, she seems overly shy. Of late, she seems to be distant in class and her work is starting to fall off.

Think for a minute about this situation, then sketch out a reflective essay with the following questions in mind: Do you think teachers should have concerns for this kind of situation? What concerns would you have for Patti? Why do you think Patti is unable to make friends? What would you do to help Patti establish a good friendship?

Approach this situation from the perspective closest to the grade level or subject area you are preparing to teach. Compare your ideas with those of the following teachers and determine how you can make your answer to this situation an exhibit for your portfolio.

(continued)

Reflections from the Classroom, (Continued)

Sandy Frederick

Apple Springs Elementary School, 3rd-5th Grade Reading Specialist
Apple Springs ISD, TX

School is often the only place where children develop social skills. Those who do not have many friends feel left out and usually have low self-esteem. Low self-esteem can be disastrous for any child. Teachers must put forth every effort to build a community within the classroom so each child can find his or her niche, feel supported, and learn important social skills.

Patti seems to overreact to new friendships because she's not secure about making and maintaining friends. Friendships don't always come about easily, and Patti needs to be given the opportunity to socialize with her classmates without the pressure of trying to make a friend.

Cooperative learning activities, paired activities, or small group games would benefit a student like Patti. She would benefit by working in a situation where each student has a specific job, leaving no opportunity for one student to dominate the group nor for any student to be left out. This will give Patti a role to play in the learning community and give her a sense of belonging. Other students will learn to work with Patti as well, and hopefully will begin to enjoy her company.

I often have students create friendly cards for each other. The children draw names from a bowl that tells them who their secret buddy will be for the activity. The card should be friendly and include at least five nice things about the student it's for and a sentence thanking that student for something he/she has done for the child who created it. It's always nice to open a card with nothing but positive things about you on it.

By keeping a class working as a team and demonstrating appreciation of one another, students learn to work together and build lasting relationships.

Jason Shotels

8th Grade

Although I feel sorry for this student and would worry that she might move into groups that don't care much about school, I don't think there is much I could do as a teacher. I am not trained to work with these kinds of problems. However, our school has an array of special programs and services to help students form friendships and get involved in extracurricular activities. One way I could help Patti would be to refer her to the counselor and have the counselor talk to her. Another way would be to recommend to Patti that she become involved in after-school activities and introduce her to the After-School Activities Coordinator. This would provide her with situations and settings in which she would meet other students. If I thought Patti's shyness was very serious, I might also treat it as a disability and consult with the special education faculty to see if Patti qualifies for special education assistance.

Chapter Review

Go back to the "Interactive and Applied Learning" feature at the beginning of the chapter for a listing of interactive and applied activities. Go to the Online Learning Center at **www.mhhe.com/arends6e** or your Interactive Student CD-ROM to take practice quizzes over the content of this chapter and receive immediate feedback. You can also review chapter content and main ideas, practice with key terms, and find annotated Web links on topics associated with this chapter.

Summary

Perspective of Classrooms As Learning Communities

- Motivating students and providing leadership for learning communities are critical leadership functions of teaching.

- A classroom community is a place in which individually motivated students and teachers respond to each other within a social setting.
- Classroom communities are social and ecological systems that include and influence the needs and motives of indi-

viduals, institutional roles, and the interaction between member needs and group norms.

- A productive learning community is characterized by an overall climate in which students feel positive about themselves and their peers, students' individual needs are satisfied so they persist in academic tasks and work cooperatively with the teacher, and students have the requisite interpersonal and group skills to meet the demands of classroom life.

Theoretical and Empirical Support

- The concept of human motivation is defined as the processes within individuals that arouse them to action.
- Psychologists make distinctions between two types of motivation: intrinsic motivation, which is sparked internally, and extrinsic motivation, which results from external or environmental factors.
- Many theories of motivation exist. Four that are particularly relevant to education include reinforcement theory, needs theories, cognitive theories, and social learning theory.
- Reinforcement theory emphasizes the importance of individuals responding to environmental events and extrinsic reinforcements.
- There are several different needs theories. In general, these theories hold that individuals strive to satisfy internal needs such as self-fulfillment, achievement, affiliation, influence, and self-determination.
- Cognitive theories of motivation stress the importance of the way people think and the beliefs and attributions they have about life's situations.
- Social learning theory posits that individuals' actions are influenced by the value particular goals hold for them and their expectations for success with particular tasks.
- Three important features that help us understand classroom communities include classroom properties, classroom processes, and classroom structures.
- Classroom properties are distinctive features of classrooms that help shape behavior. Six important properties include multidimensionality, simultaneity, immediacy, unpredictability, publicness, and history.
- Classroom processes define interpersonal and group features of classrooms and include expectations, leadership, attraction, norms, communication, and cohesiveness.
- Classroom structures are the foundations that shape particular lessons and behaviors during those lessons. Three important structures include task, goal, and participation structures.

- Some classroom features can be altered by the teacher; others cannot. Some classroom properties, such as multidimensionality and immediacy, cannot be influenced readily by the teacher. Group processes and the classroom goal, task, reward, and participation structures are more directly under the teacher's control.
- Studies on classrooms and teaching show that student motivation and learning are influenced by the types of processes and structures teachers create in particular classrooms.
- Studies have also uncovered important relationships among teacher behaviors, student engagement, and learning. In general, students react more positively and persist in academic tasks in classrooms characterized by democratic as opposed to authoritarian processes and in classrooms characterized by positive feeling tones and learning orientations.
- Influence in classrooms does not flow just from the teacher. Studies show that students influence each other and the behavior of their teachers.

Strategies for Motivating Students and Building Productive Learning Communities

- Effective teachers create productive learning communities by focusing on things that can be altered, such as increasing student motivation and encouraging group development.
- Factors associated with motivation that teachers can modify and control include the overall feeling tone of the classroom, task difficulty, students' interests, knowledge of results, classroom goal and reward structures, and students' needs for achievement, influence, affiliation, and self-determination.
- Although the use of extrinsic rewards makes good common sense, teachers should avoid overemphasizing this type of motivation.
- Teachers assist the development of their classrooms as a group by teaching students how groups grow and about the stages they go through and by helping students learn how to work in groups.
- Allocating time to building productive learning environments will reduce many of the frustrations experienced by beginning teachers and will extend teachers' abilities to win student cooperation and involvement in academic tasks.

Key Terms

achievement motives   143

affiliative motives   143

attribution theory   145

classroom activities   150

competitive goal
   structures   151

cooperative goal
   structures   151

ecological systems   147

endogenous statements   156

exogenous statements   156

extrinsic motivation   141

feedback   161

feeling tone   159

flow experiences   144

goal structures   151

group development   164

individualistic goal
   structures   151

influence   143

intrinsic motivation   141

motivation   141

needs theory   142

negative reinforcers   142

participation structures   152

positive reinforcers   142

punishments   142

reinforcement theory   141

reward structures   151

social learning theory   145

task structures   151

Portfolio and Field Experience Activities

This feature has been designed to help you learn from your field experiences and to assist you in the preparation of artifacts for your professional portfolio on topics and standards associated with Chapter 4.

1. Complete the "Reflections from the Classroom" exercise at the end of this chapter. The recommended reflective essay will provide insights into your views about a teacher's responsibilities toward the emotional and social well-being of students.

2. Get students in your field experience classroom to complete the "Classroom Life" survey—Activity 4.2 in the *Guide to Field Experiences and Portfolio Development*. Use your analysis as a portfolio artifact that examines your views about student motivation and interest.

3. Complete Activity 4.4 in the *Guide to Field Experiences and Portfolio Development* as an artifact that demonstrates your beliefs about the features of a positive learning community.

Books for the Professional

Go to the Online Learning Center at www.mhhe.com/arends6e or your Interactive Student CD-ROM for an annotated version of this list.

Csikszentmihalyi, M. (1990). *Flow: The Psychology of Optimal Experience.* New York: Harper & Row.

Johnson, D. W., and Johnson, F. P. (1999). *Joining Together: Group Theory and Group Skills* (7th ed.). Englewood Cliffs, NJ: Prentice-Hall.

Raffini, J. P. (1996). *150 Ways to Increase Intrinsic Motivation in the Classroom.* Boston: Allyn & Bacon.

Schmuck, R. A., and Schmuck, P. (2001). *Group Processes in the Classroom* (8th ed.). New York: McGraw-Hill.

Sapon-Shevin, M., and Shevin, S. (1998). *Because We Can Change the World: A Practical Guide to Building Cooperative, Inclusive Classroom Communities.* Boston: Allyn & Bacon.

Chapter Five

Classroom Management

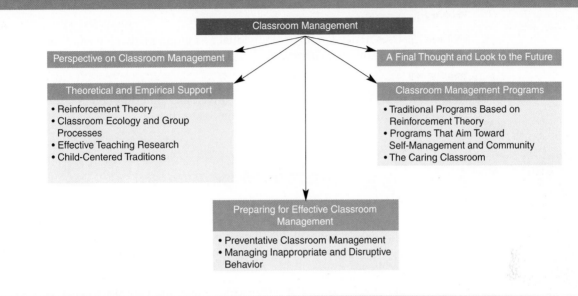

```
                         ┌─────────────────────────┐
                         │  Classroom Management    │
                         └─────────────────────────┘
```

Perspective on Classroom Management

A Final Thought and Look to the Future

Theoretical and Empirical Support

- Reinforcement Theory
- Classroom Ecology and Group Processes
- Effective Teaching Research
- Child-Centered Traditions

Classroom Management Programs

- Traditional Programs Based on Reinforcement Theory
- Programs That Aim Toward Self-Management and Community
- The Caring Classroom

Preparing for Effective Classroom Management

- Preventative Classroom Management
- Managing Inappropriate and Disruptive Behavior

Interactive **and** *Applied Learning*

Go to your Interactive Student CD-ROM to:

- Hear audio clips of Vickie Williams and Richard Beyard (ninth grade biology) talk about their overall approaches to classroom management in the *Teachers on Teaching* feature
- Watch the video clip: "Managing Classrooms"
- View examples of classroom rules and procedures

Go to the Online Learning Center at www.mhhe.com/arends6e to read *PowerWeb* articles and newsfeed updates about:

- Cheating
- Classroom climate
- Classroom management
- Cultural diversity in education
- Discipline
- Moral development
- Morality and schooling
- Nonviolent conflict resolution
- Prejudice in schools
- School discipline
- Values in education
- Violence
- Zero tolerance

Considering **Standards**

Studying this chapter will help you meet two INTASC principles:

Primary

INTASC 5: Uses understanding of individual and group motivation and behavior to create positive learning environment.

Secondary

INTASC 6: Uses knowledge of verbal and nonverbal communication to foster inquiry, collaboration, and supportive classroom interaction.

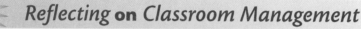

Reflecting **on** *Classroom Management*

Beginning teachers report that the most difficult aspect of their first years of teaching is classroom management. They worry about it; they even have recurring nightmares about this issue. Before you read this chapter, reflect a bit about your own student experiences with this topic. What stands out in your mind about the ways your teachers managed their classrooms?

- Think about those who were strong disciplinarians and very strict. What did they do in regard to classroom management? How did you respond to this type of teacher and classroom? How did other students respond? What were the advantages of this type of management? Disadvantages?

- Now think about teachers who were very lax. What did they do in regard to classroom management? How did you respond to this type of teacher and classroom? How did other students respond? What were the advantages of this type of management? Disadvantages?

- Finally, write down the kind of classroom manager you want to be. Will you be strict? Lax? Friendly? What about your students? Do you want them to behave because you say they should? Or have you thought about helping your students develop self-discipline?

Go to the Online Learning Center at www.mhhe.com/arends6e to respond to these questions.

When teachers talk about the most difficult problems they experienced in their first years of teaching, they mention **classroom management** and discipline most often. Although a rich knowledge base on classroom management has been developed, beginning and student teachers continue to feel insecure about managing their first classrooms, and they spend many sleepless nights worrying about this issue.

Many of these anxieties are, in fact, similar to the anxieties experienced by people in any field when they are asked to assume positions of leadership and to exert influence for the first time. Nonetheless, gaining a repertoire of basic classroom management understandings and skills will do much to reduce the anxiety that naturally accompanies one's first classroom assignment. Describing the important concepts and skills associated with classroom management is the aim of this chapter. The first section of the chapter builds on the conceptual frameworks introduced in Chapters 3 and 4 and then presents a sampling of key research studies from the classroom management literature. In the final section of the chapter are specific and concrete procedures beginning teachers can use as they prepare for effective classroom management within the context of a democratic learning community.

Perspective on Classroom Management

Although this chapter has a point of view, as you will discover, it also is eclectic in regard to the specific classroom management procedures. For example, you will find procedures that have grown out of the research that shows how effective management is connected to teachers' abilities to be "with it," to use effective instructional strategies, and to make lessons interesting for their students. At the same time, the shortcomings of this perspective are described, and approaches stemming from child-centered theorists are also presented for consideration. Multiple perspectives and approaches are provided because they exist in today's schools, and as beginning teachers, you will not always be free to choose the approach you think best. Some schools, for instance, will have a very definite behavioral approach to classroom management; all teachers will be expected to develop rules and procedures in their classrooms consistent with this approach. Other schools will foster more humanistic, child-centered approaches to classroom management. Finally, as is the case with most aspects of teaching, the most effective classroom managers are those with a repertoire of strategies and approaches that can be used with students as particular situations dictate.

Many of the ideas for understanding classroom management were presented in previous chapters and need only brief mention here. For example, the idea that the teacher's biggest job is to develop a democratic learning community where all students are valued, respect one another, and are motivated to work together remains central for thinking about classroom management. The same is true for the idea that good classroom management requires teachers who can create authentic relationships with their students and develop an "ethic of care." There are, however, two more ideas that can provide additional perspective on effective classroom management.

First, *classroom management is possibly the most important challenge facing beginning teachers.* A new teacher's reputation among colleagues, school authorities, and students will be strongly influenced by his or her ability to perform the managerial functions of teaching, particularly creating an orderly learning environment and dealing with student behavior. Sometimes, beginning teachers think this is unfair and argue that schools and principals put too much emphasis on order as contrasted to learning. Perhaps it is

Effective teachers have a repertoire of management strategies to be used as situations dictate.

Classroom management is one of the most important challenges beginning teachers face.

unfair. Nonetheless, a teacher's leadership ability is tested in the arena of management and discipline, and when something goes wrong, it is known more quickly than other aspects of teaching. More important, without adequate management, little else can occur. Dunkin and Biddle (1974) pointed out this important fact over two decades ago when they wrote that "management of the classroom . . . forms a necessary condition for cognitive learning; and if the teacher cannot solve problems in this sphere, we can give the rest of teaching away" (p. 135).

Second, *classroom management and instruction are highly interrelated.* An important perspective stressed in the first part of this chapter is what Brophy and Putnam (1979), Evertson and Emmer (2003), and Burke and Putnam (1998) have called **preventative management.** This perspective has dominated views about classroom management for over two decades. Classroom management is not an end in itself; it is merely one part of a teacher's overall leadership role. In this regard, classroom management cannot be separated from the other aspects of teaching. For example, when teachers plan carefully for lessons, as described in Chapter 3, they are doing much to ensure good classroom management. When teachers plan ways to allocate time to various learning activities or consider how space should be used in the classroom, they are again making important decisions that will affect classroom management. Similarly, all the strategies for building productive learning communities described in Chapter 4, such as helping the classroom develop as a group, attending to student motivation, and facilitating honest and open discourse, are also important components of classroom management.

Preventative management is the perspective that many classroom problems can be solved through good planning, interesting and relevant lessons, and effective teaching.

Further, each teaching model or strategy a teacher chooses to use places its own demands on the management system and influences the behaviors of both teachers and learners. The instructional tasks associated with giving a lecture, for example, call for behaviors on the part of students that are different from those needed for tasks associated with learning a new skill. Similarly, behavioral demands for students working together in groups are different from those required for working alone on a seatwork assignment. Instructional tasks are integrally related not only to the problem of instruction but also to the problems of order and management. Teachers who plan appropriate classroom activities and tasks, who make wise decisions about time and space allocation, and who have a sufficient repertoire of instructional strategies will be building a learning environment that secures student cooperation on learning tasks and minimizes discipline problems.

"I'D LIKE TO OVERWHELM THEM WITH INSTRUCTIONAL EXCELLENCE, BUT I'M NOT ABOVE WINNING THROUGH INTIMIDATION."

Source: Martha F. Campbell, Phi Delta Kappan

Check, Extend, Explore

Check
- Why do most people consider classroom management the most important challenge for beginning teachers?
- How is classroom management linked to other aspects of instruction?
- What examples can you give to demonstrate that order in the classroom is considered extremely important by most educators?

Extend
- Reflect on the kinds of worries and anxieties you experience in regard to classroom management.
- Do you agree or disagree with child-centered theorists that too much emphasis is put on controlling students? Go to the "Extend Question Poll" on the Online Learning Center to respond.

Explore
- Go to the Online Learning Center at www.mhhe.com/arends6e for links to websites related to *Classroom Management and the Beginning Teacher.*

Finally, alternative perspectives to the preventative approach exist and stem mainly from the work of child-centered theorists such as John Dewey and the Swiss educator Johann Pestalozzi, as well as an array of twentieth-century humanistic reformers such as Abraham Maslow and Carl Rogers. This perspective is critical of processes aimed at controlling students and instead focuses on the basic goodness of children and youth. Educators holding this perspective argue for treating children in schools humanely and respectfully and for creating learning communities characterized by what Nel Noddings (1992, 2001) has called an "ethic of care." These settings assist student development not only academically but also socially and emotionally.

Theoretical and Empirical Support

Three traditions have guided the theory and research on classroom management: reinforcement theory, the ecological and group processes perspective, and child-centered views. This section is organized around these three perspectives.

Reinforcement Theory

You read in Chapter 4 how **reinforcement** and behavioral theory dominated thinking about motivation in the early part of the twentieth century. This perspective has also had a strong influence on classroom management. Remember that reinforcement theory emphasizes the centrality of external events in directing behavior and the importance of positive and negative reinforcers (Skinner, 1956). Teachers who apply behavioral principles to classroom management use rewards in the form of grades, praise, and privileges to reinforce desired behavior and punishments, such as bad grades, reprimands, and loss of privileges, to discourage undesirable tendencies or actions.

Behavioral approaches often emphasize how to control the behavior of individual students as compared to considering the classroom group and overall learning situation.

Many times this approach has focused on the individual student and has sought to understand the causes of a particular student's classroom behavior rather than causes that may stem from the features of the classroom group or the teaching situation.

This tradition has been led mainly by clinical and counseling psychologists, such as Dreikurs (1968) and Dreikurs and Grey (1968), and by behavioral psychologists and those who apply behavioral theory, such as Canter and Canter (1976, 2002). Their practice has focused on such psychological causes as insecurity, need for attention, anxiety, and lack of self-discipline as well as on sociological causes such as parent overprotection, bad peer relationships, or disadvantaged backgrounds. Recommendations to teachers stemming from this research normally emphasize ways to help individual students through counseling or behavior modification and show less concern for managing the classroom group. Behavior modification programs, the use of token economies, and assertive discipline (Canter & Canter, 1976, 2002; Cohen, 1973) are formal programs that have developed based on reinforcement theory and have been used widely in classrooms during the past thirty years. Although many of the behavioral-oriented programs have shortcomings, they nonetheless are found in many schools today, and beginning teachers should be knowledgeable about them. These will be described later in the chapter in the Classroom Management Programs section.

Classroom Ecology and Group Processes

Researchers in the ecology and group process tradition are interested in how student cooperation and involvement are achieved in group settings.

Chapter 4 described several ideas that help explain classroom life from an ecological perspective, and the work of such researchers as Barker (1968), Doyle (1979, 1986), Gump (1967), and Kounin (1970) were cited. The ecological perspective addresses directly the problem of classroom control and group management procedures.

Classroom management researchers in this tradition study the way student cooperation and involvement are achieved so that important learning activities can be accomplished. The major function of the teacher from this point of view is to plan and orchestrate well-conceived group activities that flow smoothly. Misbehavior of students is conceived as actions that disrupt this activity flow. Examples of disruptions include students talking when quiet is desired, students not working on a seatwork assignment the teacher has given, or students getting out of their seats at inappropriate times. Teacher interventions in regard to student misbehavior, as will be described later, should be quick, often minor, and aimed at keeping the flow of learning activities and tasks on the right track.

Kounin's Research. The classic piece of research in the **classroom ecology** tradition was done in the late 1960s by Jacob Kounin and his colleagues. After several years of trying to understand classroom discipline, Kounin started to consider that maybe it was not the way teachers disciplined their students that was important but instead the way the classroom as a group was managed that made a difference. Kounin's work has greatly influenced the way we think about classroom management. His classic study is described in the Research Summary for this chapter. Many of Kounin's research findings are discussed in more detail later in the chapter.

Doyle and Carter's Research. Other researchers of particular interest who have used the ecological framework to guide their research are Walter Doyle and Kathy Carter (1984) at the University of Arizona. They were interested in how specific academic tasks are connected to student involvement and classroom management. To explore this topic, they observed one junior high school English teacher and the students in

Research Summary

What Do Teachers Do to Create Well-Managed Classrooms?

Kounin, J. S. (1970). *Discipline and group management in classrooms.* New York: Holt, Rinehart & Winston.

The most challenging aspect of teachers' work is developing and maintaining a well-managed classroom. This challenge has led many researchers to examine how effective teachers manage their classrooms. The interesting result that stems from all this research is that good classroom managers actually prevent problems from occurring through the way they plan for and pace their lessons and the means they use to nip misbehavior in the bud. The classic study on this topic was done by Jacob Kounin in the 1960s.

Problem and Approach: After several years of trying to understand discipline in classrooms, Jacob Kounin started to consider that perhaps the key was not so much the way teachers disciplined individual students but, instead, the way they managed the whole classroom group. So, he decided to study group management. This is an interesting and important study because Kounin was one of the first researchers to go directly into classrooms and observe exactly what was going on. His study was also one of the first to use a video camera as an observation tool.

Sample: The sample of Kounin's study reported here consisted of forty-nine teachers and their students in upper elementary classrooms.

Procedures: Kounin developed elaborate procedures for observing classrooms, including videotaping teacher and student interaction and transcript analysis. Many variables were measured in the complete study. Here, only a few of the more important variables are described.

Dependent Variables: For Kounin, managerial success was demonstrated by classrooms in which work involvement was high and student deviancy was low.

1. Work involvement fell into three categories: (a) definitely doing the assigned work, (b) probably doing the assigned work, and (c) definitely not doing the assigned work.
2. Deviancy consisted of a three-category scheme: (a) student not misbehaving, (b) student mildly misbehaving, and (c) student engaging in serious misbehavior.

Contextual Variables: Kounin observed two types of learning activities: recitations and seatwork.

Independent Variables: Kounin conceptualized eight different variables for describing the group management behavior of teachers.

1. *"With-itness."* The ability to accurately spot deviant behavior, almost before it starts.
2. *"Overlappingness."* The ability to spot and deal with deviant behavior while going right on with the lesson.
3. *Smoothness.* Absence of behaviors that interrupt the flow of activities.
4. *Momentum.* Absence of behaviors that slow down lesson pacing.
5. *Group alerting.* Techniques used by teachers to keep noninvolved students attending and forewarned of forthcoming events.
6. *Accountability.* Techniques used by teachers to keep students accountable for their performance.
7. *Challenge arousal.* Techniques used by teachers to keep students involved and enthusiastic.
8. *Variety.* The degree to which various aspects of lessons differed.

Pointers for Reading Research: Up to this point in presenting statistics, researchers depended on mean scores and used *t* tests or analysis of variance (*f* tests) to see if mean scores between two groups were significant. To understand Kounin's study, a new statistic—the *correlation coefficient*, described in the Resource Handbook section on understanding research—needs to be reviewed. Remember, correlation refers to the extent of a relationship that exists between pairs of measures. The coefficient can range from +1.00 through .00 to −1.00. The sign does not have the traditional mathematical meaning. Instead, a plus sign represents a positive relationship, a minus sign a negative relationship. A .00 means no relationship exists, +1.00 means a perfect relationship exists, and −1.00 means a reverse relationship exists. Correlations can be tested for significance just as mean scores can.

Results: Table 5.1 shows the correlations Kounin found between various aspects of teacher management behavior and children's behavior during recitation and seatwork.

(continued)

Research Summary

What Do Teachers Do to Create Well-Managed Classrooms? (Continued)

Table 5.1 *Correlation of Selected Teacher Management Behaviors and Children's Behavior in Recitation and Seatwork Settings**

	Recitation		Seatwork	
Dependent Variable	**Work Involvement**	**Freedom from Deviancy**	**Work Involvement**	**Freedom from Deviancy**
Momentum	.656	.641	.198	.490
With-itness	.615	.531	.307	.509
Smoothness	.601	.489	.382	.421
Group alerting	.603	.442	.234	.290
Accountability	.494	.385	.002	−.035
Overlappingness	.460	.362	.259	.379
Challenge arousal	.372	.325	.308	.371
Overall variety and challenge	.217	.099	.449	.194
Class size (Range = 21–39)	−.279	−.258	−.152	−.249

*N = 49 classrooms (correlation of .276 is significant at .05 level)

Source: After Kounin (1970), p. 169

Discussion and Implications Kounin's research provides a rich source of ideas for how teachers can approach the problem of classroom management. Table 5.1 shows that with-itness, momentum, overlappingness, smoothness, and group alerting all appear to increase student work involvement, particularly during recitation lessons. Similarly, with-itness and momentum decrease student deviancy. With-itness also decreases student deviancy in seatwork lessons, whereas variety appears to be the major behavior that helps promote work involvement in seatwork.

Note that all the relationships in the table, although not significant, are positive, except for the negative correlation coefficients for the relationships between accountability and freedom from deviancy during seatwork and those associated with class size. These negative correlations are small and what they mean essentially is that no relationships were found between those variables.

The implications for teacher behavior from Kounin's work are great and are described in some detail in the next section of this chapter, Effective Teaching Research.

three of her classes in a middle-class suburban school for a period of almost three months. The teacher, Mrs. Dee, was selected for study because she was an experienced teacher and she was considered to have considerable expertise in teaching writing to students.

This work is informative to the topic of classroom management because the researchers found that students had considerable influence over the task demands of the classroom. For instance, over a period of time, Mrs. Dee assigned students a variety of major and minor writing tasks. Examples include writing an essay comparing Christmas in Truman Capote's story "A Christmas Memory" with Christmas today, writing a short story report, and writing descriptive paragraphs with illustrations. In some of the writing tasks, Mrs. Dee tried to encourage student creativity and self-direction, and to do that, she left the assignments somewhat open-ended. From detailed observations of Mrs. Dee's classroom, Doyle and Carter found, however, that students pressed to reduce the amount of self-direction and independent judgment in some of the writing assignments. Students, even those considered very bright, used tactics such as asking questions or feigning confusion to force Mrs. Dee to become more and more concise and explicit. In other words, the students influenced the teacher to do more and more of their thinking.

Doyle and Carter also found that by asking questions about content and procedures, students, in addition to changing the assignment, also slowed down the pace of classroom activities. This was done to get an assignment postponed or just to use up class time. When Mrs. Dee refused to answer some of the students' delaying questions, things seemed only to get worse. Here is a direct quote from a report of what the researchers observed:

> Some students became quite adamant in their demands. . . . On such occasions, order began to break down and the normal smoothness and momentum of the classes were reinstated only when the teacher provided the prompts and resources the students were requesting. The teacher was pushed, in other words, to choose between conditions for students' self-direction and preserving order in the classroom (p. 146).

Mrs. Dee was an experienced enough teacher to know that order had to come first or everything else was lost.

Effective Teaching Research

Some classroom management researchers have been influenced by both behavioral theory and the ecological orientation. These researchers strived in the 1970s and 1980s to identify the behaviors of effective teachers, meaning teachers who could consistently produce high student engagement with academic activities. They pursued this approach because, as you read in Chapter 3, strong relationships had been found between student engagement and student achievement.

This research, which has spread over thirty years, has been led by Edmund Emmers, Carolyn Evertson, and several of their colleagues. Like Kounin before them, teacher-effectiveness researchers found strong relationships between student on-task behavior and a number of teacher behaviors. Specifically, when effective classroom managers were compared to ineffective classroom managers, the following teacher behaviors were observed:

1. The more effective classroom managers had *procedures* that governed student talk, participation, and movement; turning in work; and what to do during downtime.
2. Laboratory and group activities in the effective managers' classrooms ran smoothly and efficiently. *Instructions were clear,* and student *misbehavior was handled quickly.*
3. Effective managers had very *clear work requirements* for students and monitored student progress carefully.
4. Effective managers gave *clear presentations and explanations,* and their directions about note taking were explicit.

The implications of this research, along with recommendations for teachers, will be discussed in more detail in the next section, Preparing for Effective Classroom Management.

Child-Centered Traditions

Finally, there is a theoretical and research tradition that provides an alternative to behavioral and preventative perspectives. Relying on theories of John Dewey and humanistic

Students have been shown to disrupt instruction by pretending to be confused.

The child-centered perspective on classroom management views the chief source of the problem as irrelevant curricula and overemphasis on quietude and uniformity.

Check, Extend, Explore

Check

- What are the three major theories that have guided classroom management research practices? What are the advantages and disadvantages of each?
- How did research conducted by Kounin and Doyle and Carter demonstrate that optimal learning is most likely achieved in an orderly classroom?
- What specific teacher behaviors lead to the most effective classroom management, according to teacher effectiveness researchers?
- What are the major features of classroom management from the perspective of child-centered theorists? Contrast child-centered views with those of behaviorists.

Extend

- Do you think you will incorporate mostly behavioral or child-centered classroom management practices in your classroom? Go to the "Extend Question Poll" on the Online Learning Center to respond.

Explore

- Go to the Online Learning Center at www.mhhe.com/ arends6e for links to websites related to Approaches to Classroom Management.

psychologists, Abraham Maslow and Carl Rogers, current researchers and reformers such as Nel Noddings, Jeannie Oakes, Alfie Kohn and George Noblit argue that behavioral-minded researchers have it all wrong. Developing smooth-running classrooms or making lessons interesting, they argue, are simplistic solutions to much more complex problems. They agree with the observation made by John Dewey many years ago:

> The chief source of the "problem of discipline" in schools is that . . . a premium is put on physical quietude, on silence, on rigid uniformity of posture and movement; upon a machine-like simulation of the attitudes of intelligent interest. The teachers' business is to hold the pupils up to these requirements and to punish the inevitable deviations which occur (Dewey in Kohn, 1996, p. 7).

This perspective embraces child-centered rather than subject-centered classrooms. Misbehavior, according to Oakes and Lipton (2003), "follows from instruction that attempts to coerce students, even if it is for their own and society's good" (p. 278), or, according to Kohn (1996), from situations "where we 'manage' behavior and try to make students do what we want . . . (rather than) . . . help them become morally sophisticated people who think for themselves and care about others" (p. 62). Curriculum should *not* be prescribed by teachers but instead should aim at promoting students' development and at meeting students' social and emotional as well as academic needs.

Child-centered educators do not have a set of specific guidelines for achieving effective classroom management, nor do they offer recipes for teachers to follow. Instead, as Nel Noddings (1992) has written, "schools should be committed to a great moral purpose: to care for children so that they too will be prepared to care" (p. 65). Caring and developing democratic classrooms become the alternative to preventative management and behavioral control.

Research in this tradition is often qualitative and ethnographic. A study done by George Noblit (1995) characterizes this approach. Noblit and his colleagues studied how two experienced inner-city teachers (one white, the other African American) developed caring relationships with their students. Noblit and his colleagues spent one full day every week for over a year in these teachers' classrooms and conducted interviews with teachers and children in the school. The vignettes displayed in Figure 5.1 illustrate how these teachers dealt with problem students and what it meant to develop "caring relationships."

Preparing for Effective Classroom Management

This section focuses directly on procedures beginning teachers can use to ensure effective classroom management. It is organized around four major topics: preventative classroom management, managing inappropriate and disruptive behavior, exhibiting confidence, and working toward caring communities and self-discipline.

Preventative Classroom Management

Many of the problems associated with student misbehavior are dealt with by effective teachers through preventative approaches. Much of this section is based on the original research emanating from Kounin's work, and effective teaching research. The ideas and procedures are introduced here and revisited in later chapters in regard to management demands of particular approaches to teaching.

Robert's Story

Robert was a challenge from his first day in Martha's classroom. He was a pudgy boy who had spent the previous school year at a special school for youths with severe behavioral problems. During the two years prior to that he had continually been removed from classrooms for exhibiting "inappropriate and aggressive" behavior.

Martha invested herself in helping him. She waited daily at the classroom door to greet Robert, and she always told him goodbye in the afternoon. She spent a few moments every day talking with him about anything and everything, from TV shows to his mother. And she firmly insisted that he participate in classroom activities—especially cooperative learning groups with the other children.

Because of the attention she paid to him, Robert slowly began to realize that Martha was committed to him. By November Robert had become a marginally accepted and fairly productive member of this class. He was still ornery and still had small outbursts in class, but he responded to Martha and to the other students in much more positive ways. Not once was Robert sent to the principal or suspended, a dramatic reversal for him. Martha was able to help Robert become a more academically and socially competent person despite the stigma of being labeled behaviorally disordered.

What was significant about Martha's influence on Robert was her dogged determination that he be given the opportunities to succeed in school and to attain social competence. There were no magic tricks, no technical fixes—just consistent, day-in and day-out, hour-to-hour, even minute-to-minute reminders to Robert to complete his work and respect others. She simply refused to give up on him. Martha explained, "I have a tendency not to give up on anybody. It is my responsibility."

Martha encouraged and enhanced Robert's social and academic growth despite the system. He usually participated in classroom discussions and activities, seemed to enjoy coming to school (in fact, never missed a day!), and appeared to have made a few friends in the class, all of whom showed up for his birthday party. Martha and Robert's caring relationship set a new context for Robert as a student. And within that context he was able to improve both his behavior and his academic achievement.

John's Story

John had been mainstreamed into Pam's class. He had the unique ability of disappearing during any classroom event. He was painfully shy and would physically hide from interaction with Pam by lining up behind other students, dropping his head and shoulders below desk level, and so on. During group work, John would not talk or participate in any way beyond sitting with the other students. Pam decided it was her responsibility to help John become more a part of the class. She demanded that he take part by sitting up, attending to assigned tasks, and working with other students.

In addition to being stern with him, Pam moved his desk close to hers and kept him near her during small-group activities. She found that touching him was a key to his attending, and over time his response to her touching changed from alarm to acceptance and finally to a perception of support. Her hand on his shoulder would allow him to speak and to participate—and, by the end of the year, eye contact with Pam was sufficient assurance for him. Pam was tough but supportive in her caring for John, and he reciprocated.

Like Martha with Robert, Pam recognized John's need to become part of the class and disregarded the implicit belief that special children really do not belong in a regular classroom. Her concern for him, her fidelity to him rather than to a mandated curricular objective, guided her search for appropriate strategies to ensure his participation and inclusion in the class. Their relationship made the classroom a safe and nurturing environment for John and led him to take part in classroom activities and to complete academic work.

Figure 5.1 *Vignettes from Noblit's Study of Caring Teachers*
Source: Adapted from Noblit (1995)

Establishing Rules and Procedures. In classrooms, as in most other settings where groups of people interact, a large percentage of potential problems and disruptions can be prevented by planning rules and procedures beforehand. To understand the truth of this statement, think for a moment about the varied experiences you have had in non-school settings where fairly large numbers of people come together. Examples most people think about include driving a car during rush hour in a large city, attending a football game, going to Disneyland, or buying tickets for a movie or play. In all of these instances, established rules and procedures indicated by traffic lights and queuing stalls help people who do not even know each other to interact in regular, predictable ways. Rules such as "the right of way" and "no cutting in line" help people negotiate rather complex processes safely and efficiently.

Think for a moment about what happens when procedures or rules suddenly break down or disappear. You can probably recall an instance when a power outage caused traffic lights to stop working or when a large crowd arrived to buy tickets for an important game before the ticket sellers set up their queuing stalls. Recently, a teacher friend was in Detroit for a conference, and her return flight was booked on an airline that had merged with another airline on that particular day. When the two airlines combined their information systems, something went wrong with the computers. This computer malfunction made it impossible for the ticket agents to know who was on a particular flight and prevented them from issuing seat assignments. The result was bedlam, full of disruptive behavior. People were shoving each other as individuals tried to ensure a seat for themselves; passengers were yelling at each other and at the cabin crew. At one point, members of a normally well-disciplined crew were even speaking sharply to each other. The incident turned out okay because a seat was found for everyone. The boarding process, however, did not proceed in the usual orderly, calm manner because some well-known procedures were suddenly unavailable.

Classrooms rules specify what students are expected to do and what they are *not* to do.

Classrooms, in some ways, are similar to busy airports or busy intersections. They, too, require rules and procedures to govern important activities. As used here, **rules** are statements that specify the things students are expected to do and not do. Normally, rules are written down, made clear to students, and kept to a minimum. **Procedures,** on the other hand, are the ways of getting work and other activity accomplished. These are seldom written down, but effective classroom managers spend considerable time teaching procedures to students in the same way they teach academic matter. Student movement, student talk, and what to do with downtime are among the most important activities that require rules to govern behavior and procedures to make work flow efficiently.

Classroom procedures are established by teachers for dealing with routine tasks and coordinating student talk and movement.

Student Movement. In many secondary classrooms, such as a science laboratory, the art room, or the physical education facility, and in all elementary classrooms, students must move around to accomplish important learning activities. They need to obtain or put away materials, sharpen pencils, form small groups, and so on.

Effective classroom managers devise ways to make needed movements by students flow smoothly. They organize queuing and distribution procedures that are efficient; they establish rules that minimize disruptions and ensure safety. Examples of rules include limiting the number of students moving at any one time and specifying when to be seated. How to line up, move in the halls, and go unattended to the library are procedures that assist with student movement.

Student Talk. Students talking at inappropriate times or asking questions to slow down the pace of a lesson pose a classroom management problem that is among the most troublesome to teachers. This problem can vary in severity from a loud, generalized classroom clamor that disturbs the teacher next door to a single student talking to a neighbor when the teacher is explaining an important idea.

Effective classroom managers have a clear set of rules governing student talking. Most teachers prescribe when no talking is allowed (when the teacher is lecturing or explaining), when low talk is allowed and encouraged (during small-group work or seatwork), and when anything goes (during recess and parties). Effective classroom managers also have procedures that make classroom discourse more satisfying and productive, such as talking one at a time during a discussion, listening to other people's ideas, raising hands, and taking turns.

Downtime. A third area of classroom life for which rules and procedures are required is during **downtime.** Sometimes, lessons are completed before a period is over, and it is inappropriate to start something new. Similarly, when students are doing seatwork, some finish before others. Waiting for a film projector to arrive for a scheduled film is another example of downtime.

Downtime occurs when lessons are completed early or when students are waiting for upcoming events, such as moving to another class or going home.

Effective classroom managers devise rules and procedures to govern student talk and movement during these times. Examples include: "If you finish your work, you can get a book and engage in silent reading until the others have finished." "While we wait for the film to start, you can talk quietly to your neighbors, but you cannot move around the room." "If your work is complete, please see if your neighbor needs your help." Table 5.2 shows a set of rules developed by one teacher and her students. Notice that the list is fairly brief and that it contains examples of what students should do and of behaviors that are inappropriate.

Teaching Rules and Procedures. Rules and procedures are of little value unless participants learn and accept them. This requires active teaching. Effective classroom managers generally establish only a few rules and procedures, then teach them carefully to students and make them routine through their consistent use. In most classrooms, only a few rules are needed, but it is important for the teacher to make sure students understand the purpose of each rule and its moral or practical underpinnings. Concepts and ideas associated with rules have to be taught just the same as any other set of concepts and ideas. For instance, very young children can see the necessity for keeping talk low during downtime when the teacher explains that loud talk disturbs students in

Table 5.2 *Sample Rules for Classrooms*

Rule	Examples of Dos and Don'ts
• Be respectful of rights of others.	Treat everyone with respect. No name calling or teasing.
• Be polite and helpful.	Say please. No fighting.
• Respect the property of others.	Keep room clean. Don't use others' supplies.
• Listen to others' ideas.	Pay attention when others are talking. Don't call out or interrupt.
• Follow all school rules.	Use your hall pass. Don't run in the cafeteria.

neighboring classrooms who are still working. Taking turns strikes a chord with older students who have heightened concerns with issues of fairness and justice. Potential injury to self and others can be given as the reason why movement in a science laboratory has to be done a certain way. One point of caution about teaching rules should be noted, however. When teachers are explaining rules, they must walk a rather thin line between providing explanations that are helpful to students and sounding patronizing or overly moralistic.

As with any other subject, rules and procedures must be taught to students.

Most movement and discourse procedures have not only a practical dimension but also a skill dimension that must be taught, like academic skills. In Chapter 12, several strategies will be described for teaching students how to listen to other people's ideas and how to participate in discussions that can be used by beginning teachers to help manage student talking. Student movement skills also need to be taught. Even with college-age students, it takes instruction and two or three practices to make getting into a circle, a fishbowl formation, or small groups move smoothly. Effective classroom managers devote time in the first week or so of the school year to teaching rules and procedures and then provide periodic review as needed.

Maintaining consistency in applying rules and procedures is an aspect of classroom management that is often troublesome for beginning teachers.

Maintain Consistency. Effective classroom managers are consistent in their enforcement of rules and their application of procedures. If they are not, any set of rules and procedures soon dissolves. For example, a teacher may have a rule for student movement that says, "When you are doing seatwork and I'm at my desk, only one student at a time can come for help." If a student is allowed to wait at the desk while a first student is being helped, soon several others will be there too. If this is an important procedure for the teacher, then whenever more than one student appears, he or she must be firmly reminded of the rule and asked to sit down. If it is not important to the teacher, it should not be set forth as a rule. Another example is if a teacher has a rule that no talking is allowed when he or she is giving a presentation or explaining important ideas or procedures. If two students are then allowed to whisper in the back of the room, even if they are not disturbing others, soon many students will follow suit. Similarly, if the teacher wants students to raise their hands before talking during a discussion and then allows a few students to blurt out whenever they please, the hand-raising rule is soon rendered ineffective.

It is sometimes difficult for beginning teachers to establish consistency for at least two reasons. One, rule breaking normally occurs when more than one event is going on simultaneously. A novice teacher cannot always maintain total awareness of the complex classroom environment and thus does not always see what is occurring. Two, it takes considerable energy and even personal courage to enforce rules consistently. Many beginning teachers find it easier and less threatening to ignore certain student behavior rather than to confront and deal with it. Experienced teachers know that avoiding a difficult situation only leads to more problems later.

A dangle is when a teacher starts an activity and then leaves it in midair.

Preventing Deviant Behavior with Smoothness and Momentum. Another dimension of preventative classroom management involves pacing instructional events and maintaining appropriate **momentum.** The research by Doyle and Carter (1984) described how students can delay academic tasks, and Kounin's research (1970) pointed out the importance of keeping lessons going in a smooth fashion. Kounin also described how teachers themselves sometimes do things that interfere with the flow of activities. For example, a teacher might start an activity and then leave it in midair. Kounin labeled this type of behavior a **dangle.** A dangle occurs, for example, when a teacher asks students to hand in their notes at the end of a lecture and then suddenly decides that he or she needs to explain one more point. Teachers also slow down lessons by doing what Kounin labeled **flip-flops.** A flip-flop occurs when an activity is started and then stopped while another is begun and then the original started again. A flip-flop occurs, for example, when a teacher tells students to get out their books and start reading silently, then interrupts the reading to explain a point, and then resumes the silent reading. Dangles and flip-flops interfere with the **smoothness** of classroom activities, cause confusion on the part of some students, and most important, present opportunities for noninvolved students to misbehave.

Kounin described two frequent types of lesson slow-down behaviors—**fragmentation** and "**overdwelling.**" A teacher who goes on and on after instructions are clear to students is overdwelling. A teacher who breaks activities into overly small units, such as "sit up straight, get your papers out, pass them to the person in front, now pass them to the next person," and so on is fragmenting instructions. Slowing down momentum disrupts smoothness and gives uninvolved students opportunities to interrupt classroom activities. Table 5.3 summarizes and illustrates the common problems identified by Kounin that disrupt smoothness and momentum in lessons.

> **Fragmentation occurs when a teacher breaks a learning activity into overly small units.**

Minimizing disruptive and slow-down behaviors is difficult for beginning teachers to learn, as are many other effective management skills, because so many aspects of management are situational. Smoothness and momentum definitely vary with the nature of individual classes—what may be a dangle in one classroom may not be so in another, or what may be overdwelling with one group of students may be appropriate for another group.

> **"Overdwelling" occurs when a teacher goes on and on after a subject or a set of instructions is clear to students.**

Orchestrating Classroom Activities during Unstable Periods. Preventative classroom management also involves planning and orchestrating student behavior during unstable periods of the school day—-periods of time when order is most difficult to achieve and maintain.

Opening Class. The beginning of class, whether it is the first few minutes of the morning in an elementary classroom or the beginning of a period in secondary schools, is an unstable time. Students are coming from other settings (their homes, the playground, another class) where a different set of behavioral norms apply. The new setting has different rules and procedures as well as friends who have not been seen since the previous day. The beginning of class is also a time in most schools in which several administrative tasks are required of teachers, such as taking roll and making announcements.

Table 5.3 *Common Problems in Maintaining Smoothness and Momentum*

Problem	Definition
Dangle	Leaving a topic dangling to do something else.
Flip-flop	Starting and stopping an activity and then going back to it.
Fragmentation	Breaking instruction or activity into overly small segments.
Overdwelling	Going over and over something even after students understand it.

Effective classroom managers plan and execute procedures that help get things started quickly and surely. For example:

1. They greet their students at the door, extending welcomes to build positive feeling tones and to keep potential trouble outside the door.
2. They train student helpers to take the roll, read announcements, and perform other administrative tasks, so they can be free to start lessons.
3. They write instructions on the board or on newsprint charts so students can get started on lessons as soon as they come into the room.
4. They establish routine and ceremonial events that communicate to students that serious work is about to begin.

Transitions. Citing research of Gump (1967, 1982) and Rosenshine (1980), Doyle (1986) said that "approximately 31 major **transitions** occur per day in elementary classrooms, and they account for approximately 15 percent of classroom time" (p. 406). There are fewer transitions in secondary classrooms, but they still are numerous and take considerable time. It is during transition periods (moving from whole group to small groups, changing from listening to seatwork, getting needed materials to do an assignment, getting ready to go to recess) when many disruptions occur. Learning to handle transitions is difficult for most beginning teachers. Prior planning and the use of cuing devices are two techniques that can help.

> Transitions are the times during a lesson when the teacher is moving from one type of learning activity to another.

Planning is crucial when it comes to managing transitions. Chapter 3 described how transitions must be planned just as carefully as any other instructional activity. At first, beginning teachers should conceive of each transition as a series of steps they want students to follow. These steps should be written down in note form and, in some instances, given to the students on the chalkboard or on newsprint charts. For example, making the transition from a whole-class lecture to seatwork might include the following steps:

Step 1: Put your lecture notes away and clear your desk.
Step 2: Make sure you have pencils and a copy of the worksheet being distributed by the row monitor.
Step 3: Begin your work.
Step 4: Raise your hand if you want me to help you.

As beginning teachers become more experienced with managing transitions, they will no longer need to list the steps for minor transitions and may instead rely on clear mental images of what is required.

Cuing and signaling systems are used by effective teachers to manage difficult transition periods. The best way to understand cuing is to think of it as an alerting device similar to the yellow light on a traffic signal or the "slow" sign on a curving road. Cues are used by teachers to alert students that they are about to change activities or tasks and to start getting ready. Here are some examples of cues:

- During a small-group activity, a teacher goes around to each group and announces, "You have five minutes before returning to the whole group."
- During a discussion activity, a teacher tells students, "We must end the discussion in a few minutes, but there will be time for three more comments."
- During a laboratory experiment, the teacher says, "We have been working for twenty minutes now, and you should be at least halfway done."
- In getting ready for a guest speaker, the teacher tells the class, "Our speaker will arrive in three minutes; let's straighten up the chairs and get ready to greet her."

Many teachers also develop a signal system for alerting students to a forthcoming transition or for helping them move through the steps of a transition smoothly. Signal systems are particularly effective with younger children and in classrooms where the activities are such that it is difficult to hear the teacher. The band instructor raising his or her baton is an example of a signal for students to get quiet and ready their instruments to play the first note. Figure 5.2 shows a set of hand signals developed by one experienced teacher to alert and assist his students with difficult transitions and to check their understanding of what is being taught.

Closing Class. The closing of class is also an unstable time in most classrooms. Sometimes the teacher is rushed to complete a lesson that has run over its allocated time; sometimes materials such as tests or papers must be collected; almost always students need to get their own personal belongings ready to move to another class, the lunchroom, or the bus. Effective teachers anticipate the potential management problems associated with closing class by incorporating the following procedures into their classroom organizational patterns:

- Leaving sufficient time to complete important closing activities, such as collecting books, papers, and the like.
- Assigning homework early enough so that possible confusion can be cleared up before the last minute of class.
- Establishing routine procedures for collecting student work (such as placing a box by the door) so class time does not have to be used for this activity.
- Using alerting and cuing procedures to give students warning that the end of the class is approaching and that certain tasks need to be completed before they leave.
- Teaching older students that class will be dismissed by the teacher, not by the school bell or buzzer.

Developing Student Accountability. Every day teachers give their students assignments. Sometimes assignments are brief in duration and can be completed as seatwork. Others are more long term and require work at home. Most often, assignments provide students opportunities for practice, and this is an important aspect of the learning process, as later chapters will discuss. However, unless student work is handled consistently and unless students are held accountable for its completion, little learning will be accomplished. Therefore, an additional dimension of classroom management involves rules and procedures for managing and holding students accountable for their work. The following guidelines, which were adapted from the recommendations of Emmer, Evertson, Anderson (1980) and Evertson, Emmer, and Worsham (2002), should be incorporated into the teachers' overall preventative management plan:

1. *Communicate assignments clearly and specify work requirements.* All assignments should be communicated clearly so all students have a full understanding about what they are supposed to do. Specific requirements must be clearly described, including such things as length, due date, neatness, spelling, grading procedures, and how missed work can be made up. Verbal explanations alone usually are not sufficient for students of any age. Teachers assist clarity when they describe assignments on worksheets or post them on a chalkboard or a newsprint chart.

2. *Have procedures for monitoring student work.* It is very important for teachers to be aware of student progress once assignments have been made. For seatwork, teachers can circulate around the room to check how things are going. For longer-term assignments, breaking down the assignment into smaller parts and requiring students

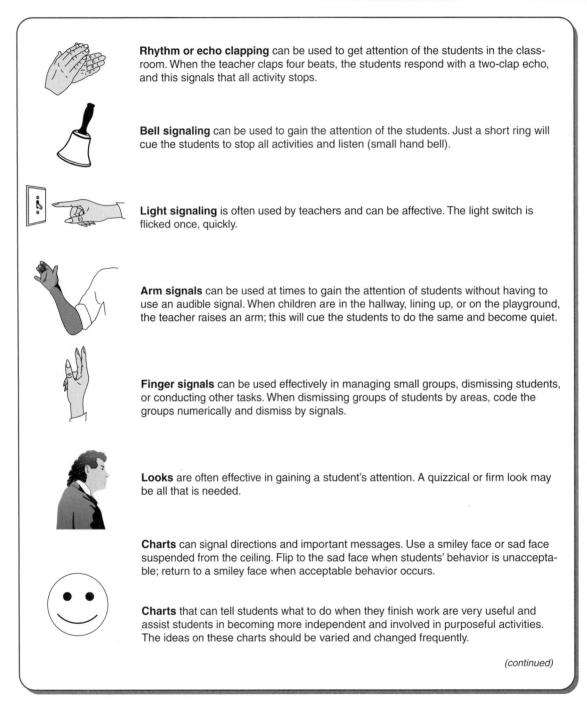

Rhythm or echo clapping can be used to get attention of the students in the classroom. When the teacher claps four beats, the students respond with a two-clap echo, and this signals that all activity stops.

Bell signaling can be used to gain the attention of the students. Just a short ring will cue the students to stop all activities and listen (small hand bell).

Light signaling is often used by teachers and can be affective. The light switch is flicked once, quickly.

Arm signals can be used at times to gain the attention of students without having to use an audible signal. When children are in the hallway, lining up, or on the playground, the teacher raises an arm; this will cue the students to do the same and become quiet.

Finger signals can be used effectively in managing small groups, dismissing students, or conducting other tasks. When dismissing groups of students by areas, code the groups numerically and dismiss by signals.

Looks are often effective in gaining a student's attention. A quizzical or firm look may be all that is needed.

Charts can signal directions and important messages. Use a smiley face or sad face suspended from the ceiling. Flip to the sad face when students' behavior is unacceptable; return to a smiley face when acceptable behavior occurs.

Charts that can tell students what to do when they finish work are very useful and assist students in becoming more independent and involved in purposeful activities. The ideas on these charts should be varied and changed frequently.

(continued)

Figure 5.2 *Examples of Signals for Communicating with Students*
Source: After Bozeman (1985)

Thumb signals can be used to respond to yes-no situations, to signal choices, and to communicate when things aren't clear.

Signal with extended thumb

Examples: Do you agree? (thumbs up); Do you disagree? (thumbs down); Not clear? (thumbs sideways)

Finger signals can be used to respond to numerical answers, multiple-choice, and true-false questions. Signal with hand against chest.

Examples: Show us how many tens are in 64.
Which word means land surrounded by water?
1. peninsula 2. island 3. continent
Which word means land surrounded by water on three sides?
1. peninsula 2. island 3. continent
Share the answer by forming the beginning symbol or letter to the answer with your fingers. (Be as creative as you can in developing signals.)

Think pads/response cards can be used to let every student answer. These responses can be written on scrap paper cut into quarters and placed in envelopes on the children's desks. Children write answers on pads or cards and hold them up to be checked by the teacher. Responses can be adapted to any subject area and any type of question. This information can serve as a pretest, a check on the prior day's work, or as a diagnostic informal assessment.

Example: Write the names of the seven (7) continents on your pads—then let me see.

Whisper signals can provide general feedback to the teacher.

Example: Point to the word as we all whisper it. Place your finger on the part that proves the answer. Whisper the number of the paragraph where the answer is found.

Head signaling can also be used to respond to a question or direction.

Example: Put your head on your desk and imagine what I am describing. Lift your head when you have the answer.

Help cards can be used to signal for assistance from the teacher or a student. When the student encounters a problem or has difficulty, he or she goes on to the next problem or activity but signals for help by placing a card on the corner of the desk. This signal will alert the teacher or a student helper to provide assistance as soon as possible. Loss of time from waiting with the hand raised is avoided and the student learns to better utilize his or her time.

Example: A student cannot spell a word, posts the help card, and continues work.

Figure 5.2 *Continued*

to file progress reports every few days helps monitor their progress. Recitations and discussions are other means for checking if students understand their assignments and if they are making satisfactory progress.

3. *Be consistent in checking students' completed work.* In most classrooms the amount of student work is enormous. Teachers need procedures for collecting assignments, such as placing baskets or trays in front of the room, and others for returning corrected work in a timely fashion. Teachers also need a system for checking all work. Sometimes, this can be accomplished by getting students to check each others' work. This is particularly appropriate for assignments for specific answers. Some assignments require careful reading by the teacher. All checking should be accomplished within a day or two after completion.

4. *Provide appropriate feedback on assignments.* Learning occurs when students receive feedback on their performance. All student work should be corrected and feedback should be given that is appropriate to the age of the students. This should occur as soon as possible after the assignment has been handed in. Often it is a good idea to spend class time going over assignments and discussing common errors or problems. Detailed guidelines for effective feedback are provided in Chapter 8.

Managing Inappropriate and Disruptive Behavior

Preventative planning and skilled orchestration of classroom activities can prevent many of the management problems faced by beginning teachers, but not all. As in other social settings, every classroom will have a few students who will choose not to involve themselves in classroom activities and, instead, be disruptive forces. Disruptions can range from students talking when they are supposed to be listening to the teacher or refusing to go along with a small-group activity to yelling at the teacher and stomping out of the room. Managing disruptive behavior calls for a special set of understandings and a special repertoire of skills.

The Causes of Misbehavior. Because beginning teachers have observed disruptive behavior in classrooms for many years as students, most can readily list the major causes of student misbehavior. These are the causes that appear on most lists: (1) students find schoolwork boring and irrelevant and try to escape it; (2) students' out-of-school lives (family or community) produce psychological and emotional problems that they play out in school; (3) students are imprisoned within schools that have authoritarian dispositions, which causes them to rebel; and (4) student rebelliousness and attention seeking are a part of the growing-up process.

Beginning teachers will want to think about the causes of inappropriate behavior, but they should beware of spending too much time on this type of analysis for two reasons. One, knowing the cause of student misbehavior, although helpful in analyzing the problem, does not necessarily lead to any change in that behavior. Two, dealing too much with psychological or sociological causes of misbehavior, particularly those that are not under the teacher's influence, can lead to acceptance and/or resignation. William Glasser (1986) made this point clearly:

> When a student is doing badly in school, we often point our fingers at a dismal home when the reason really is that the student does not find school satisfying enough for him to make an effort. There is no doubt that a student who cannot satisfy his needs at home may come to your class hungry for love and recognition and impatient that he can't quickly get what he wants. Rather than become discouraged, you should realize that if he can begin to satisfy

his needs in your class, and if you are patient enough with his impatience, he has a good chance to learn enough to lead a productive life despite his home life (p. 21).

Dealing with Misbehavior. The general approach recommended to beginning teachers for dealing with disruptive behavior is not to search zealously for causes but, instead, to focus on the misbehavior itself and to find ways to change it, at least during the period of time the student is in the classroom. This approach emphasizes the importance of teachers accurately spotting misbehavior and making quick, precise interventions.

Being With It and Overlapping. You can all remember a teacher from your own school days who seemed to have "eyes in the back of her head." Kounin calls this skill "**with-itness.**" Teachers who are with it spot deviant behavior right away and are almost always accurate in identifying the student who is responsible. Teachers who lack this skill normally do not spot misbehavior early, and they often make mistakes when assigning blame.

"**Overlappingness**" is a second skill teachers use to spot and deal with deviant behavior. Overlapping means being able to spot a student acting inappropriately and inconspicuously deal with it so the lesson is not interrupted. Moving close to an offender is one overlapping tactic effective classroom managers use. Putting a hand on the shoulder of a student who is talking to his neighbor while continuing with instructions about how to do a project is another. Integrating a question intended to delay instruction or a "smart" remark right into an explanation about Edgar Allen Poe's syntax is a third example of overlappingness.

With-it and overlapping skills are difficult to learn because they call for quick, accurate reading of classroom situations and the ability to perform several different teaching behaviors simultaneously. Once learned, however, they ensure more smoothly running lessons and classrooms.

Responding Quickly to Desist Incidences. In classrooms, just as in any social setting, there are some participants who commit deviant acts. An example of deviant behavior

Teachers who can spot disruptive student behavior quickly and accurately are called "with-it."

Enhancing Teaching with Technology

Technology as a Management Tool

Computers and recording technologies can assist teachers in achieving effective classroom management in several important ways. Computers can be used to orchestrate classroom activities during unstable periods and provide needed assistance during downtimes. Audio- and video-recording devices can help teachers identify and deal with inappropriate or disruptive classroom behavior and serve as a communication tool with parents.

Effective teachers have found that they can use the computer and projection devices to help manage students when they are moving from one type of learning activity to another. For example, the signals for communicating with students illustrated in Figure 5.2 can be programmed into the computer and flashed on a screen at an appropriate time. These electronic messages and signals are more readily observed in a busy classroom than are the teacher's voice and/or hand signals. They are also less intrusive than light and bell signals used by many teachers.

Prior to the availability of computers, teachers kept a variety of motivational books, games, and puzzles available for students who finished their work before most of their classmates because they knew that *idle hands* get in trouble quickly. Today, a favorite means of keeping students occupied during these times is to let them work on computers. A variety of educational software and websites provide learning activities students can pursue on their own. Many of these have gamelike and educational qualities. They are highly motivational and provide excellent means for students to pursue their own learning without the teacher's direct supervision.

To deal with disruptive students, teachers must become careful observers and recorders of inappropriate student behavior. This aspect of behavior management is usually recommended by special education professionals and is very important when teachers use positive and negative reinforcement. The premise is that by recording student behavior, teachers can recognize patterns of misbehavior and its relationship to certain events or times of day. This information can lead teachers to a better understanding of a student's behavior and better use of rein-

forcement schedules or more preventative management strategies.

One useful strategy for recording student behavior is an approach called *ABC* (*a*ntecedents-*b*ehaviors-*c*onsequences) analysis. Following is an example of ABC analysis provided by special educators Friend and Bursuck (2002):

Ms. Carlisle is observing Carlos. When the class is directed to form cooperative groups (*antecedent*), Carlos gets up from his seat and heads for the pencil sharpener (*behavior*). Ms. Carlisle tells Carlos to join the group (*consequence*). By keeping an ongoing ABC log of Carlos's behavior, Ms. Carlisle found out that whenever the class is transitioning from one activity to another, Carlos is likely to be off task (p. 456).

Recording student behavior with so many other things going on is burdensome for the typical classroom teacher. However, several kinds of technologies can be used to ease this burden. For instance, a file can be created on a laptop computer for keeping records and chronological ordering of ABC analysis. Event or wrist counters, such as those used to keep score in golf, can be used to keep track of particular student behaviors. For example, the teacher could click every time a student such as Carlos got out of his seat inappropriately. Similarly, a tape or video recorder can be used to record a student's inappropriate verbal behavior. This type of recording can then be used to discuss the behavior with the student and, when appropriate, with parents. However, a note of caution is in order about using recording devices—in some communities they may be negatively received.

Finally, e-mail and cell-phone technologies make communication with parents or guardians about student behavior much easier to accomplish. E-mail, for example, makes it possible to inform many parents on a moment's notice about both positive behavior and behaviors that have been disruptive. This type of parent communication and involvement, as well as other examples provided in later chapters, can increase student achievement and improve parents' relationships with the teacher and the school.

on the freeway is driving ten or fifteen miles an hour above the speed limit; in church, it might be falling asleep during the sermon; in a library, it is talking loudly while others are trying to study. Those charged with the responsibility of enforcing rules and procedures may or may not choose to respond to each occurrence of deviancy. For example, most highway patrol officers will not stop a motorist for going seventy miles an hour on the freeway where the speed limit is sixty-five; most ministers don't confront a single parishioner who falls asleep; and those who talk very softly in libraries will probably not be reprimanded by the librarian. There are times, however, when those in charge will choose to respond to deviant behaviors. Kounin called this a **desist incident,** meaning an incident serious enough that, if not dealt with, will lead to further and widening management problems. Desist incidents are identified and dealt with in the business of classroom management.

A desist incident is a classroom occurrence serious enough that if not dealt with, will lead to widening management problems.

Teachers respond to desist incidents in a variety of ways. Kounin (1970) identified several teacher **desist behaviors.** Three of these behaviors are illustrated in Table 5.4. Drawing on the work of Kounin, several different groups of procedures have been developed to deal with student misbehavior and to bring student attention back to a lesson once it has strayed. These include the Jones Model, Evertson and Emmer's model, and the LEAST model. The procedures for each model are summarized in Table 5.5. As you can see, the Jones model is primarily nonverbal and is useful for minor misbehavior. Procedures recommended by Evertson and Emmer concentrate on stopping inappropriate behaviors swiftly and making sure students understand what they are doing wrong. The LEAST model (an acronym for the steps teachers follow) includes procedures for minor misbehaviors as well as more serious problems that need to be handled over a period of time. Effective teachers create procedures that work for them, and these likely will include aspects of each of the models.

Using Rewards. A rather well-established principle in psychology is that when certain behaviors are *reinforced,* they tend to be repeated; conversely, behaviors that are not reinforced tend to decrease or disappear. This principle holds true for classrooms and provides teachers with one means for managing student behavior. The key to using **reinforcement principles** to influence student behavior obviously rests on the teacher's ability to (1) identify desirable behaviors, (2) identify appropriate reinforcers, and (3) skillfully use these reinforcers to strengthen and encourage desired behaviors.

Table 5.4 *Examples of Teacher Desist Behaviors*

Clarity—The degree to which a teacher specifies what is wrong.
Unclear desist:	"Stop that!"
Clear desist:	"Do not sharpen your pencil while I am talking."

Firmness—The degree to which a teacher communicates "I mean it."
Unfirm desist:	"Please don't do that."
Firm desist:	"I absolutely will not tolerate that from you!"

Roughness—The degree to which a teacher expresses anger.
Unrough desist:	"You shouldn't do that anymore."
Rough desist:	"When you do that, I get angry and I intend to punish you."

Table 5.5 *Three Models for Dealing with Student Misbehavior*

Jones	Evertson and Emmer	LEAST
1. Move close to where student is sitting.	1. Ask the student to stop the inappropriate behavior. Teacher maintains contact with child until appropriate behavior is correctly performed.	1. **L**eave it alone. Is the behavior going to become troublesome? If not, ignore it.
2. Make eye contact.	2. Make eye contact with student until appropriate behavior returns. This is suitable when the teacher is certain the student knows what the correct response is.	2. **E**nd the action indirectly. Distract the student from the misbehavior by giving him or her something to do, preferably in a different area.
3. Provide gentle pat on the shoulder, if needed.	3. Restate or remind the student of the correct rule or procedure.	3. **A**ttend more fully. Get to know the student better before you decide on a course of action. Is there something disturbing happening at home? Is there some kind of learning problem?
4. Keep pace and momentum of lesson going.	4. Ask the student to identify the correct procedure. Give feedback if the student does not understand it.	4. **S**pell out directions. Remind the student of what he or she should be doing. If necessary, also remind him or her about the consequences for failing to comply.
	5. Impose the consequence or penalty of rule or procedure violation. Usually, the consequence for violating a procedure is simply to perform the procedure until it is correctly done.	5. **T**rack the behavior. If this is a continuing problem, keep systematic records of the behavior and your actions to correct it. This can evolve into a contract with the student.
	6. Change the activity. Frequently, off-task behavior occurs when students are engaged too long in repetitive, boring tasks or in aimless recitations. Injecting variety is appropriate when off-task behavior spreads throughout a class.	

Praise is the reward most readily available for teachers. However, praise must be used appropriately to be effective.

Praise. The reinforcer most readily available to the classroom teacher is *praise.* However, there are important guidelines for the effective use of praise. For example, general praise, such as "great job," "oh, that's wonderful," or "excellent" is not very effective. Nor is insincere praise apt to have the desired effect. Jere Brophy reviewed a massive amount of research on the subject of praise and came up with the guidelines for teachers described in Table 5.6 (Brophy, 1981, Brophy and Good, 1986).

Table 5.6 *Guidelines for Effective Praise*

Effective Praise	Ineffective Praise
Is specific	Is global and general
Attends to students' accomplishments	Rewards mere participation
Helps students appreciate their accomplishments	Compares students with others
Attributes success to effort and ability	Attributes success to luck
Focuses attention on task-relevant behavior	Focuses attention on external authority

Rewards and Privileges. Teachers can also encourage desirable behaviors through granting *rewards* and *privileges* to students. Rewards teachers have at their disposal include:

- Points for certain kinds of work or behavior that can enhance a student's grade.
- Symbols such as gold stars, happy faces, or certificates of accomplishment.
- Special honor rolls for academic work and social conduct.

Privileges that are at the command of most teachers to bestow include:

- Serving as a class leader or helper who takes notes to the office, collects or passes out papers, grades papers, runs the movie projector, and the like.
- Extra time for recess.
- Special time to work on a special individual project.
- Being excused from some required work.
- Free reading time.

A carefully designed system of rewards and privileges can help immensely in encouraging some types of behavior and reducing others. However, rewards and privileges will not solve all classroom management problems, and beginning teachers should be given two warnings: First, what is a reward or a privilege for some students will not be perceived as such by others. The age of students obviously is a factor; family, ethnic, and geographical background are others. Effective teachers generally involve their students in identifying rewards and privileges in order to ensure their effectiveness. Second, an overemphasis on extrinsic rewards can interfere with the teacher's efforts to promote academic work for its own sake and to help students practice and grow in self-discipline and management.

> An overemphasis on external rewards can hinder student growth in self-management.

Coercive Punishment and Penalties. Rewards and privileges are used to reinforce and strengthen desirable behaviors. *Punishments* and *penalties* are used to discourage infractions of important rules and procedures. Socially acceptable punishments and penalties available to teachers are, in fact, rather limited and include:

- Taking points away for misbehavior that, in turn, affects students' grades.
- Making the student stay in from recess or after school for detention.
- Removing privileges.
- Expelling from class or sending a student to a counselor or administrator.

Beginning teachers should be careful about the types of punishments and penalties they establish. Researchers from the University of Texas offer the guidelines found in Figure 5.3.

Check, Extend, Explore

Check
- What are the major steps teachers can take to prevent classroom management problems?
- What specific classroom times seem to lead to discipline problems? Why?
- What are some actions teachers commonly practice that can disrupt the momentum of lessons?
- What is the general approach for dealing with students who are disruptive? Do you agree? Why or why not?
- What factors should a teacher consider to effectively use a reward system?

Extend
- Do you agree or disagree with the proposition that students are inherently good and that misbehavior stems from the way classrooms are structured and managed? Go to the "Extend Question Poll" on the Online Learning Center to respond.

Explore
- Go to the Online Learning Center at www.mhhe.com/arends6e for links to websites related to *Effective Classroom Management Strategies.*

1. Use reductions in grade or score for assignment- or work-related behaviors such as missing or incomplete work.
2. Use a fine or demerit system to handle repeated violations of rules and procedures, particularly those involving willful refusal to comply with reasonable requests. Given them one warning, and if the behavior persists, assess a fine or demerit.
3. If you have a student who frequently receives penalties, try to set a more positive tone. Help the student formulate a plan to stop the inappropriate behavior.
4. Limit the use of penalties such as fines or checks to easily observable behaviors that represent major or chronic infractions of rules and procedures. The reason for this limitation is that penalty systems work only when they are used consistently. In order for this to take place, you must be able to detect the misbehavior when it occurs. If you cannot, you will find yourself constantly trying to catch students who misbehave.
5. Keep your classroom positive and supportive. Penalties should serve mainly as deterrents and should be used sparingly. Try to rely on rewards and personal encouragement to maintain good behavior.

Figure 5.3 *Guidelines for the Use of Penalties*
Source: After Emmer et al. (2002)

Classroom Management Programs

Over the past two decades, a spate of classroom management programs has been developed by psychologists, researchers, and educational practitioners. These programs stem from a specific theory or perspective and require schoolwide participation. Program creators develop materials to help teachers understand the program, and they provide training on how to use it. Though the effectiveness of particular programs has not always been studied, these programs nonetheless have been adopted and used widely. Four of these programs are described here to give beginning teachers a cursory understanding of what they may be confronted with in student teaching or their first teaching position.

Traditional Programs Based on Reinforcement Theory

Assertive Discipline. Some classroom management and discipline programs have been built around the central concepts of the teacher acting in confident and assertive ways toward student misbehavior and administering predetermined penalties for infractions of classroom rules. During the past fifteen years, one of the more popular programs based on these ideas has been developed by Lee Canter and Marlene Canter (1976, 2002). Called **assertive discipline,** the Canters' program maintains that teachers can gain control of their classrooms by insisting on appropriate student behavior and by responding assertively to student infractions.

"The hardest part about goin' back to school is learning how to whisper again."

Source: ©Bill Keane, Inc. Reprinted with special permission of King Features Syndicate.

Teachers (and sometimes whole schools) trained in assertive discipline start by developing a set of classroom and school rules deemed necessary for learning to occur. Consequences for disobedience are also clearly specified in advance. Students and their parents are then given clear explanations of these rules, and the consequences for infractions are explained. The Canters stress the importance of teachers following through with their rules, being consistent with administering consequences, and expecting support from parents.

The Assertive Response Style. At the center of the Canters' approach is their belief that teachers should respond to student misbehavior with an assertive style instead of responding passively or in hostile ways. Responding to student misbehavior with a rhetorical question such as, "Why are you doing that?" is an example of a passive style. A passive teacher, according to the Canters, is not using interpersonal influence effectively and appears wishy-washy to students. A hostile teacher, on the other hand, often responds angrily to student misbehavior and makes threats such as, "You'll be sorry you did that," or tries to produce guilt such as, "You should be ashamed of yourself." Passive and hostile styles are not effective, according to the Canters. Teachers who use a passive style are not communicating clearly to students what they expect, and the hostile style often produces meaningless threats that are difficult to enforce.

The assertive style calls for teachers to be very clear about their expectations and to respond to student misbehavior firmly and confidently. Teachers are counseled to specify the misbehaving student by name and to keep eye contact with the student. The Canters maintain that teachers should not accept excuses from misbehaving students. They argue that even though students may have inadequate parenting, special health problems, or great stress in their lives, these unfortunate circumstances should not excuse students from acting appropriately in the classroom or taking responsibility for their own behavior.

Consequences. Under the Canter approach, consequences are kept simple and are designed so their implementation will not cause severe disruption to ongoing instructional

Assertive discipline is an approach to classroom management that emphasizes teachers insisting on appropriate student behavior and responding assertively to student infractions.

activities. Cangelosi (1999) reported one example of an assertive discipline program in a particular junior high school:

1. Each classroom teacher specifies for students the rules for classroom conduct.
2. The first time each day a student violates a rule during a particular class session, the teacher writes the student's name on a designated area of a chalkboard. The number of the rule that was violated is put next to the name. The teacher does not say anything.
3. The second time a student violates a rule (not necessarily the same rule), the number of that rule is added to the student's name on the board. Again, the teacher makes no other response to the off-task behavior.
4. Upon the third violation of the rules in the same class period, the student must leave the class and report to a detention room.
5. There are no penalties or requirements for students who have no more than one violation during any one class period.
6. Students with two violations are required to meet with the teacher after school to discuss the misbehavior and map out a plan for preventing recurrences.
7. The parent of students with three violations must appear at school to discuss the misbehavior and make plans for preventing recurrences (pp. 32–33).

Though the Canters' approach has been very popular, it also has its critics. Some teachers find it difficult to administer consequences without significantly disrupting their instructional programs. It takes time and energy, for instance, to write names on the chalkboard and to keep track of rule infractions. Also, some believe that the behavioristic approach behind assertive discipline puts too much emphasis on penalties and teacher-made rules and not enough emphasis on involving students in establishing their own classroom rules and learning how to be responsible for self-discipline. Finally, assertive discipline has not been evaluated thoroughly, and its effectiveness remains unclear.

Dreikurs' Logical Consequences. Chapter 4 provided a description about how people's behavior can be attributed to goal-directed activity aimed at satisfying human motives and needs. Dreikurs and his colleagues (1968, 1988), developed an approach to classroom discipline based on the idea that most student behavior, acceptable and unacceptable, stems from the fundamental need to belong and to feel worthwhile. According to Dreikurs, when the need to belong or feel worthwhile is frustrated through socially acceptable channels, students misbehave. Dreikurs categorized this misbehavior into four types: (1) attention getting, (2) power seeking, (3) revenge seeking, and (4) displays of inadequacy. Each instance requires a different response from the teacher. If a student is trying to get attention, the best thing to do, according to Dreikurs, is to ignore the behavior. If the student is trying to upstage or gain power over the teacher, the teacher should decline to get involved in the power struggle and try instead to find a way to give the student more influence and responsibility.

The Dreikurs approach is still used in some schools. Teachers trained in the approach learn how to identify the type of student misbehavior partly by getting in touch with their own emotional response. If the teacher feels "bugged," it is likely the student is seeking attention; if the teacher is getting angry, perhaps it is because the student is seeking power. Trained teachers also learn how to administer **logical consequences** according to the type of misguided goal behind the student's behavior. Logical consequences are punishments related directly to a misbehavior rather than the more general penalties of detention or reprimands used in many classrooms. Mak-

Logical consequences are punishments administered for misbehavior that are directly related to the infraction.

ing a student who wrote on the bathroom wall repaint the wall is a classic example of a logical consequence.

The Dreikurs approach emphasizes the importance of democratic classrooms in which students have a say in making the rules. Dreikurs views the logical consequence of misbehavior as more than just arbitrary punishment. He encourages teachers to administer logical consequences in a friendly and matter-of-fact manner, without elements of moral judgment. The long-range goal of this approach to discipline is to have students understand the reasons for their misbehavior and find ways to satisfy their self-worth and affiliation needs in socially acceptable ways.

The difficulties teachers have with the Dreikurs approach are twofold. Without extensive training, some find it difficult to develop the skill in identifying the specific motive that is causing the student to misbehave. Others find it difficult to identify logical consequences for many misbehaviors that occur in classrooms. For instance, what is the logical consequence for speaking out of turn? For sassing the teacher? For smoking in the halls or carrying a weapon to school? Nonetheless, some teachers who possess the necessary counseling skills have found the Dreikurs approach a powerful tool for dealing with disruptive students and helping them develop self-management skills.

Programs That Aim Toward Self-Management and Community

There are also classroom management programs that have been built on premises stemming from humanistic psychology and child-centered, constructivist principles of teaching and learning.

Glasser's Classroom Meeting. Trained first as an engineer and later as a physician and clinical psychologist, William Glasser (1969, 1986, 1992) has devoted much of his professional life to finding ways to make schools more satisfying and productive for students. Like Dreikurs, Glasser believes that most classroom problems stem from a failure to satisfy the basic need of students. In his early work, Glasser emphasized students' need for love and feelings of self-worth; in his later work, he expanded his list of basic needs to include survival and reproduction, belonging and love, power and influence, freedom and fun. Whereas Dreikurs proposes counseling and individual attention as a way to help students find ways to satisfy their needs, Glasser believes that school structures need to be modified. He proposed the **classroom meeting,** a regular thirty-minute nonacademic period in which teachers and students discuss and find cooperative solutions to personal and behavior problems and in which students learn how to take responsibility for their own behavior and their personal and social development.

> Classroom meetings are an approach to classroom management in which the teacher holds regular meetings for the purpose of helping students identify and resolve problem situations.

Running Classroom Meetings. A Glasser classroom meeting consists of six steps, or phases (see Table 5.7). Note that for each phase there are specific things teachers need to do to make the meeting go successfully. In addition, there are several aspects of the total learning environment that need attention. When the classroom meeting is first being introduced and taught to students, the teacher keeps the learning environment tightly structured. More and more freedom can be given to students as they become successful in meetings. The teacher must maintain responsibility for ensuring participation, keeping student problem solving focused, and providing overall leadership. Usually, the teacher acts as discussion leader and asks students to sit in a circle during the classroom meetings. However, with younger students, participants sometimes sit on the floor, and with older students, the role of discussion leader is sometimes assumed by a student in the class.

Table 5.7 *Syntax for the Glasser Classroom Meeting*

Phase	Teacher Behavior
Phase 1: Establish the climate.	Using many of the strategies and procedures described in Chapter 4, the teacher establishes a climate in which all students feel free to participate and to share opinions and feedback.
Phase 2: Identify problems.	Teacher asks students to sit in a circle. Either the teacher or the students can bring up problems. Teacher should make sure that problems are described fully and in nonevaluative ways. Specific examples of the problems are encouraged.
Phase 3: Make value judgments.	After a specific problem has been identified, the teacher asks students to express their own values about the problem and the behaviors associated with it.
Phase 4: Identify courses of action.	Teacher asks students to suggest alternative behaviors or procedures that might help solve the problem and to agree on one to try out.
Phase 5: Make a public commitment.	Teachers asks students to make a public commitment to try out the new behaviors or procedures.
Phase 6: Provide follow-up and assessment.	At a later meeting, the problem is again discussed to see how effectively it is being solved and whether commitments have been kept.

Suggestions for Starting and Running Classroom Meetings. Effective execution of classroom meetings requires specific teacher actions before, during, and after the meeting. As much care and concern must go into planning and executing meetings as any other aspect of instruction.

Planning. In preparation for classroom meetings, teachers need to think through what they want the meeting to accomplish and have some problems ready for discussion in case none comes from students. Most important, overall planning must allow time for classroom meetings on a regular basis.

In elementary schools, many teachers who use classroom meetings start each day with this activity; others schedule it as a way to close each day; still others schedule classroom meetings on a weekly basis. In most middle and high schools, teachers schedule meetings less frequently, perhaps thirty minutes every other Friday, with special meetings if serious problems arise. The frequency of meetings is not as important as their regularity.

Conducting the Meeting. On the surface, the classroom meeting may look fairly simple and easy to conduct. In reality, it is very complex and calls for considerable skill on the part of the teacher. If a beginning teacher is in a school where classroom meetings are common and students already understand their basic purposes and procedures, then the teacher can start meetings at the beginning of school. If not, then the recommendation is for beginning teachers to wait for a few weeks before introducing classroom meetings to students.

Most of the student and teacher skills needed for successful meetings are described elsewhere in *Learning to Teach*, particularly in Chapters 4 and 12. Some are repeated here, as they specifically relate to each phase of the classroom meeting:

1. *Establishing climate.* Before classroom meetings can be successful, the overall climate must be one that encourages participation in free and nonpunitive ways. Students also must be prepared in the appropriate mind-set to make meetings productive. Although classroom meetings can be used to build this kind of productive environment, some degree of trust must exist before meetings can be implemented. Many of the activities described in Chapter 4 are preludes to implementing classroom meetings.

2. *Identifying problems.* Students who have not been involved in classroom meetings need to be taught what constitutes a legitimate problem for the meeting. Problem-solving techniques can be taught, including giving students time to practice stating a problem, giving examples of a problem, and identifying the descriptive and value dimensions of a problem.

3. *Dealing with values.* The values surrounding most classroom behavior problems are very important, especially differences regarding the value of academic work. Put bluntly, some students do not value academic work as much as teachers do. At the same time, teachers may find an amazing similarity of values across racial, ethnic, and social-class lines regarding other aspects of classroom behavior. For example, most students, even at a very young age, see the moral and practical necessity of such rules as taking turns, listening, and showing respect to others. They also readily embrace most procedures that ensure safety and fairness. The classroom meeting can become an important forum for talking about value similarities and differences.

4. *Identifying alternative courses of action.* Except for very young children, most students can readily identify courses of action they, their teacher, or their classmates can take to resolve all kinds of classroom management problems. They know the reasons for rewarding desirable behavior and punishing disruptive behavior, and they also know the shortcomings of relying too heavily on these strategies. They even know what sort of alternative actions are available in classroom settings. During this phase of the classroom meeting, the teacher's primary role is to listen to alternative proposals, make sure everyone understands each one, and push for some type of consensus about which action students are willing to take. The teacher must also be clear and straightforward with students if a proposed action is definitely unacceptable, particularly if it goes against school policy. However, this does not exclude student efforts to get school policies changed.

5. *Making a public commitment.* A public commitment is nothing more than a promise by students, and in some instances the teacher, that certain attempts are going to be made to correct problem situations. Many teachers write these commitments on newsprint charts so that everyone in the class can remember them.

6. *Follow-up and assessment.* Once students have made a commitment to try out a new set of procedures and behaviors, it is very important that these commitments be followed and assessed. Specifically, teachers must remember the public commitments that were made and periodically come back to them in future classroom meetings. If commitments are not being kept or if the planned actions are not solving the problem, then additional time and energy must be given to the problem.

Conducting a classroom meeting calls for considerable skill on the part of teachers. The rewards of this approach, however, are worth the effort.

The Caring Classroom

Finally, programs have been developed on constructivist, child-centered principles that aim at building threat-free learning communities and helping students make their own choices and develop self-management. These programs, advocated by reformers such as Charney (1993), Kohn (1996), Noddings (1992, 2001), and Oakes and Lipton (2003), are more difficult to describe in a textbook than traditional classroom management programs. This is true because their developers emphasize no single alternative to more traditional approaches but instead argue that the alternatives are endless. Consistent with their perspective, constructivist, child-centered educators do not believe that their approach can be anchored in a set of simple recipes. However, they have enunciated principles for teachers to follow, such as those outlined by Kohn (1996):

- Act in ways that are socially just.
- Develop authentic relationships free of power and control.
- Allow students to construct moral meaning.
- Limit structures and procedures.
- Give students a say and have them solve problems together.

The meaning of teaching in socially just ways has been described by Oakes and Lipton (2003) as creating classrooms where teachers stand up for social justice and work to change the inequities that exist in the educational system. All talk and action in the classroom is aimed at understanding and working toward social justice. Here is what two teachers had to say about this perspective and its meaning for their approach to classroom management:

> I intend to break the cycle of an educational system that treats my current and future students as children who need to be controlled and "schooled." I intend to take advantage of my students' open-mindedness and susceptibility to instill in them a strong sense of social responsibility. My teaching means nothing if I am not leaving my students with unforgettable experiences and transformative dialogues through which they view themselves as conscious, competent participants in some larger reality—a community, which has the potential of being transformed only through their collaborative efforts (Oakes & Lipton, p. 32).
>
> As a first-year teacher, I also cannot get discouraged if I am not able to create a socially just and democratic classroom in two weeks, or two months. The fact that the journey is a difficult one signifies its existence. I should keep this in mind and not get discouraged or overwhelmed. If you are passionately acting towards a just and transformative ideal, then you are a social justice advocate (Oakes & Lipton, p. 33).

Developing authentic, caring relationships free of power and control is another principle that guides teachers in caring, child-centered classrooms. This means creating the type of learning community described in Chapter 4 in which teachers care for students and students care for each other in an atmosphere of participation and trust. These conditions can best be achieved if teachers limit the structure and procedures imposed on students. Kohn (1996), for example, says structures and restrictions should meet certain criteria. They are okay if they protect students, provide for flexibility, are developmentally appropriate, and lead to student involvement. They are inappropriate if they are simply to impose order or quiet voices, for adults only, or are developmentally inappropriate.

Finally, educators who argue for caring, child-centered classrooms have recommendations for dealing with disruptive and misbehaving students. Note the differences between Kohn's suggestions found in Table 5.8 and those described early in this chapter.

Kohn's suggestions emphasize the importance of building a relationship, joining in mutual problem solving, and keeping punishments to a minimum.

Table 5.8 *Kohn's Ten Suggestions for Dealing with Disruptive or Misbehaving Students*

Relationship	It is not possible to work with students who have done something wrong unless a trusting relationship has been developed.
Skills	Teachers need to help students develop the skills to solve problems and resolve conflicts. These would include listening skills and the ability to calm themselves and take another's point of view.
Diagnose	Teachers need to make sure they are accurately interpreting what is going on and are able to help students do their own analysis.
Question practices	Teachers need to look at their own practices and ask themselves if they are the cause of the misbehavior.
Maximize student involvement	Teachers need to be constantly on the lookout for ways to expand the role students play in making decisions.
Construct authentic solutions	Teachers and students need to develop real solutions to complex problems and not just a solution that can be done quickly.
Make restitution	Teachers should help students think about how they can make restitution and reparations for truly destructive actions.
Check back later	Teachers should encourage students to check back later to see if the solution and agreements are working.
Flexibility	Good problem solving for difficult situations requires flexibility about logistics and substance.
Minimize punitive impact	Sometimes there is no alternative to punishment. When that is the case, every effort should be made to minimize punishment through warm and regretful tones and confidence that problems eventually can be solved.

Source: Kohn (1996), p. 47

Check, Extend, Explore

Check
- What are the advantages and disadvantages of the assertive discipline approach in the classroom?
- How does Dreikurs explain misbehavior? In what ways do logical consequences teach a student to behave appropriately?
- What teacher activities does Glasser's classroom meeting model require for successful classroom management? What factors contribute to a favorable meeting?
- What principles guide classroom management from a child-centered perspective?
- Contrast Kohn's suggestion for dealing with disruptive behavior with the Canters' recommendations.

Extend
- What are your personal opinions about behavioral approaches such as assertive discipline?
- Do you think child-centered approaches to classroom management will work? Go to the "Extend Question Poll" on the Online Learning Center to respond.

Explore
- Go to the Online Learning Center at www.mhhe.com/arends6e for links to websites related to *Programs and Resources on Classroom Management.*

A Final Thought and Look to the Future

As with so many other aspects of teaching, approaches to classroom management are in a state of transition at the beginning of the twenty-first century. What this means for a beginning teacher is that you will likely get your first job in a school where very traditional views of learning and classroom management prevail. Perhaps students will be treated as passive receptacles for teacher-constructed knowledge, and they will be expected to do what the adults in the school tell them to do. At the same time, many of you and others like you will have been influenced by a constructivist view of teaching and learning that holds that teachers should help students take active roles in constructing their own intellectual and moral meaning. This approach to teaching requires a different kind of classroom management system. It requires developing caring, learning communities in which students have a say in what they do and how they behave. It requires spending less time controlling students and more time helping them think for themselves and care for others. This will be the challenge of teaching and providing leadership for twenty-first-century classrooms.

Reflections **from the** *Classroom*

The Out-of-Control Classroom

A teacher in the school where you have just finished your student teaching has resigned at mid-year for personal reasons. The principal has asked if you would be willing to take her place until the end of the academic year. You are pleased to have been asked, but you also know that the class has been completely out of control. You have observed students in the class fighting with one another. Other teachers have told you that the resigning teacher found the class impossible to manage: Students talk when they should be listening; they get up and move around the classroom regardless of what is going on; they are unruly and disrespectful. It is even rumored that this out-of-control situation is the reason behind the teacher's sudden departure. You know that if you take the position and are unsuccessful, your reputation and chances for future jobs will be ruined. Nonetheless, you decide that you can do it. But now you have to decide where to start and what to do.

Write a reflective essay about this situation that can be used in your portfolio to let others know your overall views and approach to classroom management. Approach this situation from the perspective closest to the grade level or subject area you are preparing to teach. Consider the following questions as you think through this problem: What are your long-range goals for this group of students? What specific problems would you tackle first? Would you lean toward dealing with this situation using behavioral approaches? Or would you strive toward working toward self-management? When you have finished your portfolio entry, compare your views with the following ideas expressed by two experienced teachers.

(continued)

Amy Callen
Lyndon Pilot School, 4th and 5th Grade
Boston, MA

Dealing with an out of control classroom can be extremely taxing for any teacher, but especially so for new teachers. In accepting this position, you have not only taken on the responsibility of teaching these students what is required of them but also teaching them how to become respectful members of the school and classroom community. It is important to walk into this situation with realistic expectations. Do not expect to work miracles overnight. Create small, achievable goals for yourself and for them.

Begin by doing your research. A good place to start is Ruth Charney's *Responsive Classroom.* This is an excellent social curriculum that clearly outlines effective management practices. Talk to the teachers who have had these students in the past and find out what has worked for them. Finally, plan your days carefully. Avoid finding yourself at 2:00 with nothing to do. It is better to have too much planned than not enough.

Your first few days should be spent creating a tone in the classroom. Do not let yourself be thrown by inappropriate and disrespectful behavior. Deal with it calmly and consistently. In some instances, you may want to ignore it. It is important to choose your battles. Academics will happen, but they should not be the focus at first. Tasks that are teacher directed are best. Whole class activities or individual seatwork (reading, writing, math, etc.) have worked really well for me in the past. Before you begin each of these activities, explicit instructions regarding what is expected will be necessary. At the end of each working session be sure to compliment those students who worked effectively.

By the end of the first week you should hope to have created a list of "rules" with the class. These rules or expectations should be displayed prominently in the classroom and always stated in the positive. Consequences for behaving outside of the expectations should be logical, fair, meaningful, and consistent to the students.

Over the course of the year, keep your assignments concise, make your expectations clear, and recognize positive behaviors. In time, the children will see that you are fair, consistent, and trustworthy and will strive to emulate the positive behavior that you are modeling.

Peter Fernandez
9th Grade

I do not know all of the reasons that this class has gotten out of control. However, I suspect three culprits—a curriculum not matched to the needs of the students, a lack of any kind of management system, and perhaps a teacher who didn't care for the students all that much. Here is what I would do. . . .

Before I accept the job, I would have a long meeting with the principal, explain my classroom management philosophy, and ask for her support. I would describe changes that would have to be made in the curriculum and in the overall structure of the classroom. If her support was not forthcoming, I would not accept the position.

If she agreed to my approach, I would do three things. First, I would tell the students that I expected to win their respect and that I think they would be happier and learn more if we all got along with each other. I would spend at least one hour every morning for as long as it takes teaching students how to talk to one another and how to resolve conflicts. I would start formal "problem-solving groups" for the purpose of giving students a say in classroom rules and in what they are expected to learn. I would spend a lot of time getting students to talk about what they think is wrong and what they think we should do about it.

Second, I would spend time talking to students, trying to discover their interests and prior knowledge. The day-to-day curriculum would then be built around their interests and knowledge.

Finally, I would ask all of the parents to come to school to discuss the class. They likely know that things have been out of control. I would explain my approach, ask for their suggestions, and then close with some concrete steps they can take at home to help their sons or daughters become more effective students.

Chapter Review

Go back to the "Interactive and Applied Learning" feature at the beginning of the chapter for a listing of interactive and applied activities. Go to the Online Learning Center at **www.mhhe.com/arends6e** or your Interactive Student CD-ROM to take practice quizzes over the content of this chapter and receive immediate feedback. You can also review chapter content and main ideas, practice with key terms, and find annotated Web links on topics associated with this chapter.

Summary

Perspective on Classroom Management

- Classroom management is not an end in itself but a part of a teacher's overall leadership role.
- Managerial and instructional aspects of teaching are highly interrelated and cannot be clearly separated in real-life teaching.
- Unless classroom management issues can be solved, the best teaching is wasted, thus making it possibly the most important challenge facing beginning teachers.

Theoretical and Empirical Support

- A well-developed knowledge base on classroom management provides guidelines for successful group management as well as ways of dealing with disruptive students.
- A large portion of disruptive student behavior can be eliminated by using preventative classroom management measures, such as clear rules and procedures and carefully orchestrated learning activities.
- "With-itness," momentum, "overlappingness," smoothness, and group alerting all increase student work involvement and decrease off-task behavior and management problems.
- Effective managers have well-defined procedures that govern student talk and movement, make work requirements clear to students, and emphasize clear explanations.
- Researchers in the child-centered tradition study how teachers develop threat-free learning communities that allow students to make choices and develop self-management.

Preparing for Effective Classroom Management

- Effective managers establish clear rules and procedures, teach these rules and procedures to students, and carefully orchestrate classroom activities during such unstable periods as the beginning and end of class and transitions.

- Effective managers develop systems for holding students accountable for their academic work and classroom behavior.
- Regardless of planning and orchestration skills, teachers are still often faced with difficult or unmotivated students who choose to be disruptive forces rather than involve themselves in academic activity.
- Effective managers have intervention skills for dealing quickly with disruptive students in direct but fair ways.
- Teachers can encourage desirable behaviors by giving praise and granting rewards and punishments.
- Specific approaches to classroom management, such as assertive discipline, emphasize the importance of being clear about expectations and consistent in administering consequences.

Classroom Management Programs

- In the long run, effective teachers find ways to reduce management and discipline problems by helping students learn self-management skills.
- As with other teaching functions, effective teachers develop an attitude of flexibility about classroom management, because they know that every class is different and plans, rules, and procedures must often be adjusted to particular circumstances.
- Although many aspects of thinking about classroom management can be learned from research, some of the complex skills of classroom orchestration will come only with extended practice and serious reflection.

A Final Thought and Look to the Future

- Approaches to classroom management may be in a state of transition. Perhaps in the future we will find teachers spending less time controlling students and more time helping them think for themselves and care for others.

Key Terms

Portfolio and Field Experience Activities

This feature has been designed to help you learn from your field experiences and to assist you in the preparation of artifacts for your professional portfolio on topics and standards associated with Chapter 5.

1. Complete the "Reflections from the Classroom" exercise at the end of this chapter. The recommended reflective essay will provide insights into your overall views and approach to classroom management.
2. Observe classroom management behaviors in a classroom using one or more of the following activities found in the *Guide to Field Experiences and Portfolio Development:* Activities 5.2, 5.3, and 5.6. Use your analysis of these observations to demonstrate your understanding and views about how to manage classroom behavior and how to respond to student misbehavior.
3. Complete Activity 5.7 in the *Guide to Field Experiences and Portfolio Development* as a means to communicate your current thinking about classroom management. How do these views relate to the views you expressed in your "Teaching Platform" (Activity 1.5 in Chapter 1)?

Books for the Professional

Go to the Online Learning Center at www.mhhe.com/arends6e or your Interactive Student CD-ROM for an annotated version of this list.

Cangelosi, J. S. (1999). *Classroom Management Strategies: Gaining and Maintaining Students' Cooperation* (4th ed.). New York: John Wiley & Sons.

Charney, R. S. (1993). *Teaching Children to Care: Management in the Responsive Classroom.* New York: Northeast Foundation for Children.

Emmer, E., Evertson, C., Clements, B., and Worsham, W. E. (2002). *Classroom Management for Secondary Teachers* (6th ed.). Englewood Cliffs, NJ: Prentice-Hall.

Evertson, C., Emmer, E., and Worsham, M. (2002). *Classroom Management for Elementary Teachers* (6th ed.). Englewood Cliffs, NJ: Prentice-Hall.

Kohn, Alfie. (1996). *Beyond Discipline: From Compliance to Community.* Alexandria, VA: Association for Supervision and Curriculum Development.

Noddings, N. (1992). *The Challenge to Care in Schools: An Alternative Approach to Education.* New York: Teachers College Press.

Weinstein, C. S. (2002). *Secondary Classroom Management: Lessons from Research and Practice* (2nd ed.). New York: McGraw-Hill.

Weinstein, C. S., and Mignano, A. J., Jr. (2002). *Elementary Classroom Management: Lessons from Research and Practice* (3rd ed.). New York: McGraw-Hill.

Chapter Six

Assessment and Evaluation

Assessment and Evaluation

Perspective on Assessment and Evaluation
- Importance of Assessment and Evaluation
- Key Assessment and Evaluation Concepts

Theoretical and Empirical Support
- Effects of Grades and Testing on Students
- Teacher Bias in Assessment and Grading

Statewide and Schoolwide Assessment Programs
- Statewide and Schoolwide Use of Standardized Tests
- Nature of Standardized Tests
- Norm-Referenced and Criterion-Referenced Tests
- Advantages and Disadvantages of Different Approaches
- Communication of Standardized Test Results

A Look to the Future of Testing and Grading
- Assessing Performance
- Authentic Assessment
- Designing and Scoring Performance and Authentic Assessments
- Student Portfolios and Narrative Descriptions
- Assessing Group Effort and Individually Contracted Work
- Experimenting with New Approaches
- Assessment Bill of Rights

Specifics of Testing and Grading
- General Principles
- Test Construction and Use
- Grading
- Summary Guidelines for Testing and Grading

A Teacher's Assessment Program
- Diagnosing Prior Knowledge
- Providing Corrective Feedback
- Testing for Summative Evaluation and Reporting
- A Special Case of Using Assessment Information to Diagnose Students with Disabilities

Interactive and Applied Learning

Go to your Interactive Student CD-ROM to:
- Hear audio clips of Sandy Frederick and Dennis Holt talk about assessment in the *Teachers on Teaching* feature
- View examples of assessment tools and materials
- View sample performance measures and scoring rubrices

Go to the Online Learning Center at www.mhhe.com/arends6e to read *PowerWeb* articles and newsfeed updates about:
- Academic performance
- Cheating
- Cheating in high school and college
- Cultural diversity in education
- Education standards
- Technology and education
- Testing and evaluation
- World Wide Web

Considering **Standards**

Studying this chapter will help you meet one INTASC principle:

Primary

INTASC #8: Understands and uses formal and informal assessment strategies to evaluate and ensure the continuous intellectual, social, and physical development of the learner.

Reflecting **on** *Assessment and Evaluation*

The best way to approach this chapter is to reflect back on your own experiences as a student with assessment and evaluation. You have been tested hundreds of times during your years in elementary and high school and college. These tests have ranged from simple pop quizzes to the high-stakes SATs and ACTs. Also you have received grades many times. Sometimes you have received grades that you deserved; others have been unfair and reflected a bias against you. What have been your experiences with tests and grades?

- How did you react to testing situations and grades? Are you the kind of student who relishes a good, hard test and who feels a real sense of accomplishment when you do well? Or are you the kind of student who tenses up in testing situations and always comes away from the experience with negative feelings?

- What do you think about standardized tests, such as IQ tests, state mastery tests, the SATs, or Praxis I and II for teachers? Do these tests ensure that students and teacher candidates learn what they are supposed to learn? Or do they simply get in the way of real learning and establish unfair barriers?

- Have you thought about what kind of assessment system you are going to establish in your classroom? Do you look forward to being the type of teacher who is considered to have tough standards and grading policies? Are you going to use these to make students work hard? Or do you dread the whole idea of making judgments about students' work and plan to do everything you can to play down competition and make sure everyone passes your classes?

Go to the Online Learning Center at www.mhhe.com/arends6e to respond to these questions.

eaders in almost all situations are responsible for assessing and evaluating the people who work for them. So, too, are teachers responsible for the assessment and evaluation of students in their classrooms—an aspect of their work that some find very difficult. Nonetheless, assessment, evaluation, and grading are of utmost importance to students and parents, and the way these processes are performed have long-term consequences. Assessment and evaluation processes also consume a fairly large portion of teachers' time. For instance, a review by Shaefer and Lissitz (1987) reported that teachers spend as much as 10 percent of their time on matters related to assessment and evaluation. Stiggins (1997) found that teachers could spend as much as one-third of their time on "assessment-related" activities. For these reasons, it is critical that beginning teachers build a repertoire of effective strategies for assessing and evaluating their students.

Although certain measurement techniques associated with assessment and evaluation are beyond the scope of this book, basic concepts and procedures are well within the grasp of the beginning teacher. The first section of this chapter provides a perspective about why assessment and evaluation are important and defines several key concepts. This is followed by a section that samples the knowledge base on this topic. The final sections describe specific procedures beginning teachers can use for developing an overall assessment plan, making tests, and grading students as well as a discussion about schoolwide assessment and evaluation processes. A discussion also is included about some newer approaches to student assessment that are emerging in some schools.

> Assessing and evaluating students is one of the things teachers do that has important and lasting consequences for students.

Perspective on Assessment and Evaluation

If you think back to your own school days, you will recall the excitement (and the anxiety) of getting back the results of a test or of receiving your report card. When these events occurred, they were almost always accompanied by the student question, "Wadja get?" You also remember (in fact, you still hear) another favorite student question, "Is it going to be on the test?" These questions and the emotion behind them highlight the importance of assessment and evaluation in the lives of students.

Importance of Assessment and Evaluation

Probably since the time the first test or the first grade was given, controversy has surrounded their use. For instance, some have argued that grades dehumanize education and establish distrust between teachers and students. Others have said that grading and comparing students lead to harmful anxiety and to low self-esteem for those who receive poor grades. Even those who acknowledge the importance of assessment and evaluation have often condemned current practices for the emphasis on testing basic skills out of context and the excessive competition that results. Still others have commented that grades are really a "rubber yardstick," measuring the whims of particular teachers rather than mastery of important educational goals. Today, teachers must test and evaluate, and they must respond to the use of standardized tests on their students and on themselves. This chapter strives to describe important contemporary features of assessment, testing, and evaluation. It also, as you will read, strives to encourage you to not accept the current situation uncritically and to consider alternative modes of assessment that may be more personalized, authentic, and fair. Regardless of the criticism and controversy surrounding this topic, the process of assessing and evaluating students has persisted and basic practices have remained essentially constant for most of the past century. In fact, the Elementary and Secondary Education Amendment (ESEA) passed by Congress in 2002 and signed by the President puts more emphasis than ever on the use of standardized tests to evaluate students and their schools. This legislation, called "Leave No Child Behind," requires schools to test children every year in grades 3 through 8 and stipulates that schools that have high proportions of failing students be put under special surveillance and allows parents of children in these schools to send them to a school of their choice. Two important conditions of schools and teaching help explain our emphasis on testing.

Sorting Function of Schools.   Sociologists have observed that schools in large, complex societies are expected to help sort people for societal roles and occupational positions. Although some may wish for the day when better and fairer means are found for making these judgments, at present, the larger society assigns the job of assessing and evaluating student growth and potential in large part to schools and teachers. How well students perform on tests, the grades they receive, and the judgments their teachers make about their potential have important, long-term consequences for students. These judgments determine who goes to college, the type of college they attend, the careers open to them, and their first jobs, as well as the lifestyles they maintain. Enduring perceptions about self-worth and self-esteem can also result from the way students are evaluated in school. For these reasons, of all the leadership aspects of teaching, assessing and evaluating student growth and potential may be the most far-reaching. Teachers who do not take this aspect of their work seriously (regardless of the reforms they may desire) are doing their students a great disservice. Still others argue that testing practices, as they have evolved in the United States, have been used to maintain the dominance of certain groups in society and prevent others from advancing. The unfairness and lack of social justice of this sorting function, criticism of current testing and grading practices, and suggested reforms will be discussed later in the chapter.

Although many wish it wasn't so, schools today help sort students for future opportunities.

Grade-for-Work Exchange.   Chapter 4 pointed out how classroom reward structures influence the overall learning community and how much of what students choose to do, or not do, is determined by what Walter Doyle labeled the "grade-for-work exchange." This idea described how students, like the rest of us, can be motivated to do certain things for extrinsic rewards. We may work hard and do what employers want so we will receive a merit raise; we may volunteer for community service hoping to receive public recognition for our work. This does not mean that our work has no intrinsic value or that altruistic reasons do not prompt us to help others. It simply means that for many people in our society, extrinsic rewards are valued and provide a strong incentive to act in particular ways.

Academic tasks such as completing assignments, studying for tests, writing papers, and carrying on classroom discourse comprise the work of students. Many teachers want their students to perform this academic work for the intrinsic value of learning itself. Although this is an admirable and, in many instances, attainable goal, grades remain important and should not be overlooked. It is important to remember that just as adults work for a salary, students work for grades. These exchanges are critically important and help explain some of classroom life.

Students work for grades just as adults work for money.

Importance of Grades to Parents.   Parents are very concerned about their children's grades because they, more than their children, understand fully the important sorting function going on in schools. Most parents can recall critical judgments made about their work and the consequences of these judgments. Similarly, they are keenly aware

"Would you rather I be the smartest kid in the dumb group or the dumbest kid in the smart group?"

Source: (c) Lo Linkert, Phi Delta Kappan (May 1998)

of the judgments being made when their child is placed in a lower-level reading group or a general math class instead of algebra.

Teachers have been known to complain about this type of parental concern, and sometimes these complaints are justified. For instance, some parents let unrealistic expectations for their children interfere with the teacher's professional judgment about the most appropriate level of work for their child. Conversely, other parents seem indifferent to their children's academic evaluation and offer little encouragement at home for doing good work or getting good grades.

Most parental concern, however, is natural and can be potentially beneficial. A growing literature (Airasian, 2001) shows that parental concern about grades and performance can be tapped and used by teachers for the purpose of enhancing student learning. For example, involving parents in appropriate ways through homework is an excellent means of extending the teacher's instructional time. Several studies (Cooper, 1989; Corno, 1996) have also shown that when teachers show regard for parental concerns by using more frequent reporting procedures and by getting parents to support the school's reward systems at home, these actions can result in more homework completed, better attendance, more academic engagement, and generally increased student output.

Key Assessment and Evaluation Concepts

Assessment and evaluation are functions carried out by teachers to gather information needed to make wise decisions, and it should be clear by now that the decisions teachers make are important to students' lives. These decisions should be based on information that is relevant and as accurate as possible. Several key concepts can help you understand this topic more fully.

Assessment. The term **assessment** usually refers to the full range of information gathered and synthesized by teachers about their students and their classrooms. Information can be gathered on students in informal ways such as through observation and verbal exchange. It can also be gathered through formal means such as homework,

Assessment is the process of collecting information about students and classrooms for the purpose of making instructional decisions.

tests, and written reports. Information about classrooms and the teacher's instruction can also be part of assessment. The range of information here can also vary from informal feedback provided by students about a particular lesson to more formal reports resulting from course evaluations and standardized tests.

Evaluation. Whereas assessment focuses on gathering and synthesizing information, the term **evaluation** usually refers to the process of making judgments, assigning value, or deciding on worth. A test, for example, is an assessment technique to collect information about how much students know on a particular topic. Assigning a grade, however, is an evaluative act, because the teacher is placing a value on the information gathered on the test.

> Evaluation is the process of making judgments or deciding on the worth of a particular approach or of a student's work.

Most evaluation specialists talk in terms of either formative or summative evaluations, depending on the use of the evaluation information. **Formative evaluations** are collected before or during instruction and are intended to inform teachers about their students' prior knowledge and skills in order to assist with planning. Information from formative evaluations is not used to make judgments about a student's work; it is used to make judgments about such matters as student grouping, unit and lesson plans, and instructional strategies. **Summative evaluations,** on the other hand, are efforts to use information about students or programs after a set of instructional activities has occurred. Its purpose is to summarize how well a particular student, group of students, or teacher performed on a set of learning goals or objectives. Summative evaluations are designed so that judgments can be made about accomplishments. Information obtained from summative evaluations is used by teachers to determine grades and to explain the reports sent to students and their parents. Table 6.1 compares key aspects of formative and summative evaluations.

Information Quality. If teachers make important decisions about students and about their teaching, it is only common sense that the information they use to make these decisions should be of high quality. Measurement and evaluation specialists use three technical terms to describe the quality of assessment information: reliability, validity, and fairness.

> A test has reliability if it produces consistent results over several administrations.

A test is said to be **reliable** when it produces dependable, consistent scores for persons who take it more than once over a period of time. For instance, if a student took a test on Friday and then the same student took the test again the next Friday and received the same score, it is likely the test is reliable. If a group of students took the test one week and repeated the same test the following week and the rankings of the vari-

Table 6.1 *Formative and Summative Evaluation*

Type of Evaluation	When Collected	Type of Information Collected	How Information Is Used
Formative	Before or during instruction	Information about student prior knowledge and/or instructional processes	To assist teacher decision making
Summative	After instruction	Information about student and/or teacher performance	To assist making judgments about student or teacher accomplishments

ous students stayed about the same, it is even more likely that the test is reliable. A reliable test, thus, is one that measures a student's ability on some topic or trait consistently over time. A reliable test gives teachers accurate and dependable assessment information; however, it is important to remember that no single test can be expected to be perfect. Factors such as student guessing, mistakes made by teachers in scoring, as well as the students' feeling of well-being on the testing day all introduce error, inconsistency, and unreliability. Later, we will describe procedures that can cut down on the amount of error in tests.

A test is said to be **valid** when it measures what it claims to measure. For example, a test that claims to measure students' attitudes toward mathematics is invalid if it really measures their attitude toward their mathematics teacher. Or, a test is invalid if its goal is to measure students' skills in higher-level thinking and instead measures the basic skill to remember and recall factual information. Obviously, if a test is not measuring what it is intended to measure, the information it produces is of no value for teacher decision making. As you will see later, it is possible to increase the validity of tests and other assessment devices.

A test is valid if it measures what it claims to measure.

Finally, a test is **fair** if it offers all students the same chance of doing well and if it does not discriminate against a particular group of students because of their race, ethnicity, or gender. A test may be unfair if individuals from one race or gender consistently score lower than individuals from other races or gender, as is the case of the SATs and some tests of general achievement. However, other factors, such as poor schools or unqualified teachers, may cause the differences in performance. Figure 6.1 illustrates the concepts of validity, reliability, and fairness.

Theoretical and Empirical Support

The knowledge base for assessment and evaluation is immense. The underlying concepts used for measuring all kinds of traits and attributes, such as academic achievement, personality, and performance, have long intellectual traditions. Similarly, technical topics associated with test construction, grading, and the use of evaluation information have been studied thoroughly for most of this century. Two lines of inquiry important to beginning teachers are sampled in this section: the effects of testing and grades on students and bias in teaching assessment.

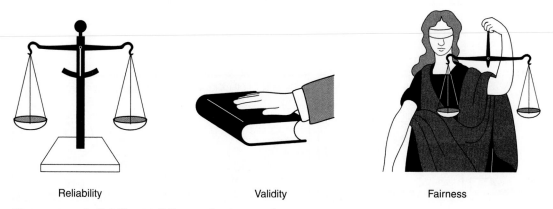

Reliability   Validity   Fairness

Figure 6.1 *Reliability, Validity, and Fairness of a Measurement*

Check, Extend, Explore

Check
- Why is assessment and evaluation of students such an important aspect of a teacher's work?
- What is meant by the "grade-for-work" exchange?
- Contrast the terms *assessment* and *evaluation* as they pertain to classroom teaching.
- What are the meanings of the terms *reliability, validity,* and *fairness*?

Extend
- Do you agree or disagree that schools should be used as a "sorting mechanism" for students? Go to the "Extend Question Poll" on the Online Learning Center to respond.

Explore
- Go to the Online Learning Center at www.mhhe.com/arends6e for links to websites related to Assessment and Evaluation.

Effects of Grades and Testing on Students

For obvious reasons, one of the most important and frequently asked questions by beginning teachers is, "Do tests, grades, and grading procedures influence student learning?" Fortunately, this has also been a question of interest to educational researchers. Much is known about the effects of grades and other **extrinsic rewards** on students. However, a note of caution is in order about this research because the issues involved are complex and intricate. As you will see, simple recipes do not exist.

One line of research stemmed from natural experiments that occurred in the late 1960s and the 1970s. During this period, several colleges and universities began the practice of giving students the choice of taking classes on a graded or a pass-fail basis. Several studies (for example, Gold et al., 1971) compared the students' performance, and the findings were pretty consistent: Students performed better in graded situations than they did in pass-fail situations.

Are Grades an Incentive? A persistent and troublesome problem for teachers is how to get students to do their homework. On the one hand, teachers would prefer that students complete assignments because of the work's intrinsic value. On the other hand, many experienced teachers would declare, "If I don't grade it, they won't do it." Francis Cullen and her colleagues (1975) conducted an interesting piece of research that shed some light on this problem.

The researchers experimentally manipulated two types of incentives (positive and negative) to see what effects they would have on getting students to complete a simple library assignment. They studied 233 students in fourteen high school classes across three suburban schools. Students in the study were asked to complete a one-page library assignment. Although the assignment varied according to the subject of the class, it was the same for all classes in terms of length and difficulty. The fourteen classes were randomly assigned to three different categories: (1) positive-incentive group, where students were told if they handed in the assignment, they would receive X number of points on their final grade. If they did not complete the assignment, no points would be taken away; (2) negative-incentive group, where students were told that if they did not hand in the assignment, they would lose X number of points on their final grade; and (3) control group, where students were told that completing or not completing the assignment would not affect their grade.

Sixty-four percent of the students in the negative-incentive group completed the assignment compared to 42 percent in the positive-incentive group and only 14 percent in the control group. These data confirmed the researchers' hypothesis that grades used as negative incentives would be more powerful than grades used as positive incentives.

PEANUTS reprinted by permission of United Feature Syndicate, Inc.

Complexity of the Influence of Grades. The Cullen study seems to show grades can be a strong incentive for performing work. A beginning teacher, however, should be careful in interpreting this finding because factors other than grades can affect performance. One key factor is how interesting or intrinsically motivating the assignment is in the first place. For example, in a rather well-known study, Lepper and her colleagues (1973) compared three groups of preschool children. Children were told they could draw pictures (an intrinsically interesting task for young children) during their free-play time. Children in one group were promised a reward if they drew a picture. Children in another group were told they would receive a surprise. Those in the third group were promised nothing. After this reward structure was introduced, the children were observed, and the amount of time they spent drawing pictures during free play was recorded. Those students who were promised a surprise or no reward at all spent almost twice as much time drawing as did students who had been promised a reward. These results, as you can see, are quite different from those of the Cullen study. Lepper and her colleagues explained their findings by pointing out that giving extrinsic rewards for something that is intrinsically interesting may actually have the opposite effect. This does not mean, however, as Lepper (1973) and others have explained, that extrinsic rewards should not be used. They are still needed for tasks that do not have high intrinsic motivation.

> A set of complex factors affects the influence of grades and extrinsic rewards on the quality of student work.

More recent studies (Milton et. al., 1986; Poullio, 1985, 1992; Tuckman, 1992) have examined the relationships among tests, grades, and student learning. In general, these studies confirm earlier research that the use of grades can increase student achievement, but the influences remain complex. Beaulieu and Uecht (1987) also conclude that student achievement on final exams improves in classes in which teachers give weekly quizzes. A caution about much of this research—it has been conducted mainly with older, college-age students and may not be valid for younger students.

Another factor that influences the effects of grades on student learning is how students themselves perceive these grades in relation to the work they have performed. You remember reading in Chapter 4 that some students attribute their success or failure to their own hard work or lack thereof, whereas other students attribute it to luck. The grade and what it means will obviously be interpreted differently by each type of student.

A student's past history with grades can also be a factor. Students who have a history of receiving high grades, for instance, have likely developed a positive view of themselves and will continue to aspire to and work for high grades. On the other hand, students who have histories of low grades come to see themselves as failures, and another low grade only confirms this perception. Obviously, the status parents and close friends attach to grades also influences students' attitudes.

Effect of Testing. As you will read in the next section, the use of standardized tests in schools is widespread today, and people in general think that if test scores are high, the school and its teachers are effective. Many instances have been reported where this is true (Education Trust, 1998; Sanders, 1996; Schmoker & Marzano, 1999). However, for a variety of reasons, the effects of standardized tests may not always be as positive as some would believe.

One reason is that most standardized tests measure only a small range of abilities, mainly those that focus on quantitative and verbal tasks. And, as you read in Chapter 1, leading educators today believe that there are various forms of intelligence, including the eight types identified by Gardner (1994). Students who possess artistic, interpersonal, or intrapersonal abilities, for example, are at a disadvantage because these abilities are not measured on standardized tests.

In any assessment situation, the possibility of teacher bias is always a worry.

Second, some educators are beginning to question whether frequent testing can actually impede meaningful education and student learning. This point of view is highlighted in the Research Summary for this chapter, which expresses a point of view in direct opposition to current state and federal policies on testing, particularly the 2002 ESEA legislation, "Leave No Child Behind."

Teacher Bias in Assessment and Grading

From your own student experiences, you undoubtedly know how important it is for teachers to be perceived as fair and impartial in their treatment of young people. Being free from bias is particularly important when teachers judge student work and assign grades. Teacher bias is also a topic that has been extensively researched. Some of the most interesting studies were done by Starch and Elliot (1912, 1913), who showed the subjectivity of teachers in assessing and assigning grades to essay exams. In their first study, the researchers asked teachers in a number of different schools to grade student-produced essay exams in English. Later the researchers asked history and mathematics teachers to perform the same task. Starch and Elliot found that teachers used many different criteria when assessing essays and, consequently, the scores or grades they gave to the same paper varied widely. On one English essay, for instance, the percentage of points awarded varied from 50 to 97. Similar studies conducted over the years continue to show that teachers hold different criteria for judging student work and that they are influenced by numerous subjective factors, such as the student's handwriting, whether or not the opinions expressed agree with those of the teacher, and the expectations teachers have for a particular student's work. (Remember the concept of self-fulfilling prophecy described in Chapter 2.) Fortunately, a number of strategies have been devised to reduce bias and subjectivity in assessment and grading. These procedures and techniques will be described more fully later in this chapter.

Statewide and Schoolwide Assessment Programs

The following sections focus on strategies teachers can use to make assessment and evaluation both fair and productive. Statewide and schoolwide standardized assessment programs are described first, followed by specific procedures teachers can use to work with the results of standardized tests and communicate these to students, parents, and members of their communities.

Statewide and Schoolwide Use of Standardized Tests

Currently, it is common practice for states to use standardized tests to diagnose and evaluate students' academic progress. Called mastery or basic competency testing, these testing programs have evolved with the accountability movement discussed in Chapter 1. Today, laws mandate that tests be administered to students in every grade. Although the tests vary from state to state, in the main they assess childrens' abilities in math, reading, and writing in the elementary grades. Grade 10 tests sometimes branch out into science, history, and geography.

The results of state tests are given to teachers, who can use them for diagnostic purposes. They are also given to students and their parents. In many states, test scores are

Check, Extend, Explore

Check
- In what ways have grades been shown to increase student performance? Why is an overemphasis on the extrinsic grade reward system possibly a disadvantage?
- What subjective criteria have been shown to influence teachers when they judge student work?

Extend
- Do you agree or disagree with the current movement to test students frequently with standardized tests? Go to the "Extend Question Poll" on the Online Learning Center to respond.
- How do your views about testing compare with those of Joseph Angaran, the author of the Research Summary?

Explore
- Go to the Online Learning Center at www.mhhe.com/arends6e for links to websites with additional research studies on *Assessment and Evaluation.*

Personal Reflections of a Third Grade Teacher

Angaran, Joseph. Reflections in an age of assessment. *Educational Leadership* March 1999, 71–72.

Most of the research summaries in *Learning to Teach* are the result of the work of professional educational researchers, mainly individuals who work in university settings and conduct their research by watching and studying what goes on in schools. The knowledge we have about teaching, however, does not come only from this source. We also have what is called the "wisdom of practice." This Research Summary contains an example of this type of knowledge. It is the personal reflections of a third-grade teacher in Eagan, Minnesota.

Problem and Approach: Joseph Angaran is concerned about what effect frequent testing and assessment may have on his students. In the twenty years he has been teaching, Angaran has observed some significant changes in the amount of time devoted to testing. He questions the usefulness and implications of the data being gathered, as well as the effect of the tests on his teaching and the learning of his students.

Reflections and Conclusions: "Every morning on my way to school, I pass by the marquee of a major entertainment complex. As I sit at the traffic light and patiently wait to begin my day, I glance at the marquee to watch announcements of upcoming events crawl across the screen in bright orange letters. I contemplate the enormity of the organization and the various set-up procedures each event must entail. . . .

"Soon, however, my thoughts become focused on the day ahead, and I wonder about the special events that dominate my date book and lesson planner. With increasing frequency, assessments are now the focus of my students' lives. When I glance at my calendar, I hardly ever see a week when I am not either preparing to test or formally assessing my students. This is a significant change since I began my teaching career nearly 20 years ago. I question the usefulness and the implications of the data we gather, as well as the effect these tests have on my teaching and on my students' learning.

"Teachers assess students by using an ever-increasing variety of tools. In my district, the average 3rd grader is evaluated with the following instruments: a national norm-referenced test for school achievement, a test to determine school ability, and two state-mandated tests in reading and math. In addition, classroom teachers are required to conduct a writing assessment and a test for oral retelling of a narrative or a descriptive text. . . .

"On some days, I merely facilitate movement among tests rather than encourage and enhance student learning. Being a teacher has been reduced to something akin to being a special events coordinator at the entertainment complex. Each test becomes another situation in which I must rearrange the classroom and its routines, coordinate test materials, and work to assuage the fears of the 8- and 9-year-olds whom I teach. The students sense underlying anxiety and apprehension despite assurances from me and their parents that we just want them to do their best. . . . Ironically, all this activity prepares them for hours of passivity. This extended amount of seat time flies in the face of what we know about how children learn. . . .

"Ostensibly, this test data will enable us to be better teachers, and it will give parents and the public a better idea of whether we are adequately preparing children for a place in society. In reality, however, the information overwhelms everyone. We now have more statistics on children than ever. Teachers are inundated with report after report, analysis after analysis, detail piled upon excruciating detail. Parents receive less information with even less interpretation of the results and, more important, no direct link to what they can do at home to help their child. The public often receives the most dramatic data taken out of context, misinterpreted, or sensationalized.

"Teachers are not provided enough time to analyze the test data and to translate the information into meaningful goals for their students. At times we seem to be putting the cart before the horse: Shouldn't we change the way we teach and then assess students? It doesn't make a lot of sense to continue to assess students when we are not given the time to modify our methodology. Without ample time to reflect and change, aren't we simply assessing either old practices or underfunded, undervalued, half-hearted attempts at educational change? . . . Without the time to examine our teaching practices and to work with our colleagues, we will continue to teach in the ways we were taught 20 or more years ago.

"In the rush to reform education, the classroom teacher's expertise and common sense have been pushed aside. . . . As professionals with extensive knowledge of child development and learning, we can determine what is best for our students. That does not mean that we will not listen to or accept information from others. It does mean, however, that we will know how to implement the most effective way to enhance student learning. After all, isn't that the goal of everyone?"

summarized by the school. Each school is compared to other schools in the state. These comparisons are published in the local newspaper. Figure 6.2 is an example of the results teachers and parents receive in one state.

The trend seems to be to make these tests more and more important in the lives of teachers and students and to use them to make high-stakes decisions. For example, schools in some communities have been taken over by the state government because their students have consistently done poorly on these tests. In some instances, students are required to pass statewide mastery tests before they are promoted to the next grade or awarded a high school diploma. Some schools require summer school for students who score below established goals.

Many school districts also have standardized testing programs. In larger school systems, whole units of specially trained personnel exist to coordinate and manage this important educational activity. It is a rare school in which students are not tested at least yearly on such topics as study skills, reading, language acquisition, mathematical operations, verbal reasoning, and concept development. Sometimes schools use tests developed and distributed by national test publishers. Others use tests developed and distributed by state or district testing authorities. The results of tests are used to make judgments about the effectiveness of schools and teachers and, most important, to decide the future educational and job opportunities available to students.

Beginning teachers will not be required to select the tests to be used on a statewide or schoolwide basis, nor will they be held responsible for the scoring or initial interpretations of these tests. They will, however, be expected to understand the nontechnical aspects of the testing program, and they will be expected to use test results and to communicate these clearly to students and their parents. In many school districts, teachers are also held accountable for their students' success on these tests.

Tests have become more and more important in the lives of students.

MASTERY TESTING PROGRAM
GRADE 8 REPORT

TEACHER:
SCHOOL:
DISTRICT:

OBJECTIVE CLUSTERS TESTED	MASTERY CRITERIA	STUDENT SCORE
WRITTEN COMMUNICATION		
1. Prewriting/referencing	11 of 15	13
2. Composing/revising	11 of 15	12
3. Editing	11 of 15	12
TOTAL NUMBER OF OBJECTIVE CLUSTERS MASTERED (out of 3)		3
READING COMPREHENSION		
1. Constructing Meaning	7 of 10	9
2. Applying Strategies	4 of 6	4
3. Analyzing, Elaborating, and Responding Critically	10 of 14	11
TOTAL NUMBER OF OBJECTIVE CLUSTERS MASTERED (out of 3)		3

WRITING SAMPLE	STUDENT SCORE
Holistic Writing Score (Goal is 8 of 12)	8

Your child has scored at or above the statewide goal in writing. Generally, students who score at this level produce fluent papers which contain somewhat well-developed responses. These papers are adequately elaborated with general and specific details. These papers show satisfactory to strong organizational strategy with a progression of ideas and transition.

DEGREES OF READING POWER (DRP)™	STUDENT SCORE
DRP Units (Goal is 64 DRP units)	78

Your child has scored at or above the statewide goal for reading. Students who score at this level possess the knowledge and skills necessary to successfully perform the tasks and assignments appropriately expected of a student at this grade level with minimal teacher assistance. Generally, students who score at this level can comprehend textbooks and other materials used at grade eight or above.

OBJECTIVES TESTED—MATHEMATICS	MASTERY CRITERIA	STUDENT SCORE
CONCEPTS		
1. Identify or extend patterns involving numbers and attributes	4 of 6	4
2. Relate fractions, decimals and percents to their pictorial representation	3 of 4	4
3. Rename fractions and mixed numbers as equivalent decimals and vice versa	3 of 4	4
4. Rename fractions and decimals as equivalent percents and vice versa	3 of 4	3
5. Identify points on number lines, scales and grids including fractions, decimals and integers	3 of 4	3
6. Estimate the magnitude of mixed numbers and decimals	3 of 4	4
COMPUTATION AND ESTIMATION		
7. Add and subtract 2-, 3- and 4-digit whole numbers, money accounts and decimals	3 of 4	4
8. Multiply and divide 2- and 3-digit whole numbers, money amounts and decimals by 1-digit whole numbers and decimals	3 of 4	4
9. Multiply and divide whole numbers and decimals by 10, 100 and 1000	3 of 4	4
10. Add and subtract fractions and mixed numbers with reasonable and appropriate denominators	3 of 4	4
11. Multiply whole numbers and fractions by fractions and mixed numbers	3 of 4	3
12. Find percents of whole numbers	3 of 4	4
13. Identify an appropriate procedure for making estimates involving whole number computation	4 of 6	6
14. Identify an appropriate procedure for making estimates involving fraction and mixed number computation	4 of 6	6
15. Identify an appropriate procedure for making estimates involving decimal computation	4 of 6	6
16. Identify an appropriate procedure for making estimates involving percents	5 of 7	6
PROBLEM SOLVING/APPLICATIONS		
17. Solve problems involving order and magnitude of fractions	3 of 4	3
18. Solve problems involving order and magnitude of whole numbers and decimals	3 of 4	4
19. Solve problems involving rounding whole numbers and decimals	3 of 4	4
20. Draw reasonable conclusions from graphs, tables and charts	3 of 4	4
21. Create graphs from data	3 of 4	4
22. Identify an appropriate number sentence to solve story problems	3 of 4	4
23. Solve or estimate a reasonable answer to problems involving whole numbers, dollar amounts, including averaging	3 of 4	3
24. Solve or estimate a reasonable answer to problems involving fractions, decimals and mixed numbers	3 of 4	3
25. Solve or estimate a reasonable answer to problems involving ratios, proportions and percents	3 of 4	3
26. Solve or estimate a reasonable answer to problems involving customary or metric units of measure	3 of 4	2
27. Solve or estimate a reasonable answer to problems involving elementary notions of probability and fairness	3 of 4	3
28. Solve or estimate a reasonable answer to problems involving means and medians of sets of data	3 of 4	4
29. Identify needed information in problem situations	3 of 4	3
30. Solve process problems involving the organization of data	3 of 4	4
MEASUREMENT/GEOMETRY		
31. Identify or draw geometric shapes and figures	3 of 4	2
32. Identify or draw geometric transformations and symmetry	3 of 4	4
33. Describe, model and classify shapes	4 of 5	5
34. Measure and determine perimeters, areas and volumes	3 of 4	4
35. Estimate lengths, areas, volumes and angle measures	3 of 4	3
36. Identify appropriate metric or customary units of measure for a given situation	3 of 4	4
ALGEBRA		
37. Solve equations involving 1 step	3 of 4	4
38. Use order of operations	3 of 4	4
39. Use formulas to evaluate expressions	3 of 4	3
40. Represent situations with algebraic expressions	3 of 4	4

Your child has scored at or above the state goal for mathematics. Students at this level possess the knowledge and skills necessary to perform the tasks and assignments expected of 8th graders with minimal teacher assistance. Generally these students demonstrate well-developed computational skills, conceptual understandings and problem solving abilities.

TOTAL NUMBER OF OBJECTIVES MASTERED = 38
TOTAL STUDENT SCORE = 154
(Goal is 130 of 172)

Figure 6.2 *Sample State Mastery Test*

Nature of Standardized Tests

Standardized tests, as contrasted to tests made by teachers, are those that have been designed and validated by professional test makers for specific purposes such as measuring academic achievement or literacy levels. They can usually be administered in many different settings and still produce reliable information. In some instances, standardized tests also provide information about how some nationwide "norm group" performed on the test, thus providing a basis of comparison for students subsequently taking the test. Examples of standardized tests include the Stanford Achievement Test, the California Achievement Test, or the well-known Scholastic Aptitude Test (SAT) used by many colleges and universities in making entrance selections. Many of you took the SAT and soon will be taking Praxis, a standardized test on teaching developed and administered by the Education Testing Service (ETS).

Norm-Referenced and Criterion-Referenced Tests

Today, two major types of standardized tests are used to measure student abilities and achievement. These are called norm-referenced and criterion-referenced tests. It is important to understand the differences between these two approaches to testing and to be able to communicate to others the assumptions, the advantages, and the disadvantages of each approach.

> Norm-referenced tests evaluate a particular student's performance by comparing it to the performance of some other well-defined group of students.

Norm-referenced tests attempt to evaluate a particular student's performance by comparing it to the performance of some other well-defined group of students on the same test. Most of the achievement tests you have taken as a student were norm-referenced. Your score told you how you performed on some specific topic or skill in comparison with students from a national population who served as the "norming" group for the test. Most norm-referenced tests produce two types of scores—a raw score and a percentile rank. The *raw score* is the number of items on the test a student answers correctly. The *percentile-rank score* is a statistical device that shows how a student compares with others, specifically the proportion of individuals who had the same or lower raw scores for a particular section of the test. Table 6.2 shows how raw scores are converted to percentile ranks on standardized, norm-referenced tests. Look at the row representing a student who answered thirty-eight out of the forty-eight test items correctly. You can see this score placed the student in the seventy-first percentile, meaning that 71 percent of the students in the norm group scored 38 or lower on the test. If you look at the row representing a student who had a raw score of 30 on the test, you can see this converts to a percentile score of 22, meaning that only 22 percent of the students in the norm group scored 30 or below.

> Criterion-referenced tests are those that evaluate a particular student's performance against a preestablished standard or criterion.

Whereas norm-referenced tests measure student performance against that of other students, **criterion-referenced tests** measure it against some agreed-upon level of performance or criterion. To show the major difference between a norm-referenced and criterion-referenced test, let us use as our example a runner's speed on the 100-yard dash. If a runner were compared to a larger group of runners using concepts from norm-referenced testing, the tester would report that a student who ran the 100-yard dash in thirteen seconds was in the sixty-fifth percentile for all other students in his or her age group. Using concepts from criterion-referenced testing, the tester would report that the established criterion for running a 100-yard dash was twelve seconds and that the student can now run it in thirteen seconds, one second short of criterion.

Generally, the content and skills measured on criterion-referenced tests are much more specific than those on norm-referenced tests. Obviously, each provides different types of information for teachers to use. Figure 6.3 compares the differences in the kinds

Table 6.2 *Conversion of Raw Scores to Percentile Ranks*

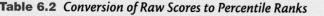

Raw Score	Percentile Rank	Raw Score	Percentile Rank
48		34	44
47		33	40
46		32	36
45	99	31	30
44	96	30	22
43	93	29	18
42	90	28	15
40	81	27	11
39	76	26	7
38	71	25	4
37	65	24	3
36	56	23	1
35	49	22	1–

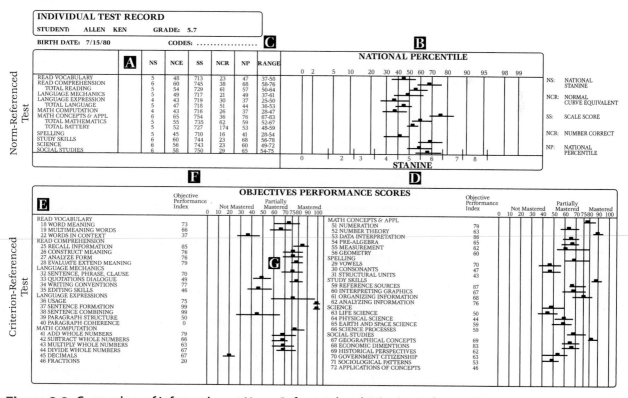

Figure 6.3 *Comparison of Information on Norm-Referenced and Criterion-Referenced Tests*

Source: California Achievement Test (1992)

of information provided by the two kinds of tests. Note that on the norm-referenced test (at the top of the figure), information is provided for more general categories, such as reading, language, and mathematics, and the student's performance is compared to national norms using percentile scores. The criterion-referenced test (at the bottom of the figure), on the other hand, indicates the level of mastery for very specific skills (such as editing skills) and reports the student's performance on an index ranging from zero (not mastered) to 100 (completely mastered). Note also that results from the norm-referenced tests are reported in percentile ranks, whereas the results of the criterion-referenced test show the degree to which a particular student has mastered a specific skill. You will read later in this chapter how those who advocate assessment procedures that are more performance-based and authentic challenge the processes associated with both norm-referenced and criterion-referenced testing. But for now, let's consider the advantages and disadvantages of the two approaches.

Advantages and Disadvantages of Different Approaches

If a teacher is interested in how his or her students compare to students elsewhere, results from norm-referenced tests are obviously called for. Norm-referenced tests allow comparisons within a particular school, district, or state. For example, achievement levels in all third grades in a particular district might be compared with those from other districts. Norm-referenced tests, however, will not tell very much about how well a specified set of school or teacher objectives are being accomplished; nor will they tell how students are currently doing in comparison to past performance on locally derived objectives.

Criterion-referenced tests, on the other hand, can provide information about a student's level of performance in relation to some specified body of knowledge or list of agreed-upon objectives or standards. This is important information to have when making judgments about the effectiveness of particular instructional programs and activities. The results of criterion-referenced tests, however, do not allow for comparing the performance of students in a particular locale with national norms. More and more schools and teachers are using criterion-referenced tests because their information is better for diagnosing student difficulties and for assessing the degree to which school-wide or systemwide purposes are being achieved.

Communication of Standardized Test Results

It is important that teachers communicate the results of standardized tests to parents and make sure they understand the limitations of these tests.

It is important that teachers be able to explain the results of both norm-referenced and criterion-referenced tests in honest and straightforward ways. They may be asked to go over test scores with students, to explain test results to parents, and to interpret test scores that are published in the newspaper. Students and their parents need to know that a single score on a test does not pretend to measure all aspects of a person's abilities. At the same time, they need to know how standardized test scores are used to make decisions that can affect students' lives.

Community members often need to be reminded of the strengths and limitations of particular testing programs and of the assumptions underlying all standardized tests. Educators have not done a very good job of explaining, in nontechnical terms, the assumptions behind norm-referenced testing and their limitations for judging the effectiveness of a particular school's educational program, nor have they explained the severe limitations of most paper-and-pencil standardized tests for making judgments about the multiple intelligences and skills of human beings. Knowledgeable teachers can find ways to communicate to parents and others that norm-referenced tests only compare students against a norm group and do not necessarily provide a good measure for how well a particular teacher, school, or system is achieving particular objectives. Teachers can also communicate to parents and the community that students' abilities and dispositions toward learning help determine how well they do on standardized tests and that a school with a predominance of less-motivated students will never perform as well as schools with a predominance of highly motivated students. Finally, teachers can remind and caution parents and others about possible test bias as well as the narrow range of objectives that are actually measured on any standardized test.

A Teacher's Assessment Program

Whereas testing specialists have the major responsibility for statewide and systemwide testing, classroom teachers are responsible for the assessment, testing, and grading related to their specific courses. In general, a teacher's assessment activities are aimed at one of the following three goals: diagnosing prior knowledge and skills, providing corrective feedback, and evaluating and grading student achievement. These three purposes have some similarities but also some important differences.

Diagnosing Prior Knowledge

To individualize instruction for specific students or to tailor instruction for a particular classroom group requires reliable information about students' capabilities and their prior knowledge. Both norm- and criterion-referenced standardized tests attempt to measure many areas of student achievement but are most highly developed and most readily available in reading, language development, and mathematics. Unfortunately, they are less available in other subject areas.

In many school systems, beginning teachers will be assisted by test and measurement personnel or by counseling and special education staff who have been specifically trained to help diagnose student capabilities and achievement. In other school systems, this type of assistance may not be available. If formal diagnostic information is not available, beginning teachers will have to rely on more informal techniques for assessing **prior knowledge.** For example, teachers can observe students closely as they approach a particular task and get some sense about how difficult or easy it is for them. Similarly, by listening carefully to students and by asking probing questions, teachers can get additional cues about students' prior knowledge on almost any topic. In fact, teacher and student questions are a major means of ascertaining student understanding. Verbal responses help teachers decide whether to move forward with the lesson or to back up and review. Nonverbal responses such as frowns, head nodding, puzzled looks, and the like also provide hints about how well students understand a topic. However, beginning teachers should be aware that sometimes these nonverbal behaviors can be misinterpreted.

Because many students will not admit their lack of knowledge or understanding in large groups, some teachers have found that interviewing students in small groups can be a good way to get the diagnostic information they need. This technique is particularly useful for getting information from students who do not participate regularly in classroom discussions or who give off few nonverbal signals. Student portfolios, described later, can also be used for diagnosing prior knowledge.

Check, Extend, Explore

Check
- How have state testing programs impacted the curriculum and the way teachers teach?
- How do norm-referenced tests and criterion-referenced tests differ? What are the advantages and disadvantages of each approach?
- Why is it important that teachers have a thorough understanding of standardized testing methods?

Extend
- Do think there are instances when parents and the community should not be apprised of test results?
- Do you agree or disagree that teachers should be evaluated based on the students' standardized test scores? Go to the "Extend Question Poll" on the Online Learning Center to respond.

Explore
- Go to the Online Learning Center at www.mhhe.com/arends6e for links to websites related to *Standardized Tests* and for *State-by-State Testing Practices.*

Prior knowledge refers to information and knowledge held by students before they receive instruction.

Providing Corrective Feedback

Corrective feedback provides students with information about how well they are doing.

A second important purpose of assessment and evaluation is to provide students with feedback on how they are doing. As with diagnosing students' prior knowledge, this is easier to do for some topics and skills than others. Test makers have developed rather sophisticated and reliable procedures for measuring discrete skills such as word recognition or simple mathematical operations. It is also quite easy to collect information on how fast a student can run the 100-yard dash or how long it takes to climb a 30-foot rope. Biofeedback techniques are also available to help students monitor their own physical reactions to stress and certain types of exertion. However, as instruction moves from a focus on such basic skills and abilities to a focus on more complex thinking and problem-solving skills, the problem of providing **corrective feedback** becomes more difficult because there are fewer reliable tests and acceptable procedures for these more complex processes.

Chapter 8 provides some principles for giving feedback to students and explains the importance of feedback for student improvement. It also emphasizes that for corrective feedback to be useful, it must be immediate, frequent, and communicated in nonjudgmental ways.

Testing for Summative Evaluation and Reporting

For most beginning teachers, the bulk of their assessment time and energy goes toward assessing student progress, determining grades, and reporting progress. Although some teachers do not like this aspect of their work and find it time-consuming, it must be done and done well for reasons enumerated earlier and reiterated here. First, students expect their work to be evaluated, and they perform academic work for grades, as you have seen. Teachers who take this work-for-grade exchange lightly or who do it poorly are normally faced with serious classroom problems. Second, the larger society has assigned the job of making judgments about student achievement and ability to teachers. It is unjust if this aspect of the job is not done well.

The key concepts and procedures associated with the three major purposes of classroom assessment are summarized in Table 6.3. The next section provides more specific information about this aspect of the teacher's assessment program.

Table 6.3 *Three Major Purposes of Classroom Assessment*

	Diagnostic	Feedback	Evaluation/Reporting
Function	Placement, planning, and determining the presence or absence of skills and prior knowledge	Feedback to student and teachers on progress	Grading of students at the end of a unit or semester
When used	At the outset of a unit, semester, or year, or during instruction when student is having problems	During instruction	At the end of a unit, quarter, or semester's work
Type of test	Standardized diagnostic tests; observations and checklists	Quizzes and special tests or homework	Final exams
Scoring	Norm- and criterion-referenced	Criterion-referenced	Norm- or criterion-referenced

A Special Case of Using Assessment Information to Diagnose Students with Disabilities

Today, beginning teachers can almost be assured that students with disabilities will be present in their regular classrooms. As you have read in previous chapters, inclusion of all students in the same classroom has many advantages. However, it also requires teachers to be able to deal with many different kinds of students and to have information about each. One set of assessment skills that is very important is in the area of diagnosis. In addition to information about academic abilities, several other kinds of assessment information are required if teachers are to work successfully with students who have special needs. These assessments are summarized in Table 6.4.

Some schools employ special educators and measurement experts, who will take the lead role in this aspect of teaching. In other schools, regular teachers will be required to participate directly in diagnosing student difficulties and using assessment information to tailor instruction for special-needs students.

Specifics of Testing and Grading

The most important aspect of student assessment and evaluation in most classrooms involves the tests teachers make and give to students. Good test construction requires both skill and a commitment to this aspect of teaching. The general principles

Table 6.4 *Type of Information Required to Assess Students with Disabilities*

Category of Disability	Type of Assessment Information Required
Mentally retarded	Degree of intellectual ability, adaptive behavior, language functioning, and medical history
Hard of hearing/deaf	Audiological, intellectual, language, speech, and social and emotional development
Speech-impaired	Audiological, articulation, fluency, voice, language, and social and emotional development
Visually handicapped	Ophthalmological, intellectual, and social and emotional development
Seriously emotionally disturbed	Intellectual, medical, and social and emotional development
Orthopedically impaired/other health impairments	Medical, motor, adaptive behavior, and social and emotional development
Deaf-blind	Audiological, ophthalmological, language, medical, and adaptive behavior
Multiply handicapped	Medical, intellectual, motor, adaptive behavior, social and emotional development, language, speech, and audiological and ophthalmological, when appropriate
Gifted	Intellectual, creative, and social and emotional development

Source: Adapted from Friend and Bursuck (2002)

Check, Extend, Explore

Check
- What are the three major purposes of a teacher's classroom assessment program?
- What methods and tools do teachers use to assess a student's prior knowledge?
- What methods and tools do teachers use to assess students with disabilities?
- In what situations is corrective feedback most effective?
- Why is the reporting of grades such a critical responsibility for a teacher?

Extend
- Have you observed instances in which a teacher had the reputation as being a "poor" or "unfair" grader? What was the consequence of this reputation?

Explore
- Go to the Online Learning Center at www.mhhe.com/arends6e for links to websites with information on *Assessment Tools and Procedures.*

that follow offer beginning teachers some much-needed guidelines for constructing their own paper-and-pencil tests. Methods that explain how to construct more complex performance tests are discussed later.

General Principles

Gronlund (1991, 1998) provided several principles that should guide teachers as they design an assessment system and create their own tests:

Assess All Instructional Objectives. An often-heard student complaint is that the test did not "cover what we covered in class." For whatever reasons, students who say this believe that they have been unfairly judged. Thus, Gronlund's first principle is that teachers should construct their test so it measures clearly the learning objectives they have communicated to students and the materials they have covered. In short, the test should be in harmony with the teacher's instructional objectives. For example, if the teacher completed a unit of work on the American colonial period and wants students to understand all aspects of this era, then the test should cover more than just the religious leaders of the period.

Cover All Cognitive Domains. Most lessons and units of instruction contain a variety of learning objectives ranging from the recall of factual information to the understanding, analysis, and creative application of specific principles. A good test does not focus entirely on one type of objective such as factual recall; rather, it measures a representative sample of the teacher's learning objectives. Measuring more complex skills such as higher-level reasoning is more difficult and time-consuming.

Gronlund's general principles provide important guidance for teachers as they develop their assessment system.

Use Appropriate Test Items. There are, as you know from your own experiences, many different kinds of test items and testing formats available to teachers. Some types of test items, such as matching or fill-in-the-blanks, are better for measuring recall of specific information; others, such as essay items, are better for tapping higher-level thinking processes and skills. A good test includes items that are most appropriate for a particular objective. More about this aspect of constructing tests is provided later.

Make Tests Valid, Reliable, and Fair. A test is considered reliable when it produces dependable, consistent scores for persons who take it more than once over a period of time. A test is said to be valid when it measures what it claims to measure. Remember, a test is fair if it offers all students the same chance of doing well and if it does not discriminate against a particular group of students because of their race, ethnicity, or gender. Teacher-made tests that are clearly written and minimize guessing are generally more reliable than ambiguous tests that encourage guessing. Likewise, tests containing a fairly large number of items are generally more reliable than those with just a few items. A test that is well planned and covers the full range of objectives and topics is most likely to ensure validity and fairness. Teaching students the necessary skills to take the test also increases validity because, in some instances, students may know the information being tested but simply cannot read or interpret the questions. No single test, however, can give a completely accurate picture of what a student knows or can do. Thus, there is always the need to interpret results with caution and to rely on multiple sources of assessment information before making final judgments about a student's work.

Use Tests to Improve Learning. This final principle is meant to remind teachers that although tests may be used primarily to diagnose or assess student achievement, they can also be learning experiences for students. Going over test results, for instance, provides teachers with opportunities to reteach important information that students may have missed. Debate and discussion over "right" answers can stimulate further study about a topic. Effective teachers integrate their testing processes into their total instructional programs for the purpose of guiding and enhancing student learning.

Although tests are used to grade students, they can also be used to improve student learning.

Test Construction and Use

Planning the Test. In almost any class, teachers attempt to teach many different things. Some of what they teach is influenced by curriculum guides that have been developed in their district and by the textbooks made available to them. Some elements that are taught stem from a teacher's own interest and judgment about what is important; still others are influenced by what students are interested in and what they choose to study. Also, the instructional objectives of a particular course can cover a range of behaviors, including important facts about a topic, major concepts and principles, simple and complex skills, appreciations, and the ability to think critically and analytically. Obviously, every piece of knowledge, skill, or cognitive process cannot be included on a particular test. Thus, teachers must make decisions about what to include and what to leave out. The **test blueprint** is a device invented by evaluation specialists to help teachers make these decisions and to determine how much space to allocate to certain kinds of knowledge and to the different levels of student cognitive processes. Table 6.5 shows a sample test blueprint using the dimensions of Bloom's Revised Taxonomy, which was introduced in Chapter 3. This table was created with the assumption that the teacher taught a unit on "Colonial Life in America" with the following six instructional objectives:

A test blueprint is a tool for constructing a test so it will have a balance of questions representing an array of instructional objectives organized around type of knowledge and cognitive processes.

Objective 1: Acquire knowledge about the workings of a New England town and a southern plantation during the sixteenth century.

Objective 2: Remember the names of four colonial figures: Cotton Mather, Anne Hutchison, Lord Calvert, and Thomas Hooker.

Objective 3: Apply knowledge by comparing life in colonial times with life in the same locale today.

Objective 4: Evaluate the actions of people in Massachusetts who were involved with the Salem witchcraft trials.

Objective 5: Create a written advertisement encouraging people in Europe to move to New England or to the South.

Objective 6: Check how the understanding of life in the colonies influences a student's own thinking about contemporary life.

At the top of the blueprint in Table 6.5, the teacher listed the six cognitive processes in Bloom's Revised Taxonomy. The four types of knowledge in the taxonomy are listed in the rows along the side of the blueprint. In the corresponding cells of the blueprint, the teacher categorized the six objectives. Notice that there is not an objective for every cell, which would be typical of most units. Finally, within the table the teacher has also listed the type and number of test items required to assess student learning for each type of knowledge and each of the cognitive processes.

Making the Test. Once the teacher has decided which types of knowledge and cognitive processes to cover on a test, the next step is to decide on the test's format and the type of

Table 6.5 *Blueprint for Assessments of Unit on Life in Colonial America using Categories of Bloom's Revised Taxonomy*

Knowledge Dimension	Remember	Understand	Apply	Analyze	Evaluate	Create
Factual Knowledge	**Objective 2** **Test item(s):** Four items asking students to match names with accomplishments					
Conceptual Knowledge	**Objective 1** **Test item(s):** Twelve true-and-false items on towns and plantations	**Objective 1** **Test item(s):** Twenty multiple-choice items on towns and plantations	**Objective 3** **Test item(s):** One essay question applying knowledge about colonial life to life today		**Objective 4** **Test item(s):** One essay question asking for reasoned judgment about witchcraft trials	
Procedural Knowledge						**Objective 5** **Test item(s):** A performance measure requiring production of an advertisement
Metacognitive Knowledge				**Objective 6** **Test item(s):** Essay question requiring reflection of student's own thinking processes		

Key to Objectives:

Objective 1: Acquire knowledge about the workings of a New England town and a southern plantation during the sixteenth century.

Objective 2: Remember the names of four colonial figures: Cotton Mather; Anne Hutchison, Lord Calvert, and Thomas Hooker.

Objective 3: Apply knowledge by comparing life in colonial times with life in the same locale today.

Objective 4: Evaluate the actions of people in Massachusetts who were involved with the Salem witchcraft trials.

Objective 5: Create a written advertisement encouraging people in Europe to move to New England or to the South.

Objective 6: Check how the understanding of life in the colonies influences a student's own thinking about contemporary life.

test items to use. In the example provided in Table 6.5, the teacher has decided to use three types of objective test items: matching, true-false, and multiple-choice. The term *objective,* as used here, means that answers to the items can be scored relatively free of bias. The teacher has also decided to use three essay questions and a performance measure. The next section, Constructing and Scoring Objective Tests, describes how to construct various types of objective and essay test items. A discussion of performance measures follows.

Constructing and Scoring Objective Tests. True-false, matching, multiple-choice, and fill-in-the-blanks are examples of test items that may be used on an **objective test.** The advantages of these types of test items are obvious. They allow greater coverage of the various topics a teacher has taught, and they can be easily and objectively scored. One disadvantage of objective tests is that it is sometimes difficult to write objective items that measure higher-level cognitive skills and processes. Another disadvantage is that good objective tests take a long time to construct. They simply cannot be put together in a few minutes the night before. Also, teachers always worry about the "guessing factor" associated with objective tests. This is particularly true when matching or true-false items are used. Finally, objective test items, regardless of how well constructed, can measure only a very limited range of understandings and skills. If a teacher decides to use the objective format, he or she must consider several factors as test items are prepared.

Tests with items that produce answers that can be scored relatively free from bias are called objective tests.

True-False Items. When the content of instruction or a learning objective calls for students to compare alternatives, true-false tests can be a useful means to measure their understanding. True-false tests are also useful as an alternative to a multiple-choice item if the teacher is having trouble coming up with several distracters. A good true-false item should be written so the choice is clear and the answer unambiguous. Look, for instance, at these examples of good and poor true-false items:

Good: An island is a land mass that is smaller than a continent and is surrounded by water.
Poor: Islands have been more important in the economic history of the world than have peninsulas.

The first example requires students to know the definition of the concept *island* as compared to other land forms. The answer is unambiguous. The second example, however, is very ambiguous. The word *important* would likely be interpreted in many different ways by students.

An obvious shortcoming with true-false test items is that students, whether they know the material or not, have a 50 percent chance of getting the correct answer.

Matching. When a teacher wants to measure student recall of a fairly large amount of factual information, matching items can be useful. Students are presented with two lists of items (concepts, dates, principles, names) and asked to select an item from one list that most closely matches an item from the other list. Most evaluation specialists caution against making either list too long—perhaps no more than six to eight items—or having more than one match for each set of items. As with true-false items, there is an element of guessing that the teacher needs to consider when choosing to use matching items. Following is an example of a matching question used by an English teacher who wanted to see if students knew the authors of the various literary works they studied.

Directions: Match the author listed in column B with the work he or she wrote, listed in column A.

Column A

1 _____ *Leaves of Grass*
2 _____ *Walden*
3 _____ *A Thousand Acres*
4 _____ *Moby Dick*
5 _____ *The Fire Next Time*
6 _____ *Jane Eyre*

Column B

A. Melville
B. Baldwin
C. Smiley
D. Bronte
E. Whitman
F. Thoreau

Fill-in-the-Blanks. A third popular objective test format is fill-in-the-blank. This kind of test is rather easy to write and it does a good job of measuring students' abilities to recall factual information. The element of guessing is virtually eliminated because choices of possible correct answers are not provided. The tricks of writing good fill-in-the-blank items are to avoid ambiguity and to make sure questions have no more than one correct response. To show how two correct answers are possible, read the following example:

The Civil War battle of Antietam was fought in _____.

Some students might write in "Maryland" (the place); others might write in "1862" (the date). Some subjects and instructional objectives lend themselves to clarity and this type of test item better than others.

Multiple-Choice. Multiple-choice items are considered by most evaluation specialists to be the best kind of objective test item. Multiple-choice items are rather robust in their use, and if carefully constructed, they minimize guessing. Also, if appropriately written, multiple-choice items can tap some types of higher-level thinking and analytical skills.

Good test items are difficult and time consuming to prepare.

Multiple-choice items consist of providing students with three types of statements: a *stem*, which poses a problem or asks a question; the *right answer*, which solves the problem or answers the question correctly; and *distracters*, statements that are plausible but wrong. Although the number of distracters can vary, normally three or four are recommended.

Good multiple-choice items are difficult to write. The stem must provide enough contextual information so students thoroughly understand the problem or question being posed. At the same time, it must be written so that the correct answer is not easily revealed. Distracters must be such that they provide plausible solutions to students who have a vague or incomplete understanding of the problem, yet they must be clearly recognized as the wrong answer by students who have command of a topic. General guidelines for writing multiple-choice items include recommendations to:

- Make the stem specific but with sufficient contextual information.
- Make all the distracters plausible and grammatically consistent with the stem.
- Make all aspects of the item clear so that students will not read more than was intended into the answer.

> **Good multiple-choice questions are difficult to write, but are considered by most as the best type of objective test item.**

Stems should be straightforward and specific but provide sufficient context. Here is an example of a good stem:

Historians attached historical significance to the Battle of Antietam because

A. So many people were killed in the bloodiest battle of the Civil War.
B. It gave Lincoln the victory he needed to issue the Emancipation Proclamation.
C. Strategically, it was the strongest victory to that point by the Confederate Army.
D. It showed how vulnerable the North was to invasion by forces from the South.

And here is an example of a poor stem:

Antietam was

A. The bloodiest battle of the Civil War.
B. The battle that gave Lincoln the victory he needed to issue the Emancipation Proclamation.
C. The strongest victory to that point by the Confederate Army.
D. The battle that showed how vulnerable the North was to invasion by forces from the South.

Most Civil War historians point out that the Battle of Antietam was tactically a draw. Strategically, however, it was a Confederate defeat, and it did give Lincoln a victory he thought he needed before formally issuing the Emancipation Proclamation. The stem in the good example alerts students that it is the "historical significance" of the battle that they should consider. Those who had a good understanding of this specific era of the Civil War would know the link between Antietam and the Emancipation Proclamation. Without that context, however, distracter A might also be a very plausible answer because the Battle of Antietam was the most costly in human life for a single day's engagement during the Civil War.

Just as the stem for a multiple-choice question needs to be carefully constructed, so too do the distracters. Teachers may make two common errors when they write distracters: lack of grammatical consistency and implausibility. Look at the following example:

Historians attached historical significance to the Battle of Antietam because

A. So many people were killed.
B. It gave Lincoln the victory he needed to issue the Emancipation Proclamation.
C. The Confederate Army.
D. Most Americans love bloody battles.

As you can see, several things are wrong with the distracters in this example. Distracters A, C, and D are much shorter than B. This may cue students to the right answer. Distracter C does not complete the sentence started in the stem; thus, it is grammatically different from B, the right answer, and distracters A and D. Finally, for the serious student, distracter D could be eliminated almost immediately.

Constructing and Scoring Essay Tests. Many teachers and test experts agree that **essay tests** do the best job of tapping students' higher-level thought processes and creativity. Obviously, this is a decided advantage of an essay test over an objective test. Another advantage is that it usually takes less time to construct. A note of caution, however. Good, clear essay questions don't just happen. And bear in mind the time it takes to construct sample answers and read and grade essay questions.

Essay tests have been criticized because they cover fewer topics than objective tests, they are difficult to grade objectively, and they may be heavily influenced by writing skills rather than knowledge of the subject. The first criticism can be resolved partially by using a combination of items—objective items to measure student understanding of basic knowledge and essay items to measure higher-level objectives.

As for grading bias, several guidelines have been developed by experienced teachers and evaluation specialists that help reduce the influence of writing prowess and grading bias.

> **Essay tests, in which students express their thoughts in writing, can tap complex ideas and concepts.**

> **Writing sample answers and using holistic scoring are two techniques teachers can use to reduce bias in grading essay tests.**

1. *Write the essay question so it is clear and explains to students what should be covered in the answer.* For example, if the teacher wants students to apply information, the questions should say that; if the teacher wants students to compare two different ideas or principles, the question should state that clearly. For instance, "Discuss the Civil War" is too broad and does not tell students what to do. Consequently, answers will vary greatly and will be difficult for the teacher to score. On the other hand, "Describe and compare economic conditions in the North and the South during the 1840s and 1850s, and explain how these conditions influenced decisions by both sides to engage in civil war" describes more clearly the topics to be covered in the essay and the type of thinking about the topic the teacher wants.

2. *Write a sample answer to the question ahead of time and assign points to various parts of the answer.* Writing a sample answer can become a criterion on which to judge each of the essays. Assigning points to various aspects of the answer (for instance, 5 points for organization, 5 points for coverage, and perhaps 5 points overall) helps deal with the problem of uneven quality that may exist within a given answer. Students should be made aware of the point distribution if this technique is used.

3. *Use scoring rubrics.* Teachers can reduce grading bias by using a scoring rubric. This device provides a rather detailed description of how a particular piece of writing or performance should look and the criteria used to judge various levels of performance. Scoring rubrics are described more fully and examples are provided in a later section, Designing and Scoring Performance and Authentic Assessments.

4. *Use techniques to reduce expectancy effects.* Chapter 2 introduced the concept of expectancy effects—a phenomenon whereby teachers expect some students to do well and others to do poorly. Having students write their names on the back of their essays is one technique that prevents this type of bias. However, this strategy has limited value because most teachers soon find they readily recognize a particular student's handwriting. If the essay test has two or three questions, reading all the responses to a single question and then shuffling the papers before reading responses to the next question is another method teachers use to reduce expectancy effects. If teachers are working in teams, checking each other's grading is also helpful.

5. *Consider using holistic scoring.* Some evaluation specialists have argued that the best procedure for scoring essay questions and other types of student writing (reports, essays, etc.) is one they have labeled **holistic scoring.** The logic behind this procedure is that the total essay written by a student is more than the sum of its parts and should be judged accordingly. Teachers who use this approach normally skim through all the essays and select samples that could be judged as very poor, average, and outstanding. These samples then become the models for judging the other papers. Some teachers use this same process but add a second procedure of stacking the papers in appropriate piles as they read—for instance, an A pile, a B pile, and so on. They then reread selected papers from the various piles to check their initial judgments and to check for comparability of papers within a given pile.

The technique for grading essay questions or other written work that emphasizes looking at the work as a whole rather than at its individual parts is called holistic scoring.

Obviously, constructing essay items and making judgments about students' work this way can be difficult and time-consuming. The use of essay questions, however, remains one of the best means for measuring the more complex and higher-level abilities of students. Subjective grading will probably always be an unattractive feature of essay testing, but by employing the safeguards described here, this factor can be greatly reduced.

Giving the Test. The format of the test and the kind of coverage it provides are important ingredients. The conditions under which students take the test are equally important. As with many other aspects of teaching, having appropriate structures and routines can help make test taking a less stressful and more productive activity for students. Several guidelines stemming from the practices of effective teachers should be considered:

1. *Find ways to deal with test anxiety.* When confronted with a test, it is normal, and even beneficial, for students to be a little bit anxious. However, some students (often more than teachers suspect) experience a degree of test anxiety that prevents them from doing as well as they could. Effective teachers learn to recognize such students and help reduce anxiety in a number of ways. One way is to simply help students relax before a testing situation. Some teachers use humor and the release from tension it provides. Other teachers use simple relaxation methods, such as a few moments for reflection or deep breathing. Sometimes anxious students lack the requisite test-taking skills. Setting aside periods of instruction to help students learn how to pace themselves, how to allocate time during a test, how to make an outline for an essay question before writing, or how to skip over objective questions for which they do not know the answers, has been shown to reduce *test anxiety* and to improve test performance.

Conditions of the testing situation are very important and can significantly influence how well students do.

2. *Organize the learning environment for conducive test taking.* In Chapter 3, you read how critical the use of space is for instruction. In Chapter 4, other aspects of the overall learning community were discussed. The physical environment for test taking should allow students ample room to do their work; this in turn helps minimize cheating. Obviously, the test environment should be quiet and free from distractions.

3. *Make routines and instructions for the test clear.* Common errors made by beginning teachers include lack of carefully developed test-taking routines and unclear instructions. Most experienced teachers routinize the process of getting started on a test. They pass out the tests face down and ask students not to start until told to do so. This procedure is important for two reasons. One, it gives each student the same amount of time to complete the test. Two, it allows the teacher a chance to go over the instructions with the whole group. In giving instructions for the test, experienced teachers know that it is important to go over each section of the test and to provide students with guidelines for how long to spend on each part. If a new format or type of question is being introduced, procedures and expectations need to be explained. Checking to make sure students understand the tasks they are to perform is another critical feature of getting students ready to take the test.

4. *Avoid undue competition and time pressures.* Unless teachers are using the cooperative learning strategies described in Chapter 10, there is always going to be some competition among students. Competition comes into focus most clearly during testing situations. Experienced teachers use a variety of means to reduce the effects of harmful competition such as grading to a criterion instead of on a curve (explained later); making the final grade for the course dependent on many samples of work, not just one or two tests; and having open discussions with students about competition and its effects on learning.

5. *Provide students with sufficient time.* Insufficient time is another factor that produces poor test performance. In fact, teachers often hear students complain, "I knew the stuff, but I didn't have enough time." Except in instances in which time is the criterion (for example, running the 100-yard dash), tests should be constructed so that students will have ample time to complete all aspects of the test. Beginning teachers often have trouble predicting the amount of time required for a particular test. Until these predictions become more accurate, a safe rule of thumb is to err on the side of having too much time. Making some of the tests "take-homes" is another way to avoid the pressures of time associated with test taking.

6. *Provide appropriate support for students with special needs.* Special-needs students, such as those who are blind or physically challenged in some other way, require special support when they are taking tests. Similarly, some otherwise capable students may have trouble reading quickly enough to complete a test in the time required. It is important for teachers to provide the special support (readers, more time, special tables) that special-needs students require.

Providing students with sufficient time to take a test is very important if teachers want students to perform well on their tests.

Grading

The logic behind norm-referenced and criterion-referenced testing also applies to the two major approaches to grading. **Grading on a curve** is a commonly used procedure in secondary schools and colleges, where students compete with each other for positions along a predetermined grading curve. A teacher following a strict interpretation of the grading-on-a-curve concept would give 10 percent of the students A's, 20 percent B's, 40 percent C's, 20 percent D's, and 10 percent F's. Under this grading scheme, even students with a high degree of mastery of the testing material sometimes fall into one of the lower grading areas and vice versa.

Grading on the curve is the practice of assigning grades so they will follow a normal curve.

An alternate approach to grading on a curve is **grading to criterion** or mastery. Teachers using this approach define rather precisely the content and skills objectives for their class and then measure student performance against those criteria. For example, in spelling, the teacher might decide that the correct spelling of 100 specified words constitutes mastery. Student grades are then determined and performance reported in terms of the percentage of the 100 words a student can spell correctly. A teacher using this approach might specify the following grading scale: A = 100 to 93 words spelled correctly; B = 92 to 85 words spelled correctly; C = 84 to 75 words spelled correctly; D = 74 to 65 words spelled correctly, and F = 64 or fewer words spelled correctly.

Grading to criterion is the practice of assigning grades according to how well students do on a pre-defined set of objectives or standards.

Table 6.6 illustrates the differences between these two approaches for a particular group of students. As you can see, the two approaches produce different grades for individuals within the same class of students. Both grading on a curve and grading on

Table 6.6 *Assigning Spelling Grades from Test Scores Using Two Approaches*

	Grading on a Curve			Grading to Criterion	
Eric	98	A		98	A
Maria	97			97	
Ruth	96	B		96	
John	96			96	
Tanisha	96			96	
Sam	95			95	
Denise	92	C		92	B
Mohammed	90			90	
Louise	90			90	
Elizabeth	90			90	
Betty	87			87	
Marcos	87			87	
Martha	86			86	
Tom	83			83	C
Chang	80	D		80	
Dick	78			78	
Beth	73			73	D
Lane	69			69	
Mark	50	F		50	F
Jordan	50			50	

mastery present some dilemmas for teachers. When grading on a curve, the teacher is confronted with questions about the relationship of grades to native ability. For example, should 10 percent of a class of very able students be given F's? Should 10 percent of a class of learning-disabled students be given A's?

Criterion testing and grading also present troublesome issues for teachers. If criterion levels are set in relation to what is realistic for a particular group of students, then able students should be expected to perform more work and at higher levels than their less-talented peers. However, when grades are assigned, the question arises: Should students who complete all work accurately, even though it is at a lower level, be given the same grade as students who complete all work accurately at a higher level?

Some schools and teachers have tried to resolve this dilemma by using a criterion-referenced report card that lists all the major objectives of the course. Rather than assigning a single grade for the entire course, the teacher assigns a number of grades or verbally describes a child's performance for each objective. This approach is also not trouble-free for teachers. Many parents are accustomed to the five-letter grading scale because it is what they experienced when they were in school. Departures are confusing to them. Also, since a student's grade point average is traditionally used to determine admission to colleges and jobs, it is difficult to report a long list of performance measures that people in the outside world can understand.

Enhancing Teaching with Technology

Test Generators and Electronic Grade Books

Most teachers today use a wide array of software programs designed to help generate and score tests, assist with authentic and performance assessment, record student performance and grades, and report results to students and their parents. Following are descriptions of how these software programs work.

Test Generators

Test generators allow teachers to create a bank of test questions that can be organized for a particular test. This makes it easy to add and delete questions from year to year, as well as create more than one version of the same test to give to students who may be absent on the day the test is given. Some test-generator software also provides printed answer keys for the test.

The test questions come from those the teacher creates, either following the guidelines provided in this chapter or from those provided by the textbook's publisher on CD-ROM or online. Some text-generator programs provide authoring software that helps teachers write and organize questions in a variety of formats: multiple-choice, true-false, matching, and completion. Software and websites are also available to help teachers develop rubrics for scoring essay questions and performance tasks. All of

these technologies allow teachers to format questions in a variety of ways and to design different tests for different classes or levels of students over the same content. Examples of test-generator software such as "Class Manager," "Easy Grade Pro," and others can be accessed from the *Learning to Teach* Online Learning Center.

Rubric Generators

Software and websites are also available to assist in the generation of scoring rubrics on a variety of topics. Most of these, such as Rubricator 4.0, help teachers align their objectives and standards to performance tasks and criteria. The websites annotated in the Online Learning Center provide examples and templates for developing rubrics on a variety of topics.

Electronic Portfolios

Computer and Web-based software can be used by students to create what has been referred to as "electronic" or "digital" portfolios (Costintino & DeLorenzo, 2002; Niguidula, 1998). In fact, you may be using such software to keep the professional portfolio required for your teacher education program. Electronic portfolios display products and artifacts of a student's work and store them on CD-ROM or on a student-produced website.

Electronic Grade Books

Keeping student attendance records and test scores is very time-consuming for teachers. It also requires great accuracy. Electronic grade books are similar to spreadsheet and database software programs. They record scores, grades, and other statistical information in a database; calculations are then performed using the spreadsheet function of the grade book. Grade-book software allows teachers to give weight to different assignments, handle missing assignments, and perform grade calculations. This software also allows teachers to create reports with charts that map a student's performance over time. This is an excellent way of generating reports for students and their parents and saves teachers many hours of work. Figure 6.4 is an example of a report generated by one grade-book software program.

THE FAMILY CIRCUS   By Bil Keane

9-24

©2002 Bil Keane, Inc.
Dist. by King Features Synd.
www.familycircus.com

"Don't open any e-mail from my teacher!
I hear it's carrying a virus."

Source: ©Bill Keane, Inc. Reprinted with special permission of King Features Syndicate.

William Course: SCID33 HIGH SCHOOL						1999/12/01 Section: 01 InteGrade Pro

#	Task Type	Task Name	Score	Out of	Percent	Percent of Sprd
1	Homework	Topic Ques. pg 416	7	10	70	4
2	lab/quiz	Extra Credit Presentations		0		0
3	lab/quiz	Constellation drawing	10	10	100	2
4	lab/quiz	Solar System Presentations	95	100	95	21
5	Homework	Topic Ques. pg 420	10	10	100	4
6	Homework	Topic Ques. pg 427	10	10	100	4
7	lab/quiz	Elipse Lab	10	10	100	2
8	Homework	Topic Ques. pg 407	5	5	50	4
9	Test	TEST-Solar System	95	100	95	60

Student' Summary Grade: 93

Missing Tasks:

#	Task Type	Task	Raw Score	Percent of Sprd
2	lab/quiz	Extra Credit Presentations	<empty>	0
		Total Percentage Missing:		0

Figure 6.4 *Grade Report by Electronic Grade Book*

Making Grades and Homework a Click Away

One way that schools, as a whole, have made use of technology is through the development of websites, which can provide a variety of information to students and their parents. One of the most interesting applications is a school-based website that posts daily grades, attendance records, summaries of lesson plans, and particular teacher's homework assignments. This is made possible with software programs that link a teacher's electronic grade book to the website. Students and parents access the site from home with a password.

These websites provide advantages for teachers, students, and parents. They allow teachers to keep everyone informed about what is going on in their classrooms by posting comments on students' work for students and their parents to see. Students no longer have excuses for not knowing when an assignment is due. Even if they have forgotten or were absent, they can find the assignment and due date on the website. Similarly, they can keep track of their grades and know where they stand in the class at all times. Parents can monitor their children's work in a much more positive atmosphere. They can follow how their child is doing in school on a regular basis, thus preventing surprises associated with the quarterly report card.

To access and learn more about this type of website, go to the *Learning to Teach* Online Learning Center, which lists addresses for ThinkWave.com, a software producer based in Sausalito, California, and others.

Summary Guidelines for Testing and Grading

This section concludes with five summary guidelines that can assist teachers as they approach the task of working out their own testing and grading procedures.

Test at All Levels. Some teachers make the common mistake of focusing most test items on simple recall of information. It is easier to write and score this type of question because there is usually a single correct answer. However, if the teacher wants to extend student thinking and to promote higher-level thought processes, then test questions must require higher-level thinking. Bloom's taxonomy and a test blueprint, described previously, are devices that can assist teachers in constructing test items at various levels.

Communicate Clearly to Students What They Will Be Tested On. A favorite question from students is, "Will we be tested on this?" Effective teachers make it very clear to students which of the ideas presented in a lecture or found in the textbook will be included on the test. Some teachers will write key ideas from a lecture on the board or give them to students in a handout. Some provide the same kind of tool for information in the text. This communicates to students exactly what they are responsible for on the test. Other teachers spend time in review, outlining key ideas to be covered on the test. Still others provide study sheets with sample questions. The goal in each case is to alert students to what is expected of them.

Effective teachers also communicate to students the various levels of knowledge they will need to demonstrate and the amount of detail expected. If the students are expected to commit a list of facts to memory, they are told so; if they are expected to evaluate one idea and contrast it with another, they are told so. Starting with the fifth or sixth grades, students can be taught Bloom's classification system and use it as a guide for their own study, just as teachers use it as a guide for test construction.

Use Multiple Measures. Today, a vast array of learning outcomes exist for most subjects taught in school. These range from knowledge of basic facts and skills to more complex learning outcomes such as critical thinking and problem solving. Some kinds of measures work very well for assessing certain kinds of outcomes, such as multiple-choice questions for testing basic information; other kinds of outcomes, however, require measures such as essay questions and performance tests to adequately assess what students know and are able to do. Effective testing and grading policies require that teachers sample a wide range of possible student performances and use multiple assessment devices to measure important outcomes.

Test Frequently. Some teachers will wait until the end of an instructional unit to test students' knowledge acquisition. It is better to test students frequently for two reasons. First, frequent tests pressure students to keep up with what they are learning and provide them with feedback on how they are doing. Second, frequent testing provides the teacher with feedback on how well students are doing on key instructional objectives and allows reteaching of ideas students are not learning.

Make Grading Procedures Explicit. Regardless of the approach a teacher chooses to use in assigning grades, the exact procedures should be written down and communicated clearly to students and to their parents. Taking the mystery out of grading is one way to help students accomplish the work expected of them and is also a means of getting students to see the "fairness" of the grading system.

Check, Extend, Explore

Check

- What are the major guidelines that teachers should follow when they construct tests?
- What purposes are served by a "test blueprint"?
- What are the advantages and disadvantages of objective tests? Of essay tests?
- What can teachers do to create an encouraging and stress-free test-taking environment?
- Contrast grading on a curve and grading to criterion.

Extend

- Do you agree or disagree with the practice of grading on a curve? Go to the "Extend Question Poll" on the Online Learning Center to respond.
- What do you think about the argument that all objective, pencil-and-paper tests should be abolished?

Explore

- Go to the Online Learning Center at www.mhhe.com/arends6e for links to websites with information on Testing and Grading.

A Look to the Future of Testing and Grading

This chapter describes the importance of assessment and evaluation mainly from the perspective of traditional practices. The effects of testing and grading on student learning have been explored, as has the importance these processes hold for parents and the long-run consequences they have for students.

This chapter has also pointed out that many aspects of testing and grading are controversial and have been for a long time. Perhaps your generation of teachers will find better and fairer ways to make judgments about the work of students. Perhaps methods will be invented that will keep the positive aspects of assessment and evaluation intact—providing feedback to students and their parents about work accomplished—but will eliminate the more destructive aspects of current practices. Some innovative processes and procedures exist. These may provide foundations on which to think about the future of assessment, evaluation, and grading.

Currently there appears to be a nationwide demand for more accountability by schools and teachers as well as a call for higher standards. There is a general belief that the emphasis over the past decade on minimal competencies measured with multiple-choice, standardized tests has raised the basic skill level of students slightly but has failed to promote and measure higher-level thinking and problem-solving skills. Many educators, parents, and test and measurement experts believe that this situation can be corrected by introducing new approaches to student assessment such as the use of authentic assessment, performance tasks, student portfolios, and grading for cooperative effort.

Assessing Performance

Instead of having students respond to multiple-choice questions on paper-and-pencil tests, advocates of **performance assessments** want students to demonstrate that they

More and more teachers require their students to demonstrate they can perform important skills.

can *perform* particular tasks, such as writing an essay, doing an experiment, interpreting the solution to a problem, playing a song, or painting a picture. Notice that the emphasis here is on testing procedural knowledge as contrasted to declarative knowledge.

Figure 6.5 compares a standardized test question and a multiday performance assessment on the concept of *volume*. Note how thoroughly the task is described and how clearly the test developers present how to score the test.

This performance test has several features that are important. It is an attempt to integrate several topics (science, writing, group work) into the assessment process rather than assessing specific skills. It requires students to perform a variety of tasks carried over several days rather than tasks that can be assessed in a few minutes. Additionally, it is an effort to measure complex intellectual skills and processes.

Authentic Assessment

Performance assessments ask students to demonstrate certain behaviors or abilities in testing situations. **Authentic assessment** takes these demonstrations a step further and

Authentic assessments have students demonstrate their abilities to perform particular tasks in real-life settings.

Standardized Test Questions on Volume

1. What is the volume of a cone that has a base area of 78 square centimeters and a height of 12 centimeters?

   a. 30 cm^3
   b. 312 cm^3
   c. 936 cm^3
   d. 2808 cm^3

2. A round and a square cylinder share the same height. Which has the greater volume?

A Multiday Performance Assessment on Volume

Background: Manufacturers naturally want to spend as little as possible not only on the product but on packing and shipping it to stores. They want to *minimize* the cost of production of their packaging, and they want to *maximize* the amount of what is packaged inside (to keep handling and postage costs down: the more individual packages you ship, the more it costs).

Setting: Imagine that your group of two or three people is one of many in the packing department responsible for m&m's candies. The manager of the shipping department has found that the cheapest material for shipping comes as a flat piece of rectangular paperboard (the piece of posterboard you will be given). She is asking each work group in the packing department to help solve this problem: *What completely closed container, built out of the given piece of paperboard, will hold the* largest volume *of m&m's for safe shipping?*

1. Prove, in a *convincing* written report to company executives, that both the *shape* and the *dimensions* of your group's container maximize the volume. In making your case, supply all important data and formulas. Your group will also be asked to make a 3-minute oral report at the next staff meeting. Both reports will be judged for *accuracy, thoroughness*, and *persuasiveness.*

2. Build a model (or multiple models) out of the posterboard of the container shape and size that you think solves the problem. The models are *not* proof; they will *illustrate* the claims you offer in your report.

Figure 6.5 *Two Approaches to Testing Volume*
Source: Wiggins (1993), p. 114

stresses the importance of the application of the skill or ability within the context of a real-life situation. Educational reformers such as Linda Darling Hammond (1996) and Jeannie Oakes (2003) argue that "meaningful performances in real-world" settings can more closely capture the richness of what students understand about how they can apply this knowledge than can testing for "bits and pieces" with conventional assessment procedures. Examples of authentic assessments include demonstrating work in exhibitions such as a science fair or art show, showing skill in a portfolio collection, performing in dance or music recitals, participating in debates, and presenting original papers to peers or parents.

Designing and Scoring Performance and Authentic Assessments

You may ask why, if performance and authentic assessments have so many advantages over more traditional approaches, these approaches aren't used more often and why it took us so long to invent them. Most measurement experts agree (as do teachers who have tried to devise and use performance assessments) that performance tests take a great deal of time to construct and administer and that, in most instances, they are much more expensive. Think, for instance, how long it would take and the cost that would be involved to administer performance assessments to cover all the traditional topics currently found on the SAT. Further, the creation of good performance assessments requires considerable technical knowledge. For teachers who choose to begin constructing their own tests to measure student performance, Linn and Gronlund (1995) and Gronlund, Linn, and Davis (1999) provided the following guidelines to improve the quality of these efforts:

1. Focus on learning outcomes that require complex cognitive skills and student performance.
2. Select or develop tasks that represent both the content and the skills that are central to important learning outcomes.
3. Minimize the dependence of task performance on skills that are irrelevant to the intended purpose of the assessment task.
4. Provide the necessary scaffolding for students to be able to understand the task and what is expected.
5. Construct task directions so that the students' task is clearly indicated.
6. Clearly communicate performance expectations in terms of the criteria by which the performance will be judged.

Many experts in authentic assessment (Wiggins, 1997, for example) argue that for authentic assessments to be effective, the criteria and standards for student work must be clear, known, and nonarbitrary. Students doing academic tasks need to know how their work will be judged in the same ways that divers and gymnasts competing in the Olympics know how their performances will be judged. Scoring rubrics is one technique assessment experts have derived to make criteria clear and nonarbitrary. A **scoring rubric** is a detailed description of some type of performance. It makes explicit the criteria that will be used to judge the performance. Rubrics can also be used to communicate criteria and standards to students before a performance. In the performing arts and sports (also in teaching), rubrics are often based on how an expert would perform. Students might be supplied with videotapes or other examples showing superior performance. Figure 6.6 provides examples of four different scoring rubrics from various grade levels.

A scoring rubric is a detailed description of some type of performance and the criteria that will be used to judge it.

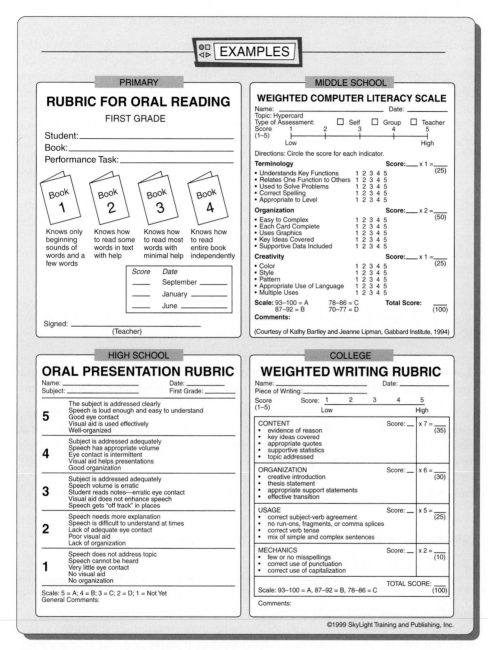

EXAMPLES

PRIMARY

RUBRIC FOR ORAL READING

FIRST GRADE

Student:_____

Book:_____

Performance Task:_____

Book 1	Book 2	Book 3	Book 4
Knows only beginning sounds of words and a few words	Knows how to read some words in text with help	Knows how to read most words with minimal help	Knows how to read entire book independently

Score	Date
_____	September _____
_____	January _____
_____	June _____

Signed: _____
                    (Teacher)

MIDDLE SCHOOL

WEIGHTED COMPUTER LITERACY SCALE

Name: _____ Date: _____

Topic: Hypercard

Type of Assessment: ☐ Self ☐ Group ☐ Teacher

Score (1–5): 1 — 2 — 3 — 4 — 5

Low / High

Directions: Circle the score for each indicator.

Terminology Score:___ x 1 =___ (25)
- Understands Key Functions   1 2 3 4 5
- Relates One Function to Others   1 2 3 4 5
- Used to Solve Problems   1 2 3 4 5
- Correct Spelling   1 2 3 4 5
- Appropriate to Level   1 2 3 4 5

Organization Score:___ x 2 =___ (50)
- Easy to Complex   1 2 3 4 5
- Each Card Complete   1 2 3 4 5
- Uses Graphics   1 2 3 4 5
- Key Ideas Covered   1 2 3 4 5
- Supportive Data Included   1 2 3 4 5

Creativity Score:___ x 1 =___ (25)
- Color   1 2 3 4 5
- Style   1 2 3 4 5
- Pattern   1 2 3 4 5
- Appropriate Use of Language   1 2 3 4 5
- Multiple Uses   1 2 3 4 5

Scale: 93–100 = A   78–86 = C   **Total Score:** ___ (100)
         87–92 = B   70–77 = D

Comments:

(Courtesy of Kathy Bartley and Jeanne Lipman, Gabbard Institute, 1994)

HIGH SCHOOL

ORAL PRESENTATION RUBRIC

Name: _____ Date: _____

Subject: _____ First Grade: _____

5
- The subject is addressed clearly
- Speech is loud enough and easy to understand
- Good eye contact
- Visual aid is used effectively
- Well-organized

4
- Subject is addressed adequately
- Speech has appropriate volume
- Eye contact is intermittent
- Visual aid helps presentations
- Good organization

3
- Subject is addressed adequately
- Speech volume is erratic
- Student reads notes—erratic eye contact
- Visual aid does not enhance speech
- Speech gets "off track" in places

2
- Speech needs more explanation
- Speech is difficult to understand at times
- Lack of adequate eye contact
- Poor visual aid
- Lack of organization

1
- Speech does not address topic
- Speech cannot be heard
- Very little eye contact
- No visual aid
- No organization

Scale: 5 = A; 4 = B; 3 = C; 2 = D; 1 = Not Yet

General Comments:

COLLEGE

WEIGHTED WRITING RUBRIC

Name: _____ Date: _____

Piece of Writing: _____

Score (1–5): 1 — 2 — 3 — 4 — 5

Low / High

CONTENT	Score: __ x 7 = __ (35)

- evidence of reason
- key ideas covered
- appropriate quotes
- supportive statistics
- topic addressed

ORGANIZATION	Score: __ x 6 = __ (30)

- creative introduction
- thesis statement
- appropriate support statements
- effective transition

USAGE	Score: __ x 5 = __ (25)

- correct subject-verb agreement
- no run-ons, fragments, or comma splices
- correct verb tense
- mix of simple and complex sentences

MECHANICS	Score: __ x 2 = __ (10)

- few or no misspellings
- correct use of punctuation
- correct use of capitalization

TOTAL SCORE: ___ (100)

Scale: 93–100 = A, 87–92 = B, 78–86 = C

Comments:

©1999 SkyLight Training and Publishing, Inc.

Figure 6.6 *Examples of Scoring Rubrics*

Source: From *The Mindful School: How to Assess Authentic Learning*, Third Edition, by Kay Burke. © 1999, 1994, 1993 SkyLight Training and Publishing, Inc. Reprinted with permission of SkyLight Professional Development, a Pearson Education Company

Student Portfolios and Narrative Descriptions

Portfolio assessment is a form of assessment that evaluates a sample of students' work and other accomplishments over time.

Closely related to performance and authentic assessment is the use of **student portfolios.** Many of you are already aware of the portfolio process in that it has been used in various fields of the visual arts for a long time. It is common practice for painters, graphic designers, and cartoonists, for example, to select illustrative pieces of their work and organize them into a portfolio that can be used to demonstrate their abilities to potential clients or employers. Often actors, musicians, and models use the same process.

Some schools, such as those in Winnetka, Illinois and Manhattan, Kansas, have students develop portfolios to both assess and report student achievement. These portfolios consist of a sample of artifacts and reflections that represent what the student has done and can do across all subject areas. Teachers in Manhattan have students include the following in their portfolios during the course of the school year: learning log entries; writing samples; spelling samples; handwriting samples; various text pages that students have mastered; audiotape recordings of readings, reports, or demonstrations; videotape recordings of readings, reports, or demonstrations; computer disks of various work; artwork; photographs; lists of books read; skills checklists; self-assessment sheets; outcome checklists; assessment narratives; and parents' reflections on the portfolio. In both Winnetka and Manhattan, students prepare their portfolios to be shared with parents and are guided by such questions as:

How has my writing changed since last year?
What do I know about numbers now that I didn't know in September?
What is unique about my portfolio?

The idea here is to have students prepare their portfolios so that they reflect on their own learning. As described in the Enhancing Teaching with Technology feature for this chapter, students today often create electronic portfolios to display artifacts of their work. In addition, the teachers in Winnetka have combined portfolios, student reflections, and their own judgments into a visual reporting device, which is illustrated in Figure 6.7.

Assessing Group Effort and Individually Contracted Work

In Chapter 10, you will read about cooperative learning procedures through which students are awarded points and grades for their work in teams and for their individual work. These procedures hold good potential for reducing the destructive process of comparing students with their peers as well as excessive competition.

Interest is also growing among educators today in using criterion-referenced evaluations. For instance, the creators and developers of mastery learning (Bloom, 1976; Guskey & Gates, 1986), the Keller (1966) plan, and individualized prescribed instruction (IPI) have shown how learning materials for some subjects can be broken down into smaller units of study and how students can be given the opportunity to work toward a specified objective (criterion) until they have mastered it. Grades under these systems are determined not by comparing students with their peers but by the number of objectives they have mastered. Systems in which teachers make contracts with individual students allow each student to compete with himself or herself on mutually agreed-upon criteria rather than to compete with others. Grading for team effort and for individually contracted work, however, are difficult processes for teachers to im-

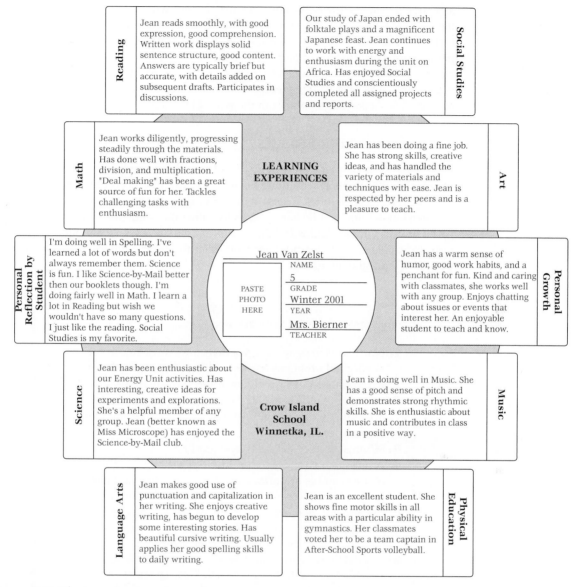

Reading

Jean reads smoothly, with good expression, good comprehension. Written work displays solid sentence structure, good content. Answers are typically brief but accurate, with details added on subsequent drafts. Participates in discussions.

Social Studies

Our study of Japan ended with folktale plays and a magnificent Japanese feast. Jean continues to work with energy and enthusiasm during the unit on Africa. Has enjoyed Social Studies and conscientiously completed all assigned projects and reports.

Math

Jean works diligently, progressing steadily through the materials. Has done well with fractions, division, and multiplication. "Deal making" has been a great source of fun for her. Tackles challenging tasks with enthusiasm.

Art

Jean has been doing a fine job. She has strong skills, creative ideas, and has handled the variety of materials and techniques with ease. Jean is respected by her peers and is a pleasure to teach.

LEARNING EXPERIENCES

Personal Reflection by Student

I'm doing well in Spelling. I've learned a lot of words but don't always remember them. Science is fun. I like Science-by-Mail better then our booklets though. I'm doing fairly well in Math. I learn a lot in Reading but wish we wouldn't have so many questions. I just like the reading. Social Studies is my favorite.

Jean Van Zelst

PASTE PHOTO HERE

NAME
5
GRADE
Winter 2001
YEAR
Mrs. Bierner
TEACHER

Personal Growth

Jean has a warm sense of humor, good work habits, and a penchant for fun. Kind and caring with classmates, she works well with any group. Enjoys chatting about issues or events that interest her. An enjoyable student to teach and know.

Science

Jean has been enthusiastic about our Energy Unit activities. Has interesting, creative ideas for experiments and explorations. She's a helpful member of any group. Jean (better known as Miss Microscope) has enjoyed the Science-by-Mail club.

Crow Island School Winnetka, IL.

Music

Jean is doing well in Music. She has a good sense of pitch and demonstrates strong rhythmic skills. She is enthusiastic about music and contributes in class in a positive way.

Language Arts

Jean makes good use of punctuation and capitalization in her writing. She enjoys creative writing, has begun to develop some interesting stories. Has beautiful cursive writing. Usually applies her good spelling skills to daily writing.

Physical Education

Jean is an excellent student. She shows fine motor skills in all areas with a particular ability in gymnastics. Her classmates voted her to be a team captain in After-School Sports volleyball.

Figure 6.7 *The Learning Experiences Form*

Source: After Hebert (1992), p. 60

plement by themselves. These experiments run strongly against current norms and traditions, and they require schoolwide policies and collegial support to be successful.

Experimenting with New Approaches

Some beginning teachers will find themselves in schools in which a great deal of experimentation is going on with alternative assessments procedures. Most will find more traditional approaches being used. Alone, without the assistance of colleagues, it is doubtful that beginning teachers can implement a complete alternative classroom assessment system. They can, however, experiment with pieces of alternative assessments. For instance, a science teacher could devise a few performance tasks, described earlier, or a language arts or English teacher could make part of a student's grade depend on the performance of particular authentic writing tasks. Some use of portfolios can benefit almost every grade level in every subject area. These steps are movements in the right direction as your generation of teachers works to find better and fairer ways to assess and make judgments about the work of students.

Assessment Bill of Rights

We conclude this chapter by returning to an admonition made at the beginning that assessment and evaluation are among the most important aspects of teachers' work and carry heavy responsibilities. Teachers must not only do this part of their job well but also must make sure that no harm comes to vulnerable students. Some assessment experts, such as Grant Wiggins (1993), have proposed an "assessment bill of rights" (illustrated in Figure 6.8) to protect students from the potential harm that may come to them from educational testing.

All students are entitled to the following:

1. Worthwhile (engaging, educative, and "authentic") intellectual problems that are validated against worthy "real-world" intellectual problems, roles, and situations.
2. Clear, apt, published, and consistently applied teacher criteria in grading work and published models of excellent work that exemplifies standards.
3. Minimal secrecy in testing and grading.
4. Ample opportunities to produce work that they can be proud of (thus, ample opportunity in the curriculum and instruction to monitor, self-assess, and self-correct their work).
5. Assessment, not just tests: multiple and varied opportunities to display and document their achievement, and options in tests that allow them to play to their strengths.
6. The freedom, climate, and oversight policies necessary to question grades and test practices without fear or retribution.
7. Forms of testing that allow timely opportunities for students to explain or justify answers marked as wrong but that they believe to be apt or correct.
8. Genuine feedback: usable information on their strengths and weaknesses and an accurate assessment of their long-term progress toward a set of exit-level standards framed in terms of essential tasks.
9. Scoring/grading policies that provide incentives and opportunities for improving performance and seeing progress against exit-level and real-world standards.

Figure 6.8 *Assessment Bill of Rights*
Source: Wiggins (1993), p. 28

Check, Extend, Explore

Check
- What are some of the controversies of testing? What solutions can be considered to remedy these problems?
- How do performance assessments and authentic assessments differ? How do they differ from standardized testing methods?
- What is a student portfolio? How can it be used in a teacher's assessment program?
- What are the primary ideas behind the "Assessment Bill of Rights" developed by Wiggins?

Extend
- Do you agree or disagree with the proposition that your generation of teachers will change the traditional ways for assessing and grading students? Go to the "Extend Question Poll" on the Online Learning Center to respond.

Explore
- Go to the Online Learning Center at www.mhhe.com/arends6e for links to websites with information about *Performance Assessment, Scoring Rubrics, and Portfolios.*

Reflections from the *Classroom*

My A, B, C's

You have just met with the principal at the school where you have been hired for your first teaching position. You asked him about the school's grading and reporting policies. He said that teachers have considerable freedom. They are required to give A's, B's, C's, D's, and F's, and they must conform to the district's grading periods. Outside, of these requirements, they can design their own system for how much weight to give to tests; quizzes, homework, participation, and the like. They can also decide whether to grade on a curve or base grades on particular standards. He told you that most students are very concerned about their grades and most already have plans to attend college. They and their parents are not afraid to complain if they believe a teacher has evaluated their work unfairly.

The principal encouraged you to talk to other teachers in the school, come up with your own approach for assessment and grading, and then discuss your plan with other teachers at your grade level or in your department. You have always believed that a teacher should have a grading system that is fair and acceptable to students. You also believe that a teacher's grading system should be one that will promote learning for all the students in a classroom.

Develop an assessment plan consistent with your teaching situation and your beliefs. Approach this situation from the perspective closest to the grade level or subject area you are preparing to teach. Address the following questions in your plan: What will be your overall approach? What weight will you give to tests, assignments, and projects? Will you give credit for participation? For effort? Will you hold all students to the same standards or will you establish different standards for gifted students and those who have learning disabilities? How will you justify your system to your students? Their parents? Before you begin, consider how your assessment plan can become an important artifact in your professional portfolio. After you finish, compare your plan to the following ideas expressed by experienced teachers.

(continued)

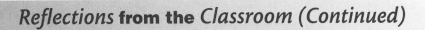

Reflections **from the** *Classroom (Continued)*

Vickie Williams

Arthur Slade Regional Catholic School, K-through 8th Grades
Glen Burnie, MD

My assessment system involves evaluating authentic performances, student participation in class, special projects or products (10% of grade, respectively), quizzes (20%), and major tests (30%). I believe my assessment system is fair, well communicated to the students and parents, and addresses multiple intelligences. Therefore, I do not feel the need to grade on a curve. However, I do include one measure of growth, a reading and writing portfolio (20%), which is evaluated each quarter according to the progress the student has made. This provides a mechanism for those with learning disabilities, as well as gifted students, to experience success based on their own baseline achievement level, rather than a mastery criterion. I have received favorable reactions to my growth portfolio from my students, as well as their parents.

I have found that the majority of students in my classes can be academically successful if I provide scoring rubrics, rating scales, and information about the quizzes and tests in advance. I make the criteria for academic success explicit and obtainable. Consistently, I make individual and aggregated assessment data available to both students and parents. I look for trends in my assessment data that might point to unfair tests, test items, or scoring criteria. If I discover items or criteria that are unfair or confusing, I change them accordingly. I do not attempt to "trick" the students or "catch them by surprise." Rather, I set reasonable expectations in advance and make adjustments when necessary to maintain an assessment system that promotes the learning success of all students.

Ellen Thomas-Covell

Timberlane Middle School, 8th Grade
Hopewell Valley School District, NJ

I teach an eighth grade Introductory Physical Science class, which is mostly laboratory-based. Students are required to write up lab reports for each experiment, and I give periodic quizzes and chapter tests. When I first began teaching, I graded each assignment on a percentage basis. At the end of the marking period, I then calculated the weighted average—making lab reports 50%, quizzes 10%, and tests 30%. For the final 10%,

I gave a grade for overall participation/preparedness/ and homework completion. However, there were two problems with my system. First, grading the lab reports was difficult because some reports were very short and to the point, while others were more lengthy and in-depth. I found myself constantly re-evaluating the overall rubric so that the longer labs were not being graded lower simply because there was more information to grade and more room for error. The second problem was that when I had special projects or any other assignments, I had to rethink the original weighting. Should I make something worth less than planned, or lump the special project in with one of the existing categories? Naturally, reassessing is part of teaching, whether you're looking at your methods, your content, your goals, or your grading. However, in this case I felt that I was unnecessarily burdening myself with the decision-making process for every new assignment collected.

I resolved this problem by going to a point system. It works very simply. Each assignment is worth a certain number of points, based on particular criteria: amount of data required, time allotted, and importance. For instance, labs are now worth from 20 points (for a one day, quick exploration) up to 100 points (for culminating, 2-week activities requiring a detailed progress log, procedural flow chart, and in-depth conclusion). The "weighting" is therefore built into each assignment! Quizzes are typically 20 to 30 points, and tests are 60 to 80 points. Special projects and graded homework are also given appropriate point values. Extra credit points for exceptional effort, marked improvement, and/or participation can be added easily to the "numerator." Penalties for missed assignments or incomplete homework can be subtracted. At any given time, students may add up their earned points and divide it by the total possible points to find their current average. I tell students that I only calculate averages for mid-term progress reports and report cards, so they need to keep a running record of their grades if they think they may want to know their average at any other time. I generated a "Marking Period Grade Sheet," which they may use for this purpose.

There are many grading plans that work. I think it is best to find a plan that works for you, but stay flexible and open-minded, and know that grading, as in all areas of teaching, is an ever-evolving skill!

🔘⊙ *Chapter Review*

Go back to the "Interactive and Applied Learning" feature at the beginning of the chapter for a listing of interactive and applied activities. Go to the Online Learning Center at **www.mhhe.com/arends6e** or your Interactive Student CD-ROM to take practice quizzes over the content of this chapter and receive immediate feedback. You can also review chapter content and main ideas, practice with key terms, and find annotated Web links on topics associated with this chapter.

Summary

Perspective on Assessment and Evaluation

- Assessment and evaluation can be defined as functions performed by teachers to make wise decisions about their instruction and about their students. A fairly large portion of a teacher's time is consumed with assessment and evaluation processes.
- The consequences of testing and grading students are immense. They can determine the colleges students attend, the careers open to them, and the lifestyles they ultimately maintain.
- Evaluation specialists make key distinctions between formative and summative evaluation. Formative evaluation information is collected before or during instruction and is used to inform teachers about their students' prior knowledge and to make judgments about lesson effectiveness. Summative evaluation information is collected after instruction and is used to summarize how students have performed and to determine grades.
- Because the decisions made are so important, it is essential that the information used by teachers to make judgments be of high quality. Measurement specialists use two technical terms to describe the quality of assessment and evaluation information: reliability and validity.
- Reliability refers to the ability of a test or measurement device to produce consistent scores or information for persons who take the test more than once over a period of time.
- Validity refers to the ability of a test or other device to measure what it claims to measure.

Theoretical and Empirical Support

- There is an extensive knowledge base about the technical aspects of assessment and evaluation.
- Studies show that external rewards, such as grades, can provide a strong incentive for students to perform work and can affect student learning.

- Studies also show that external rewards can sometimes have negative effects, particularly with tasks students find intrinsically interesting anyway.

Statewide and Schoolwide Assessment Programs

- Most states today have testing programs that measure student achievement in grades 3–8. Information from statewide tests is often used to compare how well schools are doing. In some instances, scores on statewide tests determine a student's promotion to the next grade or graduation from high school.
- Standards-based education and frequent testing are believed by many to have positive effects on student learning. Some leading educators and teachers, however, believe that frequent testing may also impede learning.
- Schoolwide assessment programs include the use of norm- and criterion-referenced tests usually chosen and administered by school district specialists.
- Norm-referenced tests evaluate a particular student's performance by comparing it to the performance of some other well-defined group of students.
- Criterion-referenced tests measure student performance against some agreed-upon criterion.
- It is important that teachers understand the advantages and disadvantages of various types of schoolwide assessment procedures and be able to communicate these to students and their parents.

A Teacher's Assessment Program

- The teacher's own classroom assessment program includes features for collecting information that can be used to diagnose students' prior knowledge and skills, to provide students with corrective feedback, and to make accurate judgments about student achievement.

- Formal tests to diagnose students' prior knowledge are more fully developed in fields such as mathematics and language arts. Asking questions, interviewing, and listening to students' responses as well as using portfolios are informal means of ascertaining what students know about a subject.
- Corrective feedback is most useful if it is immediate, frequent, and communicated in nonjudgmental ways.
- Testing students' progress and determining grades is an important aspect of teachers' work, and society expects it to be done well.

Specifics of Testing and Grading

- A variety of guidelines exist for teachers to follow as they construct tests to measure student learning and make judgments and assign grades for student work.
- General principles for test construction consist of making test items in harmony with instructional objectives, covering all learning tasks, making tests valid and reliable, interpreting test results with care, and using the appropriate test items.
- A test blueprint is a device to help teachers determine how much space to allocate to various topics covered and to measure various levels of student cognitive processes.
- Teacher-made tests can consist of true-false, matching, fill-in-the-blanks, multiple-choice, and essay items. Each type has its own advantages and disadvantages.
- Teacher bias in judging student work from essay questions is an important issue. To reduce bias, teachers should make their expectations for essay answers clear to students, write sample answers ahead of time, and use techniques to reduce expectancy effects.

- When giving tests, effective teachers find ways to reduce students' test anxiety, organize their learning environments to be conducive to test taking, make instructions clear, and avoid undue competition.
- Grading on a curve and grading to criterion or mastery are the two approaches used by classroom teachers. Each grading approach has its advantages and its shortcomings.
- Testing guidelines—making sure there is congruence between test items and what is being taught, testing frequently, testing at all levels, being fair and impartial, and communicating clearly about testing and grading procedures—help teachers devise effective assessment and evaluation programs in their classrooms.

A Look to the Future of Testing and Grading

- Currently, there appears to be a nationwide call for more accountability by schools and better and fairer ways to test and evaluate students.
- Performance and authentic assessments, as well as the use of portfolios, are likely to replace the more traditional paper-and-pencil tests in the near future.
- Performance and authentic assessments ask students to demonstrate that they can perform particular real-life tasks, such as writing an essay, doing an experiment, or playing a song.
- Developing performance and authentic assessment devices is a difficult and complex task, as is making sure these newer forms of tests are valid and reliable.
- New interest in accountability and testing has also led to the development of an "assessment bill of rights" to make sure that students are not harmed by educational testing procedures.

Key Terms

Portfolio and Field Experience Activities

This feature has been designed to help you learn from your field experiences and to assist you in the preparation of artifacts for your professional portfolio on topics and standards associated with Chapter 6.

1. Complete the "Reflections from the Classroom" exercise at the end of this chapter. The recommended assessment plan will provide evidence of your understanding and proficiency in assessment and evaluation.

2. Using Activities 6.2 and 6.4 in the *Guide to Field Experiences and Portfolio Development,* interview a teacher about his or her grading practices and critique one of his or her tests. Your analysis of the interview and critique of the test can provide evidence for your portfolio about your understanding of grading and testing.

3. Complete Activity 6.6 in the *Guide to Field Experiences and Portfolio Development* as means to communicate your ability to develop and use various kinds of assessment devices.

Books for the Professional

Go to the Online Learning Center at www.mhhe.com/ arends6e or your Interactive CD-ROM for an annotated version of this list.

Airasian, P. W. (2001). *Classroom Assessment: Concepts and Applications* (4th ed.). New York: McGraw-Hill.

Gronlund, N. E. (2002). *Assessment of Student Achievement* (7th ed.). Boston: Allyn & Bacon.

Marzano, R. J. (2000). *Transforming Classroom Grading.* Alexandria, VA: Association for Supervision and Curriculum Development.

Rothman, R. (1995). *Measuring Up: Standards, Assessment and School Reform.* San Francisco: Jossey-Bass.

Stiggins, R. (1996). *Student-Centered Classroom Assessment* (2nd ed.). New York: Prentice-Hall.

Wiggins, G. P. (1998). *Educative Assessment: Designing Assessment to Inform and Improve Student Performance.* San Francisco: Jossey-Bass.

Part 3 *The Interactive Aspects of Teaching*

Part 3 of *Learning to Teach* focuses directly on what most people think of as teaching—the actual face-to-face interaction between the teacher and the learner. Each of the six chapters in Part 3 describes one of six basic instructional approaches: (1) presenting and explaining; (2) direct instruction; (3) concept teaching; (4) cooperative learning; (5) problem-based learning; and (6) discussion. The first three models rely mainly on social learning theory and on behavioral and information-processing theories of learning and are more or less teacher-centered. The next three approaches are based on learner-centered principles. Learner-centered approaches rest on the philosophical perspective of John Dewey and other progressive educators as well as those who currently hold cognitive and contructivist perspectives of teaching and learning. As you study these approaches, you will learn that each has been designed to achieve certain learning outcomes at the expense of others, and as such, each approach has advantages and disadvantages. No one approach is necessarily better than another. Appropriate use of each depends on the nature of the students in a classroom and the type of goals the teacher wants to achieve.

The various approaches described in Part 3 are labeled *teaching models,* although other terms—such as *teaching strategies, teaching methods,* or *teaching principles*—share similar characteristics. The label *teaching model* was selected for two important reasons.

First, the concept *model* implies something larger than a particular strategy, method, or tactic. For example, as used here, the term *teaching model* encompasses a broad, overall approach to instruction rather than a specific strategy. Models of teaching have some attributes that specific strategies and methods do not have. The attributes of a model are a coherent theoretical basis—a point of view about what students should learn and how they learn, and recommended teaching behaviors and classroom structures for bringing about different types of learning.

Second, the concept of the teaching model serves as an important communication device for teachers. Joyce and Weil (1972, Joyce, Weil, and Calhoun, 2000) have classified various approaches to teaching according to their instructional goals, their syntaxes, and the nature of their learning environments. Instructional goals specify the type of *student outcomes* a model has been designed to achieve. The use of a particular model helps a teacher achieve some goals but not others. A model's *syntax* is the overall flow of a lesson's activity. The *learning environment* is the context in which any teaching act must be carried out, including the ways students are motivated and managed.

Although there is nothing magical about these words or this classification system, they provide a language for communicating about various kinds of teaching activities, when they should occur, and why.

In describing the teaching models in the chapters that follow, it may seem to suggest that there is only one correct way to use a particular model. In some respects, this is true. If teachers deviate too far from a model's syntax or environmental demands, they are not using the model. On the other hand, once teachers have mastered a particular model, they often adapt it to their own particular teaching style and to the particular group of students with whom they are working. As with most other aspects of teaching, models are guides for thinking and talking about teaching. They should not be viewed as recipes to follow.

There is a substantial knowledge base for the interactive aspects of teaching as well as wisdom that has been accumulated by experienced teachers over the years. Part of the excitement and challenge in learning to teach is in figuring out the complexities of teaching, which the organizational pattern of a book can never portray with complete accuracy.

Chapter Seven

Presenting and Explaining

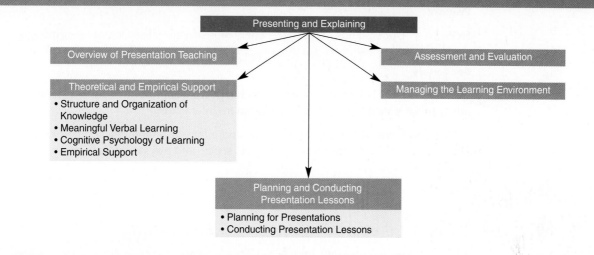

Interactive **and** *Applied Learning*

Go to your Interactive Student CD-ROM to:

- Hear audio clips of Patricia Merkel and Dennis Holt talk about the presentation model of instruction in the *Teachers on Teaching* feature
- Watch the video clip: Presentation Teaching
- Complete the Presenting and Explaining Case Exercise in the Chapter 7 *Case Exercises and Practice Tasks* area.
- Complete the Presenting and Explaining Practice Tasks in the Chapter 7 *Case Exercises and Practice Tasks* area. Plan for presentations: task analysis; differentiate guided practice for two students; assess student learning; respond to teaching dilemmas; and reflect on the use of direct instruction.

Go to the Online Learning Center at www.mhhe.com/arends6e to read *PowerWeb* articles and newsfeed updates about:

- Classroom management
- Cultural diversity in education
- Instruction
- Learning
- Technology and education
- Testing and evaluation
- World Wide Web

Considering **Standards**

Studying this chapter will help you meet three INTASC principles:

Primary

INTASC 4: Understands and uses a variety of instructional strategies to encourage student development of critical thinking, problem-solving, and performance skills.

Secondary

INTASC 6: Uses knowledge of verbal and nonverbal communication to foster inquiry, collaboration, and supportive classroom interaction.

INTASC 8: Understands and uses formal and informal assessment strategies to evaluate and ensure the continuous intellectual, social, and physical development of the learner.

Reflecting **on** *Presenting and Explaining*

Think of all the lectures you have heard in your lifetime or the many instances when a teacher or coach tried to explain something to you. You can conjure up some lectures that were stimulating, leaving you eager to learn more about the topic; others may have been boring, causing you to struggle to stay awake; still others may have been humorous and entertaining, but you didn't learn very much. You may remember some explanations that were very concise and clear, while others were ambiguous and confusing.

Before reading this chapter, take a few minutes to think about and do the following:

- *Make a list of the essential characteristics of the best lectures you have ever heard.*
- *Make a similar list of the characteristics of the worst lectures you have ever heard.*
- *Make a third list of the characteristics of clear and unclear explanations.*

Now, study your lists and consider what you think your teachers did to develop the best lectures or explanations and what they did or didn't do that produced poor lectures and unclear explanations. How did different types of lectures and explanations influence what you learned? Did you learn anything from the bad lecture or the unclear explanations? Why? Why not?

 Go to the Online Learning Center at www.mhhe.com/arends6e to respond to these questions.

Presentations (lectures) and explanations by teachers comprise one-sixth to one-fourth of all classroom time. The amount of time devoted to presenting and explaining information increases at the higher grade levels of elementary school, in middle schools, and in high schools (Dunkin & Biddle, 1974; Rosenshine & Stevens, 1986; Strange, 2002). Some educators have argued that teachers devote too much time to talking, and over the years, considerable effort has gone into creating models aimed at decreasing the amount of teacher talk and making instruction more student-centered. Nonetheless, formal presentation of information remains the most popular model of teaching, and the amount of time devoted to it has remained relatively stable over most of the twentieth century (Cuban, 1993).

The popularity of presenting and explaining is not surprising, since the most widely held objectives for education at the present time are those associated with the acquisition and retention of information. Curricula in schools are structured around bodies of information organized as science, mathematics, English, and the social sciences. Consequently, curriculum guides, textbooks, and tests routinely used by teachers are similarly organized. Further, many exams that students are required to take test primarily information. Experienced teachers know that exposition is an effective way of helping students acquire the array of information society believes it is important for them to know.

> Despite criticism, presentation, or lecture, maintains its popularity among teachers.

The purpose of this chapter is to introduce the **presentation teaching model** and to describe how to use it effectively. We cannot judge the ideal amount of time a teacher should devote to this model. Instead, the model is described as a valuable teaching approach that can be used in all subject areas and at all grade levels. The appropriate use of the presentation model is situational; that is, its use depends on the objective the teacher is striving to achieve and the particular students with whom the teacher is working.

> The appropriate use of the presentation model varies, depending on a teacher's objective and the particular students in the class.

Fortunately, the knowledge base on teacher presentation and explanation is fairly well developed. Beginning teachers can learn this model quite easily. As you read this chapter and study the model, you will find much that is familiar. You already know some of the material from speech classes in high school or college. You know some of the difficulties of presenting from informal talks or speeches you have made. Although the goals of public speaking and classroom presentations are quite different, many of the basic communication skills are the same. We first provide a general overview of the presentation model using the analytical scheme described in the introduction to Part 3; namely, that a teaching model has three features: (1) the type of learner outcomes it produces; (2) its syntax or overall flow of instructional activities; and (3) its learning environment.

Following the overview, we take a brief look at the theoretical and empirical support for the presentation model, after which we provide a detailed discussion of how to plan and conduct a presentation lesson. This same chapter structure will be followed in subsequent Part 3 chapters.

Overview of Presentation Teaching

The specific presentation model highlighted here is an adaptation of what is sometimes called the *advance organizer model*. This model requires a teacher to provide students with advance organizers before presenting new information and to make special efforts during and following a presentation to strengthen and extend student thinking. This particular approach was chosen for two reasons: One, the approach is compatible with current knowledge from cognitive psychology about the way individuals acquire, process, and retain new information. Two, various components of the model have been

> The presentation model requires a highly structured environment characterized by a teacher who is an active presenter and students who are active listeners.

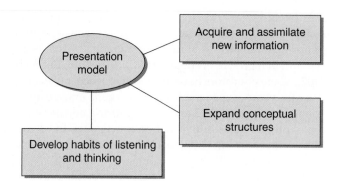

Figure 7.1 *Presentation Teaching Aims at Accomplishing Three Learner Outcomes*

carefully studied over the past forty years, thus giving the model a substantial, if not always consistent, knowledge base.

Briefly, the learning outcomes of the presentation model, shown in Figure 7.1, are rather clear and straightforward: namely, to help students acquire, assimilate, and retain new information, expand their conceptual structures, and develop particular habits of listening and for thinking about information.

Presentation is a teacher-centered model consisting of four major phases: (1) The flow proceeds from the teacher's initial attempt to clarify the aims of the lesson and to get students ready to learn, through (2) presentation of an advance organizer and (3) presentation of the new information, to (4) the conclusion with interactions aimed at checking student understanding of the new information and extending and strengthening their thinking skills. When using the presentation model, the teacher strives to structure the learning environment tightly. Except in the final phase of the model, the teacher is an active presenter and expects students to be active listeners. Use of the model requires a physical learning environment that is conducive to presenting and listening, including appropriate facilities for use of multimedia technology. More detail about the model's syntax will be provided later in the chapter in the section Conducting Presentation Lessons.

Theoretical and Empirical Support

Three complementary sets of ideas have come together to provide the theoretical and empirical support for the presentation model of teaching. These include (1) the concept of **structure of knowledge,** (2) the psychology of **meaningful verbal learning,** and (3) ideas from **cognitive psychology** on how the human memory system works and how knowledge is represented and acquired. It is important to understand the ideas underlying these three topics because they provide the basis on which teachers choose, organize, and present information to students. They also support several features of the direct instruction and concept teaching models presented in Chapters 8 and 9, respectively.

Structure and Organization of Knowledge

Knowledge of the world has been organized around various subject areas called *disciplines.* History is an example of a discipline that organizes knowledge using temporal concepts; biology organizes information and ideas about living things; and physics,

Check, Extend, Explore

Check
- What are the four phases of a presentation lesson?
- What learner outcomes characterize presentation lessons?
- What type of learning environment is required for an effective presentation?

Extend
- Many people believe that teachers spend too much time talking to students. Do you agree or disagree with this opinion? Go to the "Extend Question Poll" on the Online Learning center to respond.

Explore
- Go to the Online Learning Center at www.mhhe.com/arends6e for links to websites related to *Presenting and Explaining.*

about the physical world. The clustering of courses by academic departments in college catalogs is one illustration of the wide array of disciplines that exist. The classification of books in libraries according to subject matter under the Dewey decimal or Library of Congress system is another.

The disciplines, as they are defined at any point in time, constitute the resources on which most teachers and curriculum developers draw in making decisions about what knowledge should be taught to students. Over fifty years ago, Ralph Taylor (1949) made this observation:

> From the standpoint of the curriculum, the disciplines should be viewed primarily as a resource that can be drawn upon for the education of students. Hence, we want to understand these resources at their best. . . . These disciplines at their best are not simply an encyclopedic collection of facts to be memorized but rather they are an active effort to make sense out of some portion of the world or of life (Ford & Pugno, 1964, p. 4).

During the 1950s, several scholars and curriculum theorists started to study how disciplines were organized and what that organization meant to instruction. A book written by Jerome Bruner in 1960 called *The Process of Education* highlighted this research. This inquiry produced the idea that each discipline has a structure consisting of key concepts that define the discipline. Figure 7.2 shows a partial structure for information about American government.

Jerome Bruner was among the first to describe how important structures of knowledge are in education.

Note that the illustration shows how the structure of government can be viewed as having several major ideas with a variety of subideas, such as citizen rights, amendment processes, and the various branches of government. It is not appropriate here to go into detail about the knowledge structures of various disciplines. However, it is important to emphasize that such structures exist and that they become a means for organizing information about topics, for dividing information into various categories, and for showing relationships among various categories of information.

The teaching implications of this structuring of knowledge are clear—the key ideas supporting each structure should be taught to students instead of lists of disparate facts or bits of information. For example, Bruner (1962) argued that knowing about a house "is not a matter of knowing about a collection of nails, shingles, wallboards, and windows" (p. 77). It is the total concept of house that is significant and important. The same can be said for examples from mathematics, economics, or botany.

Meaningful Verbal Learning

David Ausubel (1963), an educational psychologist, did some interesting groundbreaking work at about the same time as Bruner. He was particularly interested in the way knowledge is organized and how the human mind organizes ideas. He explained that at any point in time, a learner has an existing "organization . . . and clarity of knowledge in a particular subject-matter field" (p. 26). He called this organization a

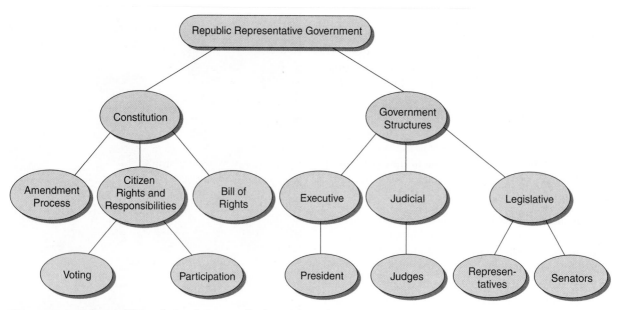

Figure 7.2 *A Partial Knowledge Structure for Representative Government*

An individual's cognitive structure determines his or her ability to deal with new information and ideas.

cognitive structure and believed that this structure determined a learner's ability to deal with new ideas and relationships. Meaning can emerge from new materials only if they tie into existing cognitive structures of prior learning.

Ausubel saw the primary function of formal education as the organizing of information for students and the presenting of ideas in clear and precise ways. The principal function of pedagogy, according to Ausubel (1963), is:

> the art and science of presenting ideas and information meaningfully and effectively—so that clear, stable and unambiguous meanings emerge and . . . [are] retained over a long period of time as an organized body of knowledge (p. 81).

For this learning to occur, according to Ausubel, the teacher should create two conditions: (1) present learning materials in a potentially meaningful form, with major and unifying ideas and principles, consistent with contemporary scholarship, highlighted rather than merely listed as facts; and (2) find ways to anchor the new learning materials to the learners' prior knowledge and ready the students' minds so that they can receive new information.

Advance organizers provide a device to help learners link new information to prior knowledge.

The major pedagogical strategy proposed by Ausubel (1963) was the use of **advance organizers.** It is the job of an advance organizer to:

> delineate clearly, precisely, and explicitly the principal similarities and differences between the ideas in a new learning passage, on the one hand, and existing related concepts in cognitive structure on the other (p. 83).

More details about how to construct and present advance organizers will be provided later in the chapter in the Using Advance Organizers section.

Cognitive Psychology of Learning

A third stream of inquiry that helps explain how information should be presented to students grew out of the rapidly expanding field of cognitive psychology, or *cognitive science* as it is sometimes called. Its frame of reference is important to teachers because it provides ways for thinking about how the mind works and how knowledge is acquired, organized, and represented in the memory system. As you read the key ideas here, you will observe how they are connected in many ways to Bruner's earlier concept of structure of knowledge (1962) and Ausubel's ideas about meaningful verbal learning (1963). However, cognitive science has expanded these earlier ideas in significant ways and has a great deal of influence on the way teaching and learning is viewed today.

Over the past decade, several cognitive psychologists (Gagné, 1985; Gagné et. al., 1993; Greeno, Collins, & Resnick, 1996; Nolan & Francis, 1992), have organized the ideas and research in the field of cognitive psychology that apply directly to teaching. The discussion that follows relies heavily on their work and their definitions of the different types of knowledge and how information is processed and represented in the memory system.

Types of Knowledge. Traditionally, learning theorists generally distinguish between two major types of knowledge: *declarative knowledge* and *procedural knowledge* (E. Gagné, 1985; E. Gagné et al., 1993; R. Gagné, 1977; Marx & Winne, 1994; and Ryle, 1949). **Declarative knowledge** is knowledge *about something* or knowledge that something is the case. **Procedural knowledge** is knowledge about *how to do something.* As described in Chapter 3, the scholars who revised Bloom's Taxonomy of Educational Objectives (Anderson et. al., 2001) expanded this category scheme to include *factual knowledge, conceptual knowledge,* and *metacognitive knowledge.* Actually, Linn and his colleagues (2001) divided declarative knowledge into two categories: factual knowledge, defined as knowing basic elements of a topic; and conceptual knowledge, knowing about the interrelationships among the basic elements. They also added a fourth dimension—metacognitive knowledge, defined as knowledge of cognition in general as well as awareness of one's own cognitive processes. For our purposes here, we will illustrate and use three types of knowledge: factual, conceptual, and procedural.

> Factual knowledge is knowing about the basic elements of a topic.
>
> Conceptual knowledge is knowing about the relationships among elements.

An example of factual knowledge is knowing that there are three branches of government defined by the Constitution, that the legislative branch has two chambers (the House and the Senate), and that representatives to the House are elected to two-year terms whereas senators are elected to six-year terms. Conceptual knowledge is understanding the relationship among the three branches, both as defined by the Constitution and as a consequence of tradition. Procedural knowledge about this same topic is knowing how to go to the polling place to vote on election day, how to write a letter to a senator, or if one is a senator, how to guide a bill through the Senate until it becomes a law. Metacognive knowledge is knowing which of many political actions might be most effective in getting a desired piece of legislation passed as well as one's own opinions and, perhaps, lack of knowledge on this whole topic. Table 7.1 summarizes the three types of knowledge and provides examples of each.

> Procedural knowledge is knowing how to do something.

In addition, knowledge can be classified, as you read in Chapter 3, according to the cognitive processes required to use the knowledge in particular ways. At the lowest level is straightforward recall of factual knowledge that one acquires and may or may not use. Recalling the rules of poetry written in iambic pentameter is an example of recalling factual knowledge. In contrast, the higher levels of cognitive processing generally involve using knowledge in some way, such as critiquing one of Robert Browning's poems or comparing and contrasting it with the work of Keats. Often, procedural knowledge requires the previous acquisition of factual or conceptual knowledge; in this case, basic concepts of poetry. Teachers want their students to have all four kinds of knowledge. They want them to acquire large bodies of basic factual knowledge; they

Table 7.1 *Four Kinds of Knowledge and Examples of Each*

Kind of Knowledge	Definition	Example
Factual	Knowing the basic elements about something	Rules of a game; definition of a triangle; definitions of the economic terms *supply* and *demand*
Conceptual	Knowing the relationships among basic elements	Relationships between supply and demand in the law of supply and demand
Procedural	Knowing how to do something	Playing basketball; using word processing; writing a letter; summarizing while reading
Metacognitive	Knowing when to use particular knowledge and awareness of one's own cognition	Knowing when to summarize when reading a passage; knowing one's own thinking or opinion on a topic

also want them to acquire important conceptual, procedural, and metacognitive knowledge so they can take action and do things effectively.

Different types of knowledge are acquired in different ways. The presentation model described in this chapter is most useful in helping students acquire straightforward, factual knowledge as well as conceptual knowledge. The direct instruction model described in Chapter 8, on the other hand, has been specifically designed to promote student learning of procedural and some types of metacognitive knowledge.

Information Processing. New knowledge (factual and conceptual) enters the mind through one of the senses—sight or hearing, for example—and is noted first by the learner's *working* or short-term memory. **Short-term memory** is the place where conscious mental work is done. For example, if you are solving the problem 26×32 mentally, you hold the intermediate products 52 and 78 in short-term memory and add them together there.

> Short-term memory is the place in the mind where conscious mental work is done.

Information in short-term memory may soon be forgotten unless stored more deeply in **long-term memory.** Long-term memory can be likened to a computer. Information must first be coded before it can be stored and, although stored for perhaps a lifetime, cannot be retrieved unless first given appropriate cues. Information or ideas stored in long-term memory must also be retrieved to working memory before they can be used.

> Long-term memory is the place in the mind where information is stored, ready for retrieval when needed.

Figure 7.3 shows how short-term and long-term memory interact in instructional settings.

Knowledge Representation. Additional cognitive psychology ideas that help explain how the presentation model works involve the way knowledge is stored and represented in memory. Cognitive psychologists use the label **schema** to define the way people organize information about particular subjects and how this organization influences their processing of new information and ideas. Individuals' schema differ in important

> An individual's schema reflects the way information has been organized and stored in memory.

Suppose that a second-grade teacher wants Joe to learn the fact that the capital of Texas is Austin. The teacher asks Joe, "What is the capital of Texas?" and Joe says, "I don't know." At the same time Joe may set up an expectancy that he is about to learn the capital of Texas, which will cause him to pay attention. The teacher then says, "The capital of Texas is Austin." Joe's ears receive this message along with other sounds such as the other pupils' speech and traffic outside the school.

All of the sounds that Joe hears are translated into electrochemical impulses and sent to the sensory register. The pattern that the capital of Texas is Austin is selected for entry into working memory, but other sound patterns are not entered.

Joe may then code the fact that the capital of Texas is Austin by associating it with other facts that he already knows about Austin (e.g., that it is a big city and that he once visited it). This coding process causes the new fact to be entered into long-term memory. If Joe has already developed special memory strategies (which is somewhat unlikely for a second grader), his executive control process would direct the coding process to use these special strategies.

The next day Joe's teacher might ask him, "What is the capital of Texas?" This question would be received and selected for entry into short-term memory. There it would provide cues for retrieving the answer from long-term memory. A copy of the answer would be used by the response generator to organize the speech acts that produce the sounds, "Austin is the capital of Texas." At this point Joe's expectancy that he would learn the capital of Texas has been confirmed.

Figure 7.3 *An Example of Short-Term and Long-Term Memory*
Source: After E. Gagné et al., (1993), p. 78.

ways, and schemata (pl.) held about various topics prepare the learner to process new information and to see relationships. The more complete a person's **prior knowledge** and schema are for a particular topic, the easier it becomes to process new information and to see more abstract relationships. Although cognitive psychologists do not always agree about the exact way knowledge is represented in the memory system, they do agree that prior knowledge definitely filters new information and thereby determines how well new information presented by a teacher will be integrated and retained by a learner (Macbeth, 2000).

> Prior knowledge refers to the information an individual has prior to instruction.

Teaching principles about presenting information growing out of ideas from cognitive psychology is important for teachers in four ways. One, it is important to know that knowledge is organized and structured around basic propositions and unifying ideas. However, individuals differ in the way their knowledge about particular topics is organized. Two, students' abilities to learn new ideas depend on their prior knowledge and existing cognitive structures. Three, the primary tasks for teachers in helping students acquire knowledge are:

1. Organizing learning materials in a thoughtful and skillful way,
2. Providing students with advance organizers that will help activate, anchor, and integrate new learning, and
3. Providing them with cues for drawing information from their long-term to their working memories.

Finally, remember that cognitive structures change as a result of new information and thus become the basis for developing new cognitive structures.

Empirical Support

The knowledge base on presenting and explaining information to learners has been developed by researchers working in several different fields, especially cognitive psychology and information processing, as described in the previous section. Other research comes from the study of teaching and has focused on such topics as set induction, use of prior knowledge, and advance organizers. Still other work has looked at teacher clarity and enthusiasm and how these attributes affect student learning. Since it is impossible to provide full coverage of this extensive research base, only selected works have been highlighted in this section.

> Establishing set is an important procedure teachers use at the beginning of a lesson for getting students ready to learn.

Prior Knowledge, Establishing Set, and Providing Cues. Research has been conducted during the past thirty years on the influence of prior knowledge for learning to read, learning to use new information, and learning to write. In general, this research points toward the importance of prior knowledge for learning new information and new skills.

One important teaching procedure for helping students use their prior knowledge is *induction,* or **establishing set,** as it will be called here. Establishing set is a technique used by teachers at the beginning of a presentation to prepare students to learn and to establish a communicative link between the learners and the information about to be presented. Several informative studies have been conducted on this topic. One of the most interesting was conducted in Australia by R. F. Schuck in the early 1980s. In a rather sophisticated experimental study, Schuck (1981) randomly assigned 120 ninth-grade biology students to two groups. Teachers for the experimental group were given four hours of training on techniques for establishing set. When the experimental students' achievement was compared to that of the control students, Schuck found that the use of establishing set had a clear impact on student achievement. This impact existed not only immediately following instruction but also when students were tested twenty-four to twenty-six weeks later.

As you will see later, establishing set is not the same as an advance organizer, although both serve the similar purpose of using students' prior knowledge. By establishing set, teachers help students retrieve appropriate information and intellectual skills from long-term memory and get it ready for use as new information and skills are introduced. More information about and examples of establishing set are provided later.

Teachers also help students activate prior knowledge by providing cues. Cues provide hints about what the students are about to experience or what they are expected to learn. Sometimes teachers cue students by telling them what they are about to see or hear. At other times, teachers cue by asking questions that evoke students' prior knowledge. There is a substantial research base about the effects of cuing spanning a twenty-year period (Guzzetti, Snyder, & Glass, 1993; Ross, 1988; Wise and Okey, 1983). More information about establishing set and using cues will be provided in the next section, Planning and Conducting Presentation Lessons.

> Teachers use advance organizers to help make information more meaningful to students by relating prior knowledge to the new lesson.

Using Advance Organizers. As you read in the previous section, Ausubel saw the use of an advance organizer as a means to help make information meaningful to students. For Ausubel, an advance organizer consists of statements made by teachers just before actual presentation of the learning materials. These statements are at a higher level of abstraction than the subsequent information. Later in this chapter, advance organizers are defined more precisely; however, here it is important to say that advance organizers help students use prior knowledge just as establishing set does. They differ, however, in that they are tied more tightly to the subsequent information and provide an anchor for later learning.

The Research Summary for this chapter (page 274) presents Ausubel's seminal work on advance organizers, first published in 1960.

Since David Ausubel first published his results, other psychologists and educational researchers have been actively testing his hypothesis. Walberg (1986) reported that from 1969 to 1979, advance organizers were the subject of thirty-two studies. Walberg also described a synthesis of research done by Luiten, Ames, and Aerson (1980) that identified over 135 studies on the effects of advance organizers. Although not all the studies show the effectiveness of advance organizers, the findings seem to be consistent enough over time to recommend that teachers use advance organizers when presenting information to students.

Teacher Clarity. Using advance organizers, establishing set, and attending to prior learning all affect student learning. Another variable associated with the presentation of information that has been shown to influence student learning is **teacher clarity.** An important early study on teacher clarity was conducted by Hiller, Gisher, and Kaess (1969). They asked teachers to deliver two different fifteen-minute presentations to

> The clarity of a presentation is a very important factor in determining how much students will learn.

Teachers show enthusiasm for their subject by using uplifting language and dramatic body movement.

their students—one on Yugoslavia and the other on Thailand. Teachers were encouraged to make the presentations in their normal fashion. They studied five teacher presentation variables: verbal fluency, amount of information, knowledge structure cues, interest, and vagueness. The researchers found significant relationships on two factors: verbal fluency (clarity) and vagueness. The researchers suggested that lack of clarity in a presentation most often indicates that the speaker does not know the information well or cannot remember the key points. This, of course, suggests several steps for teachers who are about to present information to their students: (1) make sure the content is thoroughly understood, (2) practice and commit the key ideas to memory prior to presentation, or (3) follow written notes very carefully.

In reviews of the research done over a long period of time, Rosenshine and Furst (1973) and Rosenshine and Stevens (1986) reported that "teacher clarity" has been a specific teaching trait that has shown up consistently as having an impact on student achievement.

Teacher Enthusiasm. An additional variable thought to influence teacher presentations is **teacher enthusiasm.** This is an interesting concept for two reasons. First, enthusiasm is often confused with theatrics and its associated distractions, and second, the research on the relationship between teacher enthusiasm and student learning is mixed.

Effects of Enthusiasm. In 1970, Rosenshine reviewed the research on teacher enthusiasm and reported that it

Research Summary

What Do We Know about Making Learning Meaningful?

Ausubel, D. P. (1960). The use of advance organizers in the learning and retention of meaningful verbal material. *Journal of Educational Psychology, 51,* 267–272.

A common problem facing all teachers is how to make the information they want students to learn meaningful. Questions often asked are: Does the information have to be interesting to students? Does it need to connect to something they already know? Are there little things teachers can do that will make a difference?

Problem and Approach: Over forty years ago, David Ausubel asked the question, "Does giving students an advance organizer to serve as an intellectual scaffold facilitate learning and retention of unfamiliar information?" Ausubel's study is one of the oldest included in this book. It is here because it sparked a research interest in this problem and subsequently led to a substantial knowledge base on the effects of using advance organizers and of the importance of connecting new information to what students already know. It also demonstrated that sometimes a fairly small intervention by teachers can make a big difference in what students learn.

Sample and Setting: Ausubel studied 110 senior undergraduate students (78 women and 32 men) at the University of Illinois. The students were in teacher education and were enrolled in a course in educational psychology when they were asked to participate in the study.

Procedures: The researcher designed a 2,500-word learning passage on the topic of the "metallurgical properties of carbon steel." Emphasis of the content of the learning materials, according to the researcher, was on "basic principles of the relationship between metallic grain structures, on the one hand, and temperature, carbon content, and rate of cooling on the other." This topic was chosen because it had been determined that it was one that most liberal arts and teacher education majors would not be familiar with, an important condition if the central hypothesis was to be tested. Subjects were divided into two groups, experimental and control. The groups were matched on the basis of ability to learn unfamiliar material (test score on another passage of comparable difficulty). Each group then received the following treatments:

- Experimental group. The introduction to the steel learning materials for students in the experimental group contained a 500-word introductory passage with a substantive advance organizer—background material presented at a higher level of abstraction than information in the content of the materials to follow.
- Control group. The introduction to the steel learning materials for students in the control group provided

showed pretty consistent relationships between teacher enthusiasm and student learning. Since that time, researchers have tried to study teacher enthusiasm and have developed training programs to help teachers become more enthusiastic in their presentations. For example, Collins (1978) developed and tested a training program that looked at a specific set of enthusiastic behaviors: rapid, uplifting, varied local delivery; dancing, wide-open eyes; frequent, demonstrative questions; varied, dramatic body movements; varied emotive facial expressions; selection of varied words, especially adjectives; ready, animated acceptance of ideas and feelings; and exuberant overall energy. Collins found that students in classes of enthusiasm-trained teachers did better than those in classes of untrained teachers.

However, a study conducted by Bettencourt (see Borg & Gall, 1993) could find no difference between enthusiasm-trained and untrained teachers. Therefore, at this time, it appears that we should be careful about the importance of enthusiasm. Although enthusiasm seems to make a difference, the exact nature of enthusiasm and how much of it to use remain unknown.

historically relevant material and information in a 500-word passage but no advance organizer.

Both groups studied the learning materials for thirty-five minutes and then took a test on the materials three days later. The test consisted of thirty-six multiple-choice items covering the major principles and facts in the learning materials.

Pointers for Reading Research: There are no new concepts introduced in Table 7.2. Ausubel's study is rather straightforward. However, as with many studies during this era, Ausubel's subjects were college students. Results stemming from this type of population do not necessarily generalize to younger students and those with varying backgrounds typical of most elementary and secondary schools. It was not until the 1970s that large numbers of researchers left their own college classrooms and conducted investigations in the schools. This study is included here regardless of its weaknesses because of Ausubel's close association with the advance organizer

model of teaching and because it has influenced so much later research.

Results: Table 7.2 shows the test scores of students in the experimental and control groups.

Discussion and Implications As can be observed in Table 7.2, students who were given advance organizers before they read the 2,500-word passage on steel retained more information three days later as compared to students who were introduced to the learning materials with a historical passage. The weakness in Ausubel's study, as a test for the effectiveness of the advance organizer, is that the information was given to students in text, not verbally. Nonetheless, the principle is still the same. A word of caution: Ausubel's study should not be interpreted as proof that historical information is unimportant. Historical perspectives can be used, but they are not as effective as conceptual organizers in helping students integrate and retain meaningful verbal information.

Table 7.2 *Retention Test Scores of Experimental and Control Groups on Learning Passage*

Group	Type of Introduction	Mean	Standard Deviation
Experimental	Advanced organizer	16.7*	5.8
Control	Historical overview	14.1	5.4

*Significant at the .05 level.

Planning and Conducting Presentation Lessons

Understanding the theoretical and research bases underlying the teacher presentation model is not sufficient for its effective use. That requires expert execution of particular decisions and behaviors during the preinstructional, interactive, and postinstructional phases of teaching. This section describes guidelines for using the presentation model appropriately and effectively.

Planning for Presentations

Except for people who are really shy, it is quite easy for someone to get up in front of a class of students and talk for twenty to thirty minutes. *Talking, however, is not teaching.* Making decisions about what content to include in a presentation and how to organize content so it is logical and meaningful to students takes extensive preparation by the teacher. Four planning tasks are most important: (1) choosing objectives and content for

Teaching is more than just talking. Successful presentation lessons require extensive preparation.

Check, Extend, Explore

Check
- Why is the concept of "structure of knowledge" important to presentation teaching?
- What does Ausubel mean by "meaningful verbal learning"?
- What are the four types of knowledge and why are they important to teaching?
- What is the difference between short-term and long-term memory?
- How can the research on prior knowledge, establishing set, using cues, and teacher clarity be used in planning a classroom presentation?

Extend
- As you read, the research on the effects of enthusiasm on student learning appear to produce mixed results. What are your own personal views about the use of enthusiasm? Of theatrics?

Explore
- Go to the Online Learning Center at www.mhhe.com/arends6e for links to websites containing information about the *Research Base of Presenting and Explaining.*

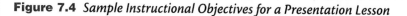

- Student will be able to describe the significance of the Fourteenth Amendment.
- Student will be able to identify the women authors of three nineteenth-century American novels.
- Student will be able to list the basic rules of ice hockey.
- Student will be able to define the meaning of photosynthesis.
- Student will be able to describe the contributions of three African Americans to United States history.

Figure 7.4 *Sample Instructional Objectives for a Presentation Lesson*

the presentation, (2) determining students' prior knowledge, (3) selecting appropriate and powerful advance organizers, and (4) planning for use of time and space.

Choosing Objectives and Content. The objectives for presentation lessons consist mainly of those aimed at the acquisition of declarative knowledge. Figure 7.4 provides examples of typical objectives teachers might choose. However, the amount of declarative knowledge in any field is endless, and several principles can assist beginning teachers as they plan particular presentations or series of presentations.

Power and Economy. In Chapter 2, the concepts of power and economy were introduced as tools for curriculum selection. These concepts can also be used by teachers as they select content to include in a presentation. Remember, the concept of power holds that only the most important and powerful concepts should be taught, rather than those of interest but not central to understanding the subject at hand. The economy concept recommends that teachers stay away from verbal clutter and limit their presentations to a minimum amount of information. Achieving economy and power in a presentation depends not so much on a teacher's delivery style as it does on planning. In fact, a carefully organized presentation read in a monotone might be more effective in producing student learning than a dynamic presentation void of powerful ideas, even though students may enjoy the latter more.

Conceptual Mapping. Another tool that is useful in deciding what to teach is that of **conceptual mapping.** Conceptual maps show relationships among ideas, and like road maps, they help users get their bearings. They also help clarify for the teacher the kinds of ideas to teach, and they provide students with a picture for understanding relationships among ideas. To make a conceptual map, you identify the key ideas associated with a topic and arrange these ideas in some logical pattern. Chapter 9 provides more detailed instructions on how to make a conceptual map and gives examples.

Determining Students' Prior Knowledge. Information given in a presentation is based on teachers' estimates of their students' existing cognitive structures and their prior knowledge of a subject. As with many other aspects of teaching, there are no clear-cut rules or easy formulas for teachers to follow. There are, however, some ideas that can serve as guides for practice as well as some informal procedures to be learned from experienced teachers.

Students' prior knowledge and interests are important when planning presentations.

Cognitive Structures. For new material to be meaningful to students, teachers must find ways to connect it to what students already know. Students' existing ideas on a particular topic determine which new concepts are potentially meaningful. Figure 7.5 illustrates how a student's cognitive structure might look in relation to certain concepts about government. Note that Figure 7.5 has the same information as Figure 7.2, but Figure 7.5 is used to show that some concepts have been learned and others have not. Note also the illustrator's judgment (shaded areas) about which concepts will be relevant because of the student's prior knowledge. (See page 280 for a discussion on adapting presentations for students of differing conceptual and ability levels.)

Intellectual Development. Cognitive structures are influenced by students' prior knowledge. They are also influenced by maturation and development. Several theorists have put forth developmental theories, including Hunt (1974), Piaget (1954, 1963), Perry (1969), and Spinthall, Spinthall and Oja (1998). Space does not allow a full discussion of the similarities and differences among developmental theorists, but they agree that learners go through developmental stages ranging from very simple and concrete structures at early ages to more abstract and complicated structures later on. It is important that teachers tailor information they present to the level of development of the learners.

Ideas about how students develop intellectually can assist teachers as they plan for a particular presentation; however, they cannot provide concrete solutions for several reasons. As experienced teachers know, development is uneven and does not occur precisely at any given age. Within any classroom, a teacher is likely to find students at extremely varied stages of development. The teacher will also find some students who have developed to a high level of abstraction in some subjects, say history, and still be at a very concrete level in another subject, such as mathematics.

Another problem facing the teacher striving to apply developmental theories to planning for a particular presentation is the problem of measuring the developmental levels of students. Most teachers must rely on informal assessments. For example,

Student's intellectual development is an important factor to consider when planning a presentation.

Teachers can successfully ascertain student understanding by asking questions and watching for nonverbal cues.

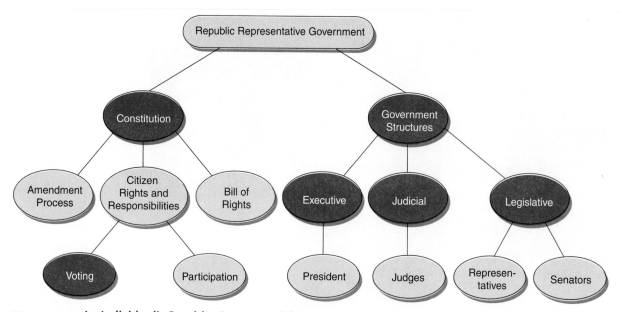

Figure 7.5 *An Individual's Cognitive Structure with Respect to Representative Government*

teachers can watch students as they approach specific problem-solving tasks and make a rough assessment of the degree to which they use concrete or abstract operations. By listening carefully to students and asking probing questions, teachers can determine whether or not the information they are presenting is meaningful. Watching for non-verbal cues during a presentation, such as silence, frowns, or expressions of interest, can provide insights into what students are picking up from the presentation. Silence, for example, can mean that students are bored; most often it means they do not understand what the teacher is saying. It may be that part of the "art of teaching" and a major difference between expert and novice teachers is expert teachers' abilities to read subtle communication cues from students and then adapt their lessons so that new learning materials become meaningful.

Advance organizers are scaffolds for new information. They are not merely a means of introducing a lesson.

Selecting Advance Organizers. The third planning task associated with the presentation model is choosing appropriate advance organizers. Remember, advance organizers become the hooks, the anchors, the "intellectual scaffolding" for subsequent learning materials. Ausubel suggested that advance organizers should be slightly more abstract than the content to be presented. Mayer (1984) suggested that concrete examples from the forthcoming lesson might work better than more abstract advance organizers. Regardless of the degree of abstraction, a good advance organizer contains materials familiar to students and is designed to relate to students' prior knowledge.

We should repeat one point here: The advance organizer *is not* the same as *other techniques* used by teachers *to introduce* a lesson, such as reviewing past work, establishing set, or giving an overview of the day's lesson. All of these are important for effective presentations, but they are not advance organizers. Following are three examples of advance organizers teachers have used in particular presentations:

Example 1. A history teacher is about to present information about the Vietnam War. After reviewing yesterday's lesson, telling students the goals of today's lesson, and asking students to recall in their minds what they already know about Vietnam (establishing set), the teacher presents the following advance organizer:

> I want to give you an idea that will help you understand why the United States became involved in the Vietnam War. *The idea is that most wars reflect conflict between peoples over one of the following: ideology, territory, or access to trade.* As I describe for you the United States' involvement in Southeast Asia between 1945 and 1965, I want you to look for examples of how conflict over ideology, territory, or access to trade may have influenced later decisions to fight in Vietnam.

Example 2. A science teacher is about to present information about foods the body needs to function well. After going over the objectives for the lesson, the teacher asks students to list all the foods they ate yesterday (establishing set) and then presents the following advance organizer:

> In a minute, I am going to give you some information about the kinds of foods the body needs to function well. Before I do that, however, *I want to give you an idea that will help you understand the different kinds of food you eat by saying they can be classified into five major food groups: fats, vitamins, minerals, proteins, and carbohydrates.* Each food group contains certain elements, such as carbon or nitrogen. Also, certain things we eat (potatoes, meat) are the sources for each of the elements in the various food groups. Now as I talk about the balanced diet the body needs, I want you to pay attention to the food group to which each thing we eat belongs.

Example 3. An art teacher is going to show and explain to students a number of paintings from different historical eras. After giving an overview of the lesson and asking students to think for a minute about changes they have observed between paintings done during different historical eras, the teacher presents the following advance organizer:

> In a minute, I am going to show and talk about several paintings—some painted in France during the early nineteenth century, others during the late nineteenth and early twentieth centuries. Before I do that I am going to give you an idea to help you understand the differences you are going to see. *That idea is that a painting reflects not only the individual artist's talent but also the times in which it is created. The "times" or "periods" influence the type of techniques an artist uses as well as what he or she paints about and the type of colors used.* As I show you the various paintings, I want you to look for differences in color, subject of the painting, and specific brush techniques used by the artists and see how they reflect the artist's time.

Planning for Use of Time and Space. Planning and managing time are very important for effective presentations. Two concerns should be foremost in teachers' minds: ensuring that allocated time matches the aptitudes and abilities of the students in the class, and motivating students so that they remain attentive and on-task throughout the lesson. Many teachers, particularly beginning teachers, underestimate the amount of time it takes to teach something well and are not always adept at checking how things are going as a lesson unfolds. Later in this chapter, assessment strategies that help teachers check for understanding are presented. Teachers use this assessment information to determine whether or not they have allocated sufficient time to a particular topic. Making sure that students understand the purposes of a presentation and tying lessons into their prior knowledge and interests are ways of increasing student attention and engagement. Guidelines for doing this also are provided in the next section, Adapting Presentations for Differing Student Abilities.

Effective presentations rely on the effective management of time and space.

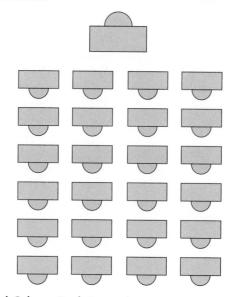

Figure 7.6 *Row-and-Column Desk Formation*

Planning and managing space is equally important for a presentation lesson. In most situations, teachers prefer the *row-and-column formation* of desks, as illustrated in Figure 7.6. This is the most traditional way of arranging classroom space, and it was so prevalent during earlier times that desks in rows were attached to the floor so they couldn't be moved. This formation is best suited to situations in which students need to focus attention on the teacher or on information displayed on the chalkboard, overhead projector, or computer projection devices.

Adapting Presentations for Differing Student Abilities. Except in rare instances, no presentation will be equally suitable for all students in a class, because students have different prior knowledge and different levels of intellectual development. They also will have differing learning styles and intelligences. Therefore, it is very important for teachers to tailor their presentations and explanations to meet the varying needs and backgrounds of the students in their class. Teachers can adapt a presentation in a variety of ways to make it relevant and meaningful to as many students as possible.

Make Ready Use of Pictures and Illustrations. There is much truth to the saying, "A picture is worth a thousand words." Pictures and illustrations can illuminate ideas and concepts in a way that words cannot, particularly for younger children and students who do not deal well with abstractions. To test this recommendation, try to explain the color green to a 3-year-old using only words. Now do it again using pictures of the color green. The Enhancing Teaching with Technology box for this chapter describes how to use computers and electronic projection devices to accompany presentations with visual and audio display.

Use Varying Cues and Examples. This chapter has emphasized the importance of prior knowledge and the way it serves as a filter through which new information must pass. Information provided to students for which they have no prior knowledge will not be

Table 7.3 *Syntax of the Presentation Model*

Phase	Teacher Behavior
Phase 1: Clarify aims and establish set.	Teacher goes over the aims of the lesson and gets students ready to learn.
Phase 2: Present advance organizer.	Teacher presents advance organizer, making sure that it provides a framework for later learning materials and is connected to students' prior knowledge.
Phase 3: Present learning materials.	Teacher presents learning materials, paying special attention to their logical ordering and meaningfulness to students.
Phase 4: Check for understanding and strengthen student thinking.	Teacher asks questions and elicits student responses to the presentation to extend student thinking and encourage precise and critical thinking.

meaningful, and it will not be learned. The use of cues and examples is one way that teachers help students to connect new information to what they already know. Since prior knowledge differs widely in most classrooms, teachers who use varying cues and examples can help make information meaningful to all students.

Be More or Less Concrete. Older and higher-achieving students can think more abstractly than can younger and most low-achieving students. When both are in the same classroom, it is important for teachers to explain ideas both concretely and abstractly to meet the needs of students of differing levels of intellectual development.

Conducting Presentation Lessons

The syntax of a presentation lesson consists of four basic phases: (1) clarifying the aims of the lesson and getting students ready to learn; (2) presenting the advance organizer; (3) presenting the new information; and (4) checking students' understanding and extending and strengthening their thinking skills. Each phase and required teacher behaviors are illustrated in Table 7.3.

Explaining Goals, Establishing Set, and Providing Cues. Effective teaching using any instructional model requires teachers to take an initial step aimed at motivating students to participate in the lesson. Behaviors consistently found effective for this purpose are sharing the goals of the lesson with students and establishing a set for learning.

Explaining Goals. In the discussion on motivation, you learned that students need a reason to participate in particular lessons and they need to know what is expected of them. Effective teachers telegraph their goals and expectations by providing abbreviated versions of their lesson plans on the chalkboard, on newsprint charts, or on electronic projection devices. Some teachers prefer newsprint charts because they can be made up the night before and posted on the wall, leaving the chalkboard free for other use; then they can be stored for future use. Effective teachers also outline the steps or

> It is important to begin a lesson with an introduction that will capture students' attention and motivate them to participate.

> **Today's Objective:** The objective of today's lesson is to help you understand how events and circumstances bring about change in the way people think about things.
>
> **Agenda**
>
> | 5 minutes | Introduction, review, and getting ready |
> |---|---|
> | 5 minutes | Advance organizer for today's lesson |
> | 20 minutes | Presentation on the demise of the battleship and the concept of decisive engagement |
> | 15 minutes | Discussion for critical thinking |
> | 5 minutes | Wrap-up and preview of tomorrow's lesson |

Figure 7.7 *Aims and Overview of Lesson on World War II*

phases of a particular lesson and the time required for each step. This allows the students to see the overall flow of a lesson and how the various parts fit together. Sharing the time parameters for the lesson also encourages students to help keep the lesson on schedule. Figure 7.7 shows how a social studies teacher shared her goals and the phases of her presentation with a group of eleventh-grade students who were studying World War II.

Making students aware of what they are going to learn will help them make connections between a particular lesson and its relevance to their own lives. This motivates students to exert more effort. It also helps them to draw prior learning from long-term memory to short-term memory, where it can be used to integrate new information provided in a presentation.

Establishing Set and Providing Cues. To get runners ready and off to an even start in a foot race, the command from the starter is "Get ready. . . . *Get set.* . . . Go!" The *get set* alerts runners to settle into their blocks, focus their attention on the track ahead, and anticipate a smooth and fast start.

Establishing set for a lesson in school is very much the same. Effective teachers have found that a brief review that gets students to recall yesterday's lesson or perhaps a question or anecdote that ties into students' prior knowledge is a good way to get started. Note the words used by the teacher in Figure 7.8 as she establishes set and provides cues for her students.

Set activities also help students get their minds off other things they have been doing (changing classes in secondary schools; changing subjects in elementary schools; lunch and recess) and begin the process of focusing on the subject of the forthcoming lesson. These activities can also serve as motivators for lesson participation. Each teacher develops his or her own style for establishing set, but no effective teacher eliminates this important element from any lesson.

Brief reviews that prompt students to reflect on a prior lesson or knowledge have been found to be an effective way to start a new lesson.

Presenting the Advance Organizer. A previous section explained the planning tasks associated with choosing an appropriate advance organizer. Now consider how an advance organizer should be presented.

Effective teachers make sure the advance organizer is set off sufficiently from the introductory activities of the lesson and from the presentation of learning materials. As with the lesson goals, it is effective to present the advance organizer to students using some type of visual format such as a chalkboard, a newsprint chart, or an overhead pro-

Figure 7.8 *Establishing Set through Review*
Source: After E. Gagné (1993)

jector. The key, of course, is that students must understand the advance organizer. It must be taught just as the subsequent information itself must be taught. This requires the teacher to be precise and clear.

> Advance organizers should be set off from introductory activities and the subsequent presentation of learning materials.

Presenting the Learning Materials. The third phase of the model is the presentation of the learning materials. Remember how important it is for a teacher to organize learning materials in their simplest and clearest form using the principles of power and economy. The key now is to present previously organized materials in an effective manner, giving attention to such matters as clarity, examples and explaining links, the rule-example-rule technique, the use of transitions, and finally, enthusiasm.

Clarity. As described previously, a teaching behavior that has consistently been shown to affect student learning is the teacher's ability to be clear and specific. Common sense tells us that students will learn more when teachers are clear and specific rather than vague. Nonetheless, researchers and observers of both beginning and experienced

1. Be clear about aims and main points.
   - State the goals of the presentation.
   - Focus on one main point at a time.
   - Avoid digressions.
   - Avoid ambiguous phrases.

2. Go through your presentation step by step.
   - Present materials in small steps.
   - Present students with an outline when material is complex.

3. Be specific and provide several examples.
   - Give detailed explanations for difficult points.
   - Provide students with concrete and varied examples.
   - Model or illustrate the idea whenever possible and remember, a picture is worth a thousand words.

4. Check for student understanding.
   - Make sure students understand one point before moving onto the next.
   - Ask questions to monitor student comprehension.
   - Ask students to summarize or paraphrase main points in their own words.
   - Reteach whenever students appear confused.

Figure 7.9 *Aspects of Clear Presentations*

teachers can find many instances of presentations that are vague and confusing. Vagueness occurs when teachers do not sufficiently understand the subjects they are teaching or when they lack sufficient examples to illuminate the subject.

Clarity of presentation is achieved through planning, organization, and lots of practice. Figure 7.9 provides suggestions to follow based on reviews of research by Rosenshine and Stevens (1986) and Cruickshank and Metcalf (1994).

> Explaining links used in presentations help learners understand cause and effect and other kinds of relationships.

Explaining Links and Examples. Effective presentations contain precise and accurate explaining links and examples. **Explaining links** are prepositions and conjunctions that indicate the cause, result, means, or purpose of an event or idea. Examples of such links include *because, since, in order to, if . . . then, therefore,* and *consequently.* Explaining links help students see the logic and relationships in a teacher's presentation and increase the likelihood of understanding.

Examples are another means used by successful presenters to make material meaningful to students. Good examples, however, are difficult for beginning teachers to think up and use. Following are guidelines that experienced teachers find useful in selecting examples:

- Identify the critical attribute(s) of the concept or idea.
- Select from students' own lives some previous knowledge or experience that exemplifies the same critical attribute.
- Check your example for distracters.
- Present the example.
- Label the critical attributes or elements in the example.
- Present exceptions.

Here is an example of an example. Say the teacher has been explaining the differences between mammals and reptiles to a group of young learners. She might proceed as follows:

- State an important generalization, such as "All mammals have warm blood."
- Then move to an example and say, "Examples of mammals you know about in your everyday lives include human beings, dogs, and cats. All of these animals are mammals with warm blood."
- Finally, conclude with, "Reptiles, on the other hand, are cold-blooded and are not mammals. One of the best-known reptiles is the snake. Can you think of others?"

Another example of a teacher using an example follows:

> There are important differences in the meanings of *climate* and *weather*. *Climate* means the overall pattern of weather a region experiences over many months and years. *Weather* is the day-to-day temperature and precipitation of a place.
> Here is an example that will show you the difference between weather and climate. When Kevin and Krista visited Boston last summer, the weather was very hot, in the high 90s. We would not, however, say that Boston has a hot climate, because the weather in the winter can be very cold.

Presenting material clearly and using precise and accurate explaining links and examples require that teachers thoroughly understand both the materials being presented and the structure of the subject area being taught. For beginning teachers having trouble, no solution exists except studying the content and the subject until they achieve mastery.

> **Understanding the subject being taught helps the presenter be more concise and complete.**

Rule-Example-Rule Technique. A third technique used by effective presenters is the **rule-example-rule technique.** To apply this technique, perform the following steps:

Step 1: State the rule, such as, "Prices in a free market are influenced by supply and demand."

Step 2: Provide examples, such as, "When Americans in the early 1980s chose to use less oil (decrease in demand) and new oil fields were opened in coastal waters (increase in supply), the price of Middle Eastern oil went down." Or, "When there was a shortage of oil in 2001 (decrease in supply), the price of oil went up."

Step 3: Summarize and restate original rule, such as, "So, as you can see, the fluctuation of supply, along with people's desire for a product, influences what the price of a product will be."

Signposts and Transitions. Particularly in longer presentations that contain several key ideas, effective presenters help learners capture main ideas and move from one part of the lesson to another by using **verbal signposts** and transitional statements. A signpost tells the learner what is important. Examples include statements such as, "This is the main point I have been trying to make," "Please remember this point," and "The most important point to remember is. . . ."

> **Signposts and transitions help learners move from one topic to another and alert them to what is important.**

Sometimes a transitional statement can be used to alert listeners to important points just made, such as, "Now let me summarize the important points for you before I move on." In other instances, a transitional statement telegraphs what is to follow; for example, "We have just covered the important eras in Hemingway's life. Let's now turn to how his involvement in the Spanish Civil War influenced his writings." Or, "Now that we know the purposes of a conjunction, let's see how they work in some sample

Enhancing Teaching with Technology

Making Presentations Interactive

Teachers can enhance their presentations and make them more interesting and thoughtful with the use of computers and interactive multimedia. Unlike presentations that use the chalkboard or the overhead projector, multimedia presentations can incorporate text, sound, pictures, graphics, and video. These computer-based presentations can also be designed to allow the listener or viewer to be much more involved. These tools are not only useful for teachers; students can also learn to use multimedia presentations to illustrate and enhance their own reports, stories, and projects.

Use by Teachers

Multimedia Presentations: "Multimedia" normally refers to integrating more than one media, such as text, graphics, audio, and video into a presentation. Today, teachers can enhance their presentations in any subject field with the use of multimedia software. On one end of the difficulty spectrum would be presentations designed to illustrate new information or ideas simply with text and pictures, perhaps using Microsoft's PowerPoint software. At the other end would be the use of hypermedia environments that allows viewers to access the information they want and to use it in ways they find most desirable. It is beyond the scope of this brief discussion to get into the details of the use of hypermedia. However, a brief description can help you get started on using multimedia to enhance your classroom

presentations. References and websites annotated in the Online Learning Center have more detailed explanations.

Several presentation software packages exist to provide assistance, including PowerPoint (Microsoft), Appleworks (Apple Computer), and KidPix (Learning Company). Whereas hypermedia presentations may take many hours to produce, a multimedia presentation to teach new ideas and concepts using text, audio, and video can be developed quite readily.

Armed with a computer and LCD*, teachers can design interesting and interactive presentations. Most of the presentation software programs allow integration of print, audio, and visual materials and provide design formats, prompts, and instant advice through wizards and auto layouts. If appropriate projectors are not available for these programs, teachers can create overhead transparencies for classroom presentations and handouts to facilitate student note taking.

A multimedia presentation, like any presentation, requires teachers to make clear decisions about content, sequencing of information and ideas, and the correct use of advance organizers and examples. However, unlike traditional presentations, a multimedia presentation requires planning for the visual aspect of the presentation. Many teachers accomplish this by using storyboards, a device for showing what information (textual and visual) goes on

*Projects that uses liquid crystal display technology.

---

sentences." Transitional statements are important because they highlight the relationships among various ideas in a presentation and they help display the internal organization of the information to learners.

Enthusiasm. As discussed in the section on Empirical Support, some evidence points to the importance of enthusiasm as an influence on student learning. However, results are somewhat contradictory.

Many teachers, particularly those in secondary schools and colleges, argue that the key to effective presentation is for the presenter to use techniques and strategies borrowed from the performing arts. In fact, books have been written describing this approach, such as Timpson and Tobin's *Teaching as Performing* (1982). Emphasis is given to wit, energy, and charisma. Presentation is full of drama, anecdotes, and humor. However, this type of presentation can produce a positive evaluation from student audiences without regard for learning outcomes. This was seen in one well-known study in which a charismatic lecturer purposely gave an entertaining lecture without any real

each slide. Putting information about each slide on a 5- × 8-inch card allows easy arrangement until the "story" is presented in the manner that makes the most sense.

Once the content of a multimedia presentation has been determined, other design issues need to be considered. Following are several, drawn mainly from Bitter and Pierson (2002, p. 267):

- Limit the amount of text on any single slide.
- Use graphics to break up large amounts of text.
- Choose a font that is legible—those between 19 and 24 points with no decorative features work best.
- Use phrases or key words.
- Don't use all capital letters—they are difficult to read. The "Wizard" in PowerPoint helps make suggestions on the use of capital letters.
- Use appropriate color. Contrast text and background (e.g., dark background, light text).
- Use graphics or sound for a real purpose, not as mere decoration.

Use by Students

Recently, teachers have seen the usefulness of having students create their own multimedia presentations that incorporate text, sound, video, and graphics. Most teachers report that this type of learning activity can help students achieve multiple learning objectives. Students are highly motivational and learn the content more thoroughly as a result of having to design a presentation and present it to others. In addition, students learn how to use technology and software widely used in the adult world. Teachers have helped students of all ages develop multimedia presentations. Obviously, younger students will require more assistance than older students and the projects they create will not be as complex as those done by older students.

Some research evidence suggests that using multimedia can be constructivist in nature and improve the self-directedness of learners. Arnold (1996), for example, placed fourth-and fifth-grade students into two heterogeneous classrooms. Each group was assigned a research project on "Immigration." One group (group A) was taught and encouraged to use technology to seek out information and to produce a multimedia report. Technology use was restricted in the other group (group B). At the end of this project the groups were assigned another project, but this time students in group B were encouraged to use technology while technology use for group B was restricted. Analysis of data at the end of both projects found that the students encouraged to use technology were more self-directed, exhibited more effective work habits, and felt more responsibility for getting their work completed. Of particular note was that students identified "at risk" were observed to be more personally involved and exhibited a higher degree of personal responsibility during the project where they were encouraged to use technology as compared to when technology use was restricted.

To see how one teacher used student-prepared Power-Point presentations in her middle-school science class, view the presentation video clip on the *Learning to Teach* Interactive Student CD-ROM.

substance and got a very positive evaluation from a student audience (Naftulin et al., 1973). Such presentations do not necessarily lead to student acquisition of important information.

Although making presentations interesting and energizing for learners is desirable, a beginning teacher who has the skills to make such presentations should consider a note of caution. Too many theatrics may, in fact, detract from the key ideas a teacher is trying to convey and focus students' attention on the entertaining aspects of the presentation. This does *not* mean that teachers should not display enthusiasm for their subjects or a particular lesson. There is a fine line between the teacher who uses humor, storytelling, and involvement to get major ideas across to students and the teacher who uses the same techniques for their entertainment value alone.

Checking for Understanding and Extending Student Thinking. The final phase of a presentation lesson is to check to see if students understand the new materials and to extend their thinking about these new ideas.

It is important to make presentations interesting and energizing.

Checking for Understanding. It is obvious that if teachers do a lot of teaching but students are not learning, nothing has been accomplished. Periodically (weekly, unit-by-unit, each quarter), effective teachers use homework, tests, and other formal devices to find out what students understand and what they don't understand. Teachers should also use informal methods to check for understanding. Watching for verbal and nonverbal cues, described earlier, is one method teachers can use. When students ask questions that don't seem to connect to the topic, they are sending a verbal signal that they are confused. Puzzled looks, silence, and frowns are nonverbal signs that students are not "getting it." Eyes wide open in amazement, smiles, and positive head nodding all signal that understanding is occurring.

Checking for understanding during presentations lets teachers know if their students are grasping the new ideas.

Experienced teachers become very effective in reading verbal and nonverbal cues; however, a surer means of **checking for understanding** is to ask students to make direct responses to statements or questions. Several easy-to-use techniques can become valuable pieces of the beginning teacher's repertoire. One is the technique of posing a question about the materials just presented and having students as a group signal their responses. Here are examples of how this works with younger students, as described by Madeline Hunter (1982):

> "Thumbs up if the statement I make is true, down if false, to the side if you're not sure."
> "Make a plus with your fingers if you agree with this statement, a minus if you don't, and a zero if you have no strong feelings."
> "Show me with your fingers if sentence 1 or sentence 2 has a dependent clause."
> "Raise your hand each time you hear (or see) an example of. . . ." (p. 60)

Note in the examples that students are encouraged to use the signal system to report confusion or things they are not quite sure of. These are areas, obviously, where teachers need to provide additional explanation. The signal system is even used at the college level, where students are appreciative of having their misconceptions cleared up immediately rather than having them revealed later on an important test. Choral responses (having students answer in unison) is another means to check for understanding, as is sampling several individuals in the class.

There are also several methods used by experienced teachers that are *not* very effective. For instance, sometimes a teacher will conclude a presentation and ask, "Now, you all understand, don't you?" Students normally perceive this as a rhetorical question and consequently do not respond. Asking more directly, "Now, does anyone have any questions?" is an equally ineffective way to check for student understanding. Most students are unwilling to admit publicly to confusion, particularly if they think they are the only ones who didn't understand what the teacher said or if they are afraid of being accused of not listening.

Extending Student Thinking. Although an effective presentation should transmit new information to students, that is not the only goal for presenting and explaining information to students. More importantly, teachers want students to use and to strengthen their existing cognitive structures and to increase their ability to monitor their own thinking. The best means for extending student thinking following a presentation of new information is through classroom discourse, primarily by asking questions and having students discuss the information. It is through this process that students integrate new knowledge with prior knowledge, build more complete knowledge structures, and come to understand more complex relationships. The techniques of asking appropriate questions and conducting effective discussions are among the most difficult for teachers to master and thus become the subject matter for Chapter 12.

Managing the Learning Environment

As described in Chapter 5, research has produced some general classroom management guidelines that apply to virtually all classrooms and all instructional models. These approaches address the way teachers strive to gain student cooperation, the means they use to motivate students, the way they establish and teach clear rules and procedures, and the actions they take to keep lessons moving smoothly and at a brisk pace. Although these general aspects of classroom management are extremely important, it is equally important for teachers to recognize that management behavior varies depending on the instructional approach a teacher is using and the type of learning tasks that derive from that approach. What might be considered "out of control" in one instance might be "in order" in another. For instance, when the teacher is using the presentation model and talking to the whole class, it is not appropriate for students to be talking to each other. Talk, however, is appropriate, even required, during a lesson using small-group discussion. In this section, we describe the unique management requirements for the presentation model.

In a presentation lesson, a teacher generally structures the learning environment very tightly. In the early stages of the lesson, the teacher is an active presenter and expects students to be active listeners. Successful use of the model requires good conditions for presenting and listening; a quiet area with good visibility including appropriate facilities for using multimedia. The success of the model also depends on students being sufficiently motivated to watch what the teacher is doing and to listen to what the teacher is saying. It is not a time for students to be sharpening pencils, talking to neighbors, or

Check, Extend, Explore

Check
- Why is prior knowledge such a critical factor in what a student learns from a presentation?
- What are the four phases of a presentation lesson? What kinds of teaching behaviors are associated with each phase?
- What are the four key features of a clear presentation?
- What role do explaining links and examples play in a presentation?
- Summarize why checking for student understanding is an important phase of a presentation lesson.

Extend
- At this point in your education, do you agree or disagree that you have enough understanding of your subject area(s) to explain it extemporaneously to others? Go to the "Extend Question Poll" on the Online Learning center to respond.

Explore
- Go to the Online Learning Center at www.mhhe.com/arends6e for links to websites related to *Planning and Conducting Presentation Lessons.*

Effective presentation depends on an environment characterized by active student listening.

Presentations break down if appropriate momentum is not maintained or if students behave in inappropriate ways.

working on other tasks. Later, when students are asked to recite or to expand on what was presented, different management concerns will surface. In essence, the presentation model requires rules governing *student talk*, procedures to ensure good *pacing*, and methods for *dealing with misbehavior*.

Students talking at inappropriate times or asking questions that slow down the pace of a lesson are among the most troublesome management concerns during a teacher presentation. This problem can vary in severity from a loud, generalized classroom clamor that disturbs the teacher next door to a single student talking to a neighbor when the teacher is explaining or demonstrating an important idea. As described in Chapter 5, teachers are well advised to have a rule that prescribes no talking when they are explaining things, and this rule must be consistently reinforced. During the recitation phase of the lesson, students must be taught to listen to other student's ideas and to take turns when participating in a recitation or a discussion.

Presentation lessons break down when the instructional events become sluggish and appropriate momentum is not maintained. In Chapter 5, you read about how students in Mrs. Dee's classroom sometimes tried deliberately to break up the pace of instruction by asking questions and feigning confusion. This resulted in the teacher reducing the amount of content being taught and doing more and more of the students' thinking for them. Effective teachers spot this type of student behavior, nip it in the bud, and move on with a well-paced and smooth-flowing presentation. When misbehavior occurs, they deal with it firmly and quickly using desist strategies described in Chapter 5.

Check, Extend, Explore

Check
- Describe the characteristics of the learning environment during a presentation lesson.
- What are the means teachers use to assess what students have learned from presentations or explanations?

Extend
- Think about the learning environments in classrooms where you have experienced effective presentation. What characterized these environments?

Explore
- Go to the Online Learning Center at www.mhhe.com/arends6e for links to websites related to *Classroom Learning Environments and Assessment.*

Assessment and Evaluation

The most important postinstructional tasks connected to the presentation model are testing and grading students on the information presented. Tests and grades are perhaps the most important feedback that teachers give to students, parents, and others associated with the schools, as you read in Chapter 6.

The presentation model is particularly adept at transmitting new information to students and at helping them retain that information. Therefore, the testing of students' knowledge acquisition and retention is the appropriate evaluation strategy for the model. This type of testing lends itself nicely to the paper-and-pencil tests with which you are familiar. In testing for student knowledge, however, several factors should be considered. Teachers should test at all levels of knowledge and not for simple recall of information. Furthermore, teachers should communicate clearly to students what they will be tested on. Finally, it is better to test frequently than to wait for midterm or final testing periods, particularly with younger students.

Reflections **from the** *Classroom*

Pleasing the Principal

You are in your first year of teaching. The principal at your school believes that teachers spend too much time talking to kids. If she walks by your room and sees you lecturing, she frowns and expresses her disapproval. At staff meetings, the principal often voices the opinion that teachers should be "facilitators of learning" and not "fountains of information." You agree that teachers should do more than just talk to students and that they should provide students with many active learning experiences. However, you also believe that you need to use presentations on a regular basis if you are going to cover all the material in the curriculum guide and if your students are going to perform well on the required standardized tests.

This situation seems to present you with a dilemma. On the one hand, you want the principal to think you are a good teacher. On the other, you feel strongly that presenting new information and ideas is central to the job of teaching.

Reflect on ways to deal with this situation. Approach it from the perspective closest to the grade level or subject area you are preparing to teach. When you have finished, write up your ideas for an exhibit in your professional portfolio and compare them with the following ideas expressed by experienced teachers who have faced the same or similar situations. You might want to consider the appropriate uses for presentation and explanation. When is this model misused?

(continued)

Reflections **from the** *Classroom (Continued)*

Jason O'Brien
Sacred Heart Academy, 3rd through 5th Grade
Diocese of St. Petersburg, FL

It is important for the administration to have confidence in the abilities of first-year teachers. That said, teachers are professionals, not technicians. Consider yourself fortunate if you have a principal that does not want you doing all the talking, or expect you to give lectures every period. If your principal is the opposite, I would explain to her that I agree that facilitation of learning is of utmost importance in teaching social studies. I would ask the principal to observe a particular lesson where I demonstrate lecturing but also where I incorporate many questions and provide for cooperative learning. Very few students are motivated enough to gain important knowledge completely on their own. Thus, it is important for the teacher to present important information followed by asking both lower- and higher-order questions. This enables students to become active participants in the presentation. As you gain teaching experience you will know when you "have" your students and when you don't. Learn from your mistakes and always try to improve the ways in which you present information. Use [hands-on material], music, and primary documents to support and make your presentations interesting and motivating. By virtue of your status as a teacher you have the responsibility to discover the most effective ways to teach your content. Sometimes you'll succeed, sometimes you'll fail, but don't be afraid to try new and creative ways of teaching.

Michael T. Girard
Bristol High School, 9th and 10th Grade
Bristol, PA

Of course, the best strategy for any teacher, novice or veteran, is to establish an open, professional relationship before she offers that frown of disapproval. Having said that, I would actively respond to the principal's reactions as soon as possible. I would set up a meeting to reassure the principal that spewing out information is not the core of my classroom instruction and that our views on how to deliver effective education actually are in harmony.

In the meeting, I would explain fully why it was necessary within the context of the lesson to present information to the class. I would bring my lesson plans so that the objectives, standards, activities, and assessments can be clearly seen and understood. I would emphasize how lecturing she observed fits within my lesson.

Next, I would invite her to my classroom to observe the follow-up activities or assessments that show the students actively learning as I help them achieve the goals of the lesson.

Chapter Review

Go back to the "Interactive and Applied Learning" feature at the beginning of the chapter for a listing of interactive and applied activities. Go to the Online Learning Center at **www.mhhe.com/arends6e** or your Interactive Student CD-ROM to take practice quizzes over the content of this chapter and receive immediate feedback. You can also review chapter content and main ideas, practice with key terms, and find annotated Web links on topics associated with this chapter.

Summary

Overview of Presentation Teaching

- Presentations, explanations, and lectures by teachers comprise a large portion of classroom time primarily because curricula in schools have been structured around bodies of information that students are expected to learn.
- The instructional goals of the presentation model are mainly to help students acquire, assimilate, and retain information.

- The general flow or syntax for a presentation lesson consists of four main phases: presenting objectives and establishing set, presenting an advance organizer, presenting the learning materials, and using processes to help extend and strengthen student thinking.
- Successful presentations require a fairly tightly structured learning environment that allows a teacher to effectively present and explain new information and the students to hear and to acquire the new information.

Theoretical and Empirical Support

- The presentation teaching model draws its rationale from three streams of contemporary thought: concepts about the way knowledge is structured, ideas about how to help students acquire meaningful verbal learning, and concepts from the cognitive sciences that help explain how information is acquired, processed, and retained.
- Bodies of knowledge have logical structures from which key concepts and ideas are drawn for teacher's presentations.
- Knowledge can be broken into three main categories: declarative knowledge, procedural knowledge, and conditional knowledge. Declarative knowledge is knowing about something or knowledge that something is the case. Procedural knowledge is knowing how to do something. Conditional knowledge is knowing when to use particular declarative or procedural knowledge.
- People take in information and knowledge through their senses and transform it into short-term and long-term memory. Meaningful verbal learning occurs when teachers present major unifying ideas in ways that connect these ideas to students' prior knowledge.
- The empirical support for the presentation model is well developed. Studies have shown the positive effects of using advance organizers, connecting new information to students' prior knowledge, and presenting the information with clarity, enthusiasm, economy, and power.

Planning and Conducting Presentation Lessons

- The planning tasks for the presentation model include carefully selecting content, creating advance organizers, and matching both to students' prior knowledge.
- Presenting information to students requires preparing students to learn from presentation as well as delivering learning materials.

- Clarity of a presentation depends on both the teacher's delivery and the teacher's general mastery of the subject matter being presented.
- Advance organizers serve as intellectual scaffolding on which new knowledge is built.
- Specific techniques used in presenting new material include explaining links, rule-example-rule, and verbal transitions.
- Teachers can help students extend and strengthen their thinking about new materials through discussion, questioning, and dialogue.

Managing the Learning Environment

- In a presentation lesson, a teacher structures the learning environment fairly tightly and makes sure students are attending to the lesson.
- Most important, presentation lessons require clear rules that govern student talk, procedures to ensure a brisk, smooth pace, and effective methods for dealing with student off-task behavior or misbehavior.

Assessment and Evaluation

- Postinstructional tasks of the presentation model consist mainly of finding ways to test for student knowledge acquisition. Because students will learn what is expected of them, it is important to test for major ideas. If testing is limited to the recall of specific ideas or information, that is what students will learn. If teachers require higher-level cognitive processing on their tests, students will also learn to do that.

Key Terms

Portfolio and Field Experience Activities

This feature has been designed to help you learn from your field experiences and to assist you in the preparation of artifacts for your professional portfolio on topics and standards associated with Chapter 7.

1. Complete the "Reflections from the Classroom" exercise at the end of this chapter and use the recommended reflective essay as an exhibit of your views about the use or misuse of presentation teaching.

2. Use Activity 7.1 in the *Guide to Field Experiences and Portfolio Development* to assess your overall skill for planning and conducting presentation lessons.

3. Use Activities 7.3 and 7.4 in the *Guide to Field Experiences and Portfolio Development* to observe a presentation by a teacher. Summarize the observations as exhibits for your portfolio to demonstrate your understanding of this model.

4. Use the case exercise on the Interactive Student CD-ROM or Activities 7.2 and 7.5 in the *Guide to Field Experiences and Portfolio Development* to create your own presentation lesson using an advance organizer. Place the product(s) of your work in your professional portfolio to demonstrate your understanding and skill to plan and conduct presentation lessons.

Books for the Professional

 Go to the Online Learning Center at www.mhhe.com/ arends6e or your Interactive Student CD-ROM for an annotated version of this list.

Bruner, J. (1960). *The Process of Education.* Cambridge, MA: Harvard University Press.

Gagné, E. D., Yekovick, C. W., and Yekovick, F. R. (1993). *The Cognitive Psychology of School Learning* (2nd ed.). New York: HarperCollins.

Joyce, Bruce, Weil, Marsha, and Calhoun, E. (2000). *Models of Teaching* (6th ed.) Boston: Allyn & Bacon.

Race, P., and Race, P. (2001). *The Lecturer's Toolkit: A Practical Guide to Learning, Teaching and Assessment* (2nd ed.). Berkeley CA: Kogan Page.

Westra, M. (1996). *Active Communication.* Pacific Grove, CA: Brooks/Cole.

Chapter Eight

Direct Instruction

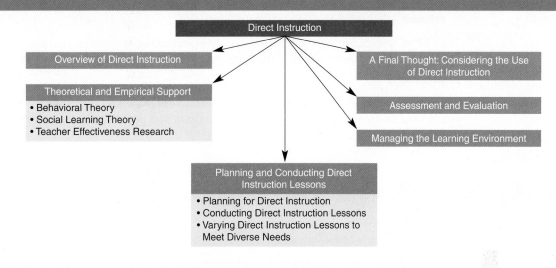

Interactive **and** Applied Learning

Go to your Interactive Student CD-ROM to:

- Hear audio clips of Dennis Walker and Angela Adams talk about the direct instruction model in the *From the Classroom* feature

- Watch the video clip: Direct Instruction

- Complete the Direct Instruction Case Exercise in the Chapter 8 *Case Exercises and Practice Tasks* area.

- Complete the Direct Instruction Practice Tasks in the Chapter 8 *Case Exercises and Practice Tasks* area. Plan for demonstration; differentiate guided practice for two students; assess student learning; respond to teaching dilemmas; and reflect on the use of direct instruction.

Go to the Online Learning Center at www.mhhe.com/arends6e to read *PowerWeb* articles and newsfeed updates about:

- Classroom management
- Cultural diversity in education
- Instruction
- Learning
- Technology and education
- Testing and evaluation
- World Wide Web

Considering **Standards**

Studying this chapter will help you meet two INTASC principles:

Primary

INTASC 4: Understands and uses a variety of instructional strategies to encourage student development of critical thinking, problem-solving, and performance skills.

Secondary

INTASC 8: Understands and uses formal and informal assessment strategies to evaluate and ensure the continuous intellectual, social, and physical development of the learner.

Reflecting **on** *Direct Instruction*

Take a minute to list the things you remember your parents or teachers doing that helped you learn the following:

- The first ten amendments to the Constitution
- How to ride a bicycle
- How to tie your shoelaces
- The fifty state capitals
- The multiplication tables

Were there particular steps or activities they used regardless of the subject? Were some things particularly helpful to your learning? What did these have in common? Were there things they did that hindered your learning?

 Go to the Online Learning Center at www.mhhe.com/arends6e to respond to these questions.

Skills—cognitive and physical—are the foundations on which more advanced learning (including learning to learn) are built. Before students can discover powerful concepts, think critically, solve problems, or write creatively, they must first acquire basic skills and information. For example, before students can acquire and process large amounts of information, they must be able to decode and encode spoken and written messages, take notes, and summarize. Before students can think critically, they must have basic skills associated with logic, such as drawing inferences from data and recognizing bias in presentation. Before students can write an eloquent paragraph, they must master basic sentence construction, correct word usage, and the self-discipline required to complete a writing task. In essence, in any field of study, we must *learn the mechanics before the magic.*

In fact, the difference between novices and experts in almost any field is that experts have mastered certain basic skills to the point where they can perform them unconsciously and with precision, even in new or stressful situations. For example, expert teachers seldom worry about classroom management, because after years of experience, they are confident of their group control skills. Similarly, top NFL quarterbacks read every move of a defense without thinking and automatically respond with skillful actions to a safety blitz or double coverage of prize receivers, something novice quarterbacks cannot do.

This chapter focuses on a teaching model that is aimed at helping students learn basic skills and knowledge that can be taught in a step-by-step fashion. For

The knowledge and skills taught in direct instruction lessons can be clearly explained or demonstrated.

our purposes here, the model is labeled the **direct instruction model.** This model does not always have the same name. Sometimes it is referred to as *active teaching* (Good, Grouws, & Ebmeier, 1983). Hunter (1982) labeled her approach the *mastery teaching model.* Rosenshine and Stephens (1986) called this approach *explicit instruction.*

This chapter begins with an overview of direct instruction, which is followed by a discussion of the theoretical and empirical support for the model. The chapter then gives concrete details about how to plan, conduct, and evaluate direct instruction lessons. Reflection and exercise materials on the Online Learning Center and the Interactive Student CD-ROM are provided to help you practice and reflect on your own approach to teaching using direct instruction.

> A major difference between novices and experts in any field is the degree to which they have mastered the basic skills of their trade.

Overview of Direct Instruction

Even though you may never have thought about direct instruction in any systematic way, you are undoubtedly familiar with certain aspects of it. The rationale and procedures underlying this model were probably used by adults to teach you to drive a car, brush your teeth, hit a solid backhand, write a research paper, or solve algebraic

> Direct instruction aims at accomplishing two major learner outcomes: mastery of well-structured academic content and acquisition of all kinds of skills.

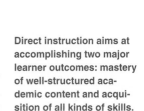

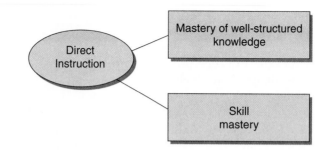

Figure 8.1 *Direct Instruction Aims at Accomplishing Two Learner Outcomes*

Check, Extend, Explore

Check
- What are the five phases of a direct instruction lesson?
- What are the learner outcomes of a direct instruction lesson?
- What type of learning environment is best for a direct instruction lesson?

Extend
- Think about a basic skill that you have mastered to the point where you can perform it more or less automatically. How long did it take? What were the defining moments when you accomplished mastery? Were you aware this was happening?

Explore
- Go to the Online Learning Center at www.mhhe.com/ arends6e for links to websites related to *Direct Instruction.*

equations. Behavioral principles on which this model rests may have been used to correct your phobia about flying or wean you from cigarettes. The direct instruction model is rather straightforward and can be mastered in a relatively short time. It is a "must" in all teachers' repertoire.

As with other teaching models, direct instruction can be described in terms of three features: (1) the type of learner outcomes it produces; (2) its syntax or overall flow of instructional activities; and (3) its learning environment.

Briefly, direct instruction was designed to promote mastery of skills (procedural knowledge) and factual knowledge that can be taught in a step-by-step fashion. These learner outcomes are shown in Figure 8.1. The model is not intended to accomplish social learning outcomes or higher-level thinking, nor is it effective for these uses. Direct instruction is a teacher-centered model that has five steps: establishing set, explanation and/or demonstration, guided practice, feedback, and extended practice. A direct instruction lesson requires careful orchestration by the teacher and a learning environment that is businesslike and task-oriented. The direct instruction learning environment focuses mainly on academic tasks and aims at keeping students actively engaged.

After taking a brief look at the theoretical and empirical support for direct instruction, we will provide a more detailed discussion on how to plan for, conduct, and evaluate direct instruction lessons.

Theoretical and Empirical Support

A number of historical and theoretical roots come together to provide the rationale and support for direct instruction. Some aspects of the model derive from training procedures developed in industrial and military settings. Barak Rosenshine and Robert Stevens (1986), for example, reported that they found a book published in 1945 entitled *How to Instruct* that included many of the ideas associated with direct instruction. For our purposes here, however, we will describe three theoretical traditions that provide the rationale for contemporary use of direct instruction: behaviorism, social learning theory, and teacher effectiveness research.

Behavioral Theory

Behavioral theories of learning have made significant contributions to direct instruction. Early behavioral theorists included the Russian physiologist Ivan Pavlov (1849–1936) and American psychologists John Watson (1878–1958), Edward Thorndike

(1874–1949), and, more recently, B. F. Skinner (1904–1990). The theory is called **behaviorism** because theorists and researchers in this tradition are interested in studying observable human behavior rather than things that cannot be observed, such as human thought and cognition. Of particular importance to teachers is B. F. Skinner's work on operant conditioning and his ideas that humans learn and act in specific ways as a result of how particular behaviors are encouraged through reinforcement. You remember from Chapter 3 that the concept of reinforcement has a special meaning in behavioral theory: consequences strengthen particular behaviors either positively by providing some type of reward or negatively by removing some irritating stimulus.

> Behavioral theories maintain that humans learn to act in certain ways in response to positive and negative consequences.

As you will read later in this chapter, teachers who teach according to behavioral principles devise objectives that describe with precision the behaviors they want their students to learn; provide learning experiences, such as practice, in which student learning can be monitored and feedback provided; and pay particular attention to how behaviors in the classroom are rewarded.

Social Learning Theory

More recently, theorists such as Albert Bandura have argued that classical behaviorism provides too limited view of learning, and they have used social learning theory to help study the unobservable aspects of human learning, such as thinking and cognition. **Social learning theory** makes distinctions between learning (the way knowledge is acquired) and performance (the behavior that can be observed). This theory also posits that much of what humans learn comes through the observation of others. According to Bandura, most human learning is done by selectively observing and placing into memory the behavior of others. Bandura (1977) wrote:

> Social learning theory posits that much of what humans learn comes through the observation of others.

> Learning would be exceedingly laborious, not to mention hazardous, if people had to rely solely on the effects of their own actions to inform them of what to do. Fortunately, most human behavior is learned observationally through modeling: from observing others one forms an idea of how new behaviors are performed, and on later occasions this coded information serves as a guide for action. Because people can learn from example what to do, at least in approximate form, before performing any behavior, they are spared needless errors (p. 22).

Unlike earlier behaviorists, social learning theorists believe that something is learned when an observer consciously attends to some behavior (e.g., striking a match) and then places that observation into long-term memory. The observer hasn't yet *performed* the observed behavior, so there have been no behavioral consequences (reinforcements), which behaviorists maintain are necessary for learning to occur. Nevertheless, as long as the memory is retained, the observer knows how to strike a match, whether or not he or she ever chooses to do so. The same claim can be said for thousands of simple behaviors such as braking a car, eating with a spoon, and opening a bottle.

According to Bandura (1986), observational learning is a three-step process: (1) the learner has to pay attention to critical aspects of what is to be learned; (2) the learner has to retain or remember the behavior; and (3) the learner must be able to reproduce or perform the behavior. Practice and mental rehearsals used in direct instruction are processes that help learners retain and produce observed behaviors. The principles of social learning translate into the following teaching behaviors:

> Learning through observation involves three steps: attention, retention, and production.

- Use strategies to gain students' attention.
- Ensure that the observation is not too complex.
- Link new skills to students' prior knowledge.

Teacher effectiveness research is an approach to studying teaching that looks at the relationship between teachers' observable behaviors and student achievement.

- Use practice to ensure long-term retention.
- Ensure a positive attitude toward the new skill so students will be motivated to reproduce or use the new behavior.

More detail on how to apply the principles stemming from social learning theory will be provided in the Conducting Direct Instruction Lessons section.

Teacher Effectiveness Research

The empirical support for the direct instruction model comes from many fields. However, the clearest empirical support for the model's classroom effectiveness comes from the **teacher effectiveness research** conducted mainly in the 1970s and 1980s, a type of research that studied the relationships between teacher behaviors and student achievement.

The study by Jane Stallings and her associates described in Chapter 3 illustrated the importance of time-on-task (Stallings & Kaskowitz, 1974). This study also contributed empirical support for the use of direct instruction. Remember that this study investigated elementary classrooms where teachers were using quite different approaches to instruction. Some teachers used highly structured and formal methods, while others used more informal teaching methods associated with the open classroom movement of the time. Stallings and her colleagues wanted to find out which of the various approaches were working best in raising student achievement. The behaviors of teachers in 166 classrooms were observed, and their students were tested for achievement gains in mathematics and reading. Although many findings emerged from this large and complex study, two of the most pronounced and long-lasting were the findings that time allocated and used for specific academic tasks was strongly related to academic achievement and that teachers who were businesslike and used teacher-directed (direct instruction) strategies were more successful in obtaining high engagement rates than those who used more informal and student-centered teaching methods.

Following this early work, literally hundreds of studies conducted between 1975 and 1990 produced essentially the same results, namely that teachers who had well-organized classrooms in which structured learning experiences prevailed produced higher student time-on-task ratios and higher student achievement than teachers who used more informal and less teacher-directed approaches. This research has been summarized on numerous occasions (see Brophy & Good, 1986; Rosenshine & Stevens, 1986; Stronge, 2002). The Research Summary for this chapter describes briefly the nature of the research that produced these findings and provides an illustration of a group of studies conducted by Tom Good and his colleagues that also provide empirical support for the direct instruction model.

Check, Extend, Explore

Check
- What are the primary features of behaviorism?
- What is the critical feature of social learning theory?
- What characterizes the methods of process-product research?
- How do most process-product researchers define achievement?

Extend
- Some people are critical of process-product research mainly because it ignores the cognitive dimension of learning. Do you agree or disagree with this perspective? Go to the "Extend Question Poll" on the Online Learning Center to respond.

Explore
- Go to the Online Learning Center at www.mhhe.com/arends6e for links to websites containing information on the Research Base of Direct Instruction and Behavioral and Social Learning.

Planning and Conducting Direct Instruction Lessons

As with any approach to teaching, expert execution of a direct instruction lesson requires specific behaviors and decisions by teachers during planning, while conducting the lesson, and while evaluating its effects. Some of these teacher actions can be found in other instructional models, and other behaviors are unique to direct instruction. The unique features of conducting a direct instruction lesson are emphasized here.

Research Summary

How Do We Study Relationships between Teacher Behavior and Student Achievement?

Good, T. L., and Grouws, D. A. (1977).
Teaching effect: A process-product study in fourth-grade mathematics classrooms. *Journal of Teacher Education, 28,* 49–54.
Good, T. L., and Grouws, D. A. (1979).
The Missouri mathematics effectiveness project: An experimental study in fourth-grade classrooms. *Journal of Educational Psychology, 71,* 355–362.

This chapter's research summary highlights, instead of a single study, a series of studies conducted by Good and his colleagues during the 1970s. Good's work is important for two reasons. One, it is a fine illustration of the process-product research, a unique approach to studying relationships between teacher behavior and student achievement. And two, it shows how knowledge is produced and refined over a number of years and through a number of studies.

Problem: Before the 1970s, many educational researchers focused mainly on teachers' personal characteristics and how they related to student learning. Researchers became disillusioned with this line of inquiry, and in the early 1970s, a new paradigm for research on teaching and learning emerged. Called **process-product research,** this approach to research had profound effects on our views of effective teaching. Process-product research was characterized both by the type of questions asked and by the methods of inquiry used by the researcher. The overriding question guiding process-product research was, "What do individual teachers do that makes a difference in their students' academic achievement?"

There are two key words in this question. One, the word *do,* suggests the importance of teachers' actions or behaviors, in contrast to earlier concerns about their personal attributes or characteristics. These teacher behaviors were labeled *process* by the researchers. The second key word is *achievement.* For the process-product researchers, achievement was the *product* of instruction. In most instances, achievement was defined as the acquisition of those skills and that knowledge that could be measured on standardized tests. Teachers were judged effective if they acted in ways that produced average to above-average achievement for students in their class.

Process-product research, thus, can be summarized as the search for those teacher behaviors (process) that led to above-average student achievement scores (product).

Process-product research was also characterized by particular methods of inquiry. Typically, process-product researchers went directly into classrooms and observed teachers in natural (regular) classroom settings. Teacher behaviors were recorded using a variety of low-inference observation devices, and student achievement was measured over several time periods, often at the beginning and end of a school year. Particular teacher behaviors were then correlated with student achievement scores, and successful and unsuccessful teacher behaviors were identified.

Procedures: Let's now look at what process-product research has contributed to our understanding of teacher effectiveness in general and to direct instruction specifically. Although hundreds of such studies were completed in the 1970s and 1980s, the work of Good and Grouws between 1972 and 1976 is illustrative of process-product research at its best, and it is illustrative of the type of evidence that supports the effectiveness of the direct instruction model.

The Initial Study: Between 1972 and 1973, Good, Grouws, and their colleagues studied over one-hundred third- and fourth-grade mathematics teachers in a school district that skirted the core of a large urban school district in the Midwest. The Iowa Test of Basic Skills was administered to students in their classrooms in the fall and spring for two consecutive years. From analyses of achievement gains made by students, the researchers were able to identify nine teachers who were relatively effective in obtaining student achievement in mathematics and nine teachers who had relatively low effectiveness. This led the researchers to plan and carry out an observational study to find out how the effective and ineffective teachers differed.

The Observational Study: To protect the identity of the "effective" and "ineffective" teachers, the researchers collected observational data from forty-one classrooms, including

(continued)

Research Summary

How Do We Study Relationships between Teacher Behavior and Student Achievement?, (Continued)

those in which the nine effective and nine ineffective teachers taught. Trained observers visited each classroom six or seven times during October, November, and December of 1974. *Process* data were collected on many variables, including how instructional time was used, teacher-student interaction patterns, classroom management, types of materials used, and frequency of homework assignments. Student achievement was measured with the Iowa Test of Basic Skills in October 1974 and in April 1975. The classroom process data were analyzed to see if there were variables on which the nine high-effective and nine low-effective teachers differed.

Results: From the comparisons, Good and Grouws concluded that teacher effectiveness was strongly associated with the following clusters of behaviors:

- *Whole-class instruction.* In general, whole-class (as contrasted to small-group) instruction was supported by this study, particularly if the teacher possessed certain capabilities such as an ability to keep things moving along.
- *Clarity of instructions and presentations.* Effective teachers introduced lessons more purposively and explained materials more clearly than ineffective teachers did.
- *High performance expectations.* Effective teachers communicated higher performance expectations to students, assigned more work, and moved through the curriculum at a brisker pace than ineffective teachers did.
- *Task-focused but productive learning environment.* Effective teachers had fewer managerial problems than in-

effective teachers. Their classrooms were task-focused and characterized by smoothly paced instruction that was relatively free of disruptions.
- *Student-initiated behavior.* Students in effective teachers' classrooms initiated more interactions with teachers than students in the classrooms of ineffective teachers did. The researchers interpreted this as students' perceiving the effective teachers as being more approachable than the ineffective teachers.
- *Process feedback (knowledge of results).* Effective teachers let their students know how they were doing. They provided students with process or developmental feedback, especially during seatwork, and this feedback was immediate and nonevaluative.
- *Praise.* Effective teachers consistently provided less praise than ineffective teachers. This reflected the nonevaluative stance of the effective teachers. This finding flew in the face of the common wisdom at that time that praise was to be used by teachers very liberally. The result of process-product research showed that praise was effective only when used under certain conditions and in particular ways and that too much praise, or praise used inappropriately, did not promote student learning.

In sum, process-product researchers found that teachers who had well-organized classrooms in which structured learning experiences prevailed produced certain kinds of student achievement better than teachers who did not use these practices.

Planning for Direct Instruction

The direct instruction approach can be used to effectively teach factual knowledge and simple and complex skills.

Chapters 2 and 7 described different kinds of knowledge. Factual knowledge, remember, was knowing the *basic element of something;* conceptual knowledge was knowing about the *relationships* among various elements; procedural knowledge was knowing *how to do something.* The direct instruction model is specifically designed to promote student learning of well-structured, factual knowledge that can be taught in a step-by-step fashion to help students master the procedural knowledge required to perform simple and complex skills.

Table 8.1 contrasts the instructional objectives aimed at promoting knowledge acquisition with those aimed at skill development. Differences can easily be observed in the two sets of objectives listed in Table 8.1. For instance, in the first set of objectives,

Table 8.1 *Contrasting Objectives for Knowledge Acquisition and Skill Development*

Knowledge Acquisition	Skill Development
1. The student will be able to list the basic rules of ice hockey.	1. The student will be able to pass while moving.
2. The student will be able to identify the subjects in the following sentences: a. Whose brother are you? b. Ralph always walked to school. c. Josie loves to read mysteries.	2. The student will supply an appropriate verb in the following sentences: a. Where _____ you? b. Ralph always _____ to school. c. _____ the apples to your sister.
3. Given the equation $y = 2.6x + 0.8$, the student will correctly select the number corresponding to the y intercept.	3. The student will be able to solve for x in the equation $9 = 2.6x + 0.8$.

the student is expected to know ice hockey rules. This is important factual knowledge for students in a physical education class. However, being able to identify the rules does not necessarily mean that the student can perform any skills associated with ice hockey, such as passing while on the move, the content of the procedural knowledge objective found in column 2. Another example illustrating the differences in the two types of objectives is from the field of music. Many people can identify a French horn; some are even familiar with the history of the instrument. Few, however, have sufficient procedural knowledge to play a French horn well.

The direct instruction model is applicable to any subject, but it is most appropriate for performance-oriented subjects such as reading, writing, mathematics, music, and physical education. It is also appropriate for the skill components of the more information-oriented subjects such as history or science. For example, direct instruction would be used to help students learn how to make or read a map, use a timeline, or adjust a microscope to focus on a slide.

Prepare Objectives. When preparing objectives for a direct instruction lesson, the more specific behavioral format described in Chapter 3 is usually the preferred approach. Remember the STP guidelines specifying that a good objective should be *student-based and specific*, specify the *testing* situation, and identify the level of expected *performance.* The major difference between writing objectives for a skill-oriented lesson, unlike lessons with more complex content, is that skill-oriented objectives usually represent easily observed behaviors that can be stated precisely and measured accurately. For example, if the objective is to have students climb a 15-foot rope in seven seconds, that behavior can be observed and timed. If the objective is to have students go to the world globe and point out Iraq, that behavior can also be observed.

Perform Task Analysis. **Task analysis** is a tool used by teachers to define with some precision the exact nature of a particular skill or well-structured bit of knowledge they want to teach. Some people believe that task analysis is something that is unreasonably difficult and complex, when in fact it is a rather straightforward and simple process, particularly for teachers who know their subjects well. The central idea behind task analysis is that complex understandings and skills cannot be learned at one time or in

Task analysis involves dividing a complex skill into its component parts so it can be taught in a step-by-step fashion.

their entirety. Instead, for ease of understanding and mastery, complex skills and understandings must first be divided into significant component parts.

Task analysis helps a teacher define precisely what it is the learner needs to do to perform a desired skill. It can be accomplished through the following steps:

Step 1: Find out what a knowledgeable person does when the skill is performed.
Step 2: Divide the overall skill into subskills.
Step 3: Put subskills in some logical order, showing those that might be prerequisites to others.
Step 4: Design strategies to teach each of the subskills and how they are combined.

Sometimes a task analysis can take the form of a flow chart. This allows the skill and the relationships among subskills to be visualized. It also can show the various steps that a learner must go through in acquiring the skill. Figure 8.2 is a task analysis done this way. It shows the steps and subskills needed to perform a set of skills associated with playing ice hockey.

It would be a mistake to believe that teachers do task analysis for every skill they teach. Effective teachers, however, rely on the main concept associated with task analysis; that is, that most skills have several subskills and that learners cannot learn to perform the whole skill well unless they have mastered the parts.

Plan for Time and Space. Planning and managing time is very important for a direct instruction lesson. The teacher must ensure that time is sufficient, that it matches the aptitudes and abilities of the students in the class, and that students are motivated to stay engaged throughout the lesson. Making sure that students understand the purposes of direct instruction lessons and tying lessons into their prior knowledge and interests are ways of increasing student attention and engagement.

Planning and managing space is also very important for a direct instruction lesson. Many teachers prefer to use the more traditional row-and-column desk formation that was illustrated in Figure 7.6. This formation, you remember, is best suited to situations in which attention needs to be focused on the teacher or on information being displayed in the front of the room. A variant on the traditional row-and-column arrangement is the horizontal row desk arrangement illustrated in Figure 8.3. Students sit quite close to each other in a fewer number of rows. This arrangement is often useful for direct instruction demonstrations in which it is important that students see what is going on or for them to be quite close to the teacher. Neither the row-and-column nor the horizontal arrangement is conducive to student-centered teaching approaches that depend on student-to-student interaction.

Conducting Direct Instruction Lessons

Although experienced teachers learn to adjust their use of direct instruction to fit various situations, most direct instruction lessons have five essential phases or steps. The lesson begins with the teacher providing a rationale for the lesson, establishing set, and getting students ready to learn. This preparational and motivational phase is then followed by presentation of the subject matter being taught or demonstration of a particular skill. The lesson then provides opportunities for guided student practice and teacher feedback on student progress. In the practice-feedback phase of this model, teachers should always try to provide opportunities for students to transfer the knowledge or skill being taught to real-life situations. Direct instruction lessons conclude

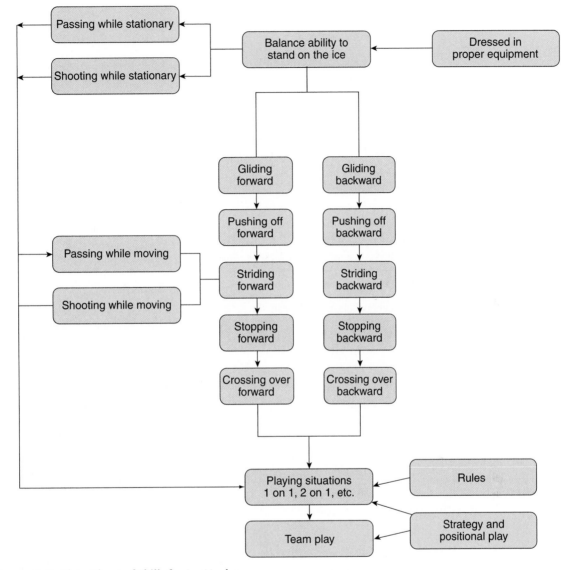

Figure 8.2 *Flow Chart of Skills for Ice Hockey*
Source: Posner and Rudnitsky (1986), p. 77

with extended practice and the transfer of skills. The five phases of the direct instruction model are summarized in Table 8.2.

Provide Objectives and Establish Set. Regardless of the instructional model being used, good teachers begin their lessons by explaining their objectives, establishing a learning set, and getting their students' attention. As previously described, an abbreviated version of the objectives should be written on the chalkboard or printed and distributed to students. This provides students with cues about what is going to happen. In addition, students should be told how a particular day's objective ties into previous ones and, in most instances, how it is a part of longer-range objectives or themes. They

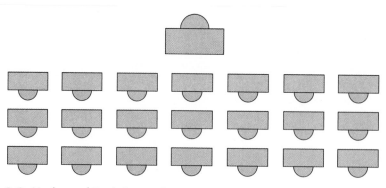

Figure 8.3 *Horizontal Desk Formation*

Table 8.2 *Syntax of the Training Model*

Phases	Teacher Behavior
Phase 1: Clarify goals and establish set.	Teacher gets students ready to learn by going over goals for the lesson, giving background information, and explaining why the lesson is important.
Phase 2: Demonstrate knowledge or skill.	Teacher demonstrates the skill correctly or presents step-by-step information.
Phase 3: Provide guided practice.	Teacher structures initial practice.
Phase 4: Check for understanding and provide feedback.	Teacher checks to see if students are performing correctly and provides feedback.
Phase 5: Provide extended practice and transfer.	Teacher sets conditions for extended practice with attention to transfer of the skill to more complex situations.

should also be informed about the flow of a particular lesson and about how much time the lesson is expected to take. Figure 8.4 shows what a science teacher provided for her students before a lesson on microscopes.

Giving the rationale and overviews for any lesson is important, but it is particularly so for skill-oriented lessons. Such lessons typically focus on discrete skills that students may not perceive as important but that require substantial motivation and commitment on their part to practice. Knowing the rationale for learning a particular skill helps to motivate and bring the desired commitment, unlike such general statements as, "It's good for you," "You'll need it to find a job," or "It is required in the curriculum guide."

Conduct Demonstrations. The direct instruction model relies heavily on the proposition that much of what is learned and much of the learner's behavioral repertoire comes from observing others. Remember, social learning theory holds that it is from watching particular behaviors that students learn to perform them and to anticipate their consequences. The behaviors of others, both good and bad, thus become guides

---

Today's objective: The objective of today's lesson is to learn how to bring into focus the lens on a compound light microscope so you can make an accurate observation of plant cells.

Agenda

5 minutes	Introduction, review, and objectives.
5 minutes	Rationale.
10 minutes	Demonstration of how to adjust lens on microscope—questions and answers.
20 minutes	Practice with your microscope (I'll come around and help).
10 minutes	Wrap-up and assignment for tomorrow.

Figure 8.4 *Aims and Overview of Today's Lesson on Microscopes*

for the learner's own behavior. This form of learning by imitation saves students much needless trial and error. It can also cause them to learn inappropriate or incorrect behaviors. To effectively demonstrate a particular concept or skill requires teachers to *acquire mastery,* or a thorough understanding, of the concept or skills before the demonstration and to carefully *rehearse* all aspects of the demonstration before the actual classroom event.

Acquiring Mastery and Understanding. To ensure that students will observe correct rather than incorrect behaviors, teachers must attend to exactly what goes into their demonstrations. The old adage often recited to children by parents, "Do as I say, not as I do," is not sufficient for teachers trying to teach precise basic information or skills. Examples abound in every aspect of human endeavor where people unknowingly perform a skill incorrectly because they observed and learned the skill from someone who was doing it wrong. The important point here is that if teachers want students to do something right, they must ensure that it is demonstrated correctly.

> Effective demonstration requires a thorough mastery of what is being taught and careful rehearsal before the classroom event.

Attend to Rehearsal. It is exceedingly difficult to demonstrate anything with complete accuracy. The more complex the information or skill, the more difficult it is to be precise in classroom demonstrations. Ensuring correct demonstration and modeling requires practice ahead of time. It also requires that the critical attributes of the skill or concept be thought through clearly and distinctly. For example, suppose you want to teach your students how to use a computerized system for locating information in the library and you are going to demonstrate how call numbers correspond to a book's location. It is important to prepare and rehearse so the numbering system demonstrated is consistent with what students will find in their particular library. If the demonstration consists of such steps as turning on the computer, punching in identifying information on the book, writing down the call number, and then proceeding to the stacks, it is important that these steps be rehearsed to the point that none (such as writing down the call number) is forgotten during the actual demonstration.

Providing Guided Practice. Common sense says that practice makes perfect. In reality, this principle does not always hold up. Everyone knows people who drive their cars

THE FAMILY CIRCUS   By Bil Keane

"I tied my shoe 'zactly right, and now I
can't even get it on."

Source: ©Bill Keane, Inc. Reprinted with special permission of King Features Syndicate.

every day but who are still poor drivers or people who have many children but who
are poor parents. All too often, the assignments teachers give students do not really
provide for the type of practice that is needed. Writing out answers to questions at the
end of a chapter, doing twenty mathematics problems, or writing an essay does not always help students master important skills.

A critical step in the direct instruction model is the way the teacher approaches
guided practice. Fortunately for teachers, a considerable amount of research evidence
now exists that can guide efforts to provide practice. For example, we know that active
practice can increase retention, make learning more automatic, and enable the learner
to transfer learning to new or stressful situations. The following principles can guide
the ways teachers provide for practice.

Assign Short, Meaningful Amounts of Practice. In most instances, particularly with a
new skill, it is important to ask students to perform the desired skill for short periods
of time and, if the skill is complex, to simplify the task at the beginning. Brevity and
simplification, however, should not distort the pattern of the whole skill.

Assign Practice to Increase Overlearning. For skills that are critical to later performance, practice must continue well beyond the stage of initial mastery. Many skills associated with the performing arts, athletics, reading, and typing have to be overlearned
so they become automatic. It is only through **overlearning** and complete mastery that a
skill can be used effectively in new situations or under stress. This ability to automatically perform a skill or combination of skills is what separates a novice from an expert
in all fields. Teachers must be careful, however, because efforts to produce overlearning
can become monotonous and actually decrease students' motivation to learn.

Be Aware of the Advantages and Disadvantages of Massed and Distributed Practice.
Many schools in the United States have homework policies—the rule of thumb is about
thirty minutes per night per subject for older students and at least a few minutes a night
for younger students. Although homework can be valuable for extending student
learning, a required amount of time each night can be harmful. The amount and tim-

Guided practice increases retention, makes skills more automatic, and pro-motes transfer to new situations.

Overlearning a skill pro-duces the automaticity needed to use it in various combinations and in both novel and stressful situations.

In general, massed prac-tice is recommended when students learn new skills. Distributed practice is rec-ommended when they re-fine existing skills.

Enhancing Teaching with Technology

Software to Assist Skill Development through Practice

The direct instruction model is used mainly to teach basic skills. Today, computer software packages exist in some quantity to assist teachers in this effort. Two major genres of software are most useful: drill and practice and tutorials.

Drill-and-practice software has been around for a good many years. Many of you probably used such programs in school or at home when you were growing up. This software does not try to teach a new skill, but instead provides students with practice opportunities and feedback on materials they have learned previously. Programs are available in mathematics, spelling, foreign languages, and other subjects in which knowledge is well structured. Recently, some very effective software packages have been developed to teach students the skills they need to operate a computer, such as keyboarding. Several examples of drill-and-practice software programs are provided on the Online Learning Center.

Drill-and-practice software can vary significantly in sophistication. Less-sophisticated programs offer practice opportunities similar to worksheets or flashcards. The practice session in this type of software provides students with a problem situation, asks them to choose a solution, and then provides them with feedback on how they are doing. Correct solutions (answers) to problem situations allow students to move on to a more difficult situation. Incorrect answers prompt remedial problems for additional practice. More sophisticated drill-and-practice software, on the other hand, includes adaptive designs that afford student practice at the appropriate level of difficulty by providing them with pretests to determine where to begin and by providing problems with the appropriate level of challenge.

Good drill-and-practice software programs and this electronic mode have been designed to be more interesting and motivating than more traditional paper-and-pencil worksheets, thus providing a unique advantage in teaching skills that might otherwise be difficult to engage students for any period of time. Programs that have effective feedback to student responses also assist teachers in performing this important teaching function and in keeping track of student progress.

Tutorials differ from drill and practice in that this software is designed to provide instruction and practice on a given skill or topic. The tutorial is based on behavioral theories of learning—a topic is presented (somewhat along the same lines as described in this chapter) with written explanations and graphic illustrations and demonstrations. The program leads students through the topic in small chunks and provides them opportunity for guided practice. The tutorial checks students' understanding and provides feedback. After several practice sessions, most tutorials end with a posttest that covers the objectives associated with the tutorial.

Sophisticated tutorials, like more sophisticated drill-and-practice software, allow students to work at their own pace. Students who are having difficulty can return to review and practice materials and those who have grasped the materials can move ahead to new materials. Also, like drill-and-practice programs, tutorials have been around for a long time. They were initially called *programmed instruction.*

In selecting drill-and-practice software, teachers should consider the issues identified in the software review form in Chapter 3. Content for all programs must be accurate, provide motivational practice opportunities, provide feedback and direct students to appropriate levels of challenge, and keep track of student progress. Today, there are many websites that provide Web-based software; most are free and cover a variety of content areas.

To date, drill-and-practice and tutorial software programs have been used more widely in the home and in industry than in classrooms. Parents, for example, have purchased software such as *Mathblaster* for their children to use, and many companies have used software programs in their employee education programs. Teachers, however, have been slower to use these tools. A number of reasons might explain this lag, such as a lack of computers in classrooms or bad experiences with early programmed instructional software that focused on superficial problems and tasks. However, contemporary drill-and-practice and tutorial software programs can be powerful and flexible tools for teachers to help their students acquire basic information and skills. Students control the instruction, learn at their own pace, and can use the programs almost anywhere there is a computer—at home, school, or work.

Some skills can be practiced with computers.

ing of practice depend on many factors. Psychologists have typically defined this issue as **massed** (continuous) **practice** versus **distributed** (divided into segments) **practice.** Although the research literature does not give direct principles that can be followed in every instance, massed practice is usually recommended for learning new skills, with the caution that long periods of practice can lead to boredom and fatigue. Distributed practice is most effective for refining already familiar skills, again with the caution that the interval of time between practice segments should not be so long that students forget or regress and have to start over again.

Attend to the Initial Stages of Practice. The initial stages of practice are particularly critical, since it is during this period that the learner can unknowingly start using incorrect techniques that later must be unlearned. It is also during the initial stages of practice that the learner will want to measure success in terms of his or her performance as contrasted to technique. This issue is described more completely in the following section.

Check Understanding and Provide Feedback. This is the phase of a direct instruction lesson that most closely resembles what is sometimes called *recitation.* It is often characterized by the teacher asking students questions and students providing answers they deem to be correct. This is a very important aspect of a direct instruction lesson, because without knowledge of results, practice is of little value to students. In fact, the most important task of teachers using the direct instruction model is providing students with meaningful feedback and **knowledge of results.** Teachers can give feedback in many ways, such as verbally, by video- or audiotaping performance, by testing, or through written comments. Without specific feedback, however, students will not learn to write well by writing, read well by reading, or run well by running. The critical question for teachers is how to provide effective feedback for large classes of students. Guidelines considered important include the following.

Guideline 1: Provide Feedback as Soon as Possible after the Practice. It is not necessary that feedback be provided instantaneously, but it should be close enough to the actual practice that students can remember clearly their own performance. This means that teachers who provide written comments on essays should be prompt in returning corrected papers. It means they should immediately correct tests gauged to measure performance and go over them with students. It also means that arrangements for verbal, video, or audio feedback should be such that delay is kept to a minimum.

Without knowledge of results (feedback), practice is of little value to students.

Guideline 2: Make Feedback Specific. In general, feedback should be as specific as possible to be most helpful to students. For example:

> "Your use of the word *domicile* is pretentious; *house* would do nicely."
> Instead of:
> "You are using too many big words."
> Or:
> "Your hand was placed exactly right for an effective backhand."
> Instead of:
> "Good backhand."
> Or:
> "Three words were spelled incorrectly on your paper: *Pleistocene, penal,* and *recommendation.*"
> Instead of:
> "Too many misspelled words."

For best results, feedback should be as specific as possible, be provided immediately following practice, and fit the developmental level of the learner.

Guideline 3: Concentrate on Behaviors and Not Intent. Feedback is most helpful and raises less defensiveness with students if it is aimed directly at some behavior rather than at one's interpretation of the intent behind the behavior. For example:

> "I cannot read your handwriting. You do not provide enough blank space between words, and you make your O's and A's identical."
> Instead of:
> "You do not work on making your handwriting neat."
> Or:
> "When you faced the class in your last speech, you spoke so softly that most students could not hear what you were saying,"
> Instead of:
> "You should try to overcome your shyness."

Guideline 4: Keep Feedback Appropriate to the Developmental Stage of the Learner. As important as knowledge of results is, feedback must be administered carefully to be helpful. Sometimes, students can be given too much feedback or feedback that is too sophisticated for them to handle. For example, a person trying to drive a car for the first time can appreciate hearing that he or she "let the clutch" out too quickly, causing the car to jerk. A beginning driver, however, is not ready for explanations about how to drop the brake and use the clutch to keep the car from rolling on a steep hill. A young student being taught the "i before e" rule in spelling probably will respond favorably to being told that he or she spelled *brief* correctly but may not be ready to consider why *receive* was incorrect.

Although incorrect performance must be corrected,
teachers should try to provide positive feedback
when students are learn-
ing new skills.

Guideline 5: Emphasize Praise and Feedback on Correct Performance. Everyone prefers to receive positive rather than negative feedback. In general, praise will be accepted whereas negative feedback may be denied. Teachers, therefore, should try to provide praise and positive feedback, particularly when students are learning new concepts and skills. However, when incorrect performance is observed, it must be corrected. Here is a sensible way to approach the problem of dealing with incorrect responses and performance:

1. Dignify the student's incorrect response or performance by giving a question for which the response would have been correct. For example, "George Washington would have been the right answer if I had asked you who was the first president of the United States."
2. Provide the student with an assist, hint, or prompt. For example, "Remember the president in 1828 had also been a hero in the War of 1812."
3. Hold the student accountable. For example, "You didn't know President Jackson today, but I bet you will tomorrow when I ask you again."

Negative feedback should
be accompanied by
demonstrations of how to
correctly perform the skill.

A combination of positive and negative feedback is best in most instances. For example, "You did a perfect job of matching subjects and verbs in this paragraph, except in the instance in which you used a collective subject." Or, "You were holding the racket correctly as you approached the ball, but you had too much of your weight on your left foot." Or, "I like the way you speak up in class, but during our last class discussion, you interrupted Ron three different times when he was trying to give us his point of view."

Guideline 6: When Giving Negative Feedback, Show How to Perform Correctly. Knowing that something has been done incorrectly does not help students do it correctly. Negative feedback should always be accompanied by teacher actions that demonstrate the correct performance. If a student is shooting a basketball with the palm of the hand, the teacher should point that out and demonstrate how to place the ball on the fingertips. If a writing sample is splattered with incorrectly used words, the teacher should pencil in words that are more appropriate. If students are holding their hands incorrectly on the computer keyboard, the teacher should model the correct placement.

Guideline 7: Help Students to Focus on Process, Not Outcomes. Many times beginners want to focus their attention on measurable performance. "I just typed thirty-five words per minute without any errors." "I wrote my essay in an hour." "I drove the golf ball 175 yards." "I cleared the bar at 4 feet, 6 inches." It is the teacher's responsibility to get students to look at the *process,* or technique, behind their performance and to help students understand that incorrect techniques may achieve immediate objectives but will probably prohibit later growth. For example, a student may type thirty-five words per minute using only two fingers but will probably never reach one hundred words per minute using this technique. Starting the approach on the wrong foot may be fine for clearing the high jump bar at 4 feet, 6 inches, but will prevent ever reaching 5 feet, 6 inches.

Guideline 8: Teach Students How to Provide Feedback to Themselves and How to Judge Their Own Performance. It is important for students to learn how to assess and judge their own performance. Teachers can help students judge their own performance in many ways. They can explain the criteria used by experts in judging performance; they can give students opportunities to judge peers and to assess their own progress in relation to others; and they can emphasize the importance of self-monitoring, goal setting, and not being satisfied with only "extrinsic" feedback from the teacher.

"And then, of course, there's the possibility of being just the slightest bit too organized."

Reprinted by permission of Glen Dines/KAPPAN.

The process of assigning practice and giving students feedback is a very important job teachers have, and it requires learning a complex set of behaviors. A learning activity in the *Field Experience and Portfolio Manual* is designed to help you observe how experienced teachers use practice and provide feedback.

Providing Extended Practice Managing the independent practice aspect of direct instruction is something that teachers need to pay particular attention to. **Independent practice,** also called *seatwork* or *homework,* provides students an opportunity to perform newly acquired skills on their own and, as such, should be viewed as a continuation of practice, not as a continuation of instruction. Also, homework and independent practice can be used as a way of extending student learning time. But teachers should not assign homework carelessly or frivolously. If a teacher doesn't value it, the students won't. Here are three general guidelines for independent practice given as homework:

> Homework is most often a continuation of practice and should involve activities that students can perform successfully.

1. *Give students homework they can perform successfully.* Homework should not involve the continuation of instruction but rather the continuation of practice or preparation for the next day's content.
2. *Inform parents about the level of involvement expected of them.* Are they expected to help their sons or daughters with answers to difficult questions or simply to provide a quiet atmosphere in which the students can complete their homework assignments? Are they supposed to check it over? Do they know the approximate frequency and duration of homework assignments?
3. *Provide feedback on the homework.* Many teachers simply check to determine whether homework was performed. What this says to the students is that it doesn't matter how it is done, as long as it is done. Students soon figure out that the task is to get something—anything—on paper, which sets a bad precedent. One method of providing feedback relatively easily is to involve students in correcting one another's homework.

Check, Extend, Explore

Check

- What are the major planning tasks associated with a direct instruction lesson?
- Why is task analysis an important planning tool for some types of direct instruction lessons?
- What are the five phases of a direct instruction lesson? What kinds of teaching behaviors are associated with each phase?
- What are the major factors teachers should consider when they assign guided practice? Independent practice?
- Summarize the guidelines for effective feedback.

Extend

- There has been considerable debate about homework. How valuable do you think homework is for increasing student learning? Go to the "Extend Question Poll" on the Online Learning Center to respond.

Explore

- Go to the Online Learning Center at www.mhhe.com/arends6e for links to websites related to *Using Direct Instruction, Practice, and Homework*.

Varying Direct Instruction Lessons to Meet Diverse Needs

Chapter 2 described many ways that children and youth can differ. These differences can include many things such as socioeconomic status, race or ethnicity, gender, ability level, prior knowledge, cognitive style, and various disabilities. Chapter 3 described how students differ in terms of their motivational needs. Because of these differences, it is safe to conclude that no single lesson will ever be equally effective with all students. This is also true with direct instruction lessons. Whereas we can provide information about how the model is supposed to work in general, it often does not work as planned in real teaching situations. Effective teachers learn how to adapt their instruction to take into account student diversity. Following are some ways that teachers can tailor direct instruction lessons:

Vary the Structure of the Lesson
- Keep lessons for younger and low-achieving students very structured; keep objectives specific; use a moderately brisk pace.
- Promote extension of basic skill instruction and provide opportunities for exploration for older and higher-achieving students.

Vary the Nature of Presentations and Demonstrations
- Highlight main ideas or procedures on the chalkboard, overhead projector, or other projection devices for younger and low-achieving students. Confine presentations to only a few points or ideas; make them short.
- Extend beyond basic ideas or skills for older and higher-achieving students.

Vary the Nature of Interaction
- Base instruction on students' prior knowledge for all students. Teaching what is already known will bore students; teaching ideas or skills for which insufficient knowledge exists is meaningless.
- Pay attention to cultural differences among racial or ethnic groups in terms of willingness to interact in front of others; do the same for gender.

Vary the Nature of Encouragement and Support
- Provide continuous encouragement and support for low-achieving and more dependent students. The less students know, the more instructional support they need.
- Allow higher-achieving and more independent students to figure things out on their own. Too much teacher encouragement can be perceived as interference. Many approaches can be successful when students know quite a bit about a subject.

Vary the Use of Practice, Seatwork, and Homework
- Make sure practice exercises are well understood and keep seatwork and homework assignments brief for lower-achieving students.
- Limit seatwork and keep homework challenging for higher-achieving, more independent students. Less review and independent practice are required.

Managing the Learning Environment

The tasks associated with managing the learning environment during a direct instruction lesson are almost identical to those used by teachers when employing the presentation model. In direct instruction, the teacher structures the learning environment very tightly, keeps an academic focus, and expects students to be keen observers, listeners, and participants. Effective teachers use the methods described in Chapter 5 to govern student talk and to ensure that lesson pace is maintained. Misbehavior that occurs during a direct instruction lesson must be dealt with accurately and quickly.

Assessment and Evaluation

Chapter 6 emphasized the importance of matching testing and evaluation strategies to the goals and objectives for particular lessons and the inherent purposes of a particular model. Since the direct instruction model is used most appropriately for teaching skills and knowledge that can be taught in a step-by-step fashion, evaluation should focus on performance tests measuring skill development rather than on paper-and-pencil tests of declarative knowledge. For example, being able to identify the characters on the typewriter's keyboard obviously does not tell us much about a person's ability to type; however, a timed typing test does. Being able to identify verbs in a column of nouns does not mean that a student can write a sentence; it takes a test that requires the student to write a sentence to enable a teacher to evaluate that student's skill. Reciting the correct steps in any of the teaching models described in this book does not tell us whether a teacher can use the model in front of thirty students; only a classroom demonstration can exhibit the teacher's mastery of that skill.

   Many times, performance tests are difficult for teachers to devise and to score with precision, and they can also be very time-consuming. However, if you want your students to master the skills you teach, nothing will substitute for performance-based evaluation procedures. Table 8.3 lists examples of the type of test items that would be included on a skills test and contrasts those with items on the same topic that one would find on a knowledge test. Note that the test items correspond to the sample objectives in Table 8.1.

Observing actual performance is the best way to assess skill development.

Table 8.3 *Items for Knowledge Test and Skill Test*

Knowledge Test	Skill Test

1. How many players are there on an ice hockey team?
  a. 6
  b. 8
  c. 10
  d. none of the above
	1. Demonstrate a pass while moving.

2. What is the subject of the following sentence? "*Mary's mother is an artist.*"
  a. Mary
  b. mother
  c. an
  d. artist
	2. Correct the verbs, as needed, in the following sentences:
	  a. Kim ran slowly to the store.
	  b. Tommy said it was time to go.
	  c. Levon sat joyfully to greet her day.
	  d. "Please be noisier," said the teacher.

3. At what point is the intercept located?
  a. 1   **c.** 3
  b. 2   **d.** 4
	3. Solve for *x* in the following equations:
	  a. $2 = x + 4$
	  b. $5x = 1 + (x/2)$
	  c. $14 = 2x + 9x$
	  d. $x/3 = 9$

A Final Thought: Considering the Use of Direct Instruction

Teacher use of direct instruction comprises a large proportion of classroom time in American classrooms. The amount of time devoted to explaining information, demonstrating, and conducting recitations increases at the higher grade levels of elementary school, in middle schools, and in high schools. It is prevalent everywhere and remains the most popular teaching model. However, the model is not without its critics, and it will be important for you to be aware of the complaints that have been lodged against direct instruction and to explore your own views and values about the model and its use in your classroom.

Because direct instruction is the most popular teaching method, teachers should be aware of problems cited by critics.

The primary criticism of direct instruction is its emphasis on teacher talk. Most observers claim that teacher talk accounts for between one-half and three-fourths of every class period, and according to Cuban (1982, 1993) this phenomenon has remained constant during most of the past one hundred years. Some educators argue that too much time is devoted to direct instruction. Others argue that the model is limited to teaching basic skills and low-level information and that it is not useful for accomplishing higher-level objectives. Still others criticize the model because of the behavioral theory underlying it. They argue that the model unavoidably supports the view that students are empty vessels to be filled with carefully segmented information rather than active learners with an innate need to acquire information and skills. Finally, there are those, including some of the model's early creators, who criticize direct instruction because of abuses in the way in which the model was implemented in many classrooms. For example, in one large public school system on the East Coast, every teacher was expected to give a direct instruction lesson every day. If a teacher used other approaches while being observed by a supervisor, the teacher received a negative evaluation. In another instance, teachers were required to write their objectives in behavioral format on the chalkboard every day, something never envisioned by the model's developers.

The continued popularity of explaining and demonstrating is not surprising, since the most widely held educational objectives are those associated with the acquisition of skills and the retention of basic information. Curricula in schools have been structured around bodies of information from the various academic disciplines—science, mathematics, English, and the social sciences. Consequently, curriculum guides, textbooks, and tests are similarly organized and are routinely used by teachers. Experienced teachers know that direct instruction is an effective way to help students acquire the array of basic information and skills believed by society to be important for students to know.

This book takes a balanced view toward direct instruction. As repeatedly stressed, direct instruction is just one of several approaches used by effective teachers. The real key to effective instruction is a teacher's ability to call on a varied repertoire of instructional approaches that permit a teacher to match instructional approaches to particular learning goals and to the needs of particular students.

Check, Extend, Explore

Check
- If you observed a direct instruction, what kind of learning environment would you likely find?
- What kinds of assessments are best to measure mastery of direct instruction objective?

Extend
- Do you agree or disagree that teachers can have a task-oriented, academic-focused learning environment, yet be positive and democratic? Go to the "Extend Question Poll" on the Online Learning Center to respond.

Explore
- Go to the Online Learning Center at www.mhhe.com/arends6e for links to websites related to *Assessment and Managing the Learning Environment.*

Reflections from the *Classroom*

Just the Basics

In your first teaching position, you find yourself in a school where the teachers were trained over ten years ago in a particular approach to direct instruction. Although there has been considerable teacher turnover in the school, the direct instruction model seems to dominate all others and is used by *all* teachers in the school. Teachers are expected to develop lesson plans using behavioral objectives and to follow the steps of the direct instruction model. The overall ethos of the school reflects an emphasis on teaching basic skills with heavy emphasis on drill and practice.

You believe in teaching basic skills to students. However, you also believe that curriculum should be individualized for your students and that students should be allowed considerable autonomy in identifying their own goals, asking their own questions, and pursuing some of their own interests.

As you reflect on this situation and your approach to teaching, consider the following:

- Think about a unit you might teach at your grade level or teaching field. What do you want your students to get out of it? Write these goals down. Ask yourself which goals are dictated

(continued)

by your school's curriculum and which are dictated by the faculty's overall approach to teaching? By your own beliefs? By those of your students? You might consider ranking these goals numerically.

- If you are in a field placement, share your goals with a fellow student or a teacher in the school. You might also discuss the goals with some students in the school. Get their opinion about which of the goals are the most important.

Now write down how you are going to approach your unit and which goals and approaches you will emphasize, remembering, of course, that your own personal views of teaching are at odds with those of the majority of teachers in your school. Approach the situation from the perspective closest to the grade level or subject area you are preparing to teach. When you have finished, include your work as an exhibit in your professional portfolio. Compare your thoughts with the following views of teachers who have faced the same or similar situation.

Kendra Ganzer

Adams Elementary School, 5th Grade
Des Moines, IA

My best advice to a new teacher is to use your professional judgment to determine what is the most appropriate course of action. As a new teacher, you know that basic skills are important, but you also know there is more than one way to help students learn. The classroom will be a new place for you so other teachers' experiences definitely warrant your attention and respect. Direct instruction does have a place in the classroom. It is an effective method when it fits the desired goals and outcomes of your lesson, but certainly you do not want to be forced to use it as your only method just because the rest of the staff prefers it.

I would plan my lessons using the instructional methods I deem most appropriate, and I would include direct instruction as one. If teachers see me using other methods, such as cooperative learning, I would tell them how I have found it to be successful when used in other classrooms. I would share with them how teacher education and instructional methods are changing. I would also share information from a research article or a textbook that supports the use of cooperative learning or other methods. However, I would not discredit my colleagues' use of direct instruction. If you ask for their advice, you could get great ideas for your lessons. You can then modify them to fit your own teaching situation. After some time, you can show examples of students' work or projects to other teachers and demonstrate how your students are learning the basic skills in the process.

Faye Airey

Thomas R. Grover Middle School, 6th through 8th Grade
West Windsor-Plainsboro, NJ

In my years of teaching, I have witnessed significant shifts of opinion about the teaching of basic skills. Should student learning focus primarily on the fundamentals or are performance-based, real-world, problem-solving tasks more important? This debate has been on-going for both inexperienced and veteran teachers alike. I support lesson design based on teaching basic skills within a practical, student-centered context, one where students become active participants engaged in tasks directly related to their everyday experiences. These settings present optimal instructional opportunities, where teaching has meaning and learning has purpose.

A practical example might be to design a simulated stock market activity in which students or small student groups invest play money and monitor daily gains/losses based on real-world company performances. What better context for teacher-directed basic-skills lessons on addition and subtraction of fractions or graphing to show stock company trends! When students are faced with a real need for a particular skill, they become active participants in the learning process. Retention is increased and the ability to make important learning connections is put into practice. Drill and practice without a purposeful context leads to student boredom and frustration; practice within real-life situations is often motivational.

Lesson design that begins by focusing on instructional goals rather than specific teaching objectives places an emphasis on individual student achievement while creating learning opportunities that cultivate natural curiosity. "How are daily stock price changes calculated?" "How can individual stock companies best share performance trends?" Few can question the enthusiasm generated in classrooms where student learning is productive and meaningful. Effective teaching requires a *balance* in which discovery, critical thinking, and questioning lead to a real understanding and mastery of essential basic skills.

⊙ *Chapter Review*

Go back to the "Interactive and Applied Learning" feature at the beginning of the chapter for a listing of interactive and applied activities. Go to the Online Learning Center at **www.mhhe.com/arends6e** or your Interactive Student CD-ROM to take practice quizzes over the content of this chapter and receive immediate feedback. You can also review chapter content and main ideas, practice the key terms, and find annotated Web links on topics associated with Chapter 8.

Summary

Overview of Direct Instruction

- Acquiring basic information and skills is an important goal for students in every subject taught in schools. In almost any field, students must learn the basics before they can go on to more advanced learning.
- The instructional effects of the direct instruction model are to promote mastery of simple and complex skills and declarative knowledge that can be carefully defined and taught in a step-by-step fashion.
- The general flow or syntax of a direct instruction lesson consists usually of five phases.
- The direct instruction model requires a highly structured learning environment and careful orchestration by the teacher. This tight structure does not mean it has to be authoritarian or uncaring.

Theoretical and Empirical Support

- The direct instruction model draws its theoretical support from behavioral theory, social learning theory, and teacher effectiveness research.
- Direct instruction has been widely used and tested in school and nonschool settings. The model has strong empirical evidence to support its use for accomplishing certain types of student learning.

Planning and Conducting Direct Instruction Lessons

- Preinstructional planning tasks associated with the model put emphasis on careful preparation of objectives and performing task analysis.
- The five phases of a direct instruction model are: (1) providing objectives and establishing set; (2) demonstrating or explaining the materials to be learned; (3) providing guided practice; (4) checking for student understanding

and providing feedback; and (5) providing for extended practice and transfer.
- Conducting a direct instruction lesson requires teachers to explain things clearly; to demonstrate and model precise behaviors; and to provide for practice, monitoring of performance, and feedback.
- The use of practice should be guided by several principles: assigning short, meaningful amounts of practice; assigning practice to increase overlearning; and making appropriate use of massed and distributed practice.

Managing the Learning Environment

- Direct instruction lessons require the unique classroom management skill of gaining students' attention in a whole-group setting and sustaining this attention for extended periods of time.
- Particular classroom management concerns include organizing the classroom setting for maximum effect; maintaining appropriate pace, flow, and momentum; sustaining engagement, involvement, and participation; and dealing with student misbehavior quickly and firmly.

Assessment and Evaluation

- Assessment tasks associated with the model put emphasis on practice and on developing and using appropriate basic knowledge and performance tests that can accurately measure simple and complex skills and provide feedback to students.

A Final Thought: Considering the Use of Direct Instruction

- Despite the variety of complaints that have been launched against direct instruction, it remains a very popular teaching model.

Key Terms

behaviorism 301

direct instruction model 299

distributed practice 312

guided practice 310

independent practice 315

knowledge of results 312

massed practice 312

overlearning 310

process-product research 304

social learning theory 301

task analysis 305

teacher effectiveness
research 302

Portfolio and Field Experience Activities

This feature has been designed to help you learn from your field experiences and to assist you in the preparation of artifacts for your professional portfolio on topics and standards associated with Chapter 8.

1. Complete the "Reflections from the Classroom" exercise at the end of this chapter and use the reflective essay as an exhibit in your portfolio of your views about direct instruction.

2. Use Activity 8.1 in the *Guide to Field Experiences and Portfolio Development* to assess your understanding and skills for using the direct instruction model.

3. Use Activities 8.3 and 8.4 in the *Guide to Field Experiences and Portfolio Development* to observe a teacher who uses direct instruction lessons. Summarize the observations as exhibits for your portfolio to demonstrate your understanding of this model.

4. Use the Direct Instruction Case Exercise on the Interactive Student CD-ROM or Activities 8.2 and 8.5 in the *Guide to Field Experiences and Portfolio Development* to create your own direct instruction lesson. Place the product(s) of your work in your professional portfolio to demonstrate your understanding and skill to plan and conduct direct instruction lessons.

Books for the Professional

Go to the Online Learning Center at www.mhhe.com/ arends6e or your Interactive Student CD-ROM for an annotated version of this list.

Feden, P. D., and Vogel, R. M. (2003). *Methods of Teaching: Applying Cognitive Science to Promote Student Learning.* New York: McGraw-Hill.

Gagne, R. M., and Wager, W. W. (1992). *Principles of Instructional Design* (5th ed.). New York: HBJ College & School Division.

Gunter, M. A., Estes, T. H., and Schwab, J. (2003). *Instruction: A Models Approach.* Boston: Allyn & Bacon.

Joyce, B., Weil, M., and Calhoun, E. (2000). *Models of Teaching* (6th ed.). Boston: Allyn & Bacon.

Posner, G. J., and Rudnitsky, A. N. (2000). *Course Design* (6th ed.). Boston: Addison-Wesley.

Chapter Nine

Concept Teaching

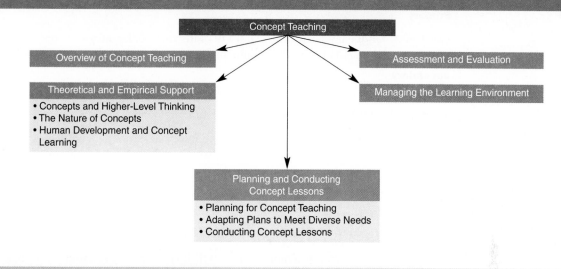

Interactive and Applied Learning

Go to your Interactive Student CD-ROM to:

- Hear audio clips of Diane Caruso (fourth/fifth grade) and Ian Call (tenth-grade world history) talk about the concept teaching in the Teachers on Teaching feature
- Complete the Concept Teaching Case Exercise in the Chapter 9 *Case Exercises and Practice Tasks* area.
- Complete the Concept Teaching Tasks in the Chapter 9 Case Exercises and Practice Tasks area. Plan for demonstration: task analysis; differentiate guided practice for two students, assess student learning, respond to teaching dilemmas, reflect on the use of concept teaching.

Go to the Online Learning Center at www.mhhe.com/arends6e to read *PowerWeb* articles and newsfeed updates about:

- Classroom management
- Cultural diversity in education
- Instruction
- Learning
- Technology and education
- Testing and evaluation
- World Wide Web

Considering **Standards** INTASC

Studying this chapter will help you meet three INTASC principles:

Primary

INTASC 4: Understands and uses a variety of instructional strategies to encourage student development of critical thinking, problem-solving, and performance skills.

Secondary

INTASC 6: Uses knowledge of verbal and nonverbal communication to foster inquiry, collaboration, and supportive classroom interaction.

INTASC 8: Understands and uses formal and informal assessment strategies to evaluate and ensure the continuous intellectual, social, and physical development of the learner.

Reflecting on *Concept Teaching*

Pick a concept from your teaching field for which you have a good understanding. Here are some examples:

- Mathematics—triangle
- Economics—scarcity
- Physical education—movement
- Literature—love

Write the concept on a piece of paper and make a web that shows other concepts that are related to the one you chose. Here is how a partial web for the concept of *scarcity* might look.

Next, consider how you might teach a young child about the concept of *scarcity*. Using a young child rather than an older one is good for this exercise because you will have to consider using means other than words to teach the concept. Think of the steps you might follow to teach the concept. In doing this, what did you learn about teaching a concept? Was it easier or more difficult than you thought it would be? What would you do differently next time?

Go to the Online Learning Center at www.mhhe.com/arends6e to respond to these questions.

M
ost experienced teachers would agree that conveying information to students is very important but that teaching students how to think is even more important. Experienced teachers also know that concepts are the basic building blocks for thinking, particularly higher-level thinking, in any subject. Concepts allow individuals to classify objects and ideas and to derive rules and principles; they provide the foundations for the idea networks that guide our thinking. The process of learning concepts begins at an early age and continues throughout life as people develop more and more complex concepts, both in school and out. The learning of concepts is crucial in schools and in everyday life because concepts allow mutual understanding among people and provide the basis for verbal interaction.

The focus of this chapter is on **concept teaching** and how teachers can help students attain and develop the basic concepts needed for further learning and higher-level thinking.

Concepts are the basic building blocks for thinking and communication.

The first section provides an overview of concept teaching, including the learning outcomes the model is designed to accomplish, the model's syntax, and the learning environment required to use the model effectively. This is followed by a discussion of the nature of concepts and the theoretical and empirical support for concept teaching. The final sections focus on the model itself and describe specific procedures used by teachers to plan, conduct, and evaluate concept teaching lessons.

Overview of Concept Teaching

"Ball." "Chair." "Box." "Table." "Crayon." Kim is naming things and placing objects into groups or classes. She is developing concepts. Combining something concrete, such as a ball, with an abstract quality, such as roundness, enables Kim to identify classes of objects, events, and ideas that differ from each other. By repeatedly sorting and classifying different balls, she can eventually form an abstract concept for these similar objects that allows her to think about them and, eventually, to communicate with others about them. But how can teachers help students learn concepts and develop conceptual understanding?

Concept teaching models have been developed primarily to teach key concepts that serve as foundations for student higher-level thinking and to provide a basis for mutual understanding and communication (see Figure 9.1). Such models are not designed

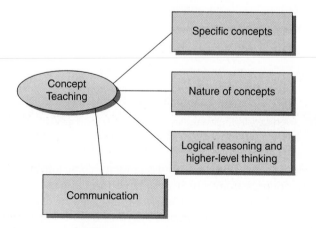

Figure 9.1 *Learner Outcomes of Concept Teaching*

to teach large amounts of information to students. However, by learning and applying key concepts within a given subject, students are able to transfer specific learnings to more general areas. In fact, without mutual understanding of certain key concepts, content learning in some subject areas is nearly impossible.

There are numerous approaches to concept teaching, but two basic ones have been selected for this chapter. These are labeled the *direct presentation* approach and the *concept attainment* approach. As will be described in detail later, the syntax for the two approaches varies slightly. Basically, however, a concept lesson consists of four major phases or steps: (1) present goals and establish set, (2) input examples and nonexamples, (3) test for concept attainment, and (4) analyze student thinking processes.

The learning environment for concept teaching might be described as moderately structured and teacher-centered. Transitions into and out of a concept lesson should be planned. The teacher makes judgments about which concepts to teach and where concept lessons should be sequenced within a larger unit of study. The teacher also selects the best examples and nonexamples of the concept based on the background and experiences of the students. During a concept lesson, there are numerous occasions when the teacher's main role becomes one of responding to student ideas, encouraging student participation, and supporting students as they develop their reasoning abilities. Checking for understanding and giving students opportunities to explore their own thinking processes also call for the teacher's support and encouragement. While a concept lesson is in progress, there is no time for casual talk with neighbors, studying other subject areas, or any other activity that might take attention away from the lesson.

> The learning environment for concept teaching is moderately structured and teacher-centered.

Theoretical and Empirical Support

The theoretical and empirical support for concept teaching and learning is very extensive and covers a wide range of topics. This is because concept development and its relation to how the mind works have held the interest of theorists, philosophers, and researchers for centuries. Recently, this work has centered mainly in psychology and includes the contributions of Jean Piaget, Jerome Bruner, David Ausubel, and Howard Gardner, among others. Their studies showed how conceptual thinking develops in children and youth and how certain approaches to concept teaching affect these learning processes. In the sections that follow, we consider the relationship between concepts and higher-level thinking, the nature of concepts, and some of the knowledge we have about how best to teach concepts to students.

Concepts and Higher-Level Thinking

Concept learning is more than simply classifying objects and forming categories. It is also more than learning new labels or vocabulary to apply to classes of objects and ideas. Instead, concept learning involves the process of constructing knowledge and organizing information into comprehensive and complex cognitive structures. Remember that "conceptual knowledge" was one of four major types of knowledge described in Chapters 3 and 7.

As has been described in Chapters 7 and 8, students come into classrooms with a variety of prior experiences from which they have formed conceptions, or schemata, about the physical and social worlds. These schemata are a student's way of looking at the world. They help students explain and interpret what is happening in their lives. Sometimes the conceptions students hold are accurate; many times they are intuitive,

Check, Extend, Explore

Check
- What are the four phases of a concept lesson?
- What are the major learner outcomes of a concept lesson?
- What type of learning environment works best for concept lessons?

Extend
- Think about lessons aimed at teaching concepts that you have experienced as a student. What were the main features of these lessons? How did you respond to the concept lesson, say in contrast to a lecture?

Explore
- Go to the Online Learning Center at www.mhhe.com/ arends6e for links to websites related to *Concept Teaching*.

naive, and, in fact, misrepresentations of reality. Misconceptions cannot be changed by simply presenting new information. Instead, change requires teaching processes that enable students to become aware of their existing schemata and help them to develop new concepts and reformulations of existing ways of thinking.

The Nature of Concepts

In everyday usage, the term **concept** is used in several ways. Sometimes it refers to an idea someone has, such as, "My concept of how a president should act is straightforward." At other times it is used as a hypothesis; for example, "My concept is that we are always in debt because we spend too much on frills." When the term *concept* is used in connection with teaching and learning, it has a more precise meaning and refers to the way knowledge and experience are categorized.

Concept learning is essentially "putting things into a class" and then being able to recognize members of that class. This requires that an individual be able to take a particular case, such as his or her pet dog Max, and place it into a general class of objects, in this case a class termed *dog*, that share certain attributes. This process requires making judgments about whether a particular case is an instance of a larger class.

Jean Piaget, a Swiss psychologist, had a lot of influence on our understanding of how conceptual thinking develops in children.

Concepts Themselves Can Be Placed into Categories. Concepts, like other objects and ideas, can be categorized and labeled. Knowing the different types of concepts is important because, as is explained later, different types of concepts require different teaching strategies. One way of classifying concepts is according to the rule structures that define their use (Table 9.1).

> Concepts are devices used to organize knowledge and experiences into categories.

Some concepts have constant rule structures. The concept of *island,* for example, always involves land surrounded by water. A *triangle* is a plane, closed figure with three sides and three angles. The rule structures for these concepts are constant. Their critical attributes are combined in an additive manner and are always the same. This type of concept is referred to as a **conjunctive concept.**

> Concepts themselves can be categorized and labeled.

Other concepts are broader and more flexible and permit alternative sets of attributes. Their rule structures are not constant. For example, the concept of a *strike* in baseball is based on a number of alternative conditions. A strike may occur when a batter swings and misses, when an umpire determines that the pitch was in the strike zone even though the batter did not swing at the ball, or when the batter hits a foul ball. This type of concept is called a **disjunctive concept**—that is, one that contains alternative sets of attributes. The concept *noun* is another example of a disjunctive concept. It may be a person, a place, or a thing, but it cannot be all three at the same time.

Table 9.1 *Three Types of Concepts*

Type	Characteristic	Example
Conjunctive	Constant rule structure	Island
Disjunctive	Alternative set of attributes	Strike in baseball
Relational	Rule structure depends on relationships	Aunt

A third type of concept is one whose rule structure depends on relationships. The concept *aunt* describes a particular relationship between siblings and their offspring. The concepts *time* and *distance* are also **relational concepts.** To understand either of these concepts, one must know the other, plus the relationship between them. For example, *week* is defined as a succession of days that has as its beginning point day one (usually Sunday) and as its ending point day seven (usually Saturday) and a duration of seven days.

Concepts Are Learned through Examples and Nonexamples. Learning particular concepts involves identifying both *examples* and *nonexamples* of a concept. For instance, a cow is an example of a mammal but is a nonexample of a reptile. Australia is an example of a country in the Southern Hemisphere, but it is a nonexample of a developing country. Cotton and silk are examples of the concept *fabric,* but leather and steel are nonexamples. As we describe later, the way examples and nonexamples are identified and used by teachers is important in a concept lesson.

Concepts Are Influenced by Social Context. The critical attributes of a conjunctive concept, such as *equilateral triangle,* are fixed across social contexts. However, disjunctive or relational concepts, such as *poverty* or *literacy rate,* change from one social context to another. For example, poverty in the United States means something much different than poverty in a developing African country. Concepts with changing critical attributes are often found in the behavioral and social sciences and need an operational definition depending on the social context or cultural environment in which they are used. Consider the concept *aunt.* In some societies, *aunt* or *auntie* refers to any adult in the society who has some responsibility for caring for a particular child and has nothing to do with actual blood relationship. Consider also the geographical concepts *north* and *south* as they relate to climate. Children in the Northern Hemisphere are taught that as one goes south, the climate gets warmer. Obviously, this conceptual relationship would not hold true for children in Australia or Argentina. The labeling of concepts is also influenced by context. In England, a car's windshield is called a *windscreen,* and the trunk is called the *boot.* In both instances, the concepts are the same; the label is what is different.

Concepts Have Definitions and Labels. All concepts have names or labels and more or less precise definitions. For example, a relatively small body of land surrounded on all sides by water is labeled an *island.* Labels and definitions permit mutual understanding and communication with others using the concept. They are prerequisites for concept teaching and learning. Labels, however, are human inventions and essentially are arbitrary. Knowing the label does not mean a student understands the concept. This is what makes teaching concepts difficult.

Concepts Have Critical Attributes. Concepts also have attributes that describe and help define them (Table 9.2). Some attributes are critical and are used to separate one concept from all others. For example, an *equilateral triangle* is a triangle with three equal sides. The **critical attributes** are that it must be a triangle and that each of the sides must be equal. Triangles without three equal sides are not equilateral triangles. In addition, if the concept is a subset of a broader concept, then it must also include the critical attributes of the broader concept. An *equilateral triangle* is a member of the class of concepts called *triangles* and thus must contain all the critical attributes of a triangle.

Teachers should provide clear examples and nonexamples of what is being taught to ensure thorough understanding of the concept.

Social context and culture influence the definition and attributes of some concepts.

A concept's critical attributes are what distinguish it from all other concepts.

Table 9.2 *Critical and Noncritical Attributes of Birds*

Critical Attributes	Noncritical Attributes
Feathers	Feather color
Warm-blooded	Ability to fly
Feet	Webbed feet

Concepts Have Noncritical Attributes. Some attributes may be found in some, but not all, members of the class. These are called **noncritical attributes.** For example, size is a noncritical attribute of an equilateral triangle. All concepts have both critical and non-critical attributes, and it is sometimes difficult for students to differentiate between the two. For example, the concept *bird* is typically associated in most people's minds with the noncritical attribute flying. Robins, cardinals, eagles, and most other birds can fly. Flying, however, is not a critical attribute of birds, since ostriches and penguins cannot fly, yet they are still classified as birds. Focusing exclusively on critical attributes and typical members of a class can sometimes cause confusion when learning new concepts. Although flying is a noncritical attribute of birds, it is nonetheless typical of most birds and must be accounted for in teaching about them.

Focusing exclusively on the critical attributes of concepts can result in confusion when learning new concepts.

Human Development and Concept Learning

Another important aspect underlying concept teaching comes from the field of human development. Research in this field, some of which dates back over half a century, has shown how age and intellectual development influence students' readiness and abilities to learn various types of concepts (Benjafield, 1992; Friedman, 1980; Piaget, 1954, 1963; Starkey, 1980; Welch & Long, 1940). This research has shown that children begin learning concepts at a very early age through object sorting and classifying activities and that concept learning continues throughout life. The way concepts are learned is affected by the learner's age, language development, and level of intellectual development. Theories of cognitive development of Jean Piaget and Jerome Bruner are important to teachers in regard to concept learning by students.

The way concepts are learned is affected significantly by the learner's age and his or her levels of intellectual development.

Swiss psychologist Jean Piaget developed a theory about how humans develop and make sense of their world. From Piaget's perspective, humans are always striving to make sense of their environment, and their biological maturation, their interaction with the environment, and their social experiences combine to influence how they think about things. The primary contribution of Piaget's ideas for teachers is his *stage theory of cognitive development.* According to Piaget, as children grow and mature, they pass through four stages of cognitive development: sensorimotor, preoperational, concrete operational, and formal operational. These stages and the kinds of thinking associated with each are illustrated in Table 9.3. As you can see, the type of learning that a person is capable of is linked to age. Younger children deal with their world in more concrete, hands-on ways, whereas older children and adults can engage in abstract problem solving.

Piaget also provided a theory for understanding how people adapt to their environment through the processes of assimilation and accommodation. When individuals experience a new idea or a new situation, they first try to make sense of the new information by using existing schemata. Remember, *schemata* refers to the way individuals store and

Check, Extend, Explore

Check
- What kind of relationships exist between concepts and higher-level thinking?
- What are the critical features of different kinds of concepts?
- What are the differences between critical and noncritical attributes?
- What are Piaget's four stages of human development?
- Name Bruner's three modes of learning.

Extend
- How might you go about teaching a child at the preoperational stage where the "sun goes at night"? To a child at the concrete operational stage? To a youth at the formal operational stage?

Explore
- Go to the Online Learning Center at www.mhhe.com/arends6e for links to websites related to *Conceptual Development*.

Assimilation occurs when individuals fit new information into existing schemata.

Accommodation occurs when individuals change existing schemata to respond to new ideas or situations.

Table 9.3 *Piaget's Stages of Cognitive Development*

Stage	Age	Kinds of Thinking Abilities
Sensorimotor	Birth–2 years	Begins to recognize objects; can imitate.
Preoperational	2–7 years	Develops use of language; begins ability to think symbolically; can see another person's point of view; lacks logical mental operations at this stage.
Concrete operational	7–11 years	Can solve concrete problems in logical fashion; able to classify.
Formal operational	11–15/adult	Can solve abstract problems in logical fashion; has concern for social issues.

organize knowledge and experiences in memory. Trying to understand the new information by adapting it to what we already know is called **assimilation.** Take the example of a young child who has a large kitty at home and sees a small puppy for the first time. She may call the puppy "kitty" because she is trying to explain the new animal with her existing schemata for animals, which up to this point only include kitties. If individuals cannot fit the new data or situation into their existing schemata, they must develop new concepts or schemata. This is called **accommodation.** In the kitty-dog example, the child has accommodated when she added the concept of *dog* and *puppy* to her schemata about animals.

Individuals are always adapting to their environment using prior knowledge and existing schemata. Concept teaching is one way to provide new ideas and expand and change existing schemata. You will read later how the processes of assimilation and accommodation influence the kinds of examples and nonexamples teachers choose to help students understand particular concepts.

An American psychologist, Jerome Bruner, also has provided a conceptualization about how children learn at different stages of maturation. Bruner (1966) identified three distinct modes of learning: (1) learning by doing, called the *enactive mode,* (2) learning by forming mental images, called the *iconic mode,* and (3) learning through a series of abstract symbols or representations, called the *symbolic mode.* As children grow older and progress through the grades, they depend less on the enactive mode and more on mental imagery and symbolic operations. In general, children under age 7 rely mainly on doing, or the enactive mode, for learning concepts. Children between the ages of 7 and 11 still rely on the enactive mode but begin learning concepts by forming mental images. Older children and early adolescents still use the iconic mode but increasingly rely on abstract symbols.

Research has shown that children can learn concepts at a fairly early age and that early concept learning facilitates what can be learned later on. A particularly interesting and important study (Novak & Musonda, 1991) on concept learning in science was selected for the Research Summary in this chapter (page 334).

Planning and Conducting Concept Lessons

This section describes procedures and guidelines for planning and conducting lessons aimed at teaching concepts and the nature of concepts.

Planning for Concept Teaching

During the planning phase of a concept lesson, teachers must make decisions about what concepts to teach and which approach to use. They must also do a thorough job of defining and analyzing concepts being taught and decide which examples and nonexamples to use and how best to present them to students during the lesson. These tasks are important and time-consuming. They make planning for a concept lesson very difficult, perhaps more so than planning for any other model of teaching.

Selecting Concepts. The curriculum is the primary source for selecting concepts to teach. Concepts may be embedded in textbooks, and the teacher's edition often provides guidance in selecting key concepts to teach. Take, for instance, the following passage on temperature and heat from a sixth-grade science textbook:

> Objects that are moving can do work. You may think of work as doing chores such as washing the car or raking leaves. Scientists, however, define *work* as a force acting on an object and causing it to move. A falling hammer, for example, can do the work of driving a nail. Such work can be done because moving objects have energy. This energy of *motion* is called *kinetic energy*. The faster an object moves, the more kinetic energy it has. . . .
>
> Molecules, like all objects, have kinetic energy because of their motion. *Temperature* is a measure of the average kinetic energy of molecules. The higher the temperature, faster the molecules in a given sample are moving, on the average (Hurd et al., 1996, pp. 82–83).

In this passage, the concepts of *work, motion, kinetic energy,* and *temperature* are described. However, it is likely that most students will not understand these concepts thoroughly unless the concepts become the subjects of particular lessons taught by the teacher.

Local curriculum guides are another source for selecting concepts for instruction. In some cases, the key concepts will be listed as vocabulary to be developed in the unit. In other cases, concepts will be found within the main ideas or generalizations for a unit of study. For example, American history courses typically contain a unit on the westward movement. In this unit, students study why people migrated westward during the early eras of the nation's history. In the process, they study such key concepts as *migration, economic gain, religious freedom,* and *political freedom.* They also examine other concepts related to the unit's objectives, such as *expansion, self-sufficiency, heterogeneity, frontier, pioneer, pluralism,* and *terrain.* Obviously, all concepts cannot be taught in a single unit, and teachers must make decisions about which ones to single out for particular lessons.

Teachers also need to make decisions about which of the new vocabulary words need to be directly taught as concepts. They must constantly judge which new terms are essential to students understanding the important ideas of a lesson or a unit. If the students don't know the key concepts within a unit, then a lesson on the unknown concepts should be taught. Concept lessons should always be taught if the materials contain unfamiliar terms, a series of steps not known to students, or the use of some "rule" that is new to students.

In the process of selecting concepts to teach, it is important to remember a point made earlier: Helping students understand a concept involves more than getting them to provide definitions of new vocabulary words.

Deciding on an Approach. A concept teaching lesson has several components. These include the name and definition of the concept, the concept's attributes (some that are critical and some that are not), and examples and nonexamples of the concept. There are

Time does not permit teaching every concept that exists in a field. Selecting appropriate concepts to teach is a major planning task for teachers.

Research Summary

Can Instruction At an Early Age Have Positive Effects on Learning Science Concepts?

Novak, J. D., and Musonda, D. (1991).
A twelve-year longitudinal study of science concept teaching. *American Educational Research Journal, 28,* 125–130.

Do we sometimes underestimate young student's abilities to learn important concepts? That is the question that Novak and Musonda set out to examine over twenty years ago. Their study is interesting for two reasons. One, it shows that if taught properly, young children can learn basic science concepts and that this learning facilitates later concept development. Two, the study illustrates what can be learned if the same subjects are studied over a span of years rather than at just one point in time.

Problem and Approach: Using qualitative and quantitative methods, Novak and Musonda explored whether first- and second-grade students could be taught basic science concepts, and if so, whether their early science learning enhanced later understanding.

Sample and Setting: From 1971 through 1973, teachers in eleven first- and second-grade classrooms taught 191 students twenty-eight science lessons that had been developed by the researchers. Each lesson required between fifteen to twenty-five minutes to teach. A similar sample of forty-eight children, all from the same school, did not participate in the science lesson program and served as a comparison sample in the study. The study was conducted in the Ithaca, New York, public schools.

Procedures: Before the study, researchers developed twenty-eight science lessons, each built around a basic science concept. Examples of lesson topics included: classification of objects; how energy is stored; air molecules and movement; change and things that change them; and energy and change. Lessons were presented with audiotapes and pictures, and students interacted with specially designed hands-on materials. Features of concept learning and the use of advance organizers were built into each science lesson. Students studied lessons one through sixteen in the first grade and lessons seventeen through twenty-eight in the second grade. The forty-eight comparison students received no science instruction during grades 1 and 2.

Students in the study were interviewed periodically, and their ideas were organized in concept maps or webs (see Figure 9.2). These maps were subsequently used by the researchers to assess changes in concept understanding from grade 1 through grade 12. As would be expected in a study of this duration, many students moved to other schools over the years, so the sample for the instructed group decreased from 191 to 38 and for the uninstructed group from 48 to 17 between grade 1 and grade 12.

Results. The results of the study reported here come primarily from data derived from the concept maps. Figure 9.2 illustrates what the concepts maps looked like; these were developed in grades 2 and 12 by Amy, one of the students in the study. As you can see, Amy's map becomes more lengthy as her understanding of science increases over the years. It also becomes more complex.

Using data available from the concepts maps for students (instructed and noninstructed) and matched according to grade point average, Novak and Musonda scored each student's science understanding at one of four different grade levels. In general, the researchers concluded that instructed students possessed more valid science concepts throughout their school years, and they held fewer misconceptions than did noninstructed students. Although wide variation existed for both groups, the instructed group consistently scored better.

Discussion and Implications The remarkable findings of this study are twofold. One, young children have much concept learning potential that is often overlooked, and two, relatively few hours of science instruction in grades 1 and 2 pay off handsomely in learning about science later on in school. The study makes a strong statement about the importance of early science instruction and how this early instruction can have lasting impact.

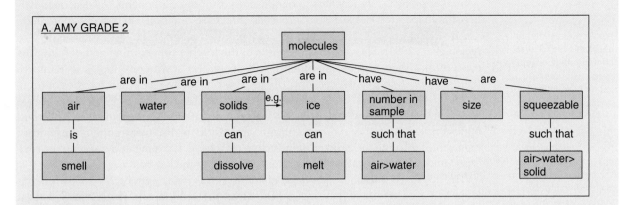

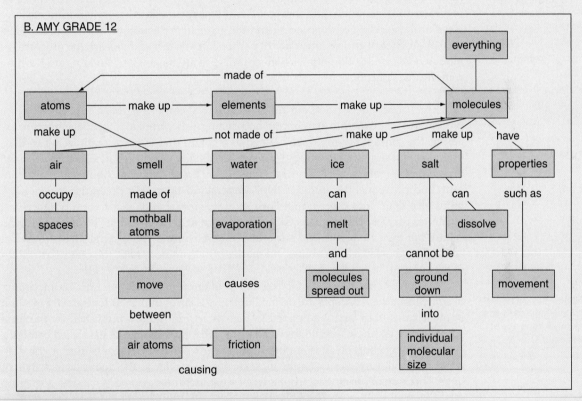

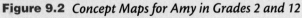

Figure 9.2 *Concept Maps for Amy in Grades 2 and 12*

Source: Novak and Musonda (1991), pp. 137–138

several approaches for teachers to handle each of these components. As described earlier, this chapter focuses on two approaches: direct presentation and concept attainment.

The **direct presentation** approach employs a deductive *rule-to-example process* (Tennyson et al., 1983). This approach consists of the teacher first naming and defining the concept and then providing students with examples and nonexamples to reinforce their understanding of the concept. The focus is on labeling and defining the concept.

The **concept attainment** approach, on the other hand, turns this sequence around and uses an inductive *example-to-rule process* (Bruner, 1956). Teachers give examples and nonexamples of a particular concept first, and students discover or attain the concept themselves through the process of inductive reasoning. Labeling and defining the concept comes at the end rather than at the beginning of the lesson.

The approach a teacher uses depends on the *goals* being sought, the *students* being taught, and the *nature* of the concept. The direct presentation approach usually is best for the development of knowledge about a concept for which students have little or no previous understanding. The concept attainment approach is best when students have some understanding of the concept and the goals of the lesson are to explore the presence or absence of critical attributes of particular concepts and to learn the processes of inductive reasoning. Sometimes both approaches are used when students are learning complicated concepts.

Defining Concepts. Critical attributes, as you read earlier, are those attributes that are present in every example of a concept and distinguish it from all other concepts. For example, the concept *tree* might be defined as a "plant that lives for many years and has a single main stem that is woody." This definition includes the critical attributes *plant, lives for many years, single main stem,* and *woody.* These critical attributes define a concept, and consequently, students must understand them. However, noncritical attributes also enter into the picture. For example, size, shape, and color are noncritical attributes of trees. Blue lagoons, sandy beaches, and palm trees may be desirable on an island, but they are noncritical attributes. When learning concepts, students must not confuse the noncritical attributes, no matter how common, with the critical attributes of the concept.

The source of the definition for a concept and its critical attributes are also important. In some instances, concepts are defined in the glossaries of the students' textbooks, but in other cases, they may be defined in the curriculum guides published by the local school districts. These definitions and critical attributes should be examined carefully. When defining concepts, it is important to recognize that some words used in the definition are irrelevant. For example, most dictionaries refer to the domesticated state of dogs. This is an interesting fact, but it is not what identifies a dog or separates dogs from cats. Essentially, there are three steps in defining a concept: (1) identify the concept's name; (2) list the critical and noncritical attributes; and (3) write a concise definition. For the *island* example, this would involve identifying the name as *island,* listing the critical attributes as landmass and water, and providing the following definition: "an island is a landmass that is smaller than a continent and is surrounded by water."

Analyzing Concepts. Once a concept has been selected and defined in terms of its critical attributes, the concept needs to be analyzed for examples and nonexamples. The selection of examples and nonexamples is probably the most difficult aspect of planning for a concept lesson. Examples serve as the connectors between the concept's abstraction and the learner's prior knowledge and experiences. Examples must be meaningful to the learner and must be as concrete as possible.

The direct presentation approach calls for teacher definition of a concept followed by appropriate provision of examples and nonexamples.

The concept attainment approach entails students deriving a concept themselves using inductive reasoning after being provided with examples and nonexamples.

Complex concepts from academic subjects need to be defined and taught appropriately for the age of the students.

Selecting good examples and nonexamples of a concept is one of the most challenging aspects of planning a concept lesson.

Table 9.4 *Analysis a Set of Concepts*

Concept	Definition	Example	Nonexample	Critical Attributes
Island	A landmass not as large as a continent, surrounded by water	Hawaii Cuba Greenland	Florida Lake Erie Australia	1. Landmass (not continent), *and* 2. Water, *and* 3. Land surrounded by water
Lake	A large inland body of water surrounded by land	Lake Huron Great Salt Lake Big Lake	Ohio River Hawaii Pond	1. Large inland body of water, *and* 2. Land, *and* 3. Water surrounded by land
Peninsula	A land area almost entirely surrounded by water but having a land connection to a larger landmass	Florida Italy Delmarva	Cuba Hudson Bay Big lake	1. Land connected to larger landmass, *and* 2. Water, *and* 3. Land surrounded almost entirely by water
Bay	A body of water partly surrounded by land but having a wide outlet to the sea	Chesapeake Bay Hudson Bay Green Bay	Florida Lake Gulf	1. Body of water connected to the sea by a wide outlet, *and* 2. Land, *and* 3. Water partly surrounded by land

Charts, diagrams, and webs as well as pictures should be used as visual examples of abstract concepts. They can also aid the teacher in analyzing the concept for instructional decisions. Table 9.4 contains an analysis of a set of concepts. Numbering the critical attributes and using the word *and* can be a reminder that all the critical attributes must be present to have an example of the concept.

Look at the example "Hawaii" in Table 9.4. It is a landmass not as large as a continent, there is a body of water nearby, and the water completely surrounds it. Each of the three critical conditions of an island is met; therefore, it is an example of the concept. Teachers might also look at Florida as a nonexample of island. Land and water are present, but the land is not completely surrounded by water. All of the criteria are not met; therefore, Florida is a nonexample.

The isolation of the attributes is critical to the analysis and teaching of concepts. The teacher needs to decide if the attributes are critical and should be presented when matching examples and nonexamples, such as Hawaii and Florida, or if the attributes are noncritical and are best used in divergent examples after clear instances of the concept are presented.

Choosing and Sequencing Examples and Nonexamples. The examples and nonexamples selected to illustrate a concept are very important. In general, it has been shown that initial examples should be familiar to the class. Students need to see typical examples clearly before they are ready to consider atypical ones. Similarly, students normally find it easier to identify a concept with its most immediate neighbors before relating it to more distant ones. If a robin is used as the best (most familiar) example of the concept *bird*, it is easier for the learner to distinguish close neighbors to robins, such

Examples that are very different from each other will enable students to focus on common attributes of the concept.

as cardinals, sparrows, or bluebirds, than to distinguish more distant members, such as ducks, chickens, or penguins.

When selecting a set of examples, teachers will often make the noncritical attributes of the concept as *different* as possible. This helps students focus on the critical attributes common to each of the examples. For instance, if teachers are developing the concept of *island,* they might include Hawaii, a tropical island, and Greenland, which has a cold climate. The obvious differences in climates will help students focus their attention on the common attributes of these two examples. Likewise, when developing a set of examples for the concept *insects,* teachers might include water bugs and ants, which live in different environments but still have the same critical attributes.

When selecting a set of matched examples and nonexamples, teachers generally attempt to make the noncritical attributes of the pairs as similar as possible. This enables students to focus on the differences between the example and the nonexample. In the case of the concept of *island,* for example, the Florida peninsula and the Cuban island could serve as a matched pair because of the similarities in climate. Examples and nonexamples should be sequenced for presentation in a logical fashion, and normally sets should be ordered from the easiest to the more difficult. Teachers may also want to give cues to focus students' thinking before each set of three or four examples.

Use of Visual Images. Using visual images affects the learning of concepts and supports the old adage that "a picture is worth a thousand words." For instance, Anderson and Smith (1987) studied how children come to understand science concepts such as *light* and *color.* They had 113 children in five classrooms study the following passage:

> Bouncing Light
>
> Have you ever thrown a rubber ball at something? If you have, you know that when the ball hits most things, it bounces off them. Like a rubber ball, light bounces off most things it hits.
>
> When light travels to something opaque, all the light does not stop. Some of this light bounces off. When light travels to something translucent or transparent, all the light does not pass through. Some of this light bounces off. When light bounces off things and travels to your eyes, you are able to see.

They found that only 20 percent of the students could understand that seeing is a process of detecting light that has been reflected off some object. However, in a second experiment, they used a visual aid such as the one illustrated in Figure 9.3. In contrast to the 20 percent who learned the concepts from reading about light, 78 percent of the students understood the concepts the teachers were trying to teach when visual aids were used to illustrate the concepts.

Graphic organizers and conceptual webs are other forms of visual representation that can be useful. These devices can help highlight the critical attributes of a concept and make the concept more concrete for students. They can also provide students with an effective means for retrieving information from long-term memory so new concepts can be more easily understood.

There are normally four steps in constructing a web for a particular concept:

Step 1: Create the core, which is the focus of the web. This would be the name of the concept.

Step 2: Construct strands branching out from the core. These strands are critical attributes of the concept.

Visual aids and pictures have been shown to greatly facilitate student understanding of complex concepts.

Graphic organizers provide visual images and are a good way for students to link new information.

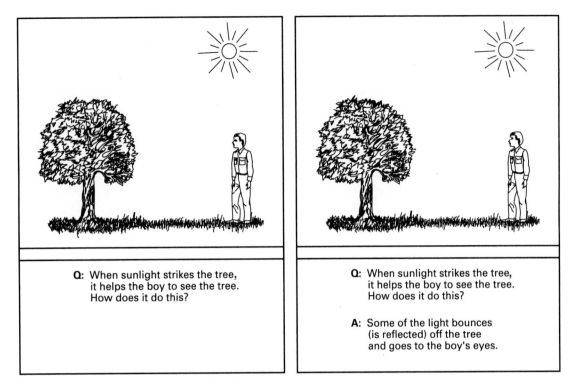

Figure 9.3 *Visual Depiction of the Role of Light in Seeing*

Source: After Richardson-Koehler (1987), p. 327

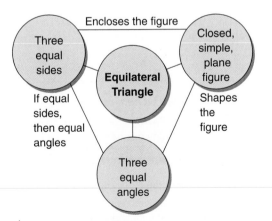

Figure 9.4 *Web of the Concept Equilateral Triangle*

Step 3: Draw strand supports, which connect the critical attributes to the concept.

Step 4: Identify the strand ties, which may show relationships among the various attributes.

Figure 9.4 is a conceptual web of the concept *equilateral triangle.*

Plan for Time and Space. Just as with previous models, deciding on how to allocate sufficient time and how to use classroom space are important planning tasks for a concept

A common mistake made by teachers is underestimating the time it will take to thoroughly teach even simple concepts.

lesson. Time requirements depend on the cognitive levels and abilities of the students as well as the complexity of the concept being taught. The most common error made by beginning teachers is underestimating the time it takes to teach even simple concepts thoroughly. Remember the earlier admonition that memorizing the definition of a concept is not the same as understanding it.

The uses of space for concept teaching are similar to those described for the presentation and direct instruction models. Since concept teaching is teacher-directed, most teachers prefer to use the more traditional row-and-column formation illustrated in Chapter 7 or the horizontal desk formation described in Chapter 8. Both of these formations keep students' attention focused on the teacher and on information being displayed in the front of the room. Unfortunately, they are not ideal for the more interactive phases of a concept lesson.

Adapting Plans to Meet Diverse Needs

Perhaps more than in any other situation, teachers must remain aware of the great diversity of their students and be ready to tailor their teaching to particular learners when they are teaching concepts. One feature of student diversity is the substantial variation in intellectual development and prior knowledge present in most classrooms. As a result, some concepts will be meaningful and appropriate for some students, while they may be too difficult for and not within the experiences of others. One way that teachers can adapt instruction to meet the needs of all learners is to consider the difficulty of the examples and nonexamples used in the concept lesson. Figure 9.5 illustrates easy, medium, and difficult examples and nonexamples for teaching the concept of *adverb*. Remember that an adverb is a word that modifies a verb, an adjective, or another adverb and functions to answer one of these questions: When? How? Where? or To what extent? The critical attributes are *modifies another word* and *function*.

Other features of diversity include the cultural backgrounds of students and the experiences they bring with them to the classroom. For example, conceptual under-

Easy Examples
1. You are so happy.
2. She has been absent lately.
3. Slowly, she walked home.
4. The train chugged loudly.

Medium Examples
5. Are you fighting mad?
6. Clouds gathered threateningly.
7. It was not difficult to explain.
8. The most dangerous weapon is a gun.

Difficult Examples
9. The small floral print looked pretty.
10. Cats are my number one favorite pet.
11. He wants the dark purple bicycle.
12. The book had three color pictures.

Easy Nonexamples
13. Sewing makes you happy.
14. She has been late.
15. She is slow.
16. The loud train chugged.

Medium Nonexamples
17. Do you fight?
18. The threatening clouds gathered.
19. It is difficult to explain that *not* is a negative word.
20. Most guns are dangerous weapons.

Difficult Nonexamples
21. The small print looked pretty.
22. One special cat is my favorite pet.
23. He wants the dark trim to match.
24. The book had three pictures.

Figure 9.5 *List of Easy, Medium, and Difficult Examples and Nonexamples of Adverbs*

standings about the relationship between latitude and temperature differ depending on the hemisphere where students live. Students in the Northern Hemisphere learn at a very early age to associate "north" with colder weather. The exact opposite is true for students who grow up in the Southern Hemisphere, where it gets colder as one goes south from the equator. Another example of differences stemming from geography is the concept of *snow.* It is reported that Eskimo languages have many words to define snow, whereas there is only one word for snow in English. As described in some detail in Chapter 2, cultural differences can also influence one's understanding and perception of a particular concept. For example, Native Americans traditionally have a much different concept of time than do Americans of European origins. There are considerable cultural differences and norms around concepts that define social relationships, verbal interaction, and social distance. Lack of experience with a particular concept or situation is one of the largest causes of variation of conceptual understanding. For example, it would be difficult to illustrate or explain the World Wide Web to an individual who has never seen a computer.

To be effective, teachers must remain aware of the vast differences among their students and never assume that any two students' understanding of a concept will be identical. As with all models of teaching, it is important that teachers consider and meet their students' diverse needs during the planning phase and design aspects of the lesson.

Conducting Concept Lessons

The four phases of a concept teaching lesson are outlined in Table 9.5. The sections that follow describe in some detail teacher and student behavior associated with each phase.

Clarifying Aims and Establishing Set. At the beginning of a concept lesson, just as with all types of lessons, the teacher needs to communicate clearly to students the aims of the lesson and how the lesson will proceed. The teacher might also go over the steps of the lesson and give students reasons why the concepts about to be taught are important to learn. Establishing set for a concept lesson requires procedures no different from those described in Chapters 7 and 8. Teachers get students ready to learn with a brief review, questions about yesterday's lesson, or an interesting anecdote that ties the forthcoming lesson into students' prior knowledge.

Establishing set and preparing a class for the lesson to be taught are important parts of concept teaching.

"CITY CHILDREN HAVE TROUBLE WITH THE CONCEPT OF HARVEST."

(© Martha Campbell, from Phi Delta Kappan)

Table 9.5 *Syntax for Concept Teaching*

Phase	Teacher Behavior
Phase 1: Clarify aims and establish set.	Teacher explains the aims and procedures for the lesson and gets students ready to learn.
Phase 2: Input examples and nonexamples.	In the direct presentation approach, teacher names the concepts, identifies the critical attributes, and illustrates with examples and nonexamples.
	In concept attainment, examples and nonexamples are given, and students inductively arrive at the concept and its attributes.
Phase 3: Test for attainment.	Teacher presents additional examples and nonexamples to test students' understanding of the concept. Students are asked to provide their own examples and nonexamples of the concept.
Phase 4: Analyze student thinking processes and integration of learning.	Teacher gets students to think about their own thinking processes. Students are asked to examine their decisions and the consequences of their choices. Teacher helps students integrate new learning by relating the concept to other concepts in a unit of study.

Input of Examples and Nonexamples and Testing for Attainment. The exact sequence for defining and labeling a concept or presenting examples and nonexamples varies according to the particular approach being used by the teacher. It is this internal arrangement and flow of activities that give each of the two approaches its unique character and allows each to accomplish the particular learning outcomes for which it was designed.

Lesson flow and sequence of concept teaching will vary depending on the topic and approach selected by the teacher.

Direct Presentation. In the direct presentation approach, the internal flow of the lesson includes the following:

1. Naming the concept and providing students with a definition.
2. Identifying the critical attributes and giving examples and nonexamples of the concept.
3. Testing for concept understanding by getting students to provide examples and nonexamples.

Taking the concept *island* as analyzed in Table 9.4, a teacher using the direct presentation approach might proceed as follows:

- Tell students that they are going to learn the concept *island* and write the name of the concept on the board so that students can see the word.
- List the critical attributes: (1) landmass (not a continent), (2) water, (3) land surrounded by water.
- Show a simple drawing that contains only the critical attributes and point out each critical attribute. This could be followed by pictures of best examples, such as Hawaii, Greenland, or Cuba. As each picture is presented, point out the critical attributes again.
- Show students both examples and nonexamples of the concept and ask questions that force judgments about whether a new instance is an example or nonexample of the concept. Have students tell why or why not. Have students come up with their own example and nonexamples.

Students learn some concepts through experimentation.

Concept Attainment. In concept attainment, students already have some grasp of a concept or set of concepts and are asked to make decisions about whether or not particular examples are instances of a class. Teachers using the concept attainment approach would use the following steps:

1. Provide students with examples, some that represent the concept and some that do not. Best examples are clearly labeled *yes,* and carefully selected nonexamples are clearly labeled *no.*
2. Urge students to hypothesize about the attributes of the concept and to record reasons for their speculation. The teacher may ask additional questions to help focus students' thinking and to get them to compare attributes of the examples and nonexamples.
3. When students appear to know the concept, they name (label) the concept and describe the process they used for identifying it. Students may guess the concept early in the lesson, but the teacher needs to continue to present examples and nonexamples until the students attain the critical attributes of the concept as well as the name of the concept.
4. The teacher checks to see if the students have attained the concept by having them identify additional examples as *yes* or *no,* tell why or why not they are examples, and generate examples and nonexamples of their own.

In the concept attainment approach, a concept is not labeled until students demonstrate understanding and have thought about critical attributes of the concept.

Concept attainment is an inductive process that assists learners in organizing data according to previously learned concepts. Unlike the direct instruction approach, the teacher provides a label and definition only after the students have engaged in the discovery of the critical attributes.

To illustrate the concept attainment approach, consider the following lesson, again using the concept *island:*

- The teacher shows a picture of an island and tells students this is an example of the concept. The teacher then shows a picture of a landform that is not an island and states that this is a nonexample of the concept.
- The teacher continues displaying pictures of islands and other landforms, telling students which are and which are not examples. Students are asked to guess what

There are many ways to help students intergrate conceptual learning.

they think the concept is. All hypotheses and ideas are listed on the chalkboard. The teacher continues to present examples and nonexamples and asks students to reconsider their original hypotheses.

- Students are asked to state a definition of the concept and, if possible, label it. They also list the critical attributes of the concept.
- The teacher then shows additional pictures of islands and other landforms and asks students to identify each as a *yes* or *no*. The teacher also asks students to provide examples of islands they know about and instances of landforms that are not islands. Students explain why or why not.

The major roles for the teacher during this aspect of a concept attainment lesson are to record student hypotheses and any critical attributes identified, to cue students, and to provide additional data if necessary.

Analyzing Thinking and Integrating Learning. The final phase of both approaches to concept teaching emphasizes teacher-directed activities aimed at helping students to analyze their own thinking processes and to integrate newly acquired conceptual knowledge. To accomplish this, teachers ask students to think back and recount what was going through their minds as they were considering the concepts. What criteria did they use for grouping items? When did they first figure out the concept? How? What was confusing in the direct presentation lesson? How does the concept relate to other concepts they know about? Were they focusing on the concept as a whole or on a particular attribute? How did noncritical attributes affect attaining the concept? If they were going to teach the concept to a younger student, what would they do?

The intent of this type of questioning is to get students to think about their own thinking (termed *metacognition* and discussed in some detail in Chapter 3) and to discover and consider the patterns they use to learn and integrate new concepts into their cognitive frameworks. This phase of a concept lesson relies, obviously, on student

Enhancing Teaching with Technology

Illustrating Concepts with CD-ROM, Simulation, and Virtual Websites

Good teachers have always known that a picture is worth a thousand words when teaching a difficult concept to students. Yet, it is often difficult to find the right picture, one that will represent an abstract concept in a meaningful way. Technology can play a significant role in helping teachers find the right pictures as well the right motion and the right sound.

Computer simulations, CD-ROMs, and virtual websites provide powerful means for bringing the outside world into the classroom and providing visual and auditory representations of abstract concepts. CD-ROM software and virtual websites are interactive and engage students by stimulating several senses through images, motion, and sound.

Let's consider an example from history. It is always difficult to get students to visualize different eras in history and concepts that help explain life in other times. *The Silk Road,* a very interesting CD-ROM program developed in Canada, does an excellent job of bringing history into the classroom. Using still photographs, video clips, other types of moving images, sound, and interesting text, *The Silk Road* shows life in thirteenth- and fourteenth-century Asia and the economic and social factors that gave rise to the rich trade route between Asia and the Middle East and Europe called the Silk Road. The software does a masterful job of holding the student's interest while illustrating the effects of early trade on the development of the modern world. The CD takes students on a trip along the Silk Road where they can view markets as they exist today as well as drawings of these markets as they were in the thirteenth and fourteenth centuries. The hypermedia environment allows students to branch into numerous topics associated with Asian and Middle Eastern regions: religion, history, customs, and geography. It was impossible to have the type of reality found in this beautiful CD a few years ago.

Similar CDs exist for just about every subject. The *National Gallery of Art CD* or *Windows on Science* use interesting collections of still photographs and video clips to illustrate hard-to-conceptualize concepts and ideas, in the visual arts and science.

Computer simulations are another type of software that can assist students as they grapple with complex concepts and ideas. Simulations are designed to replicate key elements of a real-life situation—situations that are often dangerous or difficult in real life. The design of simulations allows students to explore and manipulate aspects of the computer-based environment. The actions they choose produce results similar to those in the real environment.

You have probably played video games based on simulated situations—from assignments to James Bond to NFL football. These motivational games allow the participant to manipulate aspects of the situation. Simulations for education exist in various subject fields, for example:

- Impact of diplomatic actions on war and peace (history)
- Effect of different weather patterns on crops (geography)
- Virtual dissection of frogs (biology)

Simulations have many uses. They can be used prior to instruction on a concept or idea to enhance student interest. They can also be used after a topic has been studied to allow students to transfer acquired knowledge to a simulated situation. Simulation is most effective when used in conjunction with other methods, such as a presentation of factual and conceptual knowledge and inquiry or project-based lessons. Also, teachers need to help students understand that no matter how realistic the simulation, it is still a simulation—it is not real life or entirely accurate. Discussing and debriefing after a simulation is a critical element for helping students see the connections of the simulation to reality and to understand the consequences of their actions in the simulated environment. Experienced teachers know they must choose simulations carefully using the criteria for selection of other software described in Chapter 3. Of particular importance are the motivational qualities of the simulation and how closely the simulation reflects reality, called *fidelity.*

Finally, websites are available that take students on virtual field trips to illustrate concepts that might be difficult to reproduce by other means. For example, students who live in Minnesota could experience deserts; or students who live in Nevada could experience tundra. As with CD-ROM, these websites, which are often free, provide visual and auditory representations and many are interactive.

Check, Extend, Explore

Check

- What are the major planning tasks associated with concept teaching?
- How do inductive concept lessons differ from those that use a deductive approach?
- What are the four phases of the concept teaching model? What types of teacher behaviors are associated with each?
- What steps can teachers take to adapt concept lessons for students of differing abilities and backgrounds?
- How does the use of examples and nonexamples differ in inductive and deductive concept lessons?
- Why is it important to help students analyze their own thinking processes?

Extend

- Some teachers believe that concept teaching takes too much time and it not as efficient as simply presenting conceptual information to students. Do you agree or disagree with this perspective? Go to the "Extend Question Poll" on the Online Learning Center to respond.

Explore

- Go to the Online Learning Center at www.mhhe.com/arends6e for links to websites related to *How to Plan and Conduct Concept Lessons.*

discussion and participation. The guidelines for questioning, encouraging, and facilitating student discussion and participation provided in Chapters 4 and 12 can also be used for this final phase of a concept teaching lesson.

Managing the Learning Environment

The tasks associated with managing the learning environment during a concept teaching lesson are very similar to those used by teachers when using the presentation or direct instruction models. This is particularly true when the teacher is using the direct presentation approach to concept teaching. For this approach, effective teachers structure the learning environment fairly tightly. While the lesson is in progress, they expect students to pay close attention to the lesson—to be keen observers and good listeners. Effective teachers use the methods described in Chapter 5 to govern student talk and to ensure that the pace of the lesson is maintained. Misbehavior that occurs during the lesson is dealt with accurately and quickly, also described in Chapter 5.

In concept attainment, on the other hand, students strive to discover or attain the concept themselves, and this inductive process requires discourse and discussion. There are times when the teacher's role is to encourage interaction and to give students opportunities to explore their own thinking processes. Facilitating this student activity requires a less-structured learning environment in which students can inquire and express their ideas freely. The management system required for more student-centered instructional activities will be described in greater detail in Chapters 10, 11, and 12.

Assessment and Evaluation

Many of the same ideas and strategies used in defining and analyzing concepts can be employed in evaluating students' understanding of concepts. However, when evaluating students' understanding of a concept, it is important that teachers ask the students to do more than merely define the concept with words.

To attain the higher levels of concept learning, students should be able to (1) define the concept and know its critical attributes, (2) recognize examples and nonexamples, and (3) evaluate examples and nonexamples in terms of their critical attributes. For example, with the concept of *island,* the learner, when given examples of islands, bays, lakes, and peninsulas, will (1) properly name and identify the islands, (2) name the critical attributes of islands and discriminate them from noncritical attributes, and (3) evaluate how the islands differ from bays, lakes, and peninsulas. In terms of the critical attributes of islands, for example, peninsulas are not completely surrounded by water.

There are a number of principles that teachers should consider when constructing tests of students' behaviors in the learning of concepts. For example, test items should include examples that measure students' abilities to generalize to newly encountered examples of a concept. The test items should also assess students' abilities to discriminate among examples and nonexamples. Tests might employ different formats, such as true-false, multiple-choice, matching, short answer, or short essay. Practice assessment activities, such as a variation of the "twenty questions" game, can be used to provide practice on students' knowledge of concepts. Figure 9.6 shows examples of multiple-choice items for assessing students' understanding of the concept of *inferring.*

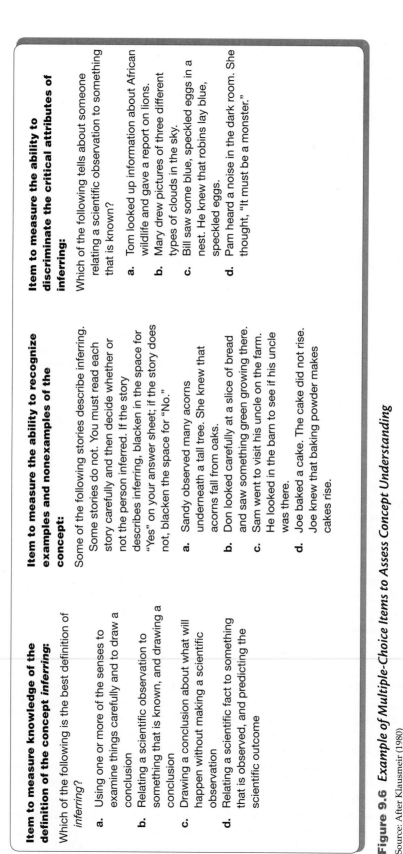

Item to measure knowledge of the definition of the concept *inferring*:

Which of the following is the best definition of *inferring*?

a. Using one or more of the senses to examine things carefully and to draw a conclusion

b. Relating a scientific observation to something that is known, and drawing a conclusion

c. Drawing a conclusion about what will happen without making a scientific observation

d. Relating a scientific fact to something that is observed, and predicting the scientific outcome

Item to measure the ability to recognize examples and nonexamples of the concept:

Some of the following stories describe inferring. Some stories do not. You must read each story carefully and then decide whether or not the person inferred. If the story describes inferring, blacken in the space for "Yes" on your answer sheet; if the story does not, blacken the space for "No."

a. Sandy observed many acorns underneath a tall tree. She knew that acorns fall from oaks.

b. Don looked carefully at a slice of bread and saw something green growing there.

c. Sam went to visit his uncle on the farm. He looked in the barn to see if his uncle was there.

d. Joe baked a cake. The cake did not rise. Joe knew that baking powder makes cakes rise.

Item to measure the ability to discriminate the critical attributes of inferring:

Which of the following tells about someone relating a scientific observation to something that is known?

a. Tom looked up information about African wildlife and gave a report on lions.

b. Mary drew pictures of three different types of clouds in the sky.

c. Bill saw some blue, speckled eggs in a nest. He knew that robins lay blue, speckled eggs.

d. Pam heard a noise in the dark room. She thought, "It must be a monster."

Figure 9.6 *Example of Multiple-Choice Items to Assess Concept Understanding*

Source: After Klausmeir (1980)

Check, Extend, Explore

Check
- What are the key features of the learning environment for concept teaching?
- What factors should teachers consider when they think about how to assess students' conceptual learning?

Extend
- Some teachers believe that only "brighter" students can benefit from concept teaching. Do you agree or disagree with this perspective? Go to the "Extend Question Poll" on the Online Learning Center to respond.

Explore
- Go to the Online Learning Center at www.mhhe.com/arends6e for links to websites related to *Learning Environments and Assessment Related to Concept Teaching.*

Reflections **from the** *Classroom*

Higher-Level Thinking—How Much?

You are in your first year of teaching and you are having a conversation with two of your teacher colleagues. The topic of teaching concepts and higher-level thinking comes up. You say that you have *not* observed many concept lessons in the classrooms the principal has asked you to observe over the past several weeks, and you wonder why. One of your colleagues responds by saying that with so much material to cover, she feels she and other teachers in the school can't justify the time it takes to plan and conduct good concept lessons. Your other colleague chimes in that many of the students in the school are of low ability and he doesn't believe that they can benefit from lessons on concepts until they have mastered basic skills, mainly through the drill-and-practice of direct instruction. You don't argue with them but their answers don't quite jibe with what you know about concept teaching and about having goals that promote meaningful learning and higher-level thinking for all students, regardless of their abilities.

Reflect on this situation and write a reflective essay about how you will approach the teaching of concepts with your students. Approach the situation from the perspective closest to the grade level or subject area you are preparing to teach. In your reflective essay, consider the following questions: Why is concept teaching important or unimportant? What kind of students benefits from concept teaching and lessons aimed at higher-level thinking? If concept lessons take more time, how can a teacher justify their use? How central will concept teaching be in your instructional repertoire? At the center? On the fringe? Depending on the students?

Compare your responses to the following provided by two experienced teachers. Include your essay as an exhibit in your professional portfolio.

Diane Caruso

Saltonstall School, 4th and 5th Grade
Salem, MA

The phrase "so much material to cover," particularly considering the constant revision of state educational frameworks, is one that is heard and repeated by thousands of teachers, both novice and experienced. It is extremely important to resist the coverage of material at the expense of concept development and understanding. Covering a topic does not insure concept mastery for *any* student, regardless of his or her strengths.

As a special needs teacher for many years, I always felt competent in my ability to challenge my students to achieve and to feel positive about themselves. Although this certainly involved the teaching and reinforcement of basic skills, other factors including the development of research techniques (simple and teacher-directed for some students), project work accompanied by clear expectations and rubrics, an exposure to/awareness of world events and hands-on experiences, and encouragement of students to express ideas and opinions through writing and discussion in a safe, accepting environment.

When I transferred to regular education almost ten years ago, one of my main concerns was being able to challenge students at the gifted end of the spectrum. I found that the methods are the same! We must observe, assess, provide activities that allow them to demonstrate success, and then lead them to that next step which will encourage them to achieve even more than they might have believed they could. Yes, concept lessons take more time, and higher order thinking strategies prolong a lesson but they also frequently lead to unanticipated teachable moments.

Believing this does not address the real and perceived pressures to cover all of the material. Diversified instructional methods—jigsaw activities, literature circles, other cooperative group practices—help to some degree. Understanding and believing that teaching children to think critically and contribute to higher-order discussions help teachers justify concept teaching. Inviting skeptics into the classroom to observe the process is also extremely helpful. Recently, the childrens' brainstorming generated a very heavy-duty discussion comparing mistreatment of poor, disenfranchised colonists during the Salem Witch Trials, Native Americans during the 1800s, and African Americans during the past century, along with other groups. An observing teacher in my class stated, "Are you sure these kids are only in fourth and fifth grade?" That's justification. Do not give up that type of educational excitement for coverage!

Ian Call
McKeel Academy, 10th Grade
Polk County, FL

All students whether they have strong or weak academic abilities, can benefit from concept lessons. One of the main reasons to include concept lessons in the curriculum for low-performing students is to create interest in the content being taught. Too often, drill and practice methods are not relevant to the students and school becomes boring and an inefficient use of their time. By utilizing concept lessons, teachers can create curriculum that interests their students in learning the material and makes their classrooms more effective.

In addition, basic skills such as reading and writing do not have to be separate from higher-order thinking. Effective concept lessons can be created to both enhance students' skills as well as promote higher-order thinking. While there is a large amount of material to cover in a school year, effective teachers can create concept lessons that not only cover the material, but also include thinking skills that students will need in the future. Students need more than just basic skills, and it is up to you to provide them with the experiences necessary to build their higher-thinking skills while they are in school.

As a first year teacher, you have a long career ahead of you, but the way you start your career will have a large impact on the many years that will follow. Planning concept lessons may take more time at the beginning, but once you get started you will find that not only do they have benefits for your students, but also yourself. Teachers who use concept lessons in their classrooms are more in tune with their students, are more intellectually challenged by the job, and are less likely to fall into the dreaded world of "Burned Out Land."

Chapter Review

Go back to the "Interactive and Applied Learning" feature at the beginning of the chapter for a listing of interactive and applied activities. Go to the Online Learning Center at **www.mhhe.com/arends6e** or your Interactive Student CD-ROM to take practice quizzes over the content of this chapter and receive immediate feedback. You can also review chapter content and main ideas, practice with key terms, and find annotated Web links on topics associated with Chapter 9.

Summary

Overview of Concept Teaching

- Concepts are the basic building blocks around which people organize their thinking and communication.

- Concept learning and logical thinking are critical goals for almost everything taught in schools. These become important scaffolding for building student understanding of school subjects. Concept learning is essentially a process of putting things into classes or categories.

- The instructional goals of concept teaching are mainly to help learners acquire conceptual understandings of the subjects they are studying and to provide a foundation for higher-level thinking.
- The general flow or syntax of a concept lesson consists of four major phases: present goals and establish set, provide examples and nonexamples, test for concept attainment, and analyze student thinking processes.
- Concept teaching requires a moderately structured learning environment.

Theoretical and Empirical Support

- The theoretical and empirical support for concept teaching and learning is very extensive and covers a wide range of topics. Studies have shown how age and intellectual development influence readiness to learn concepts. Piaget's and Bruner's developmental theories are of particular importance to concept teaching and learning.
- A concept's critical attributes help define and distinguish it from other concepts. The various kinds of concepts include conjunctive concepts, disjunctive concepts, and relationship concepts. Students grasp general concepts mainly by being presented with specific examples and nonexamples of the concept.
- Studies have also shown how examples and nonexamples should be presented to maximize students' learning and how teachers can use such specific practices as visual images and graphic organizers to support concept learning.

Planning and Conducting Concept Lessons

- Planning tasks for concept lessons include selecting concepts and choosing the most appropriate approach.
- There are several different approaches to teaching concepts. Two of the most prevalent are direct presentation and concept attainment. In direct presentation, the teacher labels and defines the concept early in the lesson and then presents the best examples through exposition. In concept

attainment, the teacher presents examples and nonexamples of a particular concept but does not define and label the concept until the end of the lesson.

- Concept analysis, selection of examples and nonexamples, and decisions regarding the sequence in which to present the examples are also important tasks teachers must perform during planning for a concept lesson.
- A concept lesson begins with the teacher telling students the aims for the lesson and getting them motivated and ready to learn.
- The exact sequencing for defining and labeling a concept and presenting examples and nonexamples varies according to the approach being used by the teacher. In direct presentation, the teacher presents the definition first, whereas in concept attainment, the teacher presents examples and nonexamples first and students discover and define the concept using an inductive process.
- Through questioning and discussion, teachers help students analyze their thinking processes and integrate new learning with old as the final phase of a concept lesson, regardless of approach.

Managing the Learning Environment

- During the presentation and attainment phases of a concept lesson, the teacher maintains a structured learning environment. However, the final phases of a concept lesson encourage student interaction and require a more flexible, student-centered learning environment.

Assessment and Evaluation

- As with other instructional models, the major postinstructional task is for teachers to match their testing programs to the model's particular goals.
- When evaluating students' understanding of a concept, it is important to ask students to do more than merely define the concept. Students should also be asked to demonstrate their knowledge of the concept's critical attributes and its relationship to other concepts.

Key Terms

Portfolio and Field Experience Activities

This feature has been designed to help you learn from your field experiences and to assist you in the preparation of artifacts for your professional portfolio on topics and standards associated with Chapter 9.

1. Complete the "Reflections from the Classroom" exercise at the end of this chapter and use the recommended reflective essay as an exhibit in your professional portfolio to show your views about concept teaching.

2. Complete Activity 9.1 in the *Guide to Field Experiences and Portfolio Development* to assess your understanding and skills to plan and conduct concept lessons.

3. Use Activity 9.2 in the *Guide to Field Experiences and Portfolio Development* to observe an experienced classroom teacher teach a concept lesson. Summarize your observation and use it as an exhibit in your professional portfolio.

4. Complete Activities 9.3 and 9.4 in the *Guide to Field Experiences and Portfolio Development* to analyze and select concepts.

5. Use Activity 9.5 in the *Guide to Field Experiences and Portfolio Development* to construct a conceptual web. Use the product of your work as an exhibit in your professional portfolio that demonstrates your webbing skills.

6. Use the Case Exercise on the Interactive Student CD-ROM to create your own concept teaching lesson. Place the product(s) of your work in your professional portfolio to demonstrate your understanding and skill in planning and conducting concept lessons.

Books for the Professional

Go to the Online Learning Center at www.mhhe.com/ arends6e or your Interactive Student CD-ROM for an annotated version of this list.

Bennett, B., and Rolheiser, C. (2001). *Beyond Monet: The Artful Science of Instructional Integration.* Toronto, Ontario: Bookation.

Blythe, T. (1997). *The Teaching for Understanding Guide.* San Francisco: Jossey-Bass.

Erickson, H. L., and Tomlinson, C. A. (2002). *Concept-based Curriculum and Instruction: Teaching Beyond the Facts.* Thousand Oaks, CA: Corwin Press.

Joyce, B., and Calhoun, E. (1998). *Learning to Teach Inductively.* Boston: Allyn & Bacon.

Tobin, K., Kahle, J. B., and Fraser, B. J. (1990). *Windows into Science Classrooms: Problems Associated with Higher-Level Cognitive Learning.* New York: Falmer Press.

Chapter Ten

Cooperative Learning

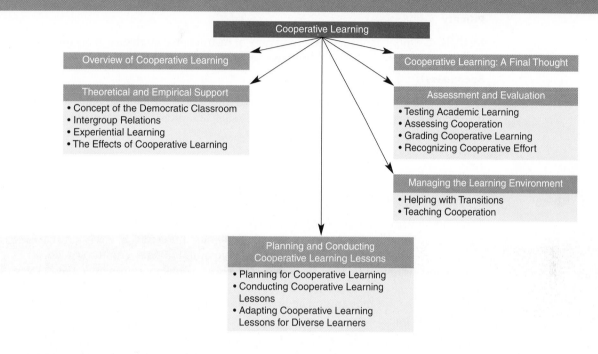

Interactive and Applied Learning

Go to your Interactive Student CD-ROM to:

- Hear audio clips of Amy Callen (fourth/fifth grade) and Jason O'Brien (fifth grade) talk about Cooperative Learning in the *Teachers on Teaching* feature
- Watch the video clip: Cooperative Learning
- Complete the Cooperative Learning Case Exercise in the Chapter 10 *Case Exercises and Practice Tasks* area
- Complete the Cooperative Learning Practice Tasks in Chapter 10 *Case Exercises and Practice Tasks* area. Plan for demonstration: task analysis; differentiate guided practice for two students; assess student learning; respond to teaching dilemmas; and reflect on the use of cooperative learning.

Go to the Online Learning Center at www.mhhe.com/arends6e to read *PowerWeb* articles and newsfeed updates about:

- Classroom management
- Cultural diversity in education
- Instruction
- Learning
- Technology and education
- Testing and evaluation
- World Wide Web

INTASC *Considering* **Standards**

Studying this chapter will help you meet two INTASC principles:

Primary

INTASC 4: Understands and uses a variety of instructional strategies to encourage student development of critical thinking, problem-solving, and performance skills.

Secondary

INTASC 8: Understands and uses formal and informal assessment strategies to evaluate and ensure the continuous intellectual, social, and physical development of the learner.

Reflecting **on** *Cooperative Learning*

Think about learning experiences you have had as a student that required you to work with other students to complete a particular assignment. The experience may have been very brief, such as working on a few math problems with the student next to you, or it might have been extensive, requiring collaboration on a major term project.

Write down your thoughts on and reactions to these experiences by considering the following questions:

- What did you like most about working on learning tasks with others? Least?
- Were the experiences you thought about valuable for you? Why? Why not?
- What do you think students learn when they work together?
- Are there some aspects of learning together that are particularly effective? What are these?
- Are there some aspects of learning together that are particularly ineffective? What are these?

Considering your answers, do you think you are a person who is prone to be positive toward cooperative learning? Or do you have some serious reservations?

> Go to the Online Learning Center at www.mhhe.com/arends6e to respond to these questions.

T he previous chapters described three models of teaching—presentation, direct instruction, and concept teaching. These models are used by teachers primarily to help students acquire new information, to learn important skills, and to think about and process information already acquired from prior learning. In essence, this is academic learning, and although this type of learning is extremely important, it doesn't represent the only goals for students. This chapter presents a model of instruction called *cooperative learning,* which goes beyond helping students learn academic content and skills to address important social and human relations goals and objectives.

The chapter begins with an overview of the instructional model, then presents its theoretical and empirical support. A section that describes the specific procedures used by teachers as they plan, conduct, and manage the learning environment during cooperative learning lessons follows. The final sections highlight the assessment and evaluation tasks associated with cooperative learning.

Overview of Cooperative Learning

All instructional models are characterized, in part, by their task structures, their goal structures, and their reward structures. **Task structures** involve the way lessons are organized and the kind of work students are asked to do. They encompass whether the teacher is working with the whole class or small groups, what students are expected to accomplish, and the cognitive and social demands placed on students as they work to accomplish assigned learning tasks. Task structures differ according to the activities involved in particular lessons. For example, some lessons require students to sit passively and receive information from a teacher's presentation. Other lessons require that students complete worksheets, and still others require discussion and debate.

A lesson's **goal structure** refers to the amount of interdependence required of students as they perform their work. Three types of goal structures have been identified. Goal structures are **individualistic** if achievement of the instructional goal requires no interaction with others and is unrelated to how well others do. **Competitive** goal structures exist when students perceive they can obtain their goals if the other students fail to obtain theirs. **Cooperative** goal structures exist when students can obtain their goal only when other students with whom they are linked can obtain theirs. These three goal structures were illustrated previously in Chapter 4.

The **reward structure** for various instructional models can also vary. Just as goal structures can be individualist, competitive, or cooperative, so too can reward structures. Individualistic reward structures exist when a reward can be achieved independently from what anyone else does. The satisfaction of running a four-minute mile is an example of an individualistic reward structure. Competitive reward structures are those for which rewards are obtained for individual effort in comparison to others. Grading on a curve is an example of a competitive reward structure, as is the way winners are defined in many track and field events. In contrast, situations in which individual effort helps others to be rewarded use cooperative reward structures. Most team sports, such as football, have a cooperative reward structure, even though teams may compete with each other.

Lessons organized around teacher-centered models are generally characterized by task structures by which teachers work mainly with a whole class of students or students work individually to master academic content. These goal and reward structures are based on individual competition and effort. In contrast, as its name implies, the

The cooperative learning model requires student cooperation and interdependence in its task, goal, and reward structures.

The terms *goal* and *reward structures* both refer to the degree of cooperation or competition required of students to achieve their goals or rewards.

cooperative learning model is characterized by cooperative task, goal, and reward structures. Students in cooperative learning situations are encouraged and/or required to work together on a common task, and they must coordinate their efforts to complete the task. Similarly, in cooperative learning, two or more individuals are interdependent for a reward they will share, if they are successful as a group. Cooperative learning lessons can be characterized by the following features:

- Students work in teams to master learning goals.
- Teams are made up of high-, average-, and low-achieving students.
- Whenever possible, teams include a racial, cultural, and gender mix.
- Reward systems are oriented to the group as well as the individual.

All these features are explained more fully later in the chapter.

The three instructional goals of cooperative learning are academic achievement, tolerance and acceptance of diversity, and development of social skills.

The cooperative learning model was developed to achieve at least three important instructional goals: academic achievement, tolerance and acceptance of diversity, and social skill development (see Figure 10.1).

Although cooperative learning encompasses a variety of social objectives, it also aims at improving student performance on important *academic tasks*. Its supporters believe that the model's cooperative reward structure raises the value students place on academic learning and changes the norms associated with achievement. Slavin (1996) noted:

> Students often do not value their peers who do well academically, while they do value their peers who excel in sports. . . . This is so because sports success brings benefits to groups (the team, the school, the town), while academic success benefits only the individual. In fact, in a class using grading on the curve or any competitive grading or incentive system, any individual's success reduces the chances that any other individual will succeed (p. 54).

Slavin, one of the founders of cooperative learning, believes that the group focus of cooperative learning can change the norms of youth culture and make it more acceptable to excel in academic learning tasks.

In addition to changing norms associated with achievement, cooperative learning can benefit both low- and high-achieving students who work together on academic tasks. Higher achievers tutor lower achievers, thus providing special help from peers who share youth-oriented interests and language. In the process, higher achievers gain academically because serving as a tutor requires thinking more deeply about the relationships of ideas within a particular subject.

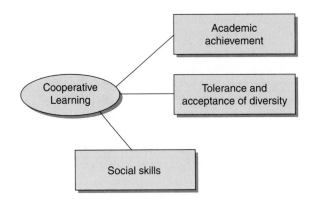

Figure 10.1 *Learner Outcomes for Cooperative Learning*

A second important effect of cooperative learning is wider tolerance and acceptance of people who are different by virtue of their race, culture, social class, or ability. Following the premises outlined by Allport (1954) over a half century ago, it is known that mere physical contact among different racial or ethnic groups or special-needs children is insufficient to reduce prejudice and stereotyping. Cooperative learning presents opportunities for students of varying backgrounds and conditions to work interdependently on common tasks and, through the use of cooperative reward structures, learn to appreciate each other.

A third and important goal for cooperative learning is to teach students skills of cooperation and collaboration. These are critical skills in a society in which much adult work is carried out in large, interdependent organizations and communities are becoming more culturally diverse and global in their orientations. Yet, many youth and adults alike lack effective social skills. This situation is evidenced by how often minor disagreements between individuals can lead to violent acts and by how often people express dissatisfaction when asked to work in cooperative situations. Cooperative learning promotes cooperation because it values and promotes the development of interpersonal intelligence, one of Gardner's eight multiple intelligences described in Chapter 2.

Six major phases or steps are involved in a cooperative learning lesson: (1) A lesson begins with the teacher going over the goals of the lesson and getting students motivated to learn. (2) This phase is followed by the presentation of information, often in the form of text rather than lecture. (3) Students are then organized into study teams. (4) In the next step, students, assisted by the teacher, work together to accomplish interdependent tasks. Final phases of a cooperative learning lesson include (5) presentation of the group's end product or testing on what students have learned and (6) recognition of group and individual efforts. The six phases of a cooperative lesson are described in more detail later in the chapter.

The learning environment for cooperative learning is characterized by democratic processes and active roles for students in deciding what should be studied and how. The teacher provides a high degree of structure in forming groups and defining overall procedures, but students are left in control of the minute-to-minute interactions within their groups.

Theoretical and Empirical Support

The cooperative learning model did not evolve from one individual's theory or from a single approach to learning. Its roots go back to the early Greeks, but its contemporary developments can be traced to the work of educational psychologists and pedagogical theorists at the beginning of the twentieth century.

Concept of the Democratic Classroom

In 1916, John Dewey wrote a book called *Democracy and Education*. Dewey's concept of education was that the classroom should mirror the larger society and be a laboratory for real-life learning. Dewey's pedagogy required teachers to create a learning environment characterized by democratic procedures and scientific processes. Their primary responsibility was to engage students in inquiry into important social and interpersonal problems. The specific classroom procedures described by Dewey (and his latter-day followers) emphasized small, problem-solving groups of students searching for their own answers and learning democratic principles through day-to-day interaction with one another.

The cooperative learning environment sets the stage for students to learn very valuable collaboration and social skills that they will use throughout their lives.

Check, Extend, Explore

Check
- What are the key characteristics of cooperative learning? How do these differ from other models of teaching?
- What are the six phases of a cooperative learning lesson?
- What are the major learner outcomes for cooperative learning?
- What type of learning environment works best for cooperative learning?

Extend
- After reading this short introduction, do you agree or disagree with the basic goals and premises of cooperative learning? Go to the "Extend Question Poll" on the Online Learning Center to respond.

Explore
- Go to the Online Learning Center at www.mhhe.com/arends6e for links to websites related to *Cooperative Learning*.

John Dewey

Many years after Dewey's initial work, Herbert Thelen (1954, 1960) developed more precise procedures for helping students work in groups. Like Dewey, Thelen argued that the classroom should be a laboratory or miniature democracy for the purpose of study and inquiry into important social and interpersonal problems. Thelen, with his interest in group dynamics, put more structure on the pedagogy of group investigation and, as is described later, provided the conceptual basis for contemporary developments in cooperative learning.

For Dewey and Thelen, the use of cooperative group work went beyond improving academic learning. Cooperative behavior and processes were considered basic to human endeavor—the foundation on which strong democratic communities could be built and maintained. The logical way to accomplish these important educational objectives, they believed, was to structure the classroom and students' learning activities so that they modeled the desired outcomes. Dewey's philosophy and pedagogy also had a strong influence on problem-based learning, a model described in Chapter 11 that has many similarities to cooperative learning.

Intergroup Relations

Dewey and Thelen viewed cooperative behavior as the foundation of democracy and saw schools as laboratories for developing democratic behavior.

In 1954, the Supreme Court issued its historic *Brown* v. *Board of Education of Topeka* decision in which the Court ruled that public schools in the United States could no longer operate under a separate-but-equal policy but must become racially integrated. This led to subsequent decisions and actions by judicial and legislative bodies all across the country demanding that public school authorities submit plans for desegregation.

At the time, thoughtful theorists and observers warned that putting people of different ethnic or racial backgrounds in the same location would not, in and of itself, counteract the effects of prejudice or promote integration and better intergroup acceptance. They knew, for example, that the cafeteria in an integrated school might still be characterized by African American students sitting on one side of the room and white students on the other. They also knew that a community might be highly integrated but still have restaurants or churches patronized by only whites or only blacks.

Interethnic contacts occurring under conditions of equal status are needed to reduce racial and ethnic prejudice.

A leading sociologist of the time, Gordon Allport, argued that laws alone would not reduce intergroup prejudice and promote better acceptance and understanding. Shlomo Sharan and his colleagues at Tel Aviv University in Israel (1984, 1999) have summarized three basic conditions required to counteract racial prejudice:

> (1) unmediated interethnic contact, (2) occurring under conditions of equal status between members of the various groups participating in a given setting, and (3) where the setting officially sanctions interethnic cooperation (p. 2).

Much of the recent interest in the cooperative learning model has grown out of attempts to structure classrooms and teaching processes according to these three conditions. Robert Slavin's work, which is described later, was conducted in part in the inner cities along the eastern seaboard as part of integration efforts. The work of Sharan and his colleagues in Israel was prompted by that country's need to find ways to promote better ethnic understanding between Jewish immigrants of European background and those of Middle Eastern background. The work of David Johnson and Roger Johnson (1979; 1998) at the University of Minnesota has explored how cooperative classroom environments might lead to better learning by and more positive regard toward students with special needs who were included in regular classrooms.

Experiential Learning

A third theoretical perspective that provides intellectual support for cooperative learning comes from theorists and researchers who are interested in how individuals learn from experience. Experience accounts for much of what people learn. For example, most people learn to ride a bicycle by riding one, and they learn about being a sister or brother by being one. Conversely, even though everyone can read books about marriage and child rearing, those who have married and raised children know that living these experiences is never the same as described in the books. Experience provides insights, understandings, and techniques that are difficult to describe to anyone who has not had similar experiences. Johnson and Johnson (1994), preeminent cooperative learning theorists, described experiential learning this way:

Experiential learning, in which individuals are personally involved in learning, provides theoretical support for cooperative learning.

> Experiential learning is based upon three assumptions: that you learn best when you are personally involved in the learning experience, that knowledge has to be discovered by yourself if it is to mean anything to you or make a difference in your behavior, and that a commitment to learning is highest when you are free to set your own learning goals and actively pursue them within a given framework (p. 7).

The Effects of Cooperative Learning

Cooperative learning has been one of the most researched teaching models. It is not possible to summarize all the research on cooperative learning here, but the following sections provide brief summaries of the model's effects on three types of learner outcomes: cooperative behavior, tolerance of diversity, and academic achievement.

Effects on Cooperative Behavior. Twenty-first century living is characterized by global, interdependent communities and by complex social institutions that require high degrees of cooperation among members. Consequently, most people prize cooperative behavior and believe it to be an important goal for education. Many of the schools' extracurricular activities, such as team sports and dramatic and musical productions, are justified on this basis. But what about activities within the classroom itself? Do certain types of activities, such as those associated with cooperative learning, have effects on students' cooperative attitudes and behaviors?

Sharan (1984, 1992, 1999) and his colleagues have sought answers to this question for over a decade. They have developed a particular approach to cooperative learning and tested it to see if its use would improve social relations among different Jewish subgroups in Israel. In one study, researchers randomly assigned thirty-three English and literature teachers to three training groups. Teachers in group 1 were taught how to fine-tune their whole-class teaching skills. Those in group 2 were taught how to use Slavin's Student Teams Achievement Divisions (STAD) (explained later), and those in group 3 were taught Sharan's Group Investigation (GI) approach to cooperative learning. The investigators collected massive amounts of information before, during, and after the experiment, including data from achievement tests, classroom observations, and cooperative behavior of students.

The majority of studies done on the effects of cooperative learning show that it produces both academic and social benefits.

For the test of cooperative behavior, students were selected from classrooms using each of the three instructional approaches and were asked to engage in a task called "Lego Man." In six-member teams (each with three European and three Middle Eastern members), students were asked to plan how they would carry out a joint task of constructing a human figure from forty-eight Lego pieces.

Cooperative learning helps students become engaged with one another.

Sharan's studies showed clearly that the instructional methods influenced the students' cooperative and competitive behavior. Cooperative learning generated more cooperative behavior, both verbal and nonverbal, than did whole-class teaching. Students from both cooperative-learning classrooms displayed less competitive behavior and more cross-ethnic cooperation than those who came from whole-class teaching classrooms.

Effects on Tolerance for Diversity. Two decades after the Supreme Court ended separate-but-equal public schools, Congress passed an equally historic piece of integration legislation in 1975. Titled the Education for All Handicapped Children Act and known as Public Law 94-142, this legislation required students with disabilities to be placed, whenever possible, into least restrictive environments. Instead of placement in special schools or classrooms (the approach used for most of the twentieth century), children with disabilities (approximately 12 percent of the student population) were to be included in regular classrooms. Obviously, this meant that regular classroom teachers now had children with physical, emotional, and mental disabilities in their classrooms.

Just as theorists knew that racial integration would not end prejudice, there was considerable evidence in 1975 that placing disabled people (who have traditionally been perceived negatively) in close proximity to others would not end negative attitudes. In fact, some researchers argued that closer contact might even increase prejudice and stereotyping. A critical factor in producing more positive attitudes and behaviors seemed to be the way the interaction between disabled and nondisabled students was structured. David Johnson, Roger Johnson (1979), and several of their colleagues at the University of Minnesota studied how goal structures influence interaction in a unique and interesting way. Their study is summarized in the Research Summary on page 362.

Studies similar to the Johnsons' research have shown that not only can cooperative learning influence tolerance and wider acceptance of students with special needs, but it also can promote better relationships among students of varying races and ethnicities.

Effects on Academic Achievement. One of the important aspects of cooperative learning is that while it is helping promote cooperative behavior and better group relations among students, it simultaneously helps students with their academic learning. Over the past decade, several researchers have reviewed and summarized the research on cooperative learning (Leinhardt, 1992; Slavin, 1995; Slavin et al., 1992; and Stronge, 2002). They reviewed studies at all grade levels and included the following subject areas: language arts, spelling, geography, social studies, science, mathematics, English as a second language, reading, and writing. Studies were conducted in urban, rural, and suburban schools in the United States, Israel, Nigeria, and Germany. Of forty-five studies reviewed, thirty-seven showed that cooperative learning classes significantly outperformed control group classes in academic achievement. Eight studies found no differences. None of the studies showed negative effects for cooperative learning.

In another experiment, Slavin (1995) and his colleagues created an elementary school based on the concepts of cooperation and cooperative learning. After the second year of implementation, students in the cooperative elementary school achieved significantly higher levels in reading vocabulary, reading comprehension, language expression, and math computation and application than did their peers in a traditional elementary school. They also displayed better social relations skills and were more accepting of disabled students.

Most developers of cooperative learning argue that learning in heterogeneous groups is beneficial for all students. It is assumed that students with lesser abilities learn more by working alongside those who have greater abilities and that the latter benefit from the process of serving as tutors to their less-able peers. However, a small body of research (Robinson, 1990, 1996) suggests that this is not always the case. Robinson reviewed the research on cooperative learning between 1967 and 1989. She concluded that intellectually gifted students do not necessarily benefit from working in heterogeneous groups. She further argues that using cooperative learning with talented students is a form of exploitation.

Although the research is not conclusive, beginning teachers who use cooperative learning should remain aware of possible unintended, negative consequences.

To summarize, a strong theoretical and empirical framework for cooperative learning reflects the perspective that humans learn from their experiences and active participation in small groups helps students learn important social skills while simultaneously developing academic skill and democratic attitudes.

Planning and Conducting Cooperative Learning Lessons

Planning for Cooperative Learning

Many of the functions of teacher planning described in previous chapters can be applied to cooperative learning. However, cooperative learning requires some unique planning tasks as well. For example, time spent organizing or analyzing specific skills required of a direct instruction lesson may instead be spent gathering resource materials, text, or worksheets so small groups of students can work on their own. Instead of planning for the smooth flow and sequencing of major ideas, the teacher can plan how to make smooth transitions from whole-class to small-group instruction. Following are some of the unique planning tasks and decisions required of teachers preparing to teach a cooperative learning lesson.

Choose an Approach. Although the basic principles of cooperative learning do not change, there are several variations of the model. Four approaches that should be part of the beginning teacher's repertoire are described here.

Student Teams Achievement Divisions. **Student Teams Achievement Divisions (STAD)** was developed by Robert Slavin and his colleagues at the Johns Hopkins University and is perhaps the simplest and most straightforward of the cooperative learning approaches (Slavin, 1995). Teachers using STAD present new academic information to students each week or on a regular basis, either through verbal presentation or text.

Check, Extend, Explore

Check
- What philosophical and theoretical contributions did John Dewey and Gordon Allport make to the development of cooperative learning?
- Why are ideas from experiential learning important to cooperative learning?
- How strong is the empirical support for cooperative learning?
- On what effects of cooperative learning do researchers seem to agree? Disagree?

Extend
- Do you agree or disagree with Robinson's assertion that the use of cooperative learning is a form of exploitation of talented and gifted students? Go to the "Extend Question Poll" on the Online Learning Center to respond.

Explore
- Go to the Online Learning Center at www.mhhe.com/arends6e for links to websites related to *Theoretical and Empirical Support for Cooperative Learning.*

In the STAD model of cooperative learning, students in heterogeneous teams help each other by using a variety of cooperative study methods and quizzing procedures.

Research Summary

What Can Make Us Cheer for Our Peers with Special Needs?

Johnson, R., Rynders, J., Johnson, D. W., Schmidt, B., and Haider, S. (1979). Interaction between handicapped and nonhandicapped teenagers as a function of situational goal structuring: Implications for mainstreaming. *American Educational Research Journal*, 16, 161–167.

Just because people who are different from one another are placed in close proximity does not mean that they will interact in positive ways or shed their prejudice and negative stereotypes. An important question for educators and teachers is, "What can we do to help students be more positive and more accepting toward peers who represent different racial backgrounds, come from different social classes, or who are disabled?" Roger Johnson and David Johnson and their colleagues addressed this question in an important study that was creative in the way it sought answers to a complex problem in a very simple setting, a bowling alley.

Problem and Approach: The researchers wanted to find out the effects of various goal structures on the interactions between nondisabled junior high students and trainable mentally challenged students in a learning situation, in this instance, bowling classes.

Sample: Subjects in the study were thirty junior high students (ages 13 to 16, including fifteen boys and fifteen girls) from three midwestern junior high schools. Nine nondisabled students came from a public junior high school; nine other nondisabled students came from a private Catholic school. The twelve disabled students were from a special school for the mentally challenged. These students were able to communicate and understand instructions and did not have any physical disabilities that would prevent them from bowling.

Procedures: Students were divided randomly into learning teams of five. Each team contained three nondisabled students and two students with disabilities. Each of the learning teams was then assigned to one of three experimental conditions:

- *Cooperative condition.* Team members were instructed to "maximize" their team's bowling score at a criterion of fifty points improvement over the previous week. They were to help each other in any way possible.
- *Individualistic condition.* Students in these teams were instructed to "maximize" their individual scores by 10 points over the previous week and to concentrate only on their own performance.
- *Laissez-faire condition.* Students were given no special instructions.

The three bowling instructors in the study were told what to say and were rotated across groups. All groups received the same amount of training over a six-week period.

Trained observers, who were kept naive about the purpose of the study, watched the students bowl and recorded interactions among students in three categories: positive, neutral, and negative. Observations focused on the period of time from when a bowler stepped up to bowl until he or she stepped down from the bowling line.

Pointers for Reading Research: The researchers used the chi square (χ^2) to test the significance of their results. This statistic is used by researchers when their data are of a particular type. It serves the same purpose as other tests of significance introduced earlier. The results as reported in this study are straightforward and easy to read and understand.

Students within a given class are divided into four- or five-member learning teams, with representatives of both sexes, various racial or ethnic groups, and high, average, and low achievers on each team. Team members use worksheets or other study devices to master the academic materials and then help each other learn the materials through tutoring, quizzing one another, or carrying on team discussions. Individually, students take weekly or biweekly quizzes on the academic materials. These quizzes are scored and each individual is given an "improvement score." This improvement score (explained later) is based not on a student's absolute score but instead on the degree to which the score exceeds a student's past averages.

Table 10.1 *Frequency of Homogeneous and Heterogeneous Interactions Within Conditions*

| | Positive | | Neutral | | Negative | | |
	Homo	Hetero	Homo	Hetero	Homo	Hetero	Total
Cooperative	495	336	67	47	4	10	959
Individualistic	243	92	61	17	15	11	439
Laissez-faire	265	136	75	49	9	6	540
Total	1,003	564	203	113	28	27	1,938

*$X^2 = 86.87, p < 01$.

Note: Homogeneous interactions took place between nondisabled students and between disabled students; heterogeneous interactions took place between disabled and nondisabled students.

Source: After R. Johnson et al. (1979), p. 165

Results: Tables 10.1 and 10.2 show the results of the bowling study. Table 10.1 displays the frequency of homogeneous and heterogeneous interactions among the students in the three conditions. Table 10.2 displays data on "group cheers" for disabled students who threw strikes and spares over the course of the study.

Discussion and Implications The data presented in Tables 10.1 and 10.2 are clear and straightforward. There were more interactions among students on the cooperative bowling team and, more important, more positive interactions that were both heterogeneous and homogeneous. Further study of the data revealed that, "Each student with a disability on the average participated in 17 positive interactions with nondisabled peers per hour in the cooperative condition, 5 in the individualistic condition, and 7 in the laissez-faire condition" (p. 164).

The number of cheers given to disabled students in the cooperative condition gives additional support to the idea that a cooperative goal structure is a means for getting positive response from nondisabled students toward their disabled peers.

Table 10.2 *Frequency of Group Cheers Within Conditions*

Condition	Frequency
Cooperative	55
Individualistic	6
Laissez-faire	3

Source: After R. Johnson et al. (1979), p. 165

This study, along with others that have produced similar results, has two important implications for teachers:

1. Individualistic and competitive goal structures associated with so many classroom learning tasks do not encourage positive interactions among people from differing backgrounds and conditions. Redefining the goal structure and making it more cooperative seems to help.
2. Severely disabled students, such as those who are mentally challenged, given the appropriate conditions, can be mainstreamed into learning settings with nondisabled students in ways that can benefit all.

Jigsaw. **Jigsaw** was developed and tested by Elliot Aronson and his colleagues (Aronson & Patnoe, 1997). Using Jigsaw, students are assigned to five- or six-member heterogeneous study teams. Academic materials are presented to the students in text form, and each student is responsible for learning a portion of the material. For example, if the textual material was on cooperative learning, one student on the team would be responsible for STAD, another for Jigsaw, another for Group Investigation, and perhaps the other two would become experts in the research base and history of cooperative learning. Members from different teams with the same topic (sometimes called the *expert group*) meet to study and help each other learn the topic. Then students return to their home teams and

In the Jigsaw model, each team member is responsible for mastering part of the learning materials and then teaching that part to the other team members.

Home Teams
(Five or six members grouped heterogeneously)

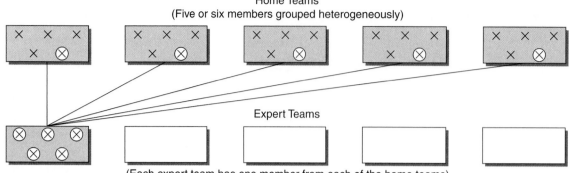

Expert Teams

(Each expert team has one member from each of the home teams)

Figure 10.2 *Jigsaw Teams*

teach other members what they have learned. Figure 10.2 illustrates the relationship between home and expert teams.

Following home team meetings and discussions, students take quizzes individually on the learning materials.

In Group Investigation, students not only work together but also help plan both the topics for study and the investigative procedure used.

Group Investigation. Many of the key features of the **Group Investigation (GI)** approach were designed originally by Herbert Thelen. More recently, this approach has been extended and refined by Sharan and his colleagues at Tel Aviv University. Group Investigation is perhaps the most complex of the cooperative learning approaches and the most difficult to implement. In contrast to STAD and Jigsaw, the GI approach involves students in planning both the topics for study and the ways to proceed with their investigations. This requires more sophisticated classroom norms and structures than do approaches that are more teacher-centered.

Teachers who use the GI approach normally divide their classes into five- or six-member heterogeneous groups. In some instances, however, groups may form around friendships or around an interest in a particular topic. Students select topics for study, pursue in-depth investigations of chosen subtopics, and then prepare and present a report to the whole class. Sharan (1984) and his colleagues described the following six steps of the GI approach:

1. *Topic selection.* Students choose specific subtopics within a general problem area, usually delineated by the teacher. Students then organize into small two- to six-member task-oriented groups. Group composition is academically and ethnically heterogeneous.
2. *Cooperative planning.* Students and the teacher plan specific learning procedures, tasks, and goals consistent with the subtopics of the problem selected in step 1.
3. *Implementation.* Pupils carry out the plan formulated in step 2. Learning should involve a wide variety of activities and skills and should lead students to different kinds of sources both inside and outside the school. The teacher closely follows the progress of each group and offers assistance when needed.
4. *Analysis and synthesis.* Pupils analyze and evaluate information obtained during step 3 and plan how it can be summarized in some interesting fashion for possible display or presentation to classmates.
5. *Presentation of final product.* Some or all of the groups in the class give an interesting presentation of the topics studied in order to get classmates involved in each other's

work and to achieve a broad perspective on the topic. Group presentations are coordinated by the teacher.

6. *Evaluation.* In cases where groups pursued different aspects of the same topic,
pupils and the teacher evaluate each group's contribution to the work of the class
as a whole. Evaluation can include either individual or group assessment, or both
(pp. 4–5).

In Chapter 11, you will discover that problem-based learning and group investigation share many of the same features. The major difference, however, is the likelihood
that heterogeneous groups will be employed in group investigation.

The Structural Approach. Another approach to cooperative learning has been developed over the past decade mainly by Spencer Kagan (1992, 1998). Although it has much
in common with other approaches, the **structural approach** emphasizes the use of particular structures designed to influence student **interaction patterns.** The structures developed by Kagan are intended to be alternatives to the more traditional classroom
structures, such as recitation, in which the teacher poses questions to the whole class
and students provide answers after raising their hands and being called on. Kagan's
structures call for students to work interdependently in small groups and are characterized by cooperative rather than individual rewards. Some structures have goals for
increasing student acquisition of academic content; other structures are designed to
teach social or group skills. *Think-pair-share* and *numbered heads together,* described here,
are two examples of structures teachers can use to teach academic content or to check
on student understanding of particular content. *Active listening* and *time tokens* are examples of structures to teach social skills and are described later in the chapter in the
social skills section.

> In the structural approach, teams may have from two to six members, and the task structure may empha-size either social or aca-demic goals.

Think-Pair-Share. The **think-pair-share** strategy has grown out of the cooperative
learning and wait-time research. The particular approach described here, initially developed by Frank Lyman (1985) and his colleagues at the University of Maryland, is an
effective way to change the discourse pattern in a classroom. It challenges the assumption that all recitations or discussions need to be held in whole-group settings, and it
has built-in procedures for giving students more time to think and to respond and to
help each other. Figure 10.3 illustrates how think-pair-share works. For instance, suppose a teacher has just completed a short presentation or students have read an assignment or a puzzling situation the teacher has described. The teacher now wants
students to consider more fully what she has explained. She chooses to use the think-
pair-share strategy rather than whole-group question and answer. She employs the following steps:

Step 1—Thinking: The teacher poses a question or an issue associated with the lesson
and asks students to spend a minute thinking alone about the answer or the issue.
Students need to be taught that talking is not part of thinking time.

Step 2—Pairing: Next, the teacher asks students to pair off and discuss what they have
been thinking about. Interaction during this period can be sharing answers if a question has been posed or sharing ideas if a specific issue was identified. Usually, teachers allow no more than four or five minutes for pairing.

Step 3—Sharing: In the final step, the teacher asks the pairs to share what they have
been talking about with the whole class. It is effective to simply go around the room
from pair to pair and continue until about a fourth or a half the pairs have had a
chance to report.

> The think-pair-share and numbered heads together techniques are alternatives to the more traditional whole-group question and answer approach.

Thinking   Pairing   Sharing

Figure 10.3 *Think-Pair-Share*

Numbered Heads Together. **Numbered heads together** is an approach developed by Spencer Kagan (1998) to involve more students in the review of materials covered in a lesson and to check their understanding of a lesson's content. Instead of directing questions to the whole class, teachers use the following four-step structure:

Step 1—Numbering: Teachers divide students into three- to five-member teams and have them number off so each student on the team has a different number between 1 and 5.

Step 2—Questioning: Teachers ask students a question. Questions can vary. They can be very specific and in question form, "How many states in the Union?" Or they can be directives, such as, "Make sure everyone knows the capitals of the states that border on the Pacific Ocean."

Step 3—Heads Together: Students put their heads together to figure out and make sure everyone knows the answer.

Step 4—Answering: The teacher calls a number and students from each group with that number raise their hands and provide answers to the whole class.

Table 10.3 summarizes and compares the four approaches to cooperative learning.

Choose Appropriate Content. As with any lesson, one of the primary planning tasks for teachers is choosing content that is appropriate for the students given their interests and prior learning. This is particularly true for cooperative learning lessons because the model requires a substantial amount of student self-direction and initiative. Without interesting and appropriately challenging content, a cooperative lesson can quickly break down.

> Because cooperative learning requires self-direction and initiative, teachers must be careful to choose content that interests students.

Veteran teachers know from past experience which topics are best suited for cooperative learning, just as they know the approximate developmental levels and interests of students in their classes. Beginning teachers must depend more on curriculum guides and textbooks for appropriate subject matter. However, there are several questions that beginning teachers can use to determine the appropriateness of subject matter:

- Have the students had some previous contact with the subject matter or will it require extended explanation by the teacher?
- Is the content likely to interest the group of students for which it is being planned?

Table 10.3 *Comparison of Four Approaches to Cooperative Learning*

	STAD	Jigsaw	Group Investigation	Structural Approach
Cognitive goals	Factual academic knowledge	Factual and academic conceptual knowledge	Conceptual academic knowledge and inquiry skills	Factual academic knowledge
Social goals	Group work and cooperation	Group work and cooperation	Cooperation in complex groups	Group and social skills
Team structure	Four- to five-member heterogeneous learning teams	Five- to six-member heterogeneous learning teams; use of home and expert teams	Five- to six-member learning groups may be homogeneous	Varies—pairs, trios, four- to six-member groups
Lesson topic selection	Usually teacher	Usually teacher	Teachers and/or students	Usually teacher
Primary task	Students may use worksheets and help each other master learning materials	Students investigate materials in expert groups; help members of home group learn materials	Students complete complex inquiries	Students do assigned tasks—social and cognitive
Assessment	Weekly tests	Varies—can be weekly tests	Completed projects and reports; can be essay tests	Varies
Recognition	Newsletters and other publicity	Newsletters and other publicity	Written and oral presentations	Varies

- If the teacher plans to use text, does it provide sufficient information on the topic?
- For STAD or Jigsaw lessons, does the content lend itself to objective quizzes that can be administered and scored quickly?
- For a Jigsaw lesson, does the content allow itself to be divided into several natural subtopics?
- For a Group Investigation lesson, does the teacher have sufficient command of the topic to guide students into various subtopics and direct them to relevant resources? Are relevant resources available?

Form Student Teams. A third important planning task for cooperative learning is deciding how student learning teams are to be formed. Obviously, this task will vary according to the goals teachers have for a particular lesson, and the racial and ethnic mix and the ability levels of students within their classes. Here are some examples of how teachers might decide to form student teams:

How student teams are formed is an important planning task for teachers.

- A fifth-grade teacher in an integrated school might use cooperative learning to help students better understand peers from different ethnic or racial backgrounds. He or she might take great care to have racially or ethnically mixed teams in addition to matching for ability levels.

- A seventh-grade English teacher in a mostly middle-class white school might form student teams according to students' achievement levels in English.
- A tenth-grade social studies teacher with a homogeneous group of students might decide to use Group Investigation and form teams according to student interest in a particular subtopic but also keep in mind mixing students of different ability levels.
- A fourth-grade teacher with several withdrawn students in her class may decide to form cooperative teams based on ability but also find ways to integrate the isolates with popular and outgoing class members.
- A teacher with several students new to the school might form learning teams on a random basis early in the year, thus ensuring opportunities for the new students to meet and work with students they don't yet know. Later, students' abilities could be used to form learning teams.

Obviously, the composition of teams has almost infinite possibilities. During the planning phase, teachers must delineate clearly their academic and social objectives. They also need to collect adequate information about their students' abilities so that if heterogeneous ability teams are desired, they will have the needed information. Finally, teachers should recognize that some features of group composition may have to be sacrificed in order to meet others.

Develop Materials. When teachers prepare for a whole-class presentation, a major task is to gather materials that can be translated into a meaningful lecture. Although teachers provide verbal information to students in a cooperative learning lesson, this information is normally accompanied by text, worksheets, and study guides.

Providing interesting and developmentally appropriate study materials is important if student teams are to work independently.

If teachers give text to students, it is important that it be both interesting and at an appropriate reading level for the particular class of students. If teachers develop study guides, these should be designed to highlight the content deemed most important. Good study guides and materials take time to develop and cannot be done well the night before a particular lesson is to begin.

If teachers are using the Group Investigation method, they will need to collect an adequate supply of materials for use by student learning teams. In some schools, a beginning teacher can rely on the school librarian and media specialists for gathering materials. This normally requires the teacher to communicate clearly about the goals and objectives of a particular lesson and to be precise about how many students will be involved. For librarians and media specialists to be of maximum assistance requires enough lead time for them to do their work. Again, a beginning teacher should be cautioned about last-minute requests. The following guidelines are offered to get maximum assistance from school support staff when planning a cooperative learning lesson:

- Meet with the school librarian and media specialists at least two weeks before the lesson and go over your lesson objectives. Ask for their ideas and assistance.
- Follow up the meeting with a brief memo summarizing ideas, time lines, and agreements.
- Check back a few days before materials are needed to see if things are coming along as you expected and offer your assistance, if needed.
- If the materials are to be used in your room, ask the specialist to help you design a system for keeping track of materials. You may also ask the specialist to come into your room and explain the system to your students.

Plan for Orienting Students to Tasks and Roles. It is important that students have a clear understanding about their roles and the teacher's expectations for them as they participate in a cooperative learning lesson. If other teachers in the school are using cooperative learning, this task will be easier because students will already be aware of the model and their role in it. In schools in which few teachers use the cooperative learning approach, beginning teachers will have to spend time describing the model to students and working with them on requisite skills. Chapters 4 and 12 describe procedures to increase communication within classroom groups, along with activities to build group cohesion. These are critical skills for students in classrooms in which teachers plan to use cooperative learning.

> If students have not had experience with cooperative learning, it is vital that the teacher orient them to its unique task, goal, and reward structures.

An important thing to remember for beginning teachers who have not used cooperative learning before and who are using it with students who are not familiar with the model is that at first, it may appear not to be working. Students will be confused about the cooperative reward structure. Parents may also object. Also, students may initially lack enthusiasm about the possibilities of small-group interactions on academic topics with their peers.

Using the cooperative learning model can be most difficult for a beginning teacher because it requires the simultaneous coordination of a variety of activities. On the other hand, this model can achieve some important educational goals that other models cannot, and the rewards of this type of teaching can be enormous for the teacher who plans carefully.

Plan for the Use of Time and Space. Another important planning task for cooperative learning is deciding how to use time and space. As described in Chapter 3, time is a scarcer commodity than most teachers realize, and cooperative learning, with its reliance on small-group interaction, makes greater demands on time resources than do some other models of instruction. Most teachers underestimate the amount of time for cooperative learning lessons. It simply takes longer for students to interact about important ideas than it does for the teacher to present the ideas directly through lecture. Making transitions from whole class to small groups can also take up valuable instructional time. Careful planning can help teachers become more realistic about time requirements and it can minimize the amount of noninstructional time.

> Cooperative learning lessons take more time than most other instructional models because they rely on small-group instruction.

Cooperative learning requires special attention to the use of classroom space, along with moveable furniture. The **cluster seating** and **swing seating** arrangements are two ways experienced teachers use space during cooperative learning.

> Cluster seating and swing seating arrangements lend themselves to cooperative learning because of their flexibility.

Cluster Seating Arrangement. Seating clusters of four or six, such as those illustrated in Figure 10.4, are useful for cooperative learning and other small-group tasks. If the cluster arrangement is used, students may have to move their chairs for lectures and demonstrations so that all students will be facing the teacher.

Swing Seating Arrangement. Lynn Newsome, a reading teacher in Howard County, Maryland, developed a particularly inventive seating approach. For cooperative learning, she uses a flexible seating arrangement that allows her to "swing" from a direct instruction lesson to a cooperative learning lesson. Her desks are arranged in a wing formation, as shown in the top of Figure 10.5. On cue, students at the shaded wing desks move their desks to the arrangement shown in the bottom of Figure 10.5. Newsome reports that in both formations, she can "maintain eye contact with all students, and the room appears spacious" (MAACIE *Cooperative News*, p. 5).

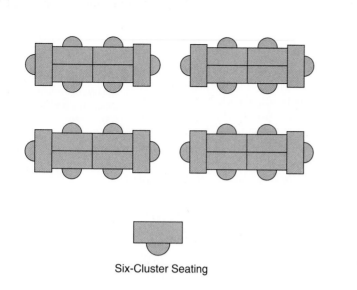

Six-Cluster Seating

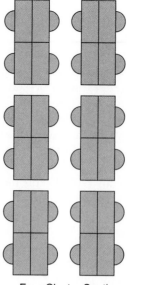

Four-Cluster Seating

Figure 10.4 *Four- and Six-Cluster Seating Arrangements*

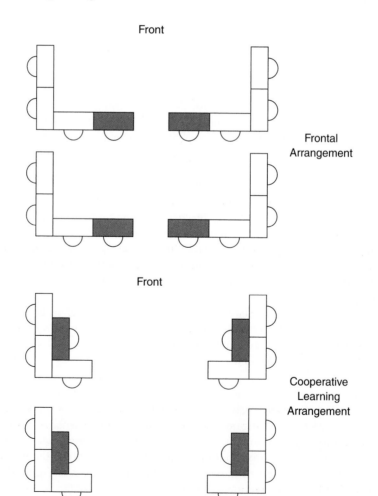

Figure 10.5 *The Swing Seating Arrangement*

Table 10.4 *Syntax of the Cooperative Learning Model*

Phases	Teacher Behavior
Phase 1: Clarify goals and establish set.	Teacher goes over goals for the lesson and establishes learning set.
Phase 2: Present information.	Teacher presents information to students either verbally or with text.
Phase 3: Organize students into learning teams.	Teacher explains to students how to form learning teams and helps groups make efficient transition.
Phase 4: Assist team work and study.	Teacher assists learning teams as they do their work.
Phase 5: Test on the materials.	Teacher tests students' knowledge of learning materials or groups present results of their work.
Phase 6: Provide recognition.	Teacher finds ways to recognize both individual and group effort and achievement.

Conducting Cooperative Learning Lessons

The six phases of a cooperative learning lesson and associated teacher behaviors for each phase are described in Table 10.4. The first four phases are discussed in this section. Testing and student recognition are described in the Assessment and Evaluation section later in the chapter.

Clarify Aims and Establish Set. Some aspects of clarifying the aims for the lesson and establishing set are no different for cooperative learning than they were for other models. Effective teachers begin all lessons by reviewing, explaining their objectives in understandable language, and showing how the lesson ties into previous learning. Because many cooperative learning lessons extend beyond a particular day or week and because the goals and objectives are multifaceted, the teacher normally puts special emphasis on this phase of instruction.

For example, when teachers introduce a group investigation lesson for the first time, they should spend sufficient time to make sure students understand the specific steps and their roles. This can also be the time when a teacher may want to talk about how students can take responsibility for their own learning and not rely solely on the teacher. It may also be a time to discuss how knowledge comes from many sources such as books, films, and one's own interactions with others.

If a teacher is about to introduce Jigsaw, he or she may want to discuss how people are required to work interdependently with others in many aspects of life and how Jigsaw gives students an opportunity to practice cooperative behaviors. Similarly, if the teacher's main objective is to improve relations between students from different ethnic backgrounds or races, he or she may want to explain this idea to students and discuss how working with people who are different from us provides opportunities to know one another better.

The important point with all these examples is that students are more likely to work toward important goals and objectives if the aims for the lesson have been explicitly

Clarifying aims for cooperative lessons is important because students must clearly understand the procedures and rules that will be involved in the lesson.

Enhancing Cooperative Interaction among Students

Critics of technology often assert that computers and the Internet isolate students from one another and from their teachers. They portray a scenario of students glued alone to a computer in a large room or at home surfing the Internet independent of family and friends. Although these situations are something to be concerned about, isolation does not necessarily have to be the case. The role of technology is under the control of the teacher. If teachers require students to work alone, they will tend to be isolated. On the other hand, if teachers require students to work together, technology can indeed enhance interaction and cooperation among students. Let's look at some ways this can happen.

Technology provides many opportunities for group work and for cooperative learning. Teachers can give students assignments and projects following several of the cooperative learning approaches described in this chapter, such as team learning, Jigsaw, and Group Investigation. Students can be encouraged (required) to use computers and the Internet to carry out tasks or investigations in interdependent ways rather than alone. Following are some examples of cooperative work using technology:

- *Create a newspaper.* Using a publication tool, students can work together to write and publish a class newspaper.

- *Create multimedia or hypermedia presentations.* In a group investigation, student groups can develop a multimedia and hypermedia presentation to display the results of their work and to explain their topic to others.
- *LOGO programming project.* Students can engage in a LOGO programming project aimed at performing a variety of age-appropriate tasks.

Technology can also provide opportunities for cognitive apprenticeships. Cognitive apprenticeships and scaffolding, as described earlier, are processes in which less-experienced students acquire knowledge and cognitive capabilities from interacting and modeling the cognitive behaviors of more-experienced adults or students. Working with CD-ROMs, exploring Web-based simulations, or developing and using databases can provide students opportunities for cognitive apprenticeships as they interact and work together. Often, these are experiences that are not available elsewhere.

As with any lesson that provides cooperative learning, those that integrate technology must be structured for task interdependence. Teachers must also help students develop social skills for working together effectively.

Finally, computers and associated technologies may also prove to be the fuel that drives school reform. Schools

discussed. It is difficult for students to perform a task well if they are unclear about why they are doing it or if the criteria for success are kept secret.

Present Information Verbally or in Text. Procedures and guidelines for presenting information to students will not be repeated here because that subject was covered extensively in Chapter 7. It is important, however, to provide some information about the use of text. Most of what is described here is not unique to the cooperative learning model and can be used by the beginning teacher in many situations involving text.

Teachers of young children know that relying on text to transmit content involves helping the children learn to read the assigned materials. Teachers in the upper grades and secondary schools (and college, for that matter) often assume their students can read and comprehend the assigned materials. Many times this is an incorrect assumption. If a cooperative learning lesson requires students to read text, then effective teachers, regardless of the age level of their students or the subject taught, will assume responsibility for helping students become better readers.

Technology provides many opportunities for cooperative learning.

have not embraced the use of technology as quickly as have other institutions in our society. Some observers—Johanssen (1996)—and Means (2000) for example, believe that traditional classrooms do not accommodate the newer technologies very well and that these technologies will not be widely used until we have major shifts in our views about learning and classrooms. The more traditional views of learning (acquiring and storing new information) and classrooms (settings with competitive reward structures and whole-class instruction) find little advantage in the newer technologies. Instead, the use of computers and the Internet, which are highly interactive and constructivist, work best in settings where students work together in small groups and where teachers serve as facilitators of student inquiry. Perhaps as cooperative learning is used more and more in American classrooms, it will serve as a catalyst for wider use of computers and telecommunication technologies.

Organize Students in Study Teams. The process of getting students into learning teams and getting them started on their work is perhaps one of the most difficult steps for teachers using cooperative learning. This is the phase in a cooperative learning lesson where bedlam can result unless the transition is carefully planned and managed. There is nothing more frustrating to teachers than transitional situations in which thirty students are moving into small groups, not sure of what they are to do and each demanding the teacher's attention and help.

> The transition from whole-class instruction to small-group work must be orchestrated carefully.

Assist Team Work and Study. Uncomplicated cooperative learning activities allow students to complete their work with minimum interruption or assistance by the teacher. For other activities, the teacher may need to work closely with each of the learning teams, reminding them of the tasks they are to perform and the time allocated for each step. When using the Group Investigation method, the teacher must remain constantly available to assist with resource identification. There is a fine line for the teacher to follow during this phase of a cooperative learning lesson. Too much interference and unrequested assistance can annoy students. It can also take

Check, Extend, Explore

Check
- What are the major planning tasks associated with cooperative learning lessons?
- How does planning for cooperative learning lessons differ from planning for direct instruction?
- What factors should teachers consider when they are choosing a particular cooperative learning approach? When choosing how to form learning groups?
- What are the six phases of a cooperative learning lesson? What kinds of teacher behaviors are associated with each phase?
- How does the teacher's role in cooperative learning differ from the teacher's role in direct instruction?

Extend
- Think about the various subjects you will be teaching. Which would lend themselves to cooperative learning lessons?
- Do you agree or disagree that it is a teacher's responsibility to teach social skills to students? Go to the "Extend Question Poll" on the Online Learning Center to respond.

Explore
- Go to the Online Learning Center at www.mhhe.com/arends6e for links to websites related to *Planning for and Using Cooperative Learning.*

away opportunities for student initiative and self-direction. At the same time, if the teacher finds that students are unclear about the directions or that they cannot complete planned tasks, then direct intervention and assistance are required.

Adapting Cooperative Learning Lessons for Diverse Learners

As with other approaches to teaching, teachers who use cooperative learning must find ways to adapt lessons to meet the needs of a diverse group of students. Many features of adapting for diversity that were described in earlier chapters hold true for cooperative learning. However, this model presents some unique opportunities and some particular challenges for teachers.

The most important opportunity inherent in cooperative learning is the chance for students with special needs and from diverse backgrounds to work together in cooperative groups and on special projects. Cooperative learning is an important way for students with disabilities to participate fully in the life of the classroom, just as it is for students from varying racial and ethnic backgrounds to develop better understanding of each other.

However, teachers must adapt cooperative learning lessons to meet the needs of all students. Some examples of appropriate adaptations include:

- Remember that before students can work effectively in cooperative learning groups, they must learn about each other and respect individual differences. Students in any class will possess varying amounts of understanding and respect, so instruction on these topics will need to vary.
- Make available more visual assists and explanations for students with disabilities to help them make transitions from whole-group to small-group work.
- Be prepared to give assistance and supportive feedback to students who may be having difficulty but who are on the right track.
- Help regular students understand how their peers with disabilities differ and what they can expect as they work together in learning groups. Point out the strengths and competencies all students bring to group tasks.
- Help all students understand cultural norms of various ethnic and racial groups and how these might affect group interaction and cooperation.
- Help all students become familiar with aids used by students with particular disabilities, such as hearing aids, sign language, and the assistive technologies described in Chapter 2.

Managing the Learning Environment

Unlike models described in the previous chapters, cooperative learning is a student-directed approach to teaching, and a cooperative learning environment requires attention to a unique set of rather difficult management tasks. For example, describing to students how to accomplish a complex group project is much more difficult than assigning them problems at the end of a textbook chapter. It is more difficult to organize students into study teams and to get them to cooperate than it is to get them to line up for recess or to sit and listen to the teacher. Consider, for example, the problems faced by Ken* when he tried to use cooperative learning as a student teacher:

*Ken's story is a true one. It was told by Ken while he was doing his student teaching and was described by Weinstein and Migano (1993).

I couldn't wait to get my students into small groups. I didn't want to be like my cooperating teacher—she does all the talking and students are never allowed to work together. They seem so passive and so isolated from one another. Although she wasn't particularly enthusiastic about small-group work, she gave me her blessing. I was really excited. I was sure that the kids would respond well if they were given the chance to be active and to interact.

I decided to use small groups in science, since my cooperating teacher has given me the most freedom in this area. (I think she doesn't like science and doesn't think it's all that important, so she lets me do whatever I want.) I told the kids that they could choose their own groups. I figured that being allowed to work with friends would be really motivating.

Well, just getting into groups was chaotic. First, we had to move the desks from rows into clusters. Then there was lots of shouting and arguing about who was going to be in which group. The whole process took about 10 minutes and was really noisy. My cooperating teacher was *not* pleased, and I was really upset when I saw what happened. My class is real heterogeneous—I've got blacks, whites, Hispanics, Asian-Americans. Well, the groups turned out really segregated. They also tended to be just about all-boy or all-girl. Even worse—I have one mainstreamed girl in my class (she's learning disabled and really hyperactive), and nobody wanted to work with her at all. I ended up *making* a group take her, and they were pretty nasty about it. And there's another kid who's real shy and quiet; I had to get him into a group, too. It was really embarrassing for both of them.

Finally, I got everyone settled down and they started to work on the assignment. We've been talking about seeds and plants, and each group was supposed to plan an experiment that they would actually carry out to demonstrate what plants needed in order to grow. I emphasized that they were supposed to work together and make sure everyone contributed to the plan.

Well, it was a real mess. A couple of the groups worked out okay, but one group argued the whole time and never got anything written. In another group—all boys—they decided to just let the kid who was smartest in science plan the experiment. He kept coming up and complaining that no one else would do any work. And it was true. The rest just sat and fooled around the whole time. Another group had three girls and one boy. The boy immediately took charge. He dominated the whole thing; the girls just sat there and let him tell them what to do.

I had pictured everyone cooperating, helping one another, contributing ideas. But it didn't work out that way at all. And the noise—it just kept getting louder and louder. I kept turning off the lights and reminding them to use their "indoor voices." For a few minutes, they'd get quieter, but then it would get loud again. Finally, my cooperating teacher stepped in and yelled at everybody. I was really humiliated. I just couldn't control them. Right now, I'm pretty turned off to using cooperative groups. I think maybe she's right. Maybe these kids just can't handle working together. Maybe I should just go back to having everyone sit and listen to me explain the lesson (Weinstein & Migano, 1993, pp. 176–177).

Many of the general management guidelines described in Chapter 5 as well as those related to presentation and direct instruction (Chapters 7 and 8) apply to cooperative learning lessons and could have assisted Ken with his management problems. When using any teaching model, it is important to have a few rules and routines that govern student talk and movement, keep lessons moving smoothly, maintain a general level of decorum in the classroom, and allow teachers to deal quickly and firmly with student misbehavior when it occurs. Management tasks unique to cooperative learning help students make the transitions from whole-class to cooperative learning groups, assist students as they work in groups, and teach students social skills and cooperative behavior.

Helping with Transitions

The process of getting students into learning groups and getting them started on their work is difficult. As Ken's story shows, this process can cause serious problems for the beginning teacher. Several simple but important strategies can be used by teachers to make transitions go smoothly:

Transition into small groups is helped by writing directions on the chalkboard, having students repeat them, and assigning each team a specific space.

1. *Write key steps on the blackboard or on charts.* Visual cues assist large groups of students as they move from one place in the room to another. Think of these as signs similar to those provided for people lining up to purchase theater tickets to a popular play or queuing procedures used at public events such as football games. Here is an example of such a display:

> *Step 1:* Move quickly to the location where your team's name has been posted on the wall.
>
> *Step 2:* Choose one team member to come up to my desk to gather needed learning materials.
>
> *Step 3:* Spend ten minutes reading your particular assignment.
>
> *Step 4:* At my signal, begin your discussions.
>
> *Step 5:* At my signal, return to your learning team and start presenting your information.

2. *State directions clearly and ask two or three students to paraphrase the directions.* Getting several students to repeat the directions helps everyone to pay attention and also gives the teacher feedback on whether or not the directions are understood.

3. *Identify and clearly mark a location for each learning team.* Left to their own devices, students at any age (even adults) will not evenly distribute themselves around a room. They will tend to cluster in areas of the room that are most easily accessible. For effective small-group work, teachers should clearly designate those parts of the room they want each team to occupy and insist that teams go to that particular location.

First attempts at group learning will likely go smoothly if the teacher defines and calls for highly structured rules and procedures.

These procedures are highly prescriptive and structured. Once teachers and students become accustomed to working in cooperative learning groups, more flexibility can be allowed. However, for beginning teachers, and in the earlier stages of using cooperative learning, tightly structured directions and procedures can make lessons move much more smoothly and prevent the frustrations and discouragement experienced by Ken.

Teaching Cooperation

In some schools, students get few opportunities to work on common tasks, and subsequently, many students do not know how to work cooperatively. To help students cooperate requires attention to the kinds of tasks assigned to small groups. It also requires teachers to teach important social and group skills, such as the ones that follow.

Structure lessons to require interdependence.

Task Interdependence. As described earlier, cooperative learning requires that task structures be interdependent rather than independent. An example of an **independent task** is when teachers give students a math worksheet, divide them into groups, tell them they can help each other, but then require each student to complete his or her own worksheet, which will be graded individually. Although students may help one another, they are *not* interdependent to accomplish the task. This same lesson would become an **interdependent task** if the teacher divided the class into groups and required

Teaching cooperation is an important aspect of cooperative learning.

each group to complete one math worksheet with all members' names on it. Many teachers using cooperative learning for the first time fail to structure tasks so that they are interdependent, and they become frustrated when their students do not cooperate or choose to work alone.

Having group members share materials, as in the previous example, is one way to structure task interdependence; having pairs of students work on assignments together is another. A third way to structure interdependence around materials is to give some students the problems and others the answers and ask them to find a match between the two through discussion. The Jigsaw cooperative learning lesson, described earlier, is another way to create interdependence as group members are dependent on each other for information.

Role differentiation is another way to structure interdependence. During a group investigation project, for instance, one student might be responsible for typing the report on his or her word processor, others for creating a Power Point to use in the presentation, and still others for delivering the actual presentation. Each group member is performing a specific task, but the success of the group as a whole depends on the cooperative and interdependent actions of all members.

Social Skills. Teachers should not assume that students have the requisite social or group skills to work cooperatively. Students may not know how to interact with one another, how to develop cooperative plans of action, how to coordinate the contributions of various group members, or how to assess group progress toward particular goals. To make cooperative learning work, teachers may need to teach a variety of group and social skills.

Social skills are those behaviors that promote successful social relationships and enable individuals to work effectively with others. Children can learn social skills from many different individuals: parents, child-care providers, neighbors, and

Teachers should not assume that all of their students possess the social skills needed to effectively work in groups. Some may need help.

teachers. Ideally, children progress from infants who possess few social skills to adults who have a rich repertoire of skills. However, many children and youth do not learn the requisite social skills to live and work together before they attend school. Skills found lacking in many children and youth include sharing skills, participation skills, and communication skills. It is important that teachers help students master these skills.

Sharing Skills. Many students have difficulty sharing time and materials. This complication can lead to serious management problems during a cooperative learning lesson. Being bossy toward other students, talking incessantly, or doing all the work for the group are examples of students' inabilities to share. Domineering students are often well intentioned and do not understand the effects of their behavior on others or on their group's work. These students need to learn the value of sharing and how to rein in their controlling behaviors. Two examples of lessons teachers can use to teach *sharing skills* are described here.

> Before students can work effectively in cooperative learning groups, they must learn about each other and respect individual differences.

1. *Round robin.* Round robin is an activity that teaches students how to take turns when working in a group. The process is quite simple. The teacher introduces an idea or asks a question that has many possible answers. The teacher then asks students to make their contributions. One student starts, making his or her contribution, and then passes the turn to the next person who does the same. Turn-taking continues until every person in the group has had a chance to talk.

2. *Pair checks.* A way to help domineering students learn sharing skills is to have them work in pairs and employ the pair checks structure. The version of pair checks described here includes the eight steps recommend by Kagan (1998):

    Step 1—Pair work: Teams divide into pairs. One student in the pair works on a worksheet or problem while the other student helps and coaches.

    Step 2—Coach checks: The student who was the coach checks the partner's work. If coach and worker disagree on an answer or idea, they may ask the advice of other pairs.

    Step 3—Coach praises: If partners agree, coach provides praise.

    Steps 4 through 6—Partners switch roles: Repeat steps 1 through 3.

    Step 7—Pairs check: All team pairs come back together and compare answers.

    Step 8—Teams celebrate: If all agree on answers, team members do team handshake or cheer.

Participation Skills. Whereas some students dominate group activity, other students may be unwilling or unable to participate. Sometimes students who avoid group work are shy. Often shy students are very bright, and they may work well alone or with one other person. However, they find it difficult to participate in a group. The rejected student may also have difficulty participating in group activity. Additionally, there is the otherwise normal student who chooses, for whatever reason, to work alone and refuses to participate in cooperative group endeavors.

Making sure that shy or rejected students get into groups with students who have good social skills is one way teachers can involve these students. Structuring task interdependence, described previously, is another means to decrease the probability of students wanting to work alone. Using planning sheets that list various group tasks along with the students responsible for completing each task is a third way to teach and ensure balanced participation among group members. *Time tokens* and *high talker tap out* are special activities that teach participation skills.

1. *Time tokens.* If the teacher has cooperative learning groups in which a few people dominate the conversation and a few are shy and never say anything, time tokens can help distribute participation more equitably. Each student is given several tokens that are worth ten or fifteen seconds of talk time. A student monitors interaction and asks talkers to give up a token whenever they have used up the designated time. When a student uses up all of his or her tokens, then he or she can say nothing more. This, of course, necessitates that those still holding tokens join the discussion.

2. *High talker tap out.* It is not uncommon to find only a small percentage of the students participating in group work or discussions. One way to produce more balanced participation is to assign one student to keep track of each student's participation. If the monitor observes a particular student talking repeatedly, he or she can pass a note asking that student to refrain from further comments until everyone has had a turn. The monitor can also encourage shy students to take a turn in the same manner.

Communication Skills. It is quite common to find both younger and older students (adults also) lacking in important **communication skills.** We all have difficulty describing our own ideas and feelings so they are accurately perceived by listeners, and we have equal difficulty in accurately hearing and interpreting what others say to us. Cooperative learning groups cannot function very effectively if the work of the group is characterized by miscommunication. The four communication skills described in Chapter 12 (paraphrasing, describing behavior, describing feelings, and checking impressions) are important and should be taught to students to ease communication in group settings.

> Teachers should help students polish communication skills to ensure success in group learning environments.

Often during classroom interaction, students are not listening to one another. Instead, they sit in the whole group with their hand in the air, waiting for their turn to speak, or in small groups where they may be talking or interrupting incessantly. One way to promote active listening during some classroom discussions (those in which the main objective is learning to listen) is to insist that before a student can speak, he or she must first paraphrase what was said by the student who just finished speaking. More on teaching active listening and paraphrasing can be found in Chapter 12.

Group Skills. Most people have had experiences working in groups in which individual members were nice people and had good social skills, yet the group as a whole did not work well. Members may have been pulling in different directions and, consequently, work was not getting done. Just as individuals must learn social skills to interact successfully in group or community settings, groups as an entity must also learn **group skills** and processes if they are to be effective. Before students can work effectively in cooperative learning groups, they must also learn about one another and respect one another's differences.

Team Building. Helping build team identity and member caring is an important task for teachers using cooperative learning groups. Simple tasks include making sure everyone knows other team members' names and having members decide on a team name. Having teams make a team banner or logo can also build esprit de corp among members. The following three activities can also be used to teach group skills and to build a positive team identity:

> Students must know and show respect for each other for cooperative learning to work.

1. *Team interviews.* Have students in the cooperative learning teams interview one another. They can find out about other members' names, places they have traveled, special interests, or a favorite sport, holiday, color, book, movie, and so forth. Teachers

Check, Extend, Explore

Check

- What are the key features of the cooperative learning environment?
- What steps can teachers take to help students make a smooth transition from large groups to small groups?
- Name the important social and group skills required of students if they are to work together effectively.

Extend

- Given the demands today to teach academic content, do you agree or disagree that using time to teach social and group skills can be justified? Go to the "Extend Question Poll" on the Online Learning Center to respond.

Explore

- Go to the Online Learning Center at www.mhhe.com/arends6e for links to websites related to *Cooperative Learning Environments and Teaching Social and Group Skills*.

can ask students to interview every student in the group and then share with the total group what they learned about group members and the group as a whole. A variation on this procedure is to have each student interview one other student in the team (or class) and then prepare an introduction for that person, which the student presents to the whole group or class.

2. *Team murals.* Teachers can ask students to use a variety of materials such as markers, crayons, chalk, paints, and pictures from magazines to make a mural illustrating how they would like their team to work together. Encourage all members to participate in making the mural. After it has been completed, have members discuss what they have done and explain their mural to members of other teams.

3. *Magic number 11.* Spencer Kagan (1998) described a team project in which students sit in a circle and hold out a clenched hand. They shake their hand up and down and say, "One, two, three." On the count of three, each student puts out so many fingers. The goal is to have all the fingers put out to add up to 11. No talking is allowed. After they succeed, the teams cheer.

Teaching Social and Group Skills. Teaching specific social and group skills is no different from teaching content-specific skills, such as map reading or how to use a microscope. Chapter 8 described the direct instruction model, which requires teachers to demonstrate and model the skill being taught and to provide time for students to practice the skill and receive feedback on how they are doing. In general, this is the model that teachers should use when teaching important social and group skills. The topic of teaching social and group skills to students is described again in Chapters 11 and 12.

Assessment and Evaluation

For each of the models of teaching described previously, we emphasized the importance of using evaluation strategies that are consistent with the goals and objectives of a particular lesson and with the model's overall theoretical framework. For example, if the teacher is using presentation and explanation to help students master important ideas and to think critically about these ideas, then test questions asking students for both recall and higher-level responses are required. If the teacher is using the direct instruction model to teach a specific skill, a performance test is required to measure student mastery of the skill and to provide corrective feedback. All the examples and suggestions given in previous chapters, however, are based on the assumption that the teacher is operating under a competitive or individualistic reward system. The cooperative learning model changes the reward system and, consequently, requires a different approach to evaluation and recognition of achievement.

Testing Academic Learning

For STAD and some versions of Jigsaw, the teacher requires students to take quizzes on the learning materials. Test items on these quizzes must, in most instances, be of an objective type, so they can be scored in class or soon after. Figure 10.6 illustrates how individual scores are determined, and Figure 10.7 gives an example of a quiz scoring sheet. Slavin (1983, 1995), the developer of this scoring system, described it this way:

> The amount that each student contributes to his or her team is determined by the amount the student's quiz score exceeds the student's own past quiz average. . . . Students with perfect papers always receive the . . . maximum, regardless of their base scores. This individual

STAD scoring procedures allow each group member to contribute proportionately based on past performance.

Step 1
Established base line.

Each student is given a base score based on averages on past quizzes.

Step 2
Find current quiz score.

Students receive points for the quiz associated with the current lesson.

Step 3
Find improvement score.

Students earn improvement points to the degree to which their current quiz score matches or exceeds their base score, using the scale provided below.

More than 10 points below base	0 points
10 points below to 1 point below base	10 points
Base score to 10 points above base	20 points
More than 10 points above base	30 points
Perfect paper (regardless of base)	30 points

Figure 10.6 *Scoring Procedures for STAD and Jigsaw*
Source: After Slavin (1995), p. 19

Student	Date: May 23 Quiz: Addition with Regrouping Base Score	Quiz Score	Improvement Points	Date: Quiz: Base Score	Quiz Score	Improvement Points	Date: Quiz: Base Score	Quiz Score	Improvement Points
Sara A.	90	100	30						
Tom B.	90	100	30						
Ursula C.	90	82	10						
Danielle D.	85	74	0						
Eddie E.	85	98	30						
Natasha F.	85	82	10						
Travis G.	80	67	0						
Tammy H.	80	91	30						
Edgar I.	75	79	20						
Andy J.	75	76	20						
Mary K.	70	91	30						
Stan L.	65	82	30						
Alvin M.	65	70	20						
Carol N.	60	62	20						
Harold S.	55	46	10						
Jack E.	55	40	0						

Figure 10.7 *Quiz Score Sheet for STAD and Jigsaw*
Source: After Slavin (1994), p. 20

improvement system gives every student a good chance to contribute maximum points to the team if (and only if) the student does his or her best, and thereby shows substantial improvement or gets a perfect paper. This improvement point system has been shown to increase student academic performance even without teams, but it is especially important as a component of STAD since it avoids the possibility that low performing students will not be fully accepted as group members because they do not contribute many points (p. 24).

A special scoring system does not exist for the Group Investigation approach. The group report or presentation serves as one basis for evaluation, and students should be rewarded for both individual contributions and the collective product.

Assessing Cooperation

Remember from earlier discussions that one of the primary goals of cooperative learning is social skill development, especially those skills that facilitate cooperation and collaboration. These skills are not as easy to assess as academic skills are, but students will not think they are important unless they are a part of the teacher's assessment system. Figure 10.8 identifies important collaborative skills that can be assessed and a rubric for doing so.

A. Works toward the achievement of group goals

4 Actively helps identify group goals and works hard to meet them.
3 Communicates commitment to the group goals and effectively carries out assigned roles.
2 Communicates a commitment to the group goals but does not carry out assigned roles.
1 Does not work toward group goals or actively works against them.

B. Demonstrates effective interpersonal skills

4 Actively promotes effective group interaction and the expression of ideas and opinions in a way that is sensitive to the feelings and knowledge base of others.
3 Participates in group interaction without prompting. Expresses ideas and opinions in a way that is sensitive to the feelings and knowledge base of others.
2 Participates in group interaction with prompting or expresses ideas and opinions without considering the feelings and knowledge base of others.
1 Does not participate in group interaction, even with prompting, or expresses ideas and opinions in a way that is insensitive to the feelings or knowledge base of others.

C. Contributes to group maintenance

4 Actively helps the group identify changes or modifications necessary in the group process and works toward carrying out those changes.
3 Helps identify changes or modifications necessary in the group process and works toward carrying out those changes.
2 When prompted, helps identify changes or modifications necessary in the group process or is only minimally involved in carrying out those changes.
1 Does not attempt to identify changes or modifications necessary in the group process, even when prompted, or refuses to work toward carrying out those changes.

Figure 10.8 *Rubric for Cooperation and Collaboration*

Source: Adapted from Marzano, Pickering, and McTighe (1993), pp. 87–88

Grading Cooperative Learning

In cooperative learning, teachers have to be careful about their reward structure. It is important for teachers to reward the group product—both the end result and the cooperative behavior that produced it. Teachers also want to assess each member's contribution to the final product. These dual assessment tasks, however, can prove troublesome for teachers when they try to assign individual grades for a group product. For instance, sometimes a few ambitious students may take on a larger portion of the responsibility for completing the group project and then be resentful toward classmates who made only minor contributions yet receive the same grade. Similarly, students who have neglected their responsibilities to the group effort may develop cynicism toward a system that rewards them for work they did not accomplish. Some experienced teachers have found a solution by providing two evaluations for students—one for the group's effort and one for each person's individual contribution.

A special challenge for cooperative learning teachers is how to grade for both team and individual effort.

Recognizing Cooperative Effort

Another important postinstructional task unique to cooperative learning is the emphasis given to recognizing student effort and achievement. Slavin and the Johns Hopkins developers created the concept of the weekly class newsletter for use with STAD and Jigsaw. The teacher (sometimes the class itself) reports on and publishes the results of team and individual learning in this newspaper.

The developers of the Group Investigation approach recognize team efforts by highlighting group presentations and by displaying the results of group investigations prominently in the room. This form of recognition can be emphasized even more by inviting guests (parents, students from another class, or the principal) to hear final reports. Newsletters summarizing the results of a class's group investigation can also be produced and sent to parents and others in the school and community. More is said about the topic of recognition in Chapter 11 on problem-based learning.

Check, Extend, Explore

Check
• What factors should teachers consider when they think about how to assess student achievement in cooperative learning?

Extend
⊛ Grading for group effort is controversial. Do you agree or disagree with this practice? Go to the "Extend Question Poll" on the Online Learning Center to respond.

Explore
⊛ Go to the Online Learning Center at www.mhhe.com/arends6e for links to websites related to Assessment and Cooperative Learning.

Cooperative Learning: A Final Thought

Cooperative learning should be a part of every beginning teacher's repertoire. Careful developmental work and empirical research have produced a model that helps to promote greater tolerance for differences, to teach important social and group skills, and to increase academic achievement. Inexperienced teachers, however, should be careful and should know about the difficulties involved in implementing cooperative learning in some settings.

In some communities, for instance, teachers may find strong resistance to the idea of cooperative reward structures. Many parents and community members value independent effort and believe these norms should be emphasized in schools to prepare youth for an adult world characterized by competition. Many students, particularly those who excel in the more traditional, individualistic reward structures, will likewise object to approaches in which interdependent activities are valued and rewards are shared.

Some educators hold high expectations for cooperative learning as an effective means to increase positive student social behavior and to correct many of the social injustices that exist in our society. The model has demonstrated success in helping to accomplish these types of goals. However, educators should be careful not to overstate the benefits of the model and to educate citizens to recognize that no approach to teaching can solve long-standing social ills overnight.

Reflections **from the** *Classroom*

Slow Down for Cooperative Learning?

In your first year of teaching, you find yourself in a school (elementary or middle) where teachers have not paid much attention to cooperative learning in the past. It is not that they are against cooperative learning; they simply have chosen to stick to more traditional, teacher-centered approaches. However, you have had extensive exposure to this model in the school where you did your student teaching and you believe strongly in the effectiveness of cooperative learning for goals you value as a teacher—teamwork and acceptance of diversity. You can't wait to get your students working in small, cooperative work groups.

During the second week of school, you introduce two cooperative learning projects in your language arts class. You choose to use STAD to teach spelling and you launch a long-term group investigation project in poetry. For spelling, you assign students to groups to ensure a good mix of abilities and ethnic-racial backgrounds; you allow the poetry groups to form according to students' interests, although you make it clear to students that you don't want any groups with all boys or all girls. You explain to your students that they will be tested in spelling weekly and that improvement and group effort will determine each student's grade. You make it clear that the group's effort in the poetry investigation will receive the highest reward.

During the first couple of weeks, you are *not* particularly happy about how things are going. Students find it difficult to settle down and work together and don't appear to be highly engaged. You have received minor complaints about your grading system; however, you haven't taken these complaints too seriously, believing that things will get better soon.

On Monday of the fourth week of school, you get a note from the principal that she wants to meet with you after school. Of course, you are curious and a little worried about why she would want this meeting. At the meeting, you are astounded—the principal tells you that a group of parents of very talented children visited the school to complain about your use of cooperative learning. They told her that their children were being penalized by having to work with less-talented students and that grading on group efforts was not fair. They expressed their belief that individuals should be rewarded for the work they produce independent of others. The principal strongly recommended that you rethink your approach.

Reflect on this situation and consider what you should do. Approach the situation from the perspective closest to the grade level or subject area you are preparing to teach. Is there a way to continue using cooperative learning without angering students, their parents, and the principal? Can you change your approach and still accomplish the teamwork and diversity goals you cherish? If you are in a field experience, share this situation with fellow students or your cooperating teachers. Then compare your thoughts with the following comments from teachers who have faced or known about similar situations. Write up your reflections on this situation as an exhibit in your professional portfolio.

Patricia A. Merkel
Eleanor Roosevelt School, Kindergarten
Pennsbury, PA

Accepting how much time is needed to establish good class rapport is not an easy task. Bravo to you for your efforts towards the cooperative learning approach. Be patient. The first few weeks of school are needed to establish guidelines for the behaviors needed in cooperative learning. The children need modeling of these behaviors and lots of practice before cooperative groups are introduced. Practice is needed in getting to the group. A timer can be used. Practice might be needed in listening and responding to individuals in the group. I assign one member of the group to be the "task master." This person's sole responsibility is to monitor the on-task behavior of other group members. Self-evaluation scales give the students an opportunity to reflect on his or her level of participation in the group. All of this takes time and practice. Do not be discouraged. Do not give up the effort towards cooperative learning. Be very specific with children regarding your expectations of them. Don't forget to "catch 'em being good."

Personally, I do not like the idea of group grades. Cooperative learning allows many social learners an opportunity to learn the way they learn best. The group product or presentation cannot be the only criterion for the individual's grade. The beauty of group activity is to encourage active learning through questions, discussions, and artistic expression. This taps into the skills held by children who might not be the ones to shine in traditional teaching and testing. Even the most successful student can use practice in the social skills needed to participate in cooperative learning.

The principal's happiness is also very important and you need him or her in your corner. Model for her what you hope to get from your students: listening, reflection, and willingness to adapt to the needs of others. No need to abandon your original, well thought out approach. As the students become successful with this model, their pleasure will be communicated to their parents. Meanwhile, you can be proactively engaged with newsletters to remind them of your efforts.

Amy Shin
8th Grade

I have seen several situations such as this one. Normally, they involve beginning teachers who want to immediately solve all of the problems in education. If I were the teacher in this situation, I would not give up on cooperative learning. Instead, I would slow down. Teachers in this middle school have not used cooperative learning in the past, so group work and grading is new to students and to their parents. Rather than implementing a full-blown STAD approach and an extended group investigation, the teacher should get students comfortable working in pairs in low-stakes situations, perhaps using "think-pair-share" after reading a particular poem. The idea of cooperative grading should also be introduced gradually. This is a topic that should be explained, discussed, and perhaps debated with parents at the school's open house and in other settings. It should also be discussed with other members of the faculty, including the principal. A teacher who wants to introduce cooperative learning in a school where it has not been used before should be prepared for the process to take as long as two or three years.

Chapter Review

Go back to the "Interactive and Applied Learning" feature at the beginning of the chapter for a listing of interactive and applied activities. Go to the Online Learning Center at **www.mhhe.com/arends6e** or your Interactive Student CD-ROM to take practice quizzes over the content of this chapter and receive immediate feedback. You can also review chapter content and main ideas, practice with key terms, and find annotated Web links on topics associated with Chapter 10.

Summary

Overview of Cooperative Learning

- Cooperative learning is unique among the models of teaching because it uses different goal, task, and reward structures to promote student learning.
- The cooperative learning task structure requires students to work together on academic tasks in small groups. The goal and reward structures require interdependent learning and recognize groups as well as individual effort.
- The cooperative learning model aims at instructional goals beyond academic learning, specifically intergroup acceptance, social and group skills, and cooperative behavior.
- The syntax for cooperative learning models relies on small-group work rather than whole-class teaching and includes six major phases: present goals and establish set; present information; organize students into learning teams; assist team work and study; test on the materials; and provide recognition.
- The model's learning environment requires cooperative rather than competitive task and reward structures. The learning environment is characterized by democratic processes in which students assume active roles and take responsibility for their own learning.

Theoretical and Empirical Support

- The intellectual roots for cooperative learning grow out of an educational tradition emphasizing democratic thought and practice, active learning, cooperative behavior, and respect for pluralism in multicultural societies.
- A strong empirical base supports the use of cooperative learning for the following educational objectives: cooperative behavior, academic learning, improved race relationships, and improved attitudes toward disabled children.

Planning and Conducting Cooperative Learning Lessons

- Planning tasks associated with cooperative learning put less emphasis on organizing academic content and more emphasis on organizing students for small-group work and collecting a variety of learning materials to be used during group work.
- One of the major planning tasks is deciding which cooperative learning approach to use. Four variations of the basic model can be used: Student Team Achievement Divisions, Jigsaw, Group Investigation, and structural approach.
- Regardless of the specific approach, a cooperative learning lesson has four essential features that must be planned: how to form heterogeneous teams, how students are to work in their groups, how rewards are to be distributed, and how much time is required.
- Conducting a cooperative learning lesson changes the teacher's role from one of center stage performer to one of choreographer of small-group activity.

Managing the Learning Environment

- Small-group work presents special management challenges to teachers.
- During cooperative learning lessons, teachers must help students make transitions to their small groups, help them manage their group work, and teach important social and group skills.

Assessment and Evaluation

- Assessment and evaluation tasks, particularly evaluation, replace the traditional competitive approaches described for earlier models with individual and group rewards, along with new forms of recognition.
- Newsletters and public forums are two devices teachers use to recognize the results of student work performed in cooperative learning lessons.
- Cooperative learning is an important approach to teaching. However, educators need to be careful and not overstate the model's benefits.

Key Terms

cluster seating 369
communication skills 379
competitive 355
cooperative 355
goal structure 355
Group Investigation (GI) 364
group skills 379
independent task 376
individualistic 355
interaction patterns 365
interdependent task 376
Jigsaw 363

Portfolio and Field Experience Activities

This feature has been designed to help you learn from your field experiences and to assist you in the preparation of artifacts for your professional portfolio on topics and standards associated with Chapter 10.

1. Complete the "Reflections from the Classroom" exercise at the end of this chapter and use the recommended reflective essay as an exhibit of your views about cooperative learning.

2. Use Activity 10.1 in the *Guide to Field Experiences and Portfolio Development* to assess your current understanding and skills to plan and conduct cooperative learning lessons. Summarize the results as an exhibit for your portfolio.

3. Use Activities 10.2, 10.3, and 10.4 in the *Guide to Field Experiences and Portfolio Development* to observe experienced teachers using cooperative learning. Summarize your observation(s) as an exhibit in your professional portfolio.

4. Use the "Case Exercise" on the Interactive Student CD-ROM and/or Activity 10.6 in the *Guide to Field Experiences and Portfolio Development* to create your own cooperative learning lesson. Place the product(s) of your work in your professional portfolio to demonstrate your understanding and skill in planning and conducting cooperative learning lessons.

Books for the Professional

Go to the Online Learning Center at www.mhhe.com/ arends6e or your Interactive Student CD-ROM for an annotated version of this list.

Aronson, E., and Patnoe, S. (1997). *The Jigsaw Classroom.* New York: Addison-Wesley Longman.

Cohen, E. (1994). *Designing Group Work: Strategies for the Heterogeneous Classroom.* New York: Teachers College Press.

Gibbs, J. (1995). *Tribes: A New Way of Learning Together.* Sausalito, CA: Center Source Systems.

Johnson, D. W., and Johnson, R. T. (1998). *Learning Together and Alone. Cooperation, Competition, and Individualization* (5th ed.). Englewood Cliffs, NJ: Prentice-Hall.

Kagan, S. (1997). *Cooperative Learning* (2nd ed.). San Juan Capistrano, CA: Resources for Teachers.

Sharan, S. (ed.). (1999). *Handbook of Cooperative Learning Methods.* Westport, CT: Praeger.

Slavin, R. (1995). *Cooperative Learning* (2nd ed.). New York: Longman.

Chapter Eleven

Problem-Based Learning

```
                        Problem-Based Learning

  Overview of Problem-Based Learning              Problem-Based Learning: A Final Thought
  • Special Features of Problem-Based
    Learning                                      Assessment and Evaluation
                                                  • Assessing Understanding
  Theoretical and Empirical Support               • Using Checklists and Rating Scales
                                                  • Assessing Adult Roles and Situations
  • Dewey and the Problem-Oriented                • Assessing Learning Potential
    Classroom                                     • Assessing Group Effort
  • Piaget, Vygotsky, and Constructivism
  • Bruner and Discovery Learning
                                                  Managing the Learning Environment
  Planning and Conducting                         • Dealing with Multitask Situations
  Problem-Based Lessons                           • Adjusting to Differing Finishing Rates
                                                  • Monitoring and Managing Student Work
  • Planning for PBL Lessons                      • Managing Materials and Equipment
  • Conducting for PBL Lessons                    • Regulating Movement and Behavior
  • Using Learning Centers for                      Outside the Classroom
    Problem-Based Learning
  • Tailoring Problem-Based Lessons for
    All Students
```

Interactive and Applied Learning

Go to your Interactive Student CD-ROM to:

- Hear audio clips of Corine Marino and Ian Call (tenth-grade world history) talk about problem-based learning in the *Teachers on Teaching* feature
- Watch the video clip: Problem-Based Learning
- Complete the Problem-Based Learning Case Exercise in the Chapter 11 *Case Exercises and Tasks* area
- Complete the Problem-Based Learning Practice Tasks in Chapter 11 *Case Exercises and Practice Tasks* area. Write objectives for a problem-based learning lesson; plan for a demonstration and guided practice; differentiate guided practice for two students; check for understanding and provide feedback; plan for extended practice; assess student learning; and reflect on planning for problem-based learning.

Go to the Online Learning Center at www.mhhe.com/arends6e to read PowerWeb articles and newsfeed updates about:

- Classroom management
- Cultural diversity in education
- Instruction
- Learning
- Technology and education
- Testing and evaluation
- World Wide Web

Considering **Standards**

Studying this chapter will help you meet two INTASC principles:

Primary

INTASC 4: Understands and uses a variety of instructional strategies to encourage student development of critical thinking, problem-solving, and performance skills.

Secondary

INTASC 8: Understands and uses formal and informal assessment strategies to evaluate and ensure the continuous intellectual, social, and physical development of the learner.

Reflecting **on** *Problem-Based Learning*

You have likely had teachers who spent a lot of time getting you to work on special projects and to take responsibility for your own learning. Instead of listening to lectures or participating in classroom discussions as a student in these teachers' classes, you were required to spend a lot of time in the library, on the Web, or out in the community. Instead of taking tests to determine your grade, you wrote reports or created other products that could be assessed. How did you react to these types of learning experiences?

- Did you enjoy them? Or did you find them uninteresting and boring?
- What did you learn from these types of experiences? What didn't you learn that you should have?
- Were there aspects of these teachers' classes that you found particularly effective for you? Ineffective?

Do the answers to these questions say anything about what you might do when you become a teacher? Will you use problem-based learning strategies? Or are you more likely to stick with more teacher-centered approaches to instruction?

 Go to the Online Learning Center at www.mhhe.com/arends6e to respond to these questions.

This chapter is about problem-based learning (PBL) and its use in promoting higher-level thinking in problem-oriented situations, including learning how to learn. The model is referred to by other names, such as *project-based instruction,* *authentic learning,* and *anchored instruction.* Unlike the presentation or direct instruction models described in Chapters 7 and 8, in which the emphasis was on teachers presenting ideas or demonstrating skills, a teacher's role in problem-based learning is to pose problems, ask questions, and facilitate investigation and dialogue. Most important, the teacher provides scaffolding—a supportive framework—that enhances inquiry and intellectual growth. Problem-based learning cannot occur unless teachers create classroom environments in which an open and honest exchange of ideas can occur. In this respect, many parallels exist among problem-based learning, cooperative learning, and classroom discussion, which is described in Chapter 12. You will note that problem-based learning shares its intellectual roots with inquiry teaching and cooperative learning. In later sections, common features of all these methods are explored in more detail.

A teacher's role in PBL is to pose authentic problems, facilitate student investigation, and support student learning.

As with previous chapters, we begin with an overview of problem-based learning and a presentation of its theoretical and empirical underpinnings. A brief discussion of the model's historical traditions is also provided. This will be followed by sections that describe the specific procedures involved in planning, conducting, and evaluating problem-based learning. The chapter concludes with a discussion of how to manage the learning environment of problem-based learning.

Overview of Problem-Based Learning

The essence of problem-based learning consists of presenting students with authentic and meaningful problem situations that can serve as springboards for investigations and inquiry. To illustrate this concept, consider the following scenario at an elementary school in a small town near Maryland's Chesapeake Bay:

> [Ten]-year old Jamel rises to speak. "The chair recognizes the delegate from Ridge School," says the chair, a student from the local high school.
>
> "I'd like to speak in favor of House Bill R130," Jamel begins. "This bill would tell farmers that they can't use fertilizer on land that is within 200 feet of the Chesapeake Bay because it pollutes the bay and kills fish. Farmers can still grow enough crops even if they don't plant close to water. We all will have a better life if we can stop pollution in the bay. I yield to questions."
>
> A hand goes up. The chair recognizes a delegate from Carver School. "How does fertilizer harm the bay?" she asks. Jamel explains how the fertilizer supplies nutrients to algae, and when too much algae grows it deprives oysters, crabs, clams, and other marine life of oxygen.
>
> A delegate from Green Holly School offers another viewpoint: "I'm a farmer," says 11-year old Maria. "I can hardly pay all my bills as it is, and I've got three kids to feed. I'll go broke if I can't fertilize my whole field" (Slavin, Madden, Dolan, & Wasik, 1994, pp. 3–4).

The essence of PBL involves the presentation of authentic and meaningful situations that serve as foundations for student investigation and inquiry.

This debate continues for over an hour as students consider the problem of pollution and its relationship to the economy from the perspectives of farmers, commercial crabbers, business owners, and citizens who see pollution ruining the local tourist industry and the value of homes in the Chesapeake region.

These students are participating in "Roots and Wings," a PBL project developed at Johns Hopkins University. The purpose of "Roots and Wings" is to help students learn academic content and problem-solving skills by engaging them in real-life problem situations. This particular program, like other PBL projects, has certain characteristics that distinguish it from other teaching approaches.

Special Features of Problem-Based Learning

Various developers of problem-based learning (Cognition & Technology Group at Vanderbilt, 1990; Gordon et. al, 2001; Krajcik, 1999; Slavin, Madden, Dolan, & Wasik, 1994; Torp & Sage, 1998) have described the instructional model as having the following features:

> **PBL lessons are organized around real-life situations that evade simple answers and invite competing solutions.**

- *Driving question or problem.* Rather than organizing lessons around particular academic principles or skills, problem-based learning organizes instruction around questions and problems that are both socially important and personally meaningful to students. They address real-life situations that evade simple answers and for which competing solutions exist.
- *Interdisciplinary focus.* Although a problem-based lesson may be centered in a particular subject (science, math, social studies), the actual problem under investigation is chosen because its solution requires students to delve into many subjects. For example, the pollution problem raised in the Chesapeake Bay lesson cuts across several academic and applied subjects—biology, economics, sociology, tourism, and government.
- *Authentic investigation.* Problem-based learning necessitates that students pursue *authentic* investigations that seek real solutions to real problems. They must analyze and define the problem, develop hypotheses and make predictions, collect and analyze information, conduct experiments (if appropriate), make inferences, and draw conclusions. The particular investigative methods used, of course, depend on the nature of the problem being studied.
- *Production of artifacts and exhibits.* Problem-based learning requires students to construct products in the form of *artifacts* and *exhibits* that explain or represent their solutions. A product could be a mock debate like the one in the "Roots and Wings" lesson. It could be a report, a physical model, a video, or a computer program. Artifacts and exhibits, as will be described later, are planned by students to demonstrate to others what they have learned and to provide a refreshing alternative to the traditional report or term paper.

> **Student collaboration in PBL encourages shared inquiry and dialogue, and the development of thinking and social skills.**

- *Collaboration.* Like the cooperative learning model described in Chapter 10, problem-based learning is characterized by students working with one another, most often in pairs or small groups. Working together provides motivation for sustained involvement in complex tasks and enhances opportunities for shared inquiry and dialogue, and for the development of social skills.

Problem-based learning was not designed to help teachers convey huge quantities of information to students. Direct instruction and lecture are better suited to this purpose. Rather, problem-based learning, as illustrated in Figure 11.1, was designed primarily to help students develop their thinking, problem-solving, and intellectual skills; learn adult roles by experiencing them through real or simulated situations; and become independent, autonomous learners. A brief discussion of these three goals follows.

> **PBL helps students develop their thinking and problem-solving skills, learn authentic adult roles, and become independent learners.**

Thinking and Problem-Solving Skills. A bewildering array of ideas and words are used to describe the way people think. But what does thinking really involve? What are thinking skills and, particularly, what are **higher-order thinking** skills? Most of the definitions that have been provided describe abstract *intellectual processes* such as the following:

- Thinking is a process involving mental operations such as induction, deduction, classification, and reasoning.

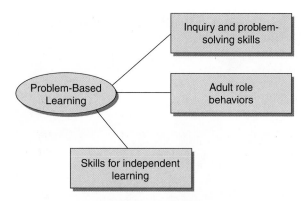

Figure 11.1 *Learner Outcomes for Problem-Based Learning*

- Thinking is a process of symbolically representing (through language) real objects and events and of using those symbolic representations to discover the essential principles of those objects and events. Such symbolic (abstract) representation is usually contrasted with mental operations that are based on the concrete level of facts and specific cases.
- Thinking is the ability to analyze, criticize, and reach conclusions based on sound inference or judgment.

Most contemporary statements about thinking recognize that higher-level thinking skills are not the same as skills associated with more routine patterns of behavior. They emphasize that even though precise definitions of higher-order thinking cannot always be found, we recognize such thinking when we see it in operation. Furthermore, higher-order thinking, unlike more concrete behaviors, is complex and not easily reduced to fixed routines. Consider the following statements of Lauren Resnick (1987) about what she defines as higher-order thinking:

- Higher-order thinking is *nonalgorithmic.* That is, the path of action is not fully specified in advance.
- Higher-order thinking tends to be *complex.* The total path is not "visible" (mentally speaking) from any single vantage point.
- Higher-order thinking often yields *multiple solutions,* each with costs and benefits, rather than unique solutions.
- Higher-order thinking involves *nuanced judgment* and interpretation.
- Higher-order thinking involves the application of *multiple criteria,* which sometime conflict with one another.
- Higher-order thinking often involves *uncertainty.* Not everything that bears on the task at hand is known.
- Higher-order thinking involves *self-regulation* of the thinking process. We do not recognize higher-order thinking in an individual when someone else "calls the plays" at every step.
- Higher-order thinking involves *imposing meaning,* finding structure in apparent disorder.
- Higher-order thinking is *effortful.* There is considerable mental work involved in the kinds of elaborations and judgments required (pp. 2–3).

Notice that Resnick used words and phrases such as *nuanced judgment, self-regulation, imposing meaning,* and *uncertainty.* Obviously, thinking processes and the skills people

Higher-order thinking skills cannot be taught by using approaches designed for teaching concrete ideas and skills.

PBL projects resemble out-of-school learning situations more closely than they do the academic lessons that characterize most school learning.

need to activate them are highly complex. Resnick also pointed out the importance of context when *thinking about thinking.* That is, although thinking processes have some similarities across situations, they also vary according to what one is thinking about. For instance, the processes we use to think about mathematics differ from those we use to think about poetry. The processes for thinking about abstract ideas differ from those used to think about real-life situations. Because of the complex and contextual nature of higher-order thinking skills, they cannot be taught using approaches suitable for teaching more concrete ideas and skills. Higher-order thinking skills and processes are, however, clearly teachable, and most programs and curricula developed for this purpose rely heavily on approaches similar to problem-based learning.

Adult Role Modeling.   Problem-based learning also aims at helping students perform in real-life situations and learn important adult roles. In "Learning in School and Out," Resnick (1987) described how school learning, as traditionally conceived, differs in four important ways from mental activity and learning that occurs outside schools. Her four comparisons are paraphrased here:

1. School learning focuses on the individual's performance, whereas out-of-school mental work involves collaboration with others.
2. School learning focuses on unaided thought processes, whereas mental activity outside school usually involves cognitive tools such as computers, calculators, and other scientific instruments.
3. School learning cultivates symbolic thinking regarding hypothetical situations, whereas mental activity outside school engages individuals directly with concrete and real objects and situations.
4. School learning focuses on general skills (reading, writing, and computing) and general knowledge (world history, chemical elements), whereas situation-specific thinking such as whether to buy or lease a new car dominates out-of-school mental activity.

Resnick's perspective provides a strong rationale for problem-based learning. She argues that this form of instruction is essential to bridge the gap between formal school learning and the more practical mental activity that occurs outside school. Note how the features of problem-based learning correspond to out-of-school mental activity:

- Problem-based learning encourages collaboration and the joint accomplishment of tasks.
- Problem-based learning has elements of an apprenticeship. It encourages observation and dialogue with others so that a student can gradually assume the observed role (scientist, teacher, doctor, artist, or historian, etc.).
- Problem-based learning engages students in self-selected investigations that enable them to interpret and explain real-world phenomena and to construct their own understanding about these phenomena.

Independent Learning. Finally, problem-based learning strives to help students become independent and **self-regulated learners.** Guided by teachers who repeatedly encourage and reward them for asking questions and seeking solutions to real problems on their own, students learn to perform these tasks independently later in life.

Problem-based learning usually consists of five major phases that begin with a teacher's orienting students to a problem situation and culminate with the presentation and analysis of student work and artifacts. When the problem is modest in scope, all five phases of the model can be covered in a few class periods. However, more complex problems may take as long as a full school year to accomplish. The five phases of the model are described in more detail later in the chapter in the Planning and Conducting Problem-Based Lessons section.

Unlike the tightly structured learning environment required for direct instruction or the careful use of small groups in cooperative learning, the learning environment and management system for problem-based instruction are characterized by open, democratic processes and by active student roles. In fact, the whole process of helping students become independent, self-regulated learners who are confident of their own intellectual skills necessitates active involvement in an intellectually safe, inquiry-oriented environment. Although the teacher and students proceed through the phases of a problem-based learning lesson in a somewhat structured and predictable fashion, the norms surrounding the lesson are those of open inquiry and freedom of thought. The learning environment emphasizes the central role of the learner, not of the teacher.

Theoretical and Empirical Support

Direct instruction, as you read in Chapter 8, draws its theoretical support from behavioral psychology and social learning theory. Teachers using direct instruction rely mainly on external stimuli, such as reinforcement, to maintain student cooperation and to keep them engaged in academic tasks. The teacher's role in a direct instruction lesson consists mainly of presenting information to students and modeling particular skills in a clear and efficient manner. Problem-based learning, on the other hand, draws on **cognitive psychology** for its theoretical support. The focus is not so much on what students are doing (their behavior) but on what they are thinking (their cognitions) while they are doing it. Although the role of a teacher in problem-based lessons sometimes involves presenting and explaining things to students, it more usually involves serving as a guide and facilitator so that students learn to think and to solve problems on their own.

Getting students to think, to solve problems, and to become autonomous learners is not a new goal for education. Teaching strategies, such as *discovery learning, inquiry*

The classroom environment of PBL is student-centered and encourages open inquiry and freedom of thought.

Check, Extend, Explore

Check
- What are the key characteristics of problem-based learning? How do these differ from other models of teaching?
- What are the major learner outcomes of problem-based learning?
- What type of learning environment works best for problem-based learning?

Extend
- Do you agree or disagree with Resnick's idea that most "in-school" learning is very different than "out-of-school" learning and that teachers should help bridge the gap between the two types of learning? Go to the "Extend Question Poll" on the Online Learning Center to respond.

Explore
- Go to the Online Learning Center at www.mhhe.com/arends6e links to websites related to *Problem-Based Learning.*

PBL draws upon cognitive psychology for theoretical support.

training, and *inductive teaching* have long and prestigious histories. The *Socratic method,* dating back to the early Greeks, emphasized the importance of inductive reasoning and of dialogue in the teaching-learning process. John Dewey (1933) described in some detail the importance of what he labeled *reflective thinking* and the processes teachers should use to help students acquire productive thinking skills and processes. Jerome Bruner (1962) emphasized the importance of discovery learning and how teachers should help learners become "constructionists" of their own knowledge. Richard Suchman (1962) developed an approach called *inquiry training* in which teachers within a classroom setting present students with puzzling situations and encourage them to inquire and seek answers. For our purposes, problem-based learning will be traced through three main streams of twentieth-century thought.

Dewey and the Problem-Oriented Classroom

> Dewey's view that schools should be laboratories for real-life problem solving provides the philosophical underpinning for PBL.

As with cooperative learning, problem-based learning finds its intellectual roots in the work of John Dewey. In *Democracy and Education* (1916), Dewey described a view of education in which schools would mirror the larger society and classrooms would be laboratories for real-life inquiry and problem solving. Dewey's pedagogy encouraged teachers to engage students in problem-oriented projects and help them inquire into important social and intellectual problems. Dewey and his disciples, such as Kilpatrick (1918), argued that learning in school should be purposeful rather than abstract and that purposeful learning could best be accomplished by having children in small groups pursue projects of their own interest and choosing. This vision of purposeful or problem-centered learning fueled by students' innate desire to explore personally meaningful situations clearly links contemporary problem-based learning with the educational philosophy and pedagogy of Dewey.

Piaget, Vygotsky, and Constructivism

Dewey provided the philosophical underpinnings for problem-based learning early in the twentieth century, but psychology provided much of its theoretical support. The European psychologists Jean Piaget and Lev Vygotsky were instrumental in developing the concept of **constructivism** on which much of contemporary problem-based learning rests.

Jean Piaget, a Swiss psychologist, spent over fifty years studying how children think and the processes associated with intellectual development. In explaining how the intellect develops in young children, Piaget confirmed that children are innately curious and are constantly striving to understand the world around them. This curiosity, according to Piaget, motivates them to actively *construct* representations in their minds about the environment they are experiencing. As they grow older and acquire more language and memory capacity, their mental representations of the world become more elaborate and abstract. At all stages of development, however, children's need to understand their environment motivates them to investigate and to construct theories that explain it.

> Constructivist theories of learning, which stress learners' need to investigate their environment and construct personally meaningful knowledge, provide the theoretical basis for PBL.

The **cognitive-constructivist perspective,** on which problem-based learning rests, borrows heavily from Piaget (1954, 1963). It posits, as did he, that learners of any age are actively involved in the process of acquiring information and constructing their own knowledge. Knowledge does not remain static but instead is constantly evolving and changing as learners confront new experiences that force them to build on and modify prior knowledge. In the words of Piaget, good pedagogy:

> must involve presenting the child with situations in which (he or she) experiments, in the broadest sense of that term—trying things out to see what happens, manipulating things, ma-

nipulating symbols, posing questions and seeking (his/her) own answers, reconciling what (he/she) finds one time with what he finds at another, comparing his finding with those of other children (Duckworth, 1991, p. 2).

Lev Vygotsky was a Russian psychologist whose work was not known to most Europeans and Americans until recently. Like Piaget, Vygotsky (1978, 1994) believed that the intellect develops as individuals confront new and puzzling experiences and as they strive to resolve discrepancies posed by these experiences. In the quest for understanding, individuals link new knowledge to prior knowledge and construct new meaning. Vygotsky's beliefs differed from those of Piaget, however, in some important ways. Whereas Piaget focused on the stages of intellectual development that all individuals go through regardless of social or cultural context, Vygotsky placed more importance on the *social aspect of learning*. Vygotsky believed that *social interaction* with others spurred the construction of new ideas and enhanced the learner's intellectual development.

A key idea stemming from Vygotsky's interest in the social aspect of learning was his concept of the **zone of proximal development.** According to Vygotsky, learners have two different levels of development: the level of actual development and the level of potential development. The *level of actual development* defines an individual's current intellectual functioning and the ability to learn particular things on one's own. Individuals also

Russian psychologist Lev Vygotsky emphasized the social aspect of learning.

have a *level of potential development*, which Vygotsky defined as the level an individual can function at or achieve with the assistance of other people, such as a teacher, parent, or more advanced peer. The zone between the learner's actual level of development and the level of potential development was labeled by Vygotsky as the *zone of proximal development*.

The importance to education of Vygotsky's ideas is clear. Learning occurs through social interaction with teachers and peers. With appropriate challenges and assistance from teachers or more capable peers, students are moved forward into their zone of proximal development where new learning occurs.

> The zone of proximal development is the label Vygotsky gave the zone between a learner's actual level of development and his or her level of potential development.

Bruner and Discovery Learning

The 1950s and 1960s saw significant curriculum reform in the United States that began in mathematics and the sciences but extended to history, the humanities, and the social sciences. Reformers strived to shift elementary and secondary curricula from a near-total focus on the transmission of established academic content to a focus on problem solving and inquiry. Pedagogy of the new curricula included activity-based and hands-on instruction in which students were expected to use their own direct experiences and observations to gain information and to solve scientific problems. Textbooks were often abandoned in favor of lab manuals. Teachers were encouraged to be facilitators and question askers rather than presenters and demonstrators of information.

Jerome Bruner, a Harvard psychologist, was one of the leaders in the curriculum reform of this era. He and his colleagues provided important theoretical support for what

> Discovery learning emphasizes active, student-centered learning experiences through which students discover their own ideas and derive their own meaning.

became known as **discovery learning,** a model of teaching that emphasized the importance of helping students understand the structure or key ideas of a discipline, the need for active student involvement in the learning process, and a belief that true learning comes through personal discovery. The goal of education was not only to increase the size of a student's knowledge base but also to create possibilities for student invention and discovery.

When discovery learning was applied in the sciences and social sciences, it emphasized the *inductive reasoning* and *inquiry processes* characteristic of the scientific method. Richard Suchman (1962) developed an approach he called **inquiry training.** When using Suchman's approach, teachers present students with puzzling situations or **discrepant events** that are intended to spark curiosity and motivate inquiry. An example of one of Suchman's inquiry lessons with a discrepant event is described here:

> The teacher holds up a pulse glass. The pulse glass consists of two small globes connected by a glass tube. It is partially filled with a red liquid. When the teacher holds one hand over the right bulb, the red liquid begins to bubble and move to the other side. If the teacher holds one hand over the left bulb, the red liquid continues to bubble but moves to the other side.
>
> The teacher asks students, "Why does the red liquid move?"
>
> As students seek answers to this question, the teacher encourages them to ask for data about the pulse glass and the moving liquid, to generate hypotheses or theories that help explain the red liquid's movement, and to think of ways they can test their hypotheses or theories.

Contemporary problem-based learning also relies on another concept from Bruner, his idea of **scaffolding.** Bruner described scaffolding as a process in which a learner is helped to master a particular problem beyond his or her developmental capacity through the assistance (scaffolding) of a teacher or more accomplished person. Note how similar Bruner's scaffolding concept is to Vygotsky's zone of proximal development concept.

The role of social dialogue in the learning process was also important to Bruner. He believed that social interactions within and outside the school accounted for much of a child's acquisition of language and problem-solving behaviors. The type of dialogue required, however, was not typically found in most classrooms. Many of the small-group strategies described in this text have grown out of the need to change the discourse structures in classrooms.

In sum, teachers using problem-based learning emphasize active student involvement, an inductive rather than a deductive orientation, and student discovery or construction of their own knowledge. Instead of giving students ideas or theories about the world, which is what teachers do when using direct instruction, teachers using inquiry or problem-based learning approaches pose questions to students and allow students to arrive at their own ideas and theories. This approach has proven to be effective, as demonstrated in this chapter's Research Summary (page 400).

Planning and Conducting Problem-Based Lessons

The problem-based learning model is quite straightforward. It is not difficult to grasp the basic ideas associated with the model. Effective execution of the model, however, is more difficult. It requires considerable practice and necessitates making specific decisions during its planning and execution. Some of the teaching principles are similar to

Check, Extend, Explore

Check
• What are the major intellectual roots of problem-based learning?
• How does the theoretical perspective of constructivism influence problem-based learning?
• What are the key ideas about problem-based learning that stem from the work of Vygotsky? Piaget? Bruner?
• What does the concept of *scaffolding* mean? How does it apply to problem-based learning?

Extend
• Some educators believe that too much emphasis is being given to constructivist principles of teaching and learning. Do you agree or disagree with this assertion? Go to the "Extend Question Poll" on the Online Learning Center to respond.

Explore
• Go to the Online Learning Center at www.mhhe.com/arends6e for links to websites related to *Information about the Theoretical and Empirical Support for Problem-Based Learning.*

those already described for presentation, direct instruction, and cooperative learning, but others are unique to problem-based instruction. In the discussion that follows, emphasis is given to the unique features of problem-based instruction.

Planning for PBL Lessons

At its most fundamental level, problem-based learning is characterized by students working in pairs or small groups to investigate ill-defined, real-life problems. Since this type of instruction is highly interactive, some believe that detailed planning is not necessary and perhaps not even possible. This simply is not true. Planning for problem-based learning, as with other interactive, student-centered approaches to teaching, requires as much, if not more, planning effort. It is the teacher's planning that facilitates smooth movement through the various phases of problem-based lessons and the accomplishment of desired instructional goals.

Because of its interactive nature, PBL requires as much, if not more, planning as compared to more teacher-centered models.

Decide on Goals and Objectives. Deciding on specific goals and objectives for a problem-based lesson is one of three important planning considerations. Previously, we described how problem-based learning was designed to help achieve such goals as enhancing intellectual and investigative skills, understanding adult roles, and helping students to become autonomous learners. Some problem-based learning lessons may be aimed at achieving all these goals simultaneously. It is more likely, however, that teachers will emphasize one or two goals in particular lessons. For instance, a teacher may design a problem-based lesson on environmental issues. However, instead of having students simulate adult roles or seek solutions to environmental problems, as was the case in the "Roots and Wings" lesson, the teacher may instead ask students to conduct an online search of the topic in order to develop this type of investigative skill. Regardless of whether a lesson is focused on a single objective or has a broad array of goals, it is important to decide on goals and objectives ahead of time so they can be communicated clearly to students.

Design Appropriate Problem Situations. Problem-based learning is based on the premise that puzzling and ill-defined problem situations will arouse students' curiosity and thus engage them in inquiry. Designing appropriate problem situations or planning ways to facilitate the planning process is a critical planning task for teachers. Some developers of problem-based instruction believe that students should have a big hand in defining the problem to be studied, because this process will foster ownership of the problem (Krajcik et al., 1994). Others, however, believe teachers should help students refine preselected problems that emanate from the school's curricula and for which the teacher has sufficient materials and equipment.

Some PBL teachers like to give students a strong hand in selecting the problem to be investigated.

A good problem situation must meet at least five important criteria. First, it should be *authentic.* This means that the problem should be anchored in students' real-world experiences rather than in the principles of particular academic disciplines. How to deal with pollution in the Chesapeake Bay is an example of a real-life problem. Learning about the effects of sunlight on nutrients and algae in warm water is an example of an academic (scientific) problem in biology. Second, the problem should be somewhat ill defined and pose a sense of mystery or puzzlement. Ill-defined problems resist simple answers and require alternative solutions, each of which has strengths and weaknesses. This, of course, provides the fodder for dialogue and debate. Third, the problem should be meaningful to students and appropriate for their level of intellectual development. Fourth, problems should be sufficiently broad to allow teachers to accomplish

Research Summary

What Do We Know about Problem-Based Learning from Combining the Results of Many Studies?

Albanese, M. A., and Mitchell, S. A. (1993).
Problem-based learning: A review of literature on its outcomes and implementation issues. *Academic Medicine, 68,* 52–81.

Bredderman, T. (1983).
Effects of activity-based elementary science on student outcomes: A quantitative synthesis. *Review of Educational Research,* 53, 499–518.

The research boxes in previous chapters have summarized the result of a single study. However, no single study on any topic or in any field provides definitive conclusions about the effects of a particular approach. The way to have confidence in conclusions is to combine the results of many studies. The process of combining results across several studies is called **meta-analysis.** Meta-analysis is a relatively new research methodology. Essentially, meta-analysis is a method of reviewing all experimental studies that have been performed over a period of time on a particular topic and then synthesizing the results of these studies. The mathematics of meta-analysis is beyond the scope of this discussion, but it involves computing what statisticians refer to as *effect size,* defined as a score that represents the strength of a treatment in an experiment or how much effect a particular approach has had. Researchers using meta-analysis examine the effect sizes from several experiments and, through this analysis, draw conclusions about particular teaching practices. Two important meta-analyses are described here to illustrate this type of research and to provide a partial picture about what kinds of instructional effects to expect from problem-based instruction.

Bredderman's Meta-Analysis

Several process- and activity-based curricula were developed during the 1960s. Three such curricula involved science instruction for elementary students: Elementary Science Study (ESS), Science—A Process Approach (SAPA), and the Science Curriculum Improvement Study (SCIS). All three of these curricula were process-oriented, meaning that the emphasis was on how to discover and construct knowledge rather than on understanding predetermined content. All three were activity-based, meaning students used their own direct experience, observation, and experimentation to gain information and to solve scientific problems. In the early 1980s, Ted Bredderman studied the effects of the elementary science projects listed here by using meta-analysis techniques.

Bredderman (1983) began his research by identifying fifty-seven studies conducted between 1967 and 1978 that compared the effects of the new process and activity-oriented curricula with the effects of more traditional (content-based) science curricula. Over nine hundred classrooms and thirteen thousand students participated in these studies. Most of the studies were conducted after teachers were given special training on the new curricula. Studies analyzed by Bredderman typically compared the trained teachers with teachers in the same school or neighboring schools where the new curricula were not being used and who had received no special training. Bredderman was able to identify nine outcome variables across the fifty-seven studies:

- Science content
- Scientific method
- Intelligence
- Creativity
- Perception
- Logical development
- Language development
- Mathematics

Bredderman's meta-analysis provided some interesting results. The use of process- and activity-oriented science programs increased student achievement in all the outcome variables except logical development. The largest effects were found in three areas: understanding of scientific methods, intelligence, and creativity. Finally, when the process- and activity-based programs were compared to traditional programs in regard to student acquisition of science content, Bredderman noted that the activity-based curriculum produced only modest increases but did not produce negative effects. This led Bredderman to conclude that "the accumulating evidence on the science curriculum reform efforts . . . consistently suggests that the more activity-process-based approaches to teaching science result in gains over traditional methods in a wide range of student outcomes" (p. 513).

Meta-Analysis of Studies in Medical Education

Since the early part of the twentieth century, medical education consisted of students spending a good portion of their early years in lecture-based instruction to learn the biological foundations of medicine. During the past twenty-five years, however, medical education has undergone some major changes. The focus of reform has been on the methods used to teach the basic sciences and the manner in which clinical education is provided. Several medical schools in the United States and Canada have experimented with problem-based instruction as an alternative to the more conventional methods. The approach to problem-based instruction in medical education is similar to the model employed in K–12 education. It involves confronting medical students with an ill-defined problem and asking them to find workable solutions. Problem solving occurs through self-study and discussion in small groups often led by a faculty facilitator. Particular problems are presented to students before formal instruction on foundational science concepts. Thus, students are required to seek and construct their own knowledge through self-study and small-group interaction. Many medical educators believe that problem-based instruction makes students take greater responsibility for their own learning and results in greater mastery of important foundational content.

In 1993, two medical researchers, Mark Albanese and Susan Mitchell, completed a meta-analysis of studies that compared the outcomes of problem-based instruction to outcomes of conventional practices. They sought studies that had investigated such outcomes as student acquisition of basic science information, clinical abilities, thought processes (thinking ability), and student and faculty satisfaction. The researchers identified slightly over one hundred studies that compared problem-based instruction in medical education with conventional methods between 1972 and 1992.

The Albanese and Mitchell meta-analysis produced some interesting findings about the effects of problem-based instruction. Medical students trained with problem-based instruction methods performed better on clinical examinations than students trained with conventional methods. They were better at problem formation and tended to engage in more productive reasoning processes. On the other hand, students trained with problem-based instruction methods scored lower on basic science examinations and viewed themselves as less prepared in the basic sciences compared to students receiving the more conventional, lecture-based instruction. This latter finding led Albanese and Mitchell to conclude that although medical students prepared with problem-based methods may be better thinkers and more clinically adept than students prepared with conventional methods, they may have deficits in basic science knowledge. They also concluded that perhaps the best approach to use in medical education is to have a balance between lecture-based, teacher-directed approaches and student-centered, problem-based approaches. Note the similarity between the conclusion reached by Albanese and Mitchell and the one expounded in this text—that is, different models of instruction are designed to accomplish different instructional goals. Good education proceeds when teachers have a rich repertoire of teaching models that can be used in a multifaceted instructional program.

their instructional goals yet sufficiently confined to make lessons feasible within time, space, and resource limitations. Finally, a good problem should benefit from group effort, not be hindered by it.

Most puzzling situations either explore the cause-and-effect relationships within a particular topic or pose "why" or "what if" questions. The number of puzzling situations in any field is endless. As you approach choosing a particular situation for a lesson, consider these points:

A good problem situation should be authentic, puzzling, open to collaboration, and meaningful to the students.

- Think about a situation involving a particular problem or topic that has been puzzling to you. The situation must pose a question or problem that requires explanation through cause-and-effect analyses and/or provides opportunities for students to hypothesize and speculate.
- Decide if a particular situation is naturally interesting to the particular group of students with whom you are working, and decide if it is appropriate for their stage of intellectual development.
- Consider whether or not you can present the problem situation in a fashion that is understandable to your particular group of students and that highlights the "puzzling" aspect of the problem.
- Consider whether working on the problem is feasible. Can students conduct fruitful investigations given the time and resources available to them?

Obviously, many problem situations can be defined and posed to students. Indeed, the list is almost limitless. Following are several examples that have been reported by teachers. Some of these are tightly focused and can be completed in rather short periods of time. Others are more complex and require a whole course of study to complete.

"Roots and Wings." Sometimes simulated problem situations are used rather than real-life problems. In "Roots and Wings," developers created an integrated problem-based approach to learning elementary science, social studies, reading, writing, and mathematics. Here are two examples of the types of problems posed to students in this program:

Sometimes simulated problem situations are more useful in the classroom than real-life problems.

- *World Lab.* Students assume the roles of various historical figures or contemporary occupational groups. They may be asked to solve the pollution problem in the Chesapeake Bay, to serve as advisors to the pharaohs of ancient Egypt, or to frame solutions to unfair taxes such as the American colonies did before the Declaration of Independence and the Revolutionary War.
- *Mathematics.* Mathematics for elementary students is moved from an abstract to a problem-solving focus. Students are asked to solve real-life math problems such as how to measure the depth of a pond or to estimate the time it would take for a ship to cross the Chesapeake Bay and are given many hands-on mathematics activities. The curriculum is also characterized by extensive use of calculators, computers, and math manipulatives.

"Learning Expeditions." Several school systems across the United States have been experimenting with a problem-based learning project called "Learning Expeditions" (see Rugen & Hart, 1994). Students involved in expeditionary learning are asked to inquire into stimulating problems and to find solutions through purposeful investigations and fieldwork. Some of the learning expeditions projects can be completed in three or four weeks; others last several months. Students are presented with ill-defined and open-ended themes or topics that cut across the traditional school subjects. Examples include such topics as urban renewal, pond life, or endangered species. From these more general topics, specific questions are posed. Examples of questions reported by teachers include the following:

- How can we tell when a community is thriving?
- What are the complex factors that influence pond life?
- How endangered are various species? How are endangered species affected by the complex interaction between humans and the environment?

As with other problem-based curricula, expeditionary learning strives to spark student interest by addressing authentic problem situations, helping students engage in field-oriented investigations, and helping them arrive at their own solutions.

Rogue Ecosystem Project. Teachers interested in environmental problems have been among the leaders in problem-based instruction. This is illustrated by the problem-based learning approach used by Hans Smith, a biology teacher at Crater High School in Central Point, Oregon.

Smith designed an interdisciplinary course in which students meet for two hours each day and receive credit for biology, government, and health. The course is centered around two environmental themes—*watersheds* and the *life cycle of the Pacific salmon* (Smith, 1995). As part of their unit on watersheds, students work on a particular project that requires them to develop a plan for a campground using their scientific knowledge about the Rogue River and the watershed area it serves. Their plan must offer a complete environmental impact study of campground construction and include interaction with the governmental agencies that approve campgrounds in the state of Oregon. Smith reported that these initial projects often prompt further inquiry and even more authentic studies such as:

> Teachers involved in environmental issues have been leaders in the use of problem-based instruction.

- Studying other rivers in the region by taking stream surveys, testing water, mapping habitats, and determining pool and riffle ratios.
- Designing and building a student-operated fish hatchery in which two thousand coho salmon are raised and released each year.

Smith's use of problem-based instruction asks students to take on very large and complex problems and involves them over a rather long period of time. Smith is an example of a creative teacher willing to give students opportunities to perform numerous out-of-school adult roles such as testing water, constructing buildings, raising fish, writing reports, interacting with government agencies, and giving presentations.

Today, the Internet is a valuable planning resource for teachers using problem-based learning. This is the topic of the Enhancing Teaching with Technology box for this chapter. The Online Learning Center also lists Web addresses for many problem-based learning sites.

Organize Resources and Plan Logistics. Problem-based learning encourages students to work with a variety of materials and tools, some of which are located in the classroom, others in the school library or computer lab, and still others outside the school. Getting resources organized and planning the logistics of student investigations are major planning tasks for PBL teachers.

In almost every instance, PBL teachers will be responsible for an adequate supply of materials and other resources for use by investigative teams. In some instances, these materials may be included in particular curriculum projects such as with the "Roots and Wings" projects. Many science classrooms contain needed supplies and equipment

Using the Web with Problem-Based Learning

Until very recently, teachers who used problem-based approaches to teaching were pretty much limited to local libraries and their local communities as sources where students could obtain information. All of this has changed dramatically over the past decade. Today, students can access information in libraries and communities all over the world through the Internet. Students involved in problem-based learning projects can use the Internet in a variety of ways, including accessing required information for PBL projects and participating with virtual problem-based learning websites. Students in a history class, for example, can visit historical sites such as Gettysburg or museums such as the Smithsonian Institution. Art students can take virtual tours of the Louvre or the East Wing of the National Gallery. Science students can tour and secure data from NASA and scientific institutes around the world.

Today, literally hundreds of websites exist that offer students virtual problem-based learning experiences or organized inquiry activities. For example, Adventure Learning Foundation provides curricula materials connected to online "Adventure Learning Expeditions." This website and its resources provide virtual cultural and travel experiences for many places in the world, such as Alaska and the Yukon; Baja California; Peru; and Oaxaca,

Mexico. As students proceed on their virtual journey, they can communicate and interact with other students from around the world who are also on the expedition. The website is packed with information, pictures, maps, and problem-based learning lesson plans for teachers. ThinkQuest is another website that helps students connect to exploration, problem-based experiences, and cultural connections including an e-pal exchange. There is a particular ThinkQuest website for individuals, such as you, who are preparing to be teachers. Addresses for these websites and several others are listed on the Online Learning Center.

Teachers need to consider three cautions when they have students use the Internet. First, although many older students can navigate the Internet quite effectively for their own personal pleasure, they may be very unsophisticated in conducting searches on academic or real-life topics. They need to be taught effective search strategies and provided lessons and assignments aimed at developing search skills.

Second, not everything found on the Internet is necessarily accurate. Information that appears in most scholarly journals and electronic databases, such as *ERIC*, is reviewed by peers, and its accuracy is checked before publication. Information that appears in mainline newspapers

to support student experiments and projects. Access in many schools to online and Internet databases and CD-ROMs also facilitates problem-based learning. When needed materials exist within the school, the primary planning task for teachers is to gather them and make them available to students. This normally requires working with school librarians and technology specialists. As described in Chapter 10, obtaining maximum assistance from librarians and technology specialists requires early notification by teachers about their plans. A series of meetings between the teacher and the specialists in which agreements are made about logistics, time lines, and rules for student conduct must be included in planning.

Projects that require out-of-school investigations or collaboration present special challenges for PBL teachers.

Sometimes students will need to do their investigative work outside the school. Students involved in the ecosystem project were encouraged to gather water samples, to present plans to local government units, and to release salmon. Some aspects of "Roots and Wings" involve interviewing local business and government leaders. Expecting students to work outside the confines of the school presents special problems for teachers and requires special planning. Teachers must plan in detail how students will be transported to desired locations and how students will be expected to behave while in nonschool settings. It also necessitates teaching students appropriate behavior for observing, interviewing, and perhaps taking photographs of people in the local community.

and magazines is reviewed by editors. Journalists are governed by a code of ethics that includes a commitment to report truthfully and accurately. However, anyone can create a website, and there are no editors or panels of peers to hold Web providers accountable. It is important that teachers point this out to their students and teach them how to evaluate the accuracy of the information they get from the Web.

Finally, there are many websites that promote hate, racism, pornography, and violence. Although there is always concern about first amendment rights, many parents do not want their children exposed to these kinds of websites. Most school districts today employ Internet-filtering software that blocks sites deemed inappropriate or unacceptable to the community. Blocked categories normally include adult content (nudity, sex, lingerie), drugs, gambling, extremist groups, and those that promote illegal activity. Many school districts also block shopping sites.

Bissell, Manring, and Roland (1999) and Bitter and Pierson (2002) offer the following advice on how to teach students to use the Internet and evaluate the information they find there:

- Choose an Internet topic or site that is likely to be motivational to your students—perhaps one that offers animations, graphic illustrations, real-time data, and simulations.

- Explore this site thoroughly for age-appropriate content before using it with students.
- Demonstrate how to access this site and discuss the kind of information found on the site.
- Assign students a topic that requires using this site as well as several others. The assignment should require collection of information and data.
- Have students report their findings and discuss which site had the most accurate and reliable information.

The World Wide Web is an excellent resource for PBL.

Conducting PBL Lessons

The five phases of problem-based learning and required teacher behaviors for each phase are summarized in Table 11.1. Desired teacher and student behaviors associated with each of these phases are described in more detail in the following sections.

Orient Students to the Problem. At the start of a problem-based learning lesson, just as with all types of lessons, teachers should communicate clearly the aims of the lesson, establish a positive attitude toward the lesson, and describe what students are expected to do. With students who are younger or who have not been involved in problem-based learning before, the teacher must also explain the model's processes and procedures in some detail. Points that need elaborating include the following:

Students need to understand that the purpose of PBL lessons is to learn how to investigate important problems and to become independent learners.

- The primary goals of the lesson are not to learn large amounts of new information but rather how to investigate important problems and how to become independent learners. For younger students, this concept might be explained as lessons in which they will be asked to figure things out on their own.
- The problem or question under investigation has no absolute "right" answer, and most complex problems have multiple and sometimes contradictory solutions.

Table 11.1 *Syntax for Problem-Based Learning*

Phase	Teacher Behavior
Phase 1: Orient students to the problem.	Teacher goes over the objectives of the lesson, describes important logistical requirements, and motivates students to engage in self-selected problem-solving activity.
Phase 2: Organize students for study.	Teacher helps students define and organize study tasks related to the problem.
Phase 3: Assist independent and group investigation.	Teacher encourages students to gather appropriate information, conduct experiments, and search for explanations and solutions.
Phase 4: Develop and present artifacts and exhibits.	Teacher assists students in planning and preparing appropriate artifacts such as reports, videos, and models, and helps them share their work with others.
Phase 5: Analyze and evaluate the problem-solving process.	Teacher helps students to reflect on their investigations and the processes they used.

- During the investigative phase of the lesson, students will be encouraged to ask questions and to seek information. The teacher will provide assistance, but students should strive to work independently or with peers.
- During the analysis and explanation phase of the lesson, students will be encouraged to express their ideas openly and freely. No idea will be ridiculed by the teacher or by classmates. All students will be given an opportunity to contribute to the investigations and to express their ideas.

One way to present problem situations for PBL is to use a discrepant event that creates a sense of mystery.

The teacher needs to present the problem situation with care or have clear procedures for involving students in problem identification. The guidelines provided in Chapter 8 on how to conduct a classroom demonstration can be helpful here. The teacher should convey the problem situation to students as interestingly and accurately as possible. Usually being able to see, feel, and touch something generates interest and motivates inquiry. Often the use of discrepant events (a situation in which the outcome is unexpected and surprising) can prick students' interest. For example, demonstrations in which water runs uphill or ice melts in very cold temperatures can create a sense of mystery and a desire to solve the problem. Short videotapes of interesting events or situations illustrating real-life problems such as pollution or urban blight are similarly motivational. The important point here is that the orientation to the problem situation sets the stage for the remaining investigation, so its presentation must capture student interest and produce curiosity and excitement.

Organize Students for Study. Problem-based learning requires teachers to develop collaboration skills among students and help them to investigate problems together. It also requires helping them plan their investigative and reporting tasks.

Study Teams. Many of the suggestions for organizing students into cooperative learning groups described in Chapter 10 pertain to organizing students into problem-based teams. Obviously, how student teams are formed will vary according to the goals teachers have for particular projects. Sometimes a teacher may decide that it is important for investigative teams to represent various ability levels and racial, ethnic, or gender diversity. If diversity is important, teachers will need to make team assignments. At other times, the teacher may decide to organize students according to mutual interests or to allow groups to form around existing friendship patterns. Investigative teams can thus form voluntarily. During this phase of the lesson, teachers should provide students with a strong rationale for the teams' organization.

> Investigative teams can be formed voluntarily around friendship patterns or according to some social or cognitive arrangements.

Cooperative Planning. After students have been oriented to the problem situation and have formed study teams, teachers and students must spend considerable time defining specific subtopics, investigative tasks, and time lines. For some projects, a primary planning task will be dividing the more general problem situation into appropriate subtopics and then helping students decide which of the subtopics they would like to investigate. For example, a problem-based lesson on the overall topic of weather might be divided into subtopics involving acid rain, hurricanes, clouds, and so forth. The challenge for teachers at this stage of the lesson is seeing that all students are actively involved in some investigation and that the sum of all the subtopic investigations will produce workable solutions to the general problem situation.

For projects that are large and complex, an important task during this phase of instruction is to help students link the investigative tasks and activities to time lines. The Gantt chart shown in Figure 11.2 provides an example of how one teacher helped her class plan for a problem-based learning project in history. As described in Chapter 2, Gantt charts allow students to plan particular tasks in relation to when each starts and ends. They are constructed by placing time across the top of the chart and then listing the tasks down the side. X's denote the specific time assigned to accomplish particular tasks.

Assist Independent and Group Investigation. Investigation, whether done independently, in pairs, or in small study teams, is the core of problem-based learning. Although every problem situation requires slightly different investigative techniques, most involve the processes of data gathering and experimentation, hypothesizing and explaining, and providing solutions.

> Most problem-based situations involve data gathering, experimentation, hypothesis development, and solution analysis.

Data Gathering and Experimentation. This aspect of the investigation is critical. It is in this step that the teacher encourages students to gather data and conduct mental or actual experiments until they fully understand the dimensions of the problem situation. The aim is for students to gather sufficient information to create and construct their own ideas. This phase of the lesson should be more than simply reading about the problem in books. Teachers should assist students in collecting information from a variety of sources, and they should pose questions to get students to think about the problem and about the kinds of information needed to arrive at defensible solutions. Students will need to be taught how to be active investigators and how to use methods appropriate for the problem they are studying: interviewing, observing, measuring, following leads, or taking notes. They will also need to be taught appropriate investigative etiquette.

> Teacher support for the free exchange of ideas and the full acceptance of ideas is imperative in the investigative phase of PBL.

Hypothesizing, Explaining, and Providing Solutions. After students have collected sufficient data and conducted experiments on the phenomena they are investigating,

This problem-based lesson has been designed to have students work in four teams for the purpose of investigating local history. The four investigative tasks are: interviewing elderly people about the community; collecting appropriate information from old newspapers in the state's historical society; studying gravestones in the local cemetery; and collecting and reading early histories written about the area.

Task	Time			
	March 10–15	March18–23	March 26–31	April 3–7
Orient students to problem situation.	xxx			
Organize study teams.	xxxxxxx			
Discuss with principal when students will be gone from school.	xx			
Gain permission from parents.	xxxxx			
Gain permission for visits from historical society.	xxx			
Have study teams plan their work.		xxxxxxxx		
Go over interviewing protocol.		xx		
Go over logistics for each type of visit.		xx		
Have teams do preliminary visit to make sure logistics are in place.		xx		
Have teams perform their investigative tasks.			xxxxxxxxx	
Have teams prepare required artifacts/exhibits.				xxxx
Share artifacts/exhibits with parents and others.				xxxx

Figure 11.2 *Gantt Chart: Eighth-Grade Local History Investigation*

they will want to start offering explanations in the form of hypotheses, explanations, and solutions. During this phase of the lesson, the teacher encourages all ideas and accepts them fully. As with the data-gathering and experimentation phases, teachers continue to pose questions that make students think about the adequacy of their hypotheses and solutions and about the quality of the information they have collected. Teachers should continue to support and model free interchange of ideas and encourage deeper probing of the problem if that is required. Questions at this stage might include, "What would you need to know in order for you to feel certain that your solution is the best?" or, "What could you do to test the feasibility of your solution?" or, "What other solutions can you propose?"

Throughout the investigative phase, teachers should provide needed assistance without being intrusive. For some projects and with some students, teachers will need to be close at hand helping students locate materials and reminding them of tasks they are to complete. For other projects and other students, teachers may want to stay out of the way and allow students to follow their own directions and initiatives.

Develop and Present Artifacts and Exhibits. The investigative phase is followed by the creation of artifacts and exhibits. **Artifacts** are more than written reports. They include such things as videotapes that show the problem situation and proposed solutions, models that comprise a physical representation of the problem situation or its solution, and computer programs and multimedia presentations. Obviously, the sophistication of particular artifacts is tied to the students' ages and abilities. A 10-year-old's poster display of acid rain will differ significantly from a high school student's design for an instrument to measure acid rain. A second-grader's diorama of cloud formations will differ from a middle school student's computerized weather program.

After artifacts are developed, teachers often organize exhibits to display students' work publicly. These exhibits should take their audiences—students, teachers, parents, and others—into account. **Exhibits** can be traditional science fairs, where each student displays his or her work for the observation and judgment of others, or verbal and/or visual presentations that exchange ideas and provide feedback. Websites also exist

PBL projects culminate in the creation and display of artifacts such as reports, posters, physical models, and videotapes.

that allow students to display the results of their work online and to enter into competition with other students if they so desire. The Online Learning Center provides addresses for these sites. The exhibition process is heightened in status if parents, students, and community members participate. It is also heightened if the exhibit demonstrates student mastery of particular topics or processes. Newsletters, such as those described in Chapter 10, offer another means to exhibit the results of students' work and to bring closure to problem-based projects.

Analyze and Evaluate the Problem-Solving Process. The final phase of problem-based learning involves activities aimed at helping students analyze and evaluate their own thinking processes as well as the investigative and intellectual skills they used. During this phase, teachers ask students to reconstruct their thinking and activity during the various phases of the lesson. When did they first start getting a clear understanding of the problem situation? When did they start feeling confidence in particular solutions? Why did they accept some explanations more readily than others? Why did they reject some explanations? Why did they adopt their final solutions? Did they change their thinking about the situation as the investigation progressed? What caused this change? What would they do differently next time?

Using Learning Centers for Problem-Based Learning*

Learning centers in elementary schools have long been a vehicle to facilitate problem-based learning and to enable younger students to work independently or in small groups on problem-based situations. Sometimes learning centers are called *learning stations, inquiry centers,* or *discovery centers.* Regardless of the label, these centers expose students to multiple experiences and hands-on activities and allow students to experience problem-based learning within the confines of the classroom environment. Learning centers are

*Thanks goes to Dr. Sharon Castle of George Mason University for her suggestion that the chapter on problem-based learning should include a discussion of learning centers and for providing materials she uses with her class to guide my discussion.

normally stocked with a variety of materials such as books, films, computer software, and audio and video recordings. These rich environments allow students of all ages and abilities to work at their own pace and often on topics of their own choosing.

According to Castle (2002), teachers can select content for learning centers in several ways. Some teachers organize centers around themes (such as fall); others around a content areas (math, literacy, science, social studies). Centers can also be organized around particular story or piece of literature, with separate stations to address literacy skills such as listening, reading comprehension, vocabulary, or writing. Other teachers organize their learning centers around Gardner's theory of multiple intelligences (described in Chapter 2). For a particular topic, teachers might have one center emphasizing the visual-spatial aspects of the topic, another focusing on the logical-mathematical, while still another might deal with the interpersonal. An example of a learning center organized around multiple intelligences can be seen on the video on the *Interactive Student CD-ROM*.

Teachers also vary in the ways they permit students to work in learning centers. Some teachers provide students with free choice. Most often, however, they provide guidelines and set conditions for students. Regardless of the exact guidelines, it is important that students make choices about their own learning and take some responsibility for managing their time and completing work on their own. Sometimes teachers organize centers to enable students to work together in small groups to develop cooperative problem-solving skills—each small group makes decisions cooperatively about how its members will work.

Successful learning centers require good organization, concise directions, and clear rules and expectations. The most common challenge for teachers in learning centers is helping students manage their time and involvement. Some students wander from center to center without focus; these students require extra guidance from the teacher. Other students rush through the work at a center without really paying much attention. Teachers need to be alert to these problems and check the work of these students work very carefully before allowing them to move on to a new learning center.

Learning centers allow students to work independently or in small groups.

Tailoring Problem-Based Lessons for All Students

Sometimes problem-based learning is viewed as a model more suited for students who are gifted and talented. This is not true. All students, regardless of their abilities, can benefit from PBL. In fact, less-talented students often do not have the skills to work independently, making it all the more important for teachers to use approaches that develop these skills. However, when using PBL with students who are learning disabled or who lack skills for working independently, teachers should strive to adapt lessons in a variety of ways:

- Provide more direct instruction on particular investigation skills such as locating information, drawing inferences from data, and analyzing rival hypotheses.
- Take more time to explain PBL lessons and expectations for student work.
- Provide more time for students at each phase of their inquiries.
- Establish more precise time lines for checking progress and holding students accountable for work.

Observing students with special needs develop inquiry and problem-solving skills and become autonomous learners can be among a teacher's most rewarding experiences.

Managing the Learning Environment

Many of the general management guidelines described in Chapter 5 apply to the management of problem-based learning. For instance, it is always important for teachers to have a clear set of rules and routines, to keep lessons moving smoothly without disruption, and to deal with misbehavior quickly and firmly. Similarly, the guidelines for how to manage group work provided in Chapter 10 on cooperative learning also apply to problem-based learning instruction. There are, however, unique management concerns for teachers using problem-based instruction, and these are described here.

Dealing with Multitask Situations

In classrooms where teachers are using problem-based learning, multiple learning tasks will be occurring simultaneously. Some student groups may be working on various subtopics in the classroom, while others may be in the library, and still others out in the community or online. Younger students may be using interest centers where students work in pairs and small groups on problems associated with science, math, language arts, and social studies before coming together to discuss their work with the whole class. To make a multitask classroom work, students must be taught to work both independently and together. Effective teachers develop cuing systems to alert students and to assist them with the transition from one type of learning task to another. Clear rules are necessary to tell students when they are expected to talk with one another and when they are expected to listen. Charts and time lines on the chalkboard should specify tasks and deadlines associated with various projects. Teachers should establish routines and instruct students how to begin and end project activities each day or period. They should also monitor the progress being made by each student or group of students during multitask situations, a skill that requires a high degree of with-itness, to use Kounin's term.

Check, Extend, Explore

Check
- What are the key planning tasks associated with problem-based learning instruction?
- What are the five phases of a PBL lesson? What kinds of teacher behaviors are associated with each phase?
- Why is orienting students to problem-based learning lessons more complicated than doing so with some other models of teaching?
- How do artifacts and exhibits differ from more traditional term papers or reports?

Extend
- Some educators argue that problem-based learning is too time consuming and that it is unrealistic to expect students to investigate issues and problems on their own. Do you agree or disagree with this assertion? Go to the "Extend Question Poll" on the Online Learning Center to respond.

Explore
- Go to the Online Learning Center at www.mhhe.com/arends6e for links to websites related to *Planning and Conducting Problem-Based Learning Lessons.*

Adjusting to Differing Finishing Rates

Special management problems of PBL include adjusting to different finishing rates, monitoring student work, managing materials and equipment, and regulating movement outside the classroom.

One of the most complex management problems faced by teachers using problem-based learning is what to do with individuals or groups who finish early or lag behind. Rules, procedures, and downtime activities are needed for students who finish early and have time on their hands. These include high-interest activities such as making available special reading materials or educational games that students can complete on their own or (for older students) procedures for moving to special laboratories to work on other projects. Effective teachers also establish the expectation that those who finish early will assist others.

Late finishers present a different set of problems. In some instances, teachers may give lagging students more time. Of course, this action results in the early finishers having even more downtime. Teachers may alternately decide to get late finishers to put in extra time after school or on the weekend. However, this action is often problematic. If students are working in teams, it could be difficult for them to get together outside school. Furthermore, students who are falling behind often are those who do not work well alone and who need a teacher's assistance to complete important tasks and assignments.

Monitoring and Managing Student Work

Unlike some other types of instruction in which all students complete the same assignment on the same date, problem-based learning generates multiple assignments, multiple artifacts, and often varying completion dates. Consequently, monitoring and managing student work is crucial when using this teaching model. Three important management tasks are critical if student accountability is to be maintained and if teachers are to keep a degree of momentum in the overall instructional process: (1) work requirements for all students must be clearly delineated, (2) student work must be monitored and feedback provided on work in progress, and (3) records must be maintained.

Many teachers manage all three of these tasks through the use of *student project forms*. Maintained on each individual, the student project form (Figure 11.3) is a written record of the work the individual or small group has agreed to complete, agreed-upon time lines for completion, and an ongoing summary of progress.

Managing Materials and Equipment

Teachers can modify lessons to adapt to the needs of disabled students.

Almost all teaching situations require some use of materials and equipment, and managing these is often troublesome for teachers. A problem-based situation, however, places greater demands on this aspect of classroom management than other teaching models because it requires the use of a rich array of materials and investigative tools. Effective teachers must develop procedures for organizing, storing, and distributing equipment and materials. Many teachers get students to help them with this process. Students can be expected to keep equipment and supplies organized in a science classroom and to distribute books and collect papers in other classrooms. Getting this aspect of management under firm control is very important because without clear procedures and routines, teachers can be overwhelmed with problem-based lesson details.

Regulating Movement and Behavior Outside the Classroom

When teachers encourage students to conduct investigations outside the classroom in such places as the library or the computer lab, they need to make sure that students un-

```
┌─────────────────────────────────────────────────────────────┐
│  Student's Name  _____ │
│  Study Team's Name_____ │
│  Project Name and Scope:  _____ │
│  _____│
│  _____│
│  _____│
│  _____│
│                                                               │
│  Particular Assignments and Deadlines                         │
│  Project 1 _____│
│  Feedback on 1  _____│
│  Project 2 _____│
│  Feedback on 2  _____│
│  Project 3 _____│
│  Feedback on 3  _____│
│  Project 4 _____│
│  Feedback on 4  _____│
│  Final artifact or exhibit_____│
│  _____│
└─────────────────────────────────────────────────────────────┘
```

Figure 11.3 *Student Project Form*

derstand schoolwide procedures for movement and use of these facilities. If hall passes are required, teachers must ensure that students use them appropriately. If movement in halls is regulated, students must understand the rules associated with this movement. Similarly, teachers must establish rules and routines to govern student behavior when they are conducting their investigations in the community. For example, students should be taught the etiquette of interviewing and the need to obtain permission before looking at certain records or taking certain kinds of pictures. Rules and regulations regarding the use of the Internet for problem-based learning were described earlier in this chapter's Enhancing Teaching with Technology box.

Assessment and Evaluation

Most of the general assessment and evaluation guidelines provided in earlier chapters also pertain to problem-based instruction. Assessment procedures must always be tailored to the instructional goals the model is intended to achieve, and it is always important for teachers to gather reliable and valid assessment information. As with cooperative learning in which the instructional intents are *not* the acquisition of declarative knowledge, assessment tasks for problem-based lessons cannot consist solely of paper-and-pencil tests. The performance assessment and evaluation procedures described in Chapter 6 are the most appropriate ones to use with problem-based instruction. The work products created by students lend themselves nicely to performance assessment using scoring rubrics such as those described in Chapter 6 or checklists and rating scales described here. Further, performance assessment can be used to measure students' problem-solving potential as well as group work.

The trend has been away from paper-and-pencil testing and toward performance assessments, which allow students to show what they can do when confronted with real problem situations.

Assessing Understanding

Problem-based learning goes beyond development of factual knowledge about a topic and aims instead at the development of rather sophisticated understandings of problems and the world that surround students. Figure 11.4 provides an example of testing for understanding rather than knowledge.

Using Checklists and Rating Scales

Finding valid and reliable measurement techniques is a challenge faced by teachers who use PBL.

Finding valid and reliable measurement techniques is one of the problems faced by teachers who want to use authentic assessment procedures. Some have turned to such fields as sports and the performing arts in which systems have been developed to measure complex performance tasks. Criterion-referenced checklists and rating scales are two devices that are often used in these fields. For example, individuals who judge diving or ice skating competitions use rating scales that compare individual performances to agreed-upon standards. Rating scales are similarly used to evaluate musical or dance performances.

Robert Rothman (1995) provided an example of a rating scale used by the teachers at Mark Twain Elementary School in Littleton, Colorado, to evaluate student work. Teachers there have developed a series of units that require students to address such real-world questions as, "How are chimpanzees and people alike?" "How are wooden baseball bats made?" "How do parrots learn to talk?" After completing their investigations, students write a report (artifact) about their topic using a computer; develop a visual representation (exhibit) of their topic; and deliver oral presentations to students, the principal, and a parent or community representative. The oral presentation is judged using the rating scale illustrated in Figure 11.5.

Assessing Adult Roles and Situations

Problem-based learning, as you read at the beginning of this chapter, strives to engage students in situations that help them to learn about adult roles and to perform some of the tasks associated with these roles. Adult situations that might be learned and how they might be assessed are presented in Figure 11.6. Most of these situations can be assessed using the performance assessment tests, checklists, and rating scales described in the previous sections.

Assessing Learning Potential

Student presentations provide one source for assessment.

Most tests, whether paper-and-pencil or performance-oriented, are designed to measure knowledge and skills at specific points in time. They do not necessarily assess learning potential or readiness to learn. Vygotsky's idea about the zone of proximal development, described earlier, has prompted measurement experts and teachers to consider how a student's learning potential might be measured, particularly potential that could be enhanced with the guidance of a teacher or more advanced peer. Readiness (learning potential) tests exist for reading and other language development areas. Assessment devices that present students with problem-solving tasks that diagnose their ability to benefit from particular kinds of instruction also exist. Assessment tasks that measure learning potential in most areas, however, are still in their infancy stage with much work yet to be done.

You are a prosecutor or a defense attorney in a trial brought by a parent group seeking to forbid purchase by your high school of a U.S. history textbook, excerpted below. (The book would be used as a *required supplement* to your current text, not in place of it.) You will present a 10-minute oral case, in pairs, to a jury, taking either side of the question, Is the book appropriate for school adoption and required reading? (supported by a written summary of your argument). You will be assessed on how well you support your claim about the accounts in the text, in response to the question, "are the accounts biased, inaccurate, or merely different from our usual viewpoint?"

On the American Revolution

As a result of the ceaseless struggle of the colonial people for their political rights, the 13 colonies practiced bourgeois representative government by setting up their own local legislatures. As electoral rights were restricted in many ways in every colony, those elected to the colonial legislatures were mostly landlords, gentry, and agents of the bourgeoisie, without any representation whatsoever from the working people. These struggles reflected the contradictions between the colonies and their suzerain state. . . .

The British administration of the colonies was completely in the interests of the bourgeoisie in Britain. . . . The British colonial rule impeded development of the national economy in North America. It forced certain businesses into bankruptcy. As a consequence, contradictions became increasingly acute between the ruling clique in Britain and the rising bourgeoisie and broad masses of the people in the colonies. . . .

Heretofore [prior to the Boston Massacre], the struggle of the colonial people had been scattered and regional. In the course of the struggle, however, they summed up their experience and came to feel it necessary to stand together for united action. Thus in November 1772, a town meeting held in Boston adopted a proposal made by Samuel Adams to create a Committee of Correspondence to exchange information with other areas, act in unison, and propagate revolutionary ideas. . . . In less than 2 months, a Committee of Correspondence was formed by more than 80 cities and towns in Massachusetts, and later became the organs of revolutionary power. . . .

The Declaration of Independence was a declaration of the bourgeois revolution. The political principles enunciated in it were aimed at protecting the system of capitalist exploitation, legitimizing the interests of the bourgeoisie. In practice, the "people" referred to in the Declaration only meant the bourgeoisie, and the "right of the pursuit of happiness" was deduced from the "right of property" and intended to stamp the mark of legitimacy on the system of bourgeois exploitation. The Declaration was signed by 56 persons, of whom 28 were bourgeois lawyers, 13 were big merchants, 8 were plantation owners and 7 were members of the free professions, but there was not one representative of the working people.

During the time of the war, America began its westward expansion on a large scale. From the first, the colonies had been founded on the corpses of the Indians. . . . In 1779 George Washington sent John Sullivan with a force of soldiers to "annihilate" the Iroquois tribe settled in northern New York.

During the war patriotic women also played a big role. While men went to the front, they took over the tasks of production. They tilled fields and wove cloth, and sent food, garments, and other articles to the front. When Washington was in a precarious situation retreating into Pennsylvania with his army, the women of Philadelphia raised a huge fund to procure winter clothes for the revolutionary army.

After the outbreak of the war, America not only failed to organize the enslaved Negroes but guarded them even more closely, thus intensifying their oppression. This seriously impeded their participation in the war and was one reason why the war for Independence was slow in achieving victory. . . .

Questions to Consider in Your Research and Presentation

1. What can be said to be the most likely political influences on the authors' point of view? What evidence is there of those influences? How do they affect the authors' choice of language?
2. Why does it make sense, given the authors' perspective, that they pay particular attention to (a) the Committee of Correspondence, (b) the contribution of women, and (c) the plight of "Indians" and "Negroes"? Are the facts accurate? Do they warrant that much attention in your view?
3. You will be judged on the accuracy, aptness, and convincing qualities of your documentation, and the rhetorical effectiveness of *your* case. Be fair, but be an effective speaker and writer!

Figure 11.4 *Example of Assessment Aimed at Understanding*

Source: Wiggins (1993), pp. 212–213

1. Student clearly describes the question and gives reasons for its importance.	Student states question but does not describe it or give reasons for its importance.	Student does not state question.
2. Evidence of preparation and organization strong.	Some evidence of prepara-tion and organization present.	No evidence of preparation or organization.
3. Delivery engaging.	Delivery somewhat engaging.	Delivery flat.
4. Sentence structure is correct.	Sentence structure is some-what correct.	Sentence structure has many errors.
5. Visual aid used to en-hance presentation.	Visual aid referred to separately.	Visual aid is not mentioned.
6. Questions from audi-ence answered clearly and with specific information.	Questions from audience somewhat answered.	Questions from audience not answered.

Figure 11.5 *Sample Rating Scale for Oral Presentations*

Source: After Rothman (1995), pp. 12–13

Student presentations are fun and also provide a rich source for assessment.

Assessing Group Effort

Chapter 10 on cooperative learning described assessment procedures used to assess and reward students for both individual and group work. These procedures can also be used for problem-based instruction. Assessing group effort reduces the harmful competition that often results from comparing students with their peers and makes school-based learning and assessment more like that found in real-life situations.

- *Attorney:* Show debate skills by playing characters in historical reenactments—Scopes trial; *Brown* v. *Board of Education.*
- *Ad agency worker:* Design advertising campaign; make book jackets.
- *Sociologist:* Design and conduct community survey; graph results.
- *Engineer:* Survey and map neighborhood.
- *Essayists:* Present conclusions in writing; write persuasive essay.
- *Historian:* Conduct oral history; critique textbooks for children.
- *Teacher:* Teach topic to a younger child.
- *Parent:* Get a young child to study.
- *Job applicant:* Prepare a portfolio, résumé.
- *Citizen:* Lead a group to closure; thoroughly rethink an issue; develop and effectively implement a plan; rate candidates; negotiate a dilemma; judge the adequacy of an emotional appeal; question the obvious.

Figure 11.6 *Professional Roles and Situations That Can Be Assessed*
Source: After Wiggins (1997)

Check, Extend, Explore

Check
- What are the key features of the learning environment for problem-based learning?
- What are the unique management concerns for teachers using problem-based learning?
- What factors should teachers consider when they think about how to assess student learning in problem-based learning?

Extend
- Do you think problem-based learning will be embraced or discarded by your generation of teachers? Go to the "Extend Question Poll" on the Online Learning Center to respond.

Explore
- Go to the Online Learning Center at www.mhhe.com/arends6e for links to websites related to *Problem-Based Learning Environments and Assessment.*

Problem-Based Learning: A Final Thought

The current interest in problem-based learning is quite extensive. The model is based on solid theoretical principles, and a modest research base supports its use. In addition, there appears to be considerable teacher and student enthusiasm for the model. It provides an attractive alternative for teachers who wish to move beyond more teacher-centered approaches to challenge students with the active-learning aspect of the model. PBL also utilizes powerful Internet resources that make its use more practical than in pre-Internet times.

There is considerable teacher and student enthusiasm for PBL.

However, problem-based learning still has some obstacles to overcome if its use is to become widespread. The organizational structures currently found in most schools are not conducive to problem-based approaches. For instance, many schools lack sufficient library and technology resources to support the investigative aspect of the model. The standard forty- or fifty-minute class period typical of most secondary schools does not allow time for students to become deeply involved in out-of-school activities. Additionally, since the model does not lend itself to coverage of a great deal of information or foundational knowledge, some administrators and teachers do not encourage its use. Drawbacks such as these cause some critics to predict that problem-based learning will fare no better than Dewey's and Kilpatrick's *project method* or the *hands-on, process-oriented* curricula of the 1960s and 1970s. That is for your generation of teachers to decide.

Reflections from the Classroom

Disappointment

You have just finished grading the history projects you assigned to your students. You sigh. Their work is very, very disappointing. Projects (research papers, video productions, portfolios, computer simulations) were supposed to be the result of a six-week, problem-based unit on local history in which students researched a variety of local historic problems, linked these to current problems, and produced interesting and engaging artifacts and exhibits. Yet, the products you have just graded are not very good. Most students prepared reports of the more traditional term paper variety. These are not carefully done; they lack depth of analysis, and they are filled with grammatical and punctuation errors. Artifacts and exhibits appear to have been done in haste. Almost all of them lack creativity.

As a beginning teacher, this is your first attempt at using problem-based learning instruction. You are puzzled about why students didn't do better, and you start thinking about what has gone wrong. You ask yourself, "Did I provide sufficient directions to students about what they were supposed to do?" "Did I help them enough as they did their inquiries?" "Did I provide sufficient motivation?" Reflect on your answers to these questions before you compare your thoughts to the following comments from experienced teachers. Approach this situation from the perspective closest to the grade level or subject area you are preparing to teach. Prepare your reflections as an exhibit in your professional portfolio.

Lynn Ciotti

Snyder-Girotti Elementary School, 6th Grade
Bristol Borough, PA

When assigning major projects to my 6th grade students I often ask myself, "Were the directions given clearly? Do the students know what is expected of them? Are the students excited and motivated to do their best work?" My main goal when assigning a major project is to give explicit details and examples so students know what is expected of them.

The first step I would take to ensure understanding is to administer detailed directions to each student with all pertinent information required to complete the project successfully. The second step would be to provide sample projects for students to review during class time. Examples of projects completed from previous year students would be beneficial so they have a concrete idea of what is expected of them.

The third step, and the most important step, would be to distribute a rubric on how the project will be evaluated. The rubric is a critical tool to show students what is expected on an assignment or project. If it is used correctly, it can be used as a checklist enabling students to verify whether they included all elements needed for a successful project. The rubric can also be used as a guideline to help students determine the grade they may receive for their project. The rubric must include ranges in effort for each domain required in the project. It is then up to the student to determine their level of effort.

If I found that projects were still done poorly after implementing these steps, I would re-teach and re-direct students in the appropriate areas. I would conference with students on an individual basis using the rubric provided to inform students of their areas of weakness. I would allow ample time for students to reflect and improve their projects making necessary corrections. Projects would then be re-evaluated and given a final grade.

Jennifer Patterson

Murdock Middle School, 8th Grade
Charlotte County, FL

When I am disappointed in the quality of work submitted by my students, I engage in the practice of self-reflection. I ask myself and reflect on the following questions: Did I set realistic expectations for my students and were they appropriate for their grade level? Were the objectives and desired outcomes clearly stated? Did I provide a clear and concise explanation and did I check to ensure that all students understood the task? Was there adequate time in and out of class for students to complete the activity? Did the assessment criteria correlate to the expectations and outcomes? In short, I ask myself whether I gave my students enough preparation and guidance, and whether I, as a teacher, was sufficiently prepared to ensure that students could complete the activity successfully.

I also encourage my students to reflect back on the project. I would ask them to discuss any problems or difficulties they encountered, and to offer suggestions that would have made the project more stimulating and meaningful. Student feedback is often as valuable as self-reflection. If necessary, I would then attempt to create an equitable solution, such as modifying the expectations and grading criteria accordingly. Another alternative is to allow students additional time to edit their work and resubmit.

There are many things a teacher can do to prevent this situation from occurring. Preparation is essential to making any student project successful. Check to make sure you fully understand the process and structure of the pedagogical strategy you employ. If you do not fully understand the nature of the strategy, do not expect your students to comprehend it either. Also, thoroughly review your expectations, objectives, and desired outcomes to make sure they are at the appropriate age and difficulty level.

Next, get your students involved and engaged in the project from the beginning. Try to pique their curiosity and interest, and make the task relevant and meaningful. Students

respond best to activities and projects that are student-centered, so try to include them in setting goals and even the criteria for assessment. This gives students a stake in their learning and this ownership will serve to motivate them. Another way to motivate students is to show them examples of work from previous students—both exemplary and poor—which will provide students with a better understanding of what is expected of them. Many times, this practice will give them the impetus to outdo former students' work.

Also, all aspects or phases of a project must be addressed. For example, if students need to use primary sources, you must make sure they understand primary sources. If the assignment requires reports to be written in a specific format, you should model this format and provide examples.

Finally, if a project is lengthy or complex, it is important for the teacher to monitor students' progress. This can be accomplished by requiring a series of due dates or "check" points for different components of the project. Above all, teachers should provide guidance and direction, while simultaneously enabling students to become self-directed learners.

Chapter Review

Go back to the "Interactive and Applied Learning" feature at the beginning of the chapter for a listing of interactive and applied activities. Go to the Online Learning Center at **www.mhhe.com/arends6e** or your Interactive Student CD-ROM to take practice quizzes over the content of this chapter and receive immediate feedback. You can also review chapter content and main ideas, practice with key terms, and find annotated Web links on topics associated with Chapter 11.

Summary

Overview of Problem-Based Learning

- Unlike other models in which the emphasis is on presenting ideas and demonstrating skills, in problem-based learning, teachers present problem situations to students and get them to investigate and find solutions on their own.
- The instructional goals of problem-based learning are threefold: to help students develop investigative and problem-solving skills, to provide students experiences with adult roles, and to allow students to gain confidence

in their own ability to think and become self-regulated learners.
- The general flow or syntax of a problem-based lesson consists of five major phases: orient students to the problem; organize students for study; assist with independent and group investigations; develop and present artifacts and exhibits; and analyze and evaluate work.
- The learning environment of problem-based learning is characterized by openness, active student involvement, and an atmosphere of intellectual freedom.

Theoretical and Empirical Support

- Problem-based learning has its intellectual roots in the Socratic method dating back to the early Greeks but has been expanded by ideas stemming from twentieth-century cognitive psychology.
- The knowledge base on problem-based learning is rich and complex. Several meta-analyses done in the last few years provide a clear picture of the model's instructional effects.
- Over the past three decades, considerable attention has been devoted to teaching approaches known by various names—discovery learning, inquiry training, higher-level thinking—all of which focus on helping students become independent, autonomous learners capable of figuring things out for themselves.

Planning and Conducting Problem-Based Lessons

- Major planning tasks associated with problem-based learning consist of communicating goals clearly, designing interesting and appropriate problem situations, and logistical preparation.
- During the investigative phase of problem-based lessons, teachers serve as facilitators and guides of student investigations.

Managing the Learning Environment

- Particular management tasks associated with problem-based learning include dealing with a multitask learning environment; adjusting to different finishing rates; finding ways to monitor student work; and managing an array of materials, supplies, and out-of-class logistics.

Assessment and Evaluation

- Assessment and evaluation tasks appropriate for problem-based learning necessitate finding alternative assessment procedures to measure such student work as performances and exhibits. These procedures go by the names of performance assessment, authentic assessment, and portfolios.

Problem-Based Learning: A Final Thought

- Teachers who use problem-based learning face many obstacles. Will the current interest in PBL continue or will the use of the model be discontinued over time.

Key Terms

artifacts 408
cognitive-constructivist perspective 396
cognitive psychology 395

constructivism 396
discovery learning 398
discrepant events 398
exhibits 409

higher-order thinking 392
inquiry training 398
meta-analysis 400
scaffolding 398

self-regulated learners 395
zone of proximal development 397

Portfolio and Field Experience Activities

This feature has been designed to help you learn from your field experiences and to assist you in the preparation of artifacts for your professional portfolio on topics and standards associated with Chapter 11.

1. Complete the "Reflections from the Classroom" exercise at the end of this chapter and use the recommended reflective essay as an exhibit of your views about how to motivate students and get quality work from them when they are involved with problem-based lessons.

2. Use Activity 11.1 in the *Guide to Field Experiences and Portfolio Development* to assess your understanding and skill for planning and conducting problem-based lessons. Summarize the results as an exhibit in your professional portfolio.

3. Use Activities 11.3 and 11.4 in the *Guide to Field Experiences and Portfolio Development* to observe and interview teachers who practice problem-based learning. Summarize your observation and/or interview and place it in your professional portfolio.

4. Complete Activity 11.5 in the *Guide to Field Experiences and Portfolio Development* to design and illustrate problem situations. Use the products of your work as an exhibit in your portfolio.

5. Use the "Case Exercise" on the Interactive Student CD-ROM to create your own problem-based lesson or practice tasks required of problem-based teaching. Place the product(s) of your work in your professional portfolio.

Books for the Professional

Go to the Online Learning Center at www.mhhe.com/arends6e or your Interactive Student CD-ROM for an annotated version of this list.

Brooks, J. G., and Brooks, M. G. (1993). *In Search of Understanding: The Case for Constructivist Classrooms.* Alexandria, VA: Association for Supervision and Curriculum Development.

Duckworth, E. (1987). *The Having of Wonderful Ideas and Other Essays on Teaching and Learning.* New York: Teachers College Press.

Fogarty, R. (1997). *Problem-Based Learning and Other Curriculum Models for the Multiple Intelligences Classroom.* Arlington Heights, IL: Skylight Professional Development.

Krajcik, J., Czerniak, C. M., and Berger, C. F. (1998). *Teaching Children Science: A Project-Based Approach.* New York: McGraw-Hill.

Lampert, M. (2001) *Teaching Problems and the Problems of Teaching.* New Haven, CT: Yale University Press.

Stepien, W. J., Senn, P. R., and Stepien, W. C. (2001). *The Internet and Problem-Based Learning: Developing Solutions Through the Web.* Tucson, AZ: Zephyr Press.

Chapter Twelve

Classroom Discussion

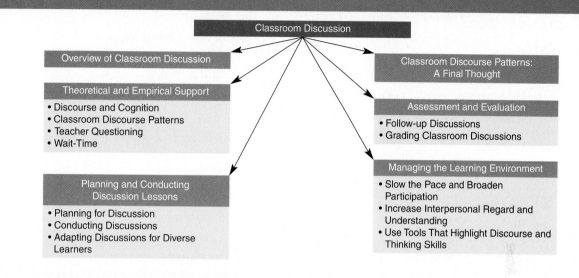

```
                          ┌─────────────────────────┐
                          │   Classroom Discussion   │
                          └─────────────────────────┘
```

Overview of Classroom Discussion

**Classroom Discourse Patterns:
A Final Thought**

Theoretical and Empirical Support
- Discourse and Cognition
- Classroom Discourse Patterns
- Teacher Questioning
- Wait-Time

Assessment and Evaluation
- Follow-up Discussions
- Grading Classroom Discussions

**Planning and Conducting
Discussion Lessons**
- Planning for Discussion
- Conducting Discussions
- Adapting Discussions for Diverse
  Learners

Managing the Learning Environment
- Slow the Pace and Broaden
  Participation
- Increase Interpersonal Regard and
  Understanding
- Use Tools That Highlight Discourse and
  Thinking Skills

Interactive **and** *Applied Learning*

Go to Your Interactive Student CD-ROM to:

- Hear audio clips of Vickie Williams (kindergarten through eighth grade reading specialist) and Ian Call (tenth grade world history) talk about the discussion model of instruction in the *Teachers on Teaching* feature
- Watch the video clip: *Classroom Discussion*
- Complete the Classroom Discussion Case Exercise in the Chapter 12 *Case Exercises and Practice Tasks* area.
- Complete the Classroom Discussion Practice Tasks in the Chapter 12 *Case Exercises and Practice Tasks* area. Write objectives for a discussion lesson; plan for demonstration and guided practice; differentiate guided practice for two students; check for understanding and provide feedback; plan for extended practice; assess student learning; and reflect on planning for discussion.

Go to the Online Learning Center at www.mhhe.com/arends6e to read *PowerWeb* articles and newsfeed updates about:

- Classroom management
- Cultural diversity in education
- Instruction
- Learning
- Technology and education
- Testing and evaluation
- World Wide Web

Considering **Standards**

Studying this chapter will help you meet three INTASC principles:

Primary

INTASC 4: Understands and uses a variety of instructional strategies to encourage student development of critical thinking, problem-solving, and performance skills.

INTASC 6: Uses knowledge of verbal and nonverbal communication to foster inquiry, collaboration, and supportive classroom interaction.

Secondary

INTASC 8: Understands and uses formal and informal assessment strategies to evaluate and ensure the continuous intellectual, social, and physical development of the learner.

Reflecting **on** *Discussion*

Surely you have had teachers during your student career who made extensive use of discussion methods. Perhaps one was the type of teacher who came to class every day and presented you with provocative questions to talk about. Perhaps another started every class with a discussion about the previous night's homework.

Consider the discussions you have participated in as a student:

- Did you participate widely in classroom discussions? Or were you a student who didn't participate much? If you didn't participate, do you know why?

- Did you think your level of participation made any difference in how much you learned? Why? Why not?

- Of the discussions you remember, which ones stand out in your mind? Which were most effective? Least effective?

- What features did the effective discussions have in common?

- What features did the ineffective discussions have in common?

- What do you think students learn during discussions? What don't they learn?

What do your answers to these questions have to say about you and your views on classroom discussion? What do they say about how you might use discussion once you have your own classroom? Will you be a teacher who uses discussions often? Or will you tend to stay away from discussions and use other approaches instead?

Go to the Online Learning Center at www.mhhe.com/arends6e to respond to these questions.

Previous chapters described specific teaching models, and you saw that at some point in most lessons, regardless of the model, dialogue or discussion was required. For instance, recitation, one type of teacher-student discourse, comes toward the end of presentation and direct instruction lessons as teachers strive to check for understanding and help students extend their thinking about particular information or concepts. Discussion occurs mainly in small groups during cooperative learning lessons, while inquiry lessons and problem-based learning demand constant dialogue to accomplish the instructional goals of the model.

This chapter focuses on *classroom discussion.* Discussion, you will find, is not exactly like the teaching models presented in previous chapters. Instead, it is a particular teaching procedure or strategy that can be used by itself or across a number of models. We will, however, use the same categories and labels to describe discussion as those used to describe previous teaching models.

This chapter begins with an overview of classroom discussion, presents its theoretical and empirical support, and examines the specific procedures involved in planning, conducting, adapting and evaluating classroom discussions. The final section highlights the importance of teaching students how to become effective participants in the classroom discourse system and describes how teachers can change some of the unproductive communication patterns that characterize many classrooms today.

> Discussion is not a full-blown teaching model; rather, it is a teaching procedure that is a crucial part of almost all teaching.

Overview of Classroom Discussion

Classroom discussion and discourse are central to all aspects of teaching. Effective use of classroom discussion requires an understanding of several important topics pertaining to classroom discourse and discussion. The dictionary definitions of *discourse* and *discussion* are almost identical: to engage in a verbal interchange and to express thoughts on particular subjects. Teachers are more likely to use the term **discussion,** since it describes the *procedures* they use to encourage verbal interchange among students. Scholars and researchers are more likely to use the term **discourse,** since it reflects their interest in the *larger patterns* of exchange and communication found in classrooms. The term *discourse* is used to provide the overall perspective about classroom communication described in the section on theoretical support. The term *discussion* is used when specific teaching procedures are described.

Sometimes discussions are confused with *recitations.* As described in more detail later, discussions are situations in which teachers and students or students and other students talk with one another and share ideas and opinions. Questions employed to stimulate discussion are usually at a higher cognitive level. **Recitations,** on the other hand, are those exchanges, such as in a direct instruction lesson, in which teachers ask students a series of lower-level or factual questions aimed at checking how well they understand a particular idea or concept.

> Recitations are question-and-answer exchanges in which teachers check how well students recall factual information or understand a concept.

Discussions are used by teachers to achieve at least three important instructional objectives, as shown in Figure 12.1. First, discussion improves students' thinking and helps them construct their own understanding of academic content. As described in previous chapters, telling students about something does not necessarily ensure their comprehension. Discussing a topic helps students strengthen and extend their knowledge of the topic and increase their ability to think about it.

Second, discussion promotes student involvement and engagement. Research, as well as the wisdom of experienced teachers, demonstrates that for true learning to take place, students must take responsibility for their own learning and not depend solely

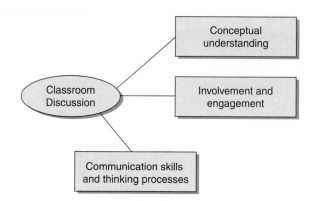

Figure 12.1 *Learner Outcomes for Discussion*

Check, Extend, Explore

Check

• What are the five phases of a classroom discussion?
• What are the major learner outcomes for classroom discussions?
• What type of learning environment works best for classroom discussions?

Extend

• Do you agree or disagree with the assertion that teachers can have effective discussions regardless of the nature of the learning environment? Go to the "Extend Question Poll" on the Online Learning Center to respond.

Explore

• Go to the Online Learning Center at www.mhhe.com/arends6e for links to websites related to *Classroom Discussion.*

on a teacher. Using discussion is one means of doing this. It gives students public opportunities to talk about and play with their own ideas and provides motivation to engage in discourse beyond the classroom.

Third, discussion is used by teachers to help students learn important communication skills and thinking processes. Because discussions are public, they provide a means for a teacher to find out what students are thinking and how they are processing the ideas and information being taught. Discussions thus provide social settings in which teachers can help students analyze their thinking processes and learn important communication skills such as stating ideas clearly, listening to others, responding to others in appropriate ways, and asking good questions.

Most discussions follow a similar pattern, but variations do exist, depending on the teacher's goals for particular lessons and the nature of the students involved. Three variations will be described later in the chapter, but essentially, all three share the same five-phase syntax: explaining the aims of the lesson, focusing and holding the discussion, bringing the discussion to a conclusion, and debriefing the discussion.

The learning environment and management system surrounding discussion are incredibly important. The environment for conducting discussions is characterized by open processes and active student roles. It also demands careful attention to the use of physical space. The teacher may provide varying degrees of structure and focus for a particular discussion, depending on the nature of the class and the learning objectives. However, in many ways, the students themselves control the specific, minute-to-minute interactions. This approach to teaching requires a large degree of student self-management and control, a topic that is explored more fully later in this chapter.

Theoretical and Empirical Support

Much of the theoretical support for the use of discussion stems from the fields in which scholars study language, communicative processes, and patterns of exchange. These studies extend to virtually every setting in which human beings come together. To consider the role of language, think for a moment about the many everyday situations in which success depends largely on the use of language and communication. Friendships, for instance, are initiated and maintained mainly through language—friends talk and share experiences with one another. Families maintain their unique histories by building patterns of discourse, sometimes even in the form of secret codes, that are nat-

Discussion provides an opportunity for students to monitor their own thinking and for teachers to correct faulty reasoning.

ural to family members but are strange to outsiders, such as new in-laws. Youth culture develops special patterns of communication that provide member identity and group cohesion. The secret codes used by gangs are an example of communication used to maintain group identity. It is difficult to imagine a cocktail party, a dinner party, a church social, or any other social event existing for very long if people could not verbally express their ideas and listen to the ideas of others. The popularity of radio talk shows and computer networking adds additional evidence to how central interaction through the medium of language is to human beings.

Language and communication are central to every aspect of human life, including life in classrooms.

Discourse through language is also central to what goes on in classrooms. Courtney Cazden (1986), one of America's foremost scholars on the topic of classroom discourse, wrote that "spoken language is the medium by which much teaching takes place and in which students demonstrate to teachers much of what they have learned" (p. 432). Spoken language provides the means for students to talk about what they already know and to form meaning from new knowledge as it is acquired. Spoken language affects the thought processes of students and provides them with their identity as learners and as members of the classroom group.

Discourse and Cognition

A strong relationship exists between language and thinking, and both lead to the ability to analyze, to reason deductively and inductively, and to make sound inferences based on knowledge.

Discourse and Thinking. Discourse is one way for students to practice their thinking processes and to enhance their thinking skills. Mary Budd Rowe (1986) summarized this important point nicely.

> To "grow," a complex thought system requires a great deal of shared experience and conversation. It is in talking about what we have done and observed, and in arguing about what we make of our experiences, that ideas multiply, become refined, and finally produce new questions and further explorations (p. 43).

In some ways, discourse can be thought of as the *externalization of thinking*—that is, exposing one's invisible thoughts for others to see. Through discussions, then, teachers are given a window for viewing the thinking skills of their students and a setting for providing correction and feedback when they observe faulty, incomplete reasoning. Thinking out loud also provides students opportunities to "hear" their own thinking and to learn how to monitor their own thinking processes. Remember, learners don't acquire knowledge simply by recording new information on a blank slate; instead, they actively build knowledge structures over a period of time as they interpret new knowledge and integrate it into prior knowledge.

Social Aspect of Discourse. One aspect of classroom discourse, then, is its ability to promote cognitive growth. Another aspect is its ability to connect and unite the cognitive and the social aspects of learning. Indeed, the classroom discourse system is central to creating positive learning environments. It helps define participation patterns and, consequently, has a great deal of impact on classroom management. The talk of teachers and students provides much of the social glue that holds classroom life together.

The cognitive-social connection is most clear in the way social participation affects thinking and cognitive growth. Lauren Resnick and Leopold Klopfer (1989) observed, for instance, that the:

> social setting provides occasions for modeling effective thinking strategies. Skilled thinkers (often the instructor, but sometimes more advanced fellow students) can demonstrate desirable ways of attacking problems, analyzing texts, or constructing argument. . . . But most important of all, the social setting may let students know that all the elements of critical thought—interpretation, questioning, trying possibilities, demanding rational justification—are *socially valued* (pp. 8–9).

Much of the work of Vygotsky and contemporary educators who hold cognitive-constructivist perspectives emphasizes the importance of social interaction in all aspects of human learning. It is through this interaction that students learn how to think and solve problems (see Hicks, 1996; Palincsar, 1986).

Classroom Discourse Patterns

Working from a variety of perspectives, researchers who study classrooms have found a discourse pattern that has remained consistent over a rather long period of time. They have also found that the traditional pattern is not necessarily the best for promoting full student participation and higher-level thinking.

We are all familiar with the basic pattern, labeled the *initiation-response-evaluation* (IRE) model by Cazden (1986, 1996) and Burbules and Bruce (2001). This exchange takes place in a whole-class setting and consists of three phases:

- Initiation: Teacher asks a question over the lesson.
- Response: Students raise their hands and reply.
- Evaluation: Teacher evaluates the response with praise or corrects the response. Teachers often answer the question themselves with a short lecture.

As you will see later, the pace of this pattern is rapid—the teacher talks most of the time and only a few students participate.

Larry Cuban (1984, 1993) documented how this pattern emerged early in the history of formal schooling and how it has persisted to the present day at all levels of schooling and across all academic subjects. Ned Flanders documented teacher dominance of

In addition to promoting cognitive growth, discussion can also be used to further a positive social environment in the classroom.

Studies have repeatedly shown that teacher talk routinely constitutes about two-thirds to three-fourths of classroom discourse.

classroom communication in the late 1960s with numerous studies on teacher-student interaction. Flanders (1970) concluded that in most classrooms, two-thirds of the talk was by teachers. John Goodlad (1984), in his extensive study of schools years later, made essentially the same observation, as did Burbules and Bruce (2001).

The pattern is still very much with us today. In the 1990s, Richard and Patricia Schmuck visited and collected information on rural schools in the United States. They studied twenty-five school districts in twenty-one states. They interviewed 212 teenagers and observed lessons in over thirty high school classrooms. In twenty-two out of the thirty classrooms, they reported seeing mainly recitation lessons. The Schmucks (1994) reported teachers talking three-fourths of the time and commented this was more than the two-thirds teacher talk Flanders observed three decades ago. Only twice did the Schmucks observe students talking in pairs, and only four times did they observe small-group interaction and exchange.

Despite its potentially harmful effects and an endless effort to modify the IRE model of discourse, recent research (Burbules, 1993; Nystrand et. al., 1997) has confirmed that most schooling continues to be based on this "transmission and recitation model of communication" (Nystrand et. al., 1997, p. xiv).

Teacher Questioning

Recitation teaching relies on teachers talking and asking questions. The ways teachers ask questions and the types of questions they ask have been the focus of considerable inquiry and concern for quite some time. Mark Gall (1970), who has on several occasions reviewed the research on questioning, highlighted how frequently questions are asked in classrooms and, like Cuban (1993), illustrated how a persistent pattern has existed over time— mainly that teachers spend a large portion of school time talking and asking questions.

Because questions are asked so often in classrooms, an obvious concern is what effects they have on student learning. In particular, what is the effect of factual and higher-order questions on student learning and thinking? For many years, the conventional wisdom held that higher-order questions lead to greater cognitive growth than that resulting from more concrete, factual questions. However, reviews of research in the early 1970s reported that no clear evidence existed one way or the other (Dunkin & Biddle, 1974; Rosenshine, 1971). By 1976, Barak Rosenshine was prepared to challenge the conventional wisdom when he concluded that "narrow" (factual) questions actually seemed to be the most useful, particularly when teachers provided immediate feedback about the correct and incorrect answers. A few years later, Redfield and Rousseau (1981) challenged the conclusion about the use of factual questions, and reported that asking higher-level and thought-provoking questions had positive effects on student achievement and thinking.

Studies have resulted in conflicting conclusions regarding the benefits of higher-order questioning over fact-based question-and-answer sessions.

During the past decade, researchers have continued to study the controversy over the effects of question types on student achievement and thinking. A consensus appears to be emerging that the type of questions teachers ask should depend on the students with whom they are working and the type of educational objectives they are trying to achieve. Gall (1984; Gall & Gall, 1990), for example, interpreted this research in the following way:

Whether teachers should ask more higher-order or lower-order questions depends on their instructional objectives and on the students being taught.

- Emphasis on fact questions is more effective for promoting young children's achievement, which involves primarily mastery of basic skills.
- Emphasis on higher cognitive questions is more effective for students when more independent thinking is required.

Traditional teacher questioning patterns may lead students to boredom and passivity.

In addition to the types of questions teachers ask, researchers have also been interested in the questions' level of difficulty and in teachers' overall pattern of questioning. **Level of difficulty** refers to students' ability to answer questions correctly regardless of cognitive level. Research on this topic has also produced mixed results. However, after a thorough review of the research, Jere Brophy and Tom Good (1986) concluded that teachers should consider three guidelines when deciding how difficult to make their questions:

- A large proportion (perhaps as high as three-fourths) of a teacher's questions should be at a level that will elicit correct answers from students in the class.
- The other one-fourth of the questions should be at a level of difficulty that will elicit some response from students, even if the response is incomplete.
- No question should be so difficult that students will not be able to respond at all.

The overall pattern of questioning is also important. All too often, the unspoken classroom discussion rules are that the teacher should ask all the questions, students should respond with right answers, and the teacher should repeat the questions if the answers are wrong. Later, you will find that this kind of discussion pattern does not promote higher-level thinking or much real engagement.

Wait-Time

Wait-time is the pause between the teacher's question and the student's response and between the student's response and the teacher's reaction.

A final, important line of research in relation to classroom discussion and discourse focuses on the pace of interchange and a variable known as *wait-time.* **Wait-time** is the pause between a teacher's question and the student's response and between the response and the teacher's subsequent reaction or follow-up question. This variable was first observed in the 1960s, when considerable effort was underway to improve curricula in almost all academic subjects. These new curricula, particularly in the sciences and the social sciences, were developed to help students learn how to inquire and discover relationships among social and/or natural phenomena. The recommended method for virtually all curricula was inquiry or discovery-oriented discussions. However, researchers found that these types of discussions were not occurring. The now classic study by Rowe on this important topic is highlighted in the Research Summary in this chapter (page 432) for two reasons. Her investigations highlighted an important problem with classroom discourse and offered a cure. They also illustrated how research in education sometimes moves from observation of teacher behavior in regular classrooms to experimentation and the testing of new practices.

Planning and Conducting Discussion Lessons

As with the teaching models described in the preceding chapters, effective discussions require that teachers perform planning, interactive, management, adaptive, and assessment tasks. Planning and interactive tasks are described in this section, followed by a discussion of management and assessment tasks.

Planning for Discussion

Two common misconceptions held by many teachers are that planning for a discussion requires less effort than planning for other kinds of teaching and that discussions cannot really be planned at all because they rely on spontaneous and unpredictable interactions among students. Both of these ideas are wrong. Planning for a discussion necessitates every bit as much effort, perhaps more, as planning for other types of lessons, and even though spontaneity and flexibility are important in discussions, it is a teacher's planning beforehand that makes these features possible.

Consider Purpose. Deciding that discussion is appropriate for a given lesson is the first planning step. Preparing the lesson and making decisions about what type of discussion to hold and specific strategies to employ are next. As described earlier, although discussions can stand alone as a teaching strategy, they are more frequently used in connection with other teaching models. Although the particular uses of discussion are practically infinite, teachers generally want their discussion to accomplish one of the three objectives: to check for student understanding of reading assignments or presentations through recitations, to teach thinking skills, or to share experiences.

Consider Students. Knowing about students' prior knowledge is just as important in planning a discussion as it is in planning other kinds of lessons. Experienced teachers know that they must also take into consideration their students' communication and discussion skills. They consider, for instance, how particular students in the class will respond differently to various kinds of questions or foci; they predict how some will want to talk all the time whereas others will be reluctant to say anything. When planning discussions, it is important to devise ways to encourage participation by as many students as possible, not just the bright ones, and to be prepared with questions and ideas that will spark the interest of a diverse student group. More is said about this aspect of discussion later.

Choose an Approach. There are several different kinds of discussions, and the approach chosen should reflect a teacher's purposes and the nature of the students involved. Three approaches are discussed here.

Recitations. Although recitation is often overused, it nonetheless has its place. One important use is when teachers ask students to listen to or read about information on a particular topic. A reading assignment in history may vary in length from a paragraph to a whole book. A teacher's talk on ecosystems may be as long as a full-hour lecture or as short as five or ten minutes. Either can cover a variety of topics. Teachers generally ask students to read or listen with a definite purpose in mind. Sometimes it is to glean important information about a topic, whereas at other times it is to become familiar with a particular author, a specific type of literature, or a point of view or particular interpretation. Brief question-and-answer sessions (recitation discussions) about assigned reading materials or a lecture can provide teachers with a means of checking student understanding. They also motivate students to complete their reading assignments or to listen carefully when the teacher is talking.

Inquiry or Problem-Based Discussion. Discussions are sometimes used to engage students in higher-order thinking and, thereby, to encourage their own intellectual investigation. Normally, such discussion is part of some type of problem-based teaching.

Check, Extend, Explore

Check
- What relationships exist among language, discourse, and thinking abilities?
- Why is the cognitive-social connection important to the understanding of classroom discussions?
- How does the use of different kinds of questions impact different types of student thinking?
- Why is the concept of wait-time important to classroom dialogue?

Extend
- What might you do as a teacher to ensure an appropriate pace in your classroom discussions?
- How do you explain the persistence of the IRE pattern of classroom discourse?

Explore
- Go to the Online Learning Center at www.mhhe.com/arends6e for links to websites related to *Theory and Research on Classroom Discussion.*

Brief question-and-answer or recitation sessions covering assigned materials are useful in checking student understanding.

Research Summary

When Can Slowing Down Increase Learning?

Rowe, M. B. (1974b).
Wait-time and rewards as instructional variables, their influence on language, logic, and fate control. Part one: Wait-time. *Journal of Research in Science Teaching,* 11, 81–94.
Could it be that the absence of talk (pauses by the teacher) does more to influence discourse and complex thinking processes than its presence? That's what Mary Budd Rowe found in a series of interesting and important studies.

Problem and Approach: In Chapter 8, process-product research was introduced to show how researchers examine existing practices in a natural setting to discover relationships between teacher behavior and student learning. Other chapters, on the other hand, described how some knowledge has resulted from experiments and comparing the effects of innovative teaching practices. Sometimes a researcher may employ both observation in natural settings and experimentation with new practices. The classic study by Rowe and her colleagues on the discourse patterns of teachers is a good example of research that moved from observation of teachers in regular classrooms to experimentation with a new procedure.

Sample and Setting: This study actually progressed through two stages: (1) systematic observation of teachers in natural settings, and (2) planned experiments in which the researchers attempted to change the natural behavior of teachers.

Natural Observations: Discussion patterns were initially analyzed from 103 tapes made by teachers using a new science curriculum. By the end of the first stage of their inquiry, they had obtained over three hundred tapes from rural, suburban, and urban areas and from a variety of grade levels. Analysis of these lessons showed that the pace of instruction in most classrooms was very fast. In all but three classrooms, out of the hundreds studied, teachers displayed the following pattern:

- Teacher asked a question. Student must respond within at least one second.
- If student did not respond in one second, teacher repeated, rephrased, asked a different question, or called on another student.
- When a student did respond, the teacher reacted or asked another question within an average of 0.9 seconds.

The investigators concluded that instruction in virtually all classrooms was very fast and without sufficient wait-time. They also concluded that in a few classrooms where they did find students engaged in inquiry, sustained conversation, speculation, and argument about ideas, the average wait-time hovered around three seconds. With this information, the researchers planned and conducted a series of controlled studies (1) to see if teachers could be taught to slow down the pace of their discussions by using wait-time, and (2) if the slower pace had an impact on discourse and cognitive processes.

Procedures for the Microstudies: Ninety-six teachers from two locations were recruited and trained to employ wait-times of at least three seconds. From a pool of lessons prepared by the researchers, teachers were asked to teach six lessons to students who were assigned to four-member learning groups. Each lesson was recorded on audiotape. Tapes were transcribed and coded. The wait-time variables were measured using the following criteria:

- **Wait-time 1:** The time between when the teacher stops speaking and when either a student responds or the teacher speaks again
- **Wait-time 2:** The time between when a student stops speaking and when the teacher speaks

Pointers for Reading Research: The results of this study are descriptive and rather straight-forward. However, Rowe's study is interesting in that it was conducted in stages. This illustrates how good research often moves from casual observations of phenomena in a natural setting to more systematic observation, and only then to intervention and manipulation of important variables in controlled settings for the purpose of seeing if things can be changed for the better.

Results: Teacher behavior changed as a result of training to use longer wait-times. Table 12.1 shows the number of questions asked and the typical distribution of question types by teachers before and after wait-time training.

Notice the sharp drop in the number of questions asked by teachers after wait-time training. Also note that the number of informational questions declined while the number of probing and thought-provoking questions increased rather dramatically.

The researchers hypothesized that if teachers could slow down their pace, this behavior would impact on the way their students responded. Table 12.1 displays the results of Rowe's wait-time studies on student outcome variables.

Table 12.2 shows these results when teachers started to use longer wait-times:

- The length of student responses increased from eight words per response under the fast pace used by teachers to twenty-seven words. This signifies considerably longer statements by students after teachers are trained to use wait-time.
- The number of unsolicited but appropriate responses increased from a mean of five to a mean of seventeen.
- Failures to respond ("I don't know" or silence) decreased. In classrooms prior to training, the "no re-

sponse" occurred as high as 30 percent of the time. This changed dramatically once teachers started to wait at least three seconds for students to think.

- When wait-time was lengthened, students provided more "evidence-type" statements to support the inferences they were making. They also asked more questions.

Discussion and Implications What is striking about this study is (1) teachers, left to their natural inclinations, pace instruction too fast to allow much careful inquiry or serious dialogue, and (2) a rather simple intervention can bring rather striking changes in discourse patterns. Learning to wait results in fewer and different types of questions by teachers and, most important, different student responses. Students in classrooms in which teachers use wait-time engage in inquiry-oriented and speculative thinking.

Table 12.1 *Number of Questions and Typical Distribution of Question Types Before and After Wait-Time Training*

	Before Training	After Training
Mean number of questions per 15 minutes of transcript	38	8
Typical questions (%)		
Rhetorical	3	2
Informational	82	34
Leading	13	36
Probing	2	28

Table 12.2 *Student Outcome Variables: Contrasts Between Tape 1 and Tape 6 of the Training Sequence for 76 of 95 Teachers Who Achieved Criterion Wait-Times of 3 Seconds or Longer*

Student Variable	Tape 1	Tape 2
Length of response		
Mean	8	27
Range	(3–12 words)	(14–39 words)
Number of unsolicited but appropriate responses		
Mean	5	17
Range	(0–17)	(12–28)
Number of failures to respond		
Mean	7	1
Range	(1–15)	(0–3)
Number of evidence-inference statements		
Mean	6	14
Range	(0–11)	(6–21)

Problem-based lessons centered around a discrepant event encourage discussion and help students become aware of their own reasoning processes.

Although a number of specific approaches have been developed, they all have a common syntax in which the teacher opens the lesson by presenting students with what Suchman (1962) labeled a *discrepant event* or what Palincsar and Brown (1989) called *mystery spots*. Both refer to puzzling situations that are not immediately explainable, such as water appearing to run uphill, metal changing shape when heated, and social data that confront conventional wisdom. Because these situations are puzzling to students and create cognitive dissonance, they provide a natural motivation to think. When using this approach, teachers encourage students to ask questions, to generate empirical data, and to formulate theories and hypotheses to explain the puzzling situation. In this type of discussion, teachers help students become conscious of their own reasoning processes and teach them to monitor and evaluate their own learning strategies.

Sharing-Based Discussion. Often teachers hold discussions for the purpose of helping students develop shared meaning from common experiences or to confront one another with differences of opinions. Younger children may be asked to talk about what they learned from their visit to the zoo or the apple farm. Older students may be asked to talk about what they learned from a science experiment they performed or from a novel they read. Important current events such as a breakthrough in an arms treaty, new abortion legislation, or a natural disaster are often discussed in the classroom so that different points of view may be explored. Unlike recitations, during which teachers ask students *to recall* specific information, or problem-based discussions, in which teachers get students *to reason,* sharing-based discussions help students *to form and express thoughts and opinions independently.* Through dialogue about shared experiences and what these experiences mean, ideas are refined or expanded and questions are raised for future study.

Make a Plan. A lesson plan for a discussion consists of a set of objectives and a content outline. The plan should include not only the targeted content but also a well-conceived focus statement, the description of a puzzling event, and/or a list of questions. If the discussion is to follow a lecture, it is likely that the teacher already has the content firmly in mind and has explored the important conceptual relationships. When the discussion follows assigned readings, experienced teachers know that they must have extensive notes not only about specific facts but, more important, about the main ideas, points of view, and key relationships highlighted in the reading.

Sometimes teachers find using the *conceptual web* technique a useful planning device. As described in Chapter 9, a web provides a visual image of the characteristics and relationships around a central idea. Remember, to make a conceptual web, you identify the key ideas associated with a particular topic and arrange them in some logical pattern.

Advance preparation and identification of questioning patterns can greatly improve the flow of a classroom discussion.

Teachers will find that careful attention to preparation will help immensely as they strive to keep details straight for students and as they facilitate student understanding and higher-order thinking. For some types of discussions, asking students questions becomes a key feature. In preparing their questioning strategy, teachers need to consider both the cognitive level of questions and their level of difficulty.

During the past three decades, many systems have been developed for classifying the cognitive level of teacher questions. Most of the classification systems are similar—all consider questions in terms of the cognitive processing they require of students. Teachers can also use Bloom's *Revised Taxonomy of Educational Objectives,* described in Chapter 3, to design questions for classroom discussions. Table 12.3 shows six cognitive categories according to Bloom's classification system and provides examples of classroom questions.

Table 12.3 *Question Types According to Bloom's Revised Taxonomy*

Cognition Process	Examples of Questions	Type of Cognition Required to Answer
Remember	In which region of the United States is Ohio? What does H_2O stand for?	Retrieving factual knowledge
Understand	What is the difference between longitude and latitude? What is the book *The Old Man and the Sea* about?	Constructing meaning
Apply	If John has 12 feet of lumber, how many 2-foot-long boards can he make? In which of the situations would Newton's second law apply?	Applying or using principles or procedures
Analyze	Why do some trees lose their leaves in winter? How does Hemingway's view of war reflect the political ideology of his time?	Explaining relationships or overall purposes
Evaluate	Which novel do you think is the best piece of literature? What do you think about the city's recycling program?	Making judgments based on criteria and standards
Create	If the North had not won the Civil War, what would life be like in the United States today? What if John Brown had succeeded at Harpers Ferry?	Generating hypotheses

Notice that questions in the "remember" and "understand" categories require students to recall information (facts, events, principles) that they have learned and to explain what it means. "Apply" and "analyze" questions require more of students and ask them to focus on the "why" of some situation and/or to apply particular kinds of knowledge. These questions are sometimes called **convergent questions** because they ask students to focus on a single, best answer or conclusion and to explain known relationships. "Evaluate" and "create" questions, on the other hand, require students to make judgments based on criteria or answer "what if" questions. These are called **divergent questions**. Divergent questions allow multiple answers, conclusions, and creativity on the part of students.

There are also questions that should be avoided in a discussion. Sandra Metts (2002) (www.cat@ilstu.edu) offered four types of questions that teachers should not ask:

- *The Dead-end Question:* A question requiring only a "yes/no" response. This question goes nowhere (e.g., "Can animals communicate?").
- *The Chameleon Question:* A question that begins in one direction and then switches to a different direction (e.g., "If language requires both symbols and rules, can animals have language? That is, if a chimpanzee can be taught to make a sign for banana, does it have language?").
- *The Fuzzy Question:* A question that is unclear or confusing (e.g., "What do you think about animals communicating?").
- *The Put-down Question:* A question that is largely rhetorical, minimizes the legitimacy of a comment, and/or closes down additional discussion (e.g., "Can we all see why Mary's solution is not feasible?").

As described earlier, the research about the effects of using various types of questions is still unclear. However, beginning teachers should keep in mind one important truth—that is, different questions require different types of thinking and a good lesson should include both lower- and higher-level questions. One way to achieve this is to start by asking questions that require recall of factual or conceptual information to see if students have grasped the basic ideas under consideration. Follow with application and analysis questions ("why" questions) and then conclude with more thought-provoking evaluation and creating ("what-if") questions.

In preparing the lesson plan and questioning strategies, remember to think through the issues associated with question difficulty. Experience helps teachers to know their students and to devise questions of appropriate difficulty. Decisions about question type and difficulty can be better made during the quiet of advanced planning than during the discussion itself.

Use Physical Space Appropriately. Another planning task involves making arrangements for appropriate use of physical space. Earlier chapters explained how different seating patterns affect communication patterns within the classroom. The best seating arrangements for discussion are the U-shape and the circle formations illustrated in Figures 12.2 and 12.3. Both seating patterns allow students to see each other, an important condition for verbal interaction. Both can be accommodated in most classrooms. Each, however, has some advantages and disadvantages that should be considered.

The **U-shaped seating pattern,** with the teacher situated in front at the open end of the U, gives a bit more authority to the teacher, an important feature when working with groups of students who lack discussion skills or where behavior management is a problem. The U-shape also allows freedom of movement for teachers. They have ready access to the chalkboard or flip charts, which may be important during the course of a discussion, and they can move into the U to make closer contact with particular students when necessary. The disadvantage of the U is that it establishes some emo-

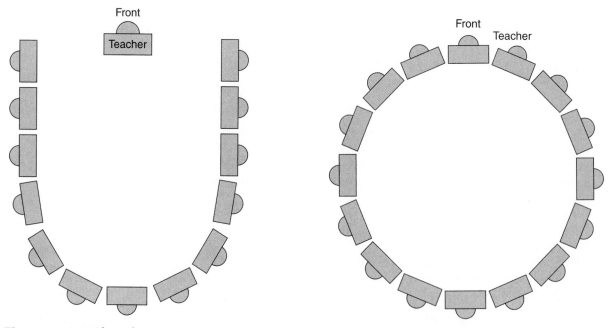

Figure 12.2 *U-Shaped Seating Arrangement*   **Figure 12.3** *Circle Seating Arrangement*

tional distance between the teacher, as discussion leader, and students. It also puts considerable physical distance between students who are sitting at the head of the U and those sitting at the end.

The **circle seating pattern,** on the other hand, minimizes both emotional and physical distance among participants and maximizes opportunities for students to talk freely with one another. The disadvantage of the circle is that it inhibits the teacher from moving freely to the chalkboard or among students.

Many elementary and secondary schools today have furniture and other features that make movement from one seating arrangement to another possible. In some instances, however, teachers will be confronted with situations that severely limit this possibility. For example, some science laboratories and shop classes have fixed tables that make moving furniture impossible. Some drama and English classes may be held in the school's theater with fixed seating. These conditions require special problem solving on the part of teachers. Some experienced science teachers have students stand in a U-shape during discussion sessions; drama teachers and some elementary teachers have their students sit on the floor. The specifics of the classroom space and the teacher's own personal preferences certainly are strong considerations when making planning decisions about use of the space prior to a discussion.

> The best seating arrangement for a discussion is either a U-shape or a circle.

Conducting Discussions

For whole-class discussions to be successful, some rather sophisticated communication and interaction skills are needed on the part of both teachers and students. It also requires norms that support open exchange and mutual respect. The syntax for most discussions consists of five phases: establishing set, focusing the discussion, holding the discussion, bringing it to a close, and debriefing. These five phases are summarized in Table 12.4. As discussion leader, a teacher also is responsible for keeping the discussion

> As discussion leader, a teacher should focus the discussion, keep it on track, encourage participation, and keep a visible record of it.

Table 12.4 *Syntax for Holding Discussion*

Phase	Teacher Behavior
Phase 1: Clarify aims and establish set.	Teacher goes over the aims for the discussion and gets students ready to participate.
Phase 2: Focus the discussion.	Teacher provides a focus for discussion by describing ground rules, asking an initial question, presenting a puzzling situation, or describing a discussion issue.
Phase 3: Hold the discussion.	Teacher monitors students' interactions, asks questions, listens to ideas, responds to ideas, enforces the ground rules, keeps records of the discussion, and expresses own ideas.
Phase 4: End the discussion.	Teacher helps bring the discussion to a close by summarizing or expressing the meaning the discussion has had for him or her.
Phase 5: Debrief the discussion.	Teacher asks students to examine their discussion and thinking processes.

PEANUTS reprinted by permission of United Feature Syndicate, Inc.

on track by refocusing student digressions, encouraging participation, and helping to keep a record of the discussions. All of these behaviors are described in some detail in the following sections.

Establish Set and Focus the Discussion. Many classroom discussions are characterized by talk and more talk, much of which has little to do with either the main aims of the lesson or with encouraging student thinking. An effective discussion, just like an effective demonstration, is clearly focused and to the point. At the beginning, teachers must explain the purposes of the discussion and get students set to participate. They should also pose a specific question, raise an appropriate issue, or present a puzzling situation associated with the topic. These activities have to be in a form students can understand and respond to. Stating the focus question or issue clearly is one key to getting a good discussion started. Another way to establish set and spark student interest is to relate the beginning discussion question or focus to students' prior knowledge or experiences. Notice how the teacher in Figure 12.4 focuses her discussion.

Hold the Discussion. As a whole-class discussion proceeds, many circumstances can get it off track. In some cases, students will purposely try to get the teacher off the topic, as, for instance, when they want to talk about last Friday's ball game instead of the causes of World War I. Talking about Friday's game is fine if that is the objective of the lesson, but it is not appropriate if the aim is to encourage student reasoning about military conflicts.

A second example of wandering is when a student expresses an idea or raises a question that has little or nothing to do with the topic. This happens often, particularly with students who have trouble concentrating in school. It is also likely to happen with younger students who have not been taught good listening and discussion skills.

> Effective discussion leaders acknowledge students' off-track remarks and then refocus their attention to the topic at hand.

In both instances, effective teachers acknowledge what students are doing—"We are talking about last Friday night's game" or, "You say your father had a good time in New York last weekend"—and then refocus the class's attention on the topic with a comment such as, "Talking about the game seems to be of great interest to all of you. I will let you do that during the last five minutes of the class period, but now I want us to get back to the question I asked you" or, "I know you are very interested in what your father did in New York, and I would love it if you would spend some time during lunch telling me more. Right now we want to talk about. . . ."

Keeping Records. Verbal exchange during a discussion proceeds more orderly if teachers keep some type of written record of the discussion as it unfolds. Writing students' main ideas or points of view on the chalkboard or flip charts provides this written record. Or it may consist of constructing conceptual webs that illustrate the various ideas and relationships.

Figure 12.4 *Focusing the discussion.*

A dilemma faced by beginning teachers in keeping a discussion record is how much detail to include and whether or not all ideas should be written down. These decisions, obviously, depend on the nature of the students involved and the purposes of the discussion. When a teacher is working with a group that lacks confidence in discourse skills, it is probably a good idea to write down as much as possible. Seeing many ideas on the chalkboard or flip chart provides a public display of the many good thoughts that exist within the group and can encourage participation. With a more experienced and confident group, the teacher may want to list only key words, thus affording a more open exchange of ideas and opinions.

If the teacher has asked students specifically for their theories or ideas about a topic, it is important to list all ideas and treat these equally, regardless of their quality. On the other hand, if questions focus on direct recall of right answers, then only right answers should be recorded.

Listening to Students' Ideas. A favorite discussion technique used by many teachers at the high school and college levels is "playing the devil's advocate." Teachers using this technique purposely take the opposite point of view from that being expressed by individual students or groups of students. Even though this approach can create lively exchange between a teacher and a few of the more verbal students, it does not work well with younger students or with many older students who lack good verbal and communication skills. Debate and argument arouse emotions, and despite their motivational potential, may divert the students' attention from the topic. They also cause many less-articulate or shy students to shrink from participation. If the teacher's goal is to help students understand a lesson and extend their thinking, then the teacher should listen carefully to each student's ideas. In this case, the teacher should remain nonjudgmental and inquiry-oriented, rather than challenging or argumentative.

> Discussion proceeds in a more orderly fashion if some type of visible written record is kept as the discussion unfolds.

> Free and open discussion is enhanced when teachers listen carefully and nonjudgmentally to students' ideas.

Enhancing Teaching with Technology
Taking Your Discussions Online

The emergence of the Internet and the World Wide Web has made it possible for people to talk with one another in ways never before imagined. Every day, literally millions of people around the world, young and old, enter "chatrooms" and "discussion forums" to talk and listen to each other. Sometimes this exchange is between people who know each other; sometimes it is between strangers. Regardless, the phenomenon highlights the centrality of discourse in human communities and the popularity of online discussions.

Teachers can use the popularity of online interaction among youth to accomplish some of the traditional goals held for classroom discussions as well as enrich their in-class discussions in ways not possible in pre-Internet times. Teachers report positive benefits of online communication and discourse. For instance, online interaction motivates some students to continue talking about important topics after the class is over. This increases learning time beyond the confines of the classroom. Online discussions can also increase participation, an important goal emphasized throughout this chapter. Some students, particularly those who are shy, say things online that they would never say in class.

E-mail is the easiest way of using the Internet in teaching to enhance classroom discussions. Its only requirement is a means to reliable e-mail access. Most students do have that access—in their homes, in public libraries, or at school. Many students are familiar with e-mail and use it on a regular basis to communicate with their friends.

Teachers who use online discussions find that students like this type of exchange. They don't have to respond im-

"For more information on what I did this summer, be sure to check out my website at www.funinsun.com."

Source: Used with permission. Phi Delta Kappan.

mediately as they do in face-to-face discussions—they can take time to think about a topic and compose their thoughts before responding. They can also engage more freely in topics that are controversial and require lively debate.

Effective online discussions and interactive learning will not, however, happen automatically. Teachers are required to encourage, guide, and facilitate online discussions just as they do face-to-face discussions. To encourage and facilitate online discussions:

In most circumstances, teachers should practice waiting at least three seconds for a student's response.

Using Wait-Time. Earlier we discussed how many teachers do not give students sufficient time to think and to respond. There are probably several reasons for this. One is the strong cultural norm in our society against silence. Silence makes many people uncomfortable and, consequently, they jump in to keep the conversation moving. Another is that waiting for student responses can be perceived by teachers as threatening to the pace and momentum of a lesson. Additionally, silence or waiting can give uninvolved students opportunities to start talking or otherwise misbehave. Although many contextual conditions influence wait-time, the general recommendations are for teachers to practice waiting at least three seconds for a student's response, to ask the question again or in a slightly different way if there is no response, and never to move on to a second question without some closure on the first. The amount of wait-time should probably be less for direct recall questions and more for questions aimed at higher-level

- *Teach students how to use online discussions.* Many students today are familiar with chatrooms and other kinds of online interactions; some are not. Just as with face-to-face discussions, students need to be taught requisite discussion skills and expectations for interacting online.
- *Deal with the logistics of online discussions.* For younger children, teachers may want to begin online discussions in their school's computer lab or in their own classrooms if several computers are available. This in-school effort then can expand slowly, perhaps with each student contributing to an online discussion at least once per week. It is reasonable to expect older students to use their own computers or those available at school or the public library and to contribute on a regular basis to discussion topics. Most teachers treat online discussions held out of class like they treat other types of homework.
- *Control the pace of online discussions and encourage broad participation.* Just as in face-to-face discussions, online discussions can become fast-paced and dominated by a few students. Reminding students to slow down and requiring those with comments to symbolize a raised hand with an asterisk are means to control pace and participation.
- *Use small groups.* Again, as with face-to-face discussions, teachers can divide the students into teams, have them work together on particular projects, and then have them communicate as a team with other teams.

Worley (2002) recommended that teachers play the following roles to promote online interactive learning:

- *Two cents.* Become another voice in the discussion. Wait until everyone else has responded to the discussion by a designated date, and then add your "two cents."
- *E-mail analysis.* Scan all the student comments, pick out one or two that bring up especially interesting issues, and respond to these. Then, send out a general e-mail to the whole class telling students to read particular comments and respond to them.
- *Student only.* Let the discussion belong only to the students and simply keep track of who has responded and how well. Give credit for quality ideas and responses.
- *Student leader.* Designate one or two students to facilitate and summarize the discussion for the class. Create a topic with the directions, "Student leader, please post topic here" and let the leader post his or her own original discussion question.
- *Water cooler.* Create one topic for the class that is totally unmoderated and "free." Simply invite your class to participate in the conversation.

Teachers need to be aware that there may be some negative aspects to online discussions. When students engage each other face-to-face, they can attend to the nuances of body language and observe the emotions that many topics generate, particularly those that are controversial and sensitive. These constraints are absent in online discussions, thus requiring "virtual etiquette." Sheila Harbet (2002) proposed the following simple rules for online discussions:

- Respect each other's viewpoints.
- Wait to be recognized to speak.
- Don't shout (ALL CAPS).
- Don't use profanity.
- Don't flame (put down someone or his or her ideas).

Finally, teachers and parents must also be aware of the potential for students to hide behind their computer monitors, never acquiring the skills to be effective in face-to-face situations.

thinking and more complex content. After a student response, teachers should also wait a sufficient time before moving on.

Responding to Student Answers. When students respond correctly to teachers' questions, effective teachers acknowledge the correct answer with brief affirmations such as, "That's right," "Okay," or "Yes." They do not spend time providing overly gushy praise. Most teachers learn these behaviors quite quickly. However, responding to incorrect or incomplete responses is a more complicated situation. The guidelines described in Chapter 8 are repeated here:

Student thinking can be extended by teacher actions that review student ideas, ask for alternative ideas, and/or seek clarification or supporting evidence.

1. *Dignify* a student's incorrect response or performance by giving a question for which the response would have been correct. For example, "George Washington would have been the right answer if I asked you who was the first president of the United States."

Being responsive to student ideas encourages participation.

2. Provide the student with an *assist*, or prompt. For example, "Remember, the president in 1828 was also a hero in the War of 1812."
3. Hold the student *accountable.* For example, "You didn't know President Jackson today, but I bet you will tomorrow when I ask you again."

Responding to Student Ideas and Opinions. Although the art of questioning is important for effective discussions, other verbal behaviors by teachers are equally important, especially those for responding to students' ideas and opinions. These are responses aimed at getting students to extend their thinking and to be more conscious of their thinking processes. Statements and questions such as the following provide illustrations on how to do this:

- Reflect on student ideas:
  "I heard you say. . . ."
  "What I think you're telling me is. . . ."
  "That's an interesting idea. I have never thought of it in quite that way. . . ."
- Get students to consider alternatives:
  "That's an interesting idea. I wonder, though, if you have ever considered this as an alternative. . . ."
  "You have provided one point of view about the issue. How does it compare with the point of view expressed by . . .?"
  "Evelyn has just expressed an interesting point of view. I wonder if someone else would like to say why they agree or disagree with her idea?"
  "Do you think the author would agree with your idea? Why? Why not?"
- Seek clarification:
  "I think you have a good idea. But I'm a bit confused. Can you expand your thought a bit to help me understand it more fully?"
- Label thinking processes and ask for supportive evidence:
  "It sounds to me like you have been performing a mental *experiment* with these data."
  "You have made a very strong *inference* from the information given you."

"Can you think of an *experiment* that would put that hypothesis to a good test?"
"What if I told you (give new information)? What would that do to your *hypothesis?*"
"That's an interesting position. What *values* led you to it?"
"If everyone held the *judgment* you just expressed, what would the result be?"

Expressing Opinions. Many beginning teachers are uncertain about whether or not they should express their own ideas and opinions during a discussion. Although teachers do not want to dominate discussions or make it appear that they are the only ones with good ideas, expressing ideas appropriately can be beneficial. It provides opportunities for teachers to model their own reasoning processes and to show students the way they tackle problems. It also communicates to students that the teacher sees himself or herself as part of a learning community interested in sharing ideas and discovering knowledge.

End the Discussion. As with other types of lessons, discussions need to be brought to proper closure. Effective teachers do this in a variety of ways. In some instances, they may choose to summarize in a few sentences what has been said and try to tie various ideas together or to relate them to the larger topic being studied. In other instances, teachers may want to close the discussion with a short presentation highlighting new or previously studied information. Some teachers ask students to summarize the discussion by posing a final question such as, "What is the main thing you got from our discussion today?" or, "What do you think was the most provocative point made during our discussion?"

Debrief the Discussion. From time to time, discussions should be debriefed. Here, the focus is not on the content of the discussion but on the way the discussion proceeded. To conduct a successful **debriefing,** teachers must teach students the differences between the discussion itself and the debriefing and then pose questions such as: "How do you think our discussion went today? Did we give everyone a chance to participate? Did we listen to one another's ideas? Were there times when we seemed to get bogged down? Why? What can we all do next time to make our discussion more stimulating or provocative?"

Adapting Discussions for Diverse Learners

Even under the best of circumstances, it is difficult to obtain good discussions characterized by open and honest communication. The fact of diversity presents a particular set of opportunities and challenges. On the one hand, when students differ in their cultural backgrounds, experiences, gender, and outlooks, classroom discussions create opportunities for them to learn from one another. What could be better? On the other hand, differences among students can also lead to silence and unproductive misunderstandings. Effective teachers know that to be successful in classroom discussions, they must be sensitive to cultural and gender differences and they must create alternatives to the traditional IRE discourse model.

Discourse Gender Differences. Gender accounts for important differences in discourse patterns in classrooms. Considerable research (Gilligan, 1982; Tannen, 1990, 1994) illustrates how men and women speak and listen in different ways and how they have different aims for their communicative acts. Males are socialized for public speaking while females are socialized for private speaking (Tannen, 1990). Girls are socialized to be passive and caring and to defer to males in public discourse. Kramarae and Treichler (1990) illustrated how this socialization finds its way into mathematics classrooms. Young women in their study were more prone to listen and to make statements about the "learning process," whereas young men talked a lot and focused their comments on ideas. Young women placed importance on "mutual support" and "collaboration" as contrasted to young men who placed priority on individual expertise, debate, right answers, and elaboration of abstract concepts. The traditional IRE discourse model, with its focus on competition and correct ideas, reflects the natural and socialized discourse patterns of males more than it does females and can make classrooms a "chilly climate" for females.

Evidence gathered over several decades, and reported previously in Chapter 2, holds that teachers (even though most are women) interact and communicate differently with boys than they do with girls (AAUW, 1992; Sadker & Sadker, 1994; Sadker, Sadker and Klein, 1991). In traditional classrooms, teachers—regardless of gender—call on boys more often than they do girls, ask them more questions, and provide them with more praise. The result is that as girls progress through the grades, they are less and less likely to contribute their ideas in discussions. By the time they reach college, they have often become invisible and silent.

Race and Class Differences. Race and class likewise account for significant differences in classroom discourse and communication. Individuals are socialized first in their families. Here, we are taught at a very early age the forms of communication politeness, the appropriateness and inappropriateness of particular gestures, as well as when and where to speak. The traditional IRE discourse pattern found in classrooms stems from middle-class, white values and it represents a discourse pattern incongruous to many Asians, African Americans, Native Americans, and students from low-SES backgrounds. Thus, many students who have been socialized with communication patterns different than the dominant form found in schools are disadvantaged and often choose to exclude themselves from the communication system altogether (see Burburles & Bruce, 2001; Delpit, 1988, 1995; Ladson-Billings, 1992, 1995). As with gender, teachers have been shown to interact differently with students who are culturally or socially different. They ask them fewer questions, give them less time to respond, and provide them with less praise and encouragement (Dayhle & Margoinis, 1995).

There are *no* simple solutions for adapting discussions to meet the diverse needs of all students, and warnings provided about cultural stereotyping in Chapter 2 need to be repeated here. Students are not just boys or girls, African Americans or Hispanic, affluent or poor. They are combinations of all these features. Remember this important fact when you consider the following guidelines:

Guideline 1: *Systematically monitor your own patterns of asking questions, using wait time and providing praise.* This is very important because teachers have been shown to be unaware of the impact of their discourse patterns on students. Most teachers say they treat all students fairly and the same. Like the case of David, described in the "Handbook on Action Research" at the end of *Learning to Teach,* teachers will continue to focus their attention in traditional ways even when confronted with data of differential treatment. Most do this *not* because they believe in differential treatment, but because they are unconscious of their actions.

Guideline 2: *Become familiar with students' backgrounds, customs, values, and dialects.* Every classroom is going to have a different mix of students, so there is no guideline to meet every situation. However, effective teachers learn about the culture of their students through study and by seeking ways of interacting in nonschool settings with parents and other adults in the school's community. Irvine and York (1995) have described communication patterns likely to be found with particular groups of students:

- African American students gain knowledge through intuition and spiral logic as contrasted to the analytical reasoning preferred by middle-class whites. Often they are more proficient in nonverbal than in verbal communications.
- Hispanic and Latino students are sensitive to the opinions of others, prefer people to ideas, and prefer close interpersonal interactions and relationships.
- Native American students prefer visual, spatial, and perceptual information rather than verbal and they prefer to learn privately rather than in public.

Guideline 3: *Explore with students what your communication and interactions mean to them.* Teachers can obtain valuable information about discourse patterns during debriefing sessions. Ask students, "What did you like and dislike about our discussion?" "Did our discussion allow you to participate on an equal footing with other students?" "What can I do to make you feel more comfortable the next time we have a discussion?"

Guideline 4: *Help each student experience communication success.* Discussion and communication skills are learned through practice just like any other skill. Using techniques such as the "fishbowl," "round-robin," or "beach ball" (described later in this chapter) help slow down the pace of discussion and allow every student practice opportunities for making contributions without having to compete with the students who are more dominant and verbal.

Guideline 5: *Create and foster alternative discourse patterns.* Unfortunately, the IRE discourse pattern is the primary contributor to teachers' differential treatment of students. Changing this traditional pattern through the use of such structures as "think-pair-share," "dyads," and "small group" will broaden participation and enhance the quality of discussions.

Managing the Learning Environment

Many of the management tasks described in previous chapters also apply to discussion lessons. For example, pacing the lesson appropriately and dealing quickly and decisively with misbehavior are both essential teacher management behaviors when conducting a discussion. However, the most important management tasks are those aimed at improving discussion and discourse patterns in the classroom: teaching students specific discussion skills and establishing classroom norms that support productive discourse patterns. Several skills and norms are critical. In this section, skills and strategies to broaden participation, to promote interpersonal regard, and to heighten classroom thinking are described. Underlying the presentation is the premise that if discussion and discourse are to improve substantially, rather dramatic changes in the classroom discourse patterns must occur.

Slow the Pace and Broaden Participation

An often-heard statement of inexperienced teachers is, "I tried to hold a discussion, but no one said anything." It is not uncommon for discussions, even those led by experienced teachers, to follow a pattern in which the teacher's questions are all answered by less than a half dozen of the twenty-five to thirty students present. Remember the rapid discourse pattern described by Rowe earlier in this chapter? To broaden participation and get real discussions going requires substantial changes to this limited pattern of discourse. The pace must be slowed down and the norms about questioning and taking turns modified. Following are strategies that work and are used by experienced teachers.

Check, Extend, Explore

Check
- What are the major planning tasks of preparing for classroom discussion?
- What are the five phases of a discussion? What kinds of teacher behaviors are associated with each?
- What significant variables should teachers consider when choosing a seating plan for discussion?
- What actions can teachers take when conducting discussions to facilitate cultural and gender differences?

Extend
- Do you agree or disagree that playing the "devil's advocate" is an effective way to have good classroom discussions? Go to the "Extend Question Poll" on the Online Learning Center to respond.

Explore
- Go to the Online Learning Center at www.mhhe.com/arends6e for links to websites related to *Planning and Conducting Discussions*.

Important management tasks faced by teachers involve the improvement of student discussion skills and controlling discourse patterns.

Think-Pair-Share.   The **think-pair-share** strategy was described in Chapter 10 as a co-operative learning structure that increased student participation. It is also an effective way to slow down the pace of a lesson and extend student thinking. This is true because it has built-in procedures for giving students more time to think and to respond and can affect the pattern of participation. For a description of the three-step think-pair-share strategy, return to Chapter 10.

To broaden participation in discussions, the pace must be slowed down, and the norms for questioning and taking turns modified.

Buzz Groups.   The use of **buzz groups** is another effective means of increasing student participation. When using buzz groups, a teacher asks students to form into groups of three to six to discuss ideas about a particular topic or lesson. Each group assigns a member to list all the ideas generated by the group. After a few minutes, the teacher asks the recorders to summarize for the whole class the major ideas and opinions expressed in their group. Buzz groups, like think-pair-share, allow for more student participation with the learning materials and make it difficult for one or a few class members to dominate discussions. Using buzz groups can change the dynamics and basic patterns of classroom discourse and are easy for most teachers to use.

Beach Ball.   A third technique, *beach ball*, is particularly effective with younger students, for broadening participation, and promoting one person to talk at a time. The teacher gives the ball to one student to start the discussion with the understanding that only the person with the ball is permitted to talk. Other students raise their hands for the ball when they want a turn. *Time tokens* and *high talker tap out*, described in Chapter 10, are two other activities teachers can use to broaden classroom participation patterns.

Increase Interpersonal Regard and Understanding

An open and honest communication process is perhaps the single most important variable for promoting positive classroom discourse and discussion. Fortunately, the way discourse occurs in classrooms can be greatly influenced by a teacher's leadership, particularly if he or she teaches skills that promote worthwhile **interpersonal communication** as well as a positive regard for it among students.

Since communication is essentially a process of sending and receiving messages, effective communication requires the sender of a message to express clearly what he or she intends to communicate and the receiver to interpret that message accurately. In reality, however, the message a person intends to send often is not the one the other person receives. The meaning intended in the sender's mind may not be accurately expressed or may be expressed in a manner that does not fit the receiver's prior experiences. Whenever either of these conditions occurs, a *communication gap* develops.

Following are four communication skills, described by Schmuck and Schmuck (2001), that people can use to make the process of sending and receiving messages more effective and thereby reduce the gap in communication. Two of these skills assist the sender; two assist the receiver.

1. **Paraphrase.**   Paraphrasing is a skill for checking whether or not you understand the ideas being communicated to you. Any means of revealing your understanding of a message constitutes a paraphrase. Paraphrasing is more than word swapping or merely saying back what another person says. It answers the question, "What exactly does the sender's statement mean to me?" and asks the sender to verify the correctness of the receiver's interpretation. The sender's statement may convey specific information, an example, or a more general idea, as shown in the following examples:

Example 1

Sender: I'd sure like to own this book.

   You: (*being more specific*) Does it have useful information in it?

Sender: I don't know about that, but the binding is beautiful.

Example 2

Sender: This book is too hard to use.

   You: (*giving an example*) Do you mean, for example, that it fails to cite research?

Sender: Yes, that's one example. It also lacks an adequate index.

Example 3

Sender: Do you have a book on teaching?

   You: (*being more general*) Do you just want information on that topic? I have several articles about it.

Sender: No, I want to find out about cooperative learning.

2. **Describe Behavior.** In using a behavior description, one person reports specific observable behaviors of another person without evaluating them or making inferences about the other's motives. If you tell me that I am rude (a trait) or that I do not care about your opinion (my motivations) when I am not trying to be rude and do care about your opinion, I may not understand what you are trying to communicate. However, if you point out that I have interrupted you several times in the last ten minutes, I would receive a clearer picture of how my actions were affecting you. Sometimes it is helpful to preface a behavior description with, "I noticed that . . ." or "I hear you say . . ." to remind yourself that you are trying to describe specific actions. Consider the following examples:

   "Jim, you've talked more than others on this topic."
   Instead of:
   "Jim, you always have to be the center of attention."
   Or:
   "Bob, I really felt good when you complimented me on my presentation before the class."
   Instead of:
   "Bob, you sure go out of your way to say nice things to people."

3. **Describe Feelings.** Although people often take pains to make sure that others understand their ideas, only rarely do they describe how they are feeling. Instead, they act on their feelings, sending messages that others draw inferences from. If you think that others are failing to take your feelings into account, it is helpful to put those feelings into words. Instead of blushing and saying nothing, try "I feel embarrassed" or "I feel pleased." Instead of "Shut up!" try "I hurt too much to hear any more" or "I'm angry with you."

4. **Check Impressions.** Checking impressions is a skill that complements describing your own feelings and involves checking your sense of what is going on inside the other person. You transform the other's expression of feelings (the blush, the silence, the tone of voice) into a tentative description of feelings and check it out for accuracy. An impression check describes what you think the other's feelings may be and does not express disapproval or approval. It merely conveys, "This is how I understand your feelings. Am I accurate?" Examples include the following:

   "I get the impression you are angry with me. Are you?"
   "Am I right that you feel disappointed that nobody commented on your suggestions?"

To improve communication, teachers can help students learn important communication skills.

Developing the four communication skills can assist the process of effectively sending and receiving messages.

> **Step 1:** Introduce and explain the four communication skills, and define a topic for students to talk about.
>
> **Step 2:** Have students get into groups of three for practice purposes. Each person in each trio is assigned a role—either sender, receiver, or observer. The sender begins a conversation and tries to describe his or her feelings or the receiver's behavior while discussing the topic. The receiver listens and either paraphrases or checks his or her impressions of the sender's feelings. The observer notes instances of communication skill use and instances where there are gaps in communication.
>
> **Step 3:** Roles are exchanged so different people become senders, receivers, and observers.
>
> **Step 4:** Finally, the teacher holds a class discussion about which skills are easy and which are difficult to learn and about how these skills can be applied in areas of classroom life as well as outside the classroom. During the discussion, the teacher should model use of the skills and encourage students to use them.

Figure 12.5 *Typical Lesson Plan for Teaching Communication Skills*

Often an impression check can be coupled easily with a behavior description, as in these examples:

> "Ellen, you've said nothing so far and seem upset with the class. Are you?"
> "Jim, you've made that proposal a couple of times. Are you feeling put down because we haven't accepted it?"

Teachers can learn and model these skills in their classrooms. They can also teach them directly to students, just as they teach many other skills. The direct instruction model described in Chapter 8 provides an appropriate strategy for teaching communication skills initially. A typical lesson is outlined in Figure 12.5.

Use Tools That Highlight Discourse and Thinking Skills

Frank Lyman and James McTighe have written extensively about the use of teaching tools, particularly visual ones, that help teachers and students learn discourse and thinking skills (Lyman, 1986; McTighe, 1998; McTighe & Lyman, 1988).

Lyman and McTighe were particularly interested in the ways that visual tools and aids can be used by teachers.

Visual Cues for Think-Pair-Share. The think-pair-share discussion strategy described previously is not easy for students to use at first. Old habits, such as responding to teacher questions before thinking or blurting out answers without waiting, are difficult to change. Lyman and teachers working with him have developed various ways of teaching students how to employ think-pair-share, particularly how and when to switch from one mode to another. A favorite strategy is to make and use **visual cuing** devices such as those illustrated in Figure 12.6.

Thinking Matrix. McTighe and Lyman (1988) also studied how to get students and their teachers to ask more questions that promote higher-level thinking and to analyze the nature of responses made to various types of questions. They created a device they

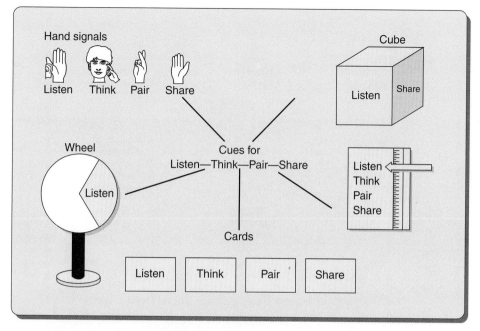

Figure 12.6 *Cues for Using Think-Pair-Share*

Source: After Lyman (1985), p. 2

call the **thinking matrix.** Lyman (1986) recommends that teachers create symbols that illustrate the various thinking processes described in Bloom's taxonomy and then construct symbol cards that can be placed on the wall or held in the teacher's hand. During a discussion, teachers point to these symbols as they ask various types of questions. They also encourage students to categorize the questions they ask and the responses they give using the symbol cards. Figure 12.7 shows the symbol system developed by Lyman and teachers who work with him.

Teaching specific discourse skills is no different from teaching content-specific skills or social skills. The direct instruction model, which requires teachers to demonstrate and model the skill being taught and to provide time for students to practice the skill and receive feedback on how they are doing, is the best approach to use.

Assessment and Evaluation

As with the other teaching approaches, there are assessment and evaluation tasks for teachers to perform following a discussion. One is considering how a particular discussion should be followed up in subsequent lessons; the other is grading.

Follow-up Discussions

Experienced teachers make both formal and mental notes for themselves following discussions. Sometimes these notes pertain to the content of the discussion and help determine subsequent lessons. For example, perhaps a discussion identifies some serious gaps in students' knowledge about a topic. Learning this might prompt a teacher to plan a presentation on a particular topic that came up in the discussion or to find suitable reading materials to assign students. A discussion can also identify aspects of a topic in which

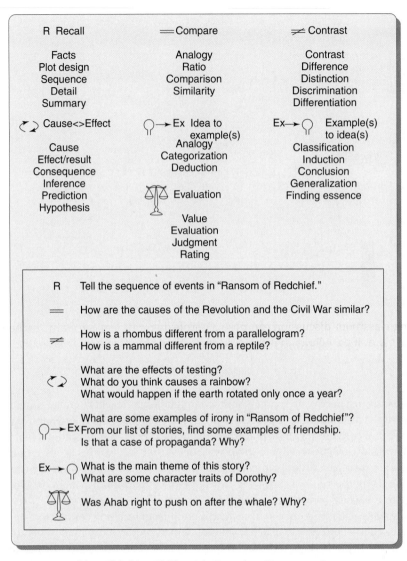

Figure 12.7 *Teaching Thinking Skills with Question-Response Cues*
Source: After Lyman (1986), p. 3

students are particularly interested. Teachers use the information they gain during discussions to plan lessons that will take advantage of this natural interest. The conduct of the discussion itself will give the teacher information about the strengths and weaknesses of students' thinking processes as well as the group's ability to engage in purposeful dialogue. Future lessons can then be planned to strengthen areas targeted for improvement.

Another aspect of following up a discussion is obtaining formal information from students about what they thought of the discussion and their role in it. The rating scale illustrated in Figure 12.8 can be an effective tool for gathering this type of assessment information.

How Did You Feel About Today's Discussion?

Class's treatment of issues

| Superficial | 1 | 2 | 3 | 4 | 5 | Thorough and deep |

Helpfulness of discussion to your understanding

| Low | 1 | 2 | 3 | 4 | 5 | High |

Your own level of engagement

| Low | 1 | 2 | 3 | 4 | 5 | High |

The class's overall level of engagement

| Low | 1 | 2 | 3 | 4 | 5 | High |

Quality of your own participation

| Poor | 1 | 2 | 3 | 4 | 5 | Excellent |

Figure 12.8 *Discussion Rating Scale*
Source: After Wiggins (1993), p. 66

Grading Classroom Discussions

Grading classroom discussion can pose a perplexing problem for many teachers. On the one hand, if participation is not graded, students may view this part of their work as less important than work for which a grade is given. Remember the "work for grade exchange" concept described in Chapters 3 and 6? On the other hand, it is difficult to quantify participation in any satisfactory way. The questions teachers are confronted with when they try to grade discussions are, "Do I reward quantity or quality?" "What constitutes a quality contribution?" "What about the student who talks all the time but says nothing?" "What about the student who is naturally shy but has good ideas?"

There are two ways experienced teachers have confronted this grading dilemma. One is to give bonus points to students who consistently appear to be prepared for discussions and who make significant contributions. If this method is used, it needs to be discussed thoroughly with the class and opportunities provided that allow each student equal access to the bonus points available.

A second way to grade discussions is to use the discussion as a springboard for a reflective writing assignment. The grade in this instance is given not for participation but for the student's ability to reflect on the discussion and put in words what the discussion meant to him or her. When students know they are responsible for a postdiscussion reflective essay, this approach, when properly conceived and managed, can heighten student attention during the discussion and extend student thinking about the discussion after it is over. The obvious disadvantage of using this type of assignment is the time required to read and assign grades to the essays.

Two ways to grade a discussion are to award bonus points for student participation and to have students do a reflective writing assignment based on the discussion.

Check, Extend, Explore

Check
- What are the key features of the learning environment for classroom discussions?
- What factors should teachers consider when they think about how to assess student learning in classroom discussions?

Extend
- Why do you think it has been so difficult to change discourse patterns in most classrooms?
- Do you think most students really want to participate in classroom discussions? Go to the "Extend Question Poll" on the Online Learning Center to respond.

Explore
- Go to the Online Learning Center at www.mhhe.com/arends6e for links to websites related to *Learning Environments and Assessment of Classroom Discussion.*

Classroom Discourse Patterns: A Final Thought

There is almost universal agreement among scholars and researchers that for real learning to occur, a different discourse pattern than the one currently found in most classrooms must be established. When asked about how they are going to teach, most beginning teachers will attest to the importance of providing opportunities for students to discuss important topics and to exchange ideas with each other and with the teacher.

Yet, year after year, classroom observers say this is not happening. Teachers continue to dominate the talk that goes on in classrooms by presenting information and giving directions for students to follow. When they ask students questions, most of them are the kind that require direct recall rather than higher-level thinking. If students don't answer immediately, the teacher asks another question or calls on another student. All of this takes place at a very rapid pace. We know from research that teacher dominance of classroom discourse patterns and the rapid pace of this discourse are harmful. We also know that slowing down the pace of discourse and using different discourse patterns such as think-pair-share will produce more and better student thinking.

If this is true, why is it so difficult to change the discourse patterns in classrooms? Are there some underlying causes for this phenomenon? Do students really want to participate in discussions? Perhaps it is easier to sit and listen. Do teachers really want to have discussions? Perhaps it is easier just to talk. Will your generation of teachers accomplish the changes so many have talked about?

Although most teachers agree that classroom discussions are an important part of the learning process, actual discussion time is often quite limited.

Reflections from the Classroom

Why Won't They Talk?

For the third day in a row, you have begun your science lesson by tossing out a provocative and challenging question. It has been your hope that you would be able to get a lively discussion going. Instead, you are met with deadly silence. Two or three students try to respond, but the others just sit there staring at you or looking down at their desks. You are embarrassed by the silence, but, more important, you are frustrated because your favorite classes when you were a student were those in which you could participate in lively debate. You believe strongly that effective teachers are those who have lively discussions in their classrooms.

You ponder this situation and ask yourself, "What's wrong? Perhaps my students are just a bunch of kids who don't care about science and care even less about talking about it. Perhaps everyone in my class is shy. Or perhaps I am doing something wrong."

Spend some time reflecting on this situation and then compare your thoughts with the following comments from experienced teachers. Approach the situation from the perspective closest to the grade level or subject area you are preparing to teach. When you are finished, write up your reflections and include them as an exhibit in your professional portfolio.

Jason O'Brien
Sacred Heart Academy, 3rd through 5th Grades
Diocese of St. Petersburg, FL

Every student, whether they admit it or not, wants to feel like he or she has a voice. If I am not getting students to respond to my questions, I would rethink the questions that I am asking. If teachers start a discussion by asking very complex questions and nobody responds, they should try starting with easier questions and working toward higher-level questions. It also helps to ask questions that are relevant to the students' lives. If you are asking a science question about the polarity of the Earth, ask students about a compass that you are holding in your hand. Once students have had success answering simple questions and you have praised them for it, they will become comfortable and less afraid to take a chance answering more difficult questions. Body language is also very important. It is crucial for students to know that you care about their answers. Do not cut off student answers. Use simple prompts such as, "Can you elaborate on that?" to facilitate higher-level thinking. If you are still getting no response, model the behavior to the students. Have them write down school-related questions for you to answer. Demonstrate what an appropriate answer looks like. A technique I sometimes employ at the beginning of the year to ensure total class participation is to hand out a token to each student. Every time a student answers a question, I take his or her token. I tell the students that I expect everyone to have given me their token by the end of class. Or you can do the opposite and devise a system of rewards for good answers. The important thing is to keep trying. With a little hard work, you can have a class full of eager respondents!

Dennis Holt
Tampa Bay Technical High School, 11th and 12th Grades
Hillsborough, FL

Classroom discussion and debate can be among the liveliest teaching experiences that you will encounter. However, on occasion, the discussion will fall flat, or worse, not occur at all. To diminish this situation, there are several actions that you can take in advance and during the discussion. First, make sure your students are prepared to discuss the subject matter. Having students complete a graphic organizer or take a short set of notes on the key points brought up in the lesson should help them focus their thoughts and facilitate discussion. You can also provide students with speaking prompts that will allow them to overcome unfamiliarity with the subject matter or just plain nervousness.

I would suggest that you consider placing students in mixed ability pairs to smooth the progress of the discussion. Begin by posing fairly simple questions to the students. Allow them time to discuss the question with each other and frame a short written response. Next, call on pairs of students at random to share their answers with the entire class. Start with fairly basic questions and spiral upwards to increasingly more difficult concepts. This allows students time to build upon their own and shared knowledge in a step-by-step manner. This method is often commonly referred to as "think, pair, share." You may also wish to provide different pairs of students with conflicting or controversial information in order to spur debate.

Whether you are engaged in a science, math, language, or social studies lesson, you will often find that the "experts" in the field have disagreements over the subject (evolution comes to mind). Providing your students with this conflicting information allows them to discover for themselves that knowledge and understanding often progress out of differences of opinion. A word of caution: in advance of any discussion or debate, particularly when the subject is controversial; make sure that your students have had a chance to practice the art of listening to each other respectfully and exchanging ideas productively. Posting and modeling classroom rules for discussion and debate can spare hurt feelings and foster an atmosphere where everyone's opinions are important.

Chapter Review

Go back to the "Interactive and Applied Learning" feature at the beginning of the chapter for a listing of interactive and applied activities. Go to the Online Learning Center at **www.mhhe.com/arends6e** or your Interactive Student CD-ROM to take practice quizzes over the content of this chapter and receive immediate feedback. You can also review chapter content and main ideas, practice with key terms, and find annotated Web links on topics associated with Chapter 12.

Summary

Overview of Classroom Discussion

- Discourse and discussion are key ingredients for enhancing student thinking and uniting the cognitive and social aspects of learning.
- When experienced teachers refer to classroom discourse, they often use the label *discussion* to describe what they are doing. Classroom discussions are characterized by students and teachers talking about academic materials and by students willingly displaying their thinking processes publicly.
- Discourse can be thought of as externalization of thinking and has both cognitive and social importance.
- The primary instructional goals of a discussion lesson are to improve student thinking, to promote involvement and engagement in academic materials, and to learn important communication and thinking skills.
- The general flow or syntax for a discussion lesson consists of five major phases: provide objectives and set; focus the discussion; hold the discussion; end the discussion; and debrief the discussion.
- The structure of the learning environment for discussion lessons is characterized by open processes and active student roles.

Theoretical and Empirical Support

- Studies for a good many years have described how discourse patterns in most classrooms do not afford effective dialogue among students or promote much discovery or higher-level thinking.
- A substantial knowledge base exists that informs teachers on how to create positive discourse systems and to hold productive discussions. Studies also provide guidelines about the types of questions to ask and how to provide appropriate pacing for students to think and to respond.
- Most classroom discourse proceeds at too rapid a pace. Teachers can obtain better classroom discourse by slowing down the pace and giving themselves and their students opportunities to think before they respond.

Planning and Conducting Discussion Lessons

- An important planning task for a discussion lesson is deciding on which approach to use. There are several kinds of discussions. Major approaches include using discussion in conjunction with other teaching models; recitation discussions; discovery or inquiry discussions; and discussions to clarify values and share personal experiences.

- Other important planning tasks for teachers to consider include determining the purposes of the discussion; being aware of students' prior knowledge and discourse skills; making plans for how to approach the discussion; and determining the type of questions to ask.
- Placing students in circles or using U-shaped seating arrangements facilitates classroom discussions.
- Primary tasks for teachers as they conduct a discussion consist of focusing the discussion; keeping the discussion on track; keeping a record of the discussion; listening to students' ideas; and providing appropriate wait-time.
- Teachers should respond with dignity to students' ideas. They should help students extend their ideas by seeking clarification, getting students to consider alternative ideas, and labeling students' thinking processes.
- Teachers must be aware of gender discourse differences as well as those that stem from race and class. To be effective, they must adapt discussions to meet the diverse language patterns of their students.

Managing the Learning Environment

- In general, discussion and classroom discourse patterns can be improved if teachers slow the pace and use methods to broaden participation and if they teach students to try to understand one another and have high interpersonal regard for each other's ideas and feelings.
- Teaching students four specific interpersonal communication skills (paraphrasing, behavior description, feeling description, and impression checking) can enhance the quality of classroom discourse and students' regard for each other.
- Specific visual tools such as the think-pair-share cuing device and the thinking matrix can help students learn discourse and thinking skills.
- For students to become effective in the discourse system and during specific discussions requires teaching student discourse skills just as directly as academic content and other academic skills are taught. The direct instruction model can be used to teach these important skills.

Assessment and Evaluation

- Assessment and evaluation tasks appropriate for discussion consist of finding ways to follow up on discussions and to grade students for their contributions.
- Teachers use two ways to grade discussions: giving bonus points to students who consistently appear to be prepared and who make contributions, and grading reflective writing assignments based on the content of the discussion.

Key Terms

buzz groups 446
circle seating pattern 437
convergent questions 435
debriefing 443
discourse 425

discussion 425
divergent questions 435
interpersonal
    communication 446
level of difficulty 430

recitations 425
think-pair-share 446
thinking matrix 449
U-shaped seating pattern 436
visual cuing 448

wait-time 430
wait-time 1 432
wait-time 2 432

Portfolio and Field Experience Activities

This feature has been designed to help you learn from your field experiences and to assist you in the preparation of artifacts for your professional portfolio on topics and standards associated with Chapter 12.

1. Complete the "Reflections from the Classroom" exercise at the end of this chapter and use the reflective essay as an exhibit of your views about how to hold effective classroom discussions.
2. Use Activity 12.1 in the *Guide to Field Experiences and Portfolio Development* to assess your understanding and skills for planning and conducting classroom discussions. Summarize the results as an exhibit for your professional portfolio.

3. Use Activities 12.2, 12.3, and 12.4 in the *Guide to Field Experiences and Portfolio Development* to observe what teachers and students do during classroom discussions. Summarize the results of your observations as an artifact for your professional portfolio.
4. Use the Case Exercise on the Interactive Student CD-ROM and/or Activity 12.5 in the *Guide to Field Experiences and Portfolio Development* to create your own discussion lesson or practice tasks required when using classroom discussion. Place the product(s) of your work in your professional portfolio.

Books for the Professional

Go to the Online Learning Center at www.mhhe.com/arends6e or your Interactive CD-ROM for an annotated version of this list.

Adger, C. T. (1995). *Engaging Students: Thinking, Talking, Cooperating.* Thousand Oaks, CA: Corwin Press.

Brookfield, S. D., and Preskill, S. (1999). *Discussion As a Way of Teaching: Tools and Techniques for the Classroom.* San Francisco: Jossey Bass.

Browne, M. N., and Keeley, S. M. (2000). *Asking the Right Questions: A Guide to Critical Thinking.* Englewood Cliffs, NJ: Prentice-Hall.

Hill, W. F. (1994). *Learning Through Discussion* (3rd ed.). Thousand Oaks, CA: Sage.

Shoop, L. L., and Wright, D. (1999). *Classroom Warm-Ups: Activities That Improve the Climate for Learning and Discussion.* Resource Publications.

Part 4 of *Learning to Teach* is devoted to the organizational aspects of teaching. Teachers, like other professionals, are expected not only to perform their primary responsibilities (in this case, providing instruction to students) but also to provide leadership to the organization as a whole. For teachers, this means working alongside others in the school—colleagues, administrators, parents, and students—to help set schoolwide expectations and gain clarity of purposes and actions.

Chapter 13 focuses on three specific aspects of schools: understanding schools as social organizations, providing leadership and working collaboratively with members of the school community, and helping schools improve. To perform these functions effectively, teachers must understand the nature of the school not only as a place where children come to learn but also as a place where adults work. Teachers also need specific organizational skills aimed at making work with others in the school productive.

As you read about and study these topics, you will discover two reasons they are so important. One, there appears to be a certain synergy at work in schools in which teachers and others have come together and made agreements about what is going to be taught. This synergy makes a difference in how much students learn. Two, your ability to provide leadership and to relate to and work with others within the school and larger professional community will have a significant impact on your career. It is in this arena that you will become known to others and will build your professional reputation. Teachers who grow and progress in their careers are those who can enter into professional and schoolwide dialogue about professional and educational issues.

School Leadership
and Collaboration

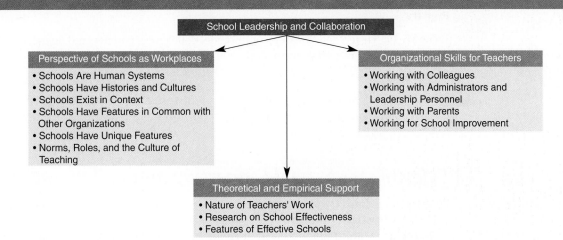

Interactive and Applied Learning

Go to your Interactive Student CD-ROM to:

- Hear audio clips of Kendra Ganzer (fifth grade) and Amy Callen talk about nonclassroom work in the Teachers on Teaching feature

Go to the Online Learning Center at www.mhhe.com/arends6e to read *PowerWeb* articles and newsfeed updates about:

- Aims of education
- Comparative education
- Cultural diversity in education
- Education
- The future of education
- Education reform
- Excellence and education
- Parents
- School integration
- School vouchers
- Urban schools
- Schools and cultural diversity
- Schools and federal policy
- School and public perceptions
- Profession of teaching
- Technology and education
- World Wide Web

Considering **Standards**

Studying this chapter will help you meet two INTASC principles:

Primary

INTASC 10: Fosters relationships with school colleagues, parents, and agencies in the larger community to support student learning and well-being.

Secondary

INTASC 9: Becomes a reflective practitioner who continually evaluates the effects of choices and actions and actively seeks out opportunities to grow professionally.

Reflecting **on** *School Leadership and Collaboration*

Before you read this chapter, consider the following situations, which are based on studies about what teachers do and how they spend their time.

Neil is a new third-grade teacher at Holbrook Elementary School. He usually arrives at school about 7:30 A.M. This particular morning, Neil opens his room, then joins other third- and fourth-grade teachers who are planning a field trip to the local airport. They discuss how each of them is going to integrate this experience into the social studies curriculum. Back in his room in time to start class at 8:35 A.M., Neil spends the rest of the morning with his third graders. He is joined at several points by other adults. The principal drops in for a few minutes to observe and see if Neil needs any help. Two mothers join the class at 9:30 A.M. to assist Neil with his reading groups, and they stay through morning recess. The school's reading specialist comes by and tests a student who Neil thinks is having a severe word recognition problem. The special education resource teacher joins Neil's classroom to work for thirty minutes with two learning-disabled students mainstreamed in Neil's room.

Over lunch, Neil talks with two second-grade teachers about students of his who were in their classrooms last year. Neil stops at the library on his way back to his classroom to pick up a film he plans to show as part of his social studies unit and to remind the librarian that he will be bringing a small group of students to the library next Tuesday.

School lets out at 2:45 P.M.; Neil drops by the reading specialist's office to discuss the results of her testing before heading to the central office to participate on a science textbook selection committee. Neil was appointed to this committee by his principal because the principal knew that he had a very strong background in science and had worked at the Marine Biology Research Center for the past two summers.

Helena teaches tenth-grade English at Cordoza High School. She, too, arrives at school about 7:30 A.M., and she meets with another new teacher to have a cup of coffee and discuss an exchange of teaching materials. Helena teaches three classes of sophomore English in the morning. Just before lunch, she is visited by her department chairperson, who is conducting one of his required formal observations of new teachers.

During her afternoon planning period, Helena and the department chair meet. He gives her feedback on her lesson, pointing out that her lecture was brilliant but that her students took a long time getting to work in the small-group exercise she had planned.

After school, Helena meets for a few minutes with members of the school's debate team for whom she serves as advisor. On this day, Helena leaves her work with the debate team early because she wants to participate in the discussion on student advising planned for this week's faculty meeting. After the faculty meeting, Helena dashes home to have a quick dinner. The school's open house is this evening, and Helena has scheduled meetings with several parents to discuss their children's work.

Analyzing these typical days in the lives of two beginning teachers illustrates that they do many things in addition to interacting with students in classrooms. They meet with students about nonacademic tasks; they meet with fellow teachers and specialists within the school; they go to meetings; they work with parents; and they attend to their own learning. What do you think of these aspects of a teacher's work? How do you see yourself relating to the rapid pace and schedule of teaching? How do you see yourself relating to the noninstructional aspects of teaching? Working with fellow teachers? With parents? In the community?

Go to the Online Learning Center at www.mhhe.com/arends6e to respond to these questions.

Previous chapters described what teachers do as they plan for and deliver instruction and manage complex classroom settings. Providing leadership and teaching students in classrooms, however, are not the only aspects of a teacher's job. Teachers are also members of an organization called *school* and, as such, are asked to perform important leadership functions at the school level, including working cooperatively with colleagues, serving on committees, and working with administrators and parents. The way these aspects of a teacher's job are performed makes a significant difference in the school's professional community and how students behave and what they learn. The way teachers carry out these functions also makes a significant difference in their own professional careers.

This chapter describes the work environment of schools and the corresponding culture of teaching. Emphasis is placed on the idea that schools are not only places where students come to learn; they are also places where adults work. After providing a conceptual framework for viewing schools as workplaces, we summarize the emerging knowledge base on the nature of teachers' work behavior and what makes some schools more effective than others. We conclude with a discussion of several important skills that beginning teachers need as they become fully involved in their first school and community.

Perspective of Schools as Workplaces

At this point in your career, it is likely that your view of schools stems mainly from many years of being a learner. You are familiar with the classroom portion of the teacher's role, with the role of student, and with the way that students and teachers interact around academic tasks. However, you may not have had much chance to observe or reflect on schools from behind the teacher's desk or as social organizations or on the nonclassroom aspects of a teacher's job. In fact, many people (including those in the media) rarely view schools from the perspective of the complex social organizations they are. This is unfortunate, because views of schools, stemming only from experi-

*A critical aspect of a
teacher's work is working
with other teachers.*

ences as students, have caused misunderstanding on the part of many—teachers, parents, and policymakers—regarding school improvement efforts. Also, unrealistic views have led to many beginning teachers' disillusionment. The section that follows provides a view of schools that extends beyond the classroom doors.

Schools Are Human Systems

In discussing schools, we take a perspective that schools are human systems that are influenced not only by the people who learn and work in them but also by the larger community and society. Schools are places where individuals do not act in totally free and disconnected ways but, instead, in more or less interdependent and predictable ways. Although individuals come together in schools to promote purposeful learning, each person does not chart his or her own course alone, nor do the actions of each have consequences only for that person. Also, as we describe later, the synergy developed by teachers acting in concert can have important consequences for student learning. To understand the human systems view of schools, think for a moment about the number of interdependent actions required to bring about a day's worth of instruction for students:

* Paper, pencils, and computers have been ordered.
* Rooms have been cleaned.
* Curriculum guides have been prepared and textbooks ordered.
* Parents have chosen to send their children to school.
* Teachers have chosen to be professionally trained.
* Buses have been driven and breakfasts and lunches prepared.
* Schedules have been determined and children assigned to classes.
* Health services for students have been planned and managed.

This list could go on and on. The point, however, is that the contemporary school is a complex human system requiring its members to perform important functions in interdependent ways.

Schools Have Histories and Cultures

Schools, like other organizations, have histories and cultures consisting of values, beliefs, and expectations that have developed and grown over time. The history of a school provides traditions and a multitude of routines—some good and some not so good—that are taken for granted by organizational members. The *culture of a school* provides the organizational arrangements that hold it together and give it power as a social entity. Lortie (1975) referred to culture as the "way members of a group think about social action; culture encompasses alternatives for resolving problems in collective life" (p. 216). Others have provided similar definitions, although they sometimes use different labels. Rutter and his colleagues (1979), for example, refer to the common values, beliefs, and ways of doing things as the school's **ethos;** Glass (1981) has called it *tone;* Joyce and his colleagues (1993) and Sergiovanni (1996) prefer the word *community.* Regardless of how it is labeled, **school culture** greatly influences what goes on in schools and determines expectations and roles for beginning teachers.

School culture consists of the ways members think about their actions and it reflects their beliefs, values, and history.

Schools Exist in Context

Context is another way to view schools and what goes on in them. The idea of context is illustrated in Figure 13.1. Notice how every activity in the concentric circles is embedded in a set of interlocking or reciprocal relationships. A particular learning task—for

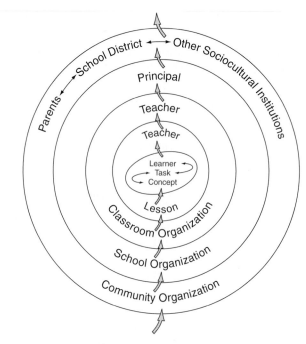

Figure 13.1 *The School in Context*

Source: From Cole and Griffin (1987) and Gallego and Cole (2001), *Handbook of Research on Teaching* (4th ed.), p. 960

instance, the task found in the inner circle, is influenced by the teacher and his or her lesson. This, in turn, is influenced by the principal and the school and ultimately by features of the larger community.

Schools Have Features in Common with Other Organizations

The primary goal of schools is to provide a purposeful environment that enhances student learning.

In some ways, schools are similar to other organizations in society. For example, as in other organizations, members are directed toward the accomplishment of some goal. In a textile plant, the goal may be the production of men's shirts; IBM says information is its business. The overriding goals for schools are to provide *purposeful learning experiences* and develop self-regulated learners. Members of schools—principals, teachers, and students—are rewarded, as are members in other organizations, when they strive for and accomplish common organizational goals. Similarly, they are punished when they fail. An example of a reward is experiments in some states in which teaching faculties are given merit increases if, as a group, they can lift achievement in their school above a set criterion. An example of punishment is instances in which teachers are dismissed if they cannot provide purposeful learning activities for their students.

Another organizational feature of schools similar to that found in other organizations is that coordination of effort is required. In addition to teachers, school staffs include curriculum coordinators, administrators, nurses, counselors, janitors, and other support personnel. Most of the people in schools, however, are students, and they too must be considered organizational members. Because school roles are specialized, routines and structures are created to help members carry out their special tasks in ways that will more or less facilitate what others are doing. The reason coordination of effort is not easy to accomplish in schools is described later.

Schools Have Unique Features

Just as schools have features in common with other organizations, they also have features that are unique. It is the special features of schools that are most important for us to understand.

Ambiguous and Conflicting Goals. It has been stated several times in this book that the overriding goals of schools are to facilitate purposive learning for students and to develop self-regulated learners. Stated at this level of abstraction, most people would readily agree with these goals. However, when people in schools speak more precisely about what purposive learning means, many of their statements may seem ambiguous and may conflict with the aims of one group or another in the community.

Goal ambiguity can be illustrated with reference to citizenship education. Most people in Western societies believe that the schools should socialize students as good citizens who accept the values of democratic political systems and who embrace some degree of freedom in their own economic activities. However, how do school people, parents, and others know whether or not this goal is being accomplished? Parents, for example, are never sure their sons or daughters are embracing the values they desire for them. Teachers seldom know how their former students behave as adult citizens. Do they vote, and are they participating community members?

As for goal conflict, do citizenship goals compete with academic learning goals? Which are most important, and how should time be allocated between the two? What constitutes good citizenship? Some argue that the most important aspect of citizenship education is the socialization of students into traditional values and beliefs. Some church-related and private schools are inclined toward this position. On the other hand, others argue that this approach to citizenship education is simply indoctrination and leads to narrowness and conformity. The good citizen, from this point of view, might be the critical thinker who questions existing values and structures and attempts to modify them.

> Goal ambiguity and conflict are more prevalent in schools than in other organizations.

Compulsory Attendance. A second special feature of schools is that their clients (the students) are compelled to be there. All states have compulsory attendance laws that require parents to send their children to school, normally until age 16. Although most people support these laws because they guarantee a minimum education for all children and help prevent forced child labor, they do create the problem of keeping unmotivated students involved in school life. Schools with large numbers of academically unmotivated students are often schools where teachers choose not to work. Recent innovations in some school systems, such as the creation of alternative and magnet schools, attempt to combat the compulsory nature of schooling by giving students and their parents more choices in the type of school the students attend. The fact still remains, however: students *must* go to school.

> The fact that students are compelled to attend school makes for a unique type of client relationship not found in most other organizations.

Political Visibility. Schools are highly visible and political in most communities. Many people take an active interest in their schools, and given local control, schools offer one of the few places where people in complex societies can have their voices heard. For example, it is quite easy in many communities to stay informed about school events since large portions of the daily newspapers are devoted to school news, including the school's budget. It is also easy to attend local school board or council meetings and voice opinions, just as it is easy to walk directly into most principals' offices without an appointment. The whole system is open and permeable. Some aspects of this situation are positive. Local control and the openness of the educational system have helped maintain strong support for education over the past century. At the same time, this situation leaves the school and those who work there vulnerable to political whims and sometimes unfair attacks.

Schools Are Communities. According to some observers, schools also differ from other organizations in that they are more like communities than modern bureaucracies (Bryk & Driscoll, 1988; Sergiovanni, 1996). Rather than being organizations governed by hierarchical control structures and formal systems of supervision, Sergiovanni argues, schools are communities built on shared purposes and mutual respect:

In some ways, schools are more like communities than they are like modern organizations.

> Communities are collections of individuals who are bonded together by natural will and who are together bound to a set of shared ideas and ideals. This bonding and binding is tight enough to transform them from a collection of "I's" into a collective we. As a "we," members are part of a tightly knit web of meaningful relationships (p. 48).

Notice some of the words used by Sergiovanni: *bonded individuals, shared ideas,* and *collective we.*

Sergiovanni argues that over the past hundred years, modern organizations in business, the military, and the health fields have been constructed around formal and contractual arrangements rather than conditions of shared values found in earlier times. Schools, he says, have mistakenly adopted these formal and contractual arrangements, and though these arrangements may make sense for businesses and hospitals, they do not work well for schools. Instead, they are the source of many of the problems found in today's school. Sergiovanni believes that schools are closer in character to the family, the neighborhood, and voluntary social groups—all organizations that have a special sense of shared values, belonging, and community.

The community metaphor for understanding schools is interesting and potentially powerful. And, as you will see later in this chapter, some research shows that schools

Schools are highly visible and political.

where teachers share a common vision and shared values and have created a collaborative professional community characterized by a dialogue and sense of belonging produce higher student learning than schools in which relationships are more formal and contractual.

Norms, Roles, and the Culture of Teaching

Another way to think about schools is to think about the norms, roles, and organizational arrangements that exist for the purpose of getting work accomplished. These will have strong influences on the experiences that beginning teachers have during both internships and their first year.

Norms. **Norms** are the expectations that people have for one another in particular social settings. They define the range of social behaviors that are allowed in given situations. Some norms are informal, such as the norm that prescribes a swimsuit rather than a cocktail dress on the beach. Some norms, however, are formal. For example, a person might not be arrested if he wore a tuxedo to the beach, but he would be if he broke a local ordinance that restricts bathing in the nude.

The expectation that educators are virtually free to teach as they please within the confines of their classrooms is known as the autonomy norm.

In schools, many formal and informal norms exist that affect teachers and students. For example, in some schools, new teachers will find norms supporting friendliness and openness that will make them feel welcome. In other schools, people may act toward one another in more reserved and formal ways. In some schools, norms to encourage experimentation may make beginning teachers feel comfortable in trying out new ideas, whereas in other schools, few risks will be encouraged. Two important norms associated with schools and the culture of teaching need highlighting, because they affect the lives of beginning teachers most directly.

Autonomy Norm. In some ways, teachers have relatively little power and influence in the larger school system. However, they do have a great deal of influence in their own classrooms, supported by what has been labeled the **autonomy norm.** Teachers, including beginning teachers, do pretty much what they want to once they are in their classrooms and their doors are closed. In many schools, they alone are responsible for the day-to-day curricula and make almost all instructional decisions for themselves.

The Hands-Off Norm. Closely paralleling the autonomy norm is a norm labeled by Lortie (1975), Sarason (1982), and Joyce, Hersh, and McKibbin (1993) as the **hands-off norm.** Not only are teachers given autonomy in their classrooms, but strong sanctions exist against interfering with other teachers in any but the most superficial ways. It is not appropriate, according to Lortie (1975), for teachers to ask for help, for example. Such a request suggests that the teacher is failing. Similarly, according to Feiman-Nemser and Floden (1986) and Little (1990), it is not permissible for teachers to tell a peer what to do or to suggest that he or she teach something differently.

The hands-off norm is the expectation in schools that teachers will not interfere in the work of other teachers.

This is not to suggest to beginning teachers that colleagues within a particular school will be unfriendly or unsupportive. Teachers socialize a great deal with one another and on an emotional level are concerned and supportive of one another. Even so, teachers often avoid talking about instructional practices. It is important to point out that many contemporary school reform projects aim at breaking down the autonomy and hands-off norms by encouraging and helping teachers work together. We return to this idea later in the chapter.

Roles. Organizations and organizational culture also describe a teacher's role. The teacher's role, for example, includes norms about how teachers should behave toward students and students toward them, how teachers should interact with each other and with the principal, and how much teachers should participate in schoolwide problem solving and decision making. People in schools learn roles through interacting with each other.

Some aspects of the teacher's role are clear and straightforward. For example, it is clear that teachers should teach academic content to students and evaluate their students' progress. Some aspects of the teacher's role, however, are not so clear and sometimes provide contradictory expectations. Contradictions in role expectations cause anxiety and trouble for beginning teachers as they enter the school for the first time.

One of the most basic contradictions in the teacher's role stems from strong expectations that teachers should treat each child as an individual even though schools are organized so that teachers must deal with students in groups. This conflict is particularly acute with secondary teachers, who face as many as 150 to 180 students a day for rather brief periods of time. This role conflict, according to Lieberman and Miller (1992) and Little and McLaughlin (1993), is what makes teaching so personal, because to deal with the contradictory demands of individualization and group instruction requires the development of a teaching style that is "individual and personal."

A second basic contradiction in the teacher's role involves the degree of distance between teacher and students. On one hand, teachers are expected to maintain a certain social distance from students so authority and discipline can be maintained. In fact, as described in Chapters 4 and 5, control is often an overriding concern for beginning teachers, since they know they are being heavily judged on this score. On the other hand, most teachers know that they must form some type of bond with students in order to motivate them and help them to learn. Beginning teachers manifest the tensions of this role contradiction in a number of ways. They worry about whether or not they should allow students to call them by their first name or how friendly they should become with a particular student they really like and so on. Such tensions are quite normal, and only experience, it seems, provides the means for dealing with the many contradictions built into the teacher's role.

Cellular Organizational Structure. Compared to most other organizations, schools are rather flat organizations. In elementary schools, there are mainly teachers and a principal, and in most secondary schools, one additional role, the department chair, is added. Some (Joyce et al., 1993; Lortie, 1975) have called this arrangement "cellular," that is, each classroom can be regarded as a cell within which the teacher is responsible for organizing the students, managing discipline, and teaching academic content. This arrangement, coupled with the hands-off norm, often creates an isolated work situation for teachers. They make independent decisions about when and how to teach each subject, and they do not ask other teachers for help. Joyce and his colleagues (1993) observed that this situation has made it customary for principals to relate to the teachers one-to-one rather than as an organized faculty prepared to take collective responsibility. This professional isolation has led some observers to refer to teaching as a "lonely profession." With the addition of many new roles in schools over the past few years, such as special teachers and lead teachers of one kind or another, and new approaches for organizing curricula, it may be that the *cellular structure* of schools is changing. Currently, it remains the most common arrangement.

Loosely Coupled Structure. The school's cellular structure also causes an organizational arrangement that has been labeled **loosely coupled** (Bohman & Deal, 1991; Weick, 1976).

Contradictions in aspects of the teacher's role often cause anxiety for beginning teachers.

School organizations are called cellular because teachers are independently responsible for organizing leadership and teaching functions within the "cells" of their own classrooms.

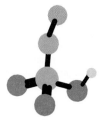

Cellular Structure

Loosely Coupled

This means that what goes on in classrooms is not very tightly connected to what goes on in other parts of the school. Teachers can and do carry out their own instructional activities independent of administrators and others. The central office may initiate new curricula or new teaching procedures, but if teachers choose to ignore these initiatives, they can. On the positive side, loose coupling allows considerable room for individual teacher decision making in situations where a substantial knowledge about "best" teaching practice is lacking. Conversely, loose coupling can stymie efforts to establish common goals and coordinated activities, something that is important for effective schooling, as you will see later.

Theoretical and Empirical Support

For many years, educators have thought about the school as a formal organization. In fact, a very important book written by Waller in 1932 on the sociology of teaching provided many important insights into the nature of schools and of teaching. However, it is only in the last three decades that educators and educational researchers have started to highlight the importance of schools as workplaces and the importance of the organizational aspects of teaching. This section provides examples from fairly recent research about the nature of the work teachers do in schools and how one way this work is done can affect what students learn.

Nature of Teachers' Work

Some people think that teachers' hours match those of the children they teach. Others think that teachers' work consists mainly of working with students. Experienced teachers do not agree with these perceptions. They know that teachers do many other things in addition to directly working with students. They also know that the time demands of teaching are quite great. Over the years, studies have supported this view.

Since 1961, the National Education Association (NEA) has surveyed teachers every five years and asked them to report the number of hours per week they spend on various teaching responsibilities. For more than thirty years, the findings of these reports have remained pretty consistent. Elementary teachers report that they work between forty-five and forty-nine hours per week, whereas secondary teachers say that they work from forty-six to fifty hours per week (Metropolitan Life, 1995). A recent survey confirmed that the majority of teachers today spend at least forty-six hours in an average week on school-related responsibilities and over a third spend more than fifty-five hours per week (Metropolitan Life, 1995). Table 13.1 shows the number of hours per week teachers spend on school-related activities.

To validate these findings and to guard against inflated self-reporting, researchers have shadowed teachers to find out precisely what kind of work they do and for how long. In one particularly interesting study, Cypher and Willower (1984) shadowed five secondary teachers. They found that teachers averaged a 48.5-hour work week, spending approximately 38 hours in school and 10.5 hours in after-school work. The findings

Check, Extend, Explore

Check
- What is meant by the saying "the school is a social system"? A community?
- How do culture, history, and ethos define many important functions and characteristics of a school?
- What features of schools make them different from other formal organizations?
- What norms tend to exist in schools that beginning teachers should anticipate?
- What aspects of a teacher's role are clear? Which tend to be more complex and contradictory?

Extend
- Teaching has been called the "lonely profession." How much will this description affect your decision to stay in teaching? Go to the "Extend Question Poll" on the Online Learning Center to respond.

Explore
- Go to the Online Learning Center at www.mhhe.com/arends6e for links to websites related to the *Nature of Schools as Workplaces.*

Teachers must be capable of juggling many different expected and unexpected activities within a typical workday.

Table 13.1 *Number of Hours per Week Spent on School-Related Responsibilities*

| | Total | Years of Teaching Experience | | Type of School | | | Size of Place | | |
		Less Than 10	10 or More	Elementary	Junior High	High School	Urban	Surburban	Rural
				Percentage					
Fewer than 40	9	8	12	12	8	9	10	10	8
41 to 45	12	10	12	11	15	9	17	10	11
46 to 50	30	30	30	31	28	29	30	28	32
51 to 55	14	15	13	16	9	14	13	15	11
More than 55	35	38	34	30	40	39	29	37	38
Median	50	54	50	51	51	55	50	55	51

Source: After Metropolitan Life (1995), p. 67

Table 13.2 *How Teachers Spend Their Time*

Activity	Total Time in Minutes	Percentage of Time
Instruction		
Direct instruction	95.4	20.6
Organizing	15.9	3.4
Reviewing	21.0	4.5
Testing	22.9	5.0
Monitoring	23.6	5.1
Other work with students		
Study hall supervision	17.4	3.8
Assemblies and clubs	5.9	1.3
Control and supervision	12.7	2.7
Interaction with colleagues and others		
Planned meetings	2.7	1.0
Unscheduled meetings	46.5	10.0
Exchanges	67.5	14.6
Desk and routine work	89.8	20.0
Travel time	24.6	5.3
Private time	16.2	3.5

Source: After Cypher and Willower (1984); Metropolitan Life (1995)

of Cypher and Willower's study combined with data from the Metropolitan Life (1995) survey are displayed in Table 13.2. Among other things, data in Table 13.2 show that most teachers spend less than 40 percent of their work week on instructional activity and that a sizable portion of their work consists of meetings and exchanges with other adults such as parents, the principal, and professional colleagues.

Helping the community is also part of a teacher's work.

Research on School Effectiveness

There is a growing belief that the overall culture and ethos of a school and what teachers do in concert contribute to what students learn as much as the performance of individual teachers. During the past two decades, researchers have begun to supply empirical evidence in support of this perspective. Sometimes this research is called **school effectiveness research;** other times it is referred to as *organizational context research.*

Regardless of the specific label, this research has demonstrated pretty consistently that school culture and community, and the collective behavior of teachers, administrators, and parents, can make an important difference in how much students learn. It points toward the importance of participants coming together and making schoolwide agreements about what should be taught, how it should be taught, and how people should relate to one another. It seems that there is a certain **synergy** working in schools that produces results that cannot be achieved when a teacher works alone on particularistic goals.

Additionally, this research emphasizes the people aspect of schooling. The quality of teaching and the professional community that exists within the school have been found to be more important than the amount of money spent on concrete, books, or paper. That does not mean that resources are not required for good schools; it just means that the amount of money spent on the school's library collection or the physical plant takes a backseat to the community that people within the school create.

Several groundbreaking studies in the late 1970s provided the first evidence on the importance of organizational features and processes. One study was done by an English child psychiatrist and his colleagues who studied twelve secondary schools in London (Rutter et al., 1979). Over a number of years, Rutter and his colleagues collected information about student behavior and achievement in and organization processes of a sample of high schools. The researchers found that student behavior and achievement varied markedly from school to school but that students were more likely to show good

School effectiveness research tries to uncover features that make some schools more effective than others.

Synergy is at work in the school, which produces results that exceed what a teacher working alone could achieve.

Behavior and achievement are strongly related to aspects of a school's social organization.

behavior and higher achievement in some schools than others. Better behavior and higher achievement were strongly related to aspects of the school's social organization, such as the degree to which a common ethos existed, the extent to which teachers held common attitudes, and the degree to which they behaved in consistent ways toward their students.

Since Rutter's study, many other researchers have conducted similar studies with elementary and secondary schools in the United States (Brookover et al., 1979; Crone & Teddie, 1995; Firestone and Rosenblum, 1988; Lee & Smith, 1996; Rosenholz, 1989). Almost all of these studies have produced similar results and conclusions, namely, that some schools develop cultures and communities that support student learning whereas other schools do not. The study by Valerie Lee and Julia Smith highlighted in the Research Summary for this chapter is an excellent example of a very recent study that illustrates the gains that can be achieved when teachers take collective responsibility for their students' learning.

Features of Effective Schools

Several researchers have summarized the research on effective schools and the effects of school processes on student learning. One of the best summaries has been provided by Joyce, Hersh, and McKibbin (1993). Their review is summarized here and then used later as an organizer for considering the organizational skills required of teachers.

Joyce and his colleagues found that features of schools that were effective can be divided into two categories: those having to do with a school's *social organization* and those having to do with the school's *instructional* and *curriculum patterns*. These features are listed in Table 13.3 and described in more detail here.

Effective school features are divided into two categories: those that deal with the social organization and those that deal with instructional and curriculum patterns.

Social Organization. Definitions of the social organizational attributes include the following:

Clear academic and social behavior goals. Academic achievement is constantly emphasized, and teachers, parents, and students share common values and understandings about the school's achievement goals.

Order and discipline. Basic rules of conduct have been agreed upon throughout the school, and teachers feel responsibility for enforcing behavioral norms both in their own particular classes and across the school.

Table 13.3 *Features of Effective Schools*

Social Organization	Instruction and Curriculum
Clear academic and social behavior goals	High academic learning time
Order and discipline	Frequent and monitored homework
High expectations	Frequent monitoring of student progress
Teacher efficacy	Coherently organized curriculum
Pervasive caring	Variety of teaching strategies
Public rewards and incentives	Opportunities for student responsibility
Administrative leadership	
Community support	

Source: After Joyce, Hersh, and McKibbin (1993)

High expectations. Teachers and other staff hold high standards for students. They convey to students an "I care" and can-do attitude and demand that each student aspire to excellence.

Teacher efficacy. Teachers also have high expectations for themselves and a strong belief that they can teach every child.

Pervasive caring. Teachers and other adults in the school develop a caring atmosphere. Their demands on students are not viewed as cruel and judgmental but as fair and caring. They communicate and celebrate student achievement.

Public rewards and incentives. Effective schools have devised ways to publicly reward student successes and achievements. Student work is displayed, honor rolls are published, and active communication exists between the school and parents.

Administrative leadership. Principals in effective schools care deeply about the school's academic programs. They support teacher and student efforts, and they help set the tone for high expectations and pervasive caring.

Community support. Staff in effective schools find ways to involve parents and community in the school's programs. This involvement goes beyond open houses to include such activities as school beautification, tutoring, and active fundraising for the school.

Instruction and Curriculum. The description of attributes associated with the instructional curriculum of effective schools includes the following:

High academic learning time. Teachers in effective schools have found ways to maximize the time devoted to academic learning. They waste little time getting classes started and move smoothly from one activity to another with minimum disruption. Schoolwide, they have found ways to keep administrative disruptions to a minimum.

Frequent and monitored homework. Homework is required and is checked by the teachers in effective schools. Checking and giving feedback to students is one way for teachers and other adults in the school to tell students they have high expectations and that they care.

Frequent monitoring of student progress. Through tests, quizzes, and informal devices, teachers keep track of student progress and give students and parents helpful feedback on this progress.

Coherently organized curriculum. The curriculum in effective schools is closely connected to the goals and objectives of the schools and is linked to the major evaluation and testing procedures. Teachers know what teachers at other levels or in other subjects are teaching and match their own instruction accordingly.

Variety of teaching strategies. Teachers in effective schools have broad repertoires of teaching strategies and employ these to help meet the school's instructional goals.

Opportunities for student responsibility. The adults in effective schools find ways to engage students in running their school through devices such as student government, and they encourage peer tutoring, hall monitoring, and other opportunities for students to engage in leadership behaviors.

Similar results have been replicated in a more recent study. Researchers McLaughlin and Talbert (2001) examined sixteen secondary schools in Michigan and California. They completed extensive and repeated observations and interviews of teachers and students. In schools where they found a high degree of student engagement and students who were "turned-on" rather than "turned-off," they also found teachers who were supported by a strong sense of school community, where subject matter was coordinated sequentially and from subject to subject, and where teachers displayed a strong commitment across the school to study and improve their teaching practices.

Check, Extend, Explore

Check
- How does a teacher's typical workday differ from that perceived by the general public?
- What types of work do teachers do in addition to direct instruction of students? What percentage of their time is spent outside of the classroom?
- What overall findings have been demonstrated by school effectiveness research?
- How do studies conducted by Rutter, Lee, Smith, and others illustrate the importance of a cohesive school culture and collaborative action on the part of teachers?

Extend
- Teachers working together has been shown to influence student learning in significant ways. To what degree are you the type of person who will enjoy working with other teachers? Go to the "Extend Question Poll" on the Online Learning Center to respond.

Explore
- Go to the Online Learning Center at www.mhhe.com/arends6e for links to websites related to *School Effectiveness and School Reform.*

Research Summary

Working Together Makes a Difference

Lee, V. E., and Smith, J. B. (1996).
Collective responsibility for learning and its effects on gains in achievement of early secondary school students. *American Journal of Education,* 104, 103–146.

The media often portray effective teachers through characters such as Jaime Escalante, of *Stand and Deliver* fame, who against great odds taught his East Los Angeles, low-academic students advanced calculus; or David Holland of *Mr. Holland's Opus,* who over a lifetime defended music education in his school and inspired his students through his singular devotion to their education and to their personal lives. It is true that individually inspiring teachers are effective, and we all remember them. At the same time, the collective, rather than individual, responsibility of teachers seems also to be crucial and provided the focus for a study by Valerie Lee and Julia Smith.

Problem and Approach: Lee and Smith began with the premise that the education of students revolves around the work done by teachers and that this work is pivotal in helping schools accomplish their main goal, student learning. But what does teachers' work consist of, and how is it organized? Specifically, what are the links between teachers' work lives and how much their students learn? These were questions that Lee and Smith set out to investigate using information from a large-scale study. The Lee and Smith study is important and was selected for inclusion here for two reasons. One, the results speak directly to the importance of the organizational aspects of teaching, and two, the study is a good illustration of how some research in education is conducted using already existing databases that are made available to the research community by governmental agencies.

Sample and Setting: The researchers used data from a nationally representative sample of 11,692 high school

sophomores and 9,904 of their teachers. The sample was drawn from 820 schools and was part of the National Educational Longitudinal Study sponsored by the National Center for Education Statistics (NELS, 1988). This study surveyed over 22,000 students in 1988 when they were in the eighth grade and then again when they were sophomores in high school in 1990. Students in the sample were surveyed and tested, as were their teachers. Of the teachers who were studied, 31 percent taught mathematics, 32 percent English, 15 percent social studies, and 22 percent science. On average, the study contained data from about twelve teachers within each of the 820 schools.

Procedures: The researchers measured learning gains made by students between the eighth and tenth grades in four subjects: mathematics, reading, history, and science. In addition, they measured three features of teachers' work:

1. *Collective responsibility for student learning.* This feature measured how much teachers in schools believed individually and collectively that they were responsible for student learning and did not attribute learning difficulties to weak students or deficient home lives.
2. *Degree of staff cooperation.* This feature measured how well teachers and administrators got along, the supportiveness of the principal, and the degree to which teachers cooperated and had clarity about the school-wide mission and goals.
3. *Amount of teacher control.* This feature measured teachers' perceptions about how much influence and control they had over conditions in their classrooms (e.g., curriculum and homework) and over policies affecting the whole school (e.g., discipline policy and the ways students were grouped).

Organizational Skills for Teachers

The perspectives and research on organizational context and effective schools are important for beginning teachers for several reasons. First, they can help round out your understanding of schools as social organizations, and second, they can serve as a reminder that your own classroom will be but part of a larger school effort. This research also draws attention to several contradictions that stem from the way schools have

Results: There were many results of this large and complex study. For our purposes here, only a few findings will be highlighted. The first and most important finding of the study was that the achievement gains made by students were significantly higher in schools where teachers took collective responsibility for their students' academic successes and failures rather than blaming students. Table 13.4 shows the gains made by students between the eighth and tenth grades in the four subject fields and compares these gains in schools with high, medium, and low levels of teachers' collective responsibility for student learning. The data in Table 13.4 show that students gained most in all subject areas in the high-responsibility schools and least in the low-responsibility schools. The researchers reported that the differences among the three types of schools were statistically significant.

The researchers also found that the amount of staff cooperation made a difference in student achievement, but not nearly so much as did collective responsibility. Interestingly, this study did not find any relationship between the dimension of teacher control and student achievement. In other words, the amount of control and influence teachers had on classroom and schoolwide policies did *not* seem to effect the achievement of their students.

Discussion and Implications This study has several important implications for teachers and for reform efforts aimed at school improvement. First, the findings emphasize the importance of teachers' work lives, particularly the beliefs they hold about their responsibility for student learning. This means that reform efforts involving new methods in classrooms or adopting new curriculum materials may not make much difference unless teachers' beliefs about their collective responsibilities for student learning also change.

Second, the results of this study provide support for the point of view that effective schools are more like caring communities than efficient bureaucracies and that caring, committed communities are more likely to occur in small settings rather than larger ones. So those school reformers who argue for making schools smaller may indeed be on the right track.

Finally, the study confirms what many people have believed for a long time—the teacher is the most important ingredient in the mix of factors that influence a child's education. What is new, however, is the study's demonstration that it is teachers working together, not alone, which seems to be the crucial reason this is true.

Table 13.4 *Mean Gains in Student Achievement for Sophomores Attending Schools with High, Medium, and Low Levels of Teachers' Responsibility for Student Learning*

Subject	High (*n* = 1,226)	Medium (*n* = 8,801)	Low (*n* = 1,665)
Math gain	6.57	5.39	4.95
Reading gain	3.70	2.51	1.61
History gain	2.95	1.51	1.26
Science gain	3.43	1.54	1.33

Level of Collective Responsibility for Learning

Source: After Lee and Smith (1996), p. 119

been organized. On one hand, it appears that effective schools are places where people have common goals, teachers have organized their curriculum coherently, and common rules and norms guide teachers' expectations for students, homework policies, and discipline. On the other hand, the cellular structure of schools and traditional norms that support teacher autonomy make it difficult for people in a school to create the conditions that will make their school effective.

The remainder of this chapter looks at specific organizational skills that will be of concern to beginning teachers. These are organized according to the other major *role holders* in schools with whom teachers are expected to work. As you read about these organizational skills, keep in mind the main idea from the effective schools research: namely, collective effort schoolwide can produce important conditions for student learning.

Working with Colleagues

Establishing good working relationships with colleagues is an important challenge for a beginning teacher. Being successful in this endeavor requires an understanding of important norms governing collegiality and specific actions that can be taken.

Norms. When beginning teachers enter their first school, they should be aware of the norms that will govern many of the relationships between themselves and their colleagues. The hands-off norm, which allows colleagues within the school to be friendly and supportive but discourages specific suggestions about instructional practices, has already been described. The beginning teacher is likely to be included in lunchroom talk about school politics and the personalities of individual students but will not find much talk about curriculum or teaching methods. Beginning teachers will find they can ask colleagues to provide assistance in finding a place to live or locating a good doctor; they will not be able to ask for help (at least not very directly), however, if they are having a classroom management problem.

The cellular structure of most schools means that beginning teachers may be expected to work alone. They will not be observed by other teachers, nor will they be invited to observe their peers. Teaching success will be known only to students, spouses, or close friends; failures will be kept secret.

Possible Actions. All schools will not reflect the norms described in exactly the same way. Some schools, in fact, may have norms that support professional collegiality. Regardless of the situation, beginning teachers do have some latitude for working with colleagues in open and constructive ways. However, it may require well-planned initiatives on their part. The following activities are usually possible.

Observing Other Teachers. This book has stressed the importance of focused observation and reflection in the process of learning to teach. This process should continue for first-year teachers. In fact, many of the observation schedules provided can be used again and again—during early field experiences, during student teaching, and in the beginning years.

Beginning teachers who want to observe other teachers should inquire early about whether or not classroom visits and observations are acceptable practice in their schools. If they are, principals, department chairs, or lead teachers can facilitate observation opportunities. If norms prevent collegial observations, it is still likely that these can be done in other schools where the beginning teacher is not known. These visits will have to be arranged by principals or by system-level curriculum specialists because they will require substitute teachers.

Discussing Educational Issues with Colleagues. Even if school norms prevent widespread collegial interaction concerning the problems of teaching, most schools have at least a handful of teachers who like more discussion and collegiality. A beginning teacher can take the initiative in seeking out these teachers and promoting this type of

New teachers can attempt to overcome autonomy norms in schools by observing, discussing, and meeting with colleagues.

exchange. Initial discussions may eventually lead to exchanges of materials and perhaps exchanges of classroom visits and observations.

Finally, beginning teachers can seek out other beginning teachers who have not yet been socialized into the hands-off norm and who are probably suffering from many of the same problems and concerns. It has happened that beginning teachers have established their own weekly study and support group where mutual concerns and teaching strategies are shared.

Working in Small Groups and at Meetings. It will be a rare school where a beginning teacher will not find at least a few meetings at which teachers come together for the purpose of mutual planning. Some beginning teachers may not feel comfortable speaking up at faculty assemblies, but they can seek out membership within numerous small groups in the school. In these small-group settings, they can promote collegial norms through modeling good group behavior, such as open communication and effective problem solving and decision making.

Working with Administrators and Leadership Personnel

A second group of people beginning teachers need to relate to is the leadership personnel within the school. School norms govern these relationships also, and specific actions are required.

Norms. Most careful observers of teachers' relationships with principals and other school leaders have pointed out that norms governing these relationships are somewhat ambiguous (Carlson, 1996; Jensen, 1989; Walcott, 1973). On one hand, the school's professional ethos supports the concept of the principal serving as the school's instructional leader and as a role model for teachers. On the other hand, the hands-off norm applies to principals and other leadership personnel as well as to other teachers. Often this norm inhibits direct participation by principals in matters of curriculum or teaching strategies. Teachers, according to Feiman-Nemser and Floden (1986), want the principal to act as a:

> buffer between themselves and outside pressures from district administrators, parents, and other community members. . . . In addition, they want the principal to be a strong force in maintaining student discipline—backing the teachers in their classroom discipline policies and maintaining consistent school-wide policies. In return for these services, the teachers are willing to cooperate with the principal's initiatives (p. 509).

In many schools, norms do not support the direct involvement and participation of the principal in instructional activities, although this may be changing.

New teachers can take several steps to build positive communication channels with the principal.

Possible Actions. Obviously, principals vary greatly in their educational beliefs and management styles. Some are very supportive, and some are not. Some have excellent organizational and interpersonal skills, and some don't. One principal's priorities and values will differ from another's. In some instances, these values and priorities will be consistent with the values and beliefs of a beginning teacher; in other cases, they will be diametrically opposed.

Several specific actions can be taken by beginning teachers to gain the support of the principal and to establish a positive working relationship, regardless of the type of person he or she turns out to be. These actions include the following:

- Initiate regular weekly meetings with the principal during the first few weeks to discuss expectations for teacher and student behavior, academic goals, and other features of the school. Find out the principal's thoughts on the attributes of effective schools and effective teaching.

- Keep the principal informed in writing about what you are doing in your classroom, particularly on such topics as special successes you have had, such as a good lesson; a complimentary note from a parent; any conflicts with students or parents; special events such as guest speakers, field trips, or parties you are planning.
- Invite the principal to your classroom, particularly for a lesson that is unique or special, and for parties in elementary schools or special celebrations in secondary schools.
- Write complimentary notes to the principal when he or she does something you like or something that is particularly helpful to you or one of your students.

All of these suggestions fall under the category of building positive communication channels between the beginning teacher and the principal. They are efforts by beginning teachers to get clear about the principal's expectations on the one hand and, on the other, to make sure the principal understands their instructional program and activities.

Other School Leaders. In many schools, beginning teachers work with other school leaders as well as the principal, including counselors, reading specialists, special education resource teachers, librarians, media specialists, and curriculum specialists. A beginning teacher should remember that roles within organizations are governed by norms that role holders shape as they interact with each other. This means that beginning teachers will have some latitude in their interactions with leadership personnel. These interactions could range from ignoring them completely to actively seeking out their support and assistance. The latter is recommended in most instances.

Beginning teachers should strive, in the very early weeks of school, to build positive working relationships with school leaders and specialists for several reasons. First, unlike teacher colleagues, leadership personnel often are expected to help beginning teachers and to provide help in confidential ways free of evaluation. Second, most counselors and resource teachers got to their current positions because they were effective classroom teachers who received advanced training. This means they probably possess important knowledge they can pass along to beginning teachers if appropriate relationships are established. Finally, resource personnel have more time to provide assistance and support than principals or other teachers in the school do. Beginning teachers should set up regular meetings with resource personnel to discuss roles and expectations, and they should try to keep these individuals informed of their classroom programs and activities.

Working with Parents

Parents are another important group in a teacher's work and professional life. For many years, educators have known that out-of-school factors, such as family and community, have strong effects on children and youth's school-related attitudes and learning. As early as 1966, Coleman and his colleagues identified the importance of family and found that family characteristics were strong predictors of student success in school. Many subsequent studies have been conducted over the past thirty years and were summarized recently by Honig, Kahne, and McLaughlin (2001). One strong conclusion stands out: *families matter.* In general, this research demonstrates that children's opportunities to learn and be successful in school are enhanced by the support and encouragement that parents (or other primary caregivers) provide them.

Working with parents and others in the community, however, is not easy for several reasons. First, the traditional norms governing parent-teacher relationships are somewhat contradictory. Teachers want their relationships with parents to include both con-

Source: The Hartford Courant, September 15, 2002, p. A7. © Pedro Molina.
Reprinted with permission.

cern for the child and support for their instructional program. At the same time, many teachers do not want parents to interfere with their classrooms (see Davies, 1991; Feiman-Nemser & Floden, 1986). Some teachers tend to keep a good distance between themselves and parents and, in fact, have little interaction with them. This is particularly true of teachers in middle and secondary schools.

Second, many schools exist in communities that are very different today than they were a century ago, when schools as we know them were established. Communities have changed and workplace demands on parents are far greater than in earlier times. Families have been reconfigured, and the nuclear family, as once defined, is no longer the norm. In many, many families today, in both affluent and impoverished neighborhoods, all of the adults work outside the home.

Finally, as described in Chapter 2, there is often a discontinuity between the school and the home. Many times the school represents a cultural background quite different from that of the parents. In general, teachers and administrators are middle class, Anglo, and monolingual speakers of English. Many students and their parents, on the other hand, are working class, members of minority groups, and speak English as a second language. Further discontinuities or mismatches between home and school exist in regard to linguistic features and value orientations. Several of these differences were identified by Corno (1989) and are listed in Table 13.5.

Table 13.5 *Differences between Culture of the Home and Culture of the School*

Culture of the Home	Culture of the School
Oral language tradition	Written language tradition
Natural	Unfamiliar
Casual	Formal
Low child-adult ratio	High child-adult ratio
Adults as nurturers	Adults as leaders or managers

Source: Adapted from "What It Means to Be Literate in Classrooms" by L. Corno (1989), in Bloom (ed.), *Classrooms and Literacy*. Norwood, NJ: Ablex

Corno (1989) observed that the differences between the home and the school, particularly the language and value differences, made communication between home and school difficult even under the best of circumstances.

Thus, working with parents, regardless of the difficulties, is important. These actions will not only affect student learning but also create a strong support system for beginning teachers in the community. It can also be a very rewarding aspect of a teacher's work. Following are several ways beginning teachers can build positive, supportive relationships with parents or other significant adults in students' lives. Remember, that guidelines for working with parents, as with other aspects of teaching, will vary from one context to another. You need to remain sensitive to the fact that in many communities, the two-parent home may no longer be the norm. You also need to recognize that even when two parents or adults live in the same home, it is likely that both are working outside the home.

Possible Actions. Teacher-parent interactions can take several forms, including reporting to parents, holding conferences with parents, and enlisting parents' help in school and at home.

Reporting to Parents. Remember the idea described in Chapter 6 that parents of children at any age want to know how their children are doing in school. The traditional report card is one means of giving parents this information. Experienced teachers, however, often use additional means to keep parents informed, because the formal report card is only issued quarterly and only summarizes progress in general terms.

Some teachers, particularly of younger children, try to make weekly or biweekly contact with parents through notes or telephone calls. Such contacts allow teachers to explain what is going on in their classrooms and how the parent's child is doing on specific lessons. Such frequent and regular contact provides the teacher with a natural means for communicating children's successes, not just their deficiencies, which often dominate more formal reports.

Another means of parent communication—one that works well for middle and high school teachers who have many students—is the use of a weekly or monthly newsletter. The use of newsletters was described in Chapter 10. Following are suggestions to guide the production and circulation of classroom or schoolwide parent newsletters adapted from Bluestein (1982), Epstein (1988), and Henderson, Marburgaer, and Ooms (1986):

> Teacher-parent interactions may include written reporting, conferencing, and requesting parent help when needed.

> Newsletters are a means of providing written updates to parents regarding activities in the classroom.

- Your newsletters can be formal or informal. They should reflect a newspaper format with headings, and they should always be neatly and carefully done.
- The language of the newsletter should be suitable for the community and chosen with the parents' backgrounds in mind.
- Newsletters should be sent home consistently. Once a month is best in most situations. They can also be shared with other teachers and with the principal.
- Newsletters should be designed to provide information parents are interested in, such as what the class is studying; changes in formats or schedules; new goals and directions for the class; new rules; routines and expectations; and upcoming projects, programs, and events.
- A portion of the newsletter should be devoted to recognitions, such as for students or teams who have done good work, for parent helpers who have made significant contributions, and for others in the community who have visited or contributed to the class.
- Newsletters should contain samples of students' work, such as writings, poems, or projects. Make sure every student's work is included eventually.
- Newsletters can be used as a way to involve parents by inviting them to participate in class activities or to serve as classroom or school helpers.

Conferences provide a valuable opportunity for parents and teachers to develop a positive working relationship.

Holding Conferences with Parents. Most beginning teachers will be involved with parent conferences. Teachers of younger children are sometimes required to make a home visit early in the school year and to hold quarterly in-school meetings with parents. Teachers of older students are normally given more latitude to initiate conferences as needed or when parents request them. In either event, holding parent conferences is an important organizational function of teaching and can provide valuable experiences for the teacher and the parents if done properly. This is also a function that some beginning teachers feel somewhat nervous about.

Using information from the New Mexico Institute for Parent Involvement, Jane Bluestein (1982) and Fuller and Olsen (1998) suggested the following strategies for teachers to use for parent conferences:

Preconference preparations include the following:

1. Notify: Purpose, place, time, length of time allotted. Consider the parent's schedule and availability; offer choices of time whenever possible.
2. Prepare: Review child's folder, gather examples of work, and prepare materials. Be very familiar with the student's performance and progress before the parent arrives.
3. Plan agenda: List items for discussion and/or presentation.
4. Arrange environment: Comfortable seating, eliminate distractions. The parent is at an immediate disadvantage by being on your "turf." To help avoid power implications, arrange the environment so that you and the parent are on equal planes (same-sized chairs), sitting side-by-side at a table, as opposed to face-to-face across your desk.

The actual conference includes the following:

1. Welcome: Establish rapport.
2. State: Purpose, time limitation, note taking, options for follow-up. This is where you share information and present data. You may find note taking during the conference useful in recording your interactions—particularly the parent's feedback and responses. In addition, discuss various avenues you (each) may follow in future dealings with the student, including directions for your instruction and expectations.

> Planning conference topics in advance can relieve the stress that beginning teachers may experience at meeting time.

3. Encourage: Information sharing, comments, questions.
4. Listen: Pause once in a while. Look for verbal and nonverbal cues. The previous two recommendations support the concept of a conference being an *exchange* between the teacher and the parent.
5. Summarize.
6. End on a positive note.

Postconference steps and recommendations include the following:

1. Review conference with child, if appropriate.
2. Share information with other school personnel, if needed.
3. Mark calendar for planned follow-up.

Enlisting Parents' Help in School and at Home. A final way that beginning teachers can work with parents is by involving them as teachers and assistants, both in school and at home. This practice is more common in elementary and middle schools than in high schools. It is also easier in communities where *not all* the parents hold jobs. Regardless of the situation, beginning teachers will always find some parents or parent surrogates willing to help if proper encouragement is given. Some guidelines for involving parents include:

Teachers can develop positive relationships with parents by asking them for assistance at work or home.

- **To assist with small groups.** Conducting small-group activities is difficult for teachers because there are so many simultaneous demands in the classroom. Effective teachers sometimes find parents who will come to the school and help on a regular basis. If beginning teachers choose to use parents in this way, they should consider the parents' schedules and plan some training so that parents know what is expected of them.
- **To assist with field trips and other special events.** Field trips and many other special events such as parties or celebrations take an extra set of hands. Again, with proper encouragement and training, parents can be most useful during these times.
- **As teacher aides.** Some teachers have found ways to use parents as aides in their classrooms, thus getting valuable assistance in correcting papers, writing and publishing class newsletters, organizing parties, and the like.
- **To help with homework.** Most parents feel a responsibility for helping their children with homework. Unfortunately, many do not know how to be helpful. Effective teachers teach parents how to teach their own children. This can also be done on a schoolwide basis. This generally requires holding special evening sessions during which the teacher explains to parents what the homework is trying to accomplish, shows them how to help students practice, and provides them with guidelines for giving students feedback. Many of the skills described in this book can be taught to parents. Teaching parents teaching skills may be time-consuming, but it can extend the teacher's influence over student learning, perhaps more than any other single action.

Working with parents can be a very rewarding aspect of a teacher's work. It can help break down the discontinuities between the home and the school and it can greatly enhance children and youth's opportunity to participate and be successful in school.

Working for School Improvement

Helping schools improve, as with other aspects of school leadership and collaboration, will not be the major concern of beginning teachers. It is, however, an area that beginners should know about. Making classrooms and schools better is a responsibility of teachers, and involvement, if only in a very small way, should start early in one's career.

Linda Darling-Hammond has been a leader in working for the professionalization of teaching and for making schools better places to work and learn.

Why Improvement? Schools, as they exist today, assumed their basic design in the late 1800s. Curiously, people are ambivalent about this design. Many citizens are comfortable with the familiar patterns of the schools they experienced as children, and they get upset with changes that challenge these basic patterns. For example, efforts to get rid of the "neighborhood school" concept, for whatever reasons, meet severe resistance in most communities. At the same time, citizens are quick to find fault with the schools when they fail to live up to contemporary expectations. Bruce Joyce and his colleagues (1993) caught the essence of this paradox when they wrote:

> Throughout history . . . [critics] . . . have found [the school] both too backward and too advanced. It falls behind the times and fails to keep us in simultaneous cadence. . . . Most citizens are cautious about educational innovation. People like the familiar old schoolhouse as much as they criticize it. They tend to believe that current problems in education are caused by changes (perceived as "lowering of standards") rather than because the old comfortable model of the school may be a little rusty and out-of-date. In fact, our society has changed a great deal since the days when the familiar and comfortable patterns of education were established, and many schools have become badly out of phase with the needs of children in today's world (pp. 3–4).

Joyce and his colleagues are right. The world has changed considerably since the idea of formal schooling was first conceived. As you know, many aspects of peoples' lives and of their social institutions have transformed dramatically over the past quarter of a century. A shrinking world produced by new communication and transportation technologies has replaced older parochial views with more cosmopolitan outlooks and interests. Shifting population patterns have made diverse, multicultural communities the norm and have greatly increased social sensitivity. New information technologies that include telecommunication satellites, word processors, microcomputers, and the Internet have substantially changed the way information can be thought about and used. The printing technologies that only came into being during the last two hundred years, making possible the current system of schools and libraries, must now compete with electronic communications. Today, every classroom and most homes have electronic access to the information and wisdom stored in the major libraries of the world. These changes provide the context in which education and schools must operate. They also influence the values and interests of the youth found in classrooms, as well as the values and beliefs you have about teaching and about schools.

Enhancing Teaching with Technology

A Look to the Future

All major innovations have both positive and negative consequences. The automobile increased individual mobility, but it also led to highway deaths, urban sprawl, and inadequate mass transit systems. The airplane has helped turn the world into a global village; it has also been used as a tool of terrorism and mass destruction. Twenty-first-century computers and related technologies hold great potential for positive effects on student learning. As described in previous chapters, research supports the use of computers (Cognition and Technology Group, 1996; Riel & Fulton, 1998) and has shown how they and related technologies can enhance not only teacher-centered instruction but also provide very strong support for activity and student-centered approaches. However, negative consequences may also occur. This final technology box discusses some societal-wide technology issues for which beginning teachers should be aware as well as some issues that pertain to your own growth as a professional in using technology to enhance student learning.

Technology-Related Issues

As described in Chapter 1, the perspective in *Learning to Teach* is one that believes technology will not take over education, replace teachers, or drastically change some of the traditional ways we have organized schooling and learning. On the other hand, beginning teachers can expect the use of technology at all grade levels to become more sophisticated and to have an increasing presence in the effective teacher's repertoire of effective practice. There will also be some important societal issues for tomorrow's educators to worry about.

Many teachers and parents believe that technology will have a negative impact on children and youth. Hours spent staring at computer monitors and playing electronic games detract youth from other endeavors—reading books, spending time with family, playing and socializing with friends. Frequent media reports of youth, such as the young men involved in the mass killings in Littleton, Colorado, being addicted to violent games and websites heighten concerns about negative aspects of computers and related technologies.

Similarly, educators and parents worry about the content of many websites and what children may be watching or to whom they may be talking. Although schools have taken steps to filter out inappropriate content, these filters exist in only one-third of homes with Internet access. In a survey of parents (Annenburg, 1999), over three-quarters of respondents expressed fear about children giving away personal information over the Internet and fear that their children would watch sexually explicit materials.

Growth in Capabilities to Use Technology

Most observers agree with Brandt (2000) that technological change in the larger society will continue at a rapid pace and these changes will demand responses by our educational institutions and by teachers. Teachers must stay abreast of technological change and continue to upgrade their skills for using technology. The International Society for Technology in Education (ISTE) has developed a set of performance technology standards for teachers (Figure 13.2). The ISTE Standards for Teachers are also included in the form of a checklist in the *Guide to Field Experiences and Portfolio Development* on the Online Learning Center so you can assess your competencies at this stage in your career.

Any new field presents many opportunities for optimism and vision. Technology is no different. Opportunities exist for you to become technology literate and competent in this rapidly revolving field. These, in turn, will help you communicate to your students a vision of a future that will require considerable skill in all realms of technology.

There are twenty-three performance technology standards for teachers organized into six broad categories.

Technology Operations and Concepts. Teachers demonstrate a sound understanding of technology operations and concepts. Teachers:

1. Demonstrate introductory knowledge, skills, and understanding of concepts related to technology (as described in the ISTE National Educational Technology Standards for Students).
2. Demonstrate continual growth in technology knowledge and skills to stay abreast of current and emerging technologies.

Planning and Designing Learning Environments and Experiences. Teachers plan and design effective learning environments and experiences supported by technology. Teachers:

1. Design developmentally appropriate learning opportunities that apply technology-enhanced instructional strategies to support the diverse needs of learners.
2. Apply current research on teaching and learning with technology when planning learning environments and experiences.
3. Identify and locate technology resources and evaluate them for accuracy and suitability.
4. Plan for the management of technology resources within the context of learning activities.
5. Plan strategies to manage student learning in a technology-enhanced environment.

Teaching, Learning, and the Curriculum. Teachers implement curriculum plans that include methods and strategies for applying technology to maximize student learning. Teachers:

1. Facilitate technology-enhanced experiences that address content standards and student technology standards.
2. Use technology to support learner-centered strategies that address the diverse needs of students.
3. Apply technology to develop students' higher-order skills and creativity.
4. Manage student learning activities in a technology-enhanced environment.

Assessment and Evaluation. Teachers apply technology to facilitate a variety of effective assessment and evaluation strategies. Teachers:

1. Apply technology in assessing student learning of subject matter using a variety of assessment techniques.
2. Use technology recourses to collect and analyze data, interpret results, and communicate findings to improve instructional practice and maximize student learning.
3. Apply multiple methods of evaluation to determine students' appropriate use of technology resources for learning, communication, and productivity.

Productivity and Professional Practice. Teachers use technology to enhance their productivity and professional practice. Teachers:

1. Use technology resources to engage in ongoing professional development and lifelong learning.
2. Continually evaluate and reflect on professional practice to make informed decisions regarding the use of technology in support of student learning.
3. Apply technology to increase productivity.
4. Use technology to communicate and collaborate with peers, parents, and the larger community in order to nurture student learning.

Social, Ethical, Legal, and Human Issues. Teachers understand the social, ethical, legal, and human issues surrounding the use of technology in PreK–12 schools and apply that understanding in practice. Teachers:

1. Model and teach legal and ethical practice related to technology use.
2. Apply technology resources to enable and empower learners with diverse backgrounds, characteristics, and abilities.
3. Identify and use technology resources that affirm diversity.
4. Promote safe and healthy use of technology resources.
5. Facilitate equitable access to technology resources for all students.

Figure 13.2 *ISTE National Educational Technology Standards for Teachers*

Social changes are also accompanied by changes in childhood and adolescence. Youth mature sooner than in earlier times, and each generation is confronted with a different set of questions and priorities that must be addressed. Some years ago, American sociologist James Coleman (1972) illustrated this problem in an article entitled "The Children Have Outgrown the Schools." In this article, he argued that schools fail students because they are pursuing the wrong goals with inappropriate experiences. Schools were created at a time when the society, according to Coleman, was "information poor and action rich." This meant that people, including youth, had plenty of things to do but little information to assist them. Over time, however, society has become "information rich but action poor"—people now have access to all kinds of information but fewer opportunities for applying and acting on the information. Coleman suggested that modern curricula should require more opportunities for active learning and involvement rather than merely providing exposure to more and more information. He argued that it is no longer sufficient to view the transmitting of information as the only purpose of schooling. Programs are needed that provide youth with realistic links between education and daily living. Don Tapscott (1998) described a similar phenomenon in his book *Growing Up Digital*—namely, that schooling is out of touch with the realities of today's "net generation." How to adapt to these changes is a difficult, perplexing problem and a challenge for your generation of teachers.

Possible Actions. As a beginning teacher encountering your first classroom, you likely will be faced with many dilemmas and unanswered questions. You also will likely be troubled by some of the discrepancies between professional ideals and the realities you find. Some beginning teachers have been known to accept these realities with a sense of resignation or defeat. Others have faced the complexities of teaching with a desire for improvement. There are some concrete things teachers can do, even in their beginning years, that will establish healthy patterns and contribute to school improvement.

Becoming a Student of One's Own Teaching. One means to improve classrooms is to become a student of one's own teaching. This type of activity is sometimes called **action research,** and it serves as a means for teachers to engage in critical inquiry into and reflection on the processes of teaching. The specifics of how to carry out action research projects are described in the Resource Handbook at the end of *Learning to Teach.*

Working on the School Level. A beginning teacher's role in schoolwide improvement efforts at first involves being a thoughtful participant in proposals that come from others. Such proposals may involve policies for beginning teacher evaluation created by the state legislature, a new science curriculum adopted by the school district, or perhaps new approaches for classroom management offered by the principal. In all these instances, beginning teachers will be primarily on the receiving end. According to Fullan (1992), when teachers are faced with proposals for reform, they should consider individually and as a faculty several issues before deciding to commit themselves to the change effort. These issues include the following:

1. *Assess the nature of the proposed change.* Teachers need to give the proposed change careful study. They need to determine if it addresses an important need and if it has been successful elsewhere. They also need to assess their own priorities. Teachers are faced with many changes all the time, and they can only put their energy into a few. In most instances, a faculty can only work on one or two improvement efforts at a time, and these are best accomplished when they are connected to the overall direction and vision of the school.
2. *Assess administrative support.* Some form of active support by administrators (superintendents and principals) is usually required for reform efforts to be successful. Although

teachers may decide to go it alone, independent of their administrators, they should do so only after careful consideration of the risks involved with this type of action.

3. *Assess support by other teachers.* Most school improvement efforts require the support of most, if not all, the teachers in a school. If a single or a few teachers choose to initiate a project, it is wise to check out colleague support first and to stimulate support if it does not already exist before moving forward. School improvement is easier in schools in which teachers have a collaborative work culture.

Exhibiting Leadership. First impressions affect the way beginning teachers are received by professional colleagues both inside and outside school. One way that beginning teachers can become known among colleagues and win their regard is to exhibit leadership potential within the school or school system. Following are some examples, reported by principals and colleagues, of what several successful beginning teachers did to exhibit leadership during their first year:

- Elaine taught on a fifth- and sixth-grade teaching team that had a weak science curriculum. Elaine had majored in biology in college and had more science background than the other, more experienced teachers on the team. She volunteered to revise the science curriculum for the team and found suitable materials for teachers to use. This leadership was applauded by team members and made Elaine a highly valued and respected team member.
- Miguel was hired as a social studies teacher in a middle school. In discussions with students and colleagues, he found that for the previous three years, no one had paid any attention to the school's drama program. Miguel had been in numerous college plays and volunteered to head up the drama club and to sponsor a spring play. The play was a huge success, and Miguel won respect for his willingness to take on this schoolwide job.
- Valerie, a high school English teacher, was upset about the hall behavior of the students in the building wing where she had been assigned. After getting things off to a good start in her own class, she began discussing the hall problem with other teachers in the wing. Under her leadership, they established a set of rules for hall behavior and together agreed on ways to monitor student behavior between classes.

Obviously, beginning teachers should not overextend themselves by assuming too many leadership responsibilities. However, it is important to pick at least one project that has the potential for schoolwide attention and devote energy to getting successful results. Meeting the leadership challenges of teaching can be among the most rewarding accomplishments of a teacher's career.

Check, Extend, Explore

Check
- What actions can beginning teachers take to facilitate positive working relationships with their colleagues?
- What actions can beginning teachers take to facilitate positive working relationships with their principals?
- What are some common parent-teacher interactions? What can a teacher do to promote optimal relationships?
- Why do schools need to improve? What actions can beginning teachers take to provide leadership for improvement?

Extend
- Do you agree or disagree that parents should be closely involved in everything that goes on in schools? Go to the "Extend Question Poll" on the Online Learning Center to respond.

Explore
- Go to the Online Learning Center at www.mhhe.com/arends6e for links to websites related to *School Improvement and Parent Involvement.*

Reflections **from the** *Classroom*

Teacher's Work

At the beginning of this chapter, you read about the busy work lives of two beginning teachers. Both are highly involved, not only with their students, but also with schoolwide activities.

Think about all aspects of a teacher's work and write a reflective essay on school leadership and collaboration. Consider the following questions: What are your views on the noninstructional aspects of a teacher's work? Are these aspects important? Or do they take valuable time that could be spent with students? What about the effective school research? Do you believe that synergy can be created and student achievement enhanced when teachers work together? Or do you believe that the best way to improve student learning is to allow maximum autonomy for teachers? When you begin your teaching career, which aspects of a teacher's work will you value the most? Which aspects will you find most troublesome? Do you look forward to working with colleagues and parents? Or do you think you will resent this type of work because it takes time away from your students? You may wish to illustrate your reflections with photographs of schools, videos, papers, and other artifacts that will demonstrate your understanding of the school as a place where teachers work and the features that make some schools more effective than others. Approach the situation from the perspective closest to the grade level you are preparing to teach. Finally, place this work in your professional portfolio and compare it with the following views of two experienced teachers.

Amy Callen

Lyndon Pilot School, 4th and 5th Grade Loop
Boston, MA

Whether you are a first-year teacher or have twenty years of experience, the day does not end when the last child steps on the school bus. There are papers to correct, bulletin boards to design, new units to research, parents to call, conferences to facilitate, meetings to attend, etc. Becoming involved in your school community is vital to your survival as a teacher. There are many ways to become involved.

However, one of the most common mistakes I have seen is taking on too many responsibilities that are not connected to your everyday work in the classroom. When I began my teaching career I volunteered for everything I could. I joined the School Site Council. I was a member of the Hiring and Evaluation Committee. I regularly attended PTO meetings, started an after-school math club, and often found myself still at school at ten o'clock at night. Because of these activities, added to my everyday classroom responsibilities, I became too busy and had no life of my own.

Teachers at the beginning of their careers should spend time outside of the classroom focusing on their practice. Attending school and district-wide professional development programs, joining study groups, observing other teachers, being observed, and attending common planning sessions are all experiences that will enhance your performance in the

classroom. Allow yourself time to get comfortable with who you are as a teacher, and begin to balance that with who you are outside of school. Do not forget that there is a life outside the school walls.

After a few years, your classroom responsibilities will seem automatic to you. You will know your curriculum inside and out, and you will be ready to share your knowledge and time with the community. This is the time to join the PTO, to start a school newspaper, write a grant, or take on a student teacher. People will appreciate your knowledge and time, and you will not become frustrated or overwhelmed with all of your responsibilities.

It is extremely tempting to involve yourself in opportunities that arise during your first year, but be patient. You have a lifetime of teaching ahead of you. Your first year is for you. Be selfish and choose only those opportunities that will support you and your growth as an educator. Also make sure you let your colleagues know that you are part of the school team.

Angela Adams

Jacksonville Middle School, 7th and 8th Grades
Jacksonville, TX

Teaching is a profession that fulfills many aspects of my life. Unfortunately, for many teachers, teaching is simply a job they think about only when inside the classroom. They rarely get involved in school-wide activities. During my first year, I wanted to be involved with everything, from science club to supporting the cheerleaders, from the band to the sports teams. I quickly realized that I had over-extended myself. Now, I choose one or two activities that I feel I can devote an adequate amount of time to and volunteer for events, depending on my schedule. When my students are involved, I also try to attend concerts, games, and plays. This is an excellent way to build positive, rewarding relationships with students and show that you support their efforts.

In addition to being involved with students, teachers should also be involved with other teachers in their school. My school allows an extra planning period so teachers can meet in departments to plan collaborative projects and lessons each day. Working with other teachers provides me with fresh ideas and new angles in which to view my subject. And, don't forget parents!

Chapter Review

Go back to the "Interactive and Applied Learning" feature at the beginning of the chapter for a listing of interactive and applied activities. Go to the Online Learning Center at **www.mhhe.com/arends6e** or your Interactive Student CD-ROM to take practice quizzes over the content of this chapter and receive immediate feedback. You can also review chapter content and main ideas, practice with key terms, and find annotated Web links on topics associated with Chapter 13.

Summary

Perspective of Schools as Workplaces

- Schools are social organizations and, as such, are adult workplaces as well as places where students come to learn.
- People in schools act not in totally free and disconnected ways but in more or less interdependent and predictable ways.
- Schools have individual histories and cultures (tone, ethos) with norms and roles that influence school goals and processes and the way people work to achieve them.
- Although schools, like other organizations, are characterized by goals and control structures, they also have special features, such as goal ambiguity, compulsory attendance, political visibility, limited resources, and sense of community.
- Two important norms that regulate the culture of teaching and behavior in schools are the autonomy norm and the hands-off norm. The autonomy norm allows teachers to do pretty much what they want inside their classrooms. The hands-off norm sanctions teachers who try to interfere with other teachers' teaching methods or processes.
- Roles also define how teachers do their work. Some aspects of a teacher's role are contradictory; for example, the need to provide individual attention to students in group settings and the need to maintain a certain amount of social distance from students.

Theoretical and Empirical Support

- Research on teachers' work lives has documented that teachers carry out many organizational functions in addition to working directly with students and that the time demands on teachers are quite extensive.
- A moderately strong knowledge base exists that helps explain why some schools are more effective than others. Some aspects of this research are still controversial.
- Research on schools has illustrated that while teaching performance in individual classrooms is very important, the way that principals, teachers, parents, and students all come together to define common goals, expectations, and procedures and the way teachers take collective responsibility for student learning have substantial impact on what students learn.
- More effective schools have processes and procedures characterized by clear goals, high expectations, pervasive caring, strong leadership, community support, high academic learning time, frequent monitoring of student progress, coherent curricula, and variety in the methods used by teachers.

Organizational Skills for Teachers

- Teachers contribute to effective schools by successfully working with colleagues; working with school leaders, such as the principal; working with parents; and providing leadership for school improvement.

- Establishing good working relationships with colleagues is very important and can be enhanced by observing other teachers in the school, volunteering to work on committees and task forces, and seeking out colleagues for discussion of educational issues.
- Teachers build good working relationships with principals and other leadership personnel by meeting with them regularly, keeping them informed about what they are doing in their classrooms, and participating in schoolwide activities.
- Parents will become partners in the teacher's classroom if they are kept informed about what is going on, made to feel welcome in the school and at conferences, and enlisted to help in their child's education at home and in school. Parent involvement can have very strong, positive effects on how well students do in school.
- Helping to improve classrooms and schools is an important aspect of the teacher's job.
- Improvement is needed because schools, in many instances, are out of phase with the needs of today's youth and do not live up to rising expectations people have for education.
- Teachers who choose to work toward school improvement can do so by becoming thoughtful and informed about change initiatives proposed by others and by helping to create and provide leadership for improvement projects.

Key Terms

action research 486	hands-off norm 467	school culture 463	synergy 471
autonomy norm 467	loosely coupled 468	school effectiveness	
ethos 463	norms 467	research 471	

Portfolio and Field Experience Activities

This feature has been designed to help you learn from your field experiences and to assist you in the preparation of artifacts for your professional portfolio on topics and standards associated with Chapter 13.

1. Complete the "Reflections from the Classroom" exercise at the end of this chapter and use the recommended reflective essay as an exhibit of your views about school leadership and collaboration.
2. Use Activity 13.1 in the *Guide to Field Experiences and Portfolio Development* to assess your workplace skills. Summarize the results as an exhibit for your portfolio.
3. Use Activities 13.3 and 13.4 in the *Guide to Field Experiences and Portfolio Development* to interview teachers about role conflict and how they work with parents. Use the recommended reflective essays to communicate your views about teaching and about working with parents as an exhibit in your professional portfolio.
4. Complete Activity 13.5 in the *Guide to Field Experiences and Portfolio Development* to develop a "platform" that describes your current thinking about effective schools. Make the product(s) of your effort into an exhibit for your professional portfolio.

Books for the Professional

Go to the Online Learning Center at www.mhhe.com/arends6e or your Interactive CD-ROM for an annotated version of this list.

Fullan, M. (2001). *The New Meaning of Educational Change* (3rd ed.). New York: Teachers College Press.

Fuller, M. L., and Olsen, G. (1998). *Home-School Relations: Working Successfully with Parents and Families.* Boston: Allyn & Bacon.

Goodlad, J. I. (1984). *A Place Called School: Prospects for the Future.* New York: McGraw-Hill.

Kohn, A. (2000). *The Schools Our Children Deserve.* New York: Houghton Mifflin.

Lieberman, A., and Miller, L. (1992). *Teachers—Their World and Their Work: Implications for School Improvement.* New York: Teachers College Press.

Sarason, S. B. (1995). *Parental Involvement and the Political Principle.* San Francisco: Jossey-Bass.

Resource Handbook

Contents

Unit 1 *Reading and Using Research*

Chapter 1 of *Learning to Teach* described the importance of the knowledge base on teaching and learning and how educational research supports the practice of teaching and frees teachers from an overreliance on earlier common-sense and rule-of-thumb approaches. As with other complex human activities, research has its own rules and specialized language, which can be very confusing to the novice. Learning to learn from research requires some understanding of the methods and language used by researchers and an awareness of where to go for research information. A broad understanding of educational research is obviously beyond the scope of this book, but certain key concepts that are important for reading and understanding research are presented in this special resource section. The aim of this section is to help beginning teachers to use research, to read research reports with a critical eye, and to locate research results that may be needed to inform the practice of teaching.

Key Research Ideas

There are several basic features of research that are important to understand in order to read and use it properly. These include the way researchers state problems, the overall conception or model that guides their research, and the way they seek to find relationships among variables.

Research Questions and Problems

Researchers and practitioners often pose their questions and problems in different ways. A problem, from the researcher's perspective, normally has three ingredients: (1) It is clearly stated in question form; (2) it focuses on relationships between two or more variables; and (3) it implies the possibility of testing from a scientific perspective. Practical problems, however, although sometimes stated in question form, rarely focus on relationships that can be clearly tested. Instead, they generally strive to state a discrepancy between the "way things are" and the way the problem solver would like them to be. To show the difference between a practical problem faced by teachers and a researchable problem posed by researchers, consider two types of questions that might be asked about student motivation. A teacher might ask a practical question such as, "How can I get my unmotivated students to do their homework each night?" A researcher, on the other hand, might ask a researchable question such as, "What are the effects of two different reward systems (free time in school versus parental praise) on time devoted to homework by unmotivated students?" Both problems are clearly stated in question form, but only the latter focuses on relationships among variables and has a built-in procedure for investigation.

Model for Research on Teaching

Educational researchers try to make sense of the world of education they study. Essentially, they try to find out what influences the very complex environment of teaching and learning. To do this, they have theories about how teaching and learning occur and they try to arrange various characteristics (variables) of this world into models that can explain teaching and learning more fully. A research **variable** is a characteristic of a person (teacher, student, parent) or some aspect of the environment (classroom, home, school, government) that can vary. Much of the research on teaching and learning during the last few decades has come from researchers who have been guided by what Robert Floden has called the "effects of teaching" model. The goal and defining characteristic of this research has been to identify the links and relationships among teachers, students, environments, and student outcomes (Floden, 2001; Gage, 1963; Mitzel, 1960; Shulman, 1986). The "effects of teaching" model has been expanded over the years and many interesting and important variables have been added. For the most part, however, the basic model has remained the same, as illustrated in Figure R1.1.

As you can see, the "effects of teaching" model organizes variables into five classes: students, teachers, context and policy, classroom, and outcomes.

1. *Student variables*—the characteristics students bring with them to the classroom, including their experiences, abilities, motivation, cognitions, and feelings.
2. *Teacher variables*—the characteristics of teachers; namely, their experiences, their training, and special properties they have such as skills, motivations, cognition, and feelings.
3. *Context and policy variables*—the larger environment to which teachers and students must adjust, such as characteristics of the community, the school and its curriculum, and local, state, and national policies.
4. *Classroom process variables*—the activities and procedures that occur in classrooms. These variables are associated with what teachers and students do. These classroom process variables are those of most concern in *Learning to Teach*.
5. *Outcome variables*—the outcomes of teaching and classroom interaction, including knowledge, skills, and attitudes. These variables can be divided into more short-term or immediate outcomes as well as long-term effects.

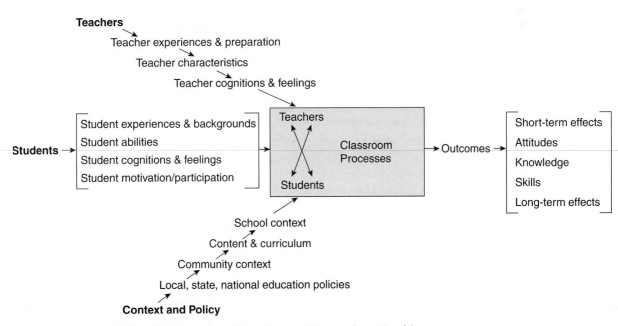

Figure R1.1 *Model for Thinking about Teaching and Research on Teaching*

Notice the arrows in the model in Figure R1.1. These show the presumed causative relationships among the variables. It is important to point out that the arrows are only predictions and are not necessarily always accurate. When discussing the model some time ago, Dunkin and Biddle (1974) explained the complexity of discovering what causes what in teaching and learning:

> For example, let us assume that teachers who come from middle-class backgrounds are known to approach pupils somewhat differently than those with lower-class backgrounds. Does this mean that social class "causes" differential classroom behavior? Indeed this interpretation might be correct. But it might also be true that teachers who come from middle- and lower-class backgrounds are more likely to attend different colleges and thus to have had different experiences in teacher training; this latter factor, then, would be the actual cause of their different behaviors in the classroom (p. 37).

Other researchers (Shulman, 1986) have taken the position that rather than assuming a causation that flows from the teacher to the learner, we should conceive of teaching as an activity involving teachers and students working jointly. Teachers learn and students teach, so the arrows in the model could go both ways. Researchers using the "effects on teaching" model strive to find relationships primarily between teacher behavior and subsequent student outcomes or they may focus on a wider array of variables and explore multiple relationships, including the cognitions and feelings of students and their teachers, as well as the multiple interactions found in classroom settings.

Other models have been developed to provide conceptual maps for the research on teaching. Although each has been constructed from its own point of view, all are attempts to show important relationships in the complex world of teaching and learning. Over the past decade, the "effects of teaching" model has been challenged. For example, some postmodern theorists have argued that any "search for firmly supported knowledge is bound to be fruitless, because all human observation and understanding are mediated by language and context" (Floden, 2001, p. 5; see also Lyotard, 1987). Hamilton and McWilliam (2001) have written that they believe the model to be "moribund." Others (Gilligan, 1982; Noddings, 1992, 2001) have argued that the dominant "effects of teaching" model has been flawed because it was conceived from the vantage point of advantaged white males and neglected views of the less privileged, such as the poor and women. For example, Nel Noddings argued that schooling and research on schooling have held that "feminine" traits such as "caring" are inferior while holding masculine traits up as models.

This brief *Resource Handbook* on how to "Read and Use Research" reflects mainly the "effects of teaching" perspective. However, as you read this handbook and as you read and use research, you should remain aware that the field of educational research today represents many scholarly traditions. Like any other human endeavor, it will change and evolve significantly over your professional lifetime.

Independent and Dependent Variables

When you read the research on teaching summarized in this book and elsewhere, you will often come across words such as *independent* and *dependent variable*. These are words used by researchers to describe a particular aspect of the variables they are studying. Strictly speaking, **independent variable** refers to a property that is the presumed *cause* of something, whereas **dependent variable** is the *consequence*. In the study of teaching, variables associated with teacher behavior (causes) are normally important independent variables, and student attitude or achievement (consequences) are important dependent variables.

Knowledge about teaching is really knowledge about the relationships between the many independent and dependent variables in the models displayed in Figure R1.1. Many of the relationships that appear to exist are only tentative and are always open to alternative interpretations. It is important to remember that an enterprise as complex as teaching does not always fall neatly into the models devised by researchers.

Approaches to Educational Research

Educational researchers use several different approaches to study problems related to teaching and learning. The critical differences among the various approaches include the assumptions researchers make about the nature of scientific knowledge and the ways they design their studies, collect information, and interpret results.

Assumptions about Scientific Knowledge

Today, researchers make different assumptions about the nature of the social world of education and about the nature of knowledge, and these assumptions influence the type of research they do. Some researchers, for instance, assume that the social world, in our case the world of schools and classrooms, has an *objective reality.* These researchers believe that schools, classrooms, teachers, and students exist independent of the researcher and that they are available for study in an objective, unbiased manner. Researchers who hold this perspective focus their research mainly on observable behaviors that can be measured. This perspective is often referred to as **positivism.** Much of the research that has been done in education over the past century rests on positivistic assumptions.

Constructivism is a different perspective about the social world and the nature of knowledge that has gained favor among the educational research community during the past thirty years. Researchers with this perspective believe that the social world does *not* exist independently but is instead constructed by the participant, mainly students, their teachers, and often the researcher himself or herself. This view of the social world is consistent with the constructivist principles of teaching and learning discussed elsewhere in *Learning to Teach.*

These perspectives about the social world and scientific knowledge are important because they influence the type of studies researchers conduct and the manner in which they analyze and report their results. Positivists, for instance, are more likely to conduct what has been labeled **quantitative research,** an approach to research that assumes an objective reality, that studies behavior in an objective fashion, and that uses statistical methods to analyze data. Constructivists, on the other hand, are more likely to conduct **qualitative research,** an approach that relies on holistic observations, reports data in narrative rather than quantitative form, and conducts the whole research process in a more personalized and interpretative fashion.

Over the years, considerable debate has occurred among researchers using these two approaches. Today, however, many of the issues have been resolved and most researchers would say that both the quantitative and qualitative methods should be used and, sometimes used together, in the same study. Both can provide valuable insights into the world of teaching and classroom practice.

Types of Research Studies

Let's now look more closely at some of the specific types of research used in education and reported in this book.

Descriptive Research

Most of you can readily cite examples of **descriptive research,** not only in the field of education but in other fields as well. On any given day, you can pick up a newspaper and read the results of a survey someone has done. A survey is one type of descriptive research. Researchers adopting this approach commonly use questionnaires or interviews to gather information about the characteristics of some phenomenon or to measure people's opinions or attitudes on some subject.

Although it is difficult to do "good" survey research, the results of such research are easily understood. In most cases, the results are presented numerically and describe the number and percentage of people who have a specific characteristic or who believe in a particular way. The part of Lortie's study summarized in Chapter 1 is an example of one type of survey research. In that instance, information was collected by interview on why people chose to go into teaching. The well-known yearly survey conducted by Gallup to get citizens' opinions about the schools is another example of survey research.

Sometimes researchers using the descriptive approach are interested in a type of problem that can best be studied using qualitative methods through direct observation of a single case or a small number of cases. These approaches take the form of case studies or, in some instances, ethnographies. **Ethnography** is a word that comes from the field of anthropology and means an extensive study of an intact group of people, such as a culture, a society, or a particular role group. Normally, what a researcher does when conducting this type of research is to select from many possibilities what might be called a typical case and then to conduct in-depth observations of that single case. The aim of a case study, or an ethnography, is to collect extensive information so that a rich description and an in-depth understanding of the research problem will result. Examples of this type of research include the work of anthropologists such as Margaret Mead, who lived with and studied the people in Samoa to discover some of the important underlying patterns of that culture, and the work of Jean Piaget, who conducted in-depth case studies of children to discover how a young child's mind develops and grows.

As a rule, researchers using observational techniques must get quite close to the subjects they are studying. In fact, some become participants themselves and try to influence the problems they are studying.

As contrasted to collecting information using questionnaires or interviews, observation allows the researcher to study the point of view of a group or person and, in turn, construct a more complete picture of the situation. A weakness of this type of research, however, is that the researcher is only studying a single case or a small number of cases. Readers or users of this research must always ask how typical or representative the researcher's case was and whether the researcher's conclusions would hold up in other cases or other settings.

Experimental Research

A second approach to research in education is the *experiment.* This is the traditional approach based on positivistic assumptions. Most readers are already familiar with the basic logic and procedures of this approach through their high school and college psychology, social science, and science classes. The results of this type of research are also frequently reported in the mass media.

The experimental study of teaching involves procedures in which the researcher, instead of describing or studying variables as they exist naturally in the world, sets up conditions so specified variables can be manipulated. Although there are over a dozen variations of educational experiments, the classical approach is for the researcher to perform three important acts: (1) to establish two groups believed to be the same; (2) to give one group (the experimental group) a special treatment and withhold the treatment from the other (the control group); and (3) to compare some measurable feature of the two groups to see if the treatment made any difference.

True experiments are difficult to do in education because many of the problems teachers and researchers are interested in are not amenable to experiments for either logistical or ethical reasons. When they can be done, however, experiments produce powerful results because they allow the researcher to draw conclusions about cause-and-effect relationships among variables. The educational problems most amenable to experimental manipulations are those associated with particular models and methods of teaching. The "bowling study" described in Chapter 10 is a good example of a cleverly constructed experiment.

Correlational Research

Because so many aspects of teaching and learning cannot be studied experimentally, a third major research approach is often employed. *Correlational* research is used when the researcher explores the relationships between two or more variables that exist naturally and tries to sort out what goes with what. This approach is also familiar to most of you. Take, for example, the now well-known correlational studies showing strong relationships between cigarette smoking and certain diseases. Over many years, medical researchers have shown that people who smoke have a higher incidence of lung cancer and heart attacks than nonsmokers have. Nonetheless, the cause-and-effect relationship remains experimentally unproven because of the ethics of setting up a true experiment in which members of one group would be given a treatment that might lead to their deaths. Much of the research on effective teaching is also correlational research. For example, the many studies that show strong relationships between certain features of classroom management and student learning, such as those described in Chapter 5, are nearly all correlational.

In the study of teaching, the researcher is usually interested in finding relationships between some type of teacher behavior and student learning. Although very useful in education, it is important to keep in mind that correlational research does not establish cause and effect among variables, only relationships. More is said about this later.

Causal-Comparative Research

Many times in education, variables of interest to the researcher cannot be manipulated, and data must be used from already defined groups. A method used to explore causal relationships in this situation is the *causal-comparative* method. In this type of research, unlike experimental research, the independent variable is not manipulated by the researcher because it already exists. Researchers compare two groups: subjects (normally in already existing groups) for whom a particular trait or pattern exists and similar subjects for whom it is absent. Two examples are given here. In both examples, the researcher studied variables that already exist and groups (classrooms) already defined.

- A researcher believes teachers are more critical toward Hispanic students than toward Anglo students. The researcher records teacher behaviors and then compares the teachers' interactions with the two groups. The independent variable in this case is ethnic origin—a trait in students that obviously already exists and is not manipulated.
- A researcher is interested in the attitudes of students toward school in two classrooms— one in which the teacher is using cooperative learning strategies, the other in which the teacher relies mainly on direct instruction. Attitudes are measured in the two classrooms and compared. Again, the independent variable (cooperative learning versus direct instruction) is a condition that already exists in the classroom and is not one the researcher manipulated.

In causal-comparative studies, differences between means are observed. The statistical tests employed are similar to those used in experimental research. This differs from correlational studies, in which the correlation coefficient is observed. Like correlational research, the results from causal-comparative studies are limited and must be interpreted with care because it is not clear whether the variables observed are a cause or a result or whether some third factor is present that may be influencing both the independent and dependent variables.

Statistical Concepts and Research Conventions

The vast majority of educational research involves measuring individual or group traits that produce quantitative data. Over the years, researchers have developed statistical procedures to help organize, analyze, and interpret their data. To read and to use research requires an understanding of some of the basic procedures and agreed-on conventions used by researchers. There is nothing magical about statistics or about symbols used by researchers. They are merely a means to communicate clearly and objectively. They may, however, appear mysterious to the novice. Brief descriptions of several key ideas can help beginning teachers understand research and perhaps motivate further study.

Sampling

Since it is obviously impossible to study all teachers or all students, educational researchers must, out of necessity, confine their studies to a small portion, or **sample,** of a total population. An example of this technique is the *sampling* done by market researchers to find out which TV shows people watch. From the millions of viewers at a given programming hour, researchers poll as few as fifteen hundred to two thousand persons selected from known segments of the viewing population. Users of market research ratings accept the results because they know that what the sample is watching represents (more or less) the habits of the total viewing audience.

The way a sample is selected is very important—if it does not accurately represent the intended larger population, the results will obviously be biased. A famous mistake in sampling occurred in the 1948 presidential election when a sample of citizens drawn from telephone directories across the country the night before the election indicated that Thomas Dewey, the Republican candidate, would be elected. The next day, however, Harry Truman, the Democratic candidate, was elected. Upon analysis, the polling firm discovered that in 1948, many voters still did not have telephones, and those without phones, who could not be included in the sample, were more prone to vote Democratic. Drawing a sample from the telephone directory was not appropriate if the pollsters wanted to know what the total population of voters was going to do. When reading reports of educational research, it is important to study carefully the sampling techniques used by the researcher.

Randomness

The concept of **randomness** is also very important in educational research. Usually random sampling or random assignment to groups means that individuals in any population have an equal chance of being selected for study. In survey research, this means that the researcher strives to define the total population of people he or she is going to study and then decides by chance which ones will be chosen for study. In experiments in which one group is to receive a special treatment and the other to serve as a control, the researcher is careful that subjects are assigned to one of the two groups on a random basis. The logic behind random sampling or random assignment to groups is that by using this procedure, the sample or the groups under investigation will have the same characteristics. This, however, is not always the case. For example, just as there is a chance, although very small, of flipping heads in a coin toss one hundred times in a row, there is also always a chance that a random sample will indeed not represent the total population or that two groups assigned at random will differ from one another in important ways.

Numbers and Conventions

Researchers also use certain conventions to organize and report the results of their work to others.

Mean Scores. In many of the research studies summarized in this book as well as elsewhere, researchers report mean scores that allow comparison of one group with another. A **mean score** is nothing more than an average score and is calculated by adding all scores and dividing by the number of cases. The reporting convention of researchers is to use the symbol $\bar{X}$ or M to designate the mean score and the symbol N to communicate to readers the number of cases used to compute a particular mean. Mean scores are used to perform many of the statistical tests employed in educational research.

Standard Deviation. Standard deviation (SD) is another statistic that provides information about a set of scores. This statistic, found in many data tables, indicates the spread of a particular set of scores from the mean. Differences in means as well as differences in standard deviation are used to compute tests of statistical significance. The symbol SD is the most common convention for reporting standard deviation.

Correlation and Correlation Coefficients. **Correlation** expresses the degree to which a relationship exists between two or more variables. Familiar examples are the relationship between student IQ and student achievement, and the relationship between particular teaching behaviors (keeping students on task) and student achievement. Another is the relationship between a person's height and his or her performance on the basketball court.

To express these relationships in mathematical terms, researchers use a statistic called the **correlation coefficient.** A correlation coefficient can range from +1.00 through .00 to −1.00. The sign does not have the traditional mathematical meaning. Instead, a plus sign represents a positive relationship, a minus sign a negative relationship. Thus, .00 means no relationship exists, +1.00 means a perfect relationship exists, and −1.00 means a perfect reverse relationship exists. As observed in many of the studies summarized in this book, few instances are found in education (or any other aspect of human behavior) where perfect positive or negative relationships exist.

As described earlier, an important thing to remember about correlational studies and correlational coefficients is that even though they may show relationships among variables, they do not explain cause and effect. As an example, many studies show a positive relationship between students' time on task and academic achievement. Consequently, it is assumed that teachers who can keep students on task more will produce superior scores on achievement tests. Although this may be true, the time-on-task principle could be turned around. It could be logically argued that it is not time on task that produces achievement, but instead it is high-achieving students who produce high time-on-task ratios.

Tests of Significance. In any empirical research on human behavior, there is always the possibility that a specific outcome is the result of chance instead of some presumed relationship that is being studied. Researchers have developed a procedure called the *test of statistical significance* to help decide whether research results are indeed true or perhaps a matter of chance. Several different tests of significance are observed in the research reports found in this book. The main idea to remember is that when researchers use the word *significance,* they are using it differently than in common usage, where it normally means *important.* In the language of researchers, **significance** means the degree of truth rather than chance that they assign to their results. In general, researchers agree that differences between two sets of scores are statistically significant if they could occur by chance only one to five times out of one hundred. When you read the research reports in this text you will often see the notation $p < .01$ or $p < .05$. This means that the probability (p) of such results could occur by chance less than ($<$) one time out of one hundred (.01) or five times out of one hundred (.05).

Reading and Keeping Abreast of Research

Reading Research with a Critical Eye

Most research in education today is subjected to a review process before it is published. Nonetheless, a teacher who is reading and using the results of research should learn to approach studies with a critical eye. Borg and Gall (1993) listed a number of weaknesses that occur in research studies and reports. Part of their list is summarized briefly here:

- *Deliberate bias.* Although the goal of research is to discover truth, sometimes research is done to convince others of a point of view or of the effectiveness of a particular educational program.
  Example: Readers of research look to see if the researcher has anything to gain if the results turn out in a particular way. If so, the possibility of bias is greatly increased, and the study has to be examined very carefully. This does not mean, however, that all inventors of new programs or approaches who also conduct research on their inventions will deliberately bias the results. In most instances, they do not.
- *Nondeliberate bias.* Sometimes bias enters into research without the researchers' being aware of it. As with many other aspects of life, distortion can exist and influence us without our knowing it.
  Example: Look for emotional language and imbalanced presentation of research studies.
- *Sampling bias.* Sampling bias is something that plagues educational research because it is so difficult to get random samples from total populations. However, as you learned in a previous section, if a sample contains bias, results can be spurious.
  Example: Studies in which volunteers have been used, where many subjects have been lost from the sample, or in which intact groups have been used for convenience purposes should raise red flags for readers and users of research.
- *Observer and measurement bias.* Human beings have a tendency to see what they want to see, hear what they want to hear, and remember what they want to remember. Even though researchers go to great lengths to guard against observer bias, they are always open to subtle error.
  Example: Looking at observation instruments or protocols to see if the researcher has included features to ensure objectivity and looking at interview questions for leading or threatening questions are means to check if observer bias has influenced the results of a study.

Reading a Research Report: An Example

It is time now to see if you can apply these research concepts to an actual research report. Read the summary of the Johnsons' study (Research Summary on page *362* and *363*) in Chapter 10. See if you can answer the following questions:

1. What assumptions about the nature of scientific knowledge are embedded in the study?
2. Is the study an example of descriptive, experimental, correlational, or causal-comparative research?
3. What variables were studied? Which variables are the independent variables? Which are the dependent variables?
4. Where would these variables fit in the model described in Figure R1.1?
5. How did the researchers use the mean statistic? From studying the scores and frequencies and tests of significance, what conclusions would you draw?
6. Based on your conclusion, what might you say about the impact of cooperative learning?
7. Which forms of bias do you find in the study? Deliberate bias? Nondeliberate bias? Observer bias? What about the sample? Is it biased?
8. What are the strengths of the study? What are the limitations?

Keeping Abreast of Research

Once one starts teaching full time, it is sometimes difficult to keep up with research. There are just so many other things to do. Fortunately, there are special services available to teachers that can cut down the time needed to keep abreast of the research on teaching and learning. Beginning in the mid-1960s, the federal government became more interested in educational research and created several services to encourage the dissemination of educational research to classroom teachers. Two of these services can be useful to the beginning teacher.

Regional Educational Laboratories. Knowing that most research and research centers were not directly applicable to classroom teachers, regional educational laboratories were created in 1964 to translate research into classroom materials and strategies and to disseminate the results to teachers. Even though their budgets do not allow direct assistance in every classroom in their region, laboratory staffs hold many useful workshops and are eager to have classroom teachers visit their labs and learn about the work they are doing. These laboratories also provide opportunities for the more energetic teachers to participate in ongoing research and development projects. A complete list of centers and regional laboratories can be obtained by visiting the *Learning to Teach* Online Learning Center.

Educational Research Information Centers. In the mid-1960s, the federal government started to put together a network of educational research information centers called ERICs. Today, there are sixteen subject-specific centers called *clearinghouses* administered by the National Library of Education (NLE). These ERIC clearinghouses are charged with three major tasks: (1) collecting the available knowledge on topics associated with various specialized areas of education; (2) organizing this information so it can be retrieved via computers from any place in the United States; and (3) summarizing these data in short bulletins and papers on topics of particular interest to teachers and other educators.

The heart of the ERIC system is the ERIC database, which contains over one million abstracts and documents on educational research and practice. This database can be accessed online via the Internet, on CD-ROM, and through abstract journals available in libraries. All libraries in major universities and many large school districts or intermediate educational agencies have direct computer connections to ERIC. To get started, you may want to contact a person in your library who can show you how to access ERIC and conduct online searches. That person will discuss the type of topic about which you would like research information and then perform an online search to give you an example of the types of articles and reports that are available.

Today, most people access the ERIC database and resources over the Internet. Individuals can visit the ERIC websites and perform online searches. AskERIC is a personalized, Internet-based service provided by the ERIC system. Users can ask questions related to education by sending an e-mail to askeric@askeric.org. Answers normally are provided within two days. Users can also use the ERIC site to obtain sample lesson plans and other products on thousands of topics, as well as for links to many other education websites and services.

ERIC clearinghouse subject areas and e-mail addresses are provided in Figure R1.2. Important ERIC and ERIC clearinghouse website addresses are provided on the Online Learning Center.

ERIC Subject Area Clearinghouses	E-mail Address
Adult, Career, and Vocational Educational	ericave@osu.edu
Assessment and Evaluation	ericae@ericae.net
Community Colleges	ericcc@ucla.edu
Counseling and Student Services	ericcass@uncg.edu
Disabilities and Gifted Education	ericec@cec.sped.org
Education Management	erice@eric.uoregon.edu
Elementary and Early Childhood Education	ericeece@uiuc.edu
Higher Education	eric-he@eric-he.edu
Information and Technology	eric@ericit.org
	askeric@asskeric.org
Languages and Linguistics	eric@cal.org
Rural Education and Small Schools	ericre@ael.org
Science, Mathematics, and	
Environmental Education	ericse@osu.edu
Social Studies/Social Science Education	ericso@indiana.edu
Teaching and Teacher Education	query@garre.org
Urban Education	eric-cue@columbia.edu

Figure R1.2 *E-Mail Addresses for ERIC Subject Area Clearinghouses*

Unit 2 *Action Research for Classroom Teachers*

Throughout *Learning to Teach,* the point of view has been that it is important for teachers to have a command of the knowledge base on teaching and that research is a valuable resource to guide teaching practices. In addition, Chapter 13 described the importance of teachers assuming responsibility and taking individual initiative for improving the classrooms and schools in which they work. A logical extension of these admonitions is the idea that teachers can become researchers for the purposes of improving their teaching and the learning environments in their classrooms. This resource unit provides the rationale for classroom research and describes how you can use action research for the purpose of improving your teaching.

Perspective and Rationale

When teachers engage in classroom research, it is commonly called **action research.** Sometimes it is referred to as **teacher research.** In many ways, action or teacher research is like any other research. It is the process of asking questions, seeking valid information, and interpreting and using the results. But it differs from some other kinds of research in that its goal is to produce valid information and knowledge that has immediate application—in this instance, for teachers or their students. And unlike some researchers, teacher researchers are more interested in knowledge about a specific situation (their own classroom) than about more general applications. In other words, action research is guided by the processes and standards of scientific inquiry, but it is not intended in most instances to inform the larger research or educational community. Instead, it is a process of acquiring information and seeking knowledge that will serve your own actions.

A Short History

Action research as conceptualized and practiced today is the outgrowth of over a half century of thought that has been most influenced by the early traditions of John Dewey, Kurt Lewin, and Les Corey and his associates at Teachers College. More recently, the field has been influenced by Donald Schön, Chris Argyris, Sharon Oja, and Marilyn Cochran-Smith. Schön's ideas about reflective practice were introduced in Chapter 1. Argyris and colleagues (1985), who studied the traditions of action research, pointed out the importance of Dewey's contributions:

> Dewey (1929, 1933) was eloquent in his criticism of the traditional separation of knowledge and action, and he articulated a theory of inquiry that was a model both for scientific method and for social practice. He hoped that the extension of experimental inquiry to social practice would lead to an integration of science and practice. He based his hope on the observation that science . . . can become a mode of directed practical doing. This observation that experimentation in science is but a special case of human beings testing their conceptions in action, is at the core of the pragmatist epistemology. For the most part, however, the modern social sciences have appropriated the model of the natural sciences in ways that have maintained the separation of science and practice that Dewey deplored. Mainstream social science is related to social practice in much the same way that the natural sciences are related to engineering. This contrasts sharply with Dewey's vision of using scientific methods in social practice (pp. 6–7).

Why Action Research?

Today, the notion of teacher as researcher has gained widespread popularity in the United States, Great Britain, Canada, and Australia. In Great Britain, much of the interest has stemmed from the work of such people as Lawrence Stenhouse (1975, 1983, 1984), who has written widely about why action research is important, and David Hopkins (1985, 2002), who has provided concrete advice to teachers about how to conduct classroom research and use the results for school improvement. In the United States, many individuals, such as Oja and Smulyan (1989), Cochran-Smith and Lytle (1993), Schmuck (1997), and Zeichner and Noffle (2001), have written about action research. In addition, the use of research and classroom teachers as action researchers has been high on the agenda of both major teacher associations, the American Federation of Teachers (AFT), and the National Education Association (NEA) (see Livingston & Castle, 1989, Ponessa, 1997). The individuals and organizations advancing worldwide action research base their argument on two common premises about the role of the teacher and the processes of improving classroom teaching.

The Autonomous Professional. Many thoughtful observers believe that the time has come for teachers to become autonomous professionals. By this, they mean that instead of teachers relying on principals, central office supervisors, or college professors to tell them what to do, they should instead have command of their own knowledge and information to support decisions they make about teaching practices. Stenhouse (1984) strongly supported this point of view:

> Good teachers are necessarily autonomous in professional judgement. They do not need to be told what to do. They are not professionally the dependents of researchers or superintendents, or innovators or supervisors. This does not mean that they do not welcome access to ideas created by other people at other places or in other times. Nor do they reject advice, consultancy or support. But they do know that ideas and people are not of much real use until they are digested to the point where they are subject of teachers' own judgement. . . (p. 7).

For Stenhouse and others, the key to becoming an autonomous professional rests on teachers' disposition and ability to engage in self-study of their teaching and testing their classroom practices to see if they work. Obviously, this has been a revolutionary view of teaching and one that departs dramatically from more traditional conceptions.

Information Is Power. In addition to the point of view that teachers should be autonomous professionals, action research is also based on several premises about the processes of school improvement and the power of valid information to bring about improvement. Change and improvement for individuals or organizations comes about only as people construct new realities to replace existing ones and thereby make proposed improvements meaningful to themselves. New realities are constructed from new information and knowledge that challenges current ways of thinking. Thus, one can think of action research as a way to help construct new realities about one's teaching. It is a way for teachers to:

- Collect *valid information* about their classrooms.
- Use this information to make *informed decisions* about teaching strategies and learning activities.
- Share the information with students in order to gain their ideas and *commitment to* specified learning activities and procedures.

Doing Action Research

To do action research requires choosing the type of inquiry in which to engage from among various forms and paying careful attention to several aspects of the action research process.

Types of Action Research

Marilyn Cochran-Smith and Susan Lytle (1993) provided a definition of teacher (action) research and categorized it into four types: journals, oral inquiries, classroom or school studies, and essays. These four types of research and what teachers do in each are described in Figure R2.1.

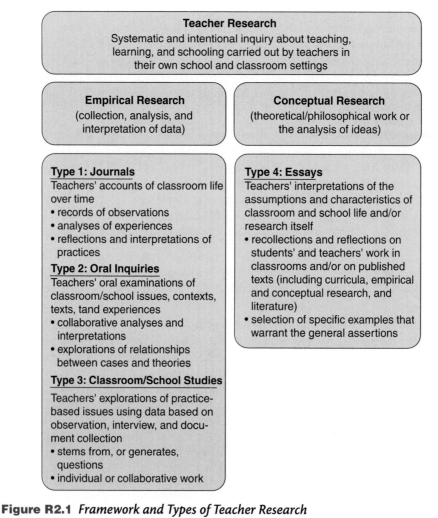

Teacher Research
Systematic and intentional inquiry about teaching, learning, and schooling carried out by teachers in their own school and classroom settings

Empirical Research
(collection, analysis, and interpretation of data)

Conceptual Research
(theoretical/philosophical work or the analysis of ideas)

Type 1: Journals
Teachers' accounts of classroom life over time
• records of observations
• analyses of experiences
• reflections and interpretations of practices

Type 2: Oral Inquiries
Teachers' oral examinations of classroom/school issues, contexts, texts, tand experiences
• collaborative analyses and interpretations
• explorations of relationships between cases and theories

Type 3: Classroom/School Studies
Teachers' explorations of practice-based issues using data based on observation, interview, and document collection
• stems from, or generates, questions
• individual or collaborative work

Type 4: Essays
Teachers' interpretations of the assumptions and characteristics of classroom and school life and/or research itself
• recollections and reflections on students' and teachers' work in classrooms and/or on published texts (including curricula, empirical and conceptual research, and literature)
• selection of specific examples that warrant the general assertions

Figure R2.1 *Framework and Types of Teacher Research*
Source: After Cochran-Smith and Lytle (1993), p. 27

Action Research Processes

In general, there is a flow, or set of steps, for initiating and completing an action research project. The three important parts of the process include deciding on problems to study and framing questions, collecting valid information, and interpreting and using this information for the purpose of improving one's teaching.

   Action research starts with classroom situations that teachers find unsatisfactory and in need of improvement. The process consists of isolating a problem for inquiry, taking action, collecting data, observing what happens, and then reflecting on the whole process before recycling into further study. Australia's Kemmis and McTaggart (1988) illustrated their view of the action research process as shown in Figure R2.2.

Problem and Question Formulation

Overall Considerations. A beginning teacher is confronted with literally hundreds of problems or questions that could be topics for action research. The most difficult part

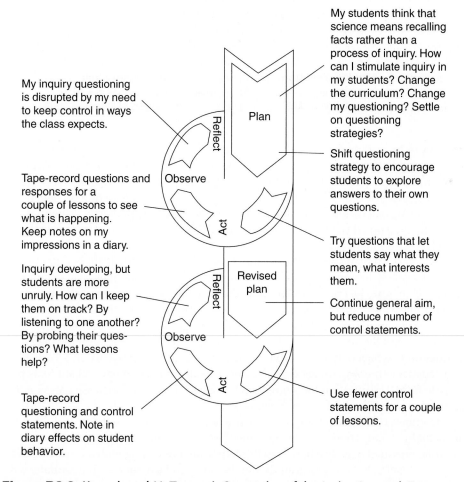

Figure R2.2 *Kemmis and McTaggart's Conception of the Action Research Process*
Source: Kemmis and McTaggart (1988)

of an action research project, however, is identifying a specific problem for study and defining carefully the variables involved. David Hopkins (1985, 2002) identified five principles to use in deciding on a problem for study:

1. *The project should not interfere with the teacher's first job, which is teaching.* Obviously, there is no easy way to say whether an action research project will disrupt teaching. Hopkins reminds us that action research is used for the purpose of understanding and improving our teaching and not for the pleasure of doing research for its own sake.

2. *Methods of collecting data should not be too demanding of the teacher's time.* This, too, is a reminder to keep projects, particularly first efforts, rather simple so that the action research does not make undue demands on already busy schedules.

3. *The methods used should produce reliable and valid information.* Even though information generated from action research is to improve a particular teacher's practice rather than more generalizable results, the validity and reliability of the information are still important. If the methods are not rigorous and the information is not reliable and valid, the results will be of little value to anyone.

4. *The problem studied should be one to which the teacher is committed and that is capable of solution.* This is a reminder that if the problem is too complex or if it is influenced by factors over which the teacher has little control, then information collected, regardless of how valid or reliable, will make little difference.

5. *Ethical standards for research govern teachers' research, just as they do any other research.* Standards such as keeping people informed about purposes of the project, obtaining authorization before collecting sensitive information, maintaining confidentiality, and respecting the rights of subjects are just as important for teacher researchers to maintain as they are for other researchers.

Getting to Specifics about Problems and Questions. As with any research, a good problem for action research is one that can be stated in a question form, focuses on the relationships among variables, and has the possibility of testing. Remember from the previous resource unit the distinctions made between independent and dependent variables. An independent variable refers to some aspect or property of the problem that is the presumed cause (teacher behavior, for instance); a dependent variable is a consequence (student engagement or learning).

Sometimes problems or questions cannot be stated very clearly in the beginning. The problem is likely to consist of a general uneasiness a teacher has about a classroom situation. Things are just not working quite the way the teacher desires. Sometimes this general uneasiness about a problem or question can be transformed into something more specific by thinking about discrepancies or gaps that exist between the "way things are" and the "way you would like them to be." For instance, a teacher may have a situation in which only four or five students out of a class of twenty-five participate in discussions (the way things are). The desired state may be to have all students participate fully. The question for study thus becomes, "How can I increase participation in my classroom during discussion periods?"

Sometimes discrepancies exist between what we think we are doing and what we are actually doing. These, too, can become the focus for inquiry. As you will see in an example provided later, teachers may think they are interacting with all students in an equitable fashion but on careful study find that they indeed interact differentially with different types or groups of students. The first question that stems from this type of problem situation is, "Do I interact differentially with different types of students?" If so, a second question for study becomes evident: "How can I change my behavior?"

In general, the recommendation for beginning teachers is to tackle problems from their own immediate experiences and concerns and ask questions that can be tested with rather straightforward plans and data collection efforts. Some of these questions will be amenable to informal data collection and testing procedures; others will require more formal methods. Here are several categories of questions that have been posed by teacher researchers during student teaching or early in their careers:

1. *Questions associated with student opinions.* Sometimes teachers are not sure what their students think about their teaching or about life in their classrooms. Questions might include the following: "Do students have high opinions of my instruction?" "Do my students find the learning environment pleasant?" "Do my students find the learning environment challenging?" "Do my students have the perception that I am treating them fairly?"

2. *Questions associated with particular teaching strategies or procedures.* Another set of questions that are amenable to action research are those that provide descriptive information about what a teacher is doing; for example, "What type of questions do I use during a discussion?" "Who talks most in my classes?" "Do I question and respond to all students in an equitable fashion?" "Do I give all students fair access to public time?" "How long do I wait for students to respond after asking a question?" "What proportion of the day is devoted to my own talking? To student talking? To seatwork?" "When I give an assignment to be completed in class, what proportion of the students are on task?"

3. *Questions comparing different approaches or variations of the same approach over time or with different groups.* Good teachers have a variety of teaching strategies and procedures at their command. As emphasized many times in this book, they match appropriate strategies to particular learning situations or groups of students. Here are some obvious questions about this matching process: What is most appropriate? What produces the best results? Here are some examples of action research questions that aim at comparing different strategies or procedures: "If I use think-pair-share (described in Chapters 10 and 12) after lecturing or showing a film in my social studies class, will it result in more student participation and learning as compared to holding a whole-class discussion?" "If I make a contract (with a reward system built in) for my uninvolved students, will this increase their engagement in learning activities as compared to not having a contract system?" "If I use manipulatives and visual graphics when teaching a particular math concept, will students' test results be better as compared to just a straight verbal presentation?" "If I use direct instruction to teach a particular skill, will five independent practices be as effective as ten in helping students acquire proficiency?" "If I increase my wait-time to four seconds, will this change the nature of the discourse patterns in my classrooms as compared to a two-second wait-time?"

Gathering Information

Once a problem or question has been identified for inquiry, the next issue to be resolved by the teacher researcher is how to gather information. There are many techniques for doing this, some quite simple and others more complex. Five specific approaches to data collection are described here. The choice of which approach to use depends on the question being asked and the time teachers have to gather and analyze the information.

Questionnaires. When teachers want information about the attitudes or opinions of their students on some aspect of their teaching or classroom, the easiest and most economical way to gather this type of information is by giving students a questionnaire to fill out. Most of you are familiar with questionnaires about teaching, because you have been asked many times to fill out course evaluations in your college classes. Many examples of this type of questionnaire can be found in the *Guide to Field Experiences and Portfolio Development.* For example, Chapter 4 has a questionnaire to get information about how students feel about life in their classrooms. Chapter 5 has an example of a questionnaire to get perceptions students have about how fairly their teacher is treating them.

Questionnaire format normally poses a question or makes a statement with which respondents can agree or disagree. For example:

My teacher treats all students the same.

| Agree strongly | Agree | Neither agree nor disagree | Disagree | Disagree strongly |

or

Does the teacher help you when you are stuck?

| All the time | Most of the time | Sometimes/ sometimes not | Hardly ever | Never |

Many of the rules for constructing questionnaire items are the same as those described in Chapter 6 for constructing multiple-choice test questions. Remember to write questions that are simple and straightforward and make sure the response categories are consistent. When constructing a questionnaire for younger children, it is normal practice to use three rather than five response categories. For very young children, the happy, neutral, or sad face response categories illustrated in Figure R2.3 can be used.

Sometimes teachers prefer more open-ended responses. In this case, asking questions such as, "What did you like best about the lesson?" or "What did you like least?" provides valuable information. This type of item will provide more in-depth information and will not be biased by the response categories. However, it can be a bit more difficult to organize and interpret the responses from this type of question as compared to questions with definite response categories.

Interviews. Whereas questionnaires have the advantage of being easier to construct and score, they also have their disadvantages. One is never sure what students are actually thinking when they check one of the response categories. It is also difficult to write good questionnaire items that explore issues in any depth. An alternative way to collect information about student attitudes and opinions is to interview them.

Information can be obtained from students either individually or in small groups through an interview. As with questionnaires, it is important to write interview questions ahead of time and keep them straightforward and directed toward the question for which answers are sought. During the interview process itself, it is important to re-

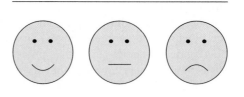

Figure R2.3 *Happy, Neutral, and Sad Face Responses*

assure students that they will not be punished for being candid, to employ good listening skills, and to emphasize how important their ideas are to you. The disadvantages of using interviews are that they are time-consuming (although the time factor can be reduced if students are interviewed in small groups), and it is frequently difficult to get students to express their true feelings and opinions candidly.

Observations. Many questions require some type of direct observation of teaching and student behavior. The procedures for observation and the recording devices can vary according to the type of question being asked. Normally, better information is acquired if a specific observation instrument is designed and used. Many specific observation instruments are provided in the accompanying manual. Their use (with adaptation) will help collect needed information for many of the questions posed by beginning teachers.

There are several ways to collect information through observation. The choice again depends on the situation. One popular way is for the teacher to ask a colleague to observe classroom interactions and collect needed information. If this approach is used, the teacher researcher needs to make sure the colleague understands the observation instrument and can use it effectively.

Another less threatening way is to make audio or video recordings of a lesson and then observe and code specific behaviors from the videotapes or audiotapes. When verbal behavior of students or teachers is the subject of inquiry, audiotapes work fine. However, subtler nonverbal behaviors require video recordings. How one teacher used both audio and video recording to study his interactions with second grade students is described later.

Notes, Diaries, and Journals. Taking careful notes or keeping a diary or journal is another way of collecting information about classroom events, your teaching, or your students' behavior. In general, observations must be committed to paper as soon as possible after an event, and they are more helpful if they are guided by a specific set of questions posed ahead of time as compared to more general observations that may come to mind. Notes and journals are particularly helpful for collecting information when the focus of inquiry is a particular student. They are also a good way to systematically study aspects of teaching that are not amenable to observation, such as your own thinking processes.

Standardized Tests. As described in Chapter 6, most states require all students to take standardized tests at various grade levels to demonstrate their mastery and achievement in reading, writing, mathematics, and often in social studies and science. To examine the effects of various approaches and practices being used in a school, teachers can use scores from these tests. For instance, teachers in a school may be disappointed by how their students are performing on the state's writing test. They decide to implement a writing-across-the-curriculum project. This approach requires teachers to have students do more writing in every subject area and to judge student work on common criteria. Obviously, student scores on the yearly standardized test would provide good insight into whether or not this new approach was making any difference.

Interpreting and Using Information from Action Research

A final step in action research is to organize the results from a project and share it with others. Some teachers share the results with colleagues and use the data they have collected as a springboard for teacher conversations about different approaches to teaching. Other teachers choose to share the results of an action research project with their students. The information collected in many projects can provide students with insights about their classroom and the teaching approaches being used by the teacher. This type of information can also help students gain commitment to learning activities found to be effective and provide a vehicle for them to think about and help plan classroom activities.

Action Research: An Example

This example is of an actual action research project done by a beginning teacher, David Weisz of Silver Spring, Maryland, while he was a student teacher in a second-grade classroom (Weisz, no date).

David's Questions

David was a very sensitive person and held strong beliefs about the importance of social justice in our society. He thought a lot about what teachers could do to promote justice and equality in their classrooms and was specifically concerned about his own treatment of students. His intentions were to treat all students equally and to communicate the same expectations to all students regardless of their abilities, ethnic background, or gender. He decided to study his use of questions and feedback in math groups from an equity perspective. He determined that the following questions would guide his action research project:

1. Do I favor students I perceive to be high achievers by directing more questions to them and by focusing high-level questions at them rather than at perceived low achievers and/or by giving them qualitatively or quantitatively better feedback?
2. Do I favor boys or girls in these same regards? (p. 2)

David explained that two things prompted his interest in this project. First, he had noticed during his student teaching the "relative ease with which a lesson can proceed if I focus exclusively or primarily on those students who appear to listen well, who have studied the materials, and who can be relied on to respond correctly or, at least, intelligently" (p. 2). He wondered if in his desire to have a smooth lesson he was favoring those whom he perceived as good students by asking them more questions and giving them more feedback and at the same time ignoring those students whom he perceived as not so good. He believed that teachers could be easily tempted into doing this as the pressures of teaching increase and wrote that he "wanted to avoid falling into this trap—or to get out of the trap if I've already fallen in it" (p. 2).

Second, David had studied gender differences in mathematics participation and written a paper on that topic for one of his college classes. He knew that some teachers show differential treatment to boys as compared to girls. He also had observed in a journal he kept that he was able to learn the names of the boys in his classes more readily than the names of the girls. So he wondered, "Will I be surprised to find that I differentiate between boys and girls in the questions I ask and the feedback I provide?" (p. 3)

David's Data Collection Methods

To carry out his study, David made five audiotapes and one videotape of lessons he identified in advance as those in which he planned to have considerable teacher-student

Table R2.1 *David's Data Sheet for Coding Particular Types of Teacher-Student Interaction*

Student's Name	Response Opportunities	Type of Questions	
		High	Low
Coding schemes:	Response opportunity:	Student was called on by teacher.	
	High questions:	Questions that required students to think.	
	Low questions:	Questions that required recall of information.	
	Type of Feedback	Teacher moved on with no response.	
	None:	Teacher praised a correct student response.	
	+ +	Teacher identified an incorrect response but dignified the error.	
	− +	Teacher identified an incorrect response and was critical of the error.	
	− −	Teacher was positive but with no effect.	
	+	Teacher was negative but with no effect.	
	−		

interaction. In addition, a week before taping, David identified the names of five students in the class whom he perceived to be high achievers and five whom he perceived to be low achievers. These perceptions were based on four weeks of experience with his students and knowing how well they did in mathematics. He reported, however, that he "quickly put this list away and tried not to think about it any more until the taping was finished" (p. 4). David knew if the names became too embedded in his mind, it could bias his interactions and diminish the value of the information he was about to collect.

Once he had his videotapes and audiotapes, David constructed and used a data sheet as shown in Table R2.1 to analyze his interaction with students.

David's Results and Interpretations

After organizing his data and putting them in table format, David found that, indeed, he was showing slight differential treatment to high achievers as contrasted to low achievers and to boys as contrasted to girls. What is most interesting about David's action research project, however, is his careful and thoughtful interpretation of these data. His own words say it better than any summary: "There were certain areas where my treatment was not equitable (high- and low-order questions and the no-response, praise, and incorrect/dignified types of feedback)" (p. 7). David did not conclude from this information, however, that his differential treatment of students was necessarily bad teaching or unfair. Instead, he thought about what it meant and posed a question that even many professional researchers have ignored: "Is differential treatment always undesirable?"

> One important question which must be dealt with at the outset is whether an equal distribution of response opportunities, types of questions, and feedback is indeed desirable when comparing my treatment of perceived high achievers and perceived low achievers. Low achievers, high achievers and midrange achievers have different needs and may therefore require some kind of differential treatment: for example, low achievers may need more response opportunities, a more judicious blend of high-order and low-order questions, more

praise—as long as it is measured and sincere—and more "dignifying" follow-up to incorrect responses. If I perceive certain students to be low achievers, would I be aiming at equal treatment of them vis-à-vis those I perceive to be high achievers, or *should I develop a more sophisticated approach to both the low achievers and the high achievers?*

A case then can be made for differential treatment of high and low achievers. The problem is, however, that when educational researchers find such differential treatment it often goes in the wrong direction—that is, it is often biased against low achievers. I refer, for example, to the work of Good and Brophy (1987). While equal treatment may not be ideal, it is nevertheless better than differential treatment that works against those who are perceived to be most in need of help (p. 11).

So, David concluded that differential treatment may be desired as long as it is meeting individual needs and not always going against those of low ability. He turned next to his differential treatment of boys and girls and in this instance reaches a different conclusion:

Differential treatment on the basis of sex would seem to be much less defensible than differential treatment for perceived high and low achievers. What is significant in my results is that even though not great, it is the fact that in each case the imbalance in my treatment favored the boys: proportionately more of the total response opportunities went to boys, proportionately more high-order questions went to boys and substantially more low-order questions went to the girls. Again, while the differential is not large, the imbalance in all three instances works to the detriment of girls. Given the generally lower participation and achievement of girls in mathematics at higher levels, *I would have felt better had the imbalance gone the other way* (p. 13).

Finally, David concluded his thoughts about his action research project and set some goals for his teaching behavior in the future:

As I teach, I do not consciously think in terms of categories such as perceived high and low achievers and boys and girls. Nevertheless, the patterns found in the types of teacher-student interaction I studied in my action research indicated that, in some cases, I am interacting with students on the basis of these categorizations rather than on the basis of the individual student and thus may be communicating to them certain expectations for their performance based on these categorizations.

I am, now, as a result of this action research, more sensitive to the many ways that this can be done. I now must work to keep this sensitivity alive and ensure that I apply it in my teaching in the years ahead (p. 13).

For those who choose to become students of their own teaching, David's action research project can be a model to follow. He chose to study a problem—differential treatment of students—that has been of concern to professional researchers for a long time. It is also a problem in which teachers, regardless of their good intentions, find discrepancies between what they believe and what they actually do. David's use of audio and video recordings, along with the rather simple but effective coding scheme, produced objective information about his teaching behavior. The limited scope of the study and its overall design conform to the principles for action research described by Hopkins (1985). Most important, David's thoughtful interpretation of his results shows the significant progress he has made in his young career toward becoming a reflective, autonomous professional.

References

Abi-Nader, J. (1991). Creating a vision of the future: Strategies for motivating minority students. *Phi Delta Kappan, 72*, 546–549.

Adelman, C. (1991). *Women at Thirty-something: Paradoxes of Attainment*. Washington, D.C.: U.S. Department of Education.

Airasian, P. W. (2001). *Classroom Assessment: Concepts and Applications* (4th ed.). New York: McGraw-Hill.

Albanese, M., and Mitchell, S. (1993). Problem-based learning: A review of literature on its outcomes and implementation issues. *Academic Medicine, 68*, 52–81.

Allen, V. (1991). Teaching bilingual and ESL children. In J. Flood, J. M. Jensen, D. Lapp, and J. R. Squire (eds.), *Handbook of Research on Teaching the English Language Arts*.

Allport, G. (1954). *The Nature of Prejudice*. Cambridge, Mass.: Addison-Wesley.

Alschuler, A. S., Tabor, D., and McIntyre, J. (1970). *Teaching Achievement Motivation: Theory and Practice in Psychological Education*. Middletown, Conn.: Education Ventures.

American Association of University Women (AAUW). (1992). *Shortchanging Girls, Shortchanging America*. Washington, D.C.: Author.

American Educational Research Association, American Psychological Association, and National Council on Measurement in Education. (1985). *Standards for Educational and Psychological Testing*. Washington, D.C.: American Psychological Association.

Anderson, L. M. (1985). What are students doing when they do all that seatwork? In C. Fisher and D. Berliner (eds.), *Perspectives on Instructional Time*. New York: Longman.

Anderson, L. M., and Smith, E. L. (1987). Teaching science. In V. Richardson-Koehler, (ed.), *Educator's Handbook: A Research Perspective*. New York: Longman.

Anderson, L. W., and Krathwohl, D. R. (eds. with P. W Airasian, K. A. Cruikshank, R. E. Mayer, P. R. Pintrich, J. Raths, and M. C. Wittrock). (2001). *A Taxonomy for Learning, Teaching, and Assessing: A Revision of Bloom's Taxonomy of Educational Objectives*. New York: Longman.

Angaran, Joseph. (1999). Reflections in an age of assessment. *Educational Leadership*, March, 71–72.

Annenburg Public Policy Center (1999). *The Internet and the Family*. Philadelphia: University of Pennsulvania. Author.

Anyon, J. (1980). Social class and the hidden curriculum of work. *Journal of Education, 162*, 67–69.

Argyris, C. (1970). *Intervention Theory and Method*. Reading, Mass.: Addison-Wesley.

Argyris, C., Putnam, R., and Smith, D. M. (1985). *Action Science*. San Francisco: Jossey-Bass.

Arithmetic Teacher. (1991). February.

Armstrong, T. (2000). *Multiple Intelligences in the Classroom* (2nd ed.). Alexandria, Va.: Association of Supervision and Curriculum Development.

Aronson, E., and Patnoe, S. (1997). *The Jigsaw Classroom*. New York: Addison-Wesley/Longman.

Ashton-Warner, S. (1963). *Teacher*. New York: Simon & Schuster.

Atkinson, J., and Feather, N. (1966). *A Theory of Achievement Motivation*. New York: Wiley.

Ausubel, D. P. (1960). The use of advance organizers in the learning and retention of meaningful verbal material. *Journal of Educational Psychology, 51*, 267–272.

Ausubel, D. P. (1963). *The Psychology of Meaningful Verbal Learning*. New York: Grune & Stratton.

Bagley, C. and Hunter, B. (1992). Restructuring contructivism and technology: Forging new relationships. *Educational Technology. 32*(7), 22–27.

Baker, D. (1986). Sex differences in classroom interaction in secondary science. *Journal of Classroom Interaction, 22*, 212–218.

Baker, E. T. (1994). Meta-analytic evidence for non-inclusive educational practices: Does educational research support current practice for special needs students. Doctoral dissertation. Temple University, Philadelphia.

Baker, E. T., Wang, M. C., and Walberg, H. (1995). Synthesis of research: The effects of inclusion on learning. *Educational Leadership, 52*, 33–34.

Baker, L., and Brown, A. (1984). Metacognitive skills and reading. In P. D. Pearson, M. Kamil, R. Barr, and P. Mosenthal (eds.). *Handbook of Reading Research*. New York: Longman.

Bandura, A. (1977). *Social Learning Theory*. Englewood Cliffs, N.J.: Prentice Hall.

Bandura, A. (1986). *Social Foundations of Thought and Action*. Englewood Cliffs, N.J.: Prentice Hall.

Banks, I. (1998). Reliance on technology threatens the essence of teaching. *The Chronicle of Higher Education*, October 16, p. B5.

Banks, J. (1995). *The Handbook of Research on Multicultural Education*. New York: Macmillan.

Banks, J. A. (1999). *An Introduction to Multicultural Education* (2nd ed.). Boston: Allyn & Bacon.

Banks, J. A. (2001). *Cultural Diversity and Education* (4th ed.). Boston: Allyn & Bacon.

Banks, J. A., and Banks, C. (eds.). (1996a). *Handbook of Research on Multicultural Education.* San Francisco: Jossey Bass.

Banks, J. A., and Banks, C. (1996b). *Teaching Strategies for Ethnic Studies* (6th ed.). Boston: Allyn & Bacon.

Barker, R. G. (1968). *Ecological Psychology.* Stanford, Calif.: Stanford University Press.

Beaulieu, R. P., and Utecht, K. M. (1987). Frequently administered formative tests and student achievement. *Journal of Instructional Psychology,* 14, 195–200.

Benjafield, J. G. (1992). *Cognitions.* Englewood Cliffs, N.J.: Prentice Hall.

Bennett, B., and Rolheiser, C. (2001). *Beyond Monet: The Artful Science of Instructional Integration.* Toronto, Ontario: Bookation, Inc.

Bennett, C. I. (1995). *Comprehensive Multicultural Education. Theory and Practice* (3rd ed.). Boston: Allyn & Bacon.

Berliner, D. C., and Biddle, B. J. (1995). *The Manufactured Crisis: Myths, Fraud, and the Attack on American Public Schools.* Reading, Mass.: Addison-Wesley.

Biklen, D. (1985). *Achieving the Complete School.* New York: Teachers College Press.

Biklen, S. K., and Pollard, D. (2001). Feminist perspectives on gender in the classroom. In V. Richardson (ed.), *Handbook of Research on Teaching.* (4th ed.). Washington, D.C.: American Educational Research Association.

Bissell, J. S., Manring, A., and Rowland, V. (1999). *CyberEducator: The Internet and World Wide Web for K-12 and Teacher Education.* Boston: McGraw-Hill.

Bitter, G., and Pierson, M. (2002). *Using Technology in the Classroom* (5th ed.). Boston: Allyn & Bacon.

Bloom, B. S. (ed.). (1956). *Taxonomy of Educational Objectives. Handbook 1: Cognitive Domain.* New York: David McKay.

Bloom, B. S. (1976). *Human Characteristics and School Learning:* New York: McGraw-Hill.

Bloom, B. S., Hastings, T. J., and Madaus, G. F. (1971). *Handbook on Formative and Summative Evaluation of Student Learning.* New York: McGraw-Hill.

Bluestein, J. (1982). *The Beginning Teacher's Resource Handbook.* Albuquerque, N.M.: Instructional Support Services.

Blythe, T. (1997). *The Teaching for Understanding Guide.* San Francisco: Jossey-Bass.

Bobbitt, F. (1918). *The Curriculum.* Boston: Houghton Mifflin.

Bohman, L. G., and Deal, T. E. (1991). *Reframing Organizations.* San Francisco: Jossey-Bass.

Borg, W. R., and Gall, M. D. (1993). *Educational Research: An Introduction* (4th ed.). New York: Longman.

Bozeman, M. (1985). *Signaling in the Classroom* (mimeographed.) Salisbury, Md.: Salisbury State College.

Brandt, R. S. (2000). *Education in a New Era.* Alexandria, Va.: Association of Supervision and Curriculum Development.

Bredderman, T. (1983). Effects of activity-based elementary science on student outcomes: A quantitative synthesis. *Review of Educational Research,* 53, 499–518.

Brenton, Myron (1970). *What's Happened to Teacher?* New York: Coward-McCann.

Brookfield, S. D., and Preskill, S. (1999). *Discussion as a Way of Teaching: Tools and Techniques in the Classroom.* San Francisco: Jossey-Bass.

Brookover, W., Beady, C., Flood, P., Schweitzer, J., and Wisenbaker, J. (1979). *School Social Systems and Student Achievement: Schools Can Make a Difference.* New York: Praeger.

Brooks, J. G., and Brook, M. G. (1993). *In Search of Understanding: The Case for Constructivist Classrooms.* Alexandria, Va.: Association for Supervision and Curriculum Development.

Brophy, J. E. (1981). Teacher praise: A functional analysis. *Review of Educational Research,* Spring, 5–32.

Brophy, J. E., and Good, T. L. (1974). *Teacher-Student Relationships: Causes and Consequences.* New York: Holt, Rinehart & Winston.

Brophy, J. E., and Good, T. L. (1986). Teacher behavior and student achievement. In M. C. Wittrock (ed.), *Handbook of Research on Teaching* (3rd ed.). New York: Macmillan.

Brophy, J. E., and Putnam, J. (1979). Classroom management in the early grades. In D. L. Duke (ed.), *Classroom Management.* Chicago: University of Chicago Press.

Brown, A., and Palincsar, A. (1985). *Reciprocal Teaching of Comprehension Strategies.* Technical Report no. 334. Champaign-Urbana, Ill.: University of Illinois.

Browne, M. N., and Keely, S. M. (2002). *Asking the Right Questions: A Guide to Critical Thinking.* Englewood Cliffs, N.J.: Prentice Hall.

Bruner, J. (1960). *The Process of Education.* Cambridge, Mass.: Harvard University Press.

Bruner, J. (1962). *On Knowing: Essays for the Left Hand.* Cambridge, Mass.: Harvard University Press.

Bruner, J. (1966). *Toward a Theory of Instruction.* Cambridge, Mass.: Harvard University Press.

Bruner, J. (1990). *Acts of Meaning.* Cambridge, Mass.: Harvard University Press.

Bruner, J. (1996). *The Culture of Education.* Cambridge, Mass.: Harvard University Press.

Bryk, A. S., and Driscoll, M. E. (1988). *The School as Community.* Madison, Wisc.: University of Wisconsin, National Center for Effective Secondary Schools.

Burbules, N. C. (1993). *Dialogue in Teaching: Theory and Practice.* New York: Teachers College Press.

Burbules, N. C., and Bruce, B. C. (2001). Theory and research on teaching as dialogue. In V. Richardson (ed.), *Handbook of Research on Teaching* (4th ed.). Washington, D.C.: American Educational Research Association.

Burke, J. B., and Putnam, J. G. (1998). *Organizing and Managing the Classroom Learning Community.* New York: McGraw-Hill.

Campbell, L., and Campbell, B. (1999). *Multiple Intelligence and Student Achievement.* Alexandria, Va.: Association of Supervision and Curriculum Development.

Cangelosi, J. S. (1999). *Classroom Management Strategies: Gaining and Maintaining Students' Cooperation* (4th ed.). New York: Longman.

Canter, L., and Canter, D. M. (1976). *Assertive Discipline.* Los Angeles: Canter and Associates.

Canter, L., and Canter, D. M. (1997). *Assertive Discipline Positive Behavior.* Santa Monica, Calif.: Canter & Associates.

Canter, L., and Canter, D. M. (2002). *Assertive Discipline: Positive Behavior Management for Today's Classroom.* Santa Monica, Calif.: Lee Canter & Associates.

Carlson, R. (1996). *Reframing and Reform.* White Plains, N.Y.: Longman.

Carnegie Corporation. (1986). *A Nation Prepared: Teachers for the Twenty-First Century.* New York: Author.

Castle, S. (2002). "Learning Centers." Working Document. Fairfax, Va.: George Mason University.

Cazden, C. B. (1972). *Child Language and Education.* New York: Holt, Rinehart & Winston.

Cazden, C. B. (1986). Classroom Discourse. In M. C. Wittrock (ed.), *Handbook of Research on Teaching* (3rd ed.). New York: Macmillan.

Cazden, C. B. (1988). *Classroom Discourse.* Portsmouth, N.H.: Heinemann.

Cazden, C. B., and Mehan, H. (1989). Principles from sociology and anthropology: Context, code, classroom, and culture. In M. C. Reynolds (ed.), *Knowledge Base for the Beginning Teacher.* New York: Pergamon Press.

Cazden, C., Cope, B., Fairclough, N., Gee, J., Kalantzis, M., Kress, G., Luke, A., Luke, C., Michaels, S., and Nakata, M., (1996). A pedagogy of multiliteracies: Designing social futures. *Harvard Educational Review.* 66, 60–92.

Claiborn, W. L. (1969). Expectancy effects in the classroom: A failure to replicate. *Journal of Educational Psychology, 60,* 377–383.

Clark, C. M., and Lampert, M. (1986). The study of teacher thinking: Implications for teacher education. *Journal of Teacher Education, 37,* 27–31.

Clark, C. M., and Yinger, R. J. (1979). *Three Studies of Teacher Planning.* East Lansing, Mich.: Institute for Research on Teaching, Michigan State University.

Cochran-Smith, M., and Lytle, S. L. (1993). *Inside Outside: Teacher Research and Knowledge.* New York: Teachers College Press.

Cognition and Technology Group at Vanderbilt. (1990). Anchored instruction. Unpublished paper. Nashville, Tenn.: Vanderbilt University.

Cognition and Technology Group at Vanderbilt. (1996a). Looking at technology in context: A framework for understanding technology and educational research. In D. Berliner and E. R. Calfee (eds.), *Handbook of Educational Psychology.* New York: Wiley.

Cognition and Technology Group at Vanderbilt. (1996b). Designing environments to reveal, support, and expand our children's potentials. In S. A. Soraci and W. Mcllvane (eds.), *Perspectives on Fundamental Processes in Intellectual Functioning.* Greenwich, Conn.: Ablex.

Cohen, E. (1994). *Designing Groupwork: Strategies for the Heterogeneous Classroom.* New York: Teachers College Press.

Cole, M., Griffin, P., and Laboratory of Comparative Cognition. (1987). *Contextual Factors in Education.* Madison, Wisc.: Wisconsin Center for Educational Research.

Coleman, J. (1961). *The Adolescent Society.* New York: Free Press.

Coleman, J. (1972). The children have outgrown the schools. *Psychology Today,* February, 72–82.

College Board. (2000). *2000 Profile of College Bound Seniors on the SAT.* New York: College Board.

Collins, M. L. (1978). Effects of enthusiasm training on preservice elementary teachers. *Journal of Teacher Education, 29,* 53–57.

Comer, J. P. (1988). Educating poor minority children. *Scientific American,* 259 (5), 42–48.

Conditions of Education. (1996). Washington, D.C.: National Center for Educational Statistics.

Conditions of Education. (1998). Washington, D.C.: National Center for Educational Statistics.

Conditions of Education. (1999). Washington, D.C.: National Center for Educational Statistics.

Conditions of Education. (2000). Washington, D.C.: National Center for Educational Statistics.

Conditions of Education. (2001). Washington, D.C.: National Center for Educational Statistics.

Conditions of Education. (2002). Washington, D.C.: National Center for Educational Statistics.

Cooper, H. (1989). *Homework.* New York: Longman.

Cooper, H. M., and Good, T. (1983). *Pygmalion Grows Up: Studies in the Expectation Communication Process.* New York: Longman.

Cooper, J. D. (1993). *Literacy: Helping Children Construct Meaning* (2nd ed.). Boston: Houghton Mifflin.

Copeland, W. D. (1980). Teaching-learning behaviors and the demands of the classroom environment. *Elementary School Journal, 80,* 163–177.

Corno, L. (1996). Homework is a complicated thing. *Educational Researcher,* 25(8), 27–30.

Corno, L. (1989). What it means to be literate in classrooms. In D. Bloome (ed.), *Classrooms and Literacy.* Norwood, N.J.: Ablex.

Costantino, P. M., and DeLorenzo, M. N. (2002). *Developing a Professional Teaching Portfolio: A Guide for Success.* Boston: Allyn & Bacon.

Crawford, J. (1997). *Best Evidence: Research Foundations of the Bilingual Education Act.* Washington, D.C.: National Clearinghouse for Bilingual Education.

Crone, L. J., and Teddie, C. (1995). Further examinations of teacher behavior in differentially effect schools: Selection and socialization process. *Journal of Classroom Interaction,* 30(1), 1–9.

Cruickshank, D., and Metcalf, K. (1994). Explaining. In T. Husen and T. N. Postlewaite (eds.), *International Encyclopedia of Education* (2nd ed.). Oxford: Pergamon.

Cruickshank, D. V., Bainer, D. L., and Metcalf, K. K. (2003). *The Act of Teaching* (2nd ed.). New York: McGraw-Hill.

Csikszentmihalyi, M. (1990). *Flow: The Psychology of Optimal Experience.* New York: Harper & Row.

Cuban, L. (1982). Persistent instruction: The high school classroom, 1900–1980. *Phi Delta Kappan,* 64, 113–118.

Cuban, L. (1984). *How Teachers Taught: Constancy and Change in American Classrooms, 1900–1980.* New York: Longman.

Cuban, L. (1993). *How Teachers Taught: Constancy and Change in American Classrooms 1890–1990.* (2nd ed.). New York: Teachers College Press.

Cullen, F. T., Cullen, J. B., Hayhow, V. L., and Plouffe, J. T. (1975). The effects of the use of grades as an incentive. *Journal of Educational Research,* 68, 277–279.

Curtis, C.K., and Shaver, J. P. (1980). Slow learners and the study of contemporary problems. *Social Education,* 44, 302–309.

Cushner, K., McClelland, A., and Safford, P. (2003). *Human Diversity in Education,* (3rd ed.). New York: McGraw-Hill.

Cypher, T., and Willower, D. J. (1984). The work behavior of secondary school teachers. *Journal of Research and Development,* 18, 17–24.

Danielson, C. (1996). *Enhancing Professional Practice: A Framework for Teaching.* Alexandria, Va.: Association for Supervision and Curriculum Development.

Darling-Hammond, L. (ed.). (1996). *What Matters Most: Teaching for America's Future.* New York: Commission on Teaching and America's Future.

Darling-Hammond, L., Wise, A. E., and Klein, S. P. (1999). *A License to Teach.* San Francisco: Jossey-Bass.

Davies, D. (1991). Schools reaching out: Family, school, and community partnerships for student success. *Phi Delta Kappan,* 72, 376–382.

Darder, A. (1991). *Culture and Power in the Classroom.* New York: Bergin and Garvey.

deCharms, R. (1976). *Enhancing Motivation.* New York: Irvington.

Deci, E., and Ryan, R. (1985). *Intrinsic Motivation and Self-Determination in Human Behavior.* New York: Plenum.

Delpit, L. (1988). The silenced dialogue. *Harvard Educational Review,* 58, 280–298.

Delpit, L. (1995). *Other People's Children: Cultural Conflict in the Classroom.* New York: The New York Press.

Denham, C., and Lieberman, A. (eds.). (1980). *Time to Learn.* Washington, D.C.: U.S. Department of Education.

Dewey, J. (1916). *Democracy and Education.* New York: Macmillan.

Dewey, J. (1933). *How We Think* (rev. ed.). Lexington, Mass.: D.C. Heath.

Dewey, J. (1938). *Experience and Education.* New York: Macmillan.

Dilworth, M. E., and Brown, C. E. (2001). Consider the difference: Teaching and learning in culturally rich schools. In V. Richardson (ed.), *Handbook of Research on Teaching.* (4th ed.). Washington, D.C.: American Educational Research Association.

Doyle, W. (1979). Classroom tasks and students' abilities. In P. L. Peterson and H. J. Walberg (eds.), *Research on Teaching: Concepts, Findings and Implications.* Berkeley, Calif.: McCutchan.

Doyle, W. (1986). Classroom organization and management. In M. C. Wittrock (ed.), *Handbook of Research on Teaching* (3rd ed.). New York: Macmillan.

Doyle, W. (1990). Themes in teacher education research. In W. R. Houston (ed.), *Handbook of Research on Teacher Education.* New York: Macmillan.

Doyle, W., and Carter, K. (1984). Academic tasks in classrooms. *Curriculum Inquiry,* 14, 129–149.

Dreikurs, R. (1968). *Psychology in the Classroom: A Manual for Teachers* (2nd ed.). New York: Harper & Row.

Dreikurs, R., and Grey, L. (1968). *A New Approach to Discipline: Logical Consequences.* New York: Hawthorne Books.

Dreikers, R. with Grunwald, B. B. and Pepper, F. C. (1998). *Maintaining Sanity in the Classroom: Classroom Management Techniques* (2nd ed.). New York: Behavioral Science Press.

Duchastel, P. C., and Brown, B. R. (1974). Incidental and relevant learning with instructional objectives. *Journal of Educational Psychology,* 66, 481–485.

Duckworth, E. (1987). *The Having of Wonderful Ideas and Other Essays on Teaching and Learning.* New York: Teachers College Press.

Duckworth, E. (1991). Twenty-four, forty-two, and I love you: Keeping it complex. In K. Jervis and C. Montag (eds.), *Progressive Education for the 1990s: Transforming Practice.* New York: Teachers College Press.

Duffy, G., and Roehler, L. (1987). Improving reading instruction through the use of responsive elaboration. *Reading Teacher,* 40, 514–520.

Dunkin, M. J., and Biddle, B. J. (1974). *The Study of Teaching.* New York: Holt, Rinehart & Winston.

Dunn, K., and Dunn, R. (1978). *Teaching Students Through Their Individual Learning Styles.* Reston, Va.: National Council of Principals.

Dunn, K., and Dunn, R. (1987). Dispelling outmoded beliefs about student learning. *Educational Leadership.* 47, 50–58.

Eby, J. W. (1992). *Reflective Planning, Teaching, and Evaluation in the Elementary School.* New York: Macmillan.

Eccles, J. S. (1989). Bringing young women to math and science. In M. Crawford and M. Gentry (eds.), *Gender and Thought: Psychological Perspectives.* New York: Springer-Veriag.

Education Trust. (1998). *Education Watch, 1998.* Washington, D.C.: Author.

Educational Leadership. (1995). January.

Educational Leadership. (1999). April.

Emmer, E., Evertson, C., Clements, B., and Worsham, W. E. (2002). *Classroom Management for Secondary School Teachers* (6th ed.). Englewood Cliffs, N.J.: Prentice Hall.

Emmer, E. T., Evertson, C., and Anderson, L. M. (1980). Effective classroom management at the beginning of the school year. *Elementary School Journal,* 80, 219–231.

Epstein, J. L. (1988). How do we improve programs for parent involvement? *Educational Horizons,* 66, 58–59.

Epstein, J. L. (1995). School/family/community partnerships: Caring for children we share. *Phi Delta Kappan,* 76, 701–712.

Erickson, H. L., and Tomlinson, C. A. (2002). *Concept-based Curriculum and Instruction: Teaching Beyond the Facts.* New York: Corwin Press.

Evertson, C., Emmer, E., and Worsham, M. (2002). *Classroom Management for Elementary School Teachers* (6th ed.). Englewood Cliffs, N.J.: Prentice Hall.

Evertson, C. M., Emmer, E. T., Sanford, J. P., and Clements, B. S. (1983). Improving classroom management: An experiment in elementary classrooms. *Elementary School Journal,* 84, 173–188.

Feden, P. R., and Vogel, R. M. (2003). *Methods of Teaching: Applying Cognitive Science to Promote Student Learning.* New York: Mc-Graw-Hill.

Feiman-Nemser, S. (1983). Learning to teach. In L. S. Shulman and G. Sykes (eds.), *Handbook of Teaching and Policy.* New York: Longman.

Feiman-Nemser, S., and Floden, R. E. (1986). In M. C. Wittrock (ed.), *Handbook of Research on Teaching* (3rd ed.). New York: Macmillan.

Fenstermacher, G. D. (1986). Philosophy of research on teaching: Three aspects. In M. C. Wittrock (ed.), *Handbook of Research on Teaching* (3rd ed.). New York: Macmillan.

Fenstermacher, G. D., and Soltis, J. F. (1986). *Approaches to Teaching.* New York: Teachers College Press.

Firestone, W. A., and Rosenblum, S. (1988). Building commitment in urban high schools. *Educational Evaluation and Policy Analysis,* 93, 285–299.

Fisher, C. W., Berliner, D., Filby, N., Marliave, R., Cahen, L., and Dishaw, M. (1980). Teaching behavior, academic learning time, and student achievement: An overview. In C. Denham and A. Lieberman (eds.), *Time to Learn.* Washington, D.C.: National Institute of Education, Department of Education.

Flanders, N. A. (1970). *Analyzing Teaching Behavior.* Reading, Mass.: Addison-Wesley.

Flavel, J. (1985). *Cognitive Development* (2nd ed.). Englewood Cliffs, N.J.: Prentice Hall.

Fleener, A. (1989). *Sample Lesson Plan Format* (mimeographed). Minneapolis, Minn.: Augsburg College.

Floden, R. E. (2001). Research on effect of teaching: A continuing model for research on teaching. *Handbook of Research on Teaching* (4th ed.). Washington, D.C.: American Educational Research Association.

Fogarty, R. (1997). *Problem-based Learning and Other Curriculum Models for the Multiple Intelligence Classroom.* Arlington Heights, Ill.: Skylight Professional Development.

Ford, G. W., and Pugno, L. (eds.). (1964). *The Structure of Knowledge and the Curriculum.* Chicago: Rand McNally.

Friedman, W. J. (1980). *The Development of Relational Understanding of Temporal and Spatial Terms.* (ERIC No. ED 178 176). Resources in Education.

Friend, M., and Bursuck, W. (1999). *Including Students with Special Needs* (2nd ed). Boston: Allyn & Bacon.

Friend, M., and Bursuck, W. (2002). *Including Students with Special Needs* (3rd ed.). Boston: Allyn & Bacon.

Fullan, M. (1992). *The New Meaning of Educational Change* (2nd ed.). New York: Teachers College Press.

Fullan, M. (2001). *The New Meaning of Educational Change.* (3rd ed.). New York: Teachers College Press.

Fuller, F. (1969). Concerns of teachers: A developmental conceptualization. *American Educational Research Journal,* 6, 207–226.

Fuller, M. L., and Olsen, G. (1998). *Home-School Relations: Working Successfully with Parents and Families.* Boston: Allyn & Bacon.

Gage, N. L. (ed.). (1963). *Handbook of Research on Teaching.* Chicago: Rand McNally.

Gage, N. L. (1978). *The Scientific Basis of the Art of Teaching.* New York: Teachers College Press.

Gage, N. L. (1984). *An Update of the Scientific Basis of the Art of Teaching* (mimeographed). Palo Alto, Calif.: Stanford University.

Gagné, E. D. (1985). *The Cognitive Psychology of School Learning.* Boston: Little, Brown.

Gagné, E. D., Yekovick, C. W., and Yekovick, F. R. (1993). *The Cognitive Psychology of School Learning* (2nd ed.). New York: HarperCollins.

Gagné, R. M. (1977). *The Conditions of Learning and Theory of Instruction* (3rd ed.). New York: Holt, Rinehart & Winston.

Gagné, R. M., and Briggs, L. J. (1980). *Principles of Instructional Design* (2nd ed.). New York: Holt, Rinehart & Winston.

Gagné, R. M., Briggs, L. J., and Wager, W. W. (1992). *Principles of Instructional Design* (5th ed.). New York: JBK College and School Division.

Gall, J., and Gall, M. (1990). Outcomes of the discussion method. In W. W. Wilen (ed.), *Teaching and Learning Through Discussion: The Theory and Practice of the Discussion Method*. Springfield, Ill.: Charles C. Thomas.

Gall, M. (1984). Synthesis of research on teachers' questioning. *Educational Leadership*, 42, 40–47.

Gall, M. D. (1970). The use of questions in teaching. *Review of Educational Research*, 40, 707–721.

Gall, M., Gall, J., and Borg, W. (2003). *Educational Research: An Introduction*. (7th ed.). Boston: Allyn and Bacon.

Gallagher, J. J., and Gallagher, S. A. (1994). *Teaching the Gifted Child* (4th ed.). Boston: Allyn & Bacon.

Gallelgo, M. A., Cole, M., and The Laboratory of Comparative Cognition. (2001). Classroom cultures and cultures in the classroom. In V. Richardson (ed.), *Handbook of Research on Teaching*. Washington, D.C.: American Educational Research Association.

Garcia, R. (1992). *Teaching in a Pluralistic Society. Concepts, Models, and Strategies*. New York: HarperCollins.

Gardner, H. (1983). *Frames of Mind*. New York: Basic Books.

Gardner, H. (1985). *The Mind's New Science*. New York: Basic Books.

Gardner, H. (1991). *The Unschooled Mind: How Children Think and How Schools Should Teach*. New York: Basic Books.

Gardner, H. (1993). *Multiple Intelligences: The Theory in Practice*. New York: Basic Books.

Gardner, H. (1994). Multiple intelligences: The theory in practice. *Teacher's College Record*, 83, 501–513.

Gardner, H. (1999). Who owns intelligence? *Atlantic Monthly*, February, 67–75.

Gardner, H., and Hatch, K. T. (1989). Multiple intelligences go to school. *Educational Researcher*, 18, 8–9.

Gersten, R., Baker, S., and Pugach, M. (2001). Contemporary research on special education. In V. Richardson (ed.), *Handbook of Research on Teaching* (4th ed.). Washington, D.C.: American Educational Research Association.

Getzels, J. W., and Thelen, H. A. (1960). The classroom group as a unique social system. In N. Henry (ed.), *The Dynamics of Instructional Groups*. Chicago: National Society for the Study of Education, 59th Yearbook, Part 2.

Gewertz, C. (2001). Study estimates 850,000 U.S. children schooled at home. *Education Week*, August 8, p. 12.

Gibbs, J. (1995). *Tribes: A New Way of Learning Together*. Sausalito, Calif.: Center Source Systems.

Gilligan, C. (1982). *In a Different Voice: Psychological Theory and Women's Development*. Cambridge, Mass.: Harvard University Press.

Glass, G. (1981). Effectiveness of special education. Paper presented at Wingspread Conference, Racine, Wis.

Glass, G. (1976). Primary, secondary, and meta-analysis of research. *Educational Researcher*. 5(10), 3–8.

Glasser, W. (1969). *Schools Without Failure*. New York: Harper & Row.

Glasser, W. (1986). *Control Theory in the Classroom*. New York: Harper & Row.

Glasser, W. (1998). *The Quality School Teacher*. New York: Harper.

Glasser, W. A. (1992). *The Quality School*. New York: HarperCollins.

Gold, R. M., Reilly, A., Silberman, R., and Lehr, R. (1971). Academic achievement declines under pass-fail grading. *Journal of Experimental Education*, 39, 17–21.

Goleman, D. (1995). *Emotional Intelligence*. New York: Bantam.

Goleman, D., McKee, A., and Boyatzis, R. E. (2002). *Primal Leadership: Realizing the Power of Emotional Intelligence*. Cambridge, MA: Harvard Business School.

Good, T. L., and Brophy, J. E. (1987). *Looking in Classrooms* (4th ed.). New York: Harper & Row.

Good, T. L., and Brophy, J. E. (2003). *Looking in Classrooms*. (9th ed.). Boston: Allyn and Bacon.

Good, T. L., and Grouws, D. A. (1977). Teaching effect: A process-product study in fourth grade mathematics classrooms. *Journal of Teacher Education*, 28, 49–54.

Good, T. L., and Grouws, D. A. (1979). The Missouri mathematics effectiveness project: An experimental study in fourth-grade classrooms. *Journal of Educational Psychology*, 71, 355–362.

Good, T. L., Grouws, D. A., and Ebmeier, H. (1983). *Active Mathematics Teaching*. New York: Longman.

Good, T. L., and Weinstein, R. (1986). Teacher expectations: A framework for exploring classrooms. In K. Zumwalt (ed.), *Improving Teaching*. Alexandria, VA: Association for Supervision and Curriculum Development.

Goodlad, J. (1984). *A Place Called School: Prospects for the Future*. New York: McGraw-Hill.

Gordon, P., Rogers, A., Comfort, M., Gavula, N., and McGee, B. (2001). A taste of problem-based learning increases achievement in urban minority middle school students. *Educational Horizons*, 79(4), 171–175.

Gould, S. J. (1996). *The Mismeasure of Man* (2nd ed.). New York: Norton.

Graham, S., and Weiner, B. (1996). Theories and principles of motivation. In D. Berliner and R. Calfee (eds.), *Handbook of Educational Psychology*. New York: Macmillan.

Grant, C. A., & Sleeter, LC. E. (1989). Race, class, gender, exceptionality, and education reform. In J. Banks & C. McGee Banks (eds.), *Multicultural Education: Issues and Perspectives*. Boston: Allyn and Bacon.

Greeno, J. G., Collins, A. M. and Resnick, L. B. (1996). Cognition and learning. In D. C. Berliner and R. C. Calfee (eds.), *Handbook of Educational Psychology*. New York: Simon and Schuster.

Griffiths, S., and Tann, S. (1992). Using reflective practice to link personal and public theories. *Journal of Education for Teaching*. 18, 69–84.

Gronlund, N. E. (1991). *Constructing Achievement Tests* (3rd ed.). Englewood Cliffs, N. J.: Prentice Hall.

Gronlund, N. E. (1999). *How to Write and Use Instructional Objectives* (6th ed.). New York: Macmillan.

Gronlund, N. E. (2002). *Assessment of Student Achievement* (7th ed.). Boston: Allyn & Bacon.

Gronlund, N. E., Linn, R. L., and Davis, K. (1999). *Measurement and Assessment in Teaching* (8th ed.). Englewood Cliffs, N.J.: Prentice Hall.

Gump, P. V. (1967). *The Classroom Behavior Setting: Its Nature and Relation to Student Behavior*. Washington, D.C.: U.S. Office of Education.

Gump, P. V. (1982). School settings and their keeping. In D. L. Duke (ed.), *Helping Teachers Manage Classrooms*. Alexandria, Va.: Association for Supervision and Curriculum Development.

Gunter, M. A., Estes, T. H., and Schwab, J. (2003). *Instruction: A Models Approach.* Boston: Allyn & Bacon.

Gurian, M. (1996). *The Wonder of Boys: What Parents, Mentors, and Educators can Do to Shape Boys into Exceptional Men.* New York: Putnam.

Guskey, T. R., and Gates, S. L. (1986). Synthesis of research on mastery learning. *Educational Leadership, 43,* 73–81.

Guthrie, G. P., and Guthrie, L. F. (1991). Streamlining interagency collaboration for youth at risk. *Educational Leadership, 49* (1), 17–22.

Guzzetti, B. J., Snyder, T. E., and Glass, G. V. (1993). Promoting conceptual change in science: A comparative meta-analysis of instructional intervention from reading and science education. *Reading Research Quarterly, 28*(2), 117–155.

Haberman, M. (1991). The pedagogy of poverty versus good teaching. *Phi Delta Kappan, 72,* 290–294.

Hallinan, M. T., and Sorensen, A. B. (1983). The formation and stability of instructional groups. *American Sociological Review, 48,* 838–851.

Halpern, D. F. (1995). Cognitive gender differences: Why diversity is a critical research issue. In H. Landrine (ed.), *Bringing Cultural Diversity to Feminist Psychology: Theory Research and Practice.* Washington, DC: American Psychological Association.

Halpern, D. F. (1996). Changing data, changing minds: What the data on cognitive sex differences tell us and what we hear. *Learning and Individual Differences, 8,* 73–82.

Hamilton, D., and McWilliam, E. (2001). Ex-centric voices that frame research on teaching. In V. Richardson (ed.), *Handbook of Research on Teaching* (4th ed.). Washington, D.C.: American Educational Research Association.

Harbet, S. (2002). "Dr. Harbert's Training Materials." (http://hhd.csun.edu/).

Hatfield, S. (1996). *Effective use of classroom computer stations across the curriculum.* ERIC Document No. ED-396704.

Heath, S. B. (1983). *Ways with Words: Language, Life and Work in Communities and Classrooms.* Cambridge, England: Cambridge University Press.

Hebert, E. A. (1992). Portfolios invite reflection—from student and staff. *Educational Leadership, 49,* 59–62.

Heider, E. R., Cazden, C. B., and Brown, R. (1968). *Social Class Differences in the Effectiveness and Style of Children's Coding Ability.* (Project Literacy Reports, No. 9). Ithaca, N.Y.: Cornell University.

Henderson, A. T., Marburgaer, C. L., and Ooms, T. (1986). *Beyond the Bake Sale: An Educator's Guide to Working with Parents.* Columbia, Mo: National Committee for Citizens in Education.

Herrnstein, R. J., and Murray, C. (1994). *The Bell Curve: Intelligence and Class Structure in American Life.* New York: Free Press.

Hicks, D. (ed.). (1996). *Discourse, Learning and Schooling.* New York: Cambridge University Press.

Hill, W. F. (1994). *Learning Through Discussion* (3rd ed.). Thousand Oaks, Calif.: Sage Publications.

Hiller, J. H., Gisher, G. A., and Kaess, W. (1969). A computer investigation of verbal characteristics of effective classroom lecturing. *American Educational Research Journal, 6,* 661–675.

Hodgkinson, H. L. (1983). Guess who's coming to college? *Higher Education, 17,* 281–287.

Hodgkinson, H. L. (1992). *A Demographic Look at the Future.* Washington, D.C.: Institute for Educational Leadership.

Honig, M. I., Kahne, J., and McLaughlin, M. W. (2001). School-community connections: Strengthening opportunity to learn and opportunity to teach. In V. Richardson (ed.), *Handbook of Research on Teaching* (4th ed.). Washington, D.C.: American Educational Research Association.

Hopkins, D. (1985). *A Teacher's Guide to Classroom Research.* Philadelphia: Open University Press.

Hopkins, D. (2002). *A Teachers Guide to Classroom Research* (2nd ed.). London: Open University Press.

Housner, L. D., and Griffey, D. C. (1985). Teacher cognition: Differences in planning and interactive decision making between experienced and inexperienced teachers. *Research Quarterly for Exercise and Sport, 56,* 45–53.

Hunt, D. (1970). A conceptual level matching model for coordinating learner characteristics with educational approaches. *Interchange: A Journal of Educational Studies, 1,* 2–16.

Hunt, D. (1974). *Matching Models in Education.* Toronto: Ontario Institute for Studies in Education.

Hunter, M. (1995). *Enhancing Teaching.* New York: Macmillan.

Hunter, M. C. (1982). *Mastery Teaching.* El Segundo, Calif.: TIP Publications.

Hurd, D., et al. (1986). *General Science: A Voyage of Exploration.* Englewood Cliffs, N.J.: Prentice Hall.

Irving, J. J., and York, D. E. (1995). Learning styles and culturally diverse students: A literature review. In Banks, J. and Banks, C. (eds.), *Handbook of Research on Multicultural Education.* New York: Macmillan.

Jackson, L. (1999). Doing school: Examining the effect of ethnic identity and school engagement in academic performance and goal attainment. Paper presented at the annual meeting of the American Educational Research Association, Montreal.

Jackson, P. W. (1968). *Life in Classrooms.* New York: Holt, Rinehart & Winston.

Jacobs, H. H. (1997). *Mapping the Big Picture.* Alexandria, Va.: Association for Supervision and Curriculum Development.

Jencks, C., Smith, M., Ackland, H., Bane, M., Cohen, D., Gintis, H., Heyns, B., and Michelson, S. (1972). *Inequality: A Reassessment of the Effect of Family and Schooling in America.* New York: Basic Books.

Jensen, A. R. (1969). How much can we boost IQ and scholastic achievement? *Harvard Education Review. 2,* 79–83.

Jensen, E. (1998). *Teaching with the Brain in Mind.* Alexandria, Va.: Association of Supervision and Curriculum Development.

Johnson, D. W., and Johnson, F. P. (1999). *Joining Together: Group Theory and Group Skills* (7th ed.). Englewood Cliffs, N.J.: Prentice Hall.

Johnson, R., Rynders, J., Johnson, D. W., Schmidt, B., and Haider, S. (1979). Interaction between handicapped and nonhandicapped teenagers as a function of situational goal structuring: Implications for mainstreaming. *American Educational Research Journal, 16,* 161–167.

Jordan, J. (1988). Nobody means more to me than you and the future life of Willie Jordan. *Harvard Educational Review, 58,* 363–374.

Joyce, B., Hersh, R., and McKibbin, M. (1993). *The Structure of School Improvement* (2nd ed.). New York: Longman.

Joyce, B., and Weil, M. (1972). *Models of Teaching.* Englewood Cliffs, N.J.: Prentice Hall.

Joyce, B., Weil, M., and Calhoun, E. (2000). *Models of Teaching* (6th ed.). Boston: Allyn & Bacon.

Kagan, S. (1992). *Cooperative Learning* (2nd ed.). San Juan Capistrano, Calif.: Resources for Teachers.

Kagan, S. (1998). *Cooperative Learning.* San Juan Capistrano, Calif.: Resources for Teachers.

Keller, F. S. (1966). A personal course in psychology. In T. Urlich, R. Stachnik, and T. Mabry (eds.), *Control of Human Behavior.* Glenview, Ill.: Scott, Foresman.

Kemmis, S., & McTaggart, R. (1998). *The Action Research Planner.* Geelong, Australia: Deakin University Press.

Kilpatrick, W. (1918). The project method. *Teachers College Record,* 19, 319–333.

Klausmeier, H. (1980). *Learning and Teaching Concepts.* New York: Academic Press.

Kleinfeld, J. (1999). Student performance: Males versus females. *The Public Interest. 134,3–20.*

Koerner, B. I. (1999). Where the boys aren't. *U.S. News & World Report,* 8 February, 46–55.

Kohn, A. (2000). *The Schools Our Children Deserve: Moving Beyond Traditional Classrooms and Tougher Standards.* New York: Marilner Books.

Kohn, Alfie. (1995). *Punishment by Rewards: The Trouble with Gold Stars, Incentive Plans, A's, Praise and Other Bribes.* Boston: Houghton Mifflin.

Kohn, Alfie. (1996). *Beyond Discipline: From Compliance to Community.* Alexandria, Va.: Association for Supervision and Curriculum Development.

Kosakowski, J. (2000). The benefits of information technology. *Education Media and Technology Yearbook,* 25.

Kotulak, R. (1996). *Inside the Brain: Revolutionary Discoveries of How the Mind Works.* Kansas City, Mo.: Andrew McMeel.

Kounin, J. S. (1970). *Discipline and Group Management in Classrooms.* New York: Holt, Rinehart & Winston.

Krajcik, J. S., Blumenfeld, P. C., Marx, R. W., and Soloway, E. (1994). A collaborative model for helping middle grade science teachers learn project-based instruction. *Elementary School Journal,* 94, 483–497.

Krajcik, J. S., Czemiak, C., and Berger, C. (2003). *Teaching Children Science: A Project-Based Approach* (2nd ed.). Boston: McGraw-Hill.

Ladson-Billings, G. (1992). Culturally relevant teachers: The key to making multicultural education work. In C. A. Grant (ed.), *Research and Multicultural Education.* London: Falmer Press.

Ladson-Billings, G. (1994). *The Dreamkeepers: Successful Teachers of African American Children.* San Francisco: Jossey-Bass.

Ladson-Billings, G. (1995). But this is just good teaching! The case for culturally relevant pedagogy. *Theory Into Practice,* 34, 161–165.

Ladson-Billngs, G. (1995). Toward a theory of culturally relevant pedagogy. *American Education Research Journal.* 32, 465–491.

Lampert, M. (2001). *Teaching Problems and the Problems of Teaching.* New Haven, Conn.: Yale University Press.

Languages spoken in U.S. homes. *Spokesman Review.* April 28, 1993, p. 2A.

Latham, A. (1999). Research link. *Educational Leadership,* November, 88–89.

Lee, V. E., and Smith, J. B. (1996). Collective responsibility for learning and its effects on gains in achievement of early secondary school students. *American Journal of Education,* 104, 1103–1146.

Leinhardt, G. (1989). Math lessons: A contrast of novice and expert competence. *Journal for Research in Mathematics Education,* 20, 52–75.

Leinhardt, G. (1992). What research on learning tells us about teaching. *Educational Leadership,* 49(7), 20–25.

Lepper, M. R., Greene, D., and Nisbett, R. (1973). Undermining children's intrinsic interest with extrinsic reward: A test of the "overjustification" hypothesis. *Journal of Personality and Social Psychology,* 28, 129–137.

Levin, H. M. (1997). Accelerated schools for disadvantaged students. *Educational Leadership,* 44, 19–21.

Lewin, K., Lippitt, R., and White, R. (1939). Patterns of aggressive behavior in experimentally created social climates. *Journal of Social Psychology,* 10, 271–299.

Lewis, O. (1965). *La Vida.* New York: Random House.

Lieberman, A. (1995). Restructuring schools: The dynamics of changing practice, structure and culture. In A. Lieberman (ed.), *The Work of Restructuring Schools: Building from the Ground Up.* New York: Teachers College Press.

Lieberman, A., and Miller, L. (1984). *Teachers, Their World, and Their Work.* Alexandria, Va.: Association of Supervision and Curriculum Development.

Lieberman, A., and Miller, L. (1992). *Teachers—Their World and Their Work: Implications for School Improvement.* New York: City College Press.

Linn, M. C., and Hyde, J. S. (1989). Gender, mathematics, and science. *Educational Researcher,* 18 (8), 17–27.

Lippitt, R., and White, R. (1963). An experimental study of leadership and group life. In E. E. Macoby, T. M. Newcomb, and F. L. Hartley (eds.), *Readings in Social Psychology.* New York: Holt, Rinehart & Winston.

Little, J. W. (1990). The persistence of privacy: Autonomy and initiative in teachers' professional relations. *Teachers College Record,* 91, 509–536.

Little, J. W., and McLaughlin, B. (eds.). (1993). *Teachers' Work: Individuals, Colleagues and Contexts.* New York: Teachers College Press.

Livingston, C., and Castle, S. (eds.). (1989). *Teachers and Research in Action.* Washington, D.C.: National Education Association.

Lortie, D. C. (1975). *School-Teacher: A Sociological Study.* Chicago: University of Chicago Press.

Lotan, R. A., and Benton, J. (1990). Finding out about complex instruction: Teaching math and science in heterogeneous classrooms. In N. Davidson (ed.), *Cooperative Learning in Mathematics: A Handbook for Teachers.* Menlo Park, Calif.: Addison-Wesley.

Luiten, J., Ames, W., and Aerson, G. (1980). A meta-analysis of advance organizers on learning and retention. *American Educational Research Journal,* 17, 211–218.

Lyman, F. (1983). *Journaling Procedures* (mimeographed). College Park, Md.: University of Maryland.

Lyman, F. (1985). *Think-Pair-Share* (mimeographed). College Park, Md.: University of Maryland.

Lyman, F. (1986). *Procedures for Using the Question/Response Cues* (mimeographed). College Park, Md.: University of Maryland and the Howard County Public Schools.

Lyotard, J. (1987). The postmodern condition. In K. Baynes, J. Bohman, and T. McCarthy (eds.), *After Philosophy: End or Transformation?* Cambridge, Mass.: MIT Press.

Lytton, H., and Romney, D. M. (1991). Parents' sex-related differential socialization of boys and girls: A meta-analytic review. *Psychological Bulletin,* 109, 267–295.

Ma, X. (1995). Gender differences in mathematics achievement between Canadian and Asian educational systems. *Journal of Educational Research.* 89, 118–127.

Macbeth, D. (2000). On an actual apparatus for conceptual change. *Science Education,* 84(2), 226–234.

Maccoby, E., Newcomb, T., and Hartley, E. (eds.). (1958). *Readings in Social Psychology* (3rd ed.). New York: Holt, Rinehart & Winston.

Macias, J. (1990). Scholastic antecedents of immigrant students: Schooling in a Mexican immigrant-sending community. *Anthropology and Education Quarterly,* 21, 291–318.

Madden, N. A., Slavin, R. E., Karweit, N. L., Dolan, L., and Wasik, B. A. (1992, April). Success for all: Longitudinal effects of a restructuring program for inner-city elementary schools. Paper presented at the annual meeting of the American Educational Research Association, San Francisco.

Mager, R. F. (1962). *Preparing Instructional Objectives.* Palo Alto, Calif.: Fearon Publishers.

Mager, R. F. (1984). *Preparing Instructional Objectives* (2nd rev. ed.). Palo Alto, Calif.: D. S. Lake.

Mager, R. F. (1997). *Preparing Instructional Objectives: A Critical Tool in the Development of Effective Instruction.* Los Angeles: Center for Effective Instruction.

Marshall, H. H. (1987). Motivational strategies of three fifth-grade teachers. *Elementary School Journal,* 88, 135–150.

Marzano, R. J. (1992). *A Different Kind of Classroom: Teaching with Dimensions of Learning.* Alexandria, Va.: Association for Supervision and Curriculum Development.

Marzano, R. J. (2000). *Transforming Classroom Grading.* Alexandria, Va.: Association for Supervision and Curriculum Development.

Marzano, R., Pickering, D., and McTighe, J. (1993). *Assessing Student Outcomes.* Alexandria, Va.: Association for Supervision and Curriculum Development.

Maslow, A. (1970). *Motivation and Personality* (2nd ed.). New York: Harper & Row.

Mayer, R. E. (1984). Aids to prose comprehension. *Educational Psychologist,* 19, 30–42.

McClelland, D. C. (1958). Methods of measuring human motivation. In J. W. Atkinson (ed.), *Motives in Fantasy, Action and Society.* New York: Van Nostrand.

McClelland, D. C. (1961). *The Achieving Society.* New York: Van Nostrand.

McClelland, D. C. (1985). *Human Motivation.* New York: Scotts Foresman.

McCown, R. R., and Roop, P. (1992). *Educational Psychology and Classroom Practice: A Partnership.* Needham Heights, Mass.: Allyn & Bacon.

McLaughlin, D. (1996). Personal narratives for school change in Navajo settings. In D. McLaughlin and W. Tierney (eds.), *Naming Silenced Lives: Personal Narratives and Processes of School Change.* London: Routledge Press.

McLaughlin, M., and Talbert, J. (2001). *Professional Communities and the Work of High School Teaching.* Chicago: University of Chicago Press.

McTighe, J., and Lyman, F. T. (1988). Cueing thinking in the classroom: The promise of theory-embedded tools. *Educational Leadership,* 45, 18–24.

Means, B. (2000). Technology in America's schools: Before and after Y2K. In R. S. Brandt (ed.), *Education in a New Era.* Alexandria, Va.: Association for Supervision and Curriculum Development.

Mercado, C. I. (2001). The learner: "Race," "ethnicity," and linquistic difference. In V. Richardson (ed.) *Handbook of Research on Teaching.* (4th ed.). Washington, D.C.: American Educational Research Association.

Merrill, M. D., and Tennyson, R. D. (1977). *Teaching Concepts: An Instructional Design Approach.* Englewood Cliffs, N.J.: Educational Technology.

Metropolitan Life Survey of the American Teacher. (1995). New York: Louis Harris & Associates.

Metts, S. (2002). "Classroom Questions." (*www.cat.ilstu.edu*).

Miles, R. (1989). *Racism.* London: Routledge.

Milton, O. et al. (1986). *Making Sense of College Grades.* San Francisco: Jossey-Bass.

Mitzel, H. (1960). Teacher effectiveness. In C. W. Harris (ed.), *Encyclopedia of Educational Research* (3rd ed.). New York: Macmillan.

Moely, B. E., et al. (1986). How do teachers teach memory skills? *Educational Psychologist,* 21, 55–72.

Monitoring the Future, 12th Grade Study: 1983, 1990, 1995, and 2000. (2000). Ann Arbor, Mich.: University of Michigan Institute of Social Research.

Naftulin, D., Ware, J., and Donnelly, F. (1973). The doctor fox lecture: A paradigm of educational seduction. *Journal of Medical Education,* 48, 630–635.

Nettles, S. M. (1991). Community involvement and disadvantaged students: A review. *Review of Educational Research,* 61, 379–406.

Newcomb, T. M. (1961). *The Acquaintance Process.* New York: Holt, Rinehart & Winston.

Niguidula, D. (1998). A richer picture of student work: The digital portfolio. In D. Allen (ed.), *Assessing Student Learning: From Grading to Understanding.* New York: Teachers College Press.

Noblit, G. (1995). In meaning: the possibilities of caring. *Phi Delta Kappan,* 77, 682.

Noddings, N. (1984). *Caring: A Feminine Approach to Ethics and Moral Education.* Berkeley, Calif.: University of California Press.

Noddings, N. (1992). *The Challenge to Care in Schools: An Alternative Approach to Education.* New York: Teachers College Press.

Noddings, N. (1995). Teaching themes of care. *Phi Delta Kappan,* 77, 676.

Noddings, N. (2001). The caring teacher. In V. Richardson (ed.), *Handbook of Research on Teaching* (4th ed.). Washington, D.C.: American Educational Research Association.

Nolan, J., and Francis, P. (1992). Changing perspectives in curriculum and instruction. In C. Glickman (ed.), *Supervision in Transition.* Alexandria, Va.: Association for Supervision and Curriculum Development.

Norton, P., and Sprague, D. (2001). *Technology for Teaching.* Boston: Allyn & Bacon.

Novak, J. D., and Musonda, D. (1991). A twelve-year longitudinal study of science concept teaching. *American Educational Research Journal,* 28, 125–130.

Nystrand, M. et al. (1997). *Opening Dialogue: Understanding the Dynamics of Language and Learning in English classrooms.* New York: Teachers College Press.

Oakes, J. (1985). *Keeping Track: How Schools Structure Inequality.* New Haven, Conn.: Yale University Press.

Oakes, J. (1992). Can tracking research inform practice? Technical, normative, and political considerations. *Educational Researcher,* 21(4), 12–21.

Oakes, J., and Lipton, M. (1999). *Teaching to Change the World.* Boston: McGraw-Hill.

Oakes, J., and Lipton, M. (2003). *Teaching to Change the World* (2nd ed.). New York: McGraw-Hill.

Ogbu, J. U. (1995). Understanding cultural diversity and learning. In Banks, J. and Banks, C. (eds.), *Handbook of Research on Multicultural Education.* New York: Macmillan.

Ogbu, J. U. (1997). Understanding the school performance of urban blacks: Some essential background knowledge. In H. Walberg, O. Reyes, and R. P. Weissberg (eds.), *Children and Youth: Interdisciplinary Perspectives.* Norwood, NJ: Ablex.

Oja, S. N., and Smulyan, L. (1989). *Collaborative Action Research: A Developmental Approach.* New York: Falmer Press.

Omi, M., and Winant, H. (1994). *Racial Formation in the United States.* New York: Routledge.

Ormund, J. E. (2000). *Educational Psychology: Developing Learners.* (3rd ed.). Upper Saddle River, NJ: Merrill.

Palincsar, A. S. (1986). The role of dialogue in providing scaffolding instruction. *Educational Psychologist,* 21, 73–98.

Palincsar, A., and Brown, A. (1989). Instruction for self-regulated reading. In L. Resnick and L. Kloper (eds.), *Toward the*

Thinking Curriculum: Current Cognitive Research. Alexandria, Va.: Association for Supervision and Curriculum Development.

Pallas, A., Natriello, G., and McDill, E. (1989). The changing nature of the disadvantaged population: Current dimensions and future trends. *Educational Researcher,* 18, 16–22.

Palloff, R. M., and Pratt, K. (1999). *Building Learning Communities in Cyberspace.* San Francisco: Jossey Bass.

Paullio, H. R. (1985). A tiger examines his stripes. *Teaching-Learning Issues,* No. 55. Knoxville, Tenn.: University of Tennessee Press.

Paullio, H. R. (1992). Learning new materials is fun—yes, but will it be on the test? *Teaching-Learning Issues,* No. 72, Knoxville, Tenn.: University of Tennessee Press.

Perelman, L. (1992). *School's Out. Hyperlearning, the New Technology and the End of Education.* New York: William Morrow.

Perkins, D. N. (1992). *Smart School: From Training Memories to Educating Minds.* New York: Free Press.

Perkins, D. N. (1995). *Outsmarting IQ: The Emerging Science of Learnable Intelligence.* New York: Free Press.

Perry, W. (1969). *Forms of Intellectual and Ethical Development During the College Years.* New York: Holt, Rinehart & Winston.

Peterson, P. L., Marx, R. W., and Clark, C. (1978). Teacher planning, teacher behavior and student achievement. *American Educational Research Journal,* 15, 417–432.

Phillips, S. (1972). Participant structures and communicative competence: Warm Springs children in community and classroom. In C. Cazden and D. Hymes (eds.), *Functions of Language in the Classroom.* New York: Teachers College Press.

Piaget, J. (1954). *The Construction of Reality in the Child.* New York: Basic Books.

Piaget, J. (1963). *Psychology of Intelligence.* Paterson, N.J.: Littlefield Adams.

Pogrow, S. (1990). Challenging at-risk students: Findings from the HOTS program. *Phi Delta Kappan,* 71, 389–397.

Pograw, S. (1990). Challenging at-risk students: Findings from the HOTS program. *Phi Delta Kappan,* January, pp. 43–47.

Pogrow, S. (1999). Systematically using powerful learning environments to accelerate the learning of disadvantaged students in grades 4–8. In C. Reigluth (ed.), *Instructional Design Theories and Models.* Hillsdale, NJ: Lawrence Erlbaum.

Pollard, D. S. (1998). The contexts of single-sex classes. *In Separated by Sex: A Critical Look at Single-Sex Education.* Washington, D.C.: American Association of University Women Education Foundation.

Portes, A., and MacLeod, D. (1996). Educational progress of children of immigrants: The roles of class, ethnicity, and school context. *Sociology of Education.* 69, 255–275.

Posner, G. J., and Rudnitsky, A. N. (2000). *Course Design* (6th ed.). New York: Addison-Wesley.

Pressley, M., et al. (1989). The challenges of classroom strategy instruction. *Elementary School Journal,* 58, 266–278.

Pressley, M., et al. (1991). *Cognitive Instruction that Really Improves Children's Academic Performance.* Cambridge, Mass.: Brookline.

Pressley, M., Woloshyn, V., and Associates. *Cognitive Strategy Instruction That Really Improves Children's Academic Performance.* Cambridge, Mass.: Brookline Books.

Putnam, J., and Burke, J. (1992). *Organizing and Managing Classroom Learning.* New York: McGraw-Hill.

Pyle, A. (1997). Attacking the textbook crisis. *Los Angeles Times.* 29 September.

Race, P., and Race, P. (2001). *The Lecturer's Toolkit: A Practical Guide to Learning, Teaching, and Assessing* (2nd ed.). Kogan Page.

"Racial Gap in Test Score Found Across New York." (2002). *New York Times,* March 28, A1, B4.

Raffini, J. P. (1996). *150 Ways to Increase Intrinsic Motivation in the Classroom.* Boston: Allyn & Bacon.

Redfield, D., and Rousseau, E. (1981). A meta-analysis of experimental research on teacher questioning behavior. *Review of Educational Research,* 51, 237–245.

Reed, S., and Sautter, R. C. (1990). Children of poverty: The status of 12 million young Americans. *Phi Delta Kappan,* 71, K1–K12.

Resnick, L. (1987a). Learning in school and out. *Educational Researcher,* 16, 13–20.

Resnick, L. B. (1987b). *Education and Learning to Think.* Washington, D.C.: National Academy Press.

Resnick, L. B., and Klopfer, L. E. (eds.). (1989). *Toward the Thinking Curriculum: Current Cognitive Research.* Alexandria, Va.: Association for Supervision and Curriculum Development.

Reynolds, M. C. (ed.). (1989). *Knowledge Base for the Beginning Teacher.* New York: Pergamon.

Richardson, V. (ed.). (2001). *Handbook of Research onTeaching* (4th ed.). Washington, D.C.: American Educational Research Association.

Richardson, V., and Placier, P. (2001). Teacher change. In V. Richardson (ed.), *Handbook of Research on Teaching* (4th ed.). Washington, D.C.: American Educational Research Association.

Richardson-Koehler, V. (ed.). (1987). *Educators' Handbook: A Research Perspective.* New York: Longman.

Riel, M., and Fulton, K. (1998). Technology in the Classroom: Tool for Doing Things Differently or Doing Different Things. Paper presented at the annual meeting of the American Educational Research Association. San Diego, Calif.

Ringstaff, C., Sandholtz, J. H., and Dwyer, D. C. (1995). Trading places: When teachers utilize student expertise in technology-intensive classrooms. In *Apple Education Research Reports.* Eugene, Oreg.: International Society for Technology in Education.

Rist, R. C. (1970). Student social class and teacher expectations: The self-fulfilling prophecy in ghetto education. *Harvard Education Review,* 40, 411–451.

Rogers, S., Ludington, J. K., and Graham, S. (1999). *Motivation and Learning.* Evergreen, Colo.: Peak Learning Systems.

Rolheiser, C., Bower, B., and Stevahn, L. (2000). *The Portfolio Organizer.* Alexandria, Va.: Association for Supervision and Curriculum Development.

Rosenbaum, J. E. (1976). *Making Equality: The Hidden Curriculum in High School Tracking.* New York: Wiley.

Rosenholz, S. (1989). *Teacher's Workplace: The Social Organization of Schools.* New York: Longman.

Rosenshine, B. (1970). Enthusiastic teaching: A research review. *School Review,* 78, 499–514.

Rosenshine, B. (1979). Content, time and direct instruction. In P. L. Peterson and H. J. Walberg (eds.), *Research on Teaching.* Berkeley, Calif.: McCutchan.

Rosenshine, B. (1980). How time is spent in elementary classrooms. In C. Denham and A. Lieberman (eds.), *Time to Learn.* Washington, D.C.: U.S. Department of Education.

Rosenshine, B., and Furst, N. (1973). The use of direct observation to study teaching. In R. M. W. Travers (ed.), *Second Handbook of Research on Teaching.* Chicago: Rand McNally.

Rosenshine, B., and Stevens, R. (1986). Teaching functions. In M. C. Wittrock (ed.), *Handbook of Research on Teaching* (3rd ed.). New York: Macmillan.

Rosenthal, R., and Jacobson, L. (1968). *Pygmalion in the Classroom.* New York: Holt, Rinehart & Winston.

Ross, J. A. (1988). Controlling variables: A meta-analysis of training studies. *Review of Educational Research,* 58(4), 405–437.

Rothman, R. (1995). *Measuring Up: Standards, Assessment and School Reform.* San Francisco: Jossey-Bass.

Rowe, M. B. (1974a). Wait-time and rewards as instructional variables, their influence on language, logic, and fate control. Part one: Wait-time. *Journal of Research in Science Teaching,* 11, 81–94.

Rowe, M. B. (1974b). Relation of wait-time and rewards to the development of language, logic, and fate control. Part II: Rewards. *Journal of Research in Science Teaching,* 11, 291–308.

Rowe, M. B. (1986). Wait time: Slowing down may be a way of speeding up. *Journal of Teacher Education,* 37, 43–50.

Rugen, L., and Hart, S. (1994). The lessons of learning expeditions. *Educational Leadership,* 52, 20–23.

Rugg, H. (1926). Curriculum-making and the scientific study of education since 1910. In H. Rugg (ed.), *Twenty-sixth Yearbook of the National Society for the Study of Education, Part I.* Bloomington, Ill.: Public Schools Publishing Co.

Russell, T., and Munby, H. (eds.). (1992). *Teachers and Teaching: From Classroom to Reflection.* New York: Falmer Press.

Rutter, M., Maughan, B., Mortimore, P., Ouston, J., and Smith, A. (1979). *Fifteen Thousand Hours: Secondary Schools and Their Effects on Children.* Cambridge, Mass.: Harvard University Press.

Ryan, K., Newman, K., Mager, G., Applegate, J., Lasley, T., Flora, R., and Johnston, J. (1980). *Biting the Apple: Accounts of First Year Teachers.* New York: Longman.

Ryle, G. (1949). *The Concept of Mind.* London: Hutchinson's University Library.

Sadker, M. (1985). *Women in Educational Administration.* Washington, D.C.: Mid-Atlantic Center for Sex Equity.

Sadker, M., and Sadker, D. (1994). *Failing in Fairness: How America's Schools Cheat Girls.* New York: Scribner.

Sadker, M., Sadker, D., and Klein, S. (1991). The issue of gender in elementary and secondary education. *Review of Research in Education,* 17, 269–334.

Sanders, W. L., and Rivers, J. C. (1996). *Cumulative and Residual Effects of Teachers on Future Student Academic Achievement* (unpublished paper). Knoxville, Tenn.: University of Tennessee.

Sandler, B. R. (1982). The Hatch Amendment: A leap backward for education. *Graduate Woman.* 76(1), 26–29.

Santrock, J. W. (1976). Affect and facilitative self-control. Influence of ecological setting, cognition, and social agent. *Journal of Educational Psychology,* 68 (5), 529–535.

Sapon-Shevin, M., and Shevin, S. (1998). *Because We Can Change the World: A Practical Guide to Building Cooperative, Inclusive Classroom Communities.* Boston: Allyn & Bacon.

Sarason, S. (1982). *The Culture of School and the Problem of Change* (2nd ed.). Boston: Allyn & Bacon.

Sarason, S. D. (1995). *Parental Involvement and the Political Principle.* San Francisco: Jossey-Bass.

Schmoker, M., and Marzano, R. (1999). Realizing the promise of standards-based education. *Educational Leadership,* 57, 177–121.

Schmuck, R. (1997). *Practical Action Research for Change.* Arlington Heights, Ill.: Skylight Professional Development.

Schmuck, R., and Schmuck, P. (2002). *Group Processes in the Classroom* (8th ed.). New York: McGraw-Hill.

Schmuck, R. A., and Schmuck, P. A. (1992). *Small Districts, Big Problems.* Newbury Park, Calif.: Corwin Press.

Schön, D. A. (1983). *The Reflective Practitioner.* San Francisco: Jossey-Bass.

Schön, D. A. (1987). *Educating the Reflective Practitioner.* San Francisco: Jossey Bass.

School choice. (1999). *Education Week,* 16 October, 1.

Schuck, R. (1981). The impact of set induction on student achievement and retention. *Journal of Educational Research,* 74, 227–232.

Schulman, L. S. (1986). Paradigms and research programs in the story of teaching: A contemporary perspective. In M. C. Wittrock (ed.), *Handbook of Research on Teaching* (3rd ed.). New York: Macmillan.

Schulman, L. S. (1987). Knowledge and teaching: Foundations of the new reform. *Harvard Education Review,* 57, 1–22.

Serbin, L., and O'Leary, D. (1975). How nursery schools teach children to shut up. *Psychology Today,* January, 56–58.

Sergiovanni, T. (1996). *Leadership for the Schoolhouse.* San Francisco: Jossey-Bass.

Shaefer, W., and Lissitz, R. (1987). Measurement training for school personnel: Recommendations and reality. *Journal of Teacher Education,* 38, 57–63.

Sharan, S., Kussell, P., Hertz-Lazarowitz, R., Bejarano, Y., Raviv, S., and Sharan, Y. (1984). *Cooperative Learning in the Classroom: Research in Desegregated Schools.* Hillsdale, N.J.: Erlbaum.

Sharon, S. (1999). *Handbook of Cooperative Learning Methods.* New York: Praeger.

Shavelson, R., and Baxter, G. (1992). What we've learned about assessing hands-on science. *Educational Leadership,* 49, 20–25.

Sharp, V. (2002). *Computer Education for Teachers* (4th ed.). New York: McGraw-Hill.

Shoop, L. L., and Wright, D. (1999). *Classroom Warm-Ups: Activities That Improve the Climate for Learning and Discussion.* SAN Jose, Calif.: Resource Publications.

Simkins, M., Cole, K., Tavalin, F., and Means, B. (2002). *Increasing Student Learning Through Multimedia Projects.* Alexandria, Va.: Association for Supervision and Curriculum Development.

Sirotnik, K. A. (1983). What you see is what you get. *Harvard Educational Review,* 54, 16–32.

Sizer, T. (1984). *Horace's Compromise: The Dilemma of the American High School.* Boston: Houghton-Mifflin.

Skinner, B. F. (1956). *Science and Human Behavior.* New York: Macmillan.

Slavin, R. (1983). *Cooperative Learning.* New York: Longman.

Slavin, R. (1986). *Student Team Learning* (3rd ed.). Baltimore: Center for Research on Elementary and Middle Schools, Johns Hopkins University.

Slavin, R. (1994). *Using Student Team Learning* (4th ed.). Baltimore: Johns Hopkins University.

Slavin, R. (1995). *Cooperative Learning* (2nd ed.). Boston: Allyn & Bacon.

Slavin, R. (1995). Cooperative learning and race relations. In Banks, J. and Banks, C. (eds.), *Handbook of Research on Multicultural Education.* New York: Macmillan.

Slavin, R. (1996). *Every Child, Every School: Success for All.* Thousand Oaks, Calif.: Corwin Press.

Slavin, R., Madden, N., Dolan, L., and Wasik, B. (1992). *Success for All.* Arlington, Va.: Educational Research Services.

Slavin, R., Madden, N., Dolan, L., and Wasik, B. (1994). Roots and wings: Inspiring academic excellence. *Educational Leadership,* 52, 10–14.

Slavin, R., Sharan, S., Kagan, S., Hertz-Lazarowitz, R., Webb, C., and Schmuck, R. (eds.). (1985). *Learning to Cooperate, Cooperating to Learn.* New York: Plenum Press.

Smith, H. (1995). Rogue eco-system project. *Educational Connection,* 1, 3–4.

Sorensen, A. B., and Hallinan, M. T. (1986). Effects of ability grouping on growth in academic achievement. *American Educational Research Journal,* 23, 519–542.

Sousa, D. A. (2001). *How the Brain Learns.* Thousand Oaks, Calif.: Corwin Press.

Spaulding, C. L. (1992). *Motivation in the Classroom.* New York: McGraw-Hill.

Sprinthall, R. C., Sprinthall, N. A., and Oja, S. N. (1998). *Educational psychology: A Developmental Approach* (7th ed.). New York: McGraw-Hill.

Stallings, J., and Kaskowitz, D. (1974). *Follow-Through Classroom Observation Evaluation 1972–1974.* (SRI project URU-7370). Stanford, Calif.: Stanford Research Institute.

Starch, D., and Elliot, E. C. (1912). Reliability of grading high school work in English. *Scholastic Review, 20,* 442–456.

Starch, D., and Elliot, E. C. (1913). Reliability of grading high school work in history. *Scholastic Review, 22,* 676–681.

Starkey, D. (1980). *The Origins of Concept Formation: Object Sorting and Object Preference in Early Infancy.* (ERIC No. ED 175555: Resources in Education).

Steele, C. M. (1992, April). Race and the schooling of Black Americans. *Atlantic Monthly,* 68–78.

Stenhouse, L. (1975). *An Introduction to Curriculum Research and Development.* London: Heinemann.

Stenhouse, L. (1983). *Authority, Education and Emancipation.* London: Heinemann.

Stenhouse, L. (1984). Artistry and teaching: The teacher as focus of research and development. In D. Hopkins and M. Wideen (eds.), *Alternative Perspectives on School Improvement.* New York: Falmer Press.

Stephen, W. J., Senn, P. R., and Stepien, W. C. (2001). *The Internet and Problem-Based Learning: Developing Solutions Through the Web.* Tucson, Ariz.: Zephyr Press.

Sternberg. R. J. (1985). *Beyond IQ: A Triarchic Theory of Human Intelligence.* New York: Cambridge University Press.

Sternberg, R. J. (1999). Ability and expertise: Its time to replace the current model of intelligence. *American Educator.* 50–51, 10–13.

Sternberg, R. J. (1999). Myths, countermyths, and truths about intelligence. In A. Woolfork (ed.), *Readings in Educational Psychology.* Boston: Allyn & Bacon.

Sternberg, R. J. (2002). *Cognitive Psychology* (3rd ed.). Belnont CA: Wadsworth Publishing Co.

Stevens, R., and Slavin, R. (1995). The cooperative elementary school: Effects on students' achievement, attitudes, and social relations. *American Educational Research Journal.* 32(2), 321–51.

Stiggins, R. (1996). *Student-Centered Classroom Assessment* (2nd ed.). Englewood Cliffs, N.J.: Prentice Hall.

Stipek, D. J. (1996). Motivation and instruction. In D. Berliner and R. Calfee (eds.), *Handbook of Educational Psychology.* New York: Macmillan.

Stipek, D. J. (2001). *Motivation to Learn: Integrating Theory and Practice* (4th ed.). Boston: Allyn & Bacon.

Stronge, J. H. (2002). *Qualities of Effective Teachers.* Alexandria, Va.: Association of Supervision and Curriculum Development.

Suchman, R. (1962). *The Elementary School Training Program in Scientific Inquiry.* Report to the U.S. Office of Education. Urbana: University of Illinois.

Swing from wings. (1990, February). Mid-Atlantic Association for Cooperation in Education Cooperative News.

Taba, H. (1996). *Teaching Strategies and Cognitive Functioning in Elementary School Children.* San Francisco: San Francisco State University.

Tannen, D. (1990). *You Just Don't Understand: Women and Men in Conversation.* New York: William Morrow.

Tannen, D. (1994). *Gender and Discourse.* New York: Oxford University Press.

Tapscott, D. (1998). *Growing Up Digital: The Rise of the Net Generation.* New York: McGraw-Hill.

Tapscott, D. (2000). The digital divide. *Jossey-Bass Reader on Technology and Learning.* San Francisco: Jossey-Bass.

Taylor, R. (1949). *Basic Principles of Curriculum and Instruction.* Chicago: University of Chicago Press.

Tennyson, R. (1978). Pictorial support and specific instructions as design variables for children's concept and rule learning. *Educational Communication and Technology: A Journal of Research and Development, 26,* 291–299.

Tennyson, R., and Cocchiarella, M. (1986). An empirically based instructional design theory for teaching concepts. *Review of Educational Research, 56,* 40–71.

Tennyson, R., Youngers, J., and Suebsonthi, P. (1983). Concept learning by children using instructional presentation forms for prototype formation and classification-skill development. *Journal of Educational Psychology, 75,* 280–290.

Terrell, S., and Rendulic, P. (1996). Using computer-managed instructional software to increase motivation and achievement in elementary school children. *Journal of Research on Computing in Education, 26*(3), 403–414.

Thelen, H. A. (1954). *Dynamics of Groups at Work.* Chicago: University of Chicago Press.

Thelen, H. A. (1960). *Education and the Human Quest.* New York: Harper & Row.

Timpson, W. M., and Tobin, D. N. (1982). *Teaching as Performing.* Englewood Cliffs, N.J.: Prentice Hall.

Tobin, K. (1992). Teacher mind frames and science learning: Beliefs about teaching and learning. In K. Tobin, J. B. Kahle, and B. J. Fraser, (eds.), *Windows into Science Classrooms: Problems Associated with Higher-Level Cognitive Learning.* New York: Falmer Press.

Tobin, K., Kahle, J. B., and Fraser, B. J. (eds.). (1992). *Windows into Science Classrooms: Problems Associated with Higher-Level Cognitive Learning.* New York: Falmer Press.

Tomlinson, C. A. (1999). *The Differentiated Classroom: Responding to the Needs of All Learners.* Alexandria, Va.: Association for Supervision and Curriculum Development.

Torp, L., and Sage, R. (1998). *Problems as Possibilities.* Alexandria, Va.: Association for Supervision and Curriculum Development.

Travers, R. M. (ed.). (1973). *Second Handbook of Research on Teaching.* Chicago: Rand McNally.

Tuckman, W. B. (1992). Does the length of the assignment or the nature of grading practices influence the amount of homework students are motivated to produce? *Journal of General Education, 41,* 190–199.

Turkle, S. (1997). *Life on the Screen: Identity in the Age of the Internet.* New York: Touchstone.

Turnbull, R., Turnbull, A., Shank, M, Smith, S., and Leal, D. (2002). *Exceptional Lives: Special Education in Today's Schools* (3rd ed.). Columbus, Ohio: Merrill/Prentice-Hall.

Tyack, D., and Cuban, L. (2000). Teaching by machine. *The Jossey-Bass Reader on Technology and Learning.* San Francisco: Jossey Bass.

Tyler, R. W. (1950). *Basic Principles of Curriculum and Instruction.* Chicago: University of Chicago Press.

U.S. Census Bureau Documents on Poverty. (2002). *www.census. gov/hhes/www/poverty.html*

U.S. Department of Education. (1998). *Conditions of Education, 1998.* Washington, D.C.: U.S. Government Printing Office.

U.S. Department of Education, Office of Bilingual Education and Minority Language Affairs. (1998). *Facts About Limited English Proficient Students.* Washington, D.C.: U.S. Government Printing Office.

Veenman, S. (1984). Perceived problems of beginning teachers. *Review of Educational Research, 54,* 143–178.

Villegas, A. M. (1991). *Culturally Responsive Teaching.* Princeton, N.J.: Educational Testing Service.

Vygotsky, L. S. (1978). *Mind in Society. The Development of Higher Psychological Processes.* Cambridge, Mass.: Harvard University Press.

Vygotsky, L. S. (1994). The problem of environment. In Rene van der Veer and J. Valsiner (eds.), *The Vygotsky Reader.* Cambridge, England: Blackwell.

Wadsworth, B. J. (1989). *Piaget's Theory of Cognitive Development* (4th ed.) New York: Longman.

Walberg, H. J. (1986). Syntheses of research on teaching. In M. C. Wittrock (ed.), *Handbook of Research on Teaching* (3rd ed.). New York: Macmillan.

Walcott, H. (1973). *The Man in the Principal's Office: An Ethnography.* New York: Holt, Rinehart & Winston.

Waller, W. (1932). *The Sociology of Teaching.* New York: Russell & Russell.

Wang, M. C., Reynolds, M., and Walberg, H. (1995). Serving students at the margin. *Educational Leadership, 52,* 12–17.

Wang, M. C., Walberg, H. J., and Reynolds, M. C. (1992). A scenario for better—not separate—special education. *Educational Leadership, 50,* 35–38.

Wapner, S., and Kemick, J. (1991). *Field-dependence-independence: Cognitive Styles Across the Life Span.* Hillsdale, NJ: Earlbaum.

War Manpower Commission (1945). *The Training Within Industry Report.* Washington, D.C.: Bureau of Training.

Warren, D. (ed.). (1989). *American Teachers: Histories of a Profession at Work.* New York: Macmillan.

Weick, K. E. (1976). Educational organizations as loosely coupled systems. *Administrative Science Quarterly, 21,* 1–19.

Weick, K. E. (1979). *The Social Psychology of Organizing* (2nd ed.). Reading, Mass.: Addison-Wesley.

Weiner, B. (ed.). (1974). *Achievement Motivation and Attribution Theory.* Morristown, N.J.: General Learning Corporation.

Weiner, B. (1986). *An Attributional Theory of Motivations and Emotion.* New York: Springer.

Weiner, B. (1992). *Human Motivation: Metaphors, Theories, and Research.* Newbury Park, CA: Sage.

Weiner, L. (1999). *Urban Teaching: The Essentials.* New York: Teachers College Press.

Weinstein, C. F., and Mayer, R. F. (1986). The teaching of learning strategies. In M. C. Wittrock (ed.), *Handbook of Research on Teaching.* New York: Macmillan.

Weinstein, C. F., and Mignano, A. J. (1993). *Elementary Classroom Management: Lessons from Research and Practice.* New York: McGraw-Hill.

Weinstein, C. F., and Mignano, A. J. (2002). *Elementary Classroom Management: Lessons from Research and Practice* (3rd ed.). New York: McGraw-Hill.

Weisz, D. n.d. *Action Research Project: Equitable Distribution of Questioning and Feedback in the Classroom* (mimeographed). College Park: University of Maryland.

Welch, L., and Long, L. (1940). The higher structural phases of concept formation. *Journal of Psychology, 9,* 59–95.

Wiggins, G., and McTighe, J. (1998). *Understanding by Design.* Alexandria, Va.: Association for Supervision and Curriculum Development.

Wiggins, G. P. (1993). *Assessing Student Performance.* San Francisco: Jossey-Bass.

Wiggins, G. P. (1997). *Educative Assessment: Designing Assessments to Inform and Improve Student Performance.* San Francisco: Jossey-Bass.

Williams, W., et al. (1996). *Practical Intelligence in Schools.* New York: HarperCollins.

Wise, A. (1995). NCATE's emphasis on performance. *NCATE Quality Teaching, 5,* 1–12.

Wise, K. C., and Okey, J. R. (1983). A meta-analysis of the effects of various science teaching strategies on achievement. *Journal of Research on Science Teaching, 20* (5), 415–524.

Wittrock, M. C. (ed.). (1986). *Handbook of Research on Teaching* (3rd ed.). New York: Macmillan.

Wolfe, P. (2001). *Brain Matters: Translating Research into Classroom Practice.* Alexandria, Va.: Association for Supervision and Curriculum Development.

Woman on Words and Images. (1975). *Dick and Jane as Victims: Sex Stereotyping in Children's Readers.* Princeton, NJ: Unpublised manuscript.

Woolfolk, A. (2001). *Educational Psychology* (8th ed.). Boston: Allyn & Bacon.

Worley, R. (2002). "Online Interactive Learning." Personal correspondence.

Yinger, R. (1980). A study of teacher planning. *Elementary School Journal, 80,* 107–127.

Zahorik, J. (1970). The effects of planning on teaching. *The Elementary School Journal, 71,* 143–151.

Zambo, R., and Hess, R. K. (1996). The gender differential effects of a procedural plan for solving mathematic word problems. *School Science and Mathematics, 96,* 362–370.

Zeichner, K., and Noffke, S. (2001). Practitioner research. In V. Richardson (ed.), *Handbook of Research on Teaching* (4th ed.). Washington, D.C.: American Educational Research Association.

Glossary

academic learning time (ALT) The amount of time a student is engaged in a particular subject or learning task at which he or she is successful.

accommodation Process of developing new concept of schemata to understand a situation that is new and can be made to fit existing schema.

accountability Holding teachers responsible for their teaching practices and for what their students learn.

achievement motivation The desire to take action and to excel for the purpose of experiencing success and feeling competent.

action research Research conducted by teachers for the purpose of improving their own teaching or schools. Also called *teacher research*.

action zone The section of the classroom (normally the front rows and center columns) where students tend to be called on most often and most verbal interaction occurs.

activity structures Patterns of behavior that characterize what teachers do as they teach and what students do as they engage in learning tasks; can be viewed as the basic unit for planning.

advance organizer A statement made by teachers before a presentation or before having students read textual materials that provides a structure for new information to be linked to students' prior knowledge.

affective domain The domain that classifies objectives in the emotional response processes.

affiliative motives The desire to take action for the purpose of experiencing friendship and close relationships with others.

analyze One of the six types of cognitive processes in Bloom's revised taxonomy and defined as being able to break materials into constituent parts and show how parts relate to one another.

analytical intelligence Defined by Robert Sternberg as the kind of intelligence that involves an individual's cognitive processes.

anticipatory set Technique used by teachers at the beginning of a lesson to prepare students to learn and to establish a communicative link between the learner's prior knowledge and the new information to be presented. Same as *establishing set* and *set induction*.

apply One of the six types of cognitive processes in Bloom's revised taxonomy and defined as being able to apply particular knowledge and carry out and implement particular procedures in a given situation.

artifacts The products produced by students in problem-based instruction, such as reports, videos, computer programs.

art of teaching A degree of accomplishment that allows basing complex decisions more on the teacher's experience than on research and scientific evidence.

assertive discipline An approach to classroom management that emphasizes teachers asserting their right to teach by insisting on appropriate student behavior and by responding assertively to student infractions.

assessment Process of collecting a full range of information about students and classrooms for the purpose of making instructional decisions.

assigning competence Drawing attention to special abilities and skills held by low-status students and bringing these to the attention of all students.

assimilation Process of understanding something new by adapting it to what is already known.

assistive technologies Special tools, mainly computer-related, to assist individuals who have special needs.

attraction The degree to which classroom participants respect and like one another.

attribution theories View of motivation that emphasizes the way individuals come to perceive and interpret the causes of their successes and failures.

authentic assessment Assessment procedures that have students demonstrate their abilities to perform particular tasks in real-life settings.

authentic relationships Relationships teachers build with their students in which both teachers and students treat each other as real and significant people.

autonomous learner A student who is motivated to take responsibility for his or her own learning and who has the skills and strategies to learn independently. See also *self-regulated learner*.

autonomy norm The expectation in many schools that teachers can do pretty much what they want within the confines of their classroom.

available time The part of the school day actually available for academic purposes.

behavioral objective A form for writing an instructional objective that emphasizes precision and careful delineation of expected student behaviors, the testing situation, and a performance criterion.

behaviorism School of psychology emphasizing the importance of behavior and the external environment as a determinant of human behavior and learning.

behavior modeling Term used in social learning theory to describe how people learn as a result of observing others.

best practice Teaching methods, processes, and procedures that have been shown to be effective for helping students learn.

buzz groups A small group technique to help broaden student participation in discussion.

causal-comparative research Research that explores causal relationships when the independent variable cannot be manipulated.

challenged A term used to refer to individuals who have special needs or disabilities.

checking for understanding Technique used by teachers to see if students have grasped newly presented information or skills.

circle seating pattern A seating arrangement used in discussion that places the teacher and students in a circle; maximizes free interchange among participants.

classroom activities Things students are expected to do in the classroom, such as listening, discussing, completing worksheets, and taking tests.

classroom ecology A way of looking at classrooms that is concerned mainly with how student cooperation and involvement are achieved.

classroom management The ways teachers organize and structure their classrooms for the purposes of maximizing student cooperation and engagement and minimizing disruptive behavior.

classroom meetings An approach to classroom management in which the teacher holds regular meetings for the purpose of helping students identify and resolve problem situations.

classroom processes Interpersonal and group processes that help classroom participants deal with issues of expectations, leadership, attraction, norms, communication, and cohesiveness.

classroom properties Distinctive features of classrooms, such as multidimensionality, simultaneity, immediacy, unpredictability, publicness, and history, that shape behavior of participants.

classroom structures The ways classrooms are organized around learning tasks and participation, and the ways goals and rewards are defined.

classroom tasks The work students are expected to do in classrooms and the cognitive and social demands placed on students as they perform particular lessons. See also *task structures*.

cluster seating A seating arrangement that puts desks in groups to facilitate cooperative learning and small-group lessons.

cognitive-constructivist perspective A view of learning that posits that learning occurs when learners are actively involved in the process of acquiring and constructing their own knowledge.

cognitive domain The domain in Bloom's taxonomy that classifies objectives in the thinking and reasoning processes.

cognitive monitoring Learners' abilities to select, to use, and to monitor appropriate learning strategies.

cognitive process dimension The dimension in Bloom's revised taxonomy that identifies the cognitive processes or thinking required of particular learning tasks.

cognitive processes The thinking engaged in by teachers and students.

cognitive psychology Psychology of learning that focuses mainly on mental processes.

cognitive strategies Complex thinking strategies associated with receiving, storing, and retrieving information.

cognitive structures The way knowledge is organized and stored in the mind.

communication skills Interpersonal skills that help facilitate the transmission and reception of verbal and non-verbal messages.

community problem solving An instructional practice that requires students to become involved in their community and help solve community problems.

competitive goal structure Goal structure where one person is successful in reaching his or her goals when others are unsuccessful.

competitive reward structure Occurs when students perceive that they can obtain their goal if, and only if, the other students with whom they work fail to obtain their goals.

concept attainment An inductive approach to teaching concepts by which students derive the meaning and attributes of a concept from examples and nonexamples of the concept given by the teacher.

concepts Ways of organizing knowledge and experiences in categories within which items have common attributes.

concept teaching Approaches to teaching in which the emphasis is on helping students learn how to make and label categories of ideas, objects, and experiences.

conceptual approach An approach to multicultural education in which teachers incorporate a series of concepts associated with cultural pluralism into ongoing lessons.

conceptual mapping A technique of visually organizing and diagraming a set of ideas or concepts in a logical pattern so relationships can be readily observed. Also called *webbing*.

conceptual knowledge One of four types of knowledge in Bloom's revised taxonomy and defined as knowing about the interrelationships among basic elements and knowing about principles, categories, theories, and models.

conceptual web See *conceptual mapping*.

conditional knowledge Knowledge about when it is appropriate to use particular declarative or procedural knowledge.

conjunctive concept A concept that has a constant rule structure.

constructivism A perspective of teaching and learning in which a learner constructs meaning from experience and interaction with others and the teacher's role is to provide meaningful experiences for students.

constructivist perspective A view that knowledge is often personal and that humans construct knowledge and meaning through experience.

control group Group of subjects that receives no special treatment during experimental research.

convergent questions Type of question that focuses on relationships and analysis of cause and effect; calls for finding single, best answer.

cooperative goal or task structures Occur when students perceive they can obtain their goal if, and only if, the other students with whom they work also obtain their goals.

cooperative learning model An approach to teaching in which students work in mixed-ability groups and are partially rewarded for group, rather than individual, effort and success.

cooperative reward structures Occur when students are interdependent for a reward they will share if they are successful as a group.

corrective feedback Information given to students about how well they are doing.

correlation A term used to express how two or more variables are related.

correlational research A type of research that investigates relationships between variables which exist naturally.

correlation coefficient Numbers ranging from $+1.00$ to -1.00 that describe the numerical relationship between variables.

create One of the six types of cognitive processes in Bloom's revised taxonomy and defined as being able to combine elements together for a coherent whole and/or reorganize elements into a new pattern.

creative intelligence Defined by Robert Sternberg as the type of intelligence that involves having insight to cope with new situations or experiences.

criterion-referenced grading A practice in which criteria for success are defined in advance and all students have an opportunity to earn any possible grade.

criterion-referenced test A test that evaluates a particular student's performance against a preestablished standard or criterion.

critical attribute Feature of a concept that distinguishes it from all other concepts.

cuing A signal from teachers to alert or to set up situations for students in order to help them get ready to make an appropriate response.

cultural deficit theory The now-discredited theory that accounts for the low achievement of minorities by postulating some defect in their culture or race.

cultural difference theory The currently accepted theory that accounts for the low achievement of minorities by postulating that the discontinuity between home culture and school culture interferes with learning.

cultural pluralism An ideology encouraging minority cultures to maintain their distinctive identities within the larger culture and to value cultural diversity within societies.

culturally relevant pedagogy Teaching practices where teachers connect the world of their students and their cultures to the world of the school and the classroom.

culture A group's total way of life; the way group members think about social action and ways to resolve issues in social collective life.

culture shock The anxious emotional response to the ambiguity and disconfirmed expectations that come from dealing with unfamiliar cultures.

curriculum mapping A technique for charting what is taught (curriculum) across grade levels and among various subjects.

dangle When a teacher starts an activity and then leaves it in midair.

debriefing Way to assess the effectiveness of a classroom discussion by asking students what they thought of the discussion.

declarative knowledge Knowledge about something or that something is the case; knowledge of facts, concepts, or principles.

demographic assumptions Assumptions made by societies about the demographic makeup of that society.

demography Study of population patterns; in education, this study is most concerned with size and distribution of school-aged children and youth.

dependent variable In research, the variable that may change as a result of the independent variable; the consequences of the independent variable.

descriptive research Research aimed at gathering detailed information about some phenonemon.

desist behavior A teaching behavior aimed at stopping disruptive student behavior.

desist incidence A classroom incident serious enough that if not dealt with will lead to widening management problems.

diagnostic test Test used by teachers to determine students' prior knowledge and level of skill development. Information used to assist in planning.

differential treatment The difference in the educational experiences of the majority race, class, culture, or gender and those of minorities; that is, differences in quality of curriculum, instruction, classroom interaction, funding, enrollment, etc.

dignifying errors Technique used by teachers when responding to student answers that are wrong.

direct instruction model An approach to teaching basic skills and sequential material in which lessons are highly goal-directed and learning environments are tightly structured by the teacher.

direct presentation One of several approaches to concept teaching.

disability A term used to refer to individuals who have special needs or challenges; the inability to do something such as hear, walk, or learn.

discontinuity A term used to describe a situation where the beliefs, values, and ways of communicating are different between one setting and another (e.g. the home and the school).

discourse The larger patterns of verbal exchange and communication that occur in classrooms.

discovery teaching or learning An approach to teaching that emphasizes encouraging students to learn concepts and principles through their own explorations and to solve problems on their own.

discrepant event A puzzling situation that sparks curiosity and motivates inquiry into cause-and-effect relationships; used by teachers to engage students.

discussion A teaching method that relies on verbal exchange of ideas among students and the teacher.

disjunctive concept A concept that contains alternative sets of attributes.

distracters Plausible but wrong answers in a multiple-choice test question.

distributed practice Practice assigned to students to be done for brief periods spread over several sessions or periods of time.

divergent questions "What-if" questions that allow multiple answers and solutions and promote creativity.

diversity Refers to the variety among people that exists in schools and society.

downtime Time in classrooms when lessons are completed early or when students are waiting for upcoming events, such as moving to another class or going home.

Ebonics A term used to refer to a dialect used by some African Americans.

ecological system A view of classrooms in which inhabitants (teachers, students, and others) interact within a highly interdependent environment.

economy Term used by Bruner to describe ways to limit the amount of materials to be taught at any one time.

emotional intelligence Defined by Goleman as an individual's ability to recognize and monitor one's emotions and be aware of the emotions of others.

encoding The process of transferring new information from short-term to long-term memory.

endogenous Qualities that are internal to a situation or have personal relevance.

engaged time The amount of time students actually spend on a particular subject or learning activity; also called *time on task.*

equity Refers to making conditions for everyone impartial, fair, just, and equal.

ESL Acronym for "English as a second language."

essay test An approach to testing in which students are required to express their thoughts in writing.

establishing set See *anticipatory set.*

ethnicity Refers to groups that have common identities such as language or nationality.

ethnography Term from the field of anthropology to describe an extensive descriptive study of a single culture, society, or particular phenonemon.

ethos Common set of values, beliefs, and ways of doing things found in particular classrooms or schools. See also *school culture.*

evaluate One of the six types of cognitive processes in Bloom's revised taxonomy and defined as being able to make judgments based on criteria or standards.

evaluation Process of judging, assigning value, or deciding on the worth of a particular program or approach or of a student's work.

example-to-rule Technique of giving examples to students, helping them to come up with the rule or principle.

exceptionality Term used to define students who have special social, mental, emotional, or physical needs.

exhibits Displays of artifacts (products) students present that show their work from a problem-based lesson.

exogenous Word used to define qualities that are external to a situation or that have external causes.

expectations The amount and quality of work and behavior expected of students in classrooms and schools.

experiential learning Theory of learning that explains how people learn from their experiences and subsequent reflections about their experiences.

experiment A type of research in which the researcher manipulates one or more variables so cause-and-effect relationships can be examined.

experimental group A group of subjects that receives a special treatment in experimental research.

expert teachers Experienced teachers who have mastered the art and science of teaching.

explaining links Prepositions or conjunctions used in a presentation that indicate the cause, result, means, or purpose of an event or idea.

extending student thinking Techniques used by teachers following a presentation to help students strengthen their understanding of the new material and to expand their cognitive structures.

extrinsic motivation Behavior caused by external factors such as rewards, punishments, or social pressures.

extrinsic reward A reward that is external to the activity itself, such as points, grades, or stars.

factual knowledge One of four types of knowledge in Bloom's revised taxonomy and defined as the basic elements, facts, and vocabulary of a topic or subject.

fairness The degree to which a test is free from bias and does not discriminate against a particular group of students because of race, ethnicity, or gender.

feedback Information given to students about their performance. Same as *knowledge of results.*

feeling tone The degree to which a learning environment or a particular learning task is perceived as pleasant or unpleasant.

field dependent Refers to individuals who tend to perceive situations "as a whole."

field independent Refers to individuals who tend to perceive the separate parts of a situation rather than the whole.

flexible grouping The teaching practice where students are put in ability groups for instruction, but the grouping remains fluid and the possibility to move from one group to another exists.

flip-flop Occurs when a teacher starts an activity, then stops and starts another one, and finally returns to the original activity.

flow experience State when individuals feel total involvement and concentration and strong feelings of enjoyment as a result of a particular experience.

formative evaluation Evaluation that occurs before or during instruction and is used to assist with planning or making adaptations.

fragmentation Occurs when a teacher breaks a learning activity into overly small units.

full bilingual program A program in which instruction is carried out equally in two languages and the goals are full oral proficiency and literacy in both.

Gantt chart A planning technique to show pieces of work in relationship to one another and when each piece is expected to start and to finish.

gender bias Views of or actions toward males and females that often favor one gender over the other.

gifted and talented Students who are identified as being very bright, creative, and/or having special talents.

goal structures The way that goals specify the degree of interdependence sought among students. There are three different types of goal structures: individualistic, competitive, and cooperative.

grading on the curve A practice of assigning grades so they will follow a normal curve.

grading to criterion Practice of assigning grades according to how well students do on a predefined set of objectives or standards.

graphic organizer A visual image presented to students to provide structure for new information about to be presented. Similar to an *advance organizer.*

group development Stages classroom groups go through in the process of developing into a cohesive and effective group.

group investigation (GI) An approach to cooperative learning in which students help define topics for study and then work together to complete their investigations.

group processes See *classroom processes.*

group skills Skills students have to participate effectively in groups.

guided practice Practice assigned to students to be completed under the guidance or watchful eye of the teacher.

handicapped A term used to refer to individuals who have special needs or challenges. Some believe it carries a negative connotation and projects a negative image toward those with special needs or challenges.

hands-off norm Expectation in many schools that teachers will not interfere in other teachers' work.

higher-order thinking Abstract intellectual process that involves analyzing, criticizing, and reaching conclusions based on sound evidence.

holistic scoring Technique for grading essay questions or other written work that emphasizes looking at the work as a whole rather than at its individual parts.

homework Assignments that students are expected to complete outside of class.

horizontal desk formation Seating arrangement in which students sit close to one another in four or five rows; useful for direct instruction lessons.

inclusion Practice of including students, regardless of their disabilities, in regular classrooms.

in-context learning style Refers to the learning style where individuals acquire understanding and skills as they are needed in real-life situations.

independent practice Practice given to students to accomplish on their own without the teacher's guidance.

independent task A situation where a learning task can be accomplished by individuals working alone.

independent variable In research, the variable that is treated and presumed to cause some change in the dependent variable.

individualistic goal structure A situation where a goal can be accomplished by individuals working or performing by themselves.

individualistic reward structure Occurs when achievement of the goal by one student is unrelated to the achievement of the goal by other students.

individualized education plan (IEP) A learning plan specifying long- and short-term educational goals for disabled students and agreed on by teachers, parents, and special educators.

inductive reasoning Process of coming up with general rules or principles based on information from specific examples or data.

inductive teaching See *inquiry teaching or training.*

influence motivation The desire to take action for the purposes of having control and a say in what's going on.

information processing The process used by the mind to take in, store, and retrieve information for use.

inquiry teaching or training An approach to teaching in which the emphasis is on helping students to inquire on their own and to develop such skills as asking questions and drawing conclusions from data.

instructional effects The learning goals a particular teaching model has been designed to achieve.

instructional aspects of teaching Those aspects of teachers' work during which they are providing face-to-face instruction to students in classrooms.

instructional objectives and goals Statements that describe a teacher's instructional intents.

intelligence Ability(ies) individuals have for solving problems and adapting to one's environment.

intelligence quotient A score that compares chronological and mental ages.

interaction patterns A term used to refer to the patterns of the verbal and nonverbal communication in classrooms.

interdependent task A situation where a learning task can only be accomplished by two or more individuals working together.

interpersonal communication skills Skills that promote honest communication and positive regard among students.

intrinsic motivation Occurs when people behave because an act brings personal satisfaction or enjoyment.

Jigsaw An approach to cooperative learning in which students work in mixed-ability groups and each student is responsible for a portion of the material.

journaling A technique of writing on a regular basis one's thoughts and reflections about teaching experiences.

knowledge acquisition The process in which students acquire and assimilate new information and knowledge.

knowledge base Information, accumulated over time from research and the wisdom of experienced teachers, that informs teaching practices.

knowledge dimension The dimension in Bloom's revised taxonomy that defines what learners know or are expected to know.

knowledge networks How information and related concepts are organized and linked together in the memory system.

knowledge of results Feedback given to students about their performance.

knowledge representation The way information is organized and stored in the memory system.

leadership aspects of teaching Aspects of teachers' work, such as providing motivation and coordinating and controlling learning environments and activities.

learning abilities Abilities individuals have for acquiring new knowledge and skills and for adapting to one's environment.

learning environment The overall climate and structures of the classroom that influence how students respond to and remain engaged in learning tasks; the context in which teaching acts are carried out.

learning preferences Preferred environments or modalities learners have toward learning and studying.

learning strategies Plans or strategies learners have for approaching particular learning tasks or studying.

learning styles Particular approaches learners have toward learning or studying.

least restrictive environment The placement situation for disabled students that is the most normal and least confining based on the student's particular needs and problems.

LEP Acronym for "limited English proficiency."

lesson plan Organization for instruction for a particular lesson or period.

lesson structures The way learning activities and series of lessons are woven together.

level of actual development A concept attributed to Lev Vygotsky that identifies a learner's level of current intellectual functioning.

level of concern The amount of stress and anxiety students experience with a particular learning task.

level of difficulty Refers to how difficult a question asked of students is to answer.

level of potential development A concept attributed to Lev Vygotsky that identifies the level at which a learner could function intellectually with the assistance of a teacher or more advanced peer.

logical consequences Punishments administered for misbehavior that are directly related to the infraction.

long-term memory Place in the mind where information is stored, ready for retrieval when needed.

loosely coupled systems An organizational arrangement in which what goes on in one part of an organization is not very connected to what goes on in other parts of the organization.

mainstreaming Placing special-needs children in regular classes for full time or part time.

massed practice Practice assigned to students to be done during a single extended period of time.

mean score The arithmetic average of a group of scores.

meaningful verbal learning The phase used by Ausubel to emphasize importance of teaching students meaningful relationships among verbal ideas and information.

melting pot Ideology of education that believes the strengths of minority cultures should be blended into a new, single, superior culture.

mental abilities Phase used to define abilities individuals have as measured by performance on particular cognitive tasks.

mental age Score in intelligence testing that designates average mental ability for a particular age group.

meta-analysis A research method that combines results across several studies.

metacognition Process of knowing and monitoring one's own thinking or *cognitive processes.*

metacognitive knowledge One of four types of knowledge in Bloom's revised taxonomy and defined as knowledge and awareness of one's own cognition.

metacognitive strategies Strategies used to recognize one's *cognitive processes* and ways to think about how information is being processed.

minority group A term used to refer to a group of people who are, or have been, disadvantaged. Does not necessarily mean numerical minority.

momentum Term used by Kounin to describe how teachers pace instruction.

motivation The process by which behavior is directed toward important human goals or toward satisfying needs and motives.

multicultural education An approach to teaching aimed at helping students recognize and value cultural diversity.

multiple intelligence Gardner's theory that states intelligence is more than a single ability and instead consists of eight different types of abilities.

needs disposition theory Theory of motivation positing that people are motivated to take action to satisfy basic and higher-level needs.

negative reinforcer A stimulus such as punishment intended to eliminate or reduce undesirable behavior.

noncritical attributes Features found in some but not all members of a category.

nonlinear model An approach to planning in which planners start with actions or activities deemed important and later attach goals to the action to help explain what happened.

norm-referenced grading A grading practice whereby students' scores are determined by comparison to others' in the class.

norm-referenced test A standardized test that evaluates a particular student's performance by comparing it to the performance of some other well-defined group of students.

norms The shared expectations students and teachers have for classroom behavior.

novice teacher A teacher who is just beginning and is still learning the art and science of teaching.

numbered heads together Small group strategies that encourage cooperation and participation.

objective tests Tests with items that produce answers that can be scored with relatively little bias.

objectivist perspective A view that knowledge consists of "truths" and an objective reality that humans have access to and can learn through discovery and inquiry.

observation A research procedure in which the researcher watches and records behaviors; a procedure for learning to teach by watching, recording, and reflecting about teacher and student behavior in classrooms.

opportunity to learn The amount of time a teacher actually spends on academic tasks or activities.

organizational aspects of teaching Those aspects of teachers' work involving interactions with other adults in the school setting for the purpose of schoolwide planning and coordination.

out-of-context learning style Learning that is not necessarily connected to real or immediate needs—the typical kind of learning required of students in schools.

overdwelling Occurs when a teacher goes on and on after a subject or a set of instructions is clear to students.

overlappingness The ability of teachers to spot disruptive behavior and to deal with it without interrupting the flow of the lesson.

overlearning Working or practicing a task or skill until it is learned completely and can be performed automatically.

participation structures The established rules and processes that determine who can say what, when, and to whom during classroom discourse.

pedagogy The study of the art and science of teaching; also refers to the methods and approaches to instruction.

performance assessment Assessment procedures that have students demonstrate their abilities to perform particular tasks in testing situations.

performance standard A standard or goal students are expected to meet.

planned academic time The amount of time that teachers set aside for different subjects and activities.

planning cycles The spans of time considered for various aspects of planning: daily, weekly, unit, term, and yearly.

portfolio A collection of a student's work that demonstrates the student's ability to perform particular tasks.

positive reinforcer A stimulus such as a reward intended to get individuals to repeat desirable behavior.

postinstructional planning Teacher planning whereby decisions are made about how to provide feedback to students and how to assess and evaluate student learning.

power Term used by Bruner to describe the process of selecting only the most important (powerful) ideas and concepts to teach to students.

practical arguments Reasoning based on knowledge and beliefs that is used by teachers as they make pedagogical decisions.

practical intelligence Defined by Robert Sternberg as the kind of abilities individuals have to adapt and reshape their environments.

praise Positive verbal and nonverbal statements offered by teachers as reinforcers to encourage and strengthen desirable student behaviors.

preinstructional planning Teacher planning conducted before instruction, during which goals, content, and approaches are decided.

presentation teaching model An approach to teaching wherein the primary emphasis is on explaining new information and ideas to students.

preventive management Perspective that effective classroom management can be achieved through good planning, interesting lessons, and effective teaching.

principle A cause-and-effect relationship between variables that has been established from results of several studies or experiments conducted over time.

prior knowledge Information and knowledge held by students before they receive instruction.

privileges Special activities and extra time bestowed by teachers to encourage desirable pupil behavior.

problem-based instruction Approach to teaching in which students investigate and study authentic and meaningful problem situations.

problem solving Finding ways to apply new solutions to complex problem situations rather than relying on fixed rules or recipes.

procedural knowledge Knowledge about how to do something. Can pertain to specific behavioral skills or to complex *cognitive strategies*.

procedures Systems established by teachers for dealing with routine tasks and coordinating student talk and movement.

process-product research Research method characterized by studying the relationships between what teachers do (process) and the effects on student achievement (product).

productions The way basic units of procedural knowledge are organized and linked in the memory system.

propositional network Units or sets of interconnected knowledge. A proposition is the basic unit in a person's *cognitive structure*.

psychomotor domain The domain in Bloom's taxonomy that classifies objectives in the physical movement and coordination processes.

punishments Penalties imposed by teachers to discourage undesirable behaviors.

race A term used to refer to a group of people who share common biological traits.

randomness Without a definite or biased pattern; the quality of being by chance.

rational-linear planning An approach to planning that focuses on setting goals and objectives first and then on selecting particular strategies or activities to accomplish these predetermined goals.

reciprocal teaching An approach to teaching reading in which peer teaching is used to help students master comprehension skills.

recitation An approach to teaching in which a teacher provides bits of information, asks questions, gets students to respond, and then provides feedback by praising or correcting.

reflection Careful and analytical thought by teachers about what they are doing and the effects of their behavior on their instruction and on student learning.

reinforcement Consequences administered by teachers to encourage and strengthen certain desirable behaviors.

relational concept A concept whose rule structure depends on its relationship to other concepts.

reliability The degree to which a test produces consistent results over several administrations.

remember One of the six types of cognitive processes in Bloom's revised taxonomy and defined as being able to recognize and recall relevant knowledge from long-term memory.

repertoire The number of teaching approaches and strategies that teachers are able to use to help students learn.

reward structures The ways in which rewards can be distributed within a classroom. There are three types: *individualistic, competitive,* and *cooperative.*

role Term used to describe a set of norms that details how various aspects of a particular job should be carried out.

row-and-column desk formation A classroom seating arrangement in which desks are organized in straight rows and columns; used effectively when a teacher is presenting or demonstrating and when student exchange is not required.

rule-example-rule technique A technique used when explaining something whereby the general principle or rule is given first, then elaborated on with specific examples, and finally summarized by a restatement of the rule.

rules for behavior Statements that specify expected classroom behaviors and define behaviors that are forbidden.

sample A group of subjects drawn from a larger population for the purpose of research.

scaffolding The process in which a learner is helped by a teacher or more accomplished person to master a particular problem beyond his or her current developmental level.

schema, schemata An individual's (teacher or student) knowledge structure or the way information has been organized and stored in memory.

school culture The ways members of a school think about social action; the embedded beliefs, values, and attitudes of members of a school. *Ethos, tone,* and *community* are often used to describe the same phenomenon.

school effectiveness research Research that tries to uncover features that make some schools more effective than others.

school improvement The process of helping schools change and adopt innovative practices.

scientific basis of teaching Teaching in which decisions are based on research and scientific evidence.

scoring rubric A detailed description of some type of performance and the criteria that will be used to judge it.

seatwork Independent work done by students, such as reading, answering questions, or completing worksheets.

self-fulfilling prophecy A situation in which teachers' expectations and predictions about student behavior or learning cause it to happen.

self-management An approach to classroom management in which teachers help students define problems, set their own goals, and monitor progress toward goal accomplishment.

self-regulated learner A learner who can diagnose a learning situation, select an appropriate learning strategy, monitor the effectiveness of the strategy, and remain engaged in the learning task until it is accomplished. See *autonomous learner.*

set induction See *anticipatory set.*

short-term memory The place in the mind where conscious mental work is done; also called *working memory.*

smoothness The smooth flow and pacing of instructional events.

social interaction The interaction and exchange among individuals; Lev Vygotsky believed that interaction and exchange spurred learning and intellectual development.

social learning theory Perspective about learning that posits that much of what humans learn is through observation of others.

social skills Skills or abilities individuals have to work or interact effectively in social and group settings.

socially just classroom Classrooms where students are engaged in the struggle for social justice in the larger society as well as in the classroom itself.

social-system perspective A way of viewing classrooms, schools, and other human organizations by considering how the various parts of the organization are interrelated and interdependent.

socioeconomic status (SES) Variations among peoples based on income, family background, and relative prestige within the society.

Socratic method An approach to teaching in which teachers help students think and inquire by asking questions that require inductive reasoning.

stages of teacher concerns A theory, attributed to Francis Fuller, explaining how teachers are concerned about different things as they learn to teach. The focus of concern is first on survival later on the teaching situation, and finally on pupil growth.

stages of teacher development A theory explaining how growth in teaching expertise occurs over time, progressing from one stage to the next stage in sequence.

standard deviation A measure that shows the spread of a set of scores from the mean.

standardized tests Tests that are normally designed by professional test makers for nationwide use and commercially distributed.

statistical test and significance Procedures used to determine whether results from research are indeed true or a result of chance.

stem A statement that poses a problem or asks a question in a multiple-choice test question.

structural approach Approach to cooperative learning attributed to Spencer Kagan.

structure of knowledge The way knowledge in particular disciplines is organized.

student accountability Holding students responsible for their learning and their behavior.

Student portfolios Portfolio assessment is a form of assessment that evaluates a sample of students' work and other accomplishments over time.

Student Teams Achievement Divisions (STADs) An approach to cooperative learning in which students work in mixed-ability groups and rewards are administered and recognized for both individual and group effort.

submersion approach The now-illegal practice of simply placing limited English proficiency students in the classroom and expecting them to pick up English on their own without any formal teaching or other support from the school.

success level The level at which students succeed in academic tasks.

summative evaluation Evaluation done after instruction to determine program effectiveness or the worth of students' work.

sustaining expectation effect Occurs when teachers do not change their previous expectations about a student, even after the student's performance has improved or regressed.

swing seating Seating plan that allows easy movement of seats during cooperative learning lessons.

synergy Positive results achieved from working together or through combined action.

syntax The overall flow, sequence, or major steps of a particular lesson.

systems analysis Study and way of thinking about the relationships that exist between the interdependent parts of some whole.

task analysis A process for breaking down complex learning tasks into fundamental parts or subdividing complex skills into specific subskills so they can be mastered one at a time.

task structures The way lessons are arranged and the learning demands that lessons place on students.

taxonomy A classification system or device that helps arrange and show relationships among objects and ideas.

taxonomy of educational objectives A system developed by Benjamin Bloom for classifying objectives into three domains: *cognitive, affective,* and *psychomotor.*

teacher clarity Phrase used to describe the process of teachers giving presentations that are clear and free of ambiguity.

teacher effectiveness research Refers to research that aims at finding relationships between teaching behavior and student achievement.

teacher enthusiasm A set of behaviors employed by teachers, such as using uplifting language and dramatic body movements, to make students interested in learning materials.

teacher expectations Beliefs, attitudes, and perceptions teachers hold about the capabilities of particular students—may or may not be accurate.

teacher research See *action research.*

teaching model A term used by Bruce Joyce to describe an overall approach or plan toward instruction. The attributes of teaching models are a coherent theoretical framework, an orientation toward what students should learn, and specific teaching procedures and structures.

test anxiety Phenomenon that occurs when students experience undue stress while taking a test and do poorly as a result.

test blueprint A tool used in constructing a test so it will have a balance of questions representing various forms of knowledge and cognitive processes.

thinking matrix A visual device to help students think about the types of questions and answers they provide during a discussion; used to teach thinking skills.

think-pair-share A technique used by teachers to slow down the pace of discourse and to increase student participation.

tiered activities A strategy for getting all students, regardless of abilities, to focus on the same understanding or skill but at different levels of abstraction or complexity.

time on task See *engaged time.*

time-tabling techniques Planning tools that chronologically map time relationships among various instructional activities.

tone See *ethos* and *school culture.*

topical approach An approach to multicultural education in which special lessons are devoted to studying heroes, holidays, art, literature, or the cuisine of a particular culture.

transfer of learning The process of applying knowledge or skills learned in one situation to new situations.

transitional bilingual programs Programs in which limited English proficiency students are initially provided instruction in their native language, with gradual increases in English until proficiency is achieved.

transitions The times during a lesson when the teacher is moving from one type of learning activity to another.

understand One of the six types of cognitive processes in Bloom's revised taxonomy and defined as being able to interpret, exemplify, classify, summarize, infer, compare, and explain knowledge.

unit An integrated plan for instruction covering several days and including several lessons aimed at a common set of goals and objectives.

U-shaped seating pattern A seating arrangement used for discussions in which students' chairs form a U and the teacher is seated at the open end of the U.

validity The degree to which a test measures what it claims to measure.

variable A characteristic of a person or a physical or social situation that can change or vary from one instance to the next.

verbal signposts Statements made by teachers when explaining something that tells the student what is important or alerts them to important points coming up.

visual cuing Use of visual devices, such as hand signals, to inform students about what they should be doing.

wait-time The time a teacher waits for a student to respond to a question and the time a teacher waits before responding back.

webbing See *conceptual mapping.*

with-itness The ability of teachers to spot disruptive student behavior quickly and accurately.

working memory See *short-term memory.*

zone of proximal development A concept attributed to Lev Vygotsky that represents the area between a learner's level of actual development and his or her level of potential development.

Credits

CHAPTER 1

p. 2, © Peter Hvizdak/The Image Works; p. 6, © Corbis; p. 11, © Bob Daemmrich; p. 16, © Elizabeth Crews; p. 27, © Bill Aron/PhotoEdit; p. 33, Alexander Turnbull Library, National Library of New Zealand, Te Puna Matauranga o Aotearoa. Photo by H G du Faur.

CHAPTER 2

p. 38, © Joel Gordon; p. 43, 58, © Bob Daemmrich/The Image Works; p. 59, © Bob Daemmrich; p. 47, Table 2.2, From Oakes and Lipton, *Teaching to Change the World*, 2nd ed; p.331. Copyright © 2003 by McGraw-Hill Higher Education. Reprinted with permission of The McGraw-Hill Companies; p. 50, © Adam Stoller. Reprinted with permission; p. 56, Figure 2.3 From Marilyn Friend & William Bursuck, *Including Students with Special Needs: A Practical Guide For Classroom Teachers*, 2nd ed.; pp. 55–56. Published by Allyn & Bacon, Boston, MA. Copyright © 1999 by Pearson Education. Reprinted by permission of the publisher; p. 86, © Elizabeth Crews.

CHAPTER 3

p. 94, © Will Hart/PhotoEdit; p. 98, © Michael Dwyer/Stock Boston; p. 104, © Elizabeth Crews; Yinger, R. J. (1980). "Study of Teacher Planning." *The Elementary School Journal*. Copyright 1980. The University of Chicago Press. Used with permission. p. 126, © Bob Daemmrich; p. 116, Table 3.8, From Lori W. Anderson, et al., *A Taxonomy for Learning, Teaching, and Assessing*, pp. 29–32. Published by Allyn & Bacon, Boston, MA. Copyright © 2001 by Pearson Education. Reprinted by permission of the publisher; p. 117, Table 3.9, From Lori W. Anderson, et al., *A Taxonomy for Learning, Teaching, and Assessing*, pp. 29–32. Published by Allyn & Bacon, Boston, MA. Copyright © 2001 by Pearson Education. Reprinted by permission of the publisher; p. 119, Table 3.10, From Lori W. Anderson, et al., *A Taxonomy for Learning, Teaching, and Assessing*, pp. 29–32. Published

by Allyn & Bacon, Boston, MA. Copyright © 2001 by Pearson Education. Reprinted by permission of the publisher; p. 120, Figure 3.10, From Lori W. Anderson, et al., *A Taxonomy for Learning, Teaching, and Assessing*, pp. 29–32. Published by Allyn & Bacon, Boston, MA. Copyright © 2001 by Pearson Education. Reprinted by permission of the publisher.

CHAPTER 4

p. 134, © Joel Gordon; p. 138, © Mary Kate Denny/PhotoEdit; p. 144, 155, 161, © Bob Daemmrich; p. 157, Table 4.3, Marshall, H.H.L. (1987). Motivational Strategies of Three Fifth-grade Teachers. *The Elementary School Journal*, 88, 135–150. Copyright 1987. The University of Chicago Press. Used with permission. p. 166, © Elizabeth Crews.

CHAPTER 5

p. 174, © Bill Bachmann/PhotoEdit; p. 178, 195, © Bob Daemmrich; p. 207, Table 5.8, From *Beyond Discipline: From Compliance to Community* by Alfie Kohn. © Alfe Kohn, 1996, pp. 120–128 and *Teaching Every Student in the Digital Age: Universal Design for Learning* by David H. Rose and Anne Meyer with Nicole Strangman and Gabrielle Rappolt, ASCD 2002, pp. 111–132. Reprinted with permission.

CHAPTER 6

p. 212, © PhotoDisc/Getty Images; p. 224, © Pauline Cutler/Getty Images/Stone; p. 236, © Elizabeth Crews; p. 245, © Sven Martson/The Image Works; p. 246, © Bob Daemmrich; p. 227, Figure 6.3, Reprinted with permission of The McGraw-Hill Companies.

CHAPTER 7

p. 262, © Bob Daemmrich; p. 267, © AP/Wide World Photos; p. 273, © Elizabeth Crews; p. 277, © Peter

Hvizdak/The Image Works; p. 288, © Will Hart/
PhotoEdit; p. 290, © Bob Krist/Corbis.

CHAPTER 8
p. 296, © Mary Kate Denny/PhotoEdit; p. 299,
© Elizabeth Crews; p. 312, © Frank Siteman/
PhotoEdit; p. 317, © Bob Daemmrich/The Image
Works.

CHAPTER 9
p. 324, © Richard Hutchings/PhotoEdit; p. 329,
© Bettmann/Corbis; p. 343, © Bob Daemmrich; p. 344,
© Bob Daemmrich/The Image Works.

CHAPTER 10
p. 352, © Syracuse Newspapers/Stephen Cannerelli/The
Image Works; p. 358, © Bettmann/Corbis; p. 360, 373,
© Bob Daemmrich; p. 377, © Eastcott-Momatiuk/The
Image Works.

CHAPTER 11
p. 388, © Bob Daemmrich; p. 394, © Bob
Daemmrich/Stock Boston; p. 397, Courtesy Davidson
Films. www.davidsonfilms.com; p. 405, 409,
© Elizabeth Crews; p. 410, © Bonnie Kamin/
PhotoEdit; p. 416, © Bob Daemmrich.

CHAPTER 12
p. 422, © Will Hart/PhotoEdit; p. 427, 430, 442,
© Elizabeth Crews; p. 433, Tables 12.1 and 12.2, Rowe,
M.B. (1974). "Wait-Time and Rewards as Instructional
Variables, Their Influence on Language, Logic and Fate
Control: Part One: Wait-time." Journal of Research in
Science Teaching, 11, 81–94. Copyright 1974. John
Wiley & Sons. Reprinted by permission of John Wiley
& Sons, Inc.

CHAPTER 13
p. 458, © Michael Newman/PhotoEdit; p. 462,
© Elizabeth Crews/The Image Works; p. 466, © Rob
Crandall/The Image Works; p. 471, © Nancy
Richmond/The Image Works; p. 481, © Bob
Daemmrich/The Image Works; p. 483, © Linda A.
Cicero/Stanford News Service; p. 485, Figure 13.2,
© 2002 ISTE 800-336-5191 (US & Canada) or 541-302-3777
(Int'l), iste@iste.org, www.iste.org. All rights reserved.
Reprinted with permission. Reprint permission does
not constitute endorsement by ISTE; p. 479, © Pedro
Molina. Reprinted with permission.

Name Index

Subject Index